Fifth Edition

Periodization

Theory and Methodology of Training

Fifth Edition

Periodization
Theory and Methodology of Training

Tudor O. Bompa, PhD
York University

G. Gregory Haff, PhD
West Virginia University

Human Kinetics

Library of Congress Cataloging-in-Publication Data

Bompa, Tudor O.
  Periodization: theory and methodology of training / Tudor O. Bompa, G. Gregory Haff.
--5th ed.
     p. cm.
  Includes bibliographical references and index.
  ISBN-13: 978-0-7360-7483-4 (hard cover)
  ISBN-10: 0-7360-7483-X (hard cover)
  1. Periodization training. 2. Weight training. I. Haff, Greg. II. Title.
  GV546.B544 2009
  613.7'11--dc22

                        2009017639

ISBN-10: 0-7360-7483-X (print)   ISBN-10: 0-7360-8547-5 (Adobe PDF)
ISBN-13: 978-0-7360-7483-4 (print)   ISBN-13: 978-0-7360-8547-2 (Adobe PDF)

Copyright © 2009 by Tudor O. Bompa and G. Gregory Haff
Copyright © 1999 by Tudor O. Bompa
Copyright © 1994, 1990, 1983 by Kendall/Hunt Publishing Company

Acquisitions Editor: Michael S. Bahrke, PhD; **Developmental Editor:** Amanda S. Ewing; **Assistant Editors:** Carla Zych, Elizabeth Watson, and Casey A. Gentis; **Copyeditor:** Julie Anderson; **Proofreader:** Joanna Hatzopoulos Portman; **Indexer:** Joan K. Griffitts; **Permission Manager:** Dalene Reeder; **Graphic Designer:** Joe Buck; **Graphic Artist:** Dawn Sills; **Cover Designer:** Bob Reuther; **Photo Asset Manager:** Laura Fitch; **Photo Production Manager:** Jason Allen; **Art Manager:** Kelly Hendren; **Associate Art Manager:** Alan L. Wilborn; **Illustrator:** Tammy Page; **Printer:** Sheridan Books

Printed in the United States of America   10 9 8 7 6 5 4 3 2 1

The paper in this book is certified under a sustainable forestry program.

Human Kinetics
Web site: www.HumanKinetics.com

United States: Human Kinetics
P.O. Box 5076
Champaign, IL 61825-5076
800-747-4457
e-mail: humank@hkusa.com

Canada: Human Kinetics
475 Devonshire Road Unit 100
Windsor, ON N8Y 2L5
800-465-7301 (in Canada only)
e-mail: info@hkcanada.com

Europe: Human Kinetics
107 Bradford Road
Stanningley
Leeds LS28 6AT, United Kingdom
+44 (0) 113 255 5665
e-mail: hk@hkeurope.com

Australia: Human Kinetics
57A Price Avenue
Lower Mitcham, South Australia 5062
08 8372 0999
e-mail: info@hkaustralia.com

New Zealand: Human Kinetics
Division of Sports Distributors NZ Ltd.
P.O. Box 300 226 Albany
North Shore City
Auckland
0064 9 448 1207
e-mail: info@humankinetics.co.nz

Contents

▼

Part III Training Methods   257

Preface

▼

The classic text *Theory and Methodology of Training* by Tudor Bompa played a large role in shaping the training practices of many coaches and athletes throughout the world. This seminal text eventually became known as *Periodization: Theory and Methodology of Training*. Since its first publication in 1983 and the fourth edition, which was published in 1999, *Periodization* has presented the latest research and practices related to training theory. The text has been translated into many languages and has become one of the major resources on periodization for sport scientists, coaches, and athletes throughout the world; in fact, the fourth edition of the text sold more than 18,000 copies and was translated into six languages. For the fifth edition of *Periodization: Theory and Methodology of Training*, Bompa teams with G. Gregory Haff to couple the classic concepts that are central to periodization and training theory with contemporary advances in sport science, physiology, and coaching. The fifth edition offers the sport scientist, coach, and athlete information central to understanding the training process while providing scientific support for the principles fundamental to periodization.

ORGANIZATION OF THE TEXT

In the fifth edition, Bompa and Haff organize the text into the three major content areas found in the fourth edition: Training Theory, Periodization Training, and Training Methods. Part I, Training Theory, contains five chapters that delve into the major concepts central to training, such as the concept of bioenergetic specificity of training (chapter 1), the importance of long-term training development (chapter 2), the development of basic characteristics associated with training (i.e., tactical, technical, physical) (chapter 3), the variables associated with developing a training plan (chapter 4), and the importance of recovery or restoration in the overall training process (chapter 5). The first five chapters give the coach, sport scientist, and athlete the concepts necessary for understanding and developing periodized training plans, which are addressed in part II.

Part II, Periodization of Training, contains four chapters that discuss many of the classic concepts found in the fourth edition. These chapters provide expanded discussions on the importance of the annual training plan (chapter 6), methods for elevating performance at appropriate times (chapter 7), methods for constructing different training cycles (chapter 8), and how to conceptualize and plan workouts (chapter 9). Chapter 7 couples the current scientific knowledge about the interrelation between training stress and performance with practical information that will allow coaches and athletes to manipulate training to ensure optimal performance during competition.

The chapters in part III, Training Methods, discuss the development of strength and power (chapter 10), endurance (chapter 11), and speed and agility (chapter 12). When examining strength and power training, chapter 10 presents information on the relationships among force, velocity, the rate of force development, and power and information on variables that can be manipulated in the construction of a strength training program. The chapters on endurance (chapter 11) and speed training (chapter 12) have been expanded to include the latest information on developing these important sport performance characteristics.

UPDATES TO THE FIFTH EDITION

The fifth edition of *Periodization: Theory and Methodology of Training* maintains several of the components of the fourth edition including sample annual training plans, microcycle loading structures, and charts for designing periodized training plans. New to the fifth edition of *Periodization* are these features:

- An expanded chapter on rest and recovery that discusses ways to facilitate recovery, including dietary supplementation, contrast baths, and massage. The latest research on recovery is accompanied by practical suggestions for the coach and athlete.

- Discussions on the importance of sequencing training and exploiting delayed training effects. Detailed physiological rationales are presented to support the contention that training must be appropriately sequenced to produce optimal performances at major competitions.

- A comprehensive update on the concept of peaking for competition. This section discusses different methods of peaking an athlete for competition and offers scientific evidence for the models presented. New figures have been created that merge contemporary scientific literature and classic literature to give the reader a visual representation of the optimal timing of a peaking cycle.

- A new chapter on the methods for developing muscular strength. This chapter discusses such concepts as conjugated sequencing and summated microcycle structures and how they can be used to maximize strength gains and better direct training.

- Expanded discussions about the development of sport-specific endurance. In this context different types of endurance and specific methods for developing endurance are presented. The physiological bases for these methods are also presented to explain how training can affect the athlete's physiology.

- Improved graphic depictions of major concepts. These new figures are based on the latest scientific literature on training and physiology.

The fifth edition of *Periodization: Theory and Methodology of Training* builds on the tradition established in previous editions of this text and expands on the current understanding of training theory and the application of periodization.

Acknowledgments

I thank Mike Bahrke and the staff at Human Kinetics for their work on this new edition.

Tudor Bompa

I thank my co-author, Tudor Bompa, for allowing me a large amount of freedom to update and modify his classic text. It truly has been an honor to work with you, Tudor, and to discuss philosophies and beliefs about training theory.

I must acknowledge the most important person in my life, my wife Erin. The sacrifices you have made to allow me to chase my dreams are too numerous to count. Over the years you have moved, packed our home, and organized my life more times than you would like. You have supported me as I have spent countless hours working in the lab and office, working with students, and traveling. As a coach, you always set me straight about the practical side of the profession and always keep me grounded. I am truly blessed to have such an amazingly talented wife. Your love, support, trust, and belief in me allow me to weather the storms that occur in the world of academics.

With great pleasure and humility I express my deepest gratitude to my mentor, Dr. Mike Stone. You are more than a mentor to me: You are one of my closest friends and confidants and the person I model myself after. I have been blessed to work with you for more than 15 years, and each day I look forward to our conversations about science and life. I am honored that you have always included me in your research journey. If I can be half the sport scientist that you are, I will have accomplished more than most.

I thank my many colleagues who over the years have supported me and given me valuable feedback. In particular I thank Chuck Dumke for his friendship and always being there to pick me up when I am down. Chuck, you are amazing, and one day we will be at the same institution working side by side again. I also acknowledge Travis Triplett; you are simply the most amazing friend and confidant. You have an extraordinary gift for analyzing situations and finding the best solutions. When I need advice, I can think of no one else I'd prefer to chat with. To my close friend Jeff McBride, I cannot express how much you have contributed to my research agenda. Your willingness to give of yourself to my lab is without a doubt the nicest thing anyone has ever done for me. I would be remiss if I did not thank my good friend Steve Plisk. You are the smartest strength coach I have ever met. Many of your ideas, philosophies, and works are quoted throughout this text. I have learned more from you than you know. To my friends in the United Kingdom, Clive Brewer and Ian Jeffreys, I thank you for all your support, for answering my multitude of questions about soccer, and for introducing me to the UKSCA.

I thank the many athletes, especially Mark Ernsting, Janna Jackson, Stephanie Hanos, Stephanie Burgess, and Domonic Van Neilen, who have trusted me with their athletic careers.

To my many students—in particular Blake Justice, Dr. Stephen Rossi, Dr. Naoki Kawamori, Mark Lehmkuhl, Dr. Alan Jung, Adam Ferrebee, Christina Harner, Dr. Tim Baghurst, Justin Kulik, Janna Jackson, David Powell, Lora McCoy, Ryan Hobbs, Kelsey Fowler, Michelle 'Meesh' Molinari, Ryan Ruben, and Adrian Whitley—I am more proud of your accomplishments than I am of my own. You have all affected my life in ways that are too numerous to count. Without your hard work and dedication, nothing could ever be accomplished.

I would like to thank our developmental editor, Amanda Ewing. I do not know how you do what you do. The process was difficult for us, and I thank you for your never-ending support and guidance. Without your help, we would never have been able to complete the final stages of this process.

Finally, I thank my parents, Guy and Sandy Haff, and my sister, Jennifer Haff. What an amazing journey it has been and continues to be. Dad, who would have thought that going to the YMCA with you to learn about lifting weights would lead to all this? Mom, thanks for always believing in me and keeping me on track. Jennifer, thank you for always challenging me to defend my beliefs.

G. Gregory Haff

Training Theory

The theoretical basis for training continues to expand as the scientific knowledge base about how the body responds to various stimuli increases. The information presented in the first five chapters establishes the foundation from which training plans can be developed. Chapter 1 explains the objectives of training, the adaptive process, and how the body supplies energy for physical activity. Chapter 2 presents the underlying basic principles of training, including the need for individualized training plans, how to develop a training model, and the importance of load progression and sequencing. Chapter 3 highlights the importance of physical, technical, tactical, and theoretical training in the overall training process. Chapter 4 examines the main variables that can be manipulated in a training plan, including volume, intensity, density, and complexity. Finally, Chapter 5 discusses the importance of rest and recovery to the training process and details the effects of overtraining and the role of recovery modalities.

CHAPTER 1

BASIS FOR TRAINING

The science of sport and the preparation of athletes is continuously evolving. This evolution is based largely upon an ever-expanding understanding of how the body adapts to different physical and psychological stressors. Contemporary sport scientists continue to explore the physiological and performance effects of different training interventions, recovery modalities, nutritional countermeasures, and biomechanical factors in order to increase the performance capacity of the modern athlete. As our understanding of the body's response to different stressors has grown, contemporary training theorists, sport scientists, and coaches have been able to expand upon the most basic concept of training.

Central to training theory is the idea that a structured system of training can be established that incorporates training activities that target specific physiological, psychological, and performance characteristics of individual sports and athletes. It follows that it is possible to modulate the adaptive process and direct specific training outcomes. This process of modulation and direction is facilitated by an understanding of the bioenergetic functions (how the body supplies energy) required to meet the physical demands of various physical activities. The coach who understands the **bioenergetic** properties of physical activity and sport as well as the impact of the timing of the presentation of training stimuli on the timeline for physical adaptation will have a greater chance of developing effective training plans.

SCOPE OF TRAINING

Athletes prepare to achieve a specific goal through structured and focused training. The intent of training is to increase the athlete's skills and work capacity to optimize athletic performance. Training is undertaken across a long period of time and involves many physiological, psychological, and sociological variables. During this time, training is progressively and individually graded. Throughout training, human physiological and psychological functions are modeled to meet demanding tasks.

Per the traditions of the ancient Olympic Games, athletes should strive to combine physical perfection with spiritual refinement and moral purity. Physical perfection signifies multilateral, harmonious development. The athlete acquires fine and varied skills, cultivates positive psychological qualities, and maintains good health. The athlete learns to cope with highly stressful stimuli in training and competitions. Physical excellence should evolve through an organized and well-planned training program based on practical experience and application of scientifically supported methods.

Paramount to training endeavors for novices and professionals is a realistic and achievable goal, planned according to individual abilities, psychological traits, and social environments. Some athletes seek to win a competition or improve previous performance; others consider gaining a technical skill or further developing a **biomotor ability**. Whatever the objective, each goal needs to be as precise and measurable as possible. In any plan, short or long term, the athlete needs to set goals and determine procedures for achieving these goals before beginning training. The deadline for achieving the final goal is the date of a major competition.

OBJECTIVES OF TRAINING

Training is a process by which an athlete is prepared for the highest level of performance possible (59, 109). The ability of a coach to direct the optimization of performance is achieved through the development of systematic training plans that draw upon knowledge garnered from a vast array of scientific disciplines, as shown in figure 1.1 (109).

The process of training targets the development of specific attributes correlated with the execution of various tasks (109). These specific attributes include: multilateral physical development, sport-specific physical development, technical skills, tactical abilities, psychological characteristics, health maintenance, injury resistance, and theoretical knowledge. The successful acquisition of these attributes is based upon utilizing means and methods that are individualized and appropriate for the athletes' age, experience, and talent level.

- *Multilateral Physical Development:* Multilateral development, or general fitness (109) as it is also known, provides the training foundation for success in all sports. This type of development targets the improvement of the basic biomotor abilities, such as endurance, strength, speed, flexibility, and coordination. Athletes who develop a strong foundation will be able to better tolerate sport-specific training activities and ultimately have a greater potential for athletic development.

- *Sport-Specific Physical Development:* Sport-specific physical development, or sport-specific fitness (109) as it is sometimes referred to, is the development of physiological or fitness characteristics that are specific to the sport. This type of training may target several specific needs of the sport such as strength, skill, endurance, speed, and flexibility (107,109). However, many sports require a blend-

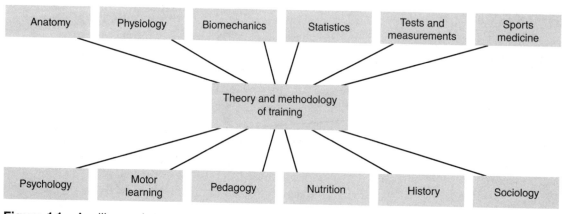

Figure 1.1 Auxiliary sciences.

ing of key aspects of performance, such as speed-strength, strength-endurance, or speed-endurance.

- **Technical Skills:** This training focuses on the development of the technical skills necessary for success in the sporting activity. The ability to perfect technical skills is based upon both multilateral and sport-specific physical development. For example, the ability to perform the iron cross in gymnastics appears to be limited by strength, one of the biomotor abilities (36). Ultimately the purpose of training that targets the development of technical skills is to perfect technique and allow for the optimization of the sport-specific skills necessary for successful athletic performance. The development of technique should occur under both normal and unusual conditions (e.g., weather, noise, etc.) and should always focus on perfecting the specific skills required by the sport.

- **Tactical Abilities:** The development of tactical abilities is also of particular importance to the training process. Training in this area is designed to improve competitive strategies and is based upon studying the tactics of opponents. Specifically, this type of training is designed to develop strategies that take advantage of the technical and physical capabilities of the athlete so that the chances of success in competition are increased.

- **Psychological Factors:** Psychological preparation is also necessary to ensure the optimization of physical performance. Some authors have also called this type of training personality development training (109); regardless of the terminology, the development of psychological characteristics such as discipline, courage, perseverence, and confidence are essential for successful athletic performance.

- **Health Maintenance:** The overall health of the athlete should be considered very important. Proper health can be maintained by periodic medical examinations and appropriate scheduling of training, including alternating between periods of hard work and periods of regeneration or restitution. Injuries and illness require specific attention and proper management of these occurrences is an important priority to consider during the training process.

- **Injury Resistance:** The best way to prevent injuries is to ensure that the athlete has developed the physical capacity and physiological characteristics necessary to participate in rigorous training and competition and to ensure appropriate application of training (61). The inappropriate application of training, which includes excessive loading, will increase the risk of injury. With young athletes it is crucial that multilateral physical development is targeted, as this allows for the development of biomotor abilities that will help decrease the potential for injury. Additionally, the management of fatigue appears to be of particular importance. When fatigue is high, the occurrence of injuries is markedly increased (103), therefore, the development of a training plans that manage fatigue should be considered to be of the utmost importance.

- **Theoretical Knowledge:** Training should increase the athletes' knowledge of the physiological and psychological basis of training, planning, nutrition, and regeneration. It is crucial that the athlete understand why certain training activities are being undertaken. This can be accomplished through discussing the training objectives established for each aspect of the training plan or by requiring the athlete to attend seminars and conferences about training. Arming the athlete with theoretical knowledge about the training process and the sport improves the likelihood that the athlete will make good personal decisions and approach the training process with a strong focus, which will allow the coach and athlete to better set training goals.

CLASSIFICATION OF SKILLS

Many ways have been suggested as methods for classifying physical activity skills. Aside from the traditional method of classifying sport actitivities into individual sports (track and field, gymnastics, boxing) and team sports (soccer, football, basketball, volleyball, rugby), a widely accepted classification uses biomotor abilities as a criterion. Biomotor abilities include strength, speed, endurance, and coordination (53). While classifying sports by biomotor abilities is very useful, other methods are also used by coaches. One popular method is to classify sporting skills as either cyclic, acyclic, or acyclic combined.

- **Cyclic skills** are used in sports such as walking, running, cross-country skiing, speedskating, swimming, rowing, cycling, kayaking, and canoeing. The main characteristic of these sports is that the motor act involves repetitive movements. Once the athlete learns one cycle of the motor act, they can duplicate it continually for long periods. Each cycle consists of distinct, identical phases that are repeated in succession. For example, the four phases of a rowing stroke; the catch, drive through the water, finish, and recovery; are part of a whole. The athlete performs them over and over in the same succession during the cyclic motion of rowing. Each cycle the athlete performs is linked; it is preceded and followed by another one.

- **Acyclic skills** show up in sports such as shot putting, discus throwing, most gymnastics, team sports, wrestling, boxing, and fencing. These skills consist of integral functions performed in one action. For instance, the skill of discus throwing incorporates the preliminary swing, transition, turn, delivery, and reverse step, but the athlete performs them all in one action.

- **Acyclic combined skills** consist of cyclic movements followed by an acyclic movement. Sports such as figure skating, diving, jumping events in track and field, and tumbling lines and vaulting in gymnastics use acyclic combined skills. Although all actions are linked, we can easily distinguish between the acyclic and cyclic movements. For instance, we can distinguish the acyclic movement of a high jumper or vaulter from the preceding cyclic approach of running.

The coach's comprehension of these skill classifications plays an important role in the selection of appropriate teaching methods. Generally, teaching the skill as a whole appears to be effective with cyclic skills, while breaking the skill into smaller pieces appears to be more effective with acyclic skills. For example, when working with javelin throwers the standing throw should be mastered prior to the three-step stride approach, the six-step approach, and the full approach (38).

SYSTEM OF TRAINING

A system is an organized, methodically arranged set of ideas, theories, or speculations. The development of a system is based upon scientific findings coupled with accumulated practical experience. A system should not be imported, although it may be beneficial to study other systems before developing one. Furthermore, in creating or developing a better system, you must consider a country's social and cultural background.

Bonderchuck (9) suggested that a system of training is constructed by observing three basic principles: 1) uncovering the system's forming factors, 2) determining the system's structure, and 3) validating the efficacy or effects of the system.

- ***Uncovering the System's Forming Factors.*** Factors that are central to the development of the training system can stem from general knowledge about the theory and methods of training, scientific findings, experiences of the nation's best coaches, and the approaches used by other countries.

- ***Determining the System's Structure.*** Once the factors central to the success of the training system are established, the actual training system can be constructed. A model for both short- and long-term training should be created. The system should be able to be applied by all coaches, but it should also be flexible enough that coaches can enrich the system's structure based upon their own experiences.

The sport scientist plays a crucial role in the establishment of a training system. Research, especially applied research, increases the knowledge base from which the training system is developed and further evolved. Additionally, the sport scientist can aid in the development of athlete-monitoring programs and talent-identification programs, the establishment of training theories, and the development of methods for dealing with fatigue and stress. While the importance of sport science to the overall training system seems apparent, this branch of science is not embraced with equal enthusiasm throughout the world. For, example Stone et al. (110) suggested that the use of sport science in the United States is on the decline, which may explain, at least in part, the decrease in performance levels evidenced by some U.S. athletes at some of the recent Olympic Games.

- ***Validating the Efficiency of the System.*** Once a training system is initiated, it should be constantly evaluated. The evaluation of the efficacy of a training system can be undertaken in a multidimensional manner. The most simplistic assessments used to validate a training system are the actual performance improvements achieved in response to the system. More complex assessments can also be used, including direct measurements of physiological adaptation, such as hormonal or cell signaling adaptations. Additionally, mechanical assessments can be quantified to determine if the training structure is working effectively; examples include the evaluation of maximal anaerobic power, maximal aerobic power, maximal force generating capacity, and peak rate of force development. Sport scientists can play a very important role in this capacity, using their expertise to evaluate the athlete and provide insight into how effective a training system is. If the training system is not optimal, then the performance enhancement team can reevaluate and modify the system.

As a whole the quality of the training system depends on direct and supportive factors (figure 1.2). Direct factors include those related to both training and evaluation, while supportive factors are related to administration and economic conditions and to professional and living styles. Although each factor in the overall system plays a role in the success of the system, it appears that the direct factors are most significant. The importance of the direct factors further strengthens the argument that the sport scientist is an important contributor to the development of a quality training system.

The development of a quality training system is essential to the optimization of performance. Training quality does not solely depend upon the coach, but upon the interaction of many factors that can impact the athlete's performance (figure 1.3). Hence, all factors that could affect the quality of training need to be effectively implemented and constantly evaluated and, when necessary, adjusted to meet the ever-changing demands of modern athletics.

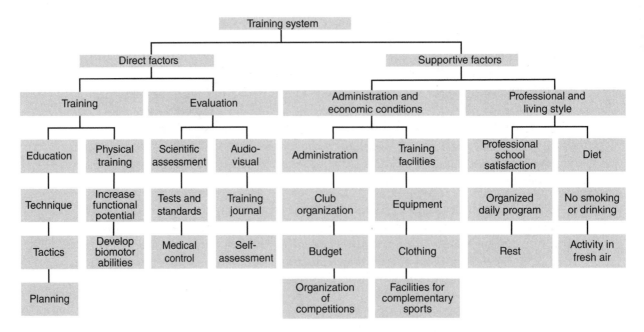

Figure 1.2 Components of a training system.

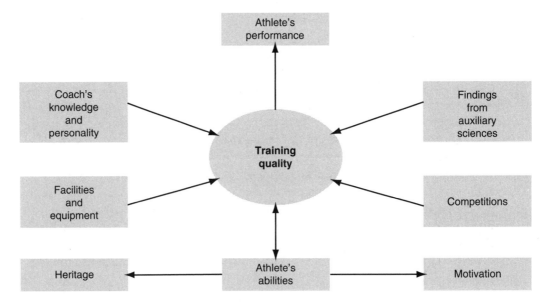

Figure 1.3 Factors that affect training quality.

ADAPTATION

Training is an organized process whereby the body and mind are constantly exposed to stressors of varied volume (quantity) and intensity. The ability of an athlete to adapt and to adjust to workloads imposed by training and competition is as important as the ability of a species to adapt to the environment in which it lives—no adaptation, no survival! For athletes, an inability to adapt to constantly varying training loads and the stressors associated with training and competition will result in critical levels of **fatigue**, **overreaching**, or even **overtraining**. In such circumstances, the athlete will be unable to achieve training goals.

A high level of performance is the result of many years of well-planned, methodical, and challenging training. During this time, the athlete tries to adapt her physiology to the specific requirements of her sport. The greater the degree of adaptation to the training process, the greater the potential for high levels of performance. Therefore, the objective of any well-organized training plan is to induce adaptations that improve performance. Improvement is possible only if the athlete observes this sequence:

Increasing stimulus (load) $\Rightarrow$ adaptation $\Rightarrow$ performance improvement.

If the load is always at the same level, adaptation occurs in the early part of training, followed by a plateau (stagnation) without any further improvement (figure 1.4):

Lack of stimulus $\Rightarrow$ plateau $\Rightarrow$ lack of improvement.

If the stimulus is excessive or overly varied, the athlete will be unable to adapt and maladaptation will occur:

Excessive stimulus $\Rightarrow$ maladaptation $\Rightarrow$ decrease in performance.

Therefore, the objective of training is to progressively and systematically increase the training stimulus (the intensity, volume of training loads, and frequency of training) to induce superior adaptation and, as a result, improve performance. These alterations in the training stimulus must include training variation to maximize the athlete's adaptation to the training plan (figure 1.5).

Training adaptations are the sum of the transformations brought about by systematically repeating bouts of exercise. These structural and physiological changes result from the specific demands that athletes place on their bodies by the activities they pursue, depending on the volume, intensity, and frequency of training. Physical training is beneficial only as long as it overloads the body in such a way that adaption is stimulated. If the stimulus does not induce a sufficient physiological challenge, no increase in adaptation can be expected. On the other hand, if the training load is very high, intolerable, and undertaken for an excessively long period of time, injury or overtraining may occur.

Specificity of Adaptation

Because adaptation is highly specific to the type of training undertaken, training must be based on the energy systems dominant in the sport, the skills of the sport, and the motor abilities required by the sport. The time required to reach a high degree

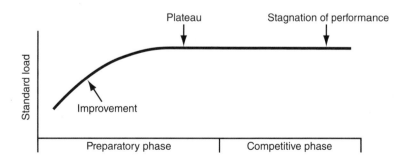

Figure 1.4 A standard load results in improvements only during the early part of the plan.

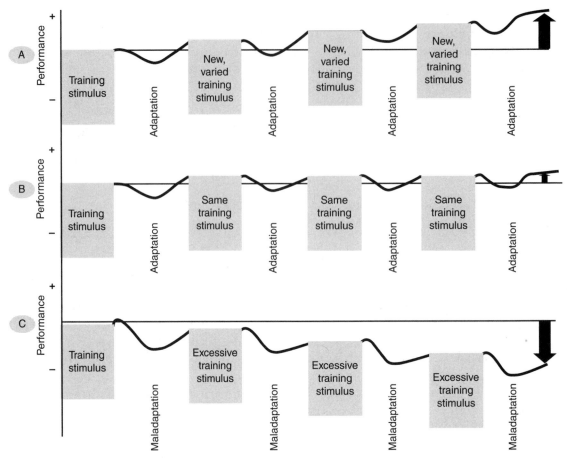

Figure 1.5 Training stimulus and adaptation.

(a) Increasing stimulus (load) ⇒ adaptation ⇒ performance improvement. *(b)* Lack of stimulus ⇒ plateau ⇒ lack of improvement. *(c)* Excessive stimulus ⇒ maladaptation ⇒ decrease in performance. ↑ = increased performance; ↓ = decreased performance.

of adaptation depends on the skill complexity and the physiological and psychological difficulty of the sport. The more complex and difficult the sport, the longer the training time required for the human body to adapt.

If an athlete expects superior performance, he must be exposed to a systematic and progressive increase in training stimuli that is designed to elevate the athlete's physiological and performance capacity (i.e., cross the threshold of adaptation). Therefore, it is of utmost importance that a systematic and well-organized training program be followed to induce superior adaptations of the main functions of the body, such as the following:

• *Neuromuscular:* Increase the efficiency of movements and coordination, increase the reflex activity of the nervous system, synchronize motor unit activity, increase recruitment of motor units, increase **motor unit** firing rate (**rate coding**), increase muscle **hypertrophy**, increase mitochondrial biogenesis, alter cell signaling pathways (19).

• *Metabolic:* Increase the muscular stores of **adenosine triphosphate** (ATP) and **phosphocreatine** (PCr), increase the capacity of muscle to store glycogen, increase the capacity of muscle to tolerate **lactic acid** buildup and delay the onset of fatigue, increase the capillary network for a superior supply of nutrients and oxygen, increase the use of fat as energy for long-duration activities, increase the efficiency of the **glycolytic energy system**, increase efficiency of the **oxidative system**, and alter specific enzymatic processes associated with the various bioenergetic systems on page 21 (87).

- *Cardiorespiratory:* Increase lung volume, increase hypertrophy of the left ventricular wall, increase volume of the left ventricle to increase stroke volume and, as a result, facilitate delivery of oxygenated blood to the working muscles, decrease heart rate, increase capillary density, increase the lactate threshold so that the athlete can perform at a higher rate of oxygen consumption, and increase $\dot{V}O_2max$ to enhance aerobic capacity for prolonged exercises.

The focus of any training program is to improve performance. This is only possible by breaking the threshold of the present level of adaptation by exposing the athlete to higher training demands (e.g., use high training loads, greater than 80% in strength training; increase duration of training or its intensity in endurance sports; or increase the percentage of maximum speed and agility through training). When an athlete achieves a new level of adaptation, her performance will improve (figure 1.6).

Adaptation is a long-term, progressive physiological response to general and sport-specific training programs with the goal of readying the athlete for the specific demands of competition. Adaptation occurs through positive changes of the main functions of the body. Training phases—preparatory and competitive—are combined with different types of adaptations:

- *Preadaptation:* gradual and temporary adaptation to training during the early part of a training plan (in this case an annual plan). If training load and the physiological stressors that result from it are not excessive, these early weeks of training will progressively lead to a more durable adaptation visible via increased work capacity and improved tolerance to higher training demand.

- *Compensation:* the body's reactions to a training program before reaching a stable adaptation. During this phase, still in the early part of the preparatory phase, the athlete experiences positive reactions to the training demand and thus improved results in testing and skills proficiency. At this time, the body can compensate for high training demands as a demonstration of the athlete's improved training potential and increased physiological efficiency.

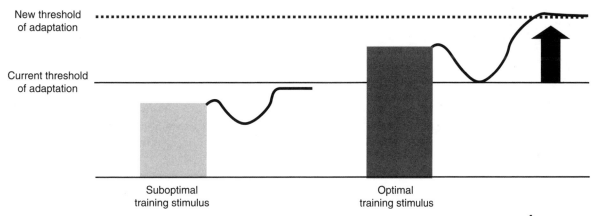

Figure 1.6 Breaking the threshold of adaptation should improve performance. ⬆ = increase in the threshold of adaptation.

• *Stable or precompetitive adaptation:* a phase of improved equilibrium between work and compensation, between high stressors and the ability to tolerate and recover from them. Many training loads and social or psychological stressors have to be planned and applied at the same levels as during competition so that the athletes can learn to react to and cope with them. Exhibition games and competitions should be used to test both technical and tactical proficiency and physiological and psychological efficiency. High levels of stability of all training factors indicate that athletes are in, or are close to reaching, the state of readiness to compete in the competitions that are scheduled for the next phase.

• *State of readiness for competitions:* the result of the athlete's training. The athlete is ready to compete with high technical efficacy, demonstrates high levels of athletic effectiveness, displays sport-specific motor skills and physical qualities, and is able to tolerate stress and adapt to it.

Training Effect

Any training program creates a certain reaction to the adaptive responses of the body; this is called a *training effect*. Since the 1960s several authors have discussed this subject, among them H.K. Cooper with his very influential work *The New Aerobics* (22).

Training effect can be classified into three categories:

•*Immediate training effect* can be detected during and immediately after a training session in the form of physiological reaction to a training load, such as increased heart rate, increased blood pressure, decreased force production as a result of fatigue, increased fatigue, and depletion of muscle glycogen depending on the intensity and volume of the training bout.

•*Delayed training effect* is the final outcome of a training session that can be long lasting. Although the immediate posttraining effect is reduced because of fatigue, the delayed training effect, meaning the positive training benefits, is apparent after the fatigue associated with training dissipates. The onset of the delayed training effect depends on the training bout: The more intense the training session, the longer the time frame before performance gains are realized (42, 43).

•*Cumulative effect* is the result of several sessions or even phases of training, which can include sessions with very challenging loads that are meant to break the threshold of adaptation of a given

OLIVIER LABALETTE/DPPI/Icon SMI

World-record holder Lance Armstrong spent many years training as a cyclist. The cumulative effect of that training was winning 7 Tour de France races.

training phase. The occurrence of the cumulative training effect often surprises coaches and athletes alike, who may not be able to anticipate or explain it ("We have worked hard and suddenly it just happened!"). Good planning of training sessions, altering high loads and intensities with compensation sessions, will allow the athlete to benefit from the cumulative training effect.

Zatsiorsky and Kraemer (119) proposed that the relationship between fatigue and training gains is a factor of 3:1, meaning that fatigue is three times shorter in duration (e.g., 24 hr) than the positive training effect (e.g., 72 hr). Certainly, the type of training can change this ratio because anaerobic training is more demanding and thus more fatiguing. In any case, the positive effects of a training session are visible after fatigue is eliminated; adaptation then can take place, accompanied by improved performance.

Cooper (22) used five categories to assess the postexercise training effect. He suggested that the athlete accumulate 30 points a week to achieve a good training effect (e.g., 2 × category 5 = 10 points; 2 × category 3 = 6 points) (table 1.1).

Thus, training effects are complex phenomena with short- and long-lasting influences that can be determined by the following:

- One's current functional or training state
- The effects of previous training bouts
- The sum of all training stimuli (loads) or their combinations, their order of application, and the interval between them

SUPERCOMPENSATION CYCLE AND ADAPTATION

The training phenomenon called *supercompensation*, also known as Weigert's law of supercompensation, was first described by Folbrot in 1941 (107) and later was discussed by Hans Selye (104), who called it the *general adaptation syndrome*. Several Russian, East German, and American (40) researchers and authors have also shed more light on this essential training concept.

Table 1.1 Cooper's Training Effect Categories

	Category	Training effect	Results
1	1.0-1.9	Minor	Develops base endurance. No improvement in maximum performance. Enhances recovery.
2	2.0-2.9	Maintenance	Maintains aerobic fitness. Does little to improve maximum performance.
3	3.0-3.9	Improvement	Improves aerobic fitness if repeated two to four times weekly.
4	4.0-4.9	Rapid improvement	Rapidly improves aerobic fitness if repeated one or two times weekly. Needs few recovery sessions.
5	5.0-up	Overreaching	Dramatically increases aerobic fitness if combined with good recovery.

From THE NEW AEROBICS by Kenneth H. Cooper, copyright © 1970 by Kenneth H. Cooper. Used by permission of Bantam Books, a division of Random House, Inc.

Selye's **general adaptive syndrome (GAS)** theory (figure 1.7) is the basis of **progressive overloading**, which if applied inappropriately can create high degrees of undesirable stress. These concepts suggest that for the best training adaptations to occur, training loads, training volumes, and bioenergetic specificity have to be systematically alternated. For example, the coach should plan training blocks that alter high, moderate, and low training intensities. These alternations of intensities allow for recovery between training sessions, and the addition of recovery time between carefully sequenced training phases is the basis for cyclical planning (known as *periodization*) and supercompensation.

Supercompensation, therefore, is a relationship between work and regeneration that leads to superior physical adaptation as well as metabolic and neuropsychological arousal before a competition. Applying the concept of supercompensation in training has many benefits:

- Helps the athlete manage stress and cope with high training intensities
- Helps coaches create structured training systems
- Avoids the onset of critical levels of fatigue and overtraining
- Makes a coach cognizant of the need to alternate intensities to facilitate the best adaptations
- Justifies the use of different types of posttraining and postcompetition recovery techniques (e.g., passive and active rest, nutrition, physiotherapy, psychological techniques)
- Facilitates precompetition training to achieve peak performance
- Uses both physiological and psychological techniques in training

When athletes train, they are exposed to a series of stimuli that alter their physiological status. These physiological responses can include acute metabolic (28, 40, 96, 113), hormonal (46, 52), cardiovascular (88), neuromuscular (32, 48, 49), and cell

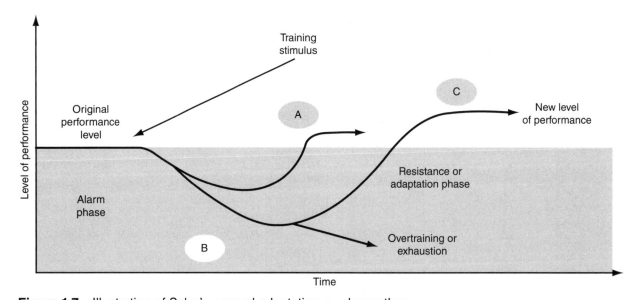

Figure 1.7 Illustration of Selye's general adaptation syndrome theory.
A = typical training; B = overtraining; C = overreaching or supercompensation.
Adapted, by permission, from A.C. Fry, 1998, The role of training intensity in resistance exercise overtraining and overreaching. In *Overtraining in sport*, edited by R.B. Kreider, A.C. Fry, and M.L. O'Toole (Champaign, IL: Human Kinetics), 114.

signaling alterations (5). These physiological responses to training are mitigated by the volume, intensity, frequency, and type of training undertaken by the athlete. The greater the volume, intensity, or duration of training, the greater the magnitude of the physiological responses to training.

The acute physiological responses to a training session will result in the accumulation of fatigue (33, 84), which can manifest itself as an inability to produce or maintain maximal voluntary force output (48, 49, 92, 93). The postexercise period also is associated with a reduction in muscle **glycogen** stores (56), lactic acid accumulation (112, 116), reductions in PCr stores (64, 72), and an increase in circulating **cortisol** levels (3, 54, 94). These physiological responses temporarily reduce the athlete's performance capacity.

Following the training session, the athlete must dissipate fatigue, restore muscle glycogen and phosphagen stores, reduce circulating cortisol levels, and deal with the lactic acid that has accumulated. The time that the athlete needs to recover is affected by many factors, which can include the training status of the athlete (49), the muscular contraction type encountered during the training session (92), the use of restoration techniques, and the nutritional status of the athlete (12). Nutritional status is of particular importance, because an inadequate diet can increase the time needed for recovery (13).

The fatigue induced by exercise results in an abrupt drop in the athlete's homeostasis curve (figure 1.8), which is coupled with a reduction in functional capacity. Following the exercise bout, the return of the athlete to homeostasis can be considered a period of compensation. The return to homeostasis, or a normal biological state, is slow and progressive, requiring several hours to several days (93). If the time between high-intensity training sessions is sufficient, the body dissipates fatigue and fully replaces the energy sources (especially glycogen), allowing the body to rebound into a state of supercompensation.

Every time supercompensation occurs, the athlete establishes a new, increased homeostatic level with positive benefits for training and performance. Consider supercompensation as the foundation of a functional increase of athletic efficiency, resulting from the body's adaptation to the training stimulus (load) and the replenishment of glycogen stores in the muscle. If the resulting phase or the time between two stimuli is too long, supercompensation will fade, leading to **involution,** or a reduction in performance capacity.

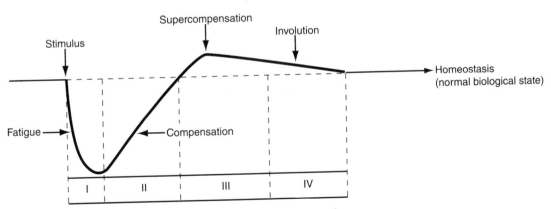

Figure 1.8   Supercompensation cycle of a training session.
Modified from N. Yakovlev, 1967, *Sports biochemistry.* Leipzig: Deutche Hochschule für Körpekultur.

Phases of Supercompensation

The *supercompensation cycle* (figure 1.9) has four phases and occurs in the following sequence.

Phase 1. Duration: 1 to 2 hr

After training, the body experiences fatigue. Exercise-induced fatigue occurs via either central or peripheral mechanisms (32). Fatigue is a multidimensional phenomenon caused by several factors:

- Reductions in neural activation of the muscle, which are generally associated with central fatigue, can occur in response to exercise (49).
- Exercise-induced central fatigue can also increase brain serotonin levels, which can lead to mental fatigue (32). This accumulated mental fatigue can affect the athlete's willingness to tolerate high levels of discomfort or pain associated with training and competition.
- Exercise can result in impairments in neuromuscular transmission and impulse propagation, impaired Ca^{2+} handling by the **sarcoplasmic reticulum**, substrate depletion, and other factors that disrupt the contractile process and are associated with exercise-induced peripheral fatigue (31).
- Exercise-induced substrate utilization occurs in response to the intensity, volume, and duration of the exercise bout. Substrates that can be significantly affected

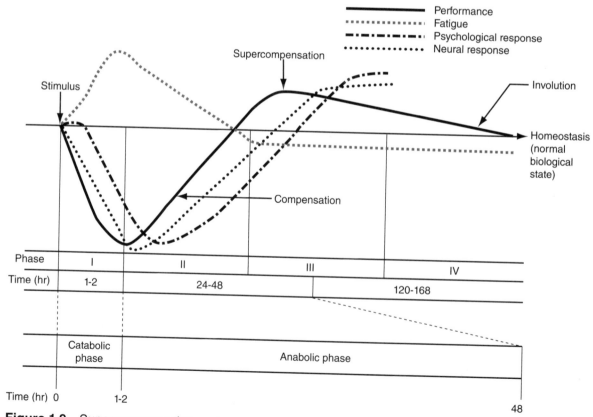

Figure 1.9 Supercompensation cycle response to a training session.

include muscle glycogen and phosphocreatine stores. Muscle glycogen can be significantly reduced in response to high-intensity interval training (11, 108), resistance training (55, 83), and endurance training (23, 27). Phosphocreatine stores can be significantly reduced in as little as 5 to 30 s and can be completely depleted after exhaustive exercise (64, 73, 74).

- The classic literature suggests that lactic acid accumulation as a result of exercise is a major player in the formation of fatigue (116). It is theorized that higher levels of lactic acid formation cause a state of acidosis, which may decrease force-generating capacity as a result of alterations in contractile properties (112, 116). Contemporary literature suggests that inorganic phosphate (P_i), which is formed from the breakdown of PCr, rather than acidosis, may be the major cause of muscle fatigue that occurs in response to exercise (116). Increased P_i concentrations appear to affect sarcoplasmic reticulum handling of Ca^{2+} (6, 30). It has also been suggested that P_i can reduce **cross-bridge** attachment force as a result of a decrease in myofibrillar Ca^{2+} sensitivity (116).

- During prolonged exercise there is an increase in glucose uptake despite a decrease in the amount of circulating insulin (75). Glucose uptake is thought to be facilitated during exercise as a result of **glucose transporter-4 (GLUT4)** (111). GLUT is contraction sensitive and facilitates the uptake of glucose by the working tissue (111).

- During exercise, whether endurance training or resistance training, significant eccentric exercise components can result in muscle damage (18). Examples of exercises that have the potential to increase muscle damage, resulting in **delayed-onset muscle soreness (DOMS)**, are downhill running and lowering weights in resistance training. Impairments in exercise performance in response to muscle damage and DOMS can last for up to 24 hr depending on the degree of muscle damage (47, 85). It has been hypothesized that the inflammation associated with muscle damage plays a role in muscle repair (18).

Phase II. Duration: 24 to 48 hr
As soon as training is terminated the compensation (rest) phase begins. During the compensation phase the following occur:

- Within 3 to 5 min of the cessation of exercise, ATP stores are completely restored (60, 66), and within 8 min PCr is completely resynthesized (60). Very high-intensity exercise may require up to 15 min of recovery after exercise for PCr to be completely restored (89). Depending on the volume, intensity, and type of training, the ATP and PCr pool may be increased above normal levels (1, 2).

- Within 2 hr after exercise bouts with large **stretch shortening cycle (SSC)** components, such as jumping, electromyographic (EMG) activity is partially restored as well as maximal voluntary contraction (MVC) (93). However, SSC-induced fatigue as indicated by depressed EMG and MVC exhibits a bimodal recovery, with the first recovery occurring within 2 hr and the final recovery taking 6 to 8 days (93).

- Muscle glycogen usually is restored to basal levels within 20 to 24 hr (13, 29). If extensive muscle damage occurs, more time is needed for muscle glycogen recovery (25). The rate at which muscle glycogen is restored is directly related to the amount of carbohydrate consumed during the compensation period (26).

- An increase in oxygen consumption following exercise, known as **excess postexercise oxygen consumption (EPOC)**, occurs in response to the exercise bout (77). Depending on the modality and intensity of the exercise bout, EPOC can remain elevated for 24 to 38 hr after the cessation of exercise (14, 77, 90).

- Resting energy expenditure is elevated as a result of a resistance training or endurance training bout. This elevation in energy expenditure can be expected to last 15 to 48 hr depending on the magnitude of the training bout (71, 91). Although the exact mechanism for stimulating an elevation in resting energy expenditure is not known, some authors have suggested that increased protein synthesis (81), increased thermogenesis from the thyroid hormones (80), and increased sympathetic nervous system activity (102) play a role in increasing the rate of energy expenditure after exercise.

- After a resistance training bout an increased protein synthesis rate occurs (17, 81). By 4 hr postexercise the muscle protein synthesis rate is increased by 50%, and by 24 hr it is elevated by 109%. The protein resynthesis rate returns to baseline by 36 hr (81). Thus, it is thought that this phase of the supercompensation cycle is the initiation of the anabolic phase.

Phase III. Duration: 36 to 72 hr

This phase of training is marked by a rebounding or supercompensation of performance.

- Force-generating capacity and muscle soreness have returned to baseline by 72 hr postexercise (118).

- Psychological supercompensation occurs, which can be marked by high confidence, feelings of being energized, positive thinking, and an ability to cope with frustrations and the stress of training.

- Glycogen stores are fully replenished, enabling the athlete to rebound (12).

Phase IV. Duration: 3 to 7 days

If the athlete does not apply another stimulus at the optimal time (during the supercompensation phase), then involution occurs, which is a decrease in the physiological benefits obtained during the supercompensation phase. By 6 to 8 days post-stretch shortening cycle (SSC) performance, the second rebound in electromyographic and maximal voluntary contraction strength occurs (93).

Following the optimal stimuli of a training session, the recovery period, including the supercompensation phase, is approximately 24 hr. Variations in the duration of the supercompensation phase depend on the type and intensity of training. For instance, following a medium-intensity aerobic endurance training session, supercompensation may occur after approximately 6 to 8 hr. On the other hand, intense activity that places a high demand on the central nervous system may require more than 24 hr, sometimes as much as 48 hr, for supercompensation to occur.

Elite athletes who follow training programs that do not allow 24 hr between training sessions do not experience supercompensation after every training session because they must undertake a second workout before supercompensation can occur. As suggested in figure 1.10, the improvement rate is higher when athletes participate in more frequent training sessions (50). When long intervals exist between training sessions, such as when training is performed three times per week (figure 1.10*a*), the athlete will experience less overall improvement than when training is undertaken more frequently (figure 1.10*b*) (50, 97). When less time exists between training sessions, the coach or athlete must alternate the intensity of the training sessions, which effectively alters the energy demands of the session, as suggested in the planning of microcycles.

If the athlete is exposed to high-intensity training sessions too frequently, the body's ability to adapt to the training stimuli will be significantly compromised and overtraining may occur (41, 44, 45). As illustrated in figure 1.11, frequent maximal-intensity stimuli can result in exhaustion or overtraining, which will lead to a decrease in performance. Recent research on the training adaptations experienced in response to resistance training supports this contention (69, 97). This research suggests that when maximal attempts are undertaken too frequently, there is a significant reduction in the athlete's ability to adapt to the training program (97). Couple this finding with previous work on high-intensity overtraining (41, 44, 45) and it is clear that training at high intensities too frequently does not maximize the athlete's performance. Some overzealous coaches, who intend to project an image of being tough and hard working, believe that athletes must reach exhaustion in each workout ("No pain, no gain!"). Under such circumstances, athletes never have time to compensate because of the high levels of fatigue generated. As fatigue increases, the athlete will require longer time for regeneration. If additional hard training sessions are added too frequently, the time for restoration continues to lengthen. Thus, a better practice is to intersperse lower-intensity training sessions into the training plan so that compensation and ultimately supercompensation can occur.

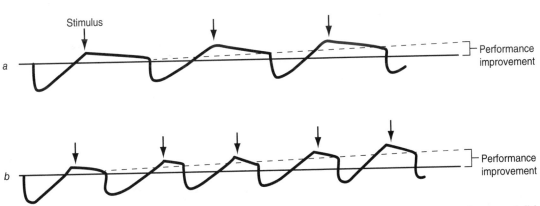

Figure 1.10   The sum of training effect. *(a)* Long intervals between training sessions and *(b)* short intervals between training sessions.
Adapted from Harre 1982 (59).

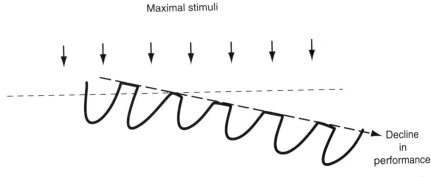

Figure 1.11   Decline in performance from prolonged maximal-intensity stimuli.

To maximize the athlete's performance the coach must regularly challenge the athlete's physiology, which elevates the ceiling of adaptation and, ultimately, performance (figure 1.12). This means that the coach must alternate high-intensity training with lower-intensity training. If done appropriately, this schedule will enhance compensation and lead to a supercompensation effect. As the athlete adapts to training, new levels of homeostasis will be achieved and higher training levels will be required for adaptation to continue (97). As the athlete adapts to new, higher levels of training, a new supercompensation cycle will begin (figure 1.13). Conversely, if the intensity of training is not planned well, the compensation curve will not surpass the previous levels of homeostasis and the athlete will not benefit from the supercompensation (figure 1.14).

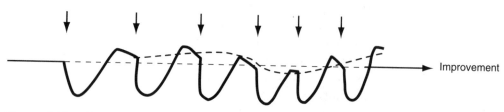

Figure 1.12 Alternating maximal- and low-intensity stimuli produces a wavelike improvement curve.

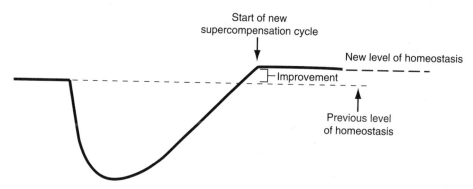

Figure 1.13 A new, higher level of homeostasis means that the next supercompensation cycle starts from that point.

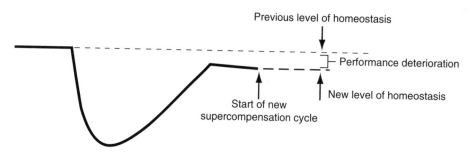

Figure 1.14 A decreased level of homeostasis means that the next supercompensation cycle starts at a point lower than the previous level.

High levels of fatigue resulting from continuous or too frequent high-intensity training will attenuate the supercompensation effects and prevent the athlete from achieving peak performance.

SOURCES OF ENERGY

Energy provides an athlete the capacity to perform work. **Work** is the application of force, that is, contracting muscles to apply force against a resistance. Energy is a prerequisite for performing physical work during training and competitions. Ultimately, we derive energy from converting foodstuff at the muscle cell level into a high-energy compound known as **adenosine triphosphate (ATP)**, which is then stored in the muscle cell. ATP, as its name suggests, consists of one molecule of adenosine and three molecules of phosphate.

Energy required for muscular contraction is released by converting high-energy ATP into ADP + P_i (adenosine diphosphate + inorganic phosphate). As one phosphate bond is broken, causing ADP and P_i to split, energy is released. The amount of ATP stored in muscle is limited, so the body must continually replenish ATP stores to enable physical activity.

The body can replenish ATP stores by any of the three energy systems, depending on the type of physical activity: the phosphagen (ATP-PC) system, the glycolytic system, and the oxidative system (figure 1.15).

Phosphagen (ATP-PC) System

The primary anaerobic energy system is the **phosphagen system (ATP-PC)**. The phosphagen system contains three basic reactions that are used in the processing of ATP. The first reaction results in the breakdown of ATP into **adenosine diphosphate (ADP)** and P_i, resulting in a release of energy. Because the skeletal muscle has limited ATP stores, further reactions are needed to maintain ATP availability. The second reaction is used to resynthesize ATP from ADP and **phosphocreatine** (creatine phosphate or **PCr**). In this scenario a phosphate is removed from the PCr, forming P_i and creatine (C). The P_i that is formed by this process is then added to ADP and an ATP molecule is formed. The final reaction that can occur breaks ADP into adenosine monophosphate and P_i, after which the P_i can again be added to ADP, resulting in the formation of ATP.

Because skeletal muscle can store only a small amount of ATP, energy depletion occurs in as little as 10 s of high-intensity work (87), whereas PCr can be decreased by 50% to 70% of initial values in as little as 5 s of high-intensity exercise and can be almost completely depleted in response to intense exhaustive exercise (64, 73, 74). Interestingly, the highest contribution to ATP production by PCr occurs in the first 2 s of the initiation of exercise; by 10 s of exercise the ability of PCr to supply ATP is decreased by 50%, and by 30 s of exercise PCr contributes very little to the supply of ATP. At around 10 s, the glycolytic system's contribution to ATP supply begins to increase (87).

The phosphagen system appears to be the primary energy source for extremely high-intensity activities, such as short sprints (e.g., 100 m dash, 40 m dash), diving, American football, weightlifting, jumping and throwing events in track and field, vaulting in gymnastics, and ski jumping.

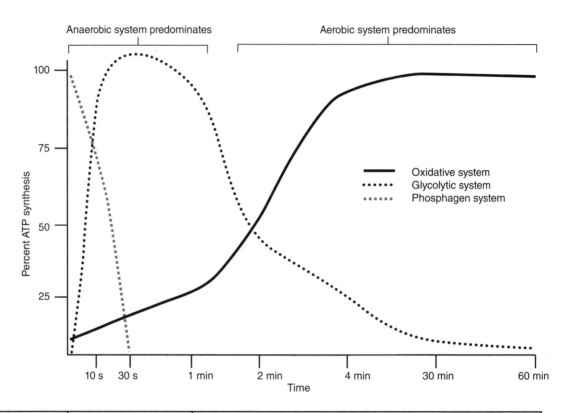

Figure 1.15 Main sources of energy in sport activity.

Adapted from McArdle, Katch, and Katch 2007 (88) and from Brooks et al. 2000 (10).

The replenishment of the phosphagen stores is usually a rapid process, with 70% restoration of ATP occurring in about 30 s and complete restoration occurring within 3 to 5 min of exercise (65). The restoration of PCr takes longer, with 2 min for 84% restoration, 4 min for 89% restoration, and 8 min for complete restoration (58, 65, 66). Restoration of the phosphagens occurs mostly via aerobic metabolism (60). However, the glycolytic system may also contribute to the restoration of the phosphagen pool after high-intensity exercise (34, 60).

Glycolytic System

The second anaerobic energy system is the **glycolytic system**, which is the prevalent energy system for activities that last from 20 s to about 2 min (87). The primary fuel

To perform well, an athlete must replenish her energy sources through proper nutrition and hydration.

for the glycolytic system comes from the breakdown of blood glucose and glycogen stores (109). Initially, the vast majority of ATP is supplied from **fast glycolysis**, and as the duration of activity approaches 2 min, the supply of ATP primarily comes from **slow glycolysis**.

Fast glycolysis results in the formation of **lactic acid**, which is rapidly converted to **lactate** (20). When glycolysis occurs at a very rapid rate, the body's ability to convert lactic acid to lactate may become impaired and lactic acid will begin to accumulate, which can result in fatigue and ultimately a cessation of activity (109). The accumulation of lactic acid is most prevalent in repeated high-intensity exercise bouts, especially those with short rest duration (63, 76). Thus, a high concentration of lactic acid may indicate a rapid energy supply.

As the duration of the activity increases toward the 2 min mark, the supply of ATP shifts from fast glycolysis to slow glycolysis. Theoretically, as the intensity of the bout of exercise is decreased and the rate of glycolytic breakdown of glucose and glycogen is slowed, thus reducing the buildup of lactic acid and allowing the body to buffer lactic acid to lactate and form pyruvate (20, 109). Once pyruvate is formed it is shuttled into the **mitochondria**, where it is used in oxidative metabolism. Lactate is also shuttled to the liver, where it is converted into glucose, or goes to active tissue such as the skeletal and heart muscle, where it is converted to pyruvate and ultimately used in oxidative metabolism (87).

The amount of glycogen available is related to the amount of carbohydrates present in the diet (26). Thus, it is easy to see that low-carbohydrate diets will result in a reduction of muscle glycogen stores, which will impair the athlete's performance (57). The utilization of glycogen during exercise and competition depends on the duration and intensity of the exercise bout (56, 105, 106). Aerobic exercise (51) and anaerobic exercise such as repeated sprint intervals (3) and resistance training (56) can significantly affect muscle and liver glycogen stores. Following exercise, one of the major concerns for athletes and coaches is the time frame for glycogen resynthesis. If the athlete does not replenish glycogen stores, performance can be significantly impaired. Inadequate muscle glycogen stores have been linked to exercise-induced muscle weakness (117), decreases in isokinetic force production (70), and decreases in isometric strength (62).

After the completion of an exercise bout, it generally takes between 20 and 24 hr for muscle glycogen to be completely restored (29). If, however, inadequate carbohydrate is present in the diet or excessive exercise-induced muscle damage occurs, the time required for glycogen restoration can be significantly extended (24, 26). In the 2 hr after the cessation of exercise, the athlete has a great opportunity to increase muscle glycogen synthesis rates. Ivy and colleagues (68) suggested that if carbohydrates are consumed within 2 hr of the completion of exercise, muscle glycogen storage can increase 45%. This may be particularly important when the athlete has only a short period of time between exercise bouts or competitive bouts on the same day (56).

Oxidative System

Much like the glycolytic system, the **oxidative system** has the ability to use blood glucose and muscle glycogen as fuel sources for producing ATP. The major difference between the glycolytic and oxidative systems is that the enzymatic reactions associated with the oxidative system occur in the presence of O_2, whereas the glycolytic system processes energy without O_2 (10). Unlike the fast glycolytic system, the oxidative system does not produce lactic acid from the breakdown of glucose and glycogen. Additionally, the oxidative system has the ability to use fats and proteins in the production of ATP (109).

At rest, the oxidative systems derives about 70% of its ATP yield from the oxidation of fats and about 30% of its ATP from the oxidation of carbohydrate (10, 109). Fuel utilization depends on the intensity of exercise. Brooks and colleagues (10) outlined what is termed the *cross-over concept*, in which lower-intensity exercise receives its ATP primarily from the oxidation of fat and some carbohydrates. As the intensity of exercise increases, the amount of carbohydrate used for ATP production increases whereas the utilization of fat to supply ATP decreases. This again gives support for the concept that higher-intensity exercise bouts use carbohydrates as a primary fuel source.

The oxidative or aerobic system is the primary source of ATP for events lasting between 2 min and approximately 3 hr (all track events of 800 m or more, cross-country skiing, long-distance speedskating). Conversely, activities that are shorter than 2 min rely on anaerobic means to meet their ATP demands (88).

The coach and athlete need to understand the bioenergetic mechanisms that supply energy for exercise and sport performance. A paradigm can be created in which the athlete is trained based on the **bioenergetics** of the sporting activity. This has been termed **bioenergetic specificity** (109). Figure 1.16 illustrates the energy sources used for specific sports and events. The coach and athlete can use the bioenergetic classification of sports, which is based on the duration, the intensity, and the fuel used by the activity, to create effective training programs for specific sports.

	ANAEROBIC PATHWAYS		AEROBIC PATHWAYS							
Energy pathways	ATP-PC	Glycolytic								
Primary energy sources	ATP PRODUCED WITHOUT THE PRESENCE OF OXYGEN		ATP PRODUCED IN THE PRESENCE OF OXYGEN							
Fuel	Phosphagens: muscular stores of ATP and PCr	Blood glucose / Liver glycogen / Muscle glycogen	Glycogen completely metabolized in the presence of oxygen					Fat		Protein
Duration	0 s — 10 s	40 s	60 s	2 min	4 min	10 min	30 min	1 hr	2 hr	3 hr
Sports events	Sprinting (<100 m)	Sprinting (200-400 m)	100 m swimming		Middle-distance track, swimming, speed skating	Long-distance track, swimming, speed skating, and canoeing				
	Throwing	Speed skating (500 m)	800 m track		1,000 m canoeing	Cross-country skiing				
	Throwing	Most gym events	500 m canoeing		Boxing	Rowing				
	Weightlifting	Track cycling	1,500 m speedskating		Wresting	Cycling: road racing				
	Ski jumping	50 m swim	Floor exercise in gymnastics		Martial arts	Marathon				
	Golf (swinging)		Alpine skiing		Figure skating	Triathlon				
	Diving		Cycling: track: 1,000 m and pursuit		Synchronized swimming					
	Vaulting in gymnastics				Cycling pursuit					
		Most team sports, racket sports, sailing								
Skills	Mostly acyclic	Acyclic and cyclic				Cyclic				

Figure 1.16 Energy sources for competitive sport.

Overlap of the Energy Systems

At all times the various energy systems contribute to the overall ATP yield. However, depending on the physiological demands associated with the exercise bout, ATP yield can be linked to a primary energy system (109). For example, very high-intensity events, such as the 100 m sprint, that occur in a short time can result in a significant reliance on the anaerobic energy systems to meet the demand for ATP (101). As the duration of the activity is extended, the reliance on oxidative mechanisms for supplying ATP increase (figure 1.17). For example, exercise bouts that last approximately 1 min will meet 70% of the body's energy demand via anaerobic mechanisms, whereas bouts of exercise that are 4 min in duration will meet 65% of the body's energy demand via the use of aerobic metabolism (101). Thus, there is a primary energy system that meets the athlete's ATP needs during a specific sporting event, and understanding this will help the coach and athlete design training programs that target specific bioenergetic needs for the sporting activity (109).

The amount of lactate in the blood gives insight into which energy system is acting as the primary energy supplier. Higher levels of lactate formation suggest that the glycolytic system is operating at a very high rate, thus creating a buildup of lactic acid and lactate. In endurance or aerobic activities, the first point at which lactate formation begins to abruptly increase is termed the **lactate threshold (LT)** and represents a shift from aerobic energy supply to anaerobic energy supply as intensity of exercise increases (109). In untrained individuals, the LT occurs somewhere between 50% and 60% of **maximal aerobic capacity** ($\dot{V}O_2$max), whereas highly trained endurance athletes demonstrate an LT as high as 80% of $\dot{V}O_2$max (16, 88). The LT of an elite endurance athlete can occur somewhere between 83% and 93% of maximal

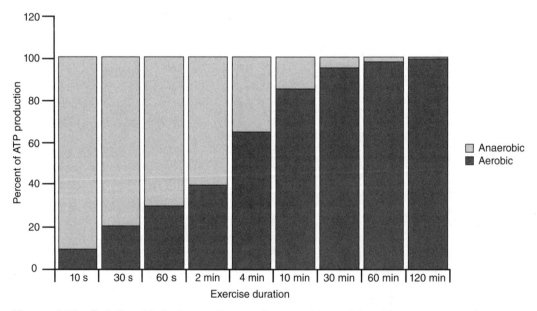

Figure 1.17 Relationship between time and anaerobic and aerobic energy supply.

heart rate (35, 67, 95). The second major increase in lactate accumulation occurs at about 4 mM and is termed the **onset of blood lactate accumulation (OBLA)** (88). In trained endurance athletes, the OBLA has been demonstrated to occur between 90% and 93% of maximum heart rate (35, 67, 95).

Several researchers have offered evidence that the time point at which the LT and OBLA occur is affected by the training stimulus (39, 78, 79). Recent work by Esfarjani and Laursen (39) suggests that performing high-intensity intervals can result in significant elevations in endurance performance and in the LT, allowing the endurance athlete to work at a higher intensity before experiencing lactic acid buildup.

Sprint interval training has been demonstrated to increase glycolytic and oxidative enzymatic activity, improve maximal short-term power output, and increase maximal aerobic power (82). It has been suggested that a high aerobic capacity enhances the recovery from high-intensity anaerobic exercise because this capacity enhances removal of lactate and PCr regeneration (114). These findings might falsely lead coaches and athletes to think that aerobic training is needed to enhance the athlete's ability to recover from repetitive bouts of high-intensity anaerobic exercise. However, several studies clearly demonstrate that maximal aerobic power or capacity is of little importance in the recovery from repetitive bouts of high-intensity anaerobic exercise (8, 15, 22, 115). The inclusion of high-intensity interval training by athletes who participate in sports that are predominated by anaerobic energy supply will result in an aerobic capacity that is high enough to enhance postexercise recovery (15). Although the inclusion of aerobic training significantly increases aerobic power and capacity, it generally decreases anaerobic performance (37). Therefore, coaches and athletes should focus on enhancing the bioenergetic profile for the sporting event.

Table 1.2 provides information regarding the bioenergetic characteristics of many sports. In interval training, the rest interval between bouts of activity can significantly affect the primary energy system stressed (109). Shorter work-to-rest intervals (such as 1:1-1:3) will selectively target the oxidative system, whereas longer work-to-rest intervals (1:12-1:20) will selectively target the phosphagen system (109). Coaches should consider modeling the intensity and time characteristics of the sporting event (99, 100). Plisk and Gambetta (100) recommended that conditioning drills model the bioenergetics of the sporting event and incorporate the tactical and technical components of the activity. If incorporated correctly, the conditioning drill will account for the time characteristics and the intensity profile of the activity. To design effective programs, the coach or athlete needs to understand the performance characteristics and bioenergetic demands of the sporting activity.

The coach or athlete should consider the durations of a rally in racket sports, a tactical segment of a game in basketball or ice hockey, and the rest interval between bouts of exercise. For example, when designing training programs for sports such as football, soccer, or rugby, the coach should consider the position the athlete plays on the team. In American football, the average play lasts between 4 and 6 s and players have rest intervals of 25 to 45 s; in addition, different positions have very different physiological challenges (98). When looking at soccer the coach should consider the distance covered by the various positions (defenders ~10 km; midfield players ~12 km; forwards ~10.5 km), because this will affect the bioenergetic stressors placed on each athlete (7). In a soccer match, high-intensity exercise that taxes the anaerobic system lasts around 7 min with an average of 19 sprints that last about 2.0 s, with the remainder of the activity taxing the aerobic system (7).

Table 1.2 Energy Delivery Systems (Ergogenesis in Percentages) for Sports

Sport	Event or position	Phosphagen	Glycolytic	Oxidative	Reference
Archery		0	0	100	Mathews and Fox (80)
Athletics (track and field)	100 m	98	2	0	Powers and Howley (95)
	200 m	38	57	5	Mader˙
	400 m	40	55	5	Powers and Howley (95)
	800 m	10	60	30	Powers and Howley (95)
	1,500 m	5	35	60	Powers and Howley (95)
	3,000 m	20	40	20	Mathews and Fox (80)
	5,000 m	2	28	70	Powers and Howley (95)
	10,000 m	5	15	80	Mathews and Fox (80)
	Marathon	0	2	100	Powers and Howley (95)
	Jumps	90	10	0	Powers and Howley (95)
	Throws	90	10	0	Powers and Howley (95)
Baseball		80	15	5	Powers and Howley (95)
Basketball		80	10	10	Powers and Howley (95)
Biathlon		0	5	95	Dal Monte (30)
Canoeing	C1: 1,000 m	25	35	40	Dal Monte (30)
	C2: 1,000 m	20	55	25	Dal Monte (30)
	C1,2: 10,000 m	5	10	85	Dal Monte (30)
Cycling	200 m track	98	2	0	Dal Monte (30)
	4,000 m pursuit	20	50	30	Dal Monte (30)
	Road racing	0	5	95	Dal Monte (30)
Diving		98	2	0	Powers and Howley (95)
Driving	Motor sports, luge	0	0-15	85-10	Dal Monte (30)
Equestrian		20-30	20-50	20-50	Dal Monte (30)
Fencing		90	10	0	Dal Monte (30)
Field hockey		60	20	20	Powers and Howley (95)
Figure skating		60-80	10-30	20	Dal Monte (30)
Football		90	10	0	Powers and Howley (95)
Golf (swinging)		100	0	0	Powers and Howley (95)
Gymnastics		90	10	0	Powers and Howley (95)
Handball		80	10	10	Dal Monte (30)
Ice hockey	Forward	80	20	0	Powers and Howley (95)
	Defense	80	20	0	Powers and Howley (95)
	Goalie	95	5	0	Powers and Howley (95)

Sport	Event or position	Phosphagen	Glycolytic	Oxidative	Reference
Judo		90	10	0	Dal Monte (30)
Kayaking	K1: 500 m	25	60	15	Dal Monte (30)
	K2,4: 500 m	30	60	10	Dal Monte (30)
	K1: 1,000 m	20	50	30	Dal Monte (30)
	K2,4: 1,000 m	20	55	25	Dal Monte (30)
	K1,2,4: 10,000 m	5	10	85	Dal Monte (30)
Rowing		20	30	50	Powers and Howley (95)
Rugby		30-40	10-20	30-50	Dal Monte (30)
Sailing		0	15	85-100	Dal Monte (30)
Shooting		0	0	100	Dal Monte (30)
Skiing	Slalom (45-50 s)	40	50	10	Alpine Canada (4)
	Giant slalom (70-90 s)	30	50	20	Alpine Canada (4)
	Super giant (80-120 s)	15	45	40	Alpine Canada (4)
	Downhill (90-150 s)	10	45	45	Alpine Canada (4)
	Nordic	0	5	95	Dal Monte (30)
Soccer	Goalie	80	20	0	Powers and Howley (95)
	Halfback	60	20	20	Powers and Howley (95)
	Striker	80	20	0	Powers and Howley (95)
	Wing	80	20	0	Powers and Howley (95)
Speedskating	500 m	95	5	0	Dal Monte (30)
	1,500 m	30	60	10	Dal Monte (30)
	5,000 m	10	40	50	Dal Monte (30)
	10,000 m	5	15	80	Dal Monte (30)
Swimming	50 m	95	5	0	Powers and Howley (95)
	100 m	80	15	5	Powers and Howley (95)
	200 m	30	65	5	Powers and Howley (95)
	400 m	20	40	40	Powers and Howley (95)
	800 m	10	30	60	Mathews and Fox (80)
	1,500 m	10	20	70	Powers and Howley (95)
Tennis		70	20	10	Powers and Howley (95)
Volleyball		90	10	0	Powers and Howley (95)
Water polo		30	40	30	Dal Monte (30)
Wrestling		45	55	0	Powers and Howley (95)

'Personal communication, 1985.

SUMMARY OF MAJOR CONCEPTS

The purpose of training is to increase athletes' working capacity, skill effectiveness, and psychological qualities to improve their performance in competitions. Training is a long-term endeavor. Athletes are not developed overnight, and a coach cannot create miracles by cutting corners and overlooking scientific and methodological theories.

As athletes train, they adapt or adjust to the training load. The better the athlete's anatomical, physiological, and psychological adaptation, the higher is the probability of improving his or her athletic performance.

Supercompensation is the most important concept in training. The dynamics of a supercompensation cycle depend on planned training intensities. Good planning must consider supercompensation, because its application in training ensures the restoration of energy and, most important, helps athletes avoid critical levels of fatigue that can result in overtraining.

To conduct an effective training program, coaches must understand energy systems, the fuel used by each system, and how much time athletes need to restore energy fuels used in training and competition. A good understanding of restoration time for an energy system is the foundation for calculating rest intervals between training activities during a workout, between workouts, and after a competition.

CHAPTER 2

PRINCIPLES OF TRAINING

Since athletic training began, more than 3,000 years ago (see *Eneida,* written by the Roman poet Virgil in the second decade BC), athletes and trainers have established and followed principles of training. These principles have evolved through the years as a result of research in the biological, pedagogical, and psychological sciences. These principles of sports training are the foundation of the theory and methodology of training.

The main objective of training is to increase the athlete's sporting skills and, ultimately, level of sporting performance. Training principles are part of a whole concept and should not be viewed in isolated units. However, they are often examined separately to better understand the basic concepts. Correct use of these training principles will result in superior training programs and well-trained athletes.

MULTILATERAL DEVELOPMENT VERSUS SPECIALIZATION

The overall development of athletes involves striking a balance between multilateral development and specialized training. In general, the early development of athletes should focus on multilateral development, which targets the overall physical development of the athletes. As the athlete becomes more developed, the proportion of specialized training, which focuses primarily on the skills needed in the targeted sport, steadily increases. In order to effectively develop the athlete, the coach must understand the importance of each of these two training stages and how the training focus changes as the athlete develops.

Multilateral Development

Support for the concept of multilateral development is found in most areas of education and human endeavors. In athletics, multilateral development, or overall physical development, is a necessity (9, 25, 84). The use of a multilateral development plan is extremely important during the early stages of an athlete's development (84). Multilateral development during the athlete's formative years lays the groundwork for later periods of training when specialization becomes a greater focus of the training plan. If properly implemented, the multilateral training phase will allow the athlete to develop the physiological and psychological basis needed to maximize performance later in his career (84).

The temptation to deviate from a multilateral development plan and begin specialized training too soon can be very great, especially when a young athlete demonstrates rapid development in a sporting activity. In such cases, it is paramount that the instructor, coach, or parent resist this temptation, because it has been well documented that a broad multilateral base of physical development is necessary to prepare the athlete for more specialized training later in her development (9, 25, 84). If training is sequenced appropriately and begins with a strong foundation of multilateral training early in the athlete's development, the athlete will be able to achieve much higher levels of physical preparation and technical mastery and ultimately will achieve higher levels of performance.

A sequential approach to an athlete's development, progressing from multilateral to specialized training as the athlete matures, appears to be a prerequisite for maximizing sporting performance (25, 79, 84). Figure 2.1 illustrates a conceptual model for a long-term sequential approach to training.

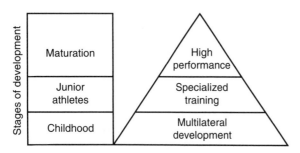

Figure 2.1 Sequential model for long-term athletic training.

The base of the pyramid in figure 2.1 represents a period of multilateral development, which is the foundation of the training program. This part of the training program includes multifaceted motor development, multisport skills, and some sport-specific skills. The variety of exercise that the athlete undertakes during this time allows for full development of the child's physiological systems. For example, in this phase of training the neuromuscular, cardiovascular, and energy systems are activated in various ways to allow for balanced development. When the athlete's development reaches an acceptable level, especially her physical development, she will progress to the second phase of development, which is marked by a greater degree of specialization.

The multilateral phase of training does not exclude specificity in the training process. On the contrary, training specificity is present in all stages of a training program but in varying proportions, as can be seen in figure 2.2. Figure 2.2 shows that during the multilateral phase of training, the percentage of specialized training is very small. As the athlete matures, the degree of specialization increases. It is believed that the multilateral base serves as a foundation for future development and helps the athlete avoid overuse injuries and staleness in training (84).

Support for the benefits of multilateral development can be seen in three longitudinal studies performed in three countries (18, 22, 46). In a 14-year study in the former East Germany (46), a large number of 9- to 12-year-olds were placed into two groups. The first group trained in a manner similar to the approach taken in North America, focusing on early specialization in a given sport. These athletes used exercises and training methods that were specific to a particular sport. The second group followed a generalized program that focused on multilateral development. This group participated in a variety of sports, learned a variety of skills, and undertook overall physical training in addition to sport-specific skills and physical training. The results of this investigation (see Comparison Between Early Specialization and

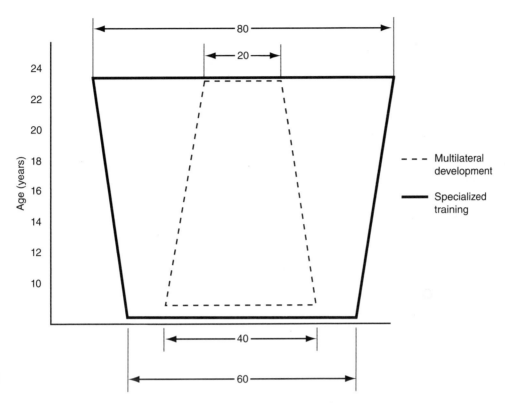

Figure 2.2   Comparison between early specialization and multilateral development.

Multilateral Development, p. 34) support the contention that a strong foundation, which is established by using a multilateral approach, leads to greater athletic success.

Russian sources (22) often refer to a survey that resulted in similar findings. This longitudinal study concluded that specialization should not start in most sports before the age of 15. Some of the major findings of this study are as follows:

- Most of the best Russian athletes had a strong multilateral foundation.
- Most athletes started training at 7 or 8 years of age. During the first few years, all athletes participated in various sports, such as soccer, cross-country skiing, running, skating, swimming, and cycling. From 10 to 13, the children also participated in team sports, gymnastics, rowing, and track and field.
- Specialized programs started at ages 15 to 17, without neglecting earlier sports and activities. Best performances were achieved after 5 to 8 years in the specialized sports.
- Athletes who specialized at a much earlier age achieved their best performances at a junior age level (<18 years). These performances were never duplicated when they became seniors (>18 years). Many retired before reaching senior levels. Only a minority of the athletes who specialized at a young age were able to improve performance at senior level.
- Many top-class athletes started to train in an organized environment at the junior level (14-18 years of age). They had never been junior champions or held national records, but at the senior age many of them achieved national- and international-class performances.
- Most athletes considered their success attributable to the multilateral foundation built during childhood and junior age.

COMPARISON BETWEEN EARLY SPECIALIZATION AND MULTILATERAL DEVELOPMENT

Early Specialization

- Quick performance improvement
- Best performances achieved at 15 to 16 years of age because of quick adaptation
- Inconsistent performance in competition
- High incidence of burnout and quitting sport by age 18
- Increased risk of injury because of forced adaptation and lack of physiological development

Multilateral Development

- Slower performance improvement
- Best performances at age 18 or older when the athlete has reached physiological and psychological maturation
- Consistent and progressive performance in competition
- Longer athletic career
- Fewer injuries as a result of more progressive loading patterns and overall physiological development

Based on Harre 1982 (46).

The third study, conducted by Carlson (18), analyzed the training background and development patterns of elite Swedish tennis players who were very successful in international competition. The subjects were divided into a study group that consisted of elite adult tennis players and a control group that was matched by age, gender, and junior rankings. The most relevant findings are shown in the summary of research on page 35. Both groups of players were equal in skills up to the age group of 12 to 14; the difference in skills between the two groups occurred after this age. Additional findings in the control group were that skill development was fast during early adolescence and these players participated in an atmosphere of high demand for success. Interestingly, the control group players specialized at age 11, whereas the study group did not begin to specialize until the age of 14. In fact, the study group participated in a wide variety of sporting activities during early adolescence, whereas the control group performed specialized, professional-like training. Although the control group demonstrated significantly greater performances as juniors, the study group demonstrated their highest levels of performance as senior athletes. The work of Carlson (18) supports the importance of a multilateral training approach that is marked by all-around sport engagement and less professional-type training during early childhood and adolescence.

The coach should consider multilateral training in the early stages of an athlete's development as the foundation for future specialization and athletic mastery (58). Multilateral training should be used mostly when training children and juniors (9, 58). In these stages of athlete development it is essential that a strong vocabulary of physical and psychological attributes be developed. Physical skill sets that are essential during this phase of training include natural movements like running, jumping, climbing, and throwing (58, 79). Additionally, the development of speed, agility, coordination, flexibility, and overall general fitness is important at this phase of development. These training goals are best accomplished through diverse activities that allow for the development of several biomotor abilities. In this process, the young athlete will be taught a diverse group of exercise techniques, which include some of the technical aspects of the selected sport. All of these skill sets will be used as the athlete becomes more developed and multilateral training becomes less of a focus.

SUMMARY OF RESEARCH EXAMINING THE EFFECTS OF EARLY SPECIALIZATION AND MULTILATERAL TRAINING ON ATHLETE DEVELOPMENT

Control Group

- Began to specialize at age 11, when multilateral training ceased
- Experienced significantly less multilateral training during early development ages
- Practiced tennis more than the study group between the ages of 13 and 15
- Tended to lose self-confidence as they progressed through training
- Developed faster during early adolescence than did the study group
- Experienced greater pressure for success during early stages of development from parents and coaches

Study Group

- Began to specialize at age 14 or older
- Experienced significantly more multilateral training during early development stages
- Practiced tennis more than the control group after the age of 15
- Tended to gain self-confidence as they progressed through training
- Developed more slowly during early adolescence than did the control group
- Experienced less pressure for success during early stages of development from parents and coaches

Adapted from Carlson 1988 (18).

All athletes should participate in multilateral training to some degree throughout their careers (figure 2.2). The greatest amount of multilateral training occurs during the early stages of development, and less focus on this type of training occurs as the athlete progresses. Multilateral development is essential to optimize the effects of specialized training later in the athlete's career.

Specialization

Whether training on a field, in a pool, or in a gymnasium, the athlete eventually will specialize in a sport or event. Training for a sport results in physiological adaptations that are specific to the activity's movement pattern, metabolic demand, force generation pattern, contraction type, and muscle recruitment pattern (28, 83, 91). The type of training used has a very specific effect on the athlete's physiological characteristics (21). For example, endurance training has the ability to stimulate both central and peripheral adaptations, which can include altering neural recruitment patterns, modifying bioenergetic or metabolic factors, and stimulating significant skeletal muscle alterations (2, 48). Conversely, resistance training results in significant alterations to the contractile machinery, neuromuscular system, and bioenergetic or metabolic pathways (1, 21). Contemporary research suggests that skeletal muscle exhibits a large amount of plasticity in response to different modalities of resistance or endurance training resulting in the activation or deactivation of different molecular signaling pathways depending on the type of training encountered (4, 6, 7, 21, 67, 68, 102). Specific adaptations are not limited to physiological responses, because technical, tactical, and psychological traits are also developed in response to specialized training. It is very likely that each sporting activity can develop attributes that allow the athlete to achieve a high level of mastery.

Specialization is a complex nonunilateral process that is based on multilateral development. As an athlete progresses from a beginner to a mature athlete who has mastered her sport, the total volume and intensity of training progressively increase, as does the degree of specialization. Several authors suggest that the best training adaptations occur in response to exercises specific to the sporting activity and exercises that target given biomotor abilities only after a multilateral foundation has been developed (22, 79). The former refers to exercises that parallel or mimic the movements of the sport, whereas the latter refers to exercises that develop strength, speed, and endurance. The ratio between these two exercise groups varies for each sport, depending on its characteristics. In long-distance running, for example, approximately 90% of the volume of training consists of sport-specific exercises. In other sports, like high jumping, these exercises represent only 40%; exercises that develop leg strength and jumping power make up the rest. When working with advanced athletes, coaches should dedicate only 60% to 80% of the total training time to sport-specific exercise (figure 2.2) and should dedicate the remainder of training to developing biomotor abilities.

Coaches should carefully plan the ratio between multilateral and specialized training, taking into consideration the modern tendency to lower the age of athletic maturation. In some sports, athletes achieve a high level of performance at young ages and thus must enter the sport at a young age (25). Examples of these sports include artistic gymnastics, gymnastics, figure skating, swimming, and diving. However, recent changes to Olympic competition rules may increase the average age for high-level gymnastics performance. For example, to compete in the Olympics a female gymnast must turn 16 during the year of the Olympic Games. During the years 2005 to 2007, the average age of competitors at the gymnastics world championships was about 18.0 (85).

Table 2.1 presents a rough guide for the age an individual can begin to train, the time when specialization may start, and the age when the highest performance is usually reached. Some authors suggest that the optimal age to begin training is

Table 2.1 Age of Starting, Specializing, and Reaching High Performance in Different Sports

Sport	Age to begin training	Age to start specialization	Age when highest performance is achieved
Archery	12-14	16-18	23-30
Athletics (track and field)			
Sprinting	10-12	14-16	22-26
Middle-distance running	13-14	16-17	22-26
Long-distance running	14-16	17-20	25-28
High jump	12-14	16-18	22-25
Triple jump	12-14	17-19	23-26
Long jump	12-14	17-19	23-26
Throws	14-15	17-19	23-27
Badminton	10-12	14-16	20-25
Baseball	10-12	15-16	22-28
Basketball	10-12	14-16	22-28
Biathlon	10-12	16-17	23-26
Bobsled	12-14	17-18	22-26

Sport	Age to begin training	Age to start specialization	Age when highest performance is achieved
Boxing	13-15	16-17	22-26
Canoeing	12-14	15-17	22-26
Chess	7-8	12-15	23-35
Continental handball	10-12	14-16	22-26
Cycling	12-15	16-18	22-28
Diving			
Women	6-8	9-11	14-18
Men	8-10	11-13	18-22
Equestrian	10-12	14-16	22-28
Fencing	10-12	14-16	20-25
Field hockey	11-13	14-16	20-25
Figure skating	7-9	11-13	18-25
Football	12-14	16-18	23-27
Gymnastics			
Women	6-8	9-10	14-18
Men	8-9	14-15	22-25
Ice hockey	6-8	13-14	22-28
Judo	8-10	15-16	22-26
Modern pentathlon	11-13	14-16	21-25
Rowing	11-14	16-18	22-25
Rugby	13-14	16-17	22-26
Sailing	10-12	14-16	22-30
Shooting	12-15	17-18	24-30
Skiing			
Alpine	7-8	12-14	18-25
Nordic	12-14	16-18	23-28
More than 30K	—	17-19	24-28
Jumping	10-12	14-15	22-26
Speedskating	10-12	15-16	22-26
Soccer	10-12	14-16	22-26
Squash and handball	10-12	15-17	23-27
Swimming			
Women	7-9	11-13	18-22
Men	7-8	13-15	20-24
Synchronized swimming	6-8	12-14	19-23
Table tennis	8-9	13-14	22-25
Tennis			
Women	7-8	11-13	20-25
Men	7-8	12-14	22-27
Volleyball	10-12	15-16	22-26
Water polo	10-12	16-17	23-26
Weightlifting	14-15	17-18	23-27
Wrestling	11-13	17-19	24-27

Adapted from Stone, Stone, and Sands 2007 (91).

between 5 and 9 (9, 12). During these early phases of training the coach should focus on developing a physical literacy that includes basic skills such as running, jumping, and throwing (9). It is important to develop these skills at the initiation of training because young athletes seem to develop these abilities at a faster rate than more mature athletes. Once the athlete develops the basics skills, he can begin some specialized training for his chosen sport. This generally occurs between the ages of 10 and 14 (9). As stated previously multilateral training is the primary focus until around the age of 14, after which more specialized training occurs.

INDIVIDUALIZATION

Individualization is one of the main requirements of contemporary training. Individualization requires that the coach consider the athlete's abilities, potential, and learning characteristics and the demands of the athlete's sport, regardless of the performance level. Each athlete has physiological and psychological attributes that need to be considered when developing a training plan.

Too often, coaches take an unscientific approach to training by literally following training programs of successful athletes or sport programs with complete disregard for the athlete's training experience, abilities, and physiological makeup. Even worse, some coaches take programs from elite athletes and apply them to junior athletes who have not yet developed the physical literacy, physiological base, or psychological skills needed to undertake these types of programs. Young athletes are not physiologically or psychologically able to tolerate programs created for advanced athletes (26, 27, 39, 101). The coach needs to understand the athlete's needs and develop training plans that meet those needs. This can be accomplished by following some guidelines:

Plan According to Tolerance Level

The training plan must be based on a comprehensive analysis of the athlete's physiological and psychological parameters, which will give the coach insight into the athlete's work capacity. An individual's training capacity can be determined by the following factors:

- *Biological and Chronological Age:* The **biological age** of an athlete is considered to be a more accurate indicator of the individual's physical performance potential than is her **chronological age** (25, 65). One of the best indicators of biological age is sexual maturation (15, 38), because it indicates an increase in circulating testosterone levels (65, 76). Athletes who are more physically mature, as indicated by a higher biological age, appear to be stronger, faster, and better at team sports than their peers who exhibit a lower biological age, even when chronological age is the same (38, 65). In general children have a greater resistance to fatigue, which may explain why they respond better to higher volumes of training (74). On the other hand, older adults appear to exhibit a decreased motivation to train intensely (93), an increased prevalence of injuries (55), and an increased occurrence of social stressors (93), all of which may contribute to a decreased ability to tolerate intense training. Most junior athletes tolerate high volumes of training with moderate loads better than high-intensity or high-load training (27, 39, 74). The combination of heavy loading and high volume is of concern with youth athletes because this practice may increase the risk of musculoskeletal injuries (39).

- *Training Age:* **Training age** is defined as the number of years an individual has been preparing for a sporting activity (12), and it is considerably different than the biological or chronological age. Athletes with a high training age have developed a substantial training base and most likely will be able to participate in a specialized training plan, especially if their early training was multilateral. An athlete who has a high chronological age in conjunction with a low training age may need more multilateral and skill acquisition training, because he lacks the training base to allow for a high degrees of specialization in his sport.

- *Training History:* The athlete's training history influences his work capacity. An athlete who has undertaken substantial multilateral training is more likely to have developed the fitness levels necessary to tolerate high training loads compared with a less-well-trained athlete (91).

- *Health Status:* An athlete who is ill or injured will have a reduced work capacity and often will not be able to tolerate the prescribed training loads (91). The type of illness or degree of injury and the physiological base converge to determine the training load that the athlete can tolerate (91). The coach must monitor the athlete's health status to determine an appropriate training load.

The age and skill level of an athlete, along with other factors, must be taken into consideration when planning training and practice sessions.

- *Stress and the Recovery Rate:* The ability to tolerate a training load is often related to all of the stressors that the athlete encounters (91). Overall stressors are considered additive, and factors that place a high demand on the athlete can alter her ability to tolerate a training load (94). For example, heavy involvement in school, work, or family activities can affect the athlete's ability to tolerate a training load. Travel to and from work, school, or training can further contribute to stress levels. Coaches should consider these factors and adjust the training load accordingly. For example, during times of high stress, such as academic examinations, a reduction in training load may be warranted.

Individualize the Training Load

The ability to adapt to a training load depends on the individual's capacity. As outlined in the preceding section, many factors contribute to the individualized response to training loads and progressions: the athlete's training history, health status, life stress, chronological age, biological age, and training age. Simply mimicking the training plans of elite athletes will not result in high levels of performance (91). Rather, the coach must address the athlete's needs and capacities by developing an individualized program, which requires detailed observations of the athlete's technical and tactical abilities, physical characteristics, strengths, and weaknesses. As discussed in the section about developing a training model later in this chapter, periodic testing of the athlete will allow for more specific and individualized training plans to be developed. Less individualization of the training plan may be needed with athletes who are roughly at the same level of development and stage of training (91).

Account for Gender Differences

Gender differences can play an important role in performance and individualized training adaptations. Prepubescent boys and girls are very similar in height, weight, girth, bone width, and skinfold thickness (101). After the onset of puberty, boys and girls begin to develop substantial differences in physical attributes. After puberty girls tend to have higher levels of body fat, lower amounts of fat-free mass, and lighter total body masses (101). From a performance perspective it is clear that men and women differ in muscle mass and strength (29, 35, 54, 95), anaerobic power and capacity (36, 64), and maximal aerobic capacity and performance (3, 19, 20, 24, 82).

Some researchers suggest that gender differences are related to anatomical or biomechanical factors (60, 66), whereas others suggest that training experiences and access to specialized training partially explain gender differences in performance (60). Support for the contention that training may partially explain the difference between the genders has been offered by Kraemer and colleagues (57), who found that differences in performance between men and women were substantially reduced when appropriate training was undertaken by women.

After looking at elite anaerobic performances (sprinting, swimming, and speedskating) from 1952 to 2006, Seiler and colleagues (81) reported that performance differences between males and females initially decreased, but more recently performances differences between the genders have ceased to narrow. Cheuvront and colleagues (19) discovered a similar trend in distance running performance when they compared performance variables between men and women.

Women are able to tolerate extensive and intensive training regimes (17). In fact, Cao (17) suggested that women are capable of handling higher volumes and intensities of resistance training than their male counterparts. However, caution should be taken when examining these data because women do have specific areas that need to be addressed. For example, women tend to be weaker in the upper body (17, 28) and trunk musculature (17). The inclusion of more exercises to strengthen these areas in female athletes may be warranted.

The performance responses of female athletes during the different phases of the menstrual cycle appear to be very individualized (101). The scientific literature suggests that in most situations, maximal and submaximal aerobic performance (53) and anaerobic performance (14, 53) are not affected by the menstrual cycle. However, the scientific literature suggests that temperature regulation is compromised during the luteal phase as a result of an increase in core temperature (53). This may be an important consideration for women who are exercising or training for extended periods of time in hot and humid conditions.

Incorporate Training Variation

Variation is one of the key components needed to induce adaptations in response to training. Skill acquisition and performance increase rapidly when novel tasks are first undertaken, but the rate of skill acquisition slows with repetition of the same training plan or loading paradigm over time (51). Stone and colleagues (87) suggested that a lack of training variation can result in what is termed **monotonous program overtraining.** This condition occurs if the same training stimulus is introduced regularly for long periods of time ultimately resulting in a reduction or plateau of performance, which could be defined as a form of overtraining. In support of this contention, O'Toole (70) suggested that the degree of monotony in the training plan is significantly related to poor performance.

Periodization of training can decrease monotony or boredom in training and ultimately induce greater physiological adaptations. Zatsiorsky (103) suggested that periodization is a balancing act between training variation and stability (monotony or repetition) of **training**. Thus variation of training is of paramount importance when considering periodization (72, 83, 91). Optimal training adaptations occur in response to a systematic variation in training load and content. If inadequate variation is provided and the program is monotonous, performance will not be optimized. This happens when the nervous system is not overloaded sufficiently to stimulate physiological adaptations (87, 91).

Variation can be incorporated into the training plan at many levels. For example, variation at the microcycle level can be added by altering training volume, intensity, frequency, and exercise selection. Stone and colleagues (91) suggested inducing variation in training through the introduction or reintroduction of novel or seminovel tasks, that is, the periodic inclusion of specific exercises (table 2.2). This plan induces greater adaptation because the tasks are removed from the training plan before complete adaptation is achieved and replaced by a task that addresses similar biomotor abilities. For example, to develop leg **strength** and **power** for volleyball, the athlete can practice back squats during the preparatory phase of training but periodically replace these exercises with 1/4 back squats to change the training stimulus while still targeting the required movement patterns and muscle groups. During the precompetition or competitive phase of training, the emphasis may shift from strength development to power-generating capacity. Therefore, the exercise program may shift as follows:

$$\text{Back squat} \Rightarrow 1/4 \text{ back squat} \Rightarrow \text{speed squat} \Rightarrow \text{jump squat}$$

Another example of this concept can be seen in the preparation of cyclists. During the off-season, cyclists typically undertake training modalities such as cross-country skiing to maintain aerobic fitness and then return to training on the bike during the preparatory phase of training. The introduction–reintroduction paradigm suggests that returning to bicycle training would rapidly increase cycling ability because the task is seminovel when reintroduced.

Table 2.2 Resistance Training Exercise Variation Via Introduction and Reintroduction

	Block 1				Block 2			
Exercise	Back squat	Back squat	Back squat	Back squat	1/3 squat	1/3 squat	1/3 squat	1/3 squat
	One-leg squat	1/4 front squat	1/4 front squat	One-leg squat	Speed squat	Jump squat	Jump squat	Speed squat
	Front squat	Overhead squat	Overhead squat	Front squat				
Week	1	2	3	4	5	6	7	8

Adapted from Stone, Stone, and Sands 2007 (91).

Changing the intensity of a training load is one way to add variation to a training plan and thus achieve greater physiological adaptations.

© Human Kinetics

Training variation can be introduced within or between microcycles. For example, on some days of the microcycle the athlete trains multiple times per day but on other days undertakes only one training session.

Multiple training sessions in the same training day have been shown to induce greater physiological adaptations than only one session per day (41). However, reducing the training density during the day can facilitate recovery, which may allow the athlete to train harder on subsequent days or microcycles.

Another way to vary the training plan is to systematically alternate the intensity of training. Alternating training intensity across the microcycle will allow for periods of stimulation and recovery, which have been suggested to induce greater physiological adaptations (91). Interestingly, alternating hard and light training sessions within the microcycle has been used to prepare endurance athletes (70) and strength and power athletes (91). Another variation strategy is to alternate both training intensity and training frequency. For example, when manipulating the training intensity within an individual training day, a morning session may occur at a high training intensity and the subsequent afternoon session may be performed at a lower intensity. On the next training day the number of sessions may be decreased to facilitate recovery or increased to increase the training stimulus.

Training variation is limited only by the coach's ability to apply scientific principles in a creative fashion. The implementation of training variation should be based on a complete understanding of the **bioenergetics** of the sport (28, 71, 91), movement patterns used in the sport (28), skills needed in the sport, and the athlete's level of development or training age (91). Advanced athletes will require more training variation than novice athletes, who have a very small training base. Novice athletes can achieve very good results with basic training models even though there is significantly less variation in the training plan.

DEVELOPMENT OF THE TRAINING MODEL

Training models, although not always well organized and often applied randomly, have been used since the 1960s (11). Although many Eastern European sport specialists acquired knowledge and experience in the use of training models, a general trend toward the use of these tools did not occur throughout the world until the 1970s (10, 16).

It is well documented that training and performance are highly related but are very individualized (5, 49). The development of a training model centers on the notion of training specificity and individualization of training programs (11, 49, 75, 92). Training models that allow for implementation, analysis, assessment, and modification of the training plan based on physiological and performance parameters are of particular use in the development of athletes (92).

The development of a training model is a long-term process that is in continual flux, because the training model will evolve in conjunction with the athlete's development. The development of a model is a labor-intensive process that relies on previous models, current athlete evaluations, and a strong scientific foundation. Although the process is time consuming, the time is well spent because the better the training model, the more likely the athlete is to achieve a high level of performance. The model must be continually evaluated and modified in response to new scientific knowledge, the athlete's level of development, and assessments of the athlete's progress. A theoretical method for developing a training model is presented in figure 2.3.

The development of a training model begins with a detailed analysis of the scientific literature regarding the sport. Understanding the physiological (e.g., bioenergetics) (75), morphological (37), anatomical, **biomotor** (56), and psychological characteristics (77) associated with a sport lays the foundation for the second phase of developing a training model. The second phase requires the development of a targeted testing program that can be used to analyze the athlete's training state. For example, the scientific literature on throwing indicates that maximal strength and explosive power are related to high levels of performance (90). Therefore, physiological tests should be developed and implemented to evaluate the athlete's force-generating capacity (peak force-generating capacity, rate of force development, maximal strength) and explosive strength (peak power assessments, power snatch 1**RM**, power clean 1RM). The athlete's tactical and technical skills must also be evaluated to delineate areas of weakness to be addressed by the training model. Tests should be developed that evaluate the athlete for areas of physical deficit or injury risk (e.g., range of motion, muscle imbalances). Other areas that can be evaluated include psychological traits (e.g., mood state), sleep status (e.g., quality of sleep), and nutritional practices. Finally, the athlete's training logs and competitive performance results should be evaluated to determine what was effective in the previous training model.

Once the evaluation of the athlete is completed, the coach interprets all the data that are collected. The training model is designed to target the athlete's needs to enhance the likelihood of a high level of performance. In this phase of the model major training factors are established. These factors include the loading progression, training intensity, volume of training, frequency of training, and the number of repetitions necessary to stimulate the appropriate physiological and psychological adaptations. Additionally, the tactical, technical, and strategic components of training model are established and integrated into the training model. The training model is very specific to the individual or team because the results of testing help

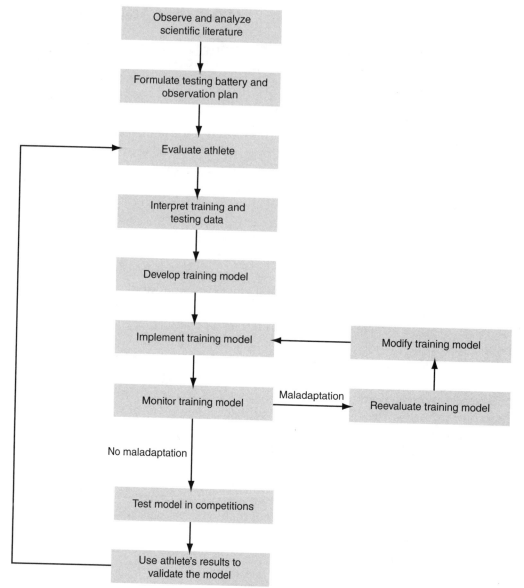

Figure 2.3 Sequence of developing a training model.

the coach establish training parameters. After the training model is developed, it is then implemented.

During the implementation phase, the athlete must be continually monitored so the coach can detect any maladaptations. A comprehensive monitoring plan includes periodic evaluation of physiological attributes (i.e., physiological testing similar to that conducted during the evaluation phase of model development), training log data, psychological status, nutritional status, and technical skill development. If during this phase the coach questions the effectiveness of the training model, it should be reevaluated and modified to ensure that performance goals are reached.

The primary test of the effectiveness of the training model is the athlete's competitive results. If the athlete achieves success in competition, the training model is considered validated. After the completion of the competitive period, specifically during the transition phase, the model continues to evolve as the athlete is reevaluated. This reevaluation includes a critical and comprehensive examination of the past training year to determine whether training goals, objectives, and performance standards were achieved. All of the testing conducted throughout the training year is evaluated to determine whether trends occurred that either increased or decreased performance. How well the athlete coped with training and competitive stress should be evaluated to determine whether improvement in this area is needed. After conducting this evaluation, the coach decides whether to use a new model for the next annual plan.

LOAD PROGRESSION

The performance results of athletes have increased during the last 50 years (80). There are many reasons for these elevations in performance, but clearly the ability to tolerate higher training loads is at the center of this phenomenon. Support for this contention is shown by the increase in training loads seen between 1975 and 2000 (table 2.3).

Improvements in performance are a direct result of the amount and quality of work the athlete achieves during training. From beginners to elite athletes, the training workload must increase gradually and be varied periodically according to each athlete's physiological capacity, psychological abilities, and work tolerance.

The training load can be thought of as a combination of intensity, duration, and frequency of training (84). The training load is determined by the degree of specificity of training and the performance development status of the athlete (83). There is a complex interaction between the athlete's fitness, the training load, and the athlete's ability to tolerate training (84).

The application of a training load results in a cascade of physiological responses that allow the athlete to adapt to the training stimulus, which elevates his fitness level and leads to a greater tolerance for training and an increase in performance capacity (84, 104). As the athlete adapts to the training load, it must increase for continued physiological adaptations to occur.

Training loads can be roughly classified as stimulating, retaining, or detraining (103, 104). A stimulating load is a training load that is heavier than the athlete's typical training load. Conversely, a detraining load is substantially lighter than usual. A detraining load ultimately results in a loss of fitness and a loss of performance capacity. In between these two loading classifications is the retaining load, which is the athlete's typical workload; the retaining load allows the athlete to maintain fitness while undergoing recovery. As the athlete adapts to a stimulating load, that load becomes the retaining load and the previous retaining load becomes a detraining

Table 2.3 Dynamics of Volume of Training From 1975 to 2000

Sport	Training volume	1975	1985	2000
Gymnastics (women)	Elements per week	3,450	6,000	5-6,000
	Routines per week	86	86	150
Rowing (women)	Kilometers per year	4,500	6,800	6,500-7,000
Fencing	Training hours per year	980	1,150	1,100-1,200
Football (soccer)	Training hours per year	460	560	500-600
Swimming (100 m)	Training hours per year	980	1,070	1,000-1,040
Boxing	Training hours per year	960	1,040	1,000-1,100

load. Thus, the loading classification is a fluid concept that changes as the athlete adapts, so the coach must pay attention to the sequence of the training loads in the periodized training plan.

A correctly sequenced training load will be increased gradually, ultimately resulting in an increase in performance capacity (84). If, however, the training load is suddenly and dramatically increased, it will take more time for the physiological adaptations to occur and performance gains to be realized (91, 97, 103, 104). The time frame needed for recovery and adaptation is directly proportional to the magnitude of the sudden increase in training load (91).

The gradual, systematic manipulation of the training load is the basis for periodization of training and is found at all levels of the training plan, from the microcycle to the Olympic cycle, in all levels of athletes. The appropriate sequencing of the training load is directly related to the athlete's performance improvements. Loading paradigms vary among different sports and geographical regions of the world. A brief examination of several loading theories is presented next.

Standard Loading

Standard loading involves the use of similar training loads and densities throughout the preparatory phase of training. When standard loading is used regularly during the preparatory phase, performance improvements occur only during the early part of this phase.

As the athlete shifts from the preparatory phase of training to the competitive phase, the training stimulus remains very similar with the exception of a reduction in training load. If standard loading is implemented in this fashion, performance plateaus during the competitive phase (see figure 1.4). This plateau in performance occurs as a result of a lack of variation in the training load. If suboptimal training loads are used during the competition phase, performance will most likely deteriorate, especially during the later part of this phase (52).

Because performance improves only during the early portion of the preparatory phase, training load must be increased each training year. Contemporary training theorists suggest that this type of loading is suboptimal in almost all situations and that strategies using step loading, summated microcycles, or conjugated sequencing may result in greater performance enhancements in the long term (72). Therefore, to optimize performance adaptations in response to the training load, the load must be increased from year to year to create the stimulus necessary for superior physiological adaptations. These enhancements will occur only if the training plan is sequenced appropriately and includes adequate periods of recovery.

Linear Loading

The linear loading of training is a concept that appears to violate many of the tenets of periodization (72, 91); however, this type of loading paradigm is very popular. According to the original proponents of this principle (50, 59), performance will increase only if the athlete trains at her maximal capacity against workloads that are gradually increased and are progressively higher than those normally encountered (8, 72, 73). Conceptually, this would lead to a loading curve that depicts a continual increase across time (figure 2.4). Although the literature has clearly demonstrated that the training load should be increased across the training cycle or the athlete's career (89, 104), this method of loading may only be useful during a short period of time (23, 31, 32, 34, 45), and periods of recovery are needed to maximize adaptive responses. If linear loading is undertaken for a long period of time, overtraining likely will result. If overtraining does occur, the athlete will exhibit physiological and psychological maladaptations, a decrease in markers of performance, and a high level of fatigue (70). Thus, linear loading in its purest sense is not an optimal way to train, except when implemented for short periods of time, because it does not allow enough time for recovery, and the potential for burnout and injury increases incrementally.

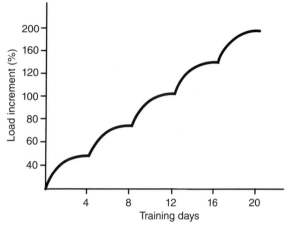

Figure 2.4 Load increments according to the overload principle.

Based on data from Hellebrandt and Houtz 1956 (50) and from Fox et al. 1989.

Step Loading

The step loading model of training allows for a progressive overload that is interspersed with periods of unloading and is sometimes referred to as a traditional or classic periodization model (62, 63, 72). The use of unloading phases or retaining loads allows for regeneration, greater physiological adaptations, and periods of psychological restoration. With the step loading paradigm (figure 2.5), a wavelike increase in training load occurs (89, 91, 98, 104). Because one training session is insufficient to provoke noticeable physiological or psychological adaptations, it is often recommended that the same training load be repeated over several training sessions. One common practice is to plan training sessions with the same characteristics for an entire microcycle and then increase the training

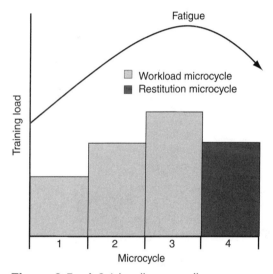

Figure 2.5 A 3:1 loading paradigm.
Adapted from Stone, Stone, and Sands 2007 (91).

load in subsequent microcycles (figure 2.5). This type of loading uses a 3:1 loading paradigm, in which the training load is increased across three microcycles and then is reduced during the fourth microcycle to allow recovery and avoid the problems typically associated with overloading.

Figure 2.5 illustrates a classic 3:1 loading paradigm. There is much evidence to support using a 4-week block of training (63, 72, 91) or a 2- to 6-week (usually 4 weeks) block of training (98, 103, 104). The load increases gradually in the first three microcycles as does the amount of accumulated fatigue, followed by an unloading phase that entails a decrease in training load and fatigue as depicted in the fourth microcycle in figure 2.5. This reduction in training load reduces fatigue, increases preparedness, and induces a series of physiological adaptations that prepare the athlete for further loading in the next series of microcycles (91). The greater the number of progressive loading steps, the longer the period of unloading needed. For example, Nádori and Granek (69) demonstrated a 4:2 paradigm approach to applying the training load where 4 weeks of increasing loads are followed by 2 unloading weeks to promote

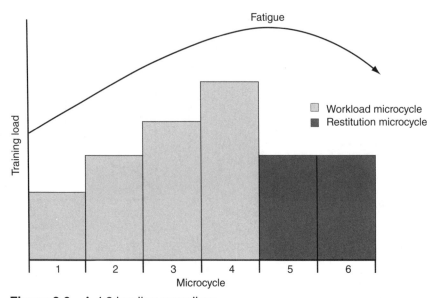

Figure 2.6 A 4:2 loading paradigm.
Based on Nádori and Granek 1989 (69) and Plisk and Stone 2003 (72).

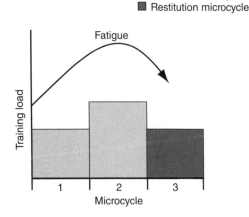

Figure 2.7 A 2:1 loading paradigm.

restoration, reduce fatigue, and increase preparedness (figure 2.6). In some situations it might be warranted to use only a few increasing steps. For example, a young athlete might use a 2:1 paradigm, with two microcycles of increasing training load followed by one microcycle of recovery (figure 2.7).

Several authors suggest that the step loading paradigm has some potential flaws especially when the same pattern of loading is used on each day of the microcycle (72, 91). These authors suggest that only 1 week of novel stimulus is presented during a 3-4 week series of microcycles, or training block, while the block itself offers a flat loading (e.g., 3-4 weeks of strength endurance training in resistance training), which can result in training monotony because of the lack of intermicrocycle variation (72). Conversely, step loading results in an intensification of workload with each progressive step, which develops a base for the next training block. This type of loading is excellent for novice athletes or those who are unaccustomed to high training intensities (72). To obviate some of the flaws associated with classic step loading paradigms, it has been suggested that more drastic intermicrocycle variations be implemented to promote a greater adaptive stimulus (72, 91) (figure 2.8). Scientific support for including more microcycle variations and periodically including submaximal training can be found in both human (30) and animal (13) studies. This literature suggests that the periodic inclusion of light training days results in a greater potential for adaptive responses, which ultimately will increase performance.

Another variation of the step loading paradigm is the summated microcyle (72, 91). In this paradigm each microcycle or week of the block of training is allocated to a performance attribute (e.g., strength endurance, maximal strength, speed strength). Across the first 3 weeks of each block of training, the volume or intensity of training is increased, with a decrease in the training load occurring during the fourth week before the initiation of the next block of training (figure 2.9). This model appears to

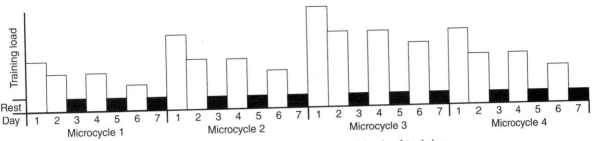

Figure 2.8 An example of intermicrocycle variation across a block of training.
White Bars = training load; Black Bars = rest
Based on Nádori and Granek 1989 (69) and Plisk and Stone 2003 (72).

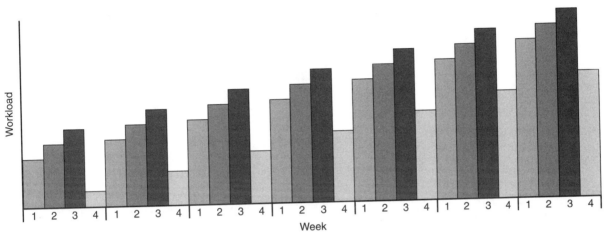

Figure 2.9 Loading paradigm for a summated microcycle model.
This depiction of a summated microcycle utilizes a 3:1 loading paradigm, with the highest level of fatigue in week 3. There is a pattern of loading, with week 1 representing strength-endurance, week 2 representing maximum strength, week 3 representing speed strength, and week 4 representing restoration training. The training stimuli are reintroduced in a cyclic pattern, allowing a specific stimulus to be reintroduced at regular intervals.
Based on Plisk and Stone 2003 (72) and Stone, Stone and Sands 2007 (91).

allow for the primary training stimulus to be reintroduced in a regular cyclic pattern (72). Proponents of this paradigm suggest that the cyclic loading pattern noted in the summated strategy allows for a large amount of contrast between each of the microcycles while decreasing the potential for overtraining or involution problems. The model has been suggested to result in a convergence of training effects, which may increase adaptation over the long term (72, 91). Furthermore, as with the basic step loading paradigm discussed earlier, the summated microcycle model can include daily variations in loading that may magnify the training stimulus and allow for further adaptations to occur. This modification to the step loading paradigm usually is best implemented with intermediate and advanced athletes (72).

Concentrated Loading

Short-term overloading is often classified as **concentrated loading** (91) or **overreaching** (61). The athlete usually can recover from this type of loading in a short period of time if she uses appropriate recovery loads (45). As a general rule, the greater the magnitude and duration of the concentrated loading phase, the more time needed for fatigue to dissipate and performance to improve (83, 91, 103, 104). Siff and Verkhoshansky (83) suggested that performance gains may occur 4 to 12 weeks after the cessation of the concentrated loading phase (figure 2.10).

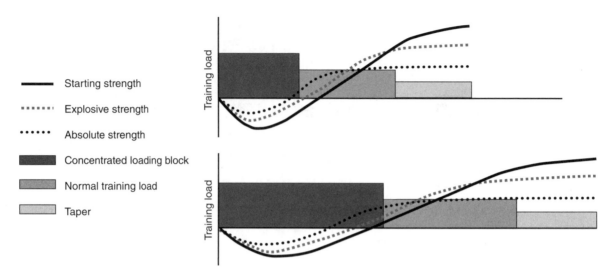

Figure 2.10 Time to adapt to concentrated loading.
Based upon Plisk and Stone 2003 (72) and Stone, Stone, and Sands 2007 (91).

Scientific support for the use of periodic concentrated loading or planned over-reaching can be seen in studies that have explored the neuroendocrine responses to overreaching (40, 42, 44). Investigators have explored the hormonal and endocrine responses to short (1 week) and long (≥3 weeks) periods of concentrated loading fol-lowed by 2 to 5 weeks of recovery. The most commonly used endocrine measure is the **testosterone/cortisol ratio (T:C ratio)**, which indicates the anabolic–catabolic balance. Although the T:C ratio is not a measure of overtraining, it does indicate **preparedness** (72, 91, 99). Thus, a high T:C ratio often corresponds to a high level of performance (33, 72).

A significant increase in training load for 3 weeks or longer results in a decrease in the basal or preexercise T:C ratio, indicating a shift toward a catabolic state that corresponds to a reduction in performance or preparedness (40, 42, 44). Conversely, if after the completion of a concentrated loading period the training load is returned to normal or lower levels, the T:C ratio and performance appear to supercompensate (40, 43). This phenomenon has also been observed in response to substantial increases in training load across one microcycle (33, 86, 99). As noted previously, the duration of the concentrated loading block corresponds to the duration of restitution needed before the supercompensation of performance occurs (figure 2.10).

Conjugated Sequence Loading Paradigm

The **conjugated sequence** paradigm is also referred to as the *coupled successive system* (96). Viru (98), Siff and Verkhoshansky (83), and Plisk and Stone (72) suggested that this method of sequencing loading allows for periods of concentrated loading or overreaching followed by periods of restitution. There are a multitude of methods for implementing this type of loading paradigm, but the most common method is to use blocks of four **microcycles** in which one primary emphasis is highlighted while maintenance loads are allocated to other areas of emphasis (72). Plisk and Stone (72) suggested that the primary goal of this type of loading is to give the athlete periods that are saturated with a specific training stimulus during which fatigue is elevated and some performance variables are decreased. For example, an athlete may undertake a concentrated loading block in which strength is the major emphasis; then during the unloading blocks, the athlete decreases her emphasis on strength while slightly increasing speed work. This pattern of loading will result in a supercompensation effect in which performance is increased dramatically (72). After completing this block, the athlete undertakes a block that imposes a progressively stronger stimulus, thus allowing the athlete to improve her performance.

The literature notes several advantages to this type of loading paradigm (72, 78, 83, 86, 94, 96-98, 100, 103). Proponents of this loading paradigm suggest that a potent stimulus can be delivered to the athlete and performance can be elevated to a higher level than with traditional loading paradigms. Additionally, this type of loading may alleviate the cumulative fatigue associated with parallel or concurrent training with traditional loading paradigms. Finally, work volumes can be reduced over the long term (72). Plisk and Stone (72) suggested that fatigue will be substantial during the accumulation or concentrated loading phase of the block, and the athlete must have the training capacity to tolerate these high training loads. Therefore, it is often recommended that this loading paradigm be used only with advanced athletes (72, 91).

A foundational concept that must be considered within the conjugated sequencing theory is that training can be sequenced in such a way that performance can be elevated at given times. Plisk and Stone (72), in their seminal article on periodization strategies, offered a preseason training example in which concentrated loading blocks of training are interspersed with periods of restitution. In this example, 3-week blocks of concentrated loading are interspersed with 4-week blocks of recovery (table 2.4). Plisk and Stone (72) suggested that by manipulating the training density and duration significantly, different training loads can be used without changing the

Table 2.4 Conjugated Sequence Model of Training and a Modified Conjugated Sequence Model of Training for the Preseason

Training variable	BLOCK OF TRAINING			
	Conjugated loading block 1	Recovery block 1	Conjugated loading block 2	Recovery block 2
CONJUGATED SEQUENCE MODEL OF TRAINING				
Duration	4 weeks	3 weeks	4 weeks	3 weeks
Strength and power training	12 total sessions 4 days/week	12 total sessions 3 days/week	12 total sessions 4 days/week	12 total sessions 3 days/week
Speed, agility, and conditioning training	6 total sessions 2 days/week	12 total sessions 3 days/week	6 total sessions 2 days/week	12 total sessions 3 days/week
MODIFIED CONJUGATED SEQUENCE CREATING MORE INTRABLOCK CONTRAST				
Duration	4 weeks	3 weeks	4 weeks	3 weeks
Strength and power training	12 total sessions 4 days/week	8 total sessions 2 days/week	12 total sessions 4 days/week	8 total sessions 2 days/week
Speed, agility, and conditioning training	6 total sessions 2 days/week	12 total sessions 3 days/week	6 total sessions 2 days/week	12 total sessions 3 days/week

Adapted from Plisk and Stone 2003 (72).

basic intensity and volume parameters. Additionally, these investigators suggested that the coach or athlete can create greater contrast between concentrated loading blocks and restitution blocks by further reducing the distribution of training during the restitution blocks.

Flat Loading

A flat loading paradigm is used only with advanced, experienced, highly trained athletes. In this model, microcycles with similar loading are blocked together followed by recovery microcycle. In the flat loading model (figure 2.11), the first three microcycles create a high physiological demand as a result of the high volume and intensity of training. After the first three microcycles, the athlete undertakes a fourth microcycle, or an unloading period. The length of the unloading period will be dependent upon the overall training load. Note that after weeks 9-11, the highest training loads in the example , there is a 2 week unloading period (weeks 12-13). Stone and O'Bryant (88) suggested that advanced athletes can tolerate this type of loading only if they have trained for many years and have developed a physiological base that allows them to train with such high volumes and intensities.

The flat loading model is suggested for the middle part of the preparatory (preseason) phase only. The step loading model can be used in conjunction with the flat loading model to progressively increase the athlete's training load. Figure 2.12 shows a preparatory phase of training in which the training load changes according to the scope of the phase of training. The program shown in figure 2.12 has three major subphases: general, specific, and precompetitive preparation.

In the general preparation subphase, two types of step loading (3:1 and 2:1) are used to stimulate physiological and psychological adaptations that will prepare the athlete for the next subphase, which entails intensive training. The training goals of general preparation are accomplished through a progressive increase in training load via the use of the step loading model. After completing the general preparation subphase, the athlete moves to the specific preparation, or accumulation, subphase of training.

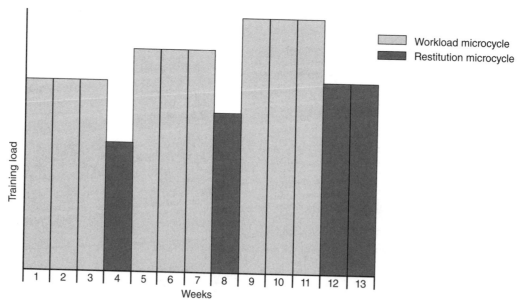

Figure 2.11   Example of a flat loading model.

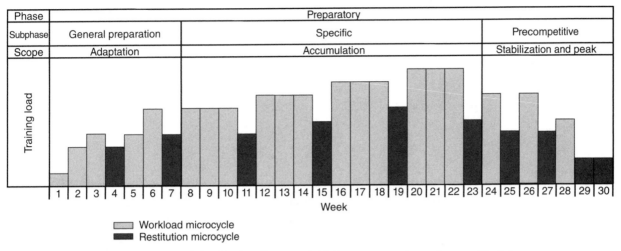

Phase	Preparatory		
Subphase	General preparation	Specific	Precompetitive
Scope	Adaptation	Accumulation	Stabilization and peak

Week

☐ Workload microcycle
■ Restitution microcycle

Figure 2.12 Implementation of the flat loading model into a preparatory phase of training.

In the specific or accumulation subphase, the primary goal is to elevate the athlete's fitness, technical proficiency, and tactical skills as much as possible. This is accomplished by exposing the athlete to high training loads for a series of microcycles followed by regenerative microcycles to offset overtraining. After the completion of this subphase, the focus of training shifts to stabilization and peaking, which comprise the precompetitive subphase. Thus, the three subphases of the preparatory phase prepare the athlete for the competitive phase of the annual training plan.

The dynamics of the loading pattern in the preparatory and competitive phases of training depend on the importance and frequency of competitions. The training loads in these phases are decreased to dissipate fatigue and begin to elevate the athlete's level of performance. Recent research suggests that higher intensities with less volume may be needed to maintain performance during the competitive phase of training (52). However, prior to major competitions, the training load will be decreased to allow the athlete to recover and, if timed correctly, supercompensate, which will maximize performance.

SEQUENCE OF THE TRAINING LOAD

One of the most important aspects of periodization of training is the sequencing of the training load. If sequenced appropriately, each block of training or phase will potentiate the next training phase. For example, research evidence supporting the idea of phase potentiation has been demonstrated for strength and power development (47). Harris and colleagues (47) demonstrated that optimal strength and power performance gains occur when basic strength development precedes the development of strength and power characteristics. Siff and Verkoshansky (83) suggested that the optimal development of medium-duration endurance for a cyclic sport occurs by sequencing training in the following fashion: general physical preparation ⇒ strength ⇒ speed ⇒ endurance (figure 2.13). As noted in figure 2.13, during the early portion of the training cycle, the athlete will undertake a large amount of aerobic training coupled with training to develop general physical attributes. After the first block of training, a block of concentrated strength development is undertaken. After completing this period of concentrated loading, the athlete shifts emphasis to speed development, with a subsequent decrease in strength development in conjunction

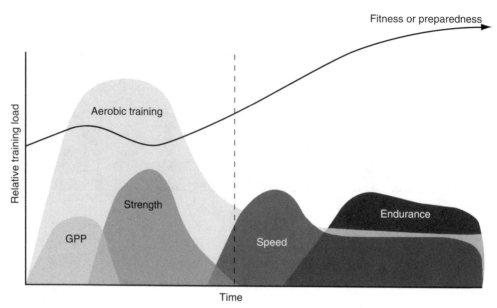

Figure 2.13 Sequential model for developing medium-duration endurance.
Aerobic training comprises approximately the first half of the cycle. In this example, general physical preparation (GPP) precedes a concentrated strength loading phase. This model uses the delayed training adaptations effect while developing speed during the third block of training. The final block is the endurance block, which is marked by specialized training for speed endurance, which specifically targets the competition.
Adapted, by permission, from M.C. Siff, 2003, *Supertraining* (Denver, CO: Supertraining International).

with a decrease in aerobic training. The collective effect of this shift in the training emphasis is a decrease in overall training stress, which allows for recovery to capitalize on the delayed training adaptations associated with concentrated loading. Finally, the athlete begins developing specialized endurance in the final block of training; this is often accomplished through competition (83).

There are endless ways to integrate the loading paradigms discussed in this chapter. For example, Stone and colleagues (91) and Plisk and Stone (72) provided a composite of different loading paradigms that together lead to the development of power (figure 2.14). In this example, the first block of training contains four microcycles that follow a 3:1 step loading model designed to emphasize strength endurance. Because the overall training load is very high in this block, fatigue will also be very high and thus this block is a concentrated loading block. The next block of training involves an overall decrease in training volume to capitalize on delayed training adaptations (83). This is accomplished by using the classic 3:1 loading paradigm and shifting training emphasis from strength endurance to the development of strength. The next three blocks of training shift emphasis to explosive strength and power development. Each block begins with a 1-week microcycle that consists of a high training volume and is then followed by two microcycles with a normal training load and one unloading microcycle. The format of this block of training is repeated two times with an increase in the overall training load in each block. To maximize the training responses, a summated microcycle model is used across all three of these blocks of training.

When choosing how to integrate the different loading models presented in this chapter, the coach must consider the training status of the athlete, the goals of the

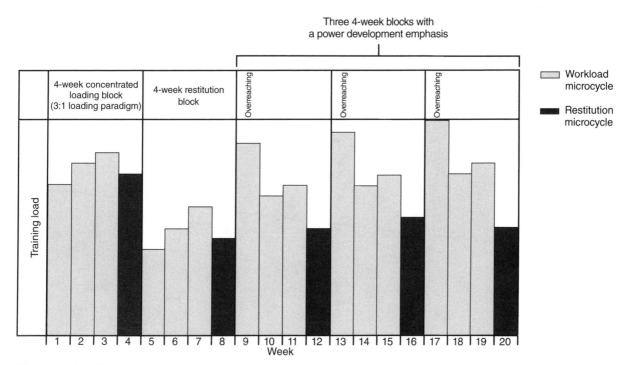

Figure 2.14 Example of the integration of multiple loading paradigms into a training cycle designed to emphasize power.
Adapted from Stone, Stone, and Sands 2007 (91) and Plisk and Stone 2003 (72).

training plan, the recovery interventions available to the athlete, the amount of time the athlete can dedicate to training, and the physiological responses to different loading models presented in the scientific literature. By using the scientific information available, the coach will be able to match the different loading models to the needs of the athlete, which will optimize training adaptations and lead to improved performance.

SUMMARY OF MAJOR CONCEPTS

Athletes must establish a strong multilateral development before specializing in a sport. If specialization occurs too soon in an athlete's development, it is likely that the athlete will achieve high levels of performance only during the junior years and will experience burnout soon after. The incorporation of a multilateral training base is especially important for young athletes. As the athlete matures, specialized training becomes more important. Such training will be dominated by drills and techniques that will lead to a faster rate of adaptations and ultimately to greater levels of performance.

A key to performance improvement is the planning of load progression. With young athletes, simple loading patterns with small amounts of variation can be very effective. However, advanced athletes require greater amounts of variation and more complex loading paradigms. Regardless of the athlete's level of development, regeneration and recovery must be included in the training program. Periods of recovery are essential to remove training-induced fatigue, replenish energy stores, and provide time for physiological and psychological adaptations to occur.

CHAPTER 3

PREPARATION FOR TRAINING

All athletic programs should address the physical, technical, tactical, psychological, and theoretical aspects of training. These factors are essential to any training program regardless of the athlete's chronological age, individual potential, level of athletic development, training age, or phase of training. However, the emphasis placed on each factor varies according to the time of year, the athlete's training age, the athlete's biological age, and the sport being trained for. Although training factors are highly interdependent, there is a specific manner in which each is developed. Physical training is the foundation on which all of the other factors related to training are developed (figure 3.1). The stronger the physical foundation, the greater the potential for developing technical, tactical, and psychological attributes.

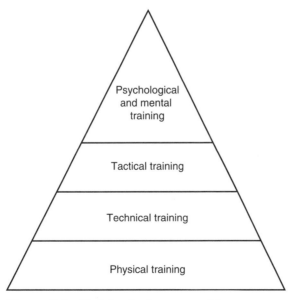

Figure 3.1 Training factors pyramid.

Coaches, especially coaches of team sports, often overlook the strong relationship between physical and technical training. If the physical training base is inadequately developed, high levels of fatigue can be generated and the athlete will be unable to develop the other training factors. This often occurs when the preparatory phase (e.g., the preseason) is too short and the appropriate physiological adaptations are not developed. When this happens, the ability to effectively develop tactical, technical, and psychological skills is impaired, which increases the risk of poor performances during competition. One can consider physical training the foundation for the development of technique, whereas technique is central to the ability to develop and use tactical skills in sport. Additionally, as one's physical capacity improves, technical and tactical capacities improve as well, which will increase self-confidence and other psychological factors. Thus, physical training capacity is a cornerstone from which all training-related factors are developed, ultimately leading to the ability to excel in sport.

PHYSICAL TRAINING

The physiological attributes necessary for sporting success are developed through appropriate physical training (31, 41). These physiological adaptations are the basis from which technical and tactical advances are established. Without the development of physical abilities, the athlete's capacity to tolerate training will be significantly impaired, resulting in an inability to develop the technical and tactical attributes necessary for sporting success. Impairments in technical and tactical development usually occur as a result of accumulated fatigue, which is easily avoided through development of the appropriate physiological base via structured physical training. These concepts are among the best-kept secrets of the Eastern European training system.

Physical training has two main goals: The first is to increase the athlete's physiological potential, and the second is to maximize sport-specific biomotor abilities. In a periodized training plan, physical training is developed in a structured, sequential pattern (figure 3.2) (27, 30, 31, 38, 41). Physical training can be broken into two interdependent parts:

- General physical training (GPT)
- Sport-Specific physical training (SSPT)

Phase of training	Preparatory phase		Competitive phase
Phase of development	1	2	3
Duration (weeks)	≥3	≥6	≥4
Objective	1. Undertake general physical training	1. Undertake sport-specific physical training 2. Perfect specific sport skills (biomotor abilities)	1. Perfect specific sport skills (biomotor abilities) 2. Maintain physiological base

Figure 3.2 A sequential approach to the development of physical training during an annual plan.

General physical training (GPT) and sport-specific physical training (SSPT) are developed during the preparatory phase of the periodized training plan. During the early part of the preparatory phase GPT is the primary emphasis, and as the athlete moves through this phase of training the emphasis shifts to SSPT. Thus GPT predominates during the early parts of the preparatory phase, whereas SSPT is dominant at the end of this phase.

GPT begins at the initiation of the preparatory phase, where the scope of training is to build a solid physiological foundation. This solid foundation is established via the use of high volumes of training performed at moderate intensities. The amount of time dedicated to GPT depends on many factors such as the athlete's training age, the athlete's needs, and the sport being trained for. The physiological adaptations established with GPT enable the athlete to tolerate the training loads encountered during SSPT.

As SSPT becomes more dominant training intensity increases, depending on the requirements of the sport. In some cases, especially at the professional level, when the preparatory phase is very short (e.g., soccer in Europe), certain elements of intensity may be emphasized during the early parts of the preparatory phase. The SSPT period builds on the physiological base established during GPT and prepares the athlete for the competitive phase of the training plan. Nádori and Granek (31) suggested that SSPT is a transition between GPT and the competitive phase of training. During the competitive period, the minimum objective of physical training is to maintain sport-specific physical development established during the preparatory phase of training (31). However, in some instances it may be possible to improve sport-specific physical development during this phase. Conversely, if training and competition are not sequenced appropriately and adequate recovery does not occur, sport-specific physical development will begin to deteriorate (31, 34, 45).

General Physical Training

The ultimate goal of GPT is to improve the athlete's working capacity and maximize physiological adaptations to prepare the athlete for future workloads. This phase of training targets the development of every component of physical fitness to increase work capacity (31). The higher the work capacity developed by the athlete during GPT, the greater her potential to adapt to the increasing physiological and psychological demands of training and competition. As stated in chapter 2, the physical development of young athletes predominantly focuses on multilateral development, which is accomplished through GPT. GPT for young athletes is rather uniform regardless of the sports being targeted in the training plan. Conversely, with advanced athletes the requirements of the sport must be addressed during GPT.

Sport-Specific Physical Training

SSPT is based on the foundation established during GPT. SSPT serves as a transition from GPT to the competitive phase (31). In this capacity, SSPT further develops the athlete's physical capacity in a fashion that is very specific to the demands of the sport. Targeting physiological adaptations that correspond to a specific sporting activity is of paramount importance when attempting to maximize competitive success (42, 45). If SSPT is sequenced and planned appropriately, the resultant physiological adaptations will increase the athlete's work capacity, which ultimately will result in higher levels of competitive performance. Well-planned SSPT will enhance the athlete's ability to recover from and adapt to the training load, which will ultimately enhance her performance capacity.

GPT and SSPT should be clearly differentiated, because the incorrect implementation of either type of training can result in inappropriate adaptations, which ultimately will decrease competitive performance. One example of an incorrect understanding of GPT and SSPT can be seen regarding the concept of endurance. The scientific literature indicates that different types of endurance are needed depending on the physiological demands of the sport (9, 45). A common misconception held by coaches is that aerobic exercise, resulting in what has been termed **low-intensity exercise endurance (LIEE)**, is important for all sports (44). Although aerobic training is a great way to improve LIEE or aerobic fitness, it generally compromises an athlete's ability to produce high forces or power outputs in a repetitive fashion, an ability required in most high-speed or strength and power–based sports (9, 44). These types of sports require a type of endurance that has been termed **high-intensity exercise endurance (HIEE)** (44). HIEE requires the athlete to sustain or repeat high-intensity exercise with exercise durations of less than 2 min (44). Therefore, for certain sports the athlete must develop appropriate endurance to maximize performance. HIEE can be developed through the performance of repeated sprints (4), sprint interval training (6, 7), and resistance training (36). Recently it has been shown that interval training has the potential to improve LIEE (6, 7, 19, 25) without compromising HIEE.

During the preparation phase, SSPT includes higher volumes of sprint or interval training and tactical drills that are specific to the sport. One strategy is to create scenarios during SSPT that model the conditions experienced in competition. For example, one might model an American football game by using 15 sprint intervals with a work to rest ratio of 1:10 (i.e., 5 s work, 50 s rest) to simulate what is encountered during competition (36). The implementation of SSPT in the preparatory phase of training depends on many factors including the athlete's training age, his chronological age, and the requirements of the sport (figure 3.3). Physiological adaptations to SSPT can occur rapidly, in as little as 2 weeks of training (6, 7, 19). SSPT may be undertaken for 2 months or more, depending on the characteristics of the sport and the athlete's level of development.

PREPARATORY PHASE		
Elite/pro athletes	General physical training	• Sport-specific training • Perfecting sport-specific biomotor abilities
Beginner to intermediate athletes	General physical training	• Sport-specific training • Perfecting sport-specific biomotor abilities
Developmental athletes	General physical training	• General physical training • Introducing sport-specific training elements

Figure 3.3 A basic representation of the duration of general physical training and sport-specific training between elite and professional athletes, beginners, and children.

EXERCISE FOR PHYSICAL TRAINING

An exercise is a motor act that can be used to target general physiological adaptations, movement patterns, or specific muscle groups that are related to the performance of the athletic skill. To simulate maximal amounts of physiological adaptation, the athlete must train for many years (ranging from 8 to 12 years) to optimize performance (28, 38). During these training years, exercises must be repeated systematically to stimulate adaptations that will improve performance.

Many training exercises are available to the coach when constructing a training plan. The coach should choose exercises that target the athlete's needs and the demands of the sport. Exercises can be classified as general or specific in regard to the development of precise biomotor abilities. Both general and specific exercises will be used throughout the training year, but their contribution to the training plan will vary between training cycles and depending on the athlete's training age (15).

Exercises for General Physical Development

Exercises for general physical development are nonspecific exercises that contribute to the athlete's physical development. These exercises develop strength, flexibility, mobility, aerobic fitness, and anaerobic capacity (15). Exercises for general physical development lay the foundation for further training by improving basic motor qualities that are central components of a multilateral program (15, 38).

Exercises that focus on general physical development are central to the training plans of children and young athletes. These exercises are also important during the early part of the preparatory phase of training (31) or with athletes who lack a solid training base. These types of exercises fall into two classifications. The first classification consists of exercises that are performed without implements (calisthenics) or are performed with objects that are not used in competition (such as stall bars, benches, skipping rope, medicine balls). The second classification includes exercises derived from the actual sport or related sporting events. A contemporary interpretation of this concept can be seen in cross-training, where during certain parts of the training year athletes participate in sporting activities that are related to the sport in which they compete (20). For example, a cyclist may participate in cross-country skiing in the off-season to develop cardiovascular fitness.

General physical development exercises are tools for developing overall fitness. Athletes need a balanced program in which muscular strength, flexibility, and endurance (HIEE or LIEE depending on the sport being trained for) are developed. For example, when strength training, an athlete can use high-volume, low-intensity training plans to target general physical development. This type of training, if done appropriately, can increase muscular strength, muscular endurance (HIEE and LIEE), and flexibility (if undertaken through a full range of motion), which can lay the foundation for specialized training that targets precise biomotor abilities.

Exercises for Specific Biomotor Development

Exercises for specific biomotor development target physiological adaptations, movement patterns, or muscle groups that are necessary for the sporting activity. This type of exercise is central to the concept of specificity of training. Specificity of training is the degree of similarity between the training exercise and the activities used in the sport (45). The more similar the characteristics of the training exercise are to the sport, the greater the transfer of training effects to the sport will be. When assessing the transferability of a training exercise to a sporting activity, the coach should consider the bioenergetics (33), movement patterns (39), and factors related to overload (45). The more similarities that are found between the training exercise and sport in regard to these factors, the greater will be the potential for the transfer of training effects.

The concept of movement pattern specificity reveals that the type of muscle action, kinematic characteristics (i.e., movement patterns), kinetic characteristics (i.e., forces, rate of force development, power output), muscle groups activated, and acceleration or velocity characteristics of the movement all contribute to the exercise's ability to transfer to the sporting activity. Particularly important to training specificity are the movement pattern and the primary muscles used in the sporting activity. For example, the primary movers related to sprinting performance are the muscles of the lower body. Therefore, a coach who works with sprinters should use exercises that target the development of lower-body muscles. However, the coach should also consider the synergistic muscles that are used in concert with the muscles of the leg. The best way to accomplish this is to target movement patterns. For example, the sprinter might use the power clean as a training exercise, because it has a power, force, and velocity profile similar to that used in sprinting. Additionally, the power clean activates the muscles of the trunk and other synergistic muscles that affect running performance. Many exercises activate the prime movers and synergistic muscles related to sprinting performance, including jumping (plyometrics), squatting (back squat, one-leg squat, front squat), and weighted sled pulling. In the scientific literature, sprinting performance has been significantly related to power clean performance (1), back squat performance (11), and vertical jumping performance (5, 11).

The use of exercises that are external to the athlete's sport is important, because sport performance alone will not give the athlete a great enough training stimulus to maximize performance gains (e.g., leg power, speed, or force-generating capacity). For example, the best high jumpers in the world do not perform more than 800 jumps per year, and this number of jumps is insufficient to develop leg power. To maximize performance gains, these athletes perform tens of thousands of exercises aimed at developing leg power (e.g., back squats, power cleans, plyometric exercises).

Sport-specific exercises are essential to maximize the transfer of training effects from training to sport performance. These exercises are very important in the preparatory phase of training but also should be considered essential components of the competitive phase of training. Some coaches and athletes exclude sport-specific exercise during the competitive phase of the periodized training plan, choosing to only perform technical training during this time. This practice is problematic because the exclusion of sport-specific training exercises during the competitive phase may lead to a loss of fitness that reduces performance as the season progresses. The coach and athlete should consider sport-specific exercises as essential components of every phase of a training plan because these exercises transfer directly to sporting performance.

TECHNICAL TRAINING

One element that discriminates various sporting activities is the technique or motor skills required. Technique encompasses all of the movement patterns, skills, and technical elements that are necessary to perform the sport. Technique can be considered the manner of performing a skill or physical exercise. Athletes must continually strive to establish perfect technique to create the most efficient movement patterns.

The more perfect or biomechanically sound the technique is, the more efficient or economical the athlete will be. For example, less energy is expended when an athlete has good running economy or technique (32). Trained runners have been reported to be more economical and to consume 20% to 30% less oxygen compared with novice runners who are running at the same submaximal speed (10, 14, 29). Biomechanists have suggested running economy is affected by stride length (8), stride rate (24), vertical stiffness (13), net vertical impulse of ground reaction forces (21), and ground contact time (32). Thus, if a runner becomes technically skilled and can optimize her stride rate, ground contact time, and stride rate, she will be more economical and thus more efficient. The relationship between technique and movement efficiency is important in all sports. Athletes must continually strive to maximize technical proficiency and therefore must incorporate technical training into their overall training plan.

AP Photo/Matt Dunham

Proper technique allows an athlete to efficiently perform a skill, so technical training must be included in training plans.

Technique and Style

Every sporting activity has a technical standard or technical model that is accepted as being perfect or as close as possible to perfect and represents the accepted model of performance (15). A model of performance must be biomechanically sound and physiologically efficient to be widely accepted. The model is generally not developed based on the technique of elite or champion athletes because their technique may not be biomechanically or physiologically sound. Therefore, simply copying the technique of a champion is not advisable.

A technical model should exhibit some flexibility, because it should be constantly updated based on new research findings. The technical model should be used as a point of comparison for an athlete's performance (15). This allows the coach to develop a training plan that targets deficiencies. Although the technical model is invaluable for training purposes, the athlete likely will develop her own individualized performance style. The structure of the skill is not different, but the athlete may make the skill look different as a result of her individual style of performance.

Individual technical styles are simply adaptations of an accepted model of performance that occur in response to technical problems in performing a motor act.

For instance, the Fosbury flop (named after the American who won the high jump at the Mexico Olympic Games in 1968) changed the technique of high jumping dramatically. This technique requires the athlete to cross over the bar by facing it with the back rather than the front part of the body. Scientific examination revealed that this technique was more mechanically efficient than the classic technique. When first introduced, this individual high jumping style was not considered the optimal technique. However, in contemporary high jumping the Fosbury flop is considered the optimal model (47). This example depicts how an individual style can become a technical model.

There are also model techniques for optimal performance in team sports (23). Things like shot distribution, execution, and rally length in net sports can all be analyzed and used to develop a model of performance (23). In team sports, the application of a model of performance can be very team specific and related to the skill set or attributes of the team. The style of performance can have tactical implications (23) and can affect how the team undertakes technical and tactical preparations.

Individualization of Technique

Not all techniques are useful for all athletes. For example, a novice athlete will use a more simplified technique than a world-class athlete (15). Therefore, when introducing technical elements to an athlete's training plan the coach must understand the individual athlete's level of development and her technical abilities and deficiencies.

In most instances technique is developed in stages, whereby simplified techniques are introduced first. After the athlete masters these basic elements, the coach then adapts the technique and adds elements that increase the technical difficulty of the training exercise. For instance, when working with a young discus thrower, a coach begins with perfecting the standing throw (17). Once the standing throw is mastered, the coach can add other elements, such as a 4/4 turn (i.e., step-in) or footwork drills, to begin teaching the athlete the rotational technique needed to be a successful discus thrower (17). Novice athletes generally use techniques that are vastly different than those of elite athletes as a result of their developmental status.

Variations can exist in the performance of a technical skill. Often these variations occur as a result of the complexity of the task or the biomechanical or physiological attributes of the athlete. Cyclic sports (e.g., running, cycling, rowing) often exhibit fewer interindividual technical differences, whereas acyclic sports (e.g., throwing, lifting, some team sports) have a greater potential for variations in technique. For example, Al Oerter tended to hold the discus in a lower position during his rotation than did most discus throwers, which is generally considered to be a technical flaw. However, this individual technical pattern was highly effective for Oerter because of his highly developed upper-body strength and fast leg speed (40). This example demonstrates that technique is developed based on the athlete's abilities, physiological and mechanical characteristics, and level of development.

When teaching a technical element or whole technique, the coach must understand the athlete's physical and psychological capacities. For example, if the thrower does not possess an adequate strength base, he may not be strong enough to keep his trunk vertical throughout the throwing movement (26). Therefore, it may not be warranted to work on the rotation portion of the throw until strength has been substantially increased. An inadequately developed physical base will limit the athlete's ability to learn technical aspects of the sport. This scenario strengthens the argument that physical training is the foundation of all training factors (figure 3.1).

Sometimes an athlete will be forced to interrupt his training schedule (e.g., because of illness or accidents). These interruptions in training generally affect the athlete's physical capacity, which may result in slight alterations in technique as a result of lost fitness. When athletes experience a decline in physical capacity, a concomitant deterioration in technique often occurs. Additionally, high levels of fatigue can negatively affect an athlete's technique or ability to perfect technique. High levels of fatigue are usually related to low levels of physical work capacity. Therefore, when physical work capacity returns to normal or fatigue is dissipated, the athlete will be able to reestablish his technique. Because of the negative effects of fatigue on technique development, some authors suggest that technical training should occur before conditioning and a heavy conditioning day should not precede a technique day (15).

Learning and Skill Formation

Learning technique is a process in which an athlete acquires mechanical skill, perfects the skill, and then ingrains the skill (38). The ability of an athlete to learn new mechanical skills depends on many factors including the athlete's current technical skill and the complexity of the skill that is being targeted (37). The athlete's physical attributes or level of development will affect her ability to learn new skills (38). However, many other factors such as the athlete's learning style or the teaching methods used can also affect how easily the athlete acquires the new skill set.

The learning of a new skill set has been suggested to be a three-part process (38), which may not always be broken into discrete parts because the steps are often blended. During the first part of learning a new skill, the athlete should receive a detailed explanation of the skill and observe the skill being performed. After the initial demonstration and explanation, the athlete begins to develop the rough technical aspects of the skill, paying particular emphasis to the most crucial phases of the movement pattern (38). During the second phase of the learning process, the athlete begins to refine the skill, a long-term process in which many repetitions of the movement are performed. During this phase technical errors are continually addressed and the athlete strives to perfect the movement pattern and minimize or eliminate technical deficiencies (38). In the third phase of learning the skill, the athlete begins to ingrain the movement pattern so that the skill is automated and happens naturally; this requires large amounts of repetitive practice undertaken for significant amounts of time.

Evolutional Character of Technique

Technique continues to evolve as technological and creative innovations are introduced into the sporting environment. Over time, training practices and techniques change and what was once an advanced technique may become outdated. Technical innovations in sport can come from the coach's imagination or from scientific inquiry into the physiological and mechanical aspects of the sport. New techniques may work well in ideal situations or in practice, but they must be translated into the competitive arena before they become accepted as a technical model. Not all new techniques or ideas will translate into the competitive arena because this environment is distinctly unique attributable to its high levels of physical and psychological stress and its random nature. When coaches and athletes attempt to improve and perfect technique, they must model the technique not only in ideal situations but also in competition.

TACTICAL TRAINING

Tactics and strategy are important concepts in coaching and athletics. Both terms are derived from the military vocabulary and have a Greek origin. The word *tactics* is derived from the Greek word *taktika,* which refers to the how things are arranged. *Strategy* comes from the Greek word *strategos,* which means "general" or "the art of the general." In the theory of warfare, strategy and tactics are categorized separately because both terms have unique dimensions. When examined in the military context, strategies focus on wide spaces, long periods, and large movements of forces, whereas tactics address smaller spaces, times, and forces. When examined in a hierarchical perspective, strategies precede war planning and the actual tactics that are used on the battlefield.

Tactics and strategies can be used during training or in a competition with direct or indirect opponents. Strategy is the organization of training, play, or competition that is based on a philosophy or way of approaching a problem (e.g., training or competition). Within the strategic framework are tactics, or the training or game plans. A good example of the interrelationship between strategies and tactics can be seen in the training process, where strength and conditioning coaches induce physiological responses by using tactics that are organized into rational systems (34). When one is attempting to understand the relationship between strategies and tactics, the simplest approach is to consider strategy as the art of projecting and directing training or competitive plans and tactics as the organization of these plans.

Tactical training refers to training offensive and defensive objectives (e.g., scoring, a specific play) that are germane to a sport. For example, in soccer, skills that are considered as part of tactical training include passing, pace of attacks, tackling, pass distribution, dribbling skills, and length of passes (23). Each sport requires certain skills, and thus tactical training may be different for each sporting activity. Tactical actions are part of the strategic framework used to train the athlete and prepare for competition. The basis of any successful tactical plan, regardless of the sporting activity, is a high level of technical proficiency. Thus, technique is a limiting factor for all tactical maneuvers, and tactics are a function of an athlete's technique. Technical abilities are based on the physiological adaptations that occur in response to physical training. Thus, physical training is the foundation for technical and tactical training (figure 3.1).

Tasks and Specificity of Tactical Training

For most elite athletes, there is very little difference between their physiological development and their technical skill (35). Often, when all other factors are held equal, the winning athlete uses more mature, advanced, and rational tactics. Even though tactical training relies heavily on physical and technical training, there appears to be an important link between psychological and tactical training (35).

Tactical mastery is founded on deep theoretical knowledge and the capacity to apply tactics appropriate for the competitive environment. Tactical training may include the following:

- Studying strategic elements of the principle sport
- Studying the rules and regulations for competition in the sport or event
- Evaluating the tactical abilities of the best athletes in the sport
- Researching the strategies used by opponents

- Evaluating the physical and psychological attributes and potential of opponents
- Evaluating the facilities and environment of competition sites
- Developing individual tactics that are based on personal strengths and weaknesses
- Critically analyzing past performances against specific opponents
- Developing an individualized tactical model with appropriate variations to meet multiple competitive demands
- Practicing a tactical model in training until it becomes ingrained

The development of tactical skills is accomplished with the same basic steps outlined in the section titled Learning and Skill Formation. Traditionally, athletes approach tactical skills training after developing the appropriate physiological basis (physical training) and technical skills. However, it is also possible to develop all three factors simultaneously as a result of proper planning and training program **integration**.

When we examine tactical training principles, it may be helpful to classify sports into general categories. Most sporting activities can be classified into five basic groups as a result of their tactical similarities.

- *Group 1:* Sports in which athletes compete separately, with no direct contact with opponents. These sports generally require athletes to perform in a predetermined order. Examples include alpine skiing, track cycling (individual events such as the 1,000 m or 4,000 m pursuit), cycling (time trial), figure skating, gymnastics, diving, in-line skating, and weightlifting.

- *Group 2:* Sports in which athletes start the competition at the same time, in either large or small groups. In these sports, some cooperation with teammates is possible, thus adding a tactical element that requires some teamwork. Examples include running events in track and field, cross-country skiing, cycling (track and road cycling), Nordic skiing, cross country running, and swimming.

- *Group 3:* Sports characterized by direct competition between two opponents. Examples include boxing, wrestling, tennis, fencing, and mixed martial arts.

- *Group 4:* Sports in which the opponents are in teams and the athletes have direct contact during the game or competition. These sports include baseball, soccer, American football, hockey, and rugby.

- *Group 5:* Sports that require athletic participation in a combination of different sporting activities. These sports are complex because they require tactics that are central to the individual sports and the general competitive plan. Sports in this group include heptathlon and decathlon in track and field, biathlon (shooting and Nordic skiing), triathlon, and modern pentathlon.

Classifying sports into broad groups helps us examine sports tactics. The innate similarities between the sports in each group can provide a deeper tactical understanding of sports with similar characteristics.

Uniform Distribution of Energy

The ability to maintain tactical proficiency under conditions of fatigue is an important determinant of competitive success. Therefore, the athlete's tactical training must include sessions that require the athlete to perform under conditions of fatigue.

© Human Kinetics

Before you can create a training program, you need to know what kinds of tactical skills are required.

The coach can create such a condition by extending practice after the athlete has become fatigued, informing the athlete either before the session begins or at some point during the session. Another possibility is to use several rested sparring partners during training, which would force the athlete or team to constantly perform at a high level. The physical training base provides the foundation for the athlete's ability to perform under conditions of fatigue: The higher the physical training base, the greater the work capacity.

Another consideration is the athlete's ability to mobilize all of her resources to finish. In close races or games, success often depends on the athlete's capacity to mobilize all forces and give everything for the final moments of the competition. The coach can create scenarios that require the athlete to maximize effort in simulated end-of-competition situations; an example is simulating the time left in a game or competition and requiring the athlete to increase the tempo of her tactical practice.

Technical Solutions to Tactical Tasks

Often athletes have to perform under adverse or unusual environmental conditions, such as on a wet field, in a strong wind, in cold water, or in a noisy environment. Such conditions require special preparation. The following guidelines may help athletes adapt to these adverse conditions.

- Perform skills and tactical maneuvers correctly and efficiently under unusual or simulated conditions.
- Organize exhibition games or competitions with partners who follow the same tactics as future opponents.
- Create unique situations that demand each athlete to independently create tactical resolutions.

The ability to demonstrate tactical discipline is essential in training. However, in competition the athlete may experience a tactical problem that was not addressed or simulated by the coach. In such a case the athlete must draw on his training and experience to create an immediate solution to the tactical problem. This process can be facilitated by exposing the athlete to various situations in training and exhibition competitions so he can create a repertoire of tactical solutions to draw on when adverse situations occur during competition.

Maximizing Teammate Cooperation

The cohesive interaction of a team is essential for success in sports classified in groups 2 and 4. Using techniques such as limiting external conditions (e.g., decreasing the available time or playing space) can force the team to interact and cooperate. Additional stress can be introduced by adding fatigue to these scenarios. These scenarios will help athletes learn how to interact and cooperate during adverse situations.

An additional strategy is to perform tactical maneuvers against a conventional opponent who is attempting to counteract the play. This scenario can be created by using an opposing team or by creating an opposing team with reserve players during training. The coach should instruct these players to behave as if they are not familiar with the applied tactics. Reserve players should participate in the preparation of game tactics, because changes in the team lineup increase the potential of a breakdown in cooperation and tactics. It is useful during practices to replace key players with spare players. This allows reserve players to become familiar with the team tactics and the other players, and it allows the existing group to see how the reserve player operates and how the team tactics will change with that player's presence. These techniques allow the team to develop new tactical combinations that can improve the team's competitive capabilities.

Perfecting the Team's Flexibility

To maximize team cooperation, the coach should introduce changes in the team's tactics that will increase its tactical flexibility. The team can use tactical flexibility to create scenarios that will surprise opponents. A plethora of tactical variations can be used, such as the following:

- Substitute different tactics at predetermined times or in response to signals from a coach or designated player (e.g., captain).
- Substitute players who bring a new and unexpected game change to the team.
- Expose the team to exhibition games against teams that use various styles of play. This allows the team to prepare for these scenarios in future games and develop tactical solutions to the style of play encountered.

Tactical Thinking and the Game Plan

A central component of tactical training is developing tactical thinking skills. The ability to think tactically is limited by the athlete's knowledge and repertoire of tactical skills. To think tactically, the athlete must learn to do the following:

- Realistically and correctly evaluate opponents as well as himself.
- Instantly recall technical skills and combinations of skills that can be used under game situations.
- Anticipate his opponent's tactics and use the appropriate tactics to counteract them.

- Disguise or conceal tactics that may prevent the opponent from sensing and counteracting the plan of attack.
- Perfectly coordinate individual actions within the team tactics.

The competition or game plan is based on analysis of tactical trends and the opponent's strengths and weakness. Components of the game plan are then integrated into the tactical training portion of the training plan. The game plan usually is progressively introduced over the last two or three microcycles so that it can be perfected by the time of competition. The game or competition plan is important for several reasons:

- To instill confidence and optimism about the upcoming competition.
- To inform the athlete about the place, facilities, and conditions under which the contest will be organized.
- To introduce the strengths and weaknesses of future opponents into each training factor.
- To use the athlete's past performance as a reference from which to build confidence. Without disregarding the athlete's weaknesses, emphasize the strong points from which to build a realistic optimism.
- To develop realistic objectives for the competition using all of the preceding factors.

The implementation of the game or competition plan occurs in several phases. First a preliminary game plan is developed. The game plan and its tactical elements are then implemented into the game situation. After the game is completed, the plan is comprehensively analyzed allowing for the further refinement of the plan and its tactical components.

Creating the Preliminary Game Plan

The first phase of game planning involves developing the preliminary game plan prior to the competition. The coach develops this plan after comprehensively analyzing potential tactical difficulties that the athlete or team is likely to encounter during the game or competition. Tactical solutions or objectives are then created in response to the potential tactical difficulties revealed during the critical analysis. In the context of the tactical plan, individual tactical objectives are assigned to players based on their strengths and weaknesses. The tactical objectives are then practiced as part of the tactical training plan.

In the days prior to the game, the athlete should avoid changing her habits because this may adversely affect game-time performance. Two or three days before the competition, the coach should reinforce the game plan and the tactics that have been developed, using structured practices that allow for the development of good technical and tactical performances. When possible, the training lesson should mirror the competitive model. The coach should acknowledge good performances to develop confidence, create motivation, and increase competitive desire.

As the competition approaches, the coach should focus only on a few major points of the game plan without overwhelming the athlete with too many instructions. No matter how detailed the preliminary game plan, there is always a potential for unforeseen technical and tactical occurrences. Therefore the plan must be flexible enough to allow the athlete to respond to these challenges.

Applying the Game Plan

The second phase of the game plan is the implementation of the general plan in an actual game situation. The initial phase of the game is generally used to test the main elements of the tactical plan. In this portion of the game, the team will strive to unveil the opponent's game plan while hiding their own plan. The athlete will need to be able to analyze and comprehend the tactical situations that arise and choose a tactical action to apply. The ability to comprehend these tactical situations will depend on the athlete's tactical knowledge, experience, team dynamics, and tactical preparation. These attributes will allow the athlete to solve problems by instantaneously working through periods of analysis, synthesis (i.e., combining separate parts into a whole), comparison, and generalization. This process allows the athlete to determine the most appropriate solutions to the tactical demands of the game. The individual decision-making processes will occur in concert with the group decision-making dynamics within the team. The coordinated efforts between each individual on the team allow for rational, original, rapid, economical, and efficient solutions to the fluctuating tactical challenges that arise during the game.

A coach needs to analyze how well a game plan is working during a competition. Is an athlete able to choose the correct tactical action to apply to a certain situation?

Analyzing the Game Plan

The third phase of game planning requires the coach to perform a systematic, critical analysis of the game plan. The coach should closely examine how the plan was developed, the effectiveness of the individual tactical roles in the plan, the success of the tactical plan, and, if the game plan did not succeed, the reasons why. The more detailed the analysis, the more it will reveal about the strengths and weakness of the plan.

The most appropriate time to analyze the game plan and discuss the results of the analysis with the athletes depends on the outcome of the game or competition. If the result was favorable, analysis of the game can occur soon after the game's completion and discussion of the results of the analysis can occur during the first practice session after the game. Conversely, if the outcome of the game is unfavorable, the analysis should be delayed to allow for a critical examination of the performance. The coach should discuss the analysis with the athletes 2 or 3 days after the competition to allow time for the psychological wounds to heal. When discussing the analysis with the athletes, the coach should be clear and reasonable and should highlight the positive aspects of the performance. The coach should also project optimism and propose a few tactical elements to emphasize in subsequent training.

Perfecting Technique and Tactical Training

Both technique and strategy in sport are in continual flux. Technical and tactical knowledge is continually changing in direct response to the evolution of sport science (50) and practical experience. This increase in technical and tactical knowledge increases the effectiveness of training. To achieve technical and tactical mastery, the coach and athlete must optimize three relationships between conflicting concepts: integration–differentiation, stability–variability, and standardization–individualization (18).

Integration–Differentiation

Learning or perfecting a skill as well as training an ability is a multifactorial process, through which the athlete can develop technical and strategic mastery. Central to the process are the concepts of integration and differentiation. **Integration** refers to combining the individual skill or tactical maneuvers into a whole process, whereas **differentiation** involves analytically processing each component of the whole process.

When learning a new technique or skill, the athlete progresses from simple technical or tactical elements to complex elements. To master a skill or tactical maneuver that has already been learned, the process is reversed: The athlete and coach must analyze the whole skill or tactical maneuver by breaking it down into subunits to determine whether technical errors exist. If the athlete and coach determine that each subunit is free of technical faults, it is likely that errors exist in how the individual subunits are unified into the whole system (e.g., connective parts or two elements in a gymnastics routine or other sport skill). If the examination of the connections between the subunits does not reveal technical errors, further differentiation of the skill is necessary to isolate the sources of error. Once the sources of error are isolated, the coach and athlete must develop strategies to eliminate the error.

The integration–differentiation process can be used to perfect or change the technical or tactical model being used. Figure 3.4 illustrates how a skill can be perfected through the use of a systematic integration (i.e. constructing whole skills) and differentiation (i.e. dissecting skill into subunits and determining where errors are) process. The outcome of this process is mastery of the skill.

If the coach determines that a technical skill or tactical maneuver is insufficient, it may be warranted to alter the performance model. The coach must determine why an error occurred and critically analyze the model to determine what components can be removed or modified (figure 3.5). Determining technical errors occurs with the same differentiation process presented earlier. Once technical errors are isolated and the coach has decided that the model of performance must be altered, the technical error must be "unlearned" and a new technical skill or element taught. Once the athlete learns the new element or skill, she must practice the skill until it becomes automatic; then the skill is reintroduced into the whole system of performance and the athlete practices the skill until it is mastered.

Stability–Variability

When training athletes there is a constant trade-off between **stability** and **variability** (45, 51). The optimal training stimulus occurs in response to a systematic variation in training load, intensity, or content (45). If, however, the training stimulus or workloads are prescribed in a monotonous fashion the athlete will experience accommodation or stagnation problems, which will halt any improvement in performance (43, 45). Therefore, the training program should include planned variation, whereby novel or

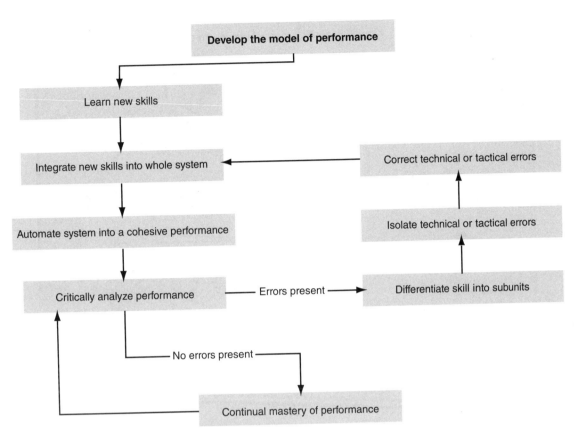

Figure 3.4 Perfecting a model of performance.
Adapted from Teodorescu and Florescu 1971 (48).

seminovel tasks are introduced or reintroduced periodically throughout the annual training plan. The introduction of novel or seminovel tasks will result in a greater stimulatory effect and greater adaptation (22), which will stabilize the athlete's skill and performance level. Therefore, variability in training (e.g., changes to volume, load, exercises, and workout density) provides a stabilizing effect in regard to performance and skill acquisition.

Standardization–Individualization

There is a constant conflict between the standardization of a skill set and the individual traits and characteristics of the athlete. The coach must develop and stabilize the athlete's technical skills while accounting for the individual's psychological and biological characteristics. In this way the coach will be able to modify the technical skill so that it becomes standardized.

Stages of Perfecting Technical and Tactical Training

The athlete's ability to perfect technique and tactics is a direct result of the coach's knowledge and teaching skill, which can include the use of preparatory and progressive drills and audiovisual aids. The athlete's ability to learn new skills is also related to her ability to process new information and her biomotor abilities. It has been suggested that athletes improve technical and tactical skills in three distinct stages (48) (figure 3.6).

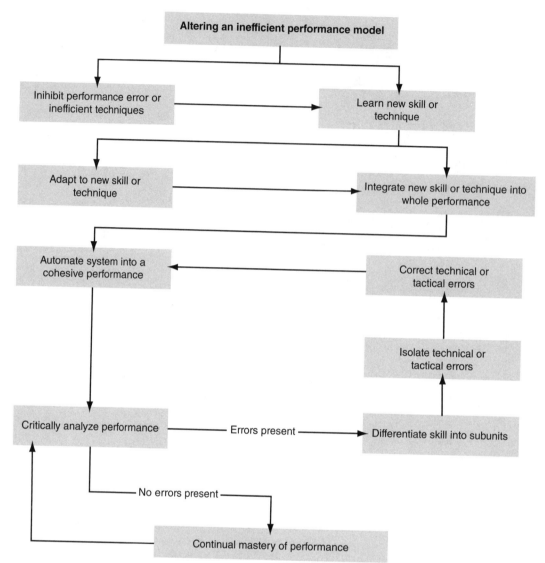

Figure 3.5 Altering an inefficient model of performance.
Adapted from Teodorescu and Florescu 1971 (48).

In the first stage, the main objective is to perfect the individual components and technical elements of a skill (differentiation). As the components are mastered, they are progressively integrated into the whole system. In concert with skill perfection are the development and perfection of the dominant or supporting biomotor abilities. The development of these biomotor abilities is essential because technique is a function of physical preparation or capacity. The acquisition of new skills and techniques is best suited for the preparatory phase of the annual plan. When skill acquisition is a central focus, it is inadvisable for the athlete to participate in competitions.

The main objective in the second stage is to perfect the whole skill under standardized conditions similar to those seen during a competition. This can be accomplished by participating in either exhibition or simulated competitions. The athlete must maintain dominant biomotor abilities during this phase so he will have an adequate physical training base to continue skill development. This stage of perfecting a skill can be integrated into the annual training plan near the end of the preparatory phase.

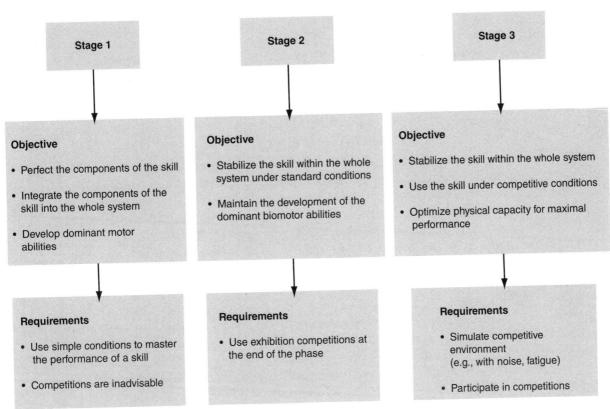

Figure 3.6 Three stages of perfecting a skill.
Adapted from Teodorescu and Florescu 1971 (48).

The final stage of perfecting a skill focuses on stabilizing the whole skill and translating it to competitive performance. The coach must create an environment (e.g., including noise, fatigue) that is as close to the actual competitive situation as possible. This stage of perfecting a skill should be implemented into the annual training plan during the competitive phase.

Correcting Technical and Tactical Errors

"If a coach fails to concentrate on correcting an athlete's technical errors, all they are doing is perfecting those errors" (3).

Often technical improvement or skill mastery is impaired because the athlete learns the skill incorrectly. If the technical skill is not taught correctly, the athlete's ability to correct technical errors is greatly impaired. The coach must strive to eliminate as many technical errors as possible to maximize the athlete's development. Technical or tactical errors can occur because of many reasons, but generally they fall into three broad areas:

• ***The athlete is performing a skill incorrectly.*** Many factors can impair an athlete's ability to learn or perfect a skill. Two interrelated factors are an insufficient physical training base and lack of correlation between biomotor abilities. A poorly developed physical training base or insufficient development of biomotor abilities can delay skill acquisition and development. For example, athletes who have not adequately developed a physical training base are more apt to develop fatigue when working on skill acquisition. Fatigue, which can result from a poor training base or a poorly implemented training plan, can impede learning or result in a deterioration of technical skills. Therefore, simply improving the athlete's physical training base may improve her ability to learn new skills. The development of biomotor abilities may also facilitate the acquisition of skills. One of the major biomotor abilities that can affect skill acquisition is strength. For example, a gymnast may not be able to learn or master a specific element (e.g., iron cross) if he does not have the appropriate level of strength to perform or practice the skill (16). Therefore, simply increasing strength as part of the physical training base will increase the athlete's ability to learn or master the targeted skill set.

- Psychological factors, such as self-confidence, morale, desire, and beliefs, appear to be significantly related to the athlete's ability to perform or develop skills (12, 49). For example, athletes who set goals that are task oriented, such as working hard to perfect a skill, generally achieve greater success than athletes who are ego driven (i.e., perform for individual notoriety) (12, 49). Athletes who are ego driven tend to perceive failure as an inability to perform a task, which may result in a withdrawal from training (12). Conversely, task-oriented athletes will respond to failure by increasing their effort in training (12) because they equate success with hard work (49).

- ***The coach's teaching method causes technical faults.*** The coach may use inappropriate teaching methods or demonstrate the technique incorrectly when introducing the skill or may fail to completely explain the technical aspects of the skill. Some coaches neglect to tailor skill instruction to the individual's learning capacity and biomotor ability. Additionally, the coach's personality, coaching style, and character can affect the athlete's ability to acquire technical skills. For example, if the coach does not allow the athlete sufficient time to learn a skill, the potential for developing technical errors is magnified.

- ***There are equipment, organizational, or environmental causes.*** The environment must foster the acquisition of proper technique, and the training session must be properly planned. Equipment must be appropriate and must function properly during each training session. Appropriate facilities (e.g., field, court) must be available for training, because an adverse environment can impair skills acquisition.

There are many ways to correct technical errors, but it is better to prevent technical errors in the first place. The best way to prevent technical errors is through the utilization of appropriate teaching methods. If technical errors do occur, it is essential that they be addressed as soon as possible. The best time to dedicate to technical or tactical corrections is the preparatory phase of the annual plan, because the stress of competition is absent during this phase and time can be dedicated to addressing technical issues.

Learning new skills or addressing technical errors should be avoided when the athlete is fatigued, because fatigue usually has a negative effect on learning. Thus it is best to address technical errors or teach new skills immediately after the warm-up. Another strategy is to increase the amount of rest between repetitions of the drills used to address errors.

The first step in addressing technical errors is to isolate the error from other technical skills. Once this is done the coach can introduce the correction or new element that will address the error. The athlete then practices the new skill. When the athlete has acquired or mastered the new skill it is integrated back into the system or whole skill. While this process is being undertaken, the athlete must maintain or develop the biomotor abilities that are necessary to support the skill being perfected.

Another issue that must be considered when addressing technical errors is the intensity or velocity at which the exercises are performed. In most cases, coaches concentrate on correcting technique with low-intensity or low-velocity movements. Although this is an important step in reeducating the athlete, sporting events often occur at higher velocities and intensities. Therefore, after the athlete becomes proficient at the new skill or corrected skill with low intensities and velocities, she must practice the skill at progressively higher velocities and intensities until the skill can be used in competition.

Visualization or mental practice is an excellent tool for correcting technical errors (46). The scientific literature has shown that athletes who use mental practice perform significantly better than those who do not (46). The coach should consider incorporating mental practice into the training plan to maximize the correction of technical errors and ultimately improve performance.

THEORETICAL TRAINING

Although it is commonly accepted that athletes need to develop physical, technical, tactical, and psychological skills, whether athletes need to understand the theoretical basis of training and sport is of great debate. Some coaches are tied to the archaic belief that they need to think for their athletes and that athletes only need to concern themselves with training and competing. In fact, approaching the development of athletes in this fashion may delay the athlete's skill and performance improvement.

The coach should consider the development of the athlete, which includes educating the athlete about the sport, training theory, and why they are doing certain things in training. To effectively educate athletes, the coach must stay up to date with theoretical knowledge by reading sport science literature, attending sport science and coaching conferences, and interacting with other coaches. The coach should educate the athlete in the following areas:

- The rules and regulations governing the sport.
- The scientific basis for understanding and analyzing the technique of the sport. Understanding basic biomechanics allows the athlete to analyze movement and ensure proper mechanics, thus decreasing the risk of injury.
- The scientific and methodological basis of biomotor abilities.
- The planning of training and how periodization of training is used to prepare the athlete for competition.
- The physiological adaptations that occur in response to training.
- The causes, methods of prevention, and basic treatments for injuries.
- The sociology of sport (i.e., intergroup relationships).
- The psychological aspects of sport, which include communication skills, behavior modification, stress management, and relaxation techniques.
- The effect of nutrition on training adaptations and how to use dietary interventions before, during, and after training or competition.

Developing the athlete's theoretical knowledge about her sport and how to prepare for her sport is an ongoing process that should include discussions before, during, and after training. The process should include things like film analysis, where the coach teaches the athlete how to critically analyze performance parameters. Athletes should be encouraged to become students of their sport. This can be accomplished through attending clinics, interacting with other coaches and athletes, reading periodicals and other pertinent texts, and engaging in detailed discussions with their personal coach.

SUMMARY OF MAJOR CONCEPTS

The preparation of athletes includes physical, technical, tactical, psychological, and theoretical training. These five factors are interrelated, with physical training being strongly linked to the development of both technical and tactical skills. Physical training is the foundation of every training program. An inadequately developed physical capacity will usually result in fatigue, which impairs technical and tactical performance during training and competition. Therefore, it is essential that the athlete's physical capacity be addressed with sound physical training.

The athlete must continually strive to attain perfect technique. The more technically proficient an athlete, the more efficient she will be and the less energy she will expend during practice and performance. Technical skills also affect the athlete's tactical capacity. Therefore, the training plan must provide for the continued development and refinement of technique.

The competitive game plan needs to be developed in advance of the competition to allow the development of the tactical training plan. The coach should integrate tactical training into the training plan to allow adequate time for the athlete to perfect the tactics prior to competition.

CHAPTER 4

VARIABLES OF TRAINING

The efficiency of a physical training program results from the manipulations of volume (duration, distance, repetitions, or volume load), intensity (load, velocity, or power output), and density (frequency), which are key variables in training. These variables should be manipulated according to the functional, physiological, and psychological requirements of the training goal or competition. Thus, when designing the training plan, the coach must first decide which variable to emphasize to meet the performance objective. The manipulations of these variables will establish distinct training-induced outcomes that can significantly affect the athlete's performance.

The training plan should emphasize training variables in proportion to the athlete's needs. The coach must continually monitor the athlete's responses to the training plan to determine whether the training variables require further adjustment. A critical analysis of annual training plans used across the athlete's career can give insight into the effectiveness of manipulations of training variables.

VOLUME

Volume is a primary component of training because it is a prerequisite for high technical, tactical, and physical achievement. The volume of training, sometimes inaccurately called the duration of training, incorporates the following integral parts:

- The time or duration of training
- The distance covered or the **volume load** in resistance training (i.e., volume load = sets × repetitions × resistance in kg)
- The number of repetitions of an exercise or technical element an athlete performs in a given time

The most simplistic definition of *volume* is the total quantity of activity performed in training. Volume can also be considered the sum of work performed during a training session or phase. The total volume of training must be quantified and monitored.

The accurate assessment of training volume depends on the sport or activity. In endurance sports (e.g., running, cycling, canoeing, cross-country skiing, and rowing), the appropriate unit for determining training volume is the distance covered (26, 61). In weightlifting or resistance training, the volume load (65, 69, 72, 79) or metric tons of training (10, 52) expressed in kilograms (volume load = sets × repetitions × resistance in kilograms) is the most appropriate method for assessing volume because **repetitions** alone are considered to be a poor estimate of work accomplished (79). The number of repetitions can be used to calculate volume in activities such as plyometrics (50) or throws in baseball (51) and track and field (49). Time seems to be a common denominator for most sports, although the proper expression of volume may be a factor of time and distance (e.g., to run 12 km in 60 min).

Two types of time-based volumes can be calculated. The first is *relative volume,* which refers to the total amount of time a group of athletes or team dedicates to training during a training lesson or phase of training. Relative volume seldom has value for an individual athlete because no information about the individual athlete's volume of work per unit time is known. A far better way to quantify the individual athlete's volume of work is *absolute volume,* which measures the amount of work that the individual performs per unit of time.

Across an athlete's career, the volume of training increases (62, 82, 83) (figure 4.1). As the athlete becomes more trained, greater training volumes are necessary to stimulate the physiological adaptations necessary to increase performance (79, 82, 83). Comparing novice and advanced athletes clearly shows that advanced athletes can tolerate much greater training volumes (65). An increase in volume over time is important for the development of aerobic athletes, strength and power athletes, and team sports athletes. An increase in technical and tactical skills training is also necessary, because high numbers of repetition are needed to improve performance.

There are many methods for increasing the athlete's volume of training. Three effective methods are

- increasing the **density** (i.e., frequency) of training,
- increasing the volume within the training session, and
- doing both.

Researchers have suggested that it is important to increase the frequency of training as much as possible without inducing overtraining (35, 78). Other researchers have definitively stated that more frequent training results in significantly greater training-induced adaptations (35, 37, 82). Increasing the number of training sessions in a single day appears to offer a physiological benefit as well (37, 82, 83). It is not uncommon for elite athletes to perform 6 to 12 training sessions per week with multiple sessions each training day (2-5, 34, 42). The athlete's ability to recover from the training volume is the most important factor dictating how much volume is used in the training plan (65). Advanced athletes can tolerate high training volumes because they can recover more quickly from the training load (65).

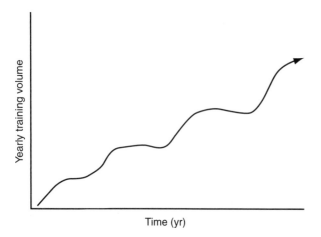

Figure 4.1 Theoretical increase in volume of training over time.

The time that athletes spend training has consistently increased over the decades. For example, Abadjiev and Faradjiev (6) reported that weightlifters in Bulgaria increased their training volume by 625% between 1966 and 1984—from 800 metric tons to 5,800 metric tons, respectively. Fiskerstrand and Seiler (28) reported that between 1970 and 2001, the volume of training increased by 22% in Norwegian international-class rowers. Although it is important to maximize training volume, it is imperative that the training volume vary according to the sport, training objectives, athlete's needs, athlete's training age, athlete's stage of development, and phase of the annual training plan.

INTENSITY

Intensity, or the qualitative component of work an athlete performs is another important training variable. Komi (43, 44) defined intensity in relation to power output (i.e., energy expenditure or work per unit of time), opposing force, or velocity of progression. According to this definition, the more work the athlete performs per unit of time, the higher the intensity (20, 69, 79). Intensity is a function of neuromuscular activation, with greater intensities (e.g., higher power outputs, higher external loads) requiring greater neuromuscular activation (36). The neuromuscular activation pattern will be dictated by the external load, the speed of performance, the amount of fatigue developed, and the type of exercise undertaken (36). An additional factor to consider is the psychological strain of an exercise. The psychological aspect of an exercise, even in the presence of a low physical strain, can have a high level of intensity, which is manifested as a result of concentration and psychological stress.

The assessment of intensity is specific to the exercise and the sport. Exercises that involve speed usually are assessed in meters per second, rate per minute, or power output (watts). When resistance is used in the activity, the intensity is typically quantified in kilograms, kilograms lifted 1 m against the force of gravity (kg/m), or power output (watts). In team sports, the intensity of play is often quantified as the average heart rate, heart rate in relation to anaerobic threshold, or percentage of maximum heart rate (13, 33, 76).

The training plan should include varied intensities within the various phases of the annual training plan, specifically at the level of the microcycle. There are many methods to quantify and establish the training intensity. For example, with exercises that are performed against a resistance or at high velocities, the training intensity can be quantified as a percentage of the best performance (68). The best performance would then represent a maximum intensity. Let's say that an athlete completes a 100 m dash in 10 s, which corresponds to a velocity of 10 m/s. If the athlete can generate a higher velocity (e.g., 10.2 m/s) over a shorter distance, the intensity would be considered supermaximal because it is more than 100% of the maximal velocity (table 4.1).

Table 4.1 Intensity Scale for Speed and Strength Exercises

Intensity zone	Percentage of maximum performance	Intensity
6	>100	Supermaximal
5	90-100	Maximum
4	80-90	Heavy
3	70-80	Medium
2	50-70	Low
1	<50	Very low

With the intensity stratification presented in table 4.1, exercises performed with resistance loads greater than 105% of maximum would most likely be either isometric or eccentric muscle actions and thus would be considered supermaximal. When training for endurance (e.g., 5,000-10,000 m), the athlete may run shorter distances at a much faster rate and thus may perform at intensities greater than 125% of the mean velocity achieved during the actual race.

An alternative method of evaluating intensity is based on the primary energy system engaged during the activity (20, 69, 74). A six-tier intensity classification can be constructed based on the biochemical responses to different types of exercise bouts (table 4.2).

- *Intensity zone 1:* Exercises in this zone of intensity rely almost exclusively on anaerobic metabolism and last for up to 6 s (e.g., snatch, clean, shot put throw, average play in American football, discuss throw). This intensity zone is marked by the highest power outputs and thus should be considered the highest intensity of exercise (20, 79). The intensity of work in this zone is substantially higher than the athlete's $\dot{V}O_2$max (maximal oxygen uptake), thus requiring any work in this zone to be supported primarily by anaerobic energy supply. The phosphagen (ATP-PC) system is the primary supplier of energy in this intensity zone. The ATP-PC system is capable of supplying energy only for very short periods of time because it relies exclusively on muscular stores of ATP and phosphocreatine (PCr) (79). The reliance on anaerobic energy supply creates a large **oxygen deficit** as a result of the rapid demand for energy that cannot be met by aerobic mechanisms (54, 79). Ultimately, an increase in oxygen consumption, or what is termed the **excess postexercise oxygen consumption (EPOC)**, occurs following exercise to replenish the ATP and PCr stores. Exercise performed in this intensity zone usually is limited by the muscular stores of ATP and PCr (79).

- *Intensity zone 2:* The second intensity zone, which is a high-intensity zone, also relies almost exclusively on anaerobic energy supply and includes activities that last between 6 and 30 s (e.g., 100 m and 200 m sprint in track and field, 100 m sprint in swimming). In this zone, like zone 1, the rate of energy supply must be very rapid and cannot be met by aerobic mechanism. Therefore, energy demand is met by a combination of the ATP-PC and the fast glycolytic system (79). The breakdown of

Table 4.2 Intensity Zones Based on Bioenergetics

Intensity zone	Event duration	Level of intensity	Primary energy system	BIOENERGETIC CONTRIBUTIONS	
				Anaerobic	Aerobic
1	<6 s	Maximum	ATP-PC	100-95	0-5
2	6-30 s	High	ATP-PC and fast glycolysis	95-80	5-20
3	30 s to 2 min	Moderately high	Fast and slow glycolysis	80-50	20-50
4	2-3 min	Moderate	Slow glycolysis and oxidative	50-40	50-60
5	3-30 min	Moderately low	Oxidative	40-5	60-95
6	>30 min	Low	Oxidative	5-2	95-98

Note: ATP-PC = Phosphagen system.

Adapted from McArdle, Katch, and Katch 2007 (54), Brooks, Fahey, White, and Baldwin 2000 (17), Stone, Stone, and Sands 2007 (79), and Conley 2000 (20).

the muscular stores of ATP occurs very rapidly, and PCr must be used to maintain the supply of energy. Within 10 s of the initiation of high-intensity exercise, the ability of PCr to maintain ATP supply is decreased by 50%, and by 30 s PCr contributes very little to ATP supply (53). Therefore, as the exercise in this intensity zone extends from 10 to 30 s in duration, the reliance on blood glucose and muscular stores of glycogen progressively increases (53). Because of the increasing reliance on fast glycolysis, there can be a substantial increase in lactic acid accumulation depending on the duration and intensity of the exercise bout (53, 79). As a result of the increased lactic acid production, a substantial EPOC can occur as a result of exercise in this intensity zone.

- **Intensity zone 3:** Activities that last from 30 s to 2 min (e.g., 400 m run, 800 m run, 1 km in track cycling) are considered moderately high-intensity activities. These activities rely predominantly on anaerobic energy supply, specifically the fast and slow glycolytic systems. As an activity's duration shifts from 30 s toward 2 min, activation of the slow glycolytic system increases. With the activities in this zone, speed and **high-intensity exercise endurance (HIEE)** are of primary concern. Depending on the duration and intensity of these activities, a large amount of lactic acid is produced in response to the metabolic challenge encountered (53). The most likely limiters of performance in this intensity zone are decreases in muscular stores of ATP, PCr, and muscle glycogen. The accumulation of **lactic acid** may also limit performance (79).

Neil Tingle/Action Plus/Icon SMI

Knowing what intensity zone your activity falls in can help you better understand what systems your body uses to provide energy for competition.

- ***Intensity zone 4:*** The fourth zone of intensity includes activities that last 2 to 3 min. The intensity in this zone is considered to be moderate and relies on a mix of slow glycolysis and oxidative **metabolism**. When an exercise reaches this zone of intensity, the body's energy supply begins to shift from reliance on anaerobic mechanisms to reliance on aerobic means. Most of the activities classified in this zone rely evenly on both the anaerobic and aerobic energy systems.

- ***Intensity zone 5:*** Activities in this zone last from 3 to 30 min (e.g., pursuit cycling, team pursuit, 2,000 m rowing, 1,500 m run, 400 m individual medley). Activities in this zone of intensity rely predominantly on the aerobic energy system and are thus of moderately low intensity. A strong cardiovascular system is essential for success in activities in this intensity zone, because oxygen supply plays a crucial role in the oxidative pathway's ability to supply energy (20). Events in this zone, especially the longer events, appear to require pacing strategies to maximize performance (79). In these events, the supply of energy (e.g., muscle and liver glycogen, fat stores) is the primary limiter of performance (79).

- ***Intensity zone 6:*** The final zone consists of the activities that are classified as low intensity because of their predominant reliance on oxidative metabolism (e.g., marathon, triathlon, road racing in cycling) (79). Conley (21) reported that power output at $\dot{V}O_2$max is about 25% to 35% of the peak power output achieved during maximal anaerobic exercise. Success in these activities relies on a strong cardiovascular system and optimal energy supply via the oxidative system. Factors that can limit performance in these activities center on energy supply. As the activity increases in duration, there is a progressive decrease in the availability of muscle glycogen, which ultimately leads to a decrease in blood glucose levels and an increased reliance on fat stores (53). As glycogen stores become depleted, it is increasingly difficult to maintain exercise intensity; therefore, the consumption of carbohydrates during exercise appears to be important to maintain performance.

When working with endurance athletes (22, 28, 66) or team sports athletes (13, 33, 76), coaches should consider using the heart rate response as an indicator of intensity. Heart rate increases linearly as both workload and oxygen consumption increase (54, 66). Because of this tight relationship, heart rate has become a popular way of quantifying exercise intensity in aerobic exercise. To maximize the effectiveness of heart rate–based training, a graded exercise test should be used to determine the athlete's maximal heart rate, anaerobic or lactate threshold, and $\dot{V}O_2$max. Although not as accurate as a graded exercise test, an age-predicted maximum can be used to estimate the athlete's maximal heart rate (66).

$$\text{Maximum heart rate} = 220 - \text{age}$$

Once the maximal heart rate is determined, heart rate training zones can be established on which to base training (tables 4.3 and 4.4). Faria and colleagues (26) suggested that the individual anaerobic threshold (IAS) is a crucial marker that can be used to determine basic and evolution heart rate training ranges (table 4.5). The basic training zone is used to stimulate increases in aerobic fitness, whereas the evolution zone is used to improve lactate tolerance (26). The basic training zone is calculated as the IAS – 50 beats per minute through the IAS – 30 beats per minute. Thus for an athlete with an IAS of 170, the basic zone would be 120 to 140 beats per minute. The evolution training zone is calculated as the IAS – 5 beats per minute through the IAS + 5 beats per minute. For example, an athlete with an IAS of 170 would have an evolution training zone of 165 to 175 beats per minute. Faria and colleagues (26) suggested that the evolution zone be used after a period of basic training and closer to competition.

In the sport of cycling you can also quantify intensity based on the measurement of power output (11, 40). When using a power-based training plan, the athlete must first determine her functional threshold, which is calculated by subtracting 5% from the average power achieved during a 20 min time trial performed on a flat surface (11). Once this is accomplished, seven distinct training zones can be established and used to develop a training plan (table 4.6).

Table 4.3   Australian Institute of Sport Heart Rate Training Zones for Male Cyclists

Training zones	Heart rate (% heart rate maximum)	Perceived exertion
Endurance 1	<75	Recovery, easy
Endurance 2	75-85	Comfortable
Endurance 3	85-92	Uncomfortable
Endurance 4	>92	Stressful

Adapted, by permission, from N. Craig et al., 2000, Protocols for the physiological assessment of high-performance track, road, and mountain cyclists. In *Physiological tests for elite athletes,* edited by C.J. Gore (Champaign, IL: Human Kinetics), 258-277.

Table 4.4   USA Cycling Heart Rate Training Zones for Cyclists

Training zones	Heart rate (% heart rate maximum)	Description of training
1	<65	Recovery ride (easy)
2	66-72	Basic endurance training
3	73-80	Tempo training
4	84-90	Anaerobic threshold training
5	91-100	Maximal efforts

Courtesy USA Cycling.

Table 4.5   Heart Rate Training Zones Based on Individual Anaerobic Threshold

Training zones	Low end	High end	
Basic training zone	HR (IAS) – 50	HR (IAS) – 30	
Evolution training zone	HR (IAS) – 5	HR (IAS) + 5	
Example			
Basic training zone	120	140	HR (IAS) = 170
Evolution training zone	165	175	

Note: HR = heart rate; IAS = individual anaerobic threshold.

Adapted from Faria, Parker, and Faria 2005 (26).

Table 4.6 Power Based Training Zones for Cycling

| Training Zone | Zone Name | PERCENTAGES | | EXAMPLE CALCULATIONS** | |
		Average Power*	Average Heart Rate*	Average Power	Average Heart Rate
1	Active recovery	<55%	<68%	<124	<121
2	Endurance	56-75%	69-83%	126-129	123-148
3	Tempo	76-90%	84-94%	171-203	150-167
4	Lactate threshold	91-105%	95-105%	205-236	169-187
5	$\dot{V}O_2$max	106-120%	>106%	239-270	>187
6	Anaerobic capacity	121-150%	N/A	272-337	N/A
7	Neuromuscular power	N/A	N/A	N/A	N/A

Based on Allen and Coggan 2006 (11).

* Based off of the functional threshold (average power for a 20 minute time trial—5%).

** Based off of a functional threshold average power of 225 and threshold heart rate of 178.

High intensities of training result in rapid progress but lead to less stable adaptation, a lower degree of consistency, a greater incidence of high-intensity overtraining, and a plateau in performance. Conversely, low-level training loads result in slower development and minimal stimulus for physiological adaptation, which correspond to a lower but more consistent performance. The training plan should systematically alter volume and intensity to maximize the physiological and performance adaptations stimulated by training.

There are two types of intensities: *absolute intensity,* which corresponds to the percentage of maximum necessary to perform the exercise, and *relative intensity,* which measures the intensity of a training session or microcycle, given the absolute intensity and the total volume of work performed in that period.

RELATIONSHIP BETWEEN VOLUME AND INTENSITY

Fundamental to the training process is the trade-off between volume and intensity (79). The interaction of these variables is the foundation for periodized training plans because of their specific effects on physiological and performance adaptations (60). Periodization of training attempts to target performance outcomes by manipulating both volume and intensity of training in a fluctuating fashion (79). The volume and intensity of training are inversely related in most instances. For example, when the intensity of training is the highest, the volume is generally low. Different physiological and performance adaptations can be stimulated by shifting the relative emphasis on these components in training. However, because training entails both a quantity and a quality, it is impractical to consider volume and intensity separately because the work accomplished is considered a good indicator of training stress (79). The greater the workload (e.g., the higher the intensity of training and the longer it is maintained) the greater the physiological stress as indicated by decreases in energetic substrates (e.g., muscle glycogen and PCr), increases in hormonal disturbances (e.g., cortisol release), and increases in neuromuscular fatigue.

High workloads develop endurance, create a work capacity base, establish the duration and stability of corresponding training effects, and serve as a foundation for intense efforts that are involved in special and technical preparation (79). Many strategies can be used to increase workload: (a) increasing the number of repetitions per set or increasing the distance with a corresponding decrease in intensity; (b) increasing the number of **sets**, exercises, or both; and (c) manipulating the **density of training** (e.g., frequency of training within the microcycle or training day). A good example of using these methods to increase workload can be seen in long-distance swimming. In the preparatory phase of training, the swimmer can increase the training volume by increasing the number, length, or distance of intervals used in training or increasing the load density (e.g., increasing the frequency of high-volume training) (62). To increase training volume, a decrease in training intensity will most likely occur. However, this low-intensity, high-volume training will serve as the base on which higher-intensity work will be built (62, 79).

The relationship between volume and intensity of training varies markedly throughout a training year depending on the focus of the phase of the annual plan (figure 4.2). With many sporting activities, these fluctuations in training can include alterations in time or emphasis on technical, tactical, and physical training. In the

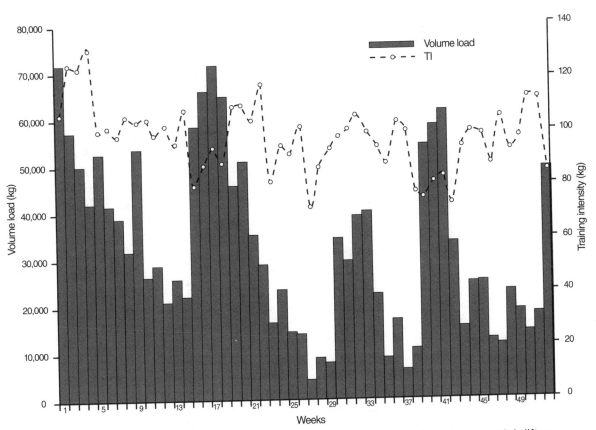

Figure 4.2 Example of fluctuations in training volume and intensity for a master's weightlifter.
Note: Volume is represented as the volume load (repetitions × sets × resistance in kg) and TI represents the average training intensity in kilograms.

preparatory phase of training, the emphasis in the early portion of the phase is on developing a physical training base with the use of high workloads. High workloads are accomplished via an increase in training **volume** with a concomitant decrease in **training intensity**. As the athlete progresses through this phase of training, the volume of physical training will progressively decrease as the training intensity increases. At the same time, more emphasis will be placed on tactical and technical training. When the workload is very high, the athlete's preparedness decreases as a result of cumulative fatigue (65, 79, 81, 82). If the athlete continually undergoes high volumes of training, performance will not be optimized even though fitness increases. However, if training intensity is not increased, the athlete will continually train at intensities below those needed for competition. Thus, to elevate performance the workload has to be decreased while intensity is increased, which ultimately increases performance. Therefore, it is important to consider the relationship between training volume and intensity in the context of the emphasis of each phase of the annual training plan.

Determining the optimal workload, which entails combinations of training volume and intensity, is a complex task that depends on many factors including the specifics of the sport, the phase of the annual training plan, and the athlete's level of development. It is much easier to quantify volume and intensity with sports that can be assessed objectively. In weightlifting, for example, it is relatively easy to determine the volume of training (e.g., multiply the sets by repetitions and resistance) and training intensity (e.g., volume load divided by total repetitions, or percentage of maximum capacity). In many team sports and sports like gymnastics, it is much more difficult to quantify these variables. One strategy is to use the total number of actions, elements, repetitions, and distances covered to determine volume. Another possibility is to quantify the duration of a training session or the number of repetitions of a skill to quantify volume. In these sports, the velocity or speed at which the athlete performs the activities of training or the average heart rate may be used to quantify the intensity of training.

Dynamics of Increasing Volume and Intensity

The amount of work that international-class athletes perform has increased markedly over the past 3 to 5 decades (6, 28). This marked increase in workload has been accomplished via an increase in training density, individual training session volume, and microcycle volume, all of which contribute to markedly greater training loads for the yearly training plan. Contemporary athletes often increase their training load by increasing training density, where training is undertaken frequently during the microcycle (8-12 sessions per week), typically with multiple (e.g., two to eight) training sessions being used in the same day (24, 34, 37, 42, 82, 83). Although distinct physiological and performance benefits can occur from increasing the density of training (35, 63, 82, 83), these increases in training load (volume and intensity) and density (frequency) must be implemented in a progressive and systematic fashion (chapter 2).

As the athlete becomes more trained, a workload that previously was considered a *stimulating load* (a training load high enough to induce physiological changes) is now a *retaining load* (a load that maintains physiological adaptations) or a *detraining load* (a load that is not high enough to maintain physiological adaptations and a loss of physiological adaptations occurs) (82, 83) (figure 4.3). For example, a novice athlete may optimize strength gains from a strength program with 3 days of training per week

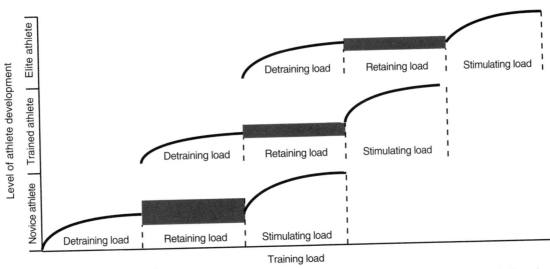

Figure 4.3   Theoretical comparison of training loads and level of athlete development. A detraining load is a suboptimal load that results in a loss of physiological adaptation. A retaining load results in maintenance of physiological adaptation. A stimulating load results in an increase in physiological adaptations.

Adapted from Zatsiorsky 1995 (82) and Zatsiorsky and Kraemer 2006 (83).

(63, 67), whereas a more advanced athlete may require more frequent (e.g., four to eight sessions per week) resistance training sessions to maximize the training stimulus. As the athlete becomes more developed she will need greater training variation, which comes from increases in training load (volume and intensity), density of training, and periodic changes in exercises or activities. These alterations in the training load should not be sudden, unless one is using planned overreaching or concentrated loading strategies (65, 69, 79). As the athlete becomes more trained and her work capacity increases, she should periodically increase the training load in a nonlinear fashion. Coaches need to be extremely careful when attempting to increase training load because most training plans entail a delay in training adaptations.

When attempting to increase training load via alterations of volume and intensity, the coach can consider several example strategies.

Strategies for altering the volume of training:

- Increase the duration of the training session. This can be a useful strategy when working with endurance athletes. For example, if the athlete is performing three sessions of 60 min duration, an increase in volume could be accomplished by increasing some of the training sessions to 90 min. This way the athlete's training volume progressively increases over time.
- Increase the density of training (i.e., frequency or number of training sessions) per week. If, for example, the athlete is performing three sessions per week, an increase to 5 days per week would increase the training density. Another possibility is to increase the number of sessions in the training day. For example, if the athlete is training 3 days per week, he could maintain a 3 day a week training plan but now include two sessions per day, for a total of six training sessions per week.
- Increase the number of repetitions, sets, drills, or technical elements per training session.
- Increase the distance traveled or the duration per repetition or drill.

Strategies for altering the intensity of training:

- Increase the velocity of movement over a given distance or the quickness or tempo of performing tactical drills.
- Increase the load (i.e., resistance or weight) in strength training.
- Increase the power output of the training activity.
- Decrease the rest interval between repetitions or tactical drills.
- Require the athlete to perform endurance, interval, or tactical work at a higher percentage of maximal heart rate.
- Increase the number of competitions in the training phase only if this fits into the training plan for the athlete and does not impede the athlete's development.

Many factors are involved in the dynamics of intensity used in training. Three factors are often talked about: (a) the characteristics of the sport, (b) the training or competitive environment, and (c) the athlete's performance level.

- *Characteristics of the Sport:* Each sporting activity stimulates distinct physiological adaptations (7, 8, 59). In sports where maximal speed, strength, or power (e.g., weightlifting, throwing, sprinting) is of primary importance, the resultant physiological stress is considered to be high in response to the activity's reliance on anaerobic energy supply. Conversely, in endurance sports (e.g., running, distance cycling, triathlon), the intensity is considered to be low as a result of the lower power outputs encountered and the reliance on aerobic energy supply (21, 79). The intensity of sporting activities that rely on technical mastery (e.g., gymnastics, diving, synchronized swimming) is determined by looking at the degree of difficulty of the individual skills performed and the predominant energy supply system. In most instances, these activities rely heavily on the anaerobic energy systems and require high power outputs or quick movements. Therefore, most of these activities fall on the high end of the intensity spectrum. The classification of team sports is often difficult because of the fluid changes in intensity that can occur. Most team sports should be considered high intensity as a result of their reliance on anaerobic energy supply (see table 1.2 on p. 28 for a summary of sporting activities and their primary energy suppliers). For any activity, the periodized training plan should include a variety of intensities because systematic variations of intensity result in superior physiological adaptations, which ultimately elevate the athlete's performance ability.

- *Training or Competitive Environment:* The training or competitive environment significantly affects the intensity of a training session. For example, running in sand or uphill can significantly increase intensity, which can be seen in an increase in the heart rate response to the training session. Using drafting strategies in cycling, running, and skating to decrease drag can significantly affect intensity. In cycling, for example, drafting behind another cyclist while riding at 39.5 km/hr has been shown to result in an approximately 7.5% reduction in average heart rate and an approximately 14% reduction in oxygen consumption ($\dot{V}O_2$) compared with cycling alone (39). Thus, drafting has the potential to decrease the intensity of the activity while maintaining a very high speed of movement. Using aerodynamic devices (e.g., aero-handlebars, disc wheels, skin suits) can reduce the drag forces encountered in cycling and thus decrease the intensity of cycling at the same absolute speed (27).

Running in the sand during training can increase the heart rate response to the training session; this is an example of the training environment affecting performance.

> • *Preparation of the Athlete's Performance Level:* The athlete's physical development appears to play a very large role in determining the content of the athlete's training program. When athletes of different training levels are introduced to the same training content (e.g., workload), differing physiological responses will most likely occur because the load represents different intensities of training for different athletes (see figure 4.3). For example, a training load that is of medium intensity for an elite athlete may be a supermaximal load for a novice athlete. Conversely, a medium load for a novice athlete may be a detraining load for an elite athlete. These contentions support the importance of using individualized training plans to optimize each athlete's physiological adaptations and ultimately her performance.

As suggested previously in this chapter, the heart rate response to training can be a useful tool for prescribing and evaluating training intensities. Heart rate may be used to compute the intensity in training as an expression of the total demand experienced during a training session. The intensity of a training session can be calculated by using the following series of equations proposed by Iliuta and Dumitrescu (41). The first step of this process is to calculate the partial intensity with the following equation:

$$\text{Partial Intensity} = \frac{\text{HR}_p \times 100}{\text{HR}_{max}}$$

In this equation, HR_p is the heart rate that results from performing the exercise for which the partial intensity is being calculated, and HR_{max} is the maximum heart rate achieved in performing the activity. Once the partial intensity is established, the intensity can be calculated with the following equations:

$$\text{Overall intensity} = \frac{\Sigma(\text{Partial intensity} \times \text{Volume of exercises})}{\Sigma(\text{Volume of exercises})}$$

Another possible use for monitoring heart rate is the concept of training impulse (TRIMP) (56, 72). TRIMP is the product of training duration and intensity, where heart rate is multiplied by a nonlinear metabolic adjustment based on the lactate curve and the training session duration (56) (for complete method of calculation, see Morton et al. 56). Although the TRIMP method of determining training stress is useful, its application is limited to aerobic training intensities that result in heart rates below maximum.

Rating the Volume and Intensity

Because the human body has the ability to adapt to a given training stimulus, actual performance can be changed in response to the training plan. Additionally, the type of training undertaken can result in very distinct genetic and molecular adaptations that underlie these performance outcomes (19, 59). To achieve the primary goal in the development of athletes, which is to maximize performance outcomes via an appropriate training stimulus, all elements of the training plan must be in line with the concept of training specificity. Coaches must consider the bioenergetic, mechanical, and movement characteristics of the sport and target these areas in the training plan. Furthermore, individualization of the training program is essential to the success of the plan. The workload should be based on the individual athlete's level of development or ability to tolerate training, the phase of the annual plan, and the ratio between the volume and intensity of training. If the appropriate workload dosage is implemented, the correct physiological responses will be stimulated and performance will improve. In training, two classifications of dosages have been established: external and internal (38, 64).

The *external dosage,* or load, is a function of the training volume and intensity. The external load is based on the relationships among the volume, intensity, and density of the training stimuli. These factors are easily monitored, and the coach and athlete should keep detailed records of what has been accomplished. The external dosage elicits the physiological and psychological adaptations that occur as a result of the training plan. These individual responses are considered the *internal dosage,* or load, and are expressed in degree and magnitude of fatigue experienced by the athlete. The magnitude and intensity of the internal dosage are direct results of the external dosage that is applied during the training plan.

Application of the same external dosage does not always result in the same physiological or psychological responses. Internal responses to training are a function of the individual athlete's response to the applied external dosage. Therefore, the internal response can only be estimated in general terms. The internal response is best tracked by using training logs or diaries and periodic physiological and psychological testing (79).

Relationship Between Volume and Adaptation

The implementation of a well-structured training plan results in very specific physiological and psychological adaptations that alter the athlete's performance capacity

(65, 72, 79). These adaptations are related to many factors, including the genetic endowment, health status, and training history of the athlete (72). The training plan is a key factor in determining performance outcomes, because training intensity, volume, and density all play a significant role in modulating the physiological adaptations that are central to performance (19, 72, 80). Of particular interest is the relationship between the dosage of training and these adaptations.

The physiological systems must be progressively overloaded to induce the adaptations necessary to improve performance. For example, a high volume of work performed by highly trained endurance athletes at a low intensity does not appear to significantly improve performance or related physiological adaptations (46). A higher work volume or intensity of work is necessary for continued adaptations to occur (16, 38, 46, 64). In another example, the volume load (i.e., volume load = sets × repetitions × resistance in kg) of training encountered in a strength training plan is strongly related to the muscular adaptations that occur in response to training. Fröböse and colleagues (30) offer evidence that the greater the volume load of training, the greater the stimulus for muscular growth and adaptation, which ultimately could have a profound effect on performance.

If the work volume, training volume, or training intensity is elevated too sharply or exceeds the athlete's work capacity, a maladaptive response can occur that can result in overtraining (see chapter 5) (31, 32, 77). If this situation occurs, performance can stagnate or even decline in response to the overtraining syndrome induced by the misapplied training stimulus. The training plan must include variations in intensity, volume, and density so the athlete alternates between stimulation and regeneration (i.e., work and rest).

The positive adaptation to a training stimulus increases the training stimulus required by the athlete in training. This increased demand for training stimulus occurs as a result of physiological adaptations that allow the athlete to tolerate greater training loads. Therefore, if the same training load is encountered again, significantly less physiological disturbance occurs, resulting in significantly less physiological adaptation. To continue to stimulate appropriate physiological adaptations, the external dosage or workload must be progressively increased, as suggested by the theory of progressive overload (29, 79). Furthermore, if the training load is substantially reduced, the training effect is diminished and an involution phase results. Although a reduction in workload is necessary when the athlete is attempting to dissipate fatigue, recover, or peak for a competition, remaining in periods of subthreshold training for too long will result in a loss of physiological adaptations and ultimately performance capacity as a result of detraining (57, 58). During the annual plan if the transition phase is too long and contains passive recovery instead of active recovery, many if not all of the adaptations stimulated by the preparatory and competitive phases of training will be lost.

DENSITY

The **density of training** can be defined as the frequency or distribution of training sessions (79) or the frequency at which an athlete performs a series of repetitions of work per unit of time (15). The density of training can be thought of as a relationship that is expressed in units of time between working and recovery phases of training. Thus, the greater the density of training, the shorter the recovery time between working phases of training. When increasing the density of training, the athlete and coach must establish a balance between work and recovery to avoid inducing excessive levels of fatigue or exhaustion, which can lead to overtraining.

It is very difficult to calculate the optimal amount of time needed between multiple training sessions (e.g., within the training day or microcycle) because many factors can contribute to the athlete's rate of recovery (see chapter 5). The intensity and volume of training encountered within the training session plays a major role in determining the amount of time needed before another training session is undertaken (79, 82). The greater the workload (i.e., intensity and volume) of the training session, the greater the amount of time needed to recover before preparedness or performance capacity is restored (82, 83). Additionally, the training status of the athlete (82, 83), chronological age of the athlete (23, 45, 71), nutritional interventions used by the athlete (18), and the use of recovery interventions (12, 55) can all affect her ability to recover from training bouts (see chapter 5 for more information). Complete recovery from a training session is not needed before the next training session. A common strategy is to increase the density of training and promote recovery by using training sessions of differing workloads within the training day or microcycle.

Two methods are commonly used to optimize the work-to-rest interval during endurance or interval-based training: (a) fixed work-to-recovery ratios (14, 47, 48, 73, 75) and (b) recovery durations that require heart rate to return to a predetermined percentage of maximum (9, 47, 48, 70).

- *Fixed Work-to-Recovery Ratios:* Several researchers have used fixed work-to-rest ratios when studying interval-based training (14, 47, 73, 75). By manipulating the work-to-rest interval, the coach and athlete can design a training plan that targets specific bioenergetic adaptations (20) (table 4.7). Work-to-rest ratios of 1:1 or 2:1 target the development of endurance characteristics, whereas ratios of 1:12 or 1:20 target strength- and power-generating characteristics.

- *Predetermined Heart Rate:* Another method for determining the length of the recovery period is to establish a heart rate that must be achieved prior to performing another work bout (9, 47, 70). One method of using this technique is to set a heart rate range of 120 to 130 beats/min as the cutoff for the initiation of the next work bout (9, 70). A second method is to set the recovery period as the time it takes the athlete's heart rate to return to 65% of maximum (47, 48).

Computing the density of a training session can be accomplished by calculating what is termed the *relative density*. The relative density is the percentage of work volume the athlete performs compared with the total volume within the training session. The relative density equation is as follows:

$$\text{Relative density} = \frac{\text{Absolute volume} \times 100}{\text{Relative volume}}$$

The absolute volume is represented by the total volume of work that the individual performs, whereas the relative volume represents the total amount of time (duration) for a training session. Let say that the absolute volume of training is 102 min and

Table 4.7 Work-to-Rest Intervals and Bioenergetic Specificity

Targeted energy system	Average work time (s)	Work-to-rest ratio
ATP-PC	5-10	1:12-1:20
Fast glycolysis	15-30	1:3-1:5
Fast and slow glycolysis and oxidative metabolism	60-180	1:3-1:4
Oxidative metabolism	>180	2:1-1:3

the relative volume is 120 min; the relative density of the training session would be calculated as follows:

$$\text{Relative density} = \frac{102 \times 100}{120} = 85\%$$

This calculated percentage suggests that the athlete worked 85% of the time. Although the relative density has some value to the athlete and coach, the absolute density of training is more important. The absolute density can be defined as the ratio between the effective work an athlete performs and the absolute volume. The absolute density or effective work is calculated by subtracting the volume of rest intervals from the absolute volume using the following equation:

$$\text{Absolute density} = \frac{(\text{Absolute volume} - \text{Volume of rest intervals}) \times 100}{\text{Absolute volume}}$$

Let's say that the volume of rest intervals is 26 min and the absolute load is 102 min. The absolute density would then be calculated as follows:

$$\text{Absolute density} = \frac{(102 - 26) \times 100}{102} = 74.5\%$$

These calculations indicate that the absolute density of training was 74.5%. Because training density is a factor of intensity, the index of absolute density could be considered medium intensity (see table 4.1). Determining the relative and absolute density of training can be useful for establishing effective training sessions.

COMPLEXITY

Complexity refers to the degree of sophistication and biomechanical difficulty of a skill. The performance of more complex skills in training can increase training intensity. Learning a complex skill may require extra work, in comparison to basic skills, especially if the athlete possesses inferior neuromuscular coordination or is not fully concentrating on the acquisition of the skill. Assigning complex skills to several individuals who have no previous experience with the skill discriminates quickly between well-conditioned and poorly conditioned athletes. Therefore, the more complex an exercise or skill, the greater the athlete's individual differences and mechanical efficiencies.

The complexity of previously learned skills may impose physiological stress even though the skills have been mastered. For example, Eniseler (25) demonstrated that heart rate and lactate accumulation are higher with tactical training compared with technical training in soccer players. In that study, the technical portion of the training session centered on skill practice without the presence of an opponent. The addition of an opponent during tactical training significantly increased the complexity of the drills and thus increased heart rate and lactate production. Additionally, when simulated games were undertaken, the complexity of the activities increased again, resulting in a concomitant increase in heart rate and lactate production. The highest heart rates and lactate levels were seen in actual games. In light of this information, the coach should consider the physiological stress of the different portions of the training session in the context of the complexity of the skills or activities used.

INDEX OF OVERALL DEMAND

Volume, intensity, density, and complexity all affect the *overall demand* an athlete encounters in training. Although these factors may complement each other, an increased emphasis on one factor may cause an increased demand on the athlete if the emphasis on the other factors is not adjusted. For instance, if the coach intends to maintain the same demand in training, and the needs of the sport require developing high-intensity endurance, the volume of training must increase. When increasing the volume, the coach must consider how this increase will affect the density of training and how much the intensity of training must be decreased.

The planning and direction of training are the primary functions of manipulations of volume, intensity, and complexity. The coach must guide the evolution of the curve of these components, especially volume and intensity, in direct relationship with the athlete's index of adaptation, phase of training, and competition schedule. The appropriate integration of these factors in the annual training plan will enhance the athlete's ability to peak at the appropriate times, thus resulting in optimal performances at these times.

The overall demand of a training plan can be calculated with the *index of overall demand* (IOD) (41). The IOD can be calculated with the equation proposed by Iliuta and Dumitrescu (41):

$$\text{Index of overall demand} = \frac{\text{OI} \times \text{AD} \times \text{AV}}{10,000}$$

For example, say the OI (overall intensity) is 63.8%, the AD (absolute density) is 74.5%, and the AV (absolute volume) is 102 min. The OI, AD, and AV can be substituted into the IOD equation as follows:

$$\text{Index of overall demand} = \frac{63.8\% \times 74.5\% \times 102}{10,000} = 48.5$$

In this example, the IOD of training is very low, slightly less than 50%.

SUMMARY OF MAJOR CONCEPTS

The amount of work encountered in training is a key variable in the success of a training plan. A large amount of work that encompasses and integrates physical, technical, and tactical training is essential to stimulate the physiological adaptations that serve as the foundation for improvements in athletic performance. The application of workload should be individualized because each athlete has a tolerance to the volume, intensity, and density of training.

The workload encountered in training has progressively increased over the past 50 years, with athletes now undertaking multiple training sessions a day and accumulating many hours of training within the microcycle. Athletes must progressively increase their training volume, intensity, and density across their athletic careers. If these factors are increased too sharply or too soon, overtraining likely will occur. Thus, an athlete's increase in workload should be individualized and progressive.

The coach must monitor training loads and performance measures to determine the effectiveness of the training plan. The coach should quantify the density of a training session or complexity of the skills practiced to account for the workload in tactical and technical training. One useful tool that has gained popularity in many sports (e.g., soccer, rugby) is heart rate monitoring, which is used to quantify training and competitive intensities. The coach should monitor factors that increase the workload or training stress and coordinate them with recovery and restoration. The coach also should consider restoration techniques and the time needed to restore energy stores (see chapter 5 for more information).

CHAPTER

5

REST AND RECOVERY

Athletes, especially elite athletes, lead very demanding lives, undergoing rigorous training regimes that push their physiological and psychological boundaries. Athletes also experience professional and social stressors, which compound the stressors typically associated with training. To maximize adaptations to training, the athlete must strike a balance between training, competition, and recovery. This can be accomplished through a balanced lifestyle in which training, social life, and recovery are held in check.

Achieving balance between training and competition stressors and recovery or restoration is of paramount importance in the maximization of an athlete's **preparedness**. When preparing an athlete for training or competition, the coach must consider how preparedness is affected by the relationship between fitness and fatigue (figure 5.1). When an athlete undertakes large volumes of training or trains at very high intensities, fitness will increase but fatigue will also increase, which can reduce preparedness. If the athlete can dissipate fatigue while maintaining fitness, her preparedness and ultimately athletic performance will improve.

The best way to increase an athlete's preparedness is to induce restoration and adaptation by implementing a properly designed periodized training program that uses logical variations in volume, intensity, and exercise selection. By including appropriate variation in the training regime, the athlete will have periods of reduced training volume, reduced training intensity, and complete rest, all of which dissipate fatigue, induce adaptations, and increase the athlete's preparedness to perform at a high level.

Many athletes, especially elite athletes, undergo rigorous, periodized training schedules that include multiple training sessions per day, but many other stressors can convene to increase an athlete's fatigue. Coupled with the high levels of training stress experienced by athletes, social stressors can compound the development of high levels of fatigue (figure 5.2), which impairs the athlete's development and ultimately performance.

The athlete may consider including specific restoration techniques as part of the periodized training regime in an attempt to speed recovery. If the athlete is able to enhance the recovery process, she may be able to tolerate greater training loads or maximize the training effects of a given training load, both of which can lead to higher levels of athletic performance (6). When an athlete must undergo multiple competitions during a very short time, the use of interventions that are specifically

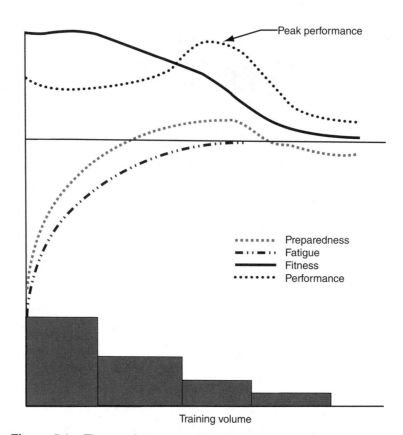

Figure 5.1 Fitness–fatigue relationship.

Adapted from Stone, Stone, and Sands 2007 (151) and Zatsiorsky and Kraemer 2006 (181).

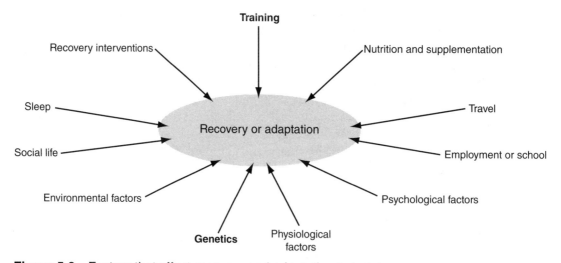

Figure 5.2 Factors that affect recovery and adaptation to training.

Adapted, by permission, from M.H. Stone, M.E. Stone, and W.A. Sands, 2007, *Principles and practice of resistance training* (Champaign, IL: Human Kinetics), 203.

designed to induce restoration and adaptation may be warranted. The athlete and coach should consider including structured recovery sessions as part of the athlete's regular training and postcompetition regime (6). To properly implement recovery strategies, the athlete and coach need to be familiar with recovery techniques and how they may be best integrated into the periodized training plan.

FATIGUE AND OVERTRAINING

Fatigue falls into two groups: acute and chronic fatigue (151). **Acute fatigue** appears to be very specific to the task being undertaken (73) and has been associated with a breakdown in excitation coupling (147), changes in the intra- and extracellular Ca^{2+} concentration (2, 147), an increase in inorganic phosphates (171), and low glycogen-induced reductions in excitation coupling and Ca^{2+} cycling regulation of the sarcoplasmic reticulum (5, 27, 92). The rate of recovery from acute fatigue can be affected by the type of training and the muscle fiber type of the athlete (141).

Chronic fatigue occurs from the convergence of physical and psychological stress, which creates a scenario in which the athlete is unable to recover from the training stimulus. The resultant decrease in performance, which can be associated with reductions in force production and rate of force development, also may be associated with a decrease in energy stores (142), hormonal alterations (23, 151), alterations to the Ca^{2+}-handling abilities of the **sarcoplasmic reticulum** (97), and neural fatigue (99). As chronic fatigue is manifested, the ability to recover from training stressors is decreased, ultimately decreasing the athlete's adaptation to training (151).

Each training session has the potential to induce symptoms of fatigue. Typically the athlete is able to recover and adapt to a training bout in a relatively short period of time (107). However, when high-volume or high-intensity training is undertaken for a microcycle, one might consider this to be an **overreaching** or concentrated loading phase of training. If this phase of high-volume or high-intensity training is extended for a long period of time, chronic fatigue likely will be induced and can lead to overtraining (figure 5.3).

Overreaching

Overreaching is a short-term decrement in performance capacity that occurs as a result of an accumulation of fatigue resulting from training and nontraining stressors (84). Overreaching usually occurs without the physiological and psychological

Fatigue	Increasing state of fatigue			
Training	Continual intensified training with inappropriate recovery			
Symptoms	Increasing severity of symptoms			
Outcome	Acute fatigue	Overreaching		Overtraining
		Functional	Nonfunctional	
Recovery	Day(s)	Days ⟶ weeks	Weeks ⟶ months	Months ⟶ ?
Performance	Increase	Temporary decrease	Decrease or no change	Decrease

Figure 5.3   Continuum of overtraining.
Adapted from Meeusen et al. 2006 (107) and Halson and Jeukendrup 2004 (57).

signs and symptoms of overtraining. Restoration of performance decrements caused by acute periods of overreaching can require several days to weeks (57, 84). Overreaching is most often planned as part of the periodized training program. After the segment of overreaching, a period of unloading or return to normal training occurs, thus potentiating a supercompensation of performance after several weeks (85). A delayed increase or supercompensation of performance usually occurs 2 to 5 weeks after the cessation of an overreaching phase of training (151). Meeusen and colleagues (107) further subdivided overreaching into two classifications, functional and nonfunctional. Functional overreaching stimulates physiological adaptations, which compensate for training-related stress; recovery can take days to weeks depending on the stimulus. Nonfunctional overreaching occurs when intensified training is continued and results in the stagnation or decreases in performance that would require longer recovery times. When nonfunctional overreaching is continued for a long period of time, the athlete eventually reaches a state of overtraining (57).

Overtraining

Overtraining is a long-term decrement in performance capacity that occurs as a result of an accumulation of training and nontraining stressors (84). Overtraining is associated with physiological and psychological signs of maladaptation such as alterations or disturbances in neural function, motor unit recruitment, hormone concentrations, excitation–contraction coupling, muscle glycogen stores, resting heart rate and blood pressure, immune function, sleep patterns, and mood (57, 151). Whereas a relatively short amount of time is necessary to restore performance after overreaching, the complete restoration of performance after overtraining can take several weeks to months (107). Overtraining can be subdivided into monotonous training and overwork (149). Overtraining that is induced by monotonous training can result in a plateau or decline in performance as a result of overadaptation of the central nervous system to the use of nonvarying motor patterns (149, 151). Conversely, chronic overwork can occur when an increased training volume or intensity is sustained for too long or repeated too frequently, thus overwhelming the athlete's ability to adapt to the training stimuli (149). Chronic overwork can result in sympathetic overwork or parasympathetic overwork. Sympathetic overwork might be considered a prolonged stress response, whereas parasympathetic overwork is an advanced stage of overtraining in which the neuroendocrine system is compromised (149). Often it is very difficult to delineate between sympathetic and parasympathetic overwork because the symptoms sometimes overlap (table 5.1).

Both volume and intensity of training can induce an overtraining stimulus (47). If, for example, a strength and power athlete goes to maximum too frequently in training (49) or an endurance athlete performs too much training volume (95), overtraining can be stimulated. The signs and symptoms of overtraining are much more severe than those seen in overreaching (57) and appear to increase with increases in intensity and volume of training (149).

Monitoring and Preventing Overtraining

Approximately 7% to 20% of elite athletes demonstrate symptoms of overtraining (102). There is no established, reliable marker for identifying overtraining, because a plethora of factors contribute to its occurrence (50, 66, 68, 94, 102). Although the best method for preventing overtraining is to use scientifically based training principles, such as periodization, the athlete also will benefit from comprehensive assessments

Table 5.1   Sports and Symptoms Associated With Sympathetic and Parasympathetic Overwork

	Sympathetic	Parasympathetic
Sports	Team sports, strength and power sports	Endurance sports
Psychological manifestations	⇓ motivation ⇑ irritability ⇑ depression	⇑ listlessness ⇑ depression ⇑ sleeping
Appetite	⇓	⇔
Cardiovascular parameters	⇑ resting, exercise, and recovery heart rate ⇑ resting, exercise, and recovery blood pressure ⇑ ECG abnormalities	⇑ resting bradycardia ⇓ ⇔ exercise heart rate ⇑ ⇔ postexercise heart rate recovery ⇓ ⇔ blood pressure response to exercise
Endocrine system	⇑ cortisol concentration ⇓ testosterone concentration ⇓ testosterone/cortisol ratio ⇑ catecholamine concentration ⇑ postexercise hormonal recovery time	⇓ responsiveness to stressors
Miscellaneous	⇓ muscle and liver glycogen stores Variable exercise-induced lactate responses	⇑ hypoglycemia during exercise ⇓ exercise and postexercise lactate concentrations
Fatigue	Chronic	⇑
Performance	⇓ ⇔	⇓ ⇔

Note: ⇑ = increased, ⇓ = decreased, ⇔ = no change; ECG = electrocardiograph.

Adapted from Stone et al. 1988 (148), Fry et al. 1991 (50), Stone et al. 2007 (151), and Mackinnon & Hooper 2000 (102).

of training stress, psychological factors such as mood state, biochemical markers of stress and recovery, and physiological responses to performance testing (see Steps to Prevent Overtraining p. 102).

The simplest method for evaluating an athlete is by using a comprehensive **training log** (102, 151). Depending on the sport, the athlete can record many different things in the training log: the volume and intensity of training, quality of sleep, body mass, resting heart rate, length of training session, rating of mood status, exercise heart rate, and injuries. The largest problem with training logs is the tediousness of the process, which often leads athletes to abandon their training logs (151). Computer technology provides a relatively easy record-keeping process that also allows for faster analysis of the training log (136).

The first sign that overtraining is a potential problem is an unexplainable stagnation or decrease in training or competitive performance (102, 107). The best way to monitor this is by using a time-series analysis, which in its simplest form can contain a graphic depiction of the results of selected performance tests. Performance tests can include competitive results or sport-specific monitoring tests.

One of the easiest tools to use in evaluating performance is a vertical jump assessment protocol. If the vertical jump test is performed on a force platform, the data collected can be very precise and yield valuable information on the training status of the athlete (151) (figure 5.4).

Another simple way to monitor the athlete is by tracking resting, exercise, and recovery heart rate variability (107, 117). Recent research suggests that monitoring heart rate during the night is a more accurate indicator of training stress than using

STEPS TO PREVENT OVERTRAINING

1. Use a periodized training program that includes the following:
    a. Periods of overreaching or concentrated loading
    b. Periods of decreased training volume and intensity to induce recovery

2. Individualize the training plan by addressing these factors:
    a. Individual training status
    b. Individual training needs

3. Integrate recovery and restoration methods into the periodized training plan.

4. Monitor athlete's performance with a comprehensive testing program that is integrated into the training plan.

5. Monitor athlete for early warning signs by assessing the following:
    a. Fatigue
    b. Total quality of recovery (TQR)
    c. Mood changes
    d. Heart rate and blood pressure
    e. Quality of sleep
    f. Irritability
    g. Occurrence of illness or injury
    h. Menstrual cycle pattern (with female athletes)
    i. Physiological responses to standardized tests, such as blood pressure, heart rate, lactate levels
    j. Immunological, biochemical, and hormonal parameters, such as the following (create a profile for each athlete):
        i. Testosterone, cortisol, and the testosterone/cortisol ratio
        ii. Catecholamine response
        iii. Markers of immune system function

6. Educate the athlete about these issues:
    a. Maintaining adequate nutrition to meet training demands (e.g., dietary carbohydrate content)
    b. Minimizing nontraining stressors
    c. Attaining adequate sleep
    d. Monitoring training and performance parameters
    e. Recognizing early warning signs of overtraining
    f. Differentiating between planned periods of overreaching and overtraining

7. Keep detailed training logs that include the following:
    a. Training volume and intensity
    b. Duration of training
    c. Weight fluctuation
    d. Ratings of well-being
    e. Ratings of sleep quality
    f. Comments on training
    g. Illness
    h. Injury

Adapted, by permission, from L.T. Mackinnon and S.L. Hooper, 2000, Overtraining and overreaching: causes, effects, and prevention. In *Exercise and sport science,* edited by W.E. Garrett and D.T. Kirkendall (Philadelphia: Lippincott Williams & Wilkins), 487-498.

only resting values (117). Therefore, it may be warranted for athletes to wear inexpensive heart rate monitors during the night to determine their average nocturnal heart rate. Nocturnal heart rate values can be graphed in a time-series fashion and compared with training volumes, allowing the coach to detect overtraining (figure 5.5).

Athletes also can use a series of scales to evaluate their mood (102) and total quality of recovery (82). The Profile of Mood States (POMS) has been used to identify athletes who are predisposed to overtraining (8, 67, 121). The total quality of recovery (TQR) scale is another subjective tool that appears to be useful in monitoring overtraining (82). This scale emphasizes the athlete's perception of fatigue and recovery, ultimately increasing self-awareness of recovery. Although both the POMS and the TQR scale are useful tools, they are probably best used as part of a comprehensive testing program that is undertaken across the different mesocycles of the training plan.

Sample time series graphs for heart rate and body weight changes can be found on page 119, while sample graphs

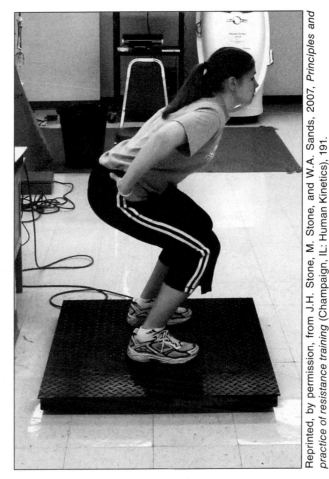

Reprinted, by permission, from J.H. Stone, M. Stone, and W.A. Sands, 2007, *Principles and practice of resistance training* (Champaign, IL: Human Kinetics), 191.

Figure 5.4 Vertical jump performed on a portable force platform.

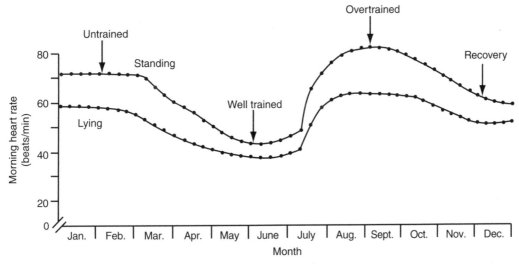

Figure 5.5 Effects of training and overtraining on early morning lying and standing heart rates.

Adapted from W. Czajkowski, 1982, A simple method to control fatigue in endurance training. In *Exercise and sports biology, international series on sports sciences* Vol. 12, edited by P.V. Komi (Champaign, IL: Human Kinetics), 210. By permission of P. Komi.

of quality and duration of sleep, sensation of tiredness, willingness to training, appetite, and muscle soreness can be found on page 122. Coaches and athletes are encouraged to make their own forms to address individual athlete needs. However a blank form has been included on page 121 to assist in the monitoring process.

RECOVERY THEORY

Recovery or regeneration is a multifactoral process that requires the coach and athlete to understand the physiological makeup of the athlete, the physiological effects of both training and recovery interventions, and the effects of integrating training and recovery strategies. A coach or athlete who understands these concepts can apply recovery interventions or training plan modifications to maximize training outcomes.

Restoration occurs at several different distinct phases: (a) **interexercise recovery**, (b) **postexercise recovery**, and (c) **long-term recovery** (140, 180).

Interexercise recovery occurs during the exercise bout and relates to the bioenergetics of the activity being undertaken. Fatigue during an exercise bout is partially related to the amount of available phosphagens. Muscular adenosine triphosphate (ATP) concentrations do not decrease by more than 45% in response to intense exercise (1, 65, 81). ATP levels are maintained as a result of the creation of ATP via the phosphagen, glycolytic, and oxidative energy systems. To maintain muscle ATP stores, phosphocreatine (PCr) can be decreased by 50% to 70% in as little as 5 s of high-intensity exercise and can be almost completely depleted with very intense exhaustive exercise (65, 81). Approximately 70% restoration of ATP occurs in about 30 s, whereas 3 to 5 min of recovery is needed to completely resynthesize ATP (70). Approximately 84% of PCr stores are restored in 2 min, 89% in 4 min, and 100% in 8 min (58, 70, 72). Phosphagens are replenished mainly via the use of aerobic metabolism (58), but fast glycolysis can contribute to recovery after high-intensity exercise (42, 58).

Postexercise recovery occurs after the cessation of exercise and is related to the removal of metabolic by-products, the replenishment of energy stores, and the initiation of tissue repair (76, 140). After the cessation of exercise the body does not immediately return to a resting state. This phenomenon is best illustrated by the elevation in oxygen consumption known as excess postexercise oxygen consumption (EPOC), seen in response to a bout of exercise (88). The magnitude and duration of EPOC are mediated by the physiological disturbance (intensity, duration, or combination) created by the exercise bout. Thus, the greater the physiological disturbance created, the larger the EPOC. Mild aerobic exercise results in a markedly smaller EPOC that reaches preexercise levels within a few minutes to several hours depending on the duration of exercise. Conversely, high-intensity anaerobic exercise such as resistance training results in a very large EPOC than can last as long as 38 hr before resting levels are achieved (88, 106). Several factors are responsible for elevating the amount of postexercise oxygen consumption: ATP and PCr resynthesis, muscle glycogen formation from lactate, oxidation of lactate to form energy, restoration of oxygen content of myoglobin and blood, thermogenic effects of elevated core temperature, thermogenic effects of hormones, and effects of elevated heart rate, ventilation, and other physiological functions (105).

Of particular interest to the coach and athlete is the restoration of muscle glycogen attributable to the link between glycogen metabolism and exercise intensity (32). Both aerobic and anaerobic exercise can significantly decrease muscle glycogen stores (54, 105). After the cessation of exercise, muscle glycogen restoration is directly related to the amount of carbohydrate consumed in the diet (35). If dietary carbohydrate intake is inadequate, the athlete's ability to recover from training sessions will decline, possibly resulting in overtraining (142). Muscle glycogen usually is restored within 20 to 24 hr of recovery (38). If inadequate carbohydrate content is present in the diet or muscle damage is excessive, muscle glycogen will be resynthesized at a slower rate, thus increasing the time needed for recovery (34, 35). Athletes do not always have 24 hr to recover before the next training session, competition, or other physical activity that requires muscle glycogen. Therefore, the athlete must maintain adequate dietary carbohydrate intake and supplement the diet with carbohydrates in the 2 hr after exercise to maximize muscle glycogen restoration.

Long-term recovery that is part of a well-planned periodized training plan can result in a supercompensation effect. Long-term recovery culminates with the peaking portion of the periodized training plan. The larger the training stimulus, the greater the accumulation of fatigue and the development of fitness, which will oppose each other and thus decrease the athlete's preparedness (figure 5.1) (151). When the athlete experiences a sudden increase in training volume or intensity, performance is significantly reduced as the result of the accumulation of fatigue (56, 151). If the athlete then returns to normal training, an increase in performance is noted and in some instances a supercompensation effect occurs. These effects have been noted in weightlifters (48, 148), cyclists (56), track athletes (162), and collegiate throwers (150) who are undergoing a period of concentrated loading or overreaching phase of training. The time required for restoration or supercompensation of performance depends on the magnitude of the concentrated loading phase (figure 5.6). Additional factors that can delay training effects include the design of the training plan, the training status of the athlete, the implementation of restorative methods, and dietary intake.

Factors Affecting Recovery

An athlete's ability to recover during training, in response to training, or over the long term can be affected by many factors (figure 5.2).

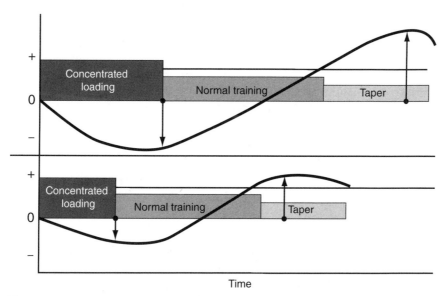

Figure 5.6   Delayed training effects of concentrated loading or overreaching. The black line indicates performance.

Adapted from D.G. Rowbottom, 2000, Periodization of training. In *Exercise and sport science,* edited by W.E. Garrett and D.T. Kirkendall (Philadelphia: Lippincott Williams & Wilkins), 499-512.

Age

Athletes older than 40 may require longer recovery periods after training than younger athletes. This is partially explained by data indicating that when older individuals perform intense exercise, especially exercise with large eccentric components, they require more time to recover their strength than do young people (41, 90) and demonstrate greater amounts of muscle damage (90, 131). Additionally, it appears that younger athletes (<18 years old) require more recovery between training sessions to realize adaptations compared with older (18-40) athletes (133). Therefore, the coach needs to consider the age of the athlete when designing a periodized plan. It may be warranted to include additional recovery or lower-intensity sessions to facilitate recovery when working with younger (<18) and older (>40) athletes.

Training Status of the Athlete

Training status affects the athlete's ability to recover from and adapt to a training stimulus. Zatsiorsky and Kraemer (181) suggested that the training load of a novice athlete may be a detraining load for an elite athlete. The beginner or novice athlete progresses at a much faster rate than his trained counterpart (151). Any reasonable training program will produce results in a novice athlete. The more experienced athlete has a much smaller window of adaptation and will require more training variation, greater training volume, and higher training intensities to create the physiological disturbance necessary to induce adaptation. The athlete must be able to recover from these increased training loads, so the coach must incorporate recovery strategies in the periodized training plan.

Time Zone Shifts

Travel can induce fatigue, which affects athletic performance and training capacity. When athletes travel they can experience what has been termed "jet lag" (128, 167). It is believed that jet lag is caused by a desynchronization between the body's circadian system and new local time, which can result in several maladies. Jet lag has been associated with sleep irregularities, bowel irregularities, loss of appetite, transient disorientation, decreases in mental performance, decreased motivation, increased occurrence of headaches, and irritability (167). These symptoms seem to be exacerbated when many time zones are crossed or when a person flies eastward (128). Several factors can affect an individual's response to travel. For example, being young and fit and having flexible sleeping habits seems to be correlated with a low incidence of travel-related difficulties (167). Some basic travel recommendations for athletes can be found in Coping With Travel.

Nutrition

Burke (20) suggested that nutrition plays a part in the recovery from exercise or competition. Of primary concern is the replenishment of muscle and liver glycogen, replacement of fluids and electrolytes, and stimulation of the tissue regeneration and repair.

When carbohydrate content of the diet is inadequate, the rate of glycogen resynthesis is impaired (35). If this scenario is coupled with multiple training sessions in 1 day or across several training days, the depletion of muscle glycogen can result in fatigue and symptoms of overtraining (143). Therefore, both endurance and strength and power athletes need to consume adequate carbohydrate to maintain training intensities. Burke (20) recommended that athletes consume 7 to 10 g of carbohydrate (CHO) per kilogram of body mass every day to ensure adequate glycogen storage.

COPING WITH TRAVEL

Before Travel

- Search for the most convenient travel schedule.
- Consider travel schedules that include a layover of a day or so because this has been shown to decrease jet lag.
- Minimize the time between proper sleep in the country being left and the first proper sleep in the destination country.
- If traveling east, go to bed 1 hr earlier in order to partially adjust to the body clock in the right direction.
- If traveling west, go to bed 1 hr later in order to partially adjust to the body clock in the right direction.
- Avoid gas-producing foods because gas expands during flight.
- When traveling to a competition, plan to arrive at least 1 day early for each time zone crossed.
- For flights that cross more than six time zones, allow 14 days for resynchronization.

- Attempt to partially synchronize sleep–wake cycles and mealtimes to those of the destination.

During Travel

- After boarding the plane, change watch to stopover or destination time.
- Drink plenty of water.
- Avoid alcohol.
- Avoid caffeinated beverages.

After Travel

- Adjust sleep–wake schedule as rapidly as possible.
- Avoid alcohol consumption.
- Avoid long naps.
- Take short power naps (20 min) if necessary.
- Undertake light-intensity exercise and moderate activity to aid resynchronization.
- Maintain regular sleep and eating times.

Adapted from Loat and Rhodes 1989 (101), Reilly and Waterhouse 2005 (129), Reilly and Edwards 2007 (125), Warden 2005 (166), and Waterhouse et al. 2007 (167).

Dehydration can have a significant negative effect on exercise performance, gastric emptying and comfort, and cognitive function (20). Thirst is generally not an adequate indicator of dehydration, so athletes must be conscious of their fluid intake. Nieman (114) recommended that athletes consume 2 cups (480 ml) of water immediately prior to exercise, 1 cup (240 ml) every 15 min during exercise, and 2 cups after the completion of exercise.

Training and nutrition are highly interrelated, and an adequate diet is necessary to provide the energy needed for rigorous training (59). Additionally, it appears that nutritional interventions can alter training-induced adaptations and speed recovery (59, 76). This suggests that including a sound dietary regime as part of the overall periodized training program is of particular importance especially when optimizing performance is the primary goal.

RECOVERY INTERVENTIONS AND MODALITIES

Athletes and coaches can use a vast array of modalities to accelerate the rate of recovery after training or competition. These modalities include complete rest, massage, cryotherapy, hydrotherapy, thermotherapy, contrast therapy, nonsteroidal anti-inflammatory drugs, compression garments, stretching, and dietary interventions. It is also possible that combinations of recovery modalities offer the most effective recovery benefits to the athlete (6, 110). For example, Monedero and Donne (110) demonstrated significantly greater rates of recovery when athletes performed a combination of active recovery techniques, followed by massage, compared with only one recovery technique.

Passive Recovery

Passive recovery techniques are the most basic of all the recovery modalities, and sleep is the main passive recovery technique (175). Sleep has a central role in aiding recovery of the athlete. When athletes experience acute or chronic sleep disturbances, both aerobic (15, 111, 118) and anaerobic performance (19, 93, 127, 145) can decrease. Sleep-induced performance decrements are noted when athletes travel across multiple time zones and are required to perform shortly after arriving at their destination. Reilly and Edwards (125) suggested that it takes 2 to 3 days for sleep quality to return to normal, 3 to 5 days for jet lag symptoms to dissipate, and 6 to 8 days for performance variables to return to normal. The more time zones that are crossed during travel, the more time needed for the athlete to return to normal sleep quality patterns. Adequate sleep appears to be integral in promoting recovery and adaptation to training and optimizing performance in competition or training. Although sleep requirements appear to vary between 5 and 10 hr a night for the nonathlete, athletes usually require greater amounts of sleep (125). Athletes should get 9 to 10 hr of sleep per day, with 80% to 90% of this sleep occurring at night. The remaining 10% to 20% sleep required by athletes can be made up with naps. Brief "power naps" lasting 10 to 15 min appear to improve alertness and performance (154) without stimulating sleep inertia, which is a period of postsleep performance impairment. Although longer naps (>30 min) also have great restorative potential, these have a greater occurrence of sleep inertia.

Active Recovery

Active recovery, or a warm-down, with light exercise is more efficient in augmenting postexercise recovery than are passive recovery strategies (110). The most noted effects of an active recovery performed at intensities less than 50% of $\dot{V}O_2$max include a significant increase in the rate of lactate clearance (104, 110, 126, 152, 168), a smoother postexercise body temperature decline (123), a dampening of the central nervous system activity (126), and a reduction in exercise-induced muscle soreness (128).

Researchers have reported that when active recovery is implemented, the typical performance deficits associated with exercise-induced fatigue are attenuated (108, 110, 128). Mika and colleagues (108) reported that an active recovery that contains very light physical activity, such as 5 min of cycling with minimal resistances, results in a more rapid restoration of maximal force-generating capacity than do passive recovery strategies. Additionally, Monedero and colleagues (110) suggested that the implementation of a 20 min active recovery session consisting of cycling at 50% of $\dot{V}O_2$max performed between two 5K bicycle time trials resulted in significantly less performance decline compared with a passive recovery strategy. Reilly and Rigby (128) examined the effects of a 12 min active recovery consisting of light jogging and stretching on the time course of recovery after a soccer game. Across a 3-day recovery period, the group that performed active recovery experienced a significantly faster rate of performance restoration and significant reduction in the onset of muscle soreness compared with the group that performed a passive recovery.

When researchers have directly compared passive recovery with active recovery strategies, massage, or other postexercise recovery modalities, they have found that passive recovery is associated with impairments in performance restoration (110), reductions in plasma lactate levels (104, 110, 168), power output during repeated cycling bouts (14), and maximal force-generating capacity (108).

Although it appears that active recovery is the most appropriate and effective postexercise recovery intervention, active recovery strategies do have a metabolic cost that some researchers suggest could impede muscle glycogen resynthesis (28) and result in a significant decrease in PCr stores (146). It appears that even when postexercise active recovery is coupled with carbohydrate consumption, muscle glycogen resynthesis rates may be slightly impaired (17) compared with when carbohydrate and passive recovery strategies are combined.

The current scientific data indicate that active recovery strategies have a great potential to facilitate postexercise recovery. Although there is limited scientific literature delineating the optional duration and intensity of an active recovery regime, it appears that light exercise performed for 10 to 20 min at less than 50% of the athlete's maximum heart rate (predicted maximum heart rate = 220 – age) (71) followed by stretching for 10 to 20 min is a prudent postexercise regime.

Massage

Massage has been used around the world for thousands of years as a rehabilitation and relaxation-inducing tool (169). Many coaches, athletes, and sports medicine professionals believe that massage can enhance recovery from training, reduce injury risk, and maintain athletic performance. Classic Western massage or Swedish massage is the most common type of massage used with athletes (103, 169). Various techniques are used in this type of massage, depending on the therapist's experience and clinical advantage desired.

The effects of massage may be stimulated by more than one mechanism. Weerapong and colleagues (169) presented a theoretical model that demonstrates how massage can affect biomechanical, physiological, neurological, and psychological mechanisms (figure 5.7). However, few empirical data are available to support these mechanisms, and substantially more research is needed. Recently, more scientific inquiry has occurred in the area of recovery and restoration techniques.

Mancinelli and colleagues (103) demonstrated that using 17 min of a classic Western massage protocol as a recovery modality during the preseason preparation of Division I women volleyball and basketball players resulted in a maintenance of shuttle run time, a decrease in perceived soreness, and an improvement in vertical jump performance when compared with a group of athletes who did not receive the massage treatment. Zainuddin and colleagues (179) reported that 10 min of massage performed 3 hr after 10 sets of six maximal isokinetic (90°/s) elbow flexions resulted in a 30% reduction of delayed-onset muscle soreness, a reduction in muscle swelling, and a significant increase in the clearance of creatine kinase compared with a passive recovery situation. Massage also may increase the rate of lactate removal (4), which may be related to the perception of recovery (62). Although it appears that massage does offer some benefit, Lane and Wenger (89) suggested that its recovery-inducing effects are equal to cold-water immersion and active recovery.

Additional support for using massage as a recovery modality comes from literature suggesting that massage reduces anxiety (96, 170, 182), tension (170), stress (130), and depression (80); improves mood (170); and increases relaxation (170), sense of well-being (11), and the perception of recovery (61, 62). Thus, it appears that massage offers significant psychological effects that may be of particular benefit to the athlete during recovery.

When implemented as part of a recovery plan, massage can be undertaken before training or competition (preparatory massage) and after competition or training

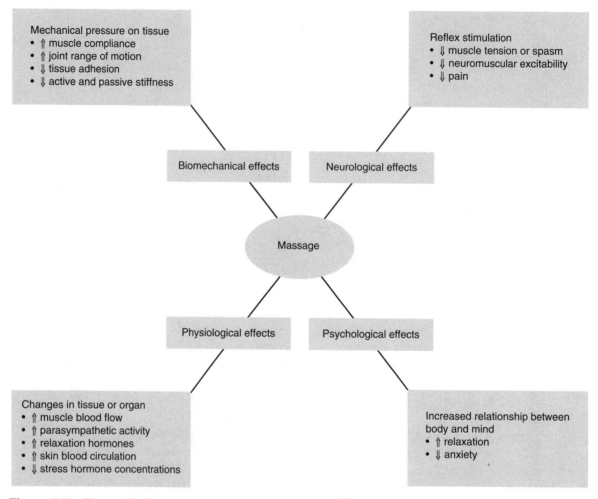

Figure 5.7 Theoretical model of massage mechanisms. ⇑ = increase; ⇓ = decrease.

Adapted, by permission, from P. Weerapong et al., 2005, "The mechanisms of massage and effects on performance, muscle recovery and injury prevention," *Sports Medicine* 35: 235-256.

(restorative massage) (3, 87, 169). A preparatory massage is generally performed for 15 to 25 min after the completion of a general warm-up and is designed to relax the body, prevent the body from cooling, and regulate preevent emotions. A restorative massage can be used after the completion of an event or training session. This type of massage is initiated 20 to 30 min after cessation of the competition or training session and can last between 7 and 12 min; a massage that takes place 1 to 2 hr after a highly fatiguing bout of exercise should last 15 to 20 min (87). If the exercise bout stimulates great fatigue, massage can be implemented several times throughout the day.

Thermotherapy

Thermotherapy entails various techniques used to heat the body, such as warm water immersion, saunas, steam baths, warm whirlpools, hydrocollator (hot) packs, paraffin baths, and infrared lamps (119, 138). Thermotherapy is believed to increase subcutaneous and cutaneous blood flow as a result of an increase in cardiac output and a lower peripheral resistance (16, 172, 173). This increase in blood flow increases cellular, lymphatic, and capillary permeability, which can increase metabolism, nutrient delivery, and waste removal from the cells (36). It is unlikely that these effects will reach the deep tissue, because the application appears to be localized at the level of the skin (119). Heat application also may increase neural transmission, muscle elasticity, joint extensibility, analgesia, and reduce muscle spasm (30, 174). Much anecdotal information can be found about the proposed benefits of thermotherapy, but little scientific research exploring its use as a recovery tool is available.

Thermotherapy does have some contraindications. The most obvious contraindication is that high temperatures can result in burns (119, 174). The application of heat also can increase inflammatory responses, swelling, and edema (119, 174). If hot water immersion is used, ectopic beats, hypotension, heat syncope, excessive tachycardia, and in rare instances death can occur (174). Coaches and athletes must be careful when using thermotherapy for athletes who have open wounds, skin conditions, peripheral vascular disease, impaired circulation, and acute musculoskeletal injuries (119).

When thermotherapy techniques are being employed as a recovery intervention, it is important to be aware that there are specific indications and contraindications for the use of each technique.

- *Sauna:* A sauna may offer some benefit as a recovery intervention. Scoon and colleagues (138) reported that when a 30 min humid sauna (89.9 ± 2 °C) was used as a recovery tool immediately after training, endurance running performance improved. Run time to exhaustion was increased by 32%, and 5K time-trial performance was increased by 1.9%. The authors suggested that the increase in performance may partially be explained by an increase in blood volume. The use of a sauna (60-140 °C; 5-15% humidity) two times a week has been recommended as a recovery intervention in response to whole-body fatigue (87).

- *Warm or hot water immersion:* Water immersion with water temperatures greater than 36 °C raises the core body temperature (174). This increase in core temperature coupled with the increased hydrostatic pressure associated with water immersion may result in a cascade of physiological responses that assist in recovery. There is very little scientific data to support the effectiveness of warm-water immersion; however a 10 to 20 min immersion has been suggested to improve recovery (18). In therapeutic settings, warm whirlpools are used for 10 to 20 min with temperatures that range from 37 to 40 °C for the leg, 37 to 45 °C for the arm or hand, and 37 to 39 °C for the whole body (119). However, for delayed-onset muscle soreness, cryotherapy or contrast therapy techniques may be more beneficial than thermotherapy (86).

Cryotherapy

Cryotherapy is a technique where cold water immersion or ice baths, ice massage, or ice packs are used to treat acute traumatic injury and facilitate postexercise or competition recovery (40). Limited information is available on the appropriate application of cryotherapy as a recovery technique (6, 12). The vast majority of research on cryotherapy has focused on its analgesic (i.e., pain-reducing) effect on localized tissue (26). The analgesic effects of cryotherapy are most likely a function of the cold temperature, which reduces the neuronal transmission rate and down-regulates the pain perception to the central nervous system (174). Although the reduction in neural transmission reduces pain, it might also result in a short-term decrease in athletic performance via the reduction of muscular contractile speed or force-generating capacity (135, 178).

Performance likely will be impaired if exercise is performed shortly after cryotherapy treatment (40, 137). Crowe and colleagues (40) offered evidence that sprint cycling performance is significantly impaired 1 hr after cold water immersion. Some investigators have reported that cryotherapy may not speed recovery (115) even though it can promote muscle relaxation and reduction of creatine kinase levels (43). It is possible the chronic use of cryotherapy as a recovery technique may reduce endurance and resistance training adaptations (176).

Cryotherapy is a useful tool for acute injury, delayed-onset muscle soreness, and pathological damages (119). When compared with no treatment or a warm whirlpool, cold whirlpool therapy has been shown to result in a greater decrease in muscle soreness (86). Additionally, the combination of cryotherapy and active recovery may restore work capacity 24 hr after treatment (177). In support of this contention, Yanagisawa and colleagues (177) demonstrated that 20 min of ice treatments followed by 20 min of active recovery exercises resulted in a greater restoration of muscular strength and reduction of muscle soreness than either ice treatments or active recovery alone. These data suggest that cryotherapy may have a place in a holistic recovery regime.

When cryotherapy techniques are being employed as a recovery intervention, it is important to be aware that there are specific indications and contraindications for the use of each technique.

© Human Kinetics

Cryotherapy techniques are used to treat injuries, although their usefulness in terms of recovery is debated.

- *Cold water immersion:* When cold water immersion is used as a cryotherapy technique, core temperature can be maintained with head-out immersion in water temperatures as low as 12 °C for around 20 to 30 min (155, 157). The literature indicates that cold water immersion can be performed for 10 to 20 min at a temperature of 12 to 18 °C as a postexercise recovery strategy. However, if the athlete has only a short time between training and competition, cold water immersion may impair performance.

Cold water immersion carries some risk for the athlete (174). Sudden cold immersion can result in hyperventilation, tachycardia, sudden loss of consciousness, convulsions, ventricular ectopy, and in rare incidents cardiac arrest and death (100). Athletes who are hypersensitive to cold can have an allergic reaction to immersion, which in the worst case can result in death (174). Wilcock and colleagues (174) recommended using cold water immersion to treat localized acute injuries and reduce inflammation rather than as a recovery strategy.

- *Ice massage:* Ice massage can be useful in treating muscle soreness following exercise (69). Treatment usually lasts for 7 to 10 min and is repeated every 20 min. The massage is performed by applying the ice to the athlete's exposed skin with circular or longitudinal strokes, with each stroke overlapping the previous stroke. Once the skin is numb, the ice massage can stop (120). Interestingly, ice massage results in a significantly faster decrease in temperature than an ice bag (183). The risk of frostbite is minimal, but if the athlete has diabetes, the duration and intensity of the cold application may need to be modified.

• *Hydrocollator (cold) pack or ice bag:* Ice bags or cold hydrocollator packs usually are used for 2 hr in a repeating pattern of 20 min of cold application followed by the removal of cold treatment for 20 min. Compared with the hydrocollator pack, an ice bag results in a colder application attributable to the melting ice (120). Prentice (119) recommended that the athlete not lie on the ice bag or hydrocollator pack during cold application.

Contrast Therapy

The alternating use of thermotherapy (heat) and cryotherapy (cold) is termed *contrast therapy* (63). Contrast therapy has been used by sports medicine professionals to treat ankle sprains as well as more generic strains and contusions of the extremities (112). Although contrast therapy commonly has been used to treat injuries, this technique is becoming more popular as a recovery tool. Contrast therapy techniques can include the combination of any thermotherapy technique with any cryotherapy technique: water immersion, ice bags, whirlpool baths, water massage, heat packs, infrared lamps, saunas, paraffin wax, and ice massage (120). Probably the most popular contrast therapy technique among coaches and athletes is hot–cold water immersion (6). Hot–cold immersion is believed to aid recovery after training or competition (29). However, athletes can use many other combinations of thermotherapy and cryotherapy techniques to induce postexercise or competition recovery. For example, a hot–cold contrast can be created by using the warm heat of a sauna and then a cold whirlpool or shower.

Contrast therapy has been suggested to result in a "muscle pumping action" as a result of the alternation between vasodilation and vasoconstriction, which is increased by the hot–cold temperature contrast (44, 63). Work by Fiscus and colleagues (44) suggested that blood flow fluctuates throughout a 4:1 (hot–cold) contrast bath session lasting 20 min. This fluctuation, or pumping action, partially explains some of the reported benefits of contrast therapy. Contrast therapy has been suggested to alter blood flow, reduce swelling, decrease inflammation and muscle spasms, change pain perception, and improve range of motion (44, 63, 112). Most of the support for the use of contrast therapy as a recovery tool comes from the combination of empirical reports (112) and contemporary scientific literature (29).

Contemporary scientific literature suggests that contrast therapy can relieve stiffness and pain (86, 159), increase creatine kinase (a marker of muscle damage) removal (52), improve neurological recovery of the peripheral nervous system through reductions in sympathetic activity (24, 55), and increase lactate removal rates (29, 156). Much more scientific research must be conducted to determine the efficacy of contrast therapy as a recovery modality and to establish the optimal ratios for hot and cold treatments.

The most common recommendations for implementing contrast therapies suggest that thermotherapy be applied three or four times longer than cryotherapy, in other words, a 3:1 or 4:1 ratio (29). It is commonly recommended that the temperature of the thermotherapy be 37 to 44 °C and the temperature of cryotherapy 7 to 20 °C (112). Contrast therapies usually last 20 to 30 min and can be repeated two or three times a day (63). It is generally recommended that contrast therapy begin with thermotherapy and end with cryotherapy to minimize the possibility of swelling and to allow for a pain-free range of motion (112).

Although it appears that contrast therapies on their own have some benefit as a recovery technique, it is likely that this technique is best used as part of a holistic approach to recovery and restoration (29). In this approach, the contrast therapy might be combined with other recovery techniques such as massage or stretching during the thermotherapy portion of the contrast. Support for a more holistic approach to recovery can be found in the study by Flannagan and colleagues (45), who used a combination of recovery modalities with soccer players. The holistic recovery strategy used in this study resulted in maintenance of sprinting speed across 6 days of competition, whereas significant reductions in performance were noted when no recovery techniques were used.

Water Immersion

Water immersion is gaining popularity as a postcompetition or posttraining recovery tool (174). Although water immersion is used most often in conjunction with thermotherapy or cryotherapy techniques, it can also be used with thermoneutral water (i.e., 16-35 °C) (174). The effects of water immersion probably are a function of the hydrostatic pressure created when the athlete is immersed in water. The increase in hydrostatic pressure associated with water immersion stimulates the displacement of fluids from the extremities toward the central cavity of the body. It is believed that water immersion provides effects similar to those of active recovery by stimulating an increase in cardiac output that increases blood flow (51, 83, 139, 174, 175). This increase in blood flow coupled with an increased diffusion gradient stimulates an increase in the rate of substrate delivery and waste clearance, which may augment the rate of recovery (174, 175). Support for this theory can be seen in the consistent increase in lactate clearance noted with water immersion (30, 113, 174).

The hydrostatic pressure noted with water immersion also has been suggested to stimulate a reduction in edema (46, 163, 174). Edema, which can occur in response to exercise or muscle damage, reduces oxygen transport to the muscle by compressing localized capillaries and increasing the transport route of blood (174). Excessive edema can result in cellular damage, which can be offset by water immersion. Water immersion increases hydrostatic pressure, which can reduce tissue degeneration, inflammation, and delayed-onset muscle soreness and improve contractile function (174, 175). Water immersion following exercise can stimulate positive psychological responses by lowering perceptions of fatigue (113). Thus, the evidence indicates that postexercise water immersion induces both physiological and psychological responses that promote recovery.

The scientific literature provides various recommendations regarding the length of water immersion needed to stimulate hydrostatic pressure–induced movement of interstitial–intravascular fluids. Investigators generally recommend that water immersion used as a postexercise recovery technique should be performed for at least 10 min (79), and most studies have used immersion periods between 15 and 20 min (174, 175). More scientific inquiry is needed to define the optimal duration of water immersion to maximize restoration.

Nonsteroidal Anti-Inflammatory Drugs

When athletes perform intense or novel exercises that require eccentric muscle actions, the occurrence of muscle dysfunction, soreness, and inflammation can increase (6). Inflammation is an integral part of the repair and adaptation responses of skeletal muscle (91). Repeated exercise with a large eccentric component usually stimulates the greatest muscular damage and concomitant inflammation. The inflammatory response begins within 24 to 48 hr of the completion of the exercise bout, with muscle soreness, stiffness, and tenderness peaking around 48 to 73 hr after exercise (159). Typical inflammation-induced responses included delayed-onset muscle soreness, reduced ranges of motion, failure of the excitation coupling or contractile mechanisms, and reductions in force-generating capacity (26). The magnitude of the exercise-induced perturbation in muscular function and resultant muscular soreness depends on the age and training status of the athlete and the magnitude of the exercise stimulus (6, 90). The more unaccustomed the athlete is to the intensity, volume, and frequency of training, the greater the potential for inducing inflammatory responses and muscular soreness.

Inflammation seems to play a major role in the athlete's adaptive responses to exercise. The chronic use of recovery methods that reduce the inflammatory response may not optimize exercise-induced adaptive responses (6). Conversely, the brief use of **nonsteroidal anti-inflammatory drugs (NSAIDs)** may stimulate short-term recovery of muscle function and dampen muscle soreness. The analgesic effectiveness of short-duration NSAID use appears to be linked to the degree of muscle soreness stimulated or the magnitude of the eccentric exercise stimulus (90).

Conversely, the repeated use of NSAIDS may attenuate the muscles'

Icon SMI

Treating inflammation and muscle soreness with drugs such as ibuprofen may provide temporary relief to muscle soreness and induce a temporary sense of recovery. However, athletes should limit their reliance on this type of recovery intervention as it may reduce training adaptations.

ability to repair and adapt to a training stimulus, ultimately decreasing the athlete's training-induced performance gains (6, 165). Large dosages of NSAIDs reduce production of myofibrillar proteins and slow the healing process (53). Evidence from animal studies suggests that NSAIDs blunt the adaptive response to eccentric exercise, reduce the repeated bout responses, and inhibit resistance training–induced muscle hypertrophy (91, 144). Additionally, over-the-counter doses of ibuprofen have been reported to blunt resistance exercise–induced protein synthesis (158).

NSAIDs can be useful for short-term inflammatory intervention, but chronic NSAID use attenuates the adaptive response of the athlete. Therefore, coaches and athletes need to be cautious when considering the use of NSAIDs as a recovery tool.

Nutritional Strategies

Training and diet are significantly interrelated. To optimize training-induced adaptations, the athlete must consume a diet that maintains the body's energy stores (37). Dietary nutrients play a key role in maintaining prolonged, intense, and intermittent exercise; assisting in the replenishment of energy reserves after a training bout or competition; and altering the adaptive response to training (60).

The metabolic stress resulting from a training bout or competition is closely associated with the intensity, volume, and type of exercise; the training and nutritional status of the athlete; and environmental factors (37). In terms of metabolic stress, the **glycogenolytic** effects of exercise are of particular interest. Muscle glycogen stores can be significantly affected by acute bouts of endurance exercise, intermittent exercise, and resistance exercise (31, 54, 164). When dietary carbohydrate intake is inadequate and frequent training is undertaken, muscle glycogen stores will not be replenished, which will result in glycogen depletion (33, 54). Muscle glycogen depletion will be accompanied by a progressive decrease in performance (21, 54). A reduction in muscle glycogen also can alter cell signaling, which can negatively influence cellular growth and adaptations (39). If chronic glycogen depletion occurs, the athlete will experience overtraining attributable to an inability to meet the energy demands of training (142).

Several nutritional strategies can be used to restore muscle **glycogen** stores and enhance muscular adaptations. Ivy and Portman (76) presented a model of nutrient timing that is designed to optimize performance and muscular adaptations. In this model, the athlete follows a combination of dietary interventions before, during, and after exercise to maximize muscle glycogen storage.

Preexercise Supplementation   The first dietary supplementation occurs before exercise. The pretraining meal or supplement will increase muscle glycogen stores if they are not fully restored, increase liver glycogen content, ensure that the athlete is well hydrated particularly when liquid sources are used, and prevent hunger (22). Burke and Deakin (22) suggested that athletes consume 1 to 4 g CHO $\times$ kg^{-1} $\times$ body weight^{-1} 1 to 4 hr before exercise begins, especially if the exercise bout is prolonged.

Supplementation During Exercise   Another strategy suggested by Ivy and Portman (76) is to consume a **carbohydrate** and **protein** beverage within 30 min of initiating exercise and then periodically throughout the exercise bout. This supplementation regime has been suggested to increase the postexercise recovery rate as a result of an increased anabolic hormone response during both resistance and endurance exercise (7, 25, 98, 109). This type of supplementation regime also has been demonstrated to result in a greater postexercise **insulin** and **growth hormone** response (25, 153), a decrease in muscle protein breakdown in conjunction with an increased postexercise muscle protein synthesis rate (122, 134), and a reduction in postexercise muscle damage and soreness (7). Additionally, this supplementation has been reported to increase exercise capacity, thus potentially enhancing the adaptive stimulus of the exercise bout (77). Ivy and Portman (76) suggested that this beverage should contain a 4:1 ratio of carbohydrate to protein. Therefore, if the athlete consumed 25 g of carbohydrate, he would concomitantly consume about 6 g of protein.

Postexercise Supplementation   The focus of postexercise supplementation is to promote glycogen resynthesis and stimulation of protein synthesis. Two important aspects of postexercise dietary supplementation are the dietary content and timing of supplementation (21, 74).

The amount of carbohydrate consumed after exercise is directly related to the amount of muscle glycogen synthesized (13, 35, 75). Approximately 1.0 to 1.85 g CHO $\times$ kg^{-1} $\times$ body weight^{-1} $\times$ h^{-1} consumed immediately after exercise appears to maximize muscle glycogen synthesis (21, 78). If less carbohydrate is consumed (0.8 g $\times$ kg^{-1} $\times$ hr^{-1}), then the addition of 0.4 g of whey protein hydrolysate plus free leucine and phenylalanine per kilogram of body weight per hour can stimulate greater glycogen synthesis (161). Conversely, the addition of amino acids and proteins does not appear to increase the rate of glycogen synthesis when high amounts of carbohydrate (>1.2 g × kg^{-1} × hr^{-1}) are consumed (78). The addition of protein does offer some benefits by stimulating an increase in circulating insulin levels (160). Increases in insulin levels have been associated with an increase in the uptake of amino acids, a stimulation of

muscle protein synthesis, a reduction in muscle protein breakdown, and an increase in protein balance (9, 10). Thus, it can be recommended that athletes consume a carbohydrate and protein beverage to stimulate muscle glycogen and increase protein synthesis rates.

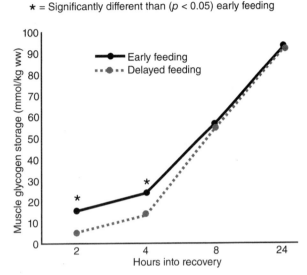

★ = Significantly different than ($p < 0.05$) early feeding

Figure 5.8   Time course of muscle glycogen resynthesis with postexercise carbohydrate supplementation.

Adapted from Ivy et al. 1988 (75), Parkin et al. 1997 (116), and Burke and Deakin 2000 (22).

The timing of supplementation can affect the rate of glycogen and protein synthesis (74). Ivy and colleagues (74) reported a 45% reduction in glycogen synthesis rates when carbohydrate was consumed 2 hr postexercise versus immediately after exercise. Conversely, Parkin and colleagues (116) reported that delaying the consumption of carbohydrates by 2 hr did not reduce muscle glycogen synthesis at 8 and 24 hr postexercise (figure 5.8).

It appears that when the time interval between training sessions or competitions is small, the athlete should consume carbohydrates and protein supplements immediately after exercise and every 60 min during the 2 hr after exercise at a rate of 0.8 to 1.0 g × kg^{-1} × hr^{-1} with 0.4 g of whey protein hydrolysate plus 0.4 g free leucine and phenylalanine per kilogram of body weight per hour. When the athlete has a long time to recover, it may not be as crucial to consume supplements immediately after exercise (22) but may be prudent to do so nonetheless.

Combination Strategies for Inducing Recovery

Many recovery strategies are available, ranging from complete rest to modalities designed to speed recovery. Combining recovery interventions appears to bring about the most rapid rates of recovery (110). There are many combinations of recovery modalities that may magnify the rate of recovery (6). For example, Monedero and Donne (110) combined 3.75 min of cycling at 50% of V̇O$_2$max followed by 7.5 min of massage to promote greater recovery of 5K time-trial performance than occurred with either active recovery or massage alone. Viitasalo and colleagues (163) combined water immersion and massage by using an underwater-jet massage, which improved recovery. Reilly and colleagues (124) reported that deep water running, a combination of active recovery with water immersion, significantly decreased muscle soreness and maintained range of motion. There are virtually infinite combinations of recovery methods that can be created, depending on the specific needs of the athlete. For example, if the athlete is attempting to recover between two competitive bouts that are separated by a short duration, a combination of active recovery and massage may be useful (see figure 5.9*a*). The combination of active recovery, water immersion, and nutritional interventions may be useful after a training bout (see figure 5.9*b*). Combining recovery methods has great potential to enhance recovery, but further research is needed to elucidate the optimal combination and sequencing of methods.

SUMMARY OF MAJOR CONCEPTS

The best way to ensure recovery and maximize training adaptations is to incorporate recovery modalities into a scientifically based periodized training plan. The scientific literature suggests that combinations of recovery techniques optimize the recovery process. The coach and athlete should consider using various techniques based on the athlete's tolerance to the modalities, which the coach determines by using a comprehensive monitoring plan. Although using a monitoring plan that is affiliated with a sport science facility is desirable, the coach can use simple strategies such as maintaining comprehensive training logs and conducting periodic testing to determine whether the athlete is responding to the training plan.

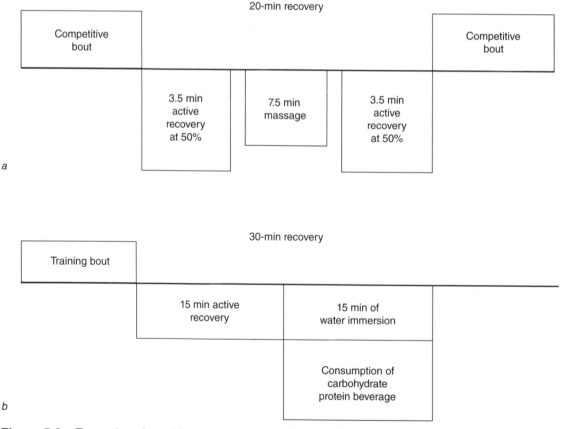

Figure 5.9 Examples of combination recovery methods. *(a)* A scenario for two competitive bouts separated by a very short period of time, based on work by Monedero and Donne (110). *(b)* A posttraining session recovery scheme that combines active recovery with water immersion.
Part *a* based on Monedero and Donne 2000 (110).

Name _____   Month _____

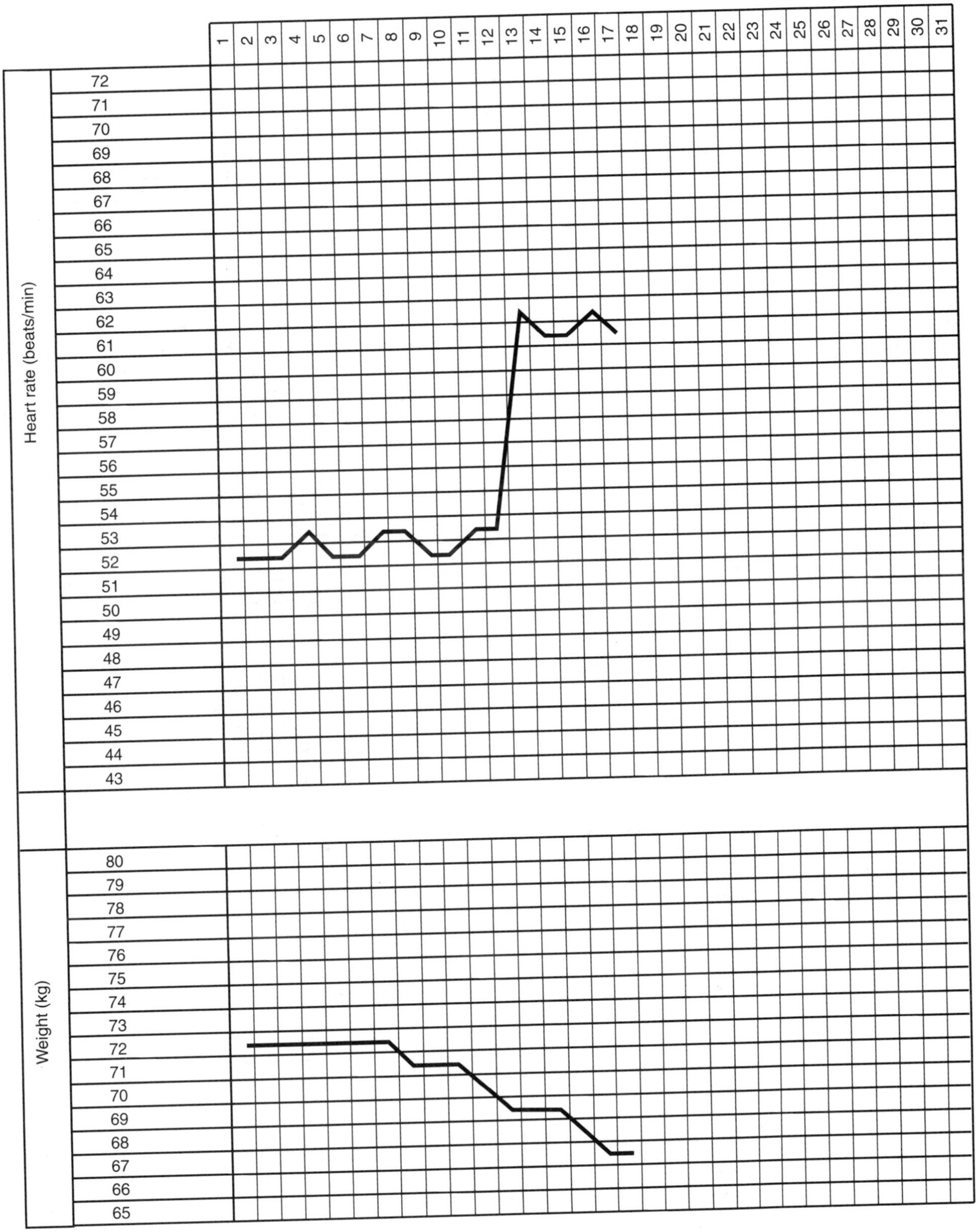

| | 1 | 2 | 3 | 4 | 5 | 6 | 7 | 8 | 9 | 10 | 11 | 12 | 13 | 14 | 15 | 16 | 17 | 18 | 19 | 20 | 21 | 22 | 23 | 24 | 25 | 26 | 27 | 28 | 29 | 30 | 31 |

Heart rate (beats/min)

72
71
70
69
68
67
66
65
64
63
62
61
60
59
58
57
56
55
54
53
52
51
50
49
48
47
46
45
44
43

Weight (kg)

80
79
78
77
76
75
74
73
72
71
70
69
68
67
66
65

		1	2	3	4	5	6	7	8	9	10	11	12	13	14	15	16	17	18	19	20	21	22	23	24	25	26	27	28	29	30	31

Length of sleep (hr)
12 / 11 / 10 / 9 / 8 / 7 / 6 / 5 / 4 / No sleep at all

Quality of sleep
Very deep / Normal / Restless / Bad with breaks / No sleep

Tiredness sensation
Very rested / Normal / Tired / Very tired / Painful tiredness

Training willingness
Very deep / Good / Poor / Unwilling / Did not train

Appetite
Very good / Good / Poor / Ate because should / Did not eat

Willingness
High / Average / Low / None at all

Muscle soreness
No pain / Little pain / Moderate pain / Severe pain

Name _____ Month _____

Heart rate

	1	2	3	4	5	6	7	8	9	10	11	12	13	14	15	16	17	18	19	20	21	22	23	24	25	26	27	28	29	30	31

Weight

	1	2	3	4	5	6	7	8	9	10	11	12	13	14	15	16	17	18	19	20	21	22	23	24	25	26	27	28	29	30	31

Name _____   Month _____

Length of sleep (hr)

	1	2	3	4	5	6	7	8	9	10	11	12	13	14	15	16	17	18	19	20	21	22	23	24	25	26	27	28	29	30	31
≥12																															
11																															
10																															
9																															
8																															
7																															
6																															
5																															
4																															
No sleep at all																															

Quality of sleep

Very deep																															
Normal																															
Restless																															
Bad with breaks																															
No sleep																															

Tiredness sensation

Very rested																															
Normal																															
Tired																															
Very tired																															
Painful tiredness																															

Training willingness

Very deep																															
Good																															
Poor																															
Unwilling																															
Did not train																															

Appetite

Very good																															
Good																															
Poor																															
Ate because should																															
Did not eat																															

Competitive willingness

High																															
Average																															
Low																															
None																															

Muscle soreness

	1	2	3	4	5	6	7	8	9	10	11	12	13	14	15	16	17	18	19	20	21	22	23	24	25	26	27	28	29	30	31
No pain																															
Little pain																															
Moderate pain																															
Severe pain																															

PART II

Periodization of Training

Periodization is one of the central concepts of training theory. This section outlines the process of developing periodized training plans. Chapter 6 highlights the importance of the annual training plan as the template from which the actual training interventions derive. A key part of developing the annual training plan is establishing when the main competitions will take place so that peaking strategies can be considered. Chapter 7 explains the peaking process and how training can be manipulated in order to increase the likelihood of high levels of performance at the appropriate times. Once the annual training plan and the timeline for the main competitive events are established, the annual training plan can be subdivided into smaller training cycles, known as macro- and microcycles. These smaller cycles are covered in chapter 8. The next step is the development of the individual workout plan. Chapter 9 presents detailed information about the development of the workout plan.

CHAPTER

6

ANNUAL TRAINING PLAN

The annual plan is the tool that guides training over a year. It is an essential component of periodization because it divides the training year into distinct phases with very specific objectives. An annual training plan is necessary to maximize physiological adaptations, which will improve performance. The annual plan directs the athlete through 12 months of training. During the last month of training the plan will vary from the rest of the training year to reduce physiological and psychological fatigue, induce regeneration, and prepare the athlete for the next year of training.

The goal of training is to induce physiological adaptations and maximize performance at specific time points, usually during the main competitions of the year. To accomplish this goal, the athlete's preparedness must increase at the appropriate time, thus ensuring a greater potential for a high level of performance. The athlete's level of preparedness is a complex interaction of developing skills, biomotor abilities, psychological traits, and the management of fatigue. The best approach for accomplishing these goals is to use periodized training that is logically constructed and appropriately sequenced.

The annual plan is the foundation for stimulating physiological and psychological adaptations while managing fatigue. In the context of this plan, the greatest challenge is peaking the athlete at the appropriate times throughout the training year. When working with inexperienced athletes, the coach will direct the training plan with little input from the athletes. Conversely, with elite athletes the coach should encourage input from the athlete when establishing the annual training plan's objectives and structure. By involving the elite athlete in the planning process, the coach can create a positive environment in which the athlete can use the planning process as a motivational tool.

PERIODIZATION

Periodization is the foundation of an athlete's training plan. The term *periodization* originates from the word *period,* which is a way of describing a portion or division of time. Periodization is a method by which training is divided into smaller, easy-to-manage segments that are typically referred to as phases of training. Periodization of training has evolved over the centuries, with many sport scientists and authors contributing to its development (6, 42, 43, 52, 53, 63, 64, 71, 72, 79, 82-85).

Periodization is not a new concept, but many people are not familiar with it or do not understand its history. The origins of periodization are unknown, but an unrefined form of the concept has existed for a long time. Evidence suggests that a simplified form of periodization was used in the ancient Olympic Games (776 BC to 393 AD). As mentioned previously in this book, Philostratus is considered one of the early proponents of periodization. Philostratus referred to the simple annual plans used by the Greek Olympians where a preparatory phase preceded the ancient Olympic Games with few informal competitions before and a rest period after the games. A similar approach has been used to prepare for the modern Olympic Games by both U.S. and European athletes.

Planning for the European competitions at the beginning of the 20th century followed a similar pattern. However, planned periodization became more sophisticated, culminating with the German program for the 1936 Olympic Games, when coaches used a 4-year plan composed of annual training plans. After World War II, the Soviets started a state-funded sports program, using athletics as a means to demonstrate the superiority of their political system.

In 1965, Lenoid P. Matveyev, a Russian sport scientist, published a model of an annual plan based on a questionnaire that asked Russian athletes how they trained before the 1952 Olympic Games in Helsinki, Finland. He borrowed the term *periodization* from history, where historians refer to the periods or phases of human development. Matveyev analyzed the data collected on the Russian athletes and produced a model of an annual training plan that was divided into phases, subphases, and training cycles. Some call this the classic model of periodization. However, the true classic model could be considered the works of Philostratus. In the 1950's and 1960's, Russian, German, Romanian, and Hungarian sport scientists published books about the evolution of periodization from ancient times to the post–World War II period, whereas their Western counterparts were slow to adopt the concept of periodization.

Matveyev structured training to culminate with only one competitive phase (44). However, this practice did not meet the needs of all sports. Thus, as the theory of periodization evolved, training plans were adapted to meet the competitive needs of athletes who participated in more than one major competition per year. Annual training plans were developed where two main competitions per year (bi-cycle plans), three main competitions per year (tri-cycle plans), and multiple peak plans were developed. Additionally, the concept of periodization of main motor abilities was developed as a tool for improving skills and maximizing athletic performance (2-5).

Periodization can be examined in the context of two important aspects of training:

1. Periodization divides the annual training plan into smaller training phases, making it easier to plan and manage the training program and ensure that peak performance occurs at the main competition.

2. Periodization structures the training phases to target biomotor abilities, which allows the athlete to develop the highest levels of speed, strength, power, agility, and endurance possible.

Many are unaware of the difference between periodization as a division of the annual plan and periodization of biomotor abilities. In most sports, the annual training plan is divided into three main phases: preparatory, competitive, and transition. The preparatory and competitive phases are divided into two subphases, which are classified as general and specific because of their differing tasks. The focus of the general subphase is to develop a physiological base by using many nonspecific training methods. The specific subphase is used to develop characteristics needed for a sport by using sport-specific modalities. The competitive phase of training is subdivided into precompetitive and competitive phases. Each phase of the annual plan contains macrocycles and microcycles. Each of these subunits has objectives that contribute to objectives of the annual training plan. Figure 6.1 illustrates the division of the annual training plan into phases and cycles.

Athletic performance depends on the athlete's physiological adaptations and psychological adjustments to training combined with the ability to develop and master skills and abilities required of the sport. The duration of each phase of the annual plan depends on the time necessary to increase the athlete's training status and elevate preparedness. The main determinant of the duration of each phase of training is the competitive schedule. To optimize performance at the appropriate time (i.e., for major competitions), athletes undergo several months of training. The training plan must be well organized and must sequentially develop physiological adaptations as well as manage fatigue to elevate preparedness, which increases the athlete's performance ability. The optimal periodization model for each sport and the time required for an optimal increase in training status and preparedness have yet to be elucidated. Confounding the coach's ability to optimally dose training is the individual athlete's ability to tolerate and adapt to a training plan, which is influenced by many factors including genetic endowment, psychological traits, training status, diet, social stressors, and recovery methods used. Because of this individuality of response to training, programs must be tailored to meet the individual needs as well as the demands of the sporting activity.

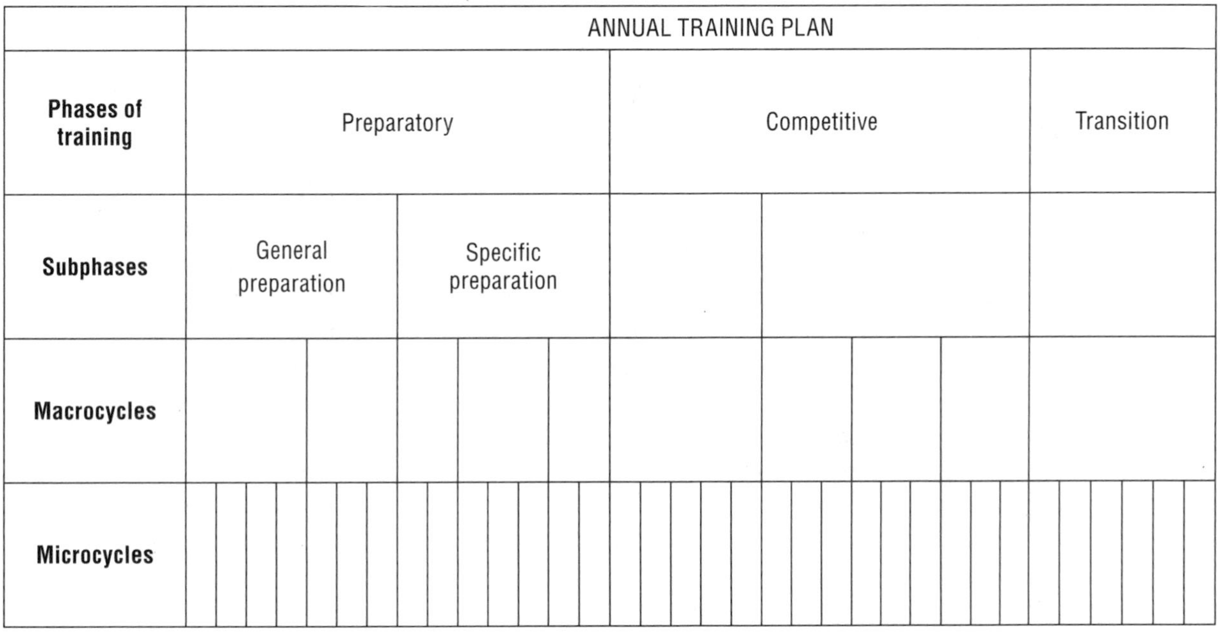

Figure 6.1   Divisions of an annual plan into phases and cycles of training.

Needs of Periodization

The phases of training are structured to stimulate physiological and psychological adaptations and are sequenced to progressively develop specific components of performance (physical, technical, and tactical) while elevating the athlete's performance capacity. A sequential approach to developing the athlete's potential is necessary because it is not possible to maintain the athlete's physiological and psychological abilities at maximal capacity throughout the entire training year. Additionally, preparedness will vary depending on the phase of training and type of training, psychological, and social stress encountered by the athlete. Therefore, the annual training plan must be subdivided into phases that sequentially develop specific aspects required to maximize performance.

The preparatory phase is the time when the physiological foundation for performance is established, whereas the competitive phase is the time when performance capacity is maximized. If the preparatory phase is inadequate, performance will not be maximized during the competitive phase because the physiological adaptations necessary for optimum performance have not been developed. After the competitive phase is completed, a transition phase is necessary to remove fatigue developed across the competitive season and enable the athlete to recover from the physiological and psychological stresses of competition. Additionally, the transition phase allows the athlete to relax and prepare psychologically for the next annual training plan, which will commence shortly. This phase of training is a transition, not an off-season. The term *off-season* is inappropriate because serious athletes do not have an off-season; rather, they transition from one annual training plan to another. Therefore, the transition is an important link between annual training plans.

The development of skills, strategic maneuvers, and biomotor abilities requires a special approach that is unique to each phase of training. Technical skill sets and tactical maneuvers are learned over time in a sequential fashion across the phases of training. The athlete attempts to perfect his technical capabilities, and as his skill level increases the complexity of tactical training can also increase. The sequential approach is also essential for the development and perfection of biomotor abilities. When attempting to improve biomotor abilities and stimulate physiological adaptations, the coach must alternate the volume and intensity of training, as proposed in the principle of load progression. Training should not occur in a linear fashion, and periodization is truly a nonlinear approach to training (70).

Climatic conditions and the seasons influence the duration of training phases within a periodized training plan. For example, seasonal sports such as skiing, rowing, and soccer are restricted by climate. In a periodized plan the phases of training are tailored to meet the individual needs of the sport, and this will account for the climatic conditions. In soccer and rowing, the preparatory phase of training occurs during the winter, and the competitive phase typically occurs in the spring, summer, or fall. The reverse is true for winter sports such as speedskating, ice hockey, and skiing.

Competition and intense training create a large amount of physiological stress and cumulative fatigue. If this stress is applied for too long, overtraining can occur and performance capacity will decrease. Therefore stressful training or competition phases should be alternated with periods of recovery and regeneration. These types of phases are transition phases that will decrease fatigue and allow the athlete to prepare for the next phase of training.

Classifying Annual Plans

Figures 6.2 through 6.5 illustrate different models of annual training plans. Figure 6.2 represents the original annual training plans presented by Matveyev (44). Although dated, this model is still promoted by several authors, especially those in the United States. Careful examination of the model reveals several characteristics:

- It is a monocycle and therefore is appropriate for seasonal sports with one major contest.
- The model is based on the specifics of training for speed and power sports such as sprinting, jumping, and throwing events in track and field.
- The volume and intensity curves may not be appropriate for sports that are dominated by endurance.

Annual training plans differ according to the requirements of the sport, and the classification of these plans largely depends on the number of competitive phases. Seasonal sports such as skiing, canoeing, and soccer and other sports with one major competition during the year usually require one competitive phase. These annual training plans can be classified as *monocycles,* because they contain only one competitive phase and one major peak (figures 6.6 and 6.7). These plans are divided into three major phases: preparatory, competitive, and transition phases. The monocycle plans shown in figures 6.6 and 6.7 include a preparatory phase in both general and specific phases of preparation. In figure 6.6, note the relationship between general and specific preparation: As one decreases, the other increases substantially. In some instances, such as in soccer, the general preparatory phase can be very short or can be eliminated altogether.

The competitive phase in figures 6.6 and 6.7 is divided into several smaller subphases. The precompetitive subphase, which usually includes exhibition competitions

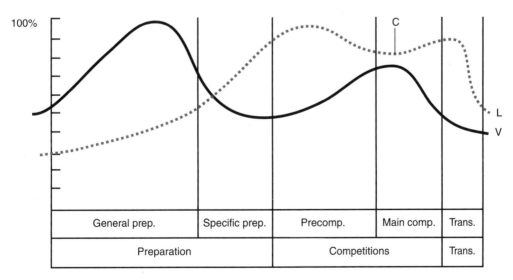

Figure 6.2 Original periodization model presented by Matveyev. C = competition; I = intensity; V = volume.

Matveyev model 1965 (44).

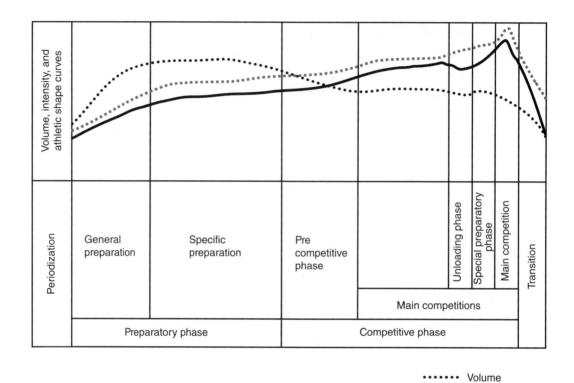

Figure 6.3 Annual plan based on a monocycle.
Adapted from Ozolin 1971 (55).

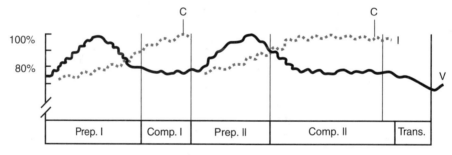

Figure 6.4 Annual plan presented by Bondarchuk. C =
volume; I = intensity.
Adapted from Bondarchuk 1986 (6).

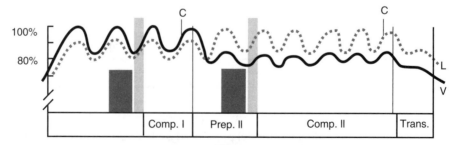

Figure 6.5 Annual plan. C = competition; V = volume; I = intensity.
Based on Tschiene 1989 (81).

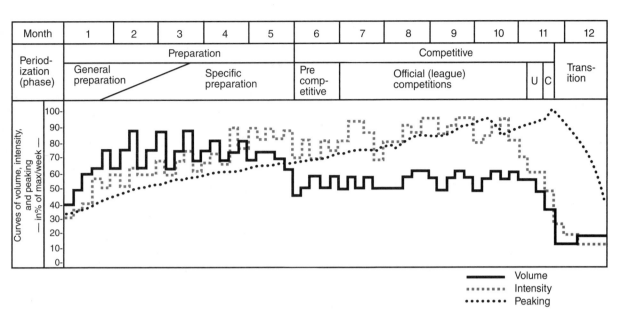

Figure 6.6 Monocycle for a speed and power sport.

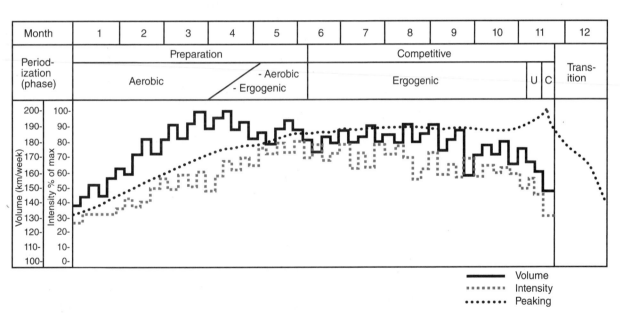

Figure 6.7 Monocycle for a sport in which endurance is the main requirement. U = unloading phase; C = competition.

only, comes before the main competition subphase in which all official competitions are scheduled. Before the most important competition of the year, two shorter sub-phases should be planned. The first is an unloading phase or taper, which is generally marked by lower volumes and intensities of training (see chapter 7). This phase allows for the removal of fatigue and an elevation in preparedness, which creates a performance supercompensation effect. After this subphase a special preparation phase follows, during which technical and tactical changes can be made. This subphase can occur in conjunction with the unloading phase or can be a separate subphase.

The preparatory and competitive phases of the annual training plans are marked by some specific characteristics. During the preparatory phase and early competitive phase, training volume is emphasized with lower intensities according to the specifics of the sport. During the preparatory phase, the quantity of work is very high and the intensity of work is low. As the competitive phase approaches, the training volume decreases while the intensity curve increases (figures 6.6 and 6.7). Thus the competitive phase has a higher emphasis on intensity or quality of work. This type of monocycle model is typical for sports dominated by speed and power because as the volume curve decreases fatigue also decreases and the training emphasis can shift toward speed and power development.

The monocycle model illustrated in figure 6.6 is an example of an annual training plan for a speed and power sport and would be inappropriate for endurance-based sports because the development of specific endurance would be insufficient and performance would be negatively affected. For sports where the bioenergetic contribution is 50%:50% (anaerobic/aerobic) or is dominated by aerobic metabolism, the training volume curve must be high throughout the competitive phase. Therefore, a different annual training plan model can be generated for these types of sports (figure 6.7). The division of the annual training plan is based on the type of endurance training the athlete will perform. Additionally, note the high volume of training, which is typical for the training plan of endurance athletes.

When working with sports that have two separate seasons, such as track and field, which has an indoor and outdoor season, a completely different approach is used to develop the annual training plan. Because there are two distinct competitive phases, an annual training plan that contains two peaks, or a bi-cycle, is used. Figure 6.8 gives an example of an annual training plan with a bi-cycle structure that incorporates the following phases:

- *Preparatory phase I:* The first preparatory phase, which should be the longest, lasts approximately 3 months and is broken into general and specific subphases.

- *Competition phase I:* The first competitive phase lasts about 2 1/2 months and brings the athlete to a peak performance.

- *Transition phase I:* The first transition phase lasts approximately 1 to 2 weeks and is marked by a period of unloading to recover the athlete. This phase leads into the second preparatory phase.

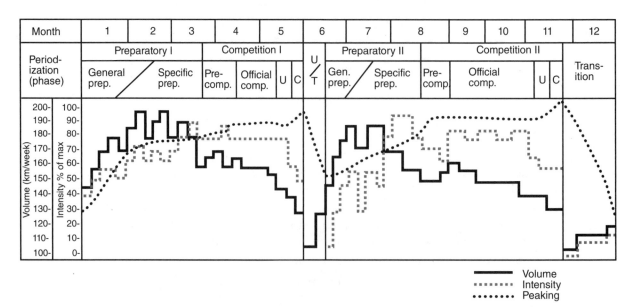

Figure 6.8 Bi-cycle plan for a sport (track and field) in which speed and power dominate.

- *Preparatory phase II:* The second preparatory phase is shorter than the first preparatory phase, lasting approximately 2 months. This phase has a much shorter general preparatory subphase, with most of the training being performed in the specific preparatory subphase.

- *Competition phase II:* The second competitive phase is slightly longer, about 3 1/2 months, and brings the athlete to a peak performance.

- *Transition Phase II:* The second transition phase is approximately 1 1/2 months long and is used to unload and recover the athlete. This phase links to the next annual training plan.

A bi-cycle plan contains two short monocycles that are linked by a very short unloading and transition phase. The approach is similar for each cycle except that the training volume in preparatory phase I is much greater than that in preparatory phase II. Additionally, the level of preparedness will be lower during competitive phase I. For example, in track and field, the outdoor championships are considered to be more important that the indoor competitions, and so the second competitive phase of the annual plan should target this major competition. Thus, it is warranted to bring the athlete's preparedness to its highest level of the year in the second competitive phase.

Although the bi-cycle annual training plan is useful for some sports, other sports such as boxing, wrestling, and gymnastics may have three major competitions during the annual plan (e.g., national championships, a qualifying meet, and the competition itself). Assuming each competition is 3 or 4 months apart the athlete would have three competitive phases, which would create a tri-cycle annual training plan structure. As illustrated in figure 6.9, a tri-cycle plan incorporates the following sequence of training:

- *Preparatory phase I:* Preparatory phase I is the longest preparatory phase of the annual training plan, lasting around 2 months. It contains both general and specific preparatory subphases.

- *Competition phase I:* Competitive phase I is the shortest of the three competitive phases in the annual training plan, lasting around 1 1/2 months.

- *Transition Phase I:* The first transition phase is very short and links the first competitive phase with the second preparatory phase. As with all transition phases, there is a period of unloading to allow the athlete to recover.

- *Preparatory phase II:* Preparatory phase II is shorter than the first preparatory phase, lasting around 1 1/2 months. This preparatory phase only contains a specific preparatory phase.

- *Competition phase II:* Competitive phase II is longer than the first competitive phase, lasting approximately 1 3/4 months.

- *Transition phase II:* The second transition phase contains a short period of unloading designed to allow the athlete to recover from competition. This transition is also short because it links competitive phase II to preparation phase III.

- *Preparatory phase III:* This preparatory phase is a short preparatory phase lasting only about 1 1/2 months. As with the second preparatory phase, only the specific preparatory subphase is used.

- *Competitive phase III:* This competitive phase is the longest of the three competitive phases contained in the tri-cycle annual training plan (~2 months). As such this phase should peak the athlete for the most major competition of the year.

- *Transition phase III:* This transition phase is the longest transition phase contained in the annual training plan lasting approximately 1 month. It serves an important role in inducing recovery and preparing the athlete for the next annual training plan.

In a tri-cycle plan, the most important competition of the three should occur during the last cycle of the year. The first of the three preparatory phases should be the longest, during which the athlete builds the technical, tactical, and physical foundation from which the next two cycles are built. Because this type of plan is typically used with advanced athletes only, the first preparatory phase contains the general preparation subphase.

In an annual plan with a tri-cycle structure, the volume curve is the highest in the first preparatory phase. This highlights the importance of training volume in this phase. The intensity curve depicted in the tri-cycle structure (figure 6.9) follows a pattern similar to that seen in a monocycle. Both the volume and intensity curves decrease slightly for each of the three unloading phases that precede the main competitions. Within the annual training plan, the highest level of preparedness should be planned for the third competitive phase to allow for the highest performances to occur at the main competition of the year.

Although the bi-cycle and tri-cycle structures are useful for many sports, other sports such as tennis, martial arts, and boxing may have four or more competitions that require peak performance (figure 6.10). In these situations the preparatory phase, which is crucial for the development of technical and tactical skills as well as biomotor abilities, is shortened significantly. Advanced athletes who have developed a strong foundation of training during the early years of their athletic development may find it easier to cope with such a heavy competitive schedule; young athletes may not. This may be a reason why so many young tennis players burn out before winning a major tournament.

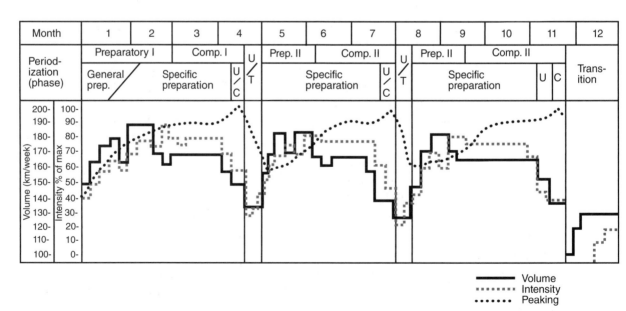

Figure 6.9 Annual training plan with tri-cycle structure.
Comp. = competition.

Month	1	2	3	4	5	6	7	8	9	10	11	12
Type of training	1		2	3	4	1		2	3	4	1		2	3	4

Figure 6.10   Four-peak annual training plan. 1 = preparatory phase; 2 = intensification, or concentrated, specific training for competition; 3 = unloading for supercompensation; 4 = recovery.

Developing a multiple-cycle of four or more competitive phases (figure 6.10) is a challenging task. This is especially true if the athlete skips a preparatory phase that focuses on regeneration and improvement of biomotor skills in a nonstressful environment. This scenario is often seen in tennis where many players are injured or withdraw from tournaments because of physical stress and mental exhaustion.

Selective Periodization

Far too often the annual training plans developed for elite athletes are used for young athletes who lack the training experience and physiological maturity to tolerate intensive competitive schedules. This is one reason why periodization of training should be individualized. The coach should consider the athlete's readiness for intensive competitive schedules, using the following guidelines:

- A monocycle is strongly suggested as the basic annual training model for novice and junior athletes. Such a plan has a long preparatory phase during which the athlete can develop foundational technical, tactical, and physical elements without the major stress of competitions. The monocycle is the typical annual plan for seasonal sports and sports for which endurance is the dominant biomotor ability (e.g., Nordic skiing, rowing, cycling, long-distance running).
- The bi-cycle annual training plan is typically used for advanced or elite athletes who can qualify for national championships. Even in this scenario, the preparatory phase should be as long as possible to allow for the development of fundamental skills.
- The multiple-peak annual training plan is recommended for advanced or international-level athletes. Presumably, these athletes have a solid foundation that allows them to handle an annual plan that contains three or more peaks.

The duration of the training phases depends largely on the competitive schedule. Table 6.1 for provides guidelines for distributing the training weeks contained in each training phase.

Table 6.1   Guidelines for the Distribution of Weeks for Each Training Phase Contained in the Classic Types of Annual Training Plans

Annual plan structure	Total weeks per cycle	NUMBER OF WEEKS PER PHASE		
		Preparatory	Competitive	Transition
Monocycle	52	≥32	10-15	5
Bi-cycle	26	13	5-10	3
Tri-cycle	17-18	≥8	3-5	2-3

Stress: Planning and Periodization

The ability to manage the stress that accumulates as a result of training and competition is an important factor that underlies successful athletic performances. Training-induced stress can be considered a summation of both physiological and psychological stressors and can be elicited by both internal and adverse external influences. Therefore it may be warranted to focus on the training effects induced by the training plan rather than the work being completed. The training plan must consider the development of fatigue, which is a by-product of training, and how to monitor or evaluate its effect on performance.

Periodization is an important tool in the management of fatigue that accumulates in response to physiological, psychological, and sociological stressors resulting from training and competition. In creating the annual plan, the coach needs to consider the effects of both training and competition on the development of fatigue and the level of stress experienced by the athlete. If structured correctly, the annual plan will manage this fatigue and reduce levels of fatigue during major competitions, when stress can be very high. Figure 6.11 shows how stress may vary across an annual training plan. Note that stress does not have the same magnitude throughout the annual plan, which is a distinct advantage of periodized training.

The stress curve in figure 6.11 parallels the intensity curve in that the higher the intensity, the higher the level of stress. The shape of the stress curve also indicates that stress is lowest during the transition phase and increases throughout the preparatory phase. In the competitive phase of training, levels of stress will fluctuate in response to competitive stress and short periods of regeneration. During the preparatory phase, the magnitude of the stress curve is a result of the relationship between training volume and intensity. Although the volume or quantity of training is high, the intensity is low because it is difficult to emphasize a high amount of work and an elevated intensity simultaneously (with the exception of weightlifting).

Training intensity is a prime contributor to stress. Therefore, the coach should consider decreasing the athlete's level of stress during the preparatory phase by emphasizing volume more than intensity. However, it is likely that the high volumes of training typically seen in the preparatory phase also produce a significant amount

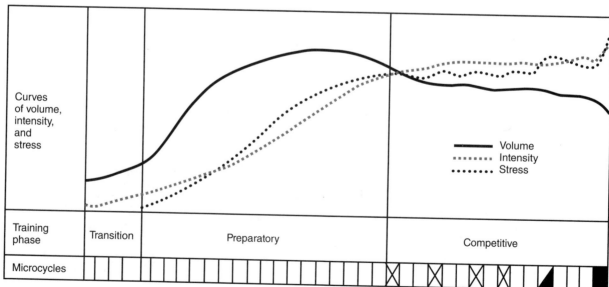

Figure 6.11 Stress curve for a monocycle.

of metabolic stress (45, 46, 79) and large hormonal disturbances (36), which can result in high levels of fatigue, a form of stress.

The stress curve throughout the competitive phase undulates in accordance with competitive, developmental, and regeneration microcycles. The number and frequency of competitions during the competitive phase clearly can have a negative impact on the athlete's level of stress. Frequent competitions can increase the athlete's level of stress, and the coach must allow a few days of regeneration following these competitions. To further deal with the stress of the competitive phase, a short period (2 or 3 days) of unloading prior to the competition may be warranted.

In addition to alternating high- and low-stress activities, the athlete can use relaxation techniques to deal with stress. The ability to tolerate stress is highly individual, and athletes who have difficulty dealing with stress may need to use motivational and relaxation techniques. The athlete's ability to tolerate stress depends largely on the training plan. The coach must structure the training plan to include phases of regeneration that use relaxation and visualization techniques to help the athlete tolerate training and competitive stress.

The athlete's psychological state depends largely on her physiological status (17, 69). If the athlete is experiencing high levels of fatigue, this accumulated stress appears to negatively affect psychological status. The better physiologically prepared the athlete, the greater the likelihood that she has a positive psychological status. A periodized training program that is structured correctly will ensure superior physiological preparedness, psychological readiness, stress management, and mental training.

PERIODIZATION OF BIOMOTOR ABILITIES

The concept of periodization is not limited to the structure of a training plan or the type of training included in a given training phase. Periodization is a concept that applies to the development of dominant biomotor abilities for a chosen sport. Because an in-depth discussion about the periodization and development of biomotor abilities is provided in later chapters, the present discussion centers on topics related to the development of the annual training plan.

Some sports, mostly individual, have a loose structure of periodization, especially regarding endurance. However, in most team sports the periodization of dominant abilities allows room for improvement. In many sports, the dominant biomotor ability is power. Recognizing this, some coaches use exercises aimed specifically at developing power throughout the year, from the early preparatory phase to the beginning of the competitive phase. This type of approach stems from a misunderstanding of periodization and the principles of specificity. Power is a function of maximal strength and speed, so it is better to develop maximal strength during the early part of the preparatory phase and then convert that strength gain into power-generating capacity in the competitive phase (figure 6.12). Several examples of periodization of dominant abilities are presented in figures 6.13 through 6.17.

PERIODIZATION OF STRENGTH TRAINING

The objectives, content, and methods of a strength training program will change throughout the phases of an annual training plan. These changes need to reflect the type of strength that a sport, event, or individual athlete requires for optimum performance (figure 6.12). These changes also depend on the phase of the annual training program and the targeted physiological adaptations for that phase.

	PREPARATORY		COMPETITIVE			TRANSITION
	General preparatory	**Specific preparatory**	**Precompetitive**	**Main competition**		**Transition**
Strength	Anatomical adaptation	Maximum strength	Conversion • Power • Muscular endurance • Both	Maintenance • Maximum strength • Power	Cessation	Compensation
Endurance	Aerobic endurance	• Aerobic endurance • Specific endurance (ergogenesis)	Sport- or event-specific endurance (ergogenesis)			Aerobic endurance
Speed	Aerobic and anaerobic endurance	HIT • Anaerobic power • Anaerobic endurance • Lactate tolerance	Specific speed Agility Reaction time Speed endurance			

Figure 6.12 Periodization of main biomotor abilities.

1. HIT= high-intensity training, typically interval-based training that models the sport or activity targeted by the training plan.
2. The training phases are not limited to a specific duration. Rather, the focus is the sequence and the proportions between the training phases.

Dates	Sept.	Oct.	Nov.	Dec.	Jan.	Feb.	March	April	May		June	July	Aug.
Competitions					Detroit	L.A.	Toronto	Prov. Orillia	Nat. championships Vancouver				
Periodization	Preparatory				Competition							Transition	
	General prep.		Specific prep.		Precomp.		Main competition					Transition	
Period of strength	Anat. adapt.		Maximum strength		Conversion to power		Maintenance (maximum strength and power)					Regeneration	

Figure 6.13 Moncycle periodization model of strength training for gymnastics.

Dates	June	July	Aug.	Sept.	Oct.	Nov.	Dec.	Jan.	Feb.	Mar.	Apr.	May
Competitions								Division champ.	Nat. champ.	World champ.		
Periodization	Preparatory				Competition						Transition	
	General prep.		Specific prep.		Precomp.		Main competition				Transition	
Period of endurance	General end. (run, bicycle)		Specific endurance (run, skate)				Specific endurance				General endurance	
Period of strength	Anat. adapt.		Maximum strength		Conversion to power		Maintenance (maximum strength and power)				Regeneration	

Figure 6.14 Monocycle periodization model for dominant abilities for figure skating.

Dates	Sept.	Oct.	Nov.	Dec.	Jan.	Feb.	Mar.	Apr.	May	June	July	Aug.
Competitions						Provincial champ.		Div. champ.		World champ.		
Periodization	Preparatory					Competition					Transition	
	General prep.	Specific prep.			Precomp.	Main competition					Transition	
Period of endurance	Anaerobic endurance	Specific endurance (swim, apnea)			Specific endurance						General endurance	
Period of strength	Anatomical adaptation	Maximum strength		Conversion –Musc. end. –Power	Maintenance						Regeneration	

Figure 6.15 Monocycle periodization model for dominant abilities in synchronized swimming.

Dates	Nov.	Dec.	Jan.	Feb.	Mar.	Apr.	May	June	July	Aug.	Sept.	Oct.
Competitions								League games				
Periodization	Preparatory						Competition					Transition
	Gen. prep.		Specific prep.			Prec.	League games					Transition
Period of strength	Anatomical adaptation		Maximum strength			Conversion – Musc. end. –Power		Maintenance Power Musc. end.				Regeneration
Period of speed	Aerobic endurance	Anaerobic endurance	Specific need			Specific speed, reaction time, and agility						
Period of endurance	Specific endurance						Perfect specific endurance					Aerobic endurance

Figure 6.16 Monocycle periodization model for dominant abilities for a baseball team.

Dates	Nov.	Dec.	Jan.	Feb.	Mar.	Apr.	May	June	July	Aug.	Sept.	Oct.
Competitions					Winter champ.						Summer champ.	
Periodization	Preparatory I			Comp. I		T	Preparatory II			Comp. II		Trans.
	General prep.		Specific prep.	Precomp.	Main. comp.	T	Gen. prep.	Spec. prep.		Precomp.	Main. comp.	Trans.
Period of strength	Anatomical adaptation		Maximum strength	Conv.: –Power –Musc. end.	Maintain: –Power –Musc. end.	Anat. adapt.	Max strength		Conv.: –Power –Musc. end.	Maintain: –Power –Musc. end.		Regen.
Period of speed	Aerobic endurance		Anaero. end. and ergogenesis	Specific speed and ergogenesis		Aerobic endurance			Anaer. end. and ergogenesis	Specific speed and ergogenesis		Games

Figure 6.17 Bi-cycle periodization model for dominant abilities in swimming (200 m) with winter and summer national championships.

T = transition.

Anatomical Adaptations

After the transition phase, when most athletes do very little strength training, it is advisable to begin a strength program to build a foundation from which future training practices are developed. This is typically accomplished during the anatomical adaptation phase of a strength training program. This phase is sometimes referred to as the hypertrophy phase (71, 79) or strength endurance phase (58). In this early preparatory phase, several key objectives are targeted:

- Stimulate increases in lean body mass, decreases in fat mass, and alterations to the connective tissue (68, 71).
- Increase short-term work capacity, which will reduce fatigue in the later stages of training when intensity of training and the volume of technique-oriented work are high (71).
- Lay a neuromuscular and conditioning foundation, which helps prevent injury. When the preparatory phase, specifically the anatomical adaptation subphase, is inadequate, the risk of injury increases.
- Develop neuromuscular balance, which decreases injury risk.

This phase of a strength training program is a crucial part of the general preparation subphase of the preparatory phase. This phase is marked by a high volume of work (e.g., two or three sets of 8-12 repetitions) performed at low intensities (40-65% of 1RM) (71, 79). The number of exercises performed will depend on the type of exercises that are selected and the goals of the training program. The use of multijoint, large-mass exercises (e.g., back squats, power cleans, snatches) requires fewer exercises, whereas the use of small-mass, machine-based exercise would require many more exercises. This subphase should last around 4 to 6 weeks (58, 71) to achieve the physiological adaptations targeted. For junior athletes or those who do not possess a strength training background, a longer anatomical adaptation phase (9-12 weeks) may be warranted.

Maximum Strength Phase

All sports require power (e.g., long jump), muscular endurance (e.g., 800-1,500 m), or some combination. Both muscular power and endurance depend directly on maximal strength (56, 74, 75, 77, 78). In support of this contention it has been shown that stronger athletes generally produce higher power outputs (74) and express higher levels of muscular endurance (47). It appears that maximal strength must be elevated before power-generating capacity can be increased because power is the product of both maximal force and speed.

The maximum strength phase has been called the basic strength phase by some authors (58, 71, 73, 79). This phase is a crucial component of the preparatory phase of the annual training plan (71). This phase is also a critical component of the special preparation phase because it builds on the general adaptations stimulated in the anatomical adaptation phase and develops the neuromuscular attributes necessary for the development of muscular power (58, 79).

The maximum strength phase can range from 1 to 3 months depending on the sport, the athlete's needs, and the annual training plan. For athletes whose sports depend heavily on maximal strength, such as American football or shot put, this phase can be on the longer end of the spectrum (3 months). In a sport for which maximal strength is the foundation, such as cycling or cross country running, this phase can be shorter (1 month). The development of maximum strength is best accomplished by three to five sets of four to six repetitions with training loads between 75% and 85% of maximal capacity (1RM).

Conversion Phase

The conversion phase, termed the strength power phase by some authors (58, 71, 73, 79), provides a transition between the preparatory phase and competitive phase (73, 71). Because this phase links the preparatory phase and competitions, some authors have suggested that this phase is an important part of the later stages of the preparatory, precompetitive, and competitive phases of the annual training plan (58).

The athlete will gradually convert the strength developed in the maximum strength phase into the type of power needed for the targeted sport (e.g., speed training, plyometrics). This is accomplished by using the appropriate strength power training methods. Maximal strength levels must be maintained during this phase, because if they decline the ability to maximize power-generating capacity will also decline. If this occurs during the competitive phase, speed and agility also will decrease.

The physiological characteristics of the sport dictate the type of power or endurance that needs to be developed during this phase of training. Because most sports require some combination of power and endurance, the ratio between these two characteristics must match the demands of the sport. For example, the ratio may be almost equal for a wrestler, but power would dominate for a canoeist (200 and 500 m), and muscular endurance should prevail for a rower (race duration 6-8 min) or for swimming events of longer duration (400-1,500 m).

Maintenance Phase

This phase of the annual training plan is designed to maintain the physiological and performance standards achieved during previous phases. It is very difficult to maintain these gains, and strength has been shown to decrease across the competitive season, especially when inappropriate training methods are used (34). The maintenance phase must contain a high enough intensity to maintain strength gains while avoiding the development of high levels of fatigue (65). Because the primary objective during the competitive phase is not the development of strength, the coach must develop an efficient training program that maintains the gains achieved during previous phases of training.

The maintenance program depends largely on the physiological requirements of the sport being trained for. Thus the ratio of strength, power, and muscular endurance must reflect these needs. For example, an American football player or shot putter would focus his strength training on maximum strength and power development, whereas an endurance athlete would focus on power and endurance development. The breakdown of training sessions that target these attributes is difficult to recommend because they depend on the competitive season. Generally, the maintenance phase contains a small number of exercises (two to four large-mass exercises) that are performed for one to three sets of one to three repetitions, with a wide range of training intensities (30-100% of 1RM) (71). The frequency of training during this phase can range from 1 to 5 days per microcycle depending on the design of the training plan and the competitive schedule.

Cessation Phase

It is usually recommended that the strength training program end 5 to 7 days prior to the main competition. This reduces the athlete's level of cumulative fatigue, decreases levels of stress, and facilitates physiological and psychological supercompensation or elevates preparedness, both of which increase the athlete's potential for high-level performance. However, this recommendation may not be adequate for all sports. For example, weightlifters would not be able to remove strength training the week before competition because this would impair their performance. Athletes in sports with a high strength or strength power requirement may benefit from simply reducing the number of sessions during the week prior to the major competition. Such a program would contain a very low volume and a moderate intensity.

Compensation Phase

The compensation phase completes the annual training plan and coincides with the transition phase. The main objective of the transition phase is to remove fatigue and allow the athlete to recover, via the use of active rest, before initiating the next annual training plan. Additionally, this phase is designed to induce regeneration, which is a very complex undertaking (see chapter 5). For injured athletes, this phase is used for rehabilitation and restoration of movement capacity. When this is necessary, the athletic trainer, physical therapist, or physiotherapist should work in conjunction with the coach to treat the athlete.

During this phase, regardless of injury or rehabilitation status, all athletes should consider an active rest training plan that includes some resistance training. This training should address the stabilizing musculature and target areas of weakness that could increase the athlete's potential risk for injury.

PERIODIZATION OF ENDURANCE

Endurance is developed in several distinct phases across the annual training plan. Within an annual training plan that contains one peak, endurance would be developed in three phases: aerobic (oxidative) endurance, aerobic and specific endurance (ergogenesis), and then specific endurance (ergogenesis) (see figure 6.12).

Aerobic Endurance

Aerobic or oxidative endurance is developed throughout the transition phase and the early preparatory phase (1-3 months). Although each sport requires slight alterations, aerobic endurance can be achieved via the use of a uniform and steady method with moderate intensities (e.g., long slow distance) and high-intensity interval training (see chapter 11). The development of aerobic endurance provides the following benefits (40, 80, 88):

Enhanced cardiorespiratory function

- Increased capillarization, which allows for an increase in oxygen and nutrient delivery
- Increased hemoglobin concentration, red blood cell number, and blood volume
- Decreased submaximal heart rate and resting blood pressure

- Increased maximal aerobic power ($\dot{V}O_2$max)
- Increased cardiac output
- Increased stroke volume
- Increased blood flow to working muscles
- Increased oxygen exchange at the lungs
- Decreased submaximal respiratory rate

Enhanced musculoskeletal system function

- Increased Type I fiber content
- Increased oxidative enzyme capacity
- Increased mitochondrial density and size
- Increased myoglobin concentration
- Increased muscular endurance capacity

These adaptations improve endurance capacity as a result of more efficient use of fuel substrates (carbohydrate and fat). These adaptations are stimulated in response to the workload, especially the training volume.

Aerobic and Specific Endurance

Aerobic endurance and specific endurance training are the components of endurance training. The training plan should introduce elements that target the energy systems used in the sport (see table 1.2 on p. 28). Endurance is developed in this phase of training through the use of uniform, alternative, and interval training (short, medium, and long duration). During the early part of this phase the emphasis is on aerobic endurance, whereas in the later portion the emphasis shifts to the development of specific endurance with the use of high-intensity interval training or sport-specific interval-based training methods (27). The shift to specific endurance development allows for a transfer of training effects, which enhances performance gains during the competitive phase of the annual training plan.

Specific Endurance Training

The development of event- or sport-specific endurance training coincides with the precompetitive and competitive phases of the annual training plan. The appropriate training method depends on the bioenergetic characteristics of the sport and the needs of the individual athlete. For many sports, the coach must emphasize training intensity so that it often exceeds competition or game intensity. One tool that may be useful for team sports like soccer is the use of small-group play and a soccer-specific "dribbling track" (figure 6.18) that can be used to couple tactical and conditioning activities in one training session (27). Alternating intensities facilitates recovery between training sessions, leading to an optimal peak at the main competition.

PERIODIZATION OF SPEED

The periodization of speed depends on the characteristics of the sport including the performance level and the competitive schedule. The development of speed for a team sport athlete is very different from that of a sprinter. Team sport athletes usually follow a monocycle annual plan, whereas sprinters usually undergo a bi-cycle

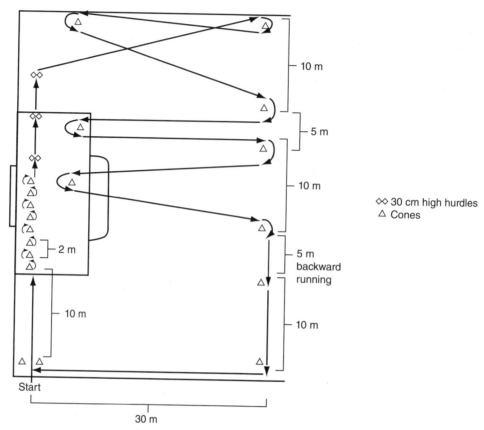

Figure 6.18 Dribbling track for developing soccer-specific endurance.

The dribble track requires the athlete to dribble a ball around the course. The athlete should gradually increase intensity until achieving a heart rate between 90% and 95% of maximum and hold that heart rate for 4 min. After the 4 min time period is completed, the athlete performs 4 min of exercise at 70% of maximal heart rate. The circuit can be completed two to four times depending on the phase of the periodized training plan. Athletes must dribble around the cones and lift the ball over the hurdles.

Adapted from *British Journal of Sports Medicine,* J.U. Hoff et al., 2002, "Soccer specific aerobic endurance training," 36: 218-221, © 2002, with permission from BMJ Publishing Group Ltd.

annual training plan as a result of having both indoor and outdoor championship competitions. Regardless of the type of individual or team sport, the periodization of speed training may follow several distinct subphases: an aerobic and anaerobic endurance phase; a maximum speed and anaerobic endurance phase; a specific speed phase; and a specific speed, agility, and reactive agility phase.

Aerobic and Anaerobic Endurance Phase

The first step in developing speed is to establish a physiological base that provides the athlete with the technical skills needed for moving fast (10). This type of training is typical of the general preparation phase of the annual training plan and is designed to elevate aerobic, anaerobic, and general endurance capacity (15). There are many methods by which to develop a physiological base for sprinting, including extensive tempo and intensive tempo training (15).

Extensive tempo training involves multiple repetitions of distances greater than 200 m performed at less than 70% of maximum speed, with 45 s between repetitions and less than 2 min between sets. This type of tempo training tends to develop aerobic capacity and aerobic power. Intensive tempo training involves higher intensities

(80-90% of maximum) and a wider range of distances (>80 m) with 30 s to 5 min recovery between repetitions and 3 to 10 min between sets. The intensive tempo method improves anaerobic capacity and targets a mix of energy systems. This type of training has also been termed *high-intensity interval training* by some authors (40). These methods create the appropriate physiological adaptations necessary for the development of high-intensity exercise endurance (79).

The metabolic adaptations induced by tempo training have a great degree of sport specificity and translate to many individual and team sports (57). The use of interval-based training methods has been reported to enhance both anaerobic and aerobic metabolism (40). Conversely, using traditional long slow distance–based training has been shown to compromise anaerobic metabolic function (79). Because speed of movement or sprinting ability depends largely on the rate of energy supply, the use of methods that compromise anaerobic function is not recommended (62).

In addition to extensive and intensive tempo training, speed endurance training may be warranted. This type of training can be performed with distances ranging from 50 to 150 m, with high intensities (90-100% of maximum), and with a wide range of recovery between repetitions (1-10 min) and sets (3-4 min) (15). This is also a form of interval training that creates a large amount of physiological stress, establishing a foundation from which to develop further speed.

As training progresses from the general preparatory to specific preparatory phase of training, additional sport-specific activities, including speed training with various intensities, are incorporated. For team sports training, tactical drills of 2 to 5 min can be performed nonstop to develop sport-specific endurance (41). In soccer this may be accomplished via the use of small-sided games in which fewer players participate in a game simulation (i.e. 2 versus 2; 3 versus 3; 5 versus 5 etc.) or a soccer-specific dribble track (figure 6.18), as recent research suggests that this practice effectively develops soccer-specific endurance capacity (27).

Maximum Speed and Anaerobic Endurance Phase

As the competitive phase approaches, training becomes more intensive, event-specific, refined, and specialized. Training will include work designed to maximize speed and continue to develop speed endurance (15).

Speed can be developed with short-distance sprints (20-80 m) performed at high intensities (90-100% of maximum) with longer rest intervals between repetitions (3-5 min) and sets (6-8 min) (15). This type of training will stress the anaerobic systems, especially the phosphagen system.

Speed endurance training, as noted previously, uses various distances and rest intervals. These different interval structures can be used to target physiological adaptations. For example, the glycolytic system and lactate tolerance can be targeted via the use of high-intensity (95-100% maximum) short-distance sprints (<80 m) performed with short rest intervals between repetitions (1 min) and longer repetitions between sets (4 min).

Specific Speed Phase

The specific speed phase can incorporate some or all the speed components and various bioenergetic-specific training methods (phosphagen and glycolytic) depending on the specifics of the sport. This phase may be ideal for the use of sport-specific training practices such as small-sided games (41) or skill-based conditioning activities (18). This phase should contain drills for developing agility and reaction time, especially for team sports, martial arts, and combat sports. At this time, the plan should begin to incorporate agility and reaction time drills.

Specific Speed, Agility, and Reactive Agility Phase

This phase of training uses methods and drills to develop speed and refine related abilities, such as agility and reaction time. Speed development is essential to the development of agility (90). However, simply working on straight-line speed will not maximize an athlete's agility (90, 91). Techniques that involve agility must also be developed (90). If the training phases are planned correctly, the speed that is developed in the previous phases will be translated into agility, which will improve sports performance.

Another component of agility is perceptual decision making, which is related to reaction time or visual scanning, anticipation, pattern recognition, and knowledge of situations (90). This has been termed *reactive agility* and is marked by the ability to react to a situation, which appears to differentiate players of different levels in various sports (12, 61). Specific drills are needed to develop this type of agility. For example, it has been suggested that reactive agility drills can increase mental processing and decrease response time to a stimulus (87). If implemented correctly, this type of training should improve an athlete's ability to react to events on the field of play.

INTEGRATED PERIODIZATION

One of the most important factors that must be considered when constructing a periodized training plan is the integration of training factors. Too often sport scientists, coaches, and practitioners isolate training factors instead of integrating all the factors into the training plan. To maximize the coach's ability to construct and deliver appropriately designed training plans, an interdisciplinary team of experts may be needed (54). This group can be considered a sports enhancement team and can include sport scientists, sport psychologists, nutritionists, biomechanists, and sports medicine professionals. Given the rapidly evolving nature of sport science (89), the team approach may be necessary to most effectively interpret, develop, and implement new training methods in the context of a periodized training plan.

The integration of all training components into a comprehensive annual training plan requires the coach and sports enhancement team to evaluate the athlete and the training goals, which will allow them to appropriately sequence training factors. Depending on the phase of the periodization plan, the training emphasis will shift to develop specific characteristics and manage fatigue. A truly comprehensive plan includes dietary recommendations and psychological training. An example of an integrated periodization plan is presented in figure 6.19. If the training plan is not completely integrated, the likelihood that the athlete will achieve successful results is significantly decreased.

ANNUAL TRAINING PLAN PHASES AND CHARACTERISTICS

The annual training plan should contain at least three training phases: preparatory, competitive, and transition phases. The number of times these three phases are performed will depend on the type of cycle that is used (e.g., monocycle, bi-cycle, tri-cycle). The objectives and characteristics of these phases remain consistent regardless of how

Months	1	2	3	4	5	6	7	8	9	10	11	12
TRAINING PHASES	PREPARATORY					COMPETITIVE						TRANSITION
Subphases	Preparatory		Specific	Precompetitive		Official and league competitions					Unloading	Transition
Speed	Anaerobic and aerobic endurance		• Maximum speed • Anaerobic endurance	• Maximum speed • Specific speed • Agility • Reactive agility		• Sport-specific preparations • Specific speed • Agility • Reactive agility					Unloading	Play, fun
Strength	Anatomical adaptation		Maximal strength	Power / Maximal strength	Maximal strength / Conversion of power	Maintenance of power or maximal strength						Compensation
Mental training	• Evaluate mental skills • Learn new mental skills • Practice relaxation		• Mental training • Visualization • Imagery • Relaxation • Energy management	• Mental rehearsal • Energizing • Positive self-talk • Visualization • Focus plans • Simulation • Coping		• Mental skills to cope with opponents • Stress management • Relaxation • Focus plans • Mental rehearsal • Motivation • Positive self-talk					• Mental skills to aid regeneration, relaxation, stress management • Positive self-talk • Visualization	• Active rest • De-stress
Nutrition	• High carbohydrate • Moderate protein		• High protein • Moderate carbohydrate	• High carbohydrate	• High carbohydrate • Moderate protein	• High carbohydrate • Moderate protein	Fluctuates according to the competitive schedule				High carbohydrate	Balanced diet

Left margin label: Periodization

Figure 6.19 Integrated periodization plan.

147

many times they are repeated throughout the annual training plan. To optimize the athlete's development throughout the annual training plan and elevate preparedness and performance to its highest levels at the appropriate time, each training phase must be correctly sequenced, completely integrated, and properly structured.

Preparatory Phase

The preparatory phase is probably the most important phase of the annual training plan. This phase establishes the physical, technical, and psychological base from which the competitive phase is developed. The adaptations developed as a result of the increased volume of training in this phase will allow the athlete to better tolerate the increase in training intensity that occurs in the competitive phase. However, if the preparatory phase is inadequate, the athlete's ability to tolerate training and maximize performance during the competitive phase will be compromised. The preparatory phase has the following objectives:

- To acquire and improve general physical training capacity
- To improve the biomotor abilities required by the sport
- To cultivate psychological traits
- To develop, improve, or perfect technique
- To familiarize athletes with the basic strategic maneuvers mastered in the following phases
- To teach athletes the theory and methodology of training specific to the sport

The preparatory phase lasts 3 to 6 months depending on the climate, sport, and type of annual plan used (e.g., monocycle, bi-cycle, tri-cycle). For individual sports the preparatory phase is approximately two times as long as the competitive phase, whereas for team sports the preparatory phase may be somewhat shorter, but not less than 2 to 3 months. The preparatory phase is specific to each sport and distinctive for each subphase (table 6.2). For any sport, the preparatory phase should be divided into two subphases: general and specific preparation.

General Preparatory Subphase

The general preparatory subphase is used to elevate the athlete's working capacity, increase general physical preparation, improve technical elements, and enhance basic tactical abilities. The primary emphasis of this subphase is to establish a high level of physical conditioning, which will improve the athlete's physiological and psychological capacity to tolerate the demands of both training and competition. Regardless of the sport, a sound physical base is an essential component for the athlete. Typically, the base is established through the use of general and sport-specific exercises rather than a reliance on sport-specific skill development. For instance, a gymnastics coach may dedicate the first two or three microcycles to the development of general and specific strength needed to master a certain technical element in the following cycles. This concept is valid for other sports in which certain physical attributes can limit technical progress. Many times the inability to develop technical skill is the result of an inadequately developed physical base. Therefore it may be warranted to determine whether the athlete possesses adequate physical support for the technical performance of an element or skill (11).

Throughout this subphase the plan includes a high training volume, consisting of exercises that require both general and specific effort. The goal is to improve working

Table 6.2   Training Objectives for Each Subphase of the Preparatory Phase

Sport	Dominant training factor	SUBPHASE	
		General preparation	**Specific preparation**
Gymnastics	Physical	General and maximal strength	Specific strength and power
	Technical	Technical elements	Elements, half and skeleton of full routine
Rowing	Physical	Aerobic endurance	Anaerobic endurance
		Anatomical adaptation	Aerobic endurance
		Maximal strength	Muscular endurance
		Muscular endurance	
Swimming (100 m)	Physical	Aerobic endurance	Anaerobic endurance
		Anatomical adaptation	Aerobic endurance
		Maximal strength	Maximal strength
			Maximal power
Swimming (800 m)	Physical	Aerobic endurance	Aerobic endurance
		Anatomical adaptation	Anaerobic endurance
		Maximal strength	Muscular endurance
Team sports	Technical	Technical elements	Apply technical elements in game situations
	Tactical	Individual and simple team tactics	Team tactics
	Physical	High intensity exercise endurance	Anaerobic endurance
		General and maximal strength	Power development

capacity and psychological drive (determination, perseverance, and willpower) necessary for the sport. For example, the development of aerobic endurance is the main objective for sports in which endurance is the dominant ability or a major contributor to performance (e.g., running, swimming, rowing, Nordic skiing). For these sports 70% to 80% of the total training time may be devoted to the development of aerobic endurance, which can be seen in the kilometers covered in training. In sports for which strength, power, and speed are important attributes, this subphase will focus on the development of anatomical adaptations and maximal strength. Increasing the weight lifted or the volume load of training is an objective way to increase working capacity and induce adaptations necessary for the sporting activity.

The process is somewhat different for team sport athletes in that while developing the physical base these athletes must also spend substantial time developing technical and tactical skills. Although technical and tactical improvements are important aspects of the training process, the plan must not neglect the development of high intensity exercise endurance, strength, and speed because these components of the physical base lay the groundwork for future performance accomplishments.

In most sports, the type of training used in the preparatory phase, especially the general subphase, plays a major role in determining the athlete's performance capacity

© Human Kinetics

Establishing a high level of physical conditioning is important before beginning specific training tasks.

during the competitive phase. Insufficient emphasis on training volume during this subphase may account for poor performances, lack of consistency, and a decrease in performance capacity during the later portion of the competitive phase. Consequently, 15% to 25% of the training for the preparatory phase should be allocated to this subphase, with the rest of the preparatory phase consisting of sport-specific preparatory activities. The duration of the general preparatory phase will be longer with novice athletes and should be progressively reduced for advanced athletes.

Increasing training volume during the general preparatory subphase is the primary emphasis; although training intensity is important, it is a secondary factor in the preparatory phase. Intensive training can be undertaken but should not exceed 40% of the total amount of training in this subphase, particularly for beginners and juniors. It is important to remember the objective of increasing working capacity during this subphase. With the increases in training, volume fatigue will increase markedly and thus preparedness will decrease greatly, reducing performance capacity. Therefore, it is inadvisable to compete during this subphase because the athlete will have a high level of fatigue, which will reduce performance capacity and increase the risk for injury (59, 60). When the athlete is highly fatigued as a result of training, technical skills will be relatively unstable and the athlete's ability to perform specific tactical maneuvers will decrease. Competition during this subphase also can negatively affect the athlete's psychological status, and it decreases the amount of time that can be dedicated to developing the physiological base needed to expand the athlete's capabilities.

Specific Preparatory Subphase

The specific preparatory subphase, or the second part of the preparatory phase, represents a transition from an emphasis on physical development to an emphasis on competition. Like the general preparatory subphase, the specific preparatory subphase has the objective of increasing the athlete's working capacity. However, in this subphase the emphasis in training is on sport-specific activities. Although the volume of work is high during this subphase, the primary emphasis (70-80% of total work) is on specific exercises related to the skills or technical elements of the sport. Toward the end of this phase the volume begins to progressively decrease, allowing for a gradual increase in the training intensity.

For sports in which intensity is important (e.g., sprinting, jumping, and team sports) the training volume may be lowered by as much as 40% in the later portions of this subphase. A different approach would be taken for sports that rely on technical mastery and coordinated movements, such as figure skating, diving, and gymnastics. In these sports it is essential that the athlete continue to perfect and develop the technical proficiency necessary for success during the competitive phase. Similarly, in team sports, racket sports, and martial arts, the specific preparatory subphase should focus on the development and improvement of sport-specific technical and tactical elements. This is accomplished with specific exercises that target the prime movers, movement patterns, and technical skills required by the sport. These exercises must be performed in such a way as to create a link between the physical attributes developed in the general preparatory subphase and the technical and tactical skills necessary for successful competition. Although the major emphasis is on technical and tactical skill development, a secondary emphasis should be on maintaining general physical development. This secondary focus should contain only a few exercises for general development (a maximum of 20%) that contribute to the athlete's multilateral development.

As the athlete's training shifts toward specialized training, there should be progressive improvement in performance-based testing and athletic performance. In the later stages of this subphase, competitions can be used as evaluative tools that provide feedback about the athlete's preparation for competition, specifically her technical and tactical development. Information garnered from these competitions can be used to modify training plans to address specific deficiencies.

Competitive Phase

Among the main tasks of the competitive phase is the perfection of all training factors, which enables the athlete to compete successfully in the main competitions or championships targeted by the annual training plan. Several general objectives are addressed during the competitive phase, regardless of the sport:

- Continued improvement or maintenance of sport-specific biomotor abilities
- Enhancing psychological traits
- Perfecting and consolidating technique
- Elevating performance to the highest level
- Dissipating fatigue and elevating preparedness
- Perfecting technical and tactical maneuvers
- Gaining competitive experience
- Maintaining sport-specific fitness

As the athlete progresses to the competitive phase, it is important that the level of physical development established during the preparatory phase be maintained. Maintenance of the physical attributes developed in previous phases is important because they support the other training factors that are developed during the competitive phase. This can be accomplished by dedicating 90% of the total physical preparation activities to sport-specific activities such as skill-based conditioning exercises (19) or small-sided games in team sports (41). The remaining 10% of the planned physical preparation activities can come from nonspecific or indirect activities, such as active rest or game-based activities that are not directly related to the sport being trained.

The objectives established for the competitive phase are met by the use of sport-specific training activities that can include technical and tactical exercises. Included in this process may be the use of simulated, exhibition, and actual competitive events. It is essential that the training activities are sport specific to stimulate performance improvement, stabilization, and consistency. As the athlete progresses through the competitive phase, training becomes more intensive while training volume is decreased. For sports dominated by speed, power, and maximum strength (e.g., sprinting, jumping, throwing, weightlifting) training intensity can increase dramatically while the volume of training is progressively decreased. In endurance sports (e.g., distance running, swimming, cross-country skiing, canoeing, rowing) training volume can be maintained or only slightly lower than that seen in the preparatory phase. An exception to this practice occurs during the competitive microcycle, when intensity decreases according to the number of races and the level of competition.

As the athlete progresses through the competitive phase, the alterations to the training plan should elevate preparedness and increase performance. The structure of the training plan will play a large role in stimulating these effects; if the plan is structured correctly, the athlete will optimize performance at the appropriate time. If performance begins to decline or becomes stagnant, it is likely that the amount of work was decreased too much, reducing physical capacity, or that the work was maintained at too high a level and fatigue is masking the potential performance gains. The modulation between work and performance appears to be an art based on science, and the integration of athlete monitoring and coaching experience will guide the decisions made during this phase of training.

The length of the competitive phase depends on the sport and the type of annual training plan. Long competitive phases are typically seen in team sports as a result of the set league schedules. Conversely, athletes in individual sports have more freedom in determining their competitive schedule, allowing for more control over the length of the competitive phase and the structure of training leading into the major competition of the year. Regardless of the sport, one of the most important factors in determining the duration and structure of the competitive phase is the phase's start date. When structuring the competitive phase and its start date consider the following parameters:

AP Photo/Gerry Broome/FILE

Annual training plans should be structured to account for the possibility of reaching a major championship competition.

- The number of competitions required to reach the highest performance. On average it takes between 7 and 10 competitions to achieve the highest performance results.
- The amount of time or interval between competitions.
- The duration of eventual qualifying meets.
- The time required for special preparation before the main competition of the year.
- The time needed for recovery and regeneration.

When structuring the competitive phase of the annual training plan it may be warranted to divide the phase into two subphases: the precompetitive phase and the main competitive phase.

Precompetitive Subphase

The precompetitive phase generally contains unofficial competitions or, in the case of team sports, exhibition games. Although this subphase is an integral part of the competitive phase, the objective is not to achieve the highest level of competition. This subphase should serve as a training tool in which the athlete participates in exhibitions or unofficial competitions as a means of preparing for later events. One of the main reasons for the use of exhibition or unofficial contests is to allow for objective feedback about the athlete's training level and preparedness for future contests. These competitions will allow for the evaluation of all technical, tactical, and physical skills under competitive conditions. Exhibitions and unofficial competitions should not significantly alter the training program, especially for elite athletes, because these contests provide a testing ground for the main competitive subphase, when the official contests begin.

Main Competitive Subphase

The main competitive subphase is dedicated strictly to maximizing preparedness, thus allowing for superior performances at the main contests. The number of training sessions contained in this subphase should reflect whether athletes are participating in a loading or regeneration (unloading) microcycle. A loading microcycle may have 10 to 14 sessions per week, whereas an unloading microcycle will contain much fewer sessions, thus facilitating a decrease in fatigue and an elevation in preparedness prior to the competition. The training content of this subphase should be centered on sport-specific methods and the maintenance of specific physical development.

Although the training volume may still be high for endurance sports, the coach can reduce the training volume to 50% to 75% of the level of the preparatory phase for sports that require technical mastery, speed, strength or power. While volume is decreasing the intensity of training gradually increases, with the highest levels occurring 2 or 3 weeks prior to the main competition. During this subphase, training sessions with maximal intensity should not occur more than two or three times per week. In the last 8 to 14 days (one or two microcycles) prior to the competition, a taper or unloading period should be used (see chapter 7 for more information).

The stress curve will be elevated during the competitive phase as a result of the increased intensity of training and the participation in competitions. The stress curve should have an undulating shape, reflecting the fluctuations between stressful activities (competitions and intense training sessions) and short periods of regeneration. The harder a competition or training session, the higher the stress curve and the longer the compensation phase needed to reduce the amount of accumulated stress or fatigue.

If possible, the coach should arrange competitions progressively in order of importance, concluding with the main competitions. Another organizational strategy is to introduce main competitions interspersed with lesser competitions that allow the athlete to continue to train drastically altering the training plan. This second strategy is possible with individual sports but may not be feasible with team sports and a set league schedule.

Six to eight microcycles prior to the main competition, focus the training program and daily cycle on the specific requirements of the competition. This will maximize the athlete's physical, technical, tactical, and psychological preparations for the main competition. Preparing the athlete for the specific competitive environment and demands will prevent any surprises and enhance the athlete's performance. In this portion of the competitive phase, 8 to 14 days of unloading will be used to peak the athlete (see chapter 7).

Unloading or Tapering Subphase   The unloading or tapering phase is the best way to elevate the athlete's preparedness and stimulate a supercompensation of performance that will increase the athlete's performance potential during the competition. Peaking is accomplished via manipulating both volume and intensity to reduce the accumulated fatigue stimulated from previous training and competition, which will allow the athlete to rest and regenerate before the major competition.

The unloading or tapering subphase should last 8 to 14 days and can use various methods of reducing volume and training intensity (see figures 7.3 and 7.4 on pp. 190 and 193 and chapter 7 for more details). The strategy used for unloading during this subphase depends largely on the type of training undertaken and the individual sport. Classically, for endurance sports, some suggest reducing intensity and maintaining volume, because endurance athletes were thought to tolerate high-volume training better than high-intensity training (figure 6.20). However, contemporary literature suggests that it may be warranted to reduce training volume and maintain training intensity (8, 31, 37, 48). During the first microcycle of unloading, the process will involve reducing the number of daily training sessions and modulating training intensity to begin the recovery process. The coach should eliminate all extraneous activities that can contribute to the athlete's fatigue and encourage the athlete to use free time to rest and recover for the pending competition. In this portion of the unloading period, it may be warranted to reduce the volume and frequency (two sessions per week) of strength training. Further reductions in the volume and intensity of training may be planned during the second microcycle of the unloading period. This can be accomplished by limiting strength training to one or two sessions or removing strength training completely depending on the sport. The volume and intensity of other training factors also should be reduced.

The same unloading approach is used for sports dominated by speed, power, or technical proficiency. In the first microcycle the training volume is reduced by 40%

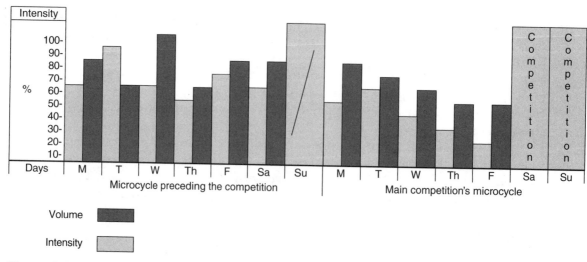

Figure 6.20   Unloading phase for an endurance sport.

to 50%, depending on the level of training undertaken prior to the taper. This period should include several short but high-intensity sessions to maintain the adaptations induced by previous training phases (figure 6.21). A two-peak microcycle structure may be used during the first microcycle of this subphase, but long rest intervals need to be included between repetitions to help dissipate fatigue and stress. During the high-intensity training session, all exercises should be dynamic and of short duration and should contain medium- to high-intensity loading. The other sessions in the microcycle should alternate submaximal intensities between low and very low intensities. With these types of sports, the volume and frequency of strength training should be reduced while maintaining moderate to high intensities. Complete removal of strength training may not be warranted because power and speed are highly dependent on strength levels.

During the second microcycle of this subphase, in which the main competition occurs, the coach continues to reduce training volume and the intensity of training.

Only one peak occurs during the early portion of this microcycle. Across this microcycle the objective is to maximally reduce fatigue and stress while increasing preparedness and maintaining the physiological adaptations that have been established.

A slightly different approach may be used when working with team sports where both training volume and intensity are equally important. During the first microcycle of the unloading phase, the coach should reduce the work volume to produce the unloading effect (figure 6.22). This can be accomplished by progressively reducing intensity across the microcycle while having two intense training sessions of 50% to 60% of maximum. During the second microcycle of this subphase, the coach should continue to reduce the volume and intensity of training, reducing volume to a greater extent than intensity. This subphase can include a two-peak microcycle, the first peak of which is performed at higher intensity than the second (15-20% less than the first peak). Two days prior to the competition, the athlete should undergo short training sessions of low to very low intensities (figure 6.22). For more details on tapering or peaking athletes for competition, refer to chapter 7.

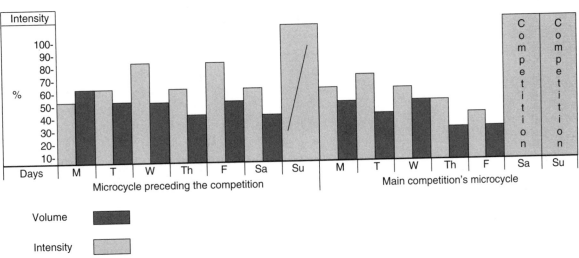

Figure 6.21   Unloading phase for a speed- or power-dominated sport.

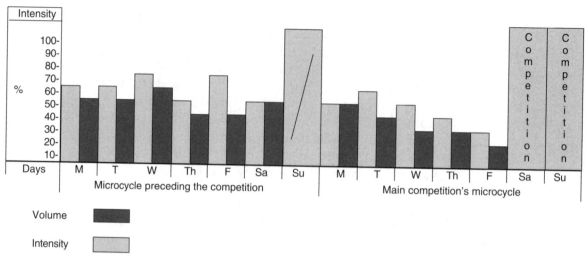

Figure 6.22 Unloading phase for a team sport.

Special Preparation Period The special preparation period can be organized separately or in concert with the unloading phase and contains activities designed to enhance performance in the most important competition in the competitive phase. The special preparation period can last between 3 and 7 days, depending on the characteristics of the competition. During this phase certain training aspects, especially tactical elements, are altered according to the latest information on opponents or the competitive schedule. The vast majority of the training in this phase follows the model concept, with the purpose of enhancing preparation for the upcoming competition. One aspect that has important implications for the final result is the special psychological preparations that target relaxation, confidence building, and motivation. However, these techniques should be used cautiously because overemphasis on psychological elements can impair performance. Each athlete is different and will require specific preparation activities to meet her individual needs.

Transition Phase

After long periods of preparation, hard work, and stressful competitions, in which both physiological and psychological fatigue can accumulate, a transition period should be used to link annual training plans or preparation for another major competition, as in the case of the bi-cycle, tri-cycle, and multicycle annual training plan. The transition phase serves an important role in preparing the athlete for the next training cycle. The athlete should start the new preparatory phase only when fully recovered from the previous competitive season (10). If the athlete initiates a new preparatory phase without full recovery, it is likely that performances will be impaired in future competitive cycles and the risk of injury will increase (10).

The transition phase, often inappropriately called the off-season, links two annual training plans. This phase facilitates psychological rest, relaxation, and biological regeneration while maintaining an acceptable level of general physical preparation (40-50% of the competitive phase). Training should be low key; all loading factors should be reduced, with the main training components centering on general training, with minimal, if any, technical or tactical development (10, 39). The transition phase generally should last 2 to 4 weeks but could be extended to 6 weeks (10, 39). Under normal circumstances the transition phase should not last longer than 6 weeks.

There are two common approaches to the transition phase. The first and incorrect approach encourages complete rest with no physical activity; the term *off-season* fits perfectly. This abrupt interruption of training and the complete inactivity can lead to significant detraining even if only undertaken for a short period of time (<4 weeks) (49, 50). This detraining effect can cause a substantial loss in the physiological adaptations established in the previous months of training.

Some authors have suggested that an abrupt cessation of training by highly trained athletes creates a phenomenon known as detraining syndrome (or relaxation syndrome) (49, 50), exercise abstinence, or exercise dependency syndrome (38). This type of detraining appears to occur in athletes who either intentionally cease training or are forced to stop training in response to an injury (38). Detraining syndrome can be characterized by many symptoms including insomnia, anxiety, depression, alterations to cardiovascular function, and a loss of appetite (see the bottom of this page for additional symptoms). These symptoms usually are not pathological and can be reversed if training is resumed within a short time. If the cessation of training is prolonged, these symptoms can become more pronounced indicating that the athlete's body is unable to adapt to this sudden inactivity. The time frame in which these symptoms manifest themselves is highly specific to the individual athlete but can occur within 2 to 3 weeks of inactivity and will vary in severity.

Simply decreasing the level of training can also stimulate a detraining effect that will decrease physiological (table 6.3) and performance capacity (49, 50). The magnitude of the detraining effects will be related to the duration of the detraining period. Short-term detraining, which occurs in less than 4 weeks, can result in some significant decreases in endurance (49) and strength performance (32, 49).

In endurance athletes, short-term detraining has been reported to result in a 4% to 25% decrease in time to exhaustion and a substantial reduction in endurance performance (49). It has been postulated that the reductions in endurance performance are largely dictated by the decline in cardiorespiratory fitness noted in response to short-term detraining (30). Maximal aerobic capacity can be reduced by 4% in as little as 4 days of detraining (86), decreased by 7% within 3 weeks of the cessation of training (9), and reduced by 14% in as little as 4 weeks of detraining (49). If the detraining period is extended to 8 weeks, aerobic capacity can continue to decrease up to 20% of predetraining values (50). These reductions in aerobic capacity are most likely related to specific alterations to the cardiorespiratory system including decreases in blood volume, stroke volume, and maximal cardiac output (table 6.3). These detraining-induced physiological alterations appear to occur progressively and proportionally

POTENTIAL SYMPTOMS OF DETRAINING SYNDROME

- Increased occurrence of dizziness and fainting
- Nonsystematic precordial disturbances
- Increased sensation or occurrence of cardiac arrhythmias
- Occurrence of extrasystolia and palpitations

- Increased incidence of headaches
- Loss of appetite
- Increased incidence of insomnia
- Occurrence of anxiety and depression
- Profuse sweating
- Gastric disturbances

Adapted from Mujika and Padilla 2000 (49).

Table 6.3 Short-Term (<4 Weeks) and Long-Term (>4 Weeks) Detraining Effects

Physiological factors altered by detraining	Detraining characteristics	Short term (<4 weeks)	Long term (>4 weeks)
Cardiorespiratory	Maximal oxygen uptake	⇓	⇓
	Blood volume	⇑	⇑
	Submaximal heart rate	⇑	⇑
	Recovery heart rate	⇑	⇑
	Stroke volume during exercise	⇓	⇓
	Maximal cardiac output	⇓	⇓
	Ventricular mass and dimension	⇓	⇓
	Mean blood pressure	⇑	⇑
	Maximal ventilatory volume	⇓	⇓
	Submaximal ventilatory volume	⇑	⇑
	Oxygen pulse	⇓	⇓
	Ventilatory equivalent	⇑	⇑
	Endurance performance	⇓	⇓
Skeletal muscle	Capillary density	⇓	⇓
	Arterial-venous oxygen difference	—	⇓
	Fiber type distribution	—	Altered
	Fiber cross-sectional area	⇓	⇓
	Type II:I area ratio	—	⇓
	Muscle mass	—	⇓
	EMG activity	⇓	⇓
	Strength power performance	⇓	⇓
	Oxidative enzyme capacity	⇓	⇓
	Glycogen synthase activity	⇓	—
	Mitochondrial ATP production	⇓	—
Metabolic characteristics	Maximal respiratory exchange ratio	⇑	⇑
	Submaximal respiratory exchange ratio	⇑	⇑
	Insulin-mediated glucose uptake	⇓	⇓
	Muscle GLUT4 protein content	⇓	⇓
	Muscle lipoprotein lipase activity	⇓	⇓
	Postprandial lipemia	⇑	—
	High-density lipoprotein cholesterol	⇓	⇓
	Low-density lipoprotein cholesterol	⇓	⇓
	Submaximal blood lactate	⇑	⇑
	Lactate threshold	⇓	⇓
	Bicarbonate level	⇓	⇓
	Muscle glycogen level	⇓	⇓
	Adrenaline-stimulated lipolysis	⇓	⇓

Adapted from Mujika and Padilla 2000 (49, 50).

⇓ = decrease, ⇑ = increase, — = no data available; EMG = electromyographic; ATP = adenosine triphosphate; GLUT4 = glucose transporter-4.

to the training status of the athlete, thus suggesting that highly trained endurance athletes will experience a greater magnitude of decline in both physiological and performance capacity.

Short-term and long-term detraining can also produce marked alterations in strength and power performance. For example, 4 weeks of detraining in which strength training is completely removed from the training plan results in a 6% to 10% reduction in maximal muscular strength (23, 32) and a 14% to 17% decrease in maximal power generation capacity (32). These reductions in strength power performance may be related to preferential atrophy of Type II muscle fibers (29, 67) and a reduction in neural drive (1, 22-24). The reduction in the ability to express muscular strength and power characteristics depends on the magnitude of the reduction of muscle cross-sectional area and electromyographic activity.

The extent of strength and power performance and physiological detraining-induced maladaptations depends on several factors including the duration of detraining and the training status of the athlete. Although the largest decrease in the expression of muscular strength occurs during the first 4 weeks (10% decrease), extending the detraining period to 8 weeks will result in a continued performance reduction (11-12% decrease) (23, 49, 50). These reductions in performance appear to occur at a greater rate and magnitude in highly trained individuals compared with recreational athletes and untrained people, because the latter appear able to maintain both strength and power performance in response to 2 to 3 weeks of detraining (29, 35, 51).

If training completely stops during the transition phase, it is likely, depending on the length of the phase, that the athlete will lose a substantial amount of the physiological adaptations gained from the previous training period. When this occurs, the athlete will spend a large portion of the next preparatory phase attempting to reestablish the physiological adaptations that were gained in the previous training period, which limits the athlete's ability to continue to improve. Conversely, if the athlete uses an active rest period during the transition phase, she will retain a larger portion of her physiological adaptations and continue to develop both physiological and performance capacities during the next general preparation phase.

In the second approach to the transition phase, active rest is used to minimize the loss of physiological function that occurs when passive methods are used. Active rest refers to participating in a compatible sport or using a period of low-volume and low-intensity training within the athlete's sport (71). By using this approach, the athlete will be able to minimize the loss of physiological adaptation and maintain some level of general fitness.

The transition phase begins immediately after the completion of the main competition and can last between 2 and 4 weeks. During the first week after the competition, active or passive rest can be used. Passive rest may be necessary if the athlete has injuries. If active rest is used during this microcycle, the volume and intensity of training are substantially reduced and may target movement patterns or activities that are not used in training. During the second to fourth microcycle of the transition phase (in a 4-week transition), the volume and intensity of training can remain low or can increase slightly. The activity used for active rest must match the bioenergetic characteristics of the sport being trained for. For example, a cyclist may use cross-country skiing or running as a transition activity, whereas a volleyball player may use basketball. The transition phase is a period during which the athlete can recover physically and psychologically while minimizing the loss of fitness.

The transition phase has an additional purpose. During this phase, the coach and athlete should analyze the training program, performance results, and testing outcomes. This is an essential task because it will allow the coach and athlete to make specific changes to the athlete's next annual training plan.

CHART OF THE ANNUAL TRAINING PLAN

Now that the basic concept of periodization and the main objectives of each training phase and subphase have been presented, an annual training plan can be constructed. Charting an annual training plan requires an understanding of the relationships between the training components and stress that these factors impart upon the athlete. During this process decisions must be made about when the major competitions are, the ratio of training factors contained in each phase, and the sequencing of the training phases. Successful training planners are able to use their knowledge about training and its physiological responses to develop training plans that will induce specific outcomes.

Annual training plans for all athletes are constructed with the same basic steps, but each plan, and thus the chart, must be individualized to the sport and the athlete's needs. Several examples of annual training plan charts are provided in this text (see the following sections), and readers can either adapt these examples or create their own charts.

Chart of a Monocycle Annual Training Plan

The first annual training plan presented (figure 6.23) is a monocycle, which is the simplest form of an annual training plan. Although figure 6.23 is structured for rowing, the format can be used as a template when creating an annual training plan for any sport that uses a monocycle model.

The top part of the chart contains a list of the athletes' names, followed by objectives that are generated by the coach alone or through consultation with the athlete. The first objective set is for performance, which should be a measurable performance (such as a time or distance), a ranking to achieve, or a combination of both performance and ranking (e.g., win six games and place fourth at the junior championships). Objectives for tests and standards should be described briefly, as suggested in the section on training parameters. After this is completed, objectives should be set for each of the training factors (e.g., physical, technical, tactical, and psychological preparation). The objectives of each training factor should emphasize the improvement and perfection of areas of weakness that have been noted from previous testing and performance analysis. The objectives of the training factors, tests, standards, and performance should all be interrelated. Achieving the objectives set for the training factors and tests and standards should increase the athlete's likelihood of achieving performance objectives at the appropriate time.

Below the objectives section is the schedule of competitions, which is the most important training parameter needed when establishing the annual training plan. This is why each sport governing body, collegiate sport conference, and national sports federation should set its competitive schedule immediately after the current year's championship. Without the competitive schedule, coaches cannot appropriately structure the annual training plan.

The coach should construct the chart from right to left around the competition dates by placing the main competition, be it provincial, national, world champion-

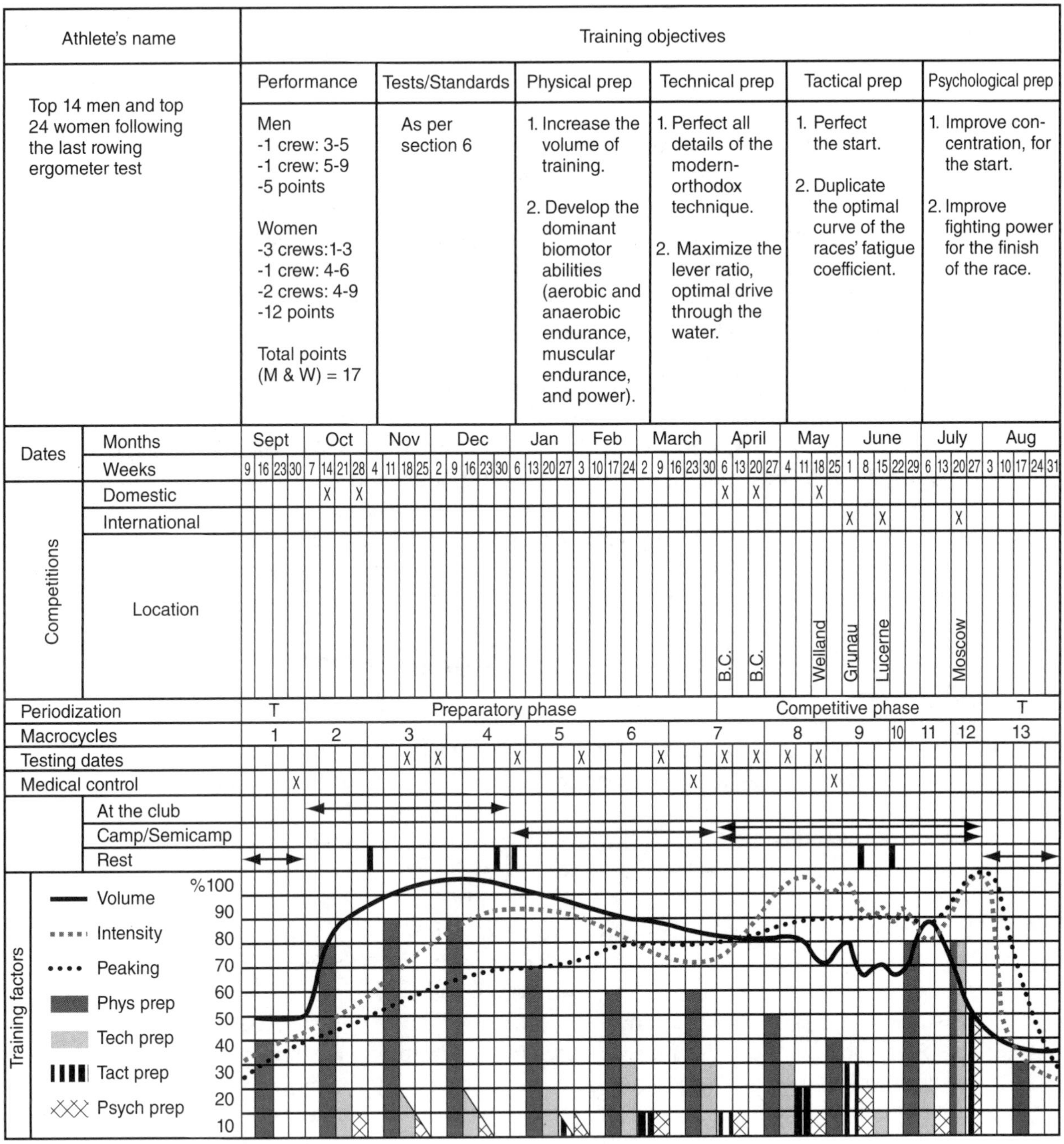
Athlete's name
Training objectives
Top 14 men and top 24 women following the last rowing ergometer test
Performance
Tests/Standards
Physical prep
Technical prep
Tactical prep
Psychological prep
Men
-1 crew: 3-5
-1 crew: 5-9
-5 points
Women
-3 crews:1-3
-1 crew: 4-6
-2 crews: 4-9
-12 points
Total points (M & W) = 17
As per section 6
1. Increase the volume of training.
2. Develop the dominant biomotor abilities (aerobic and anaerobic endurance, muscular endurance, and power).
1. Perfect all details of the modern-orthodox technique.
2. Maximize the lever ratio, optimal drive through the water.
1. Perfect the start.
2. Duplicate the optimal curve of the races' fatigue coefficient.
1. Improve concentration, for the start.
2. Improve fighting power for the finish of the race.
Dates
Months
Sept
Oct
Nov
Dec
Jan
Feb
March
April
May
June
July
Aug
Weeks
9 16 23 30 7 14 21 28 4 11 18 25 2 9 16 23 30 6 13 20 27 3 10 17 24 2 9 16 23 30 6 13 20 27 4 11 18 25 1 8 15 22 29 6 13 20 27 3 10 17 24 31
Competitions
Domestic
International
Location
B.C.
B.C.
Welland
Grunau
Lucerne
Moscow
Periodization
T
Preparatory phase
Competitive phase
T
Macrocycles
1 2 3 4 5 6 7 8 9 10 11 12 13
Testing dates
Medical control
At the club
Camp/Semicamp
Rest
Training factors
Volume
Intensity
Peaking
Phys prep
Tech prep
Tact prep
Psych prep
%100
90
80
70
60
50
40
30
20
10

Figure 6.23 Annual training plan for the 1980 Olympic Games.
T = transition, prep = preparation.

ship, or Olympic Games, on the right-hand side of the chart and allowing room (4-6 weeks) for the transition phase. In figure 6.23 the major competition occurs on July 20. This date dictates how to list the remaining months and weekends in the planning chart. There should be 52 boxes; one for each weekend when, in most cases, competitions are organized. In figure 6.23, the Olympic finals are scheduled on July 20, so the transition phase is placed to the right of that date and corresponds to the month of August. All other months are then listed from right to left, suggesting that under normal circumstances the preparatory phase may commence in September of the previous year. To the left of the main competition of the year, all other contests that the athlete will participate in are listed. Symbols or color are used to differentiate main, important, and exhibition competitions. The coach should indicate whether the competition is domestic or international and place the location of the competition in the space provided.

Once the dates and locations of the competitions are recorded on the training chart, the annual training plan can be divided into training phases, working from right to left. In figure 6.23, the line for periodization contains the three classic phases (preparatory, competitive, and transition phases). The transition phase is planned for August, whereas the competitive phase is 16 weeks long, from April 6 to July 20. The remaining weeks are used for the preparatory phase (October 7 to March 30) and an initial transition phase (September 9-30). Either a color code or lines can be used to indicate where each phase begins or ends.

After establishing the training phase, the coach divides the annual training plan into individual macrocycles based on the schedule of competitions, the objectives of training, and the similarities of the methods used to achieve the objectives. In figure 6.23 the transition phases (September and August) are considered as separate macrocycles. Although the main competition or tournament is of short duration, the optimization (peaking) of preparedness during the days or week(s) prior to the competition warrants a separate macrocycle. Furthermore, the period preceding the main competition (three microcycles in this example), when preparedness is elevated, is a separate macrocycle.

Another short macrocycle is specified for the week following the two competitions in Europe, namely Grünau and Lucerne. After these competitions against some of the finest competitors in the world, competition- and travel-induced fatigue will be high and a recovery macrocycle is planned before the next macrocycle, which leads into the Olympics. A 4-week macrocycle is used for these two international competitions because they are approached in a cyclical fashion, each having one microcycle for training and one for unloading and competition. Another 4-week macrocycle, containing three microcycles of specialized training and one microcycle of unloading, is planned to precede the time-trial race in Welland.

The longest macrocycle (six microcycles) of the annual plan will precede the three microcycles of specialized training. During these six microcycles, the main objective is to develop aerobic endurance. During this cycle the athletes participate in two long-distance regattas in British Columbia (BC). The macrocycle from February to March is also long (five microcycles) and is designed to convert maximal strength to muscular endurance. The two macrocycles prior to this macrocycle (December to January) have some similarities (developing maximal strength and aerobic endurance). Throughout most of December, the athletes will work on developing aerobic endurance through rowing ergometer work, running, and cross-country skiing. General development, building the foundation for strength training, and aerobic endurance are among the main objectives of both cycles. Finally, after dividing the annual training plan into macrocycles, the coach can number them from left to right (first to last). Each macrocycle is referred to by number.

After determining and numbering the macrocycles, the coach determines the dates for testing and medical controls. The first test should be conducted during the microcycle prior to the first macrocycle of the preparatory phase, especially for prospective athletes. The results of these tests will be used to compute optimal load, number of repetitions, and amount of work planned for training. It is a recommended that all athletes be tested prior to initiating a new training program so the coach can gauge their training status. During the preparatory phase, it may be advisable to test the athlete at the end of each macrocycle to assess progress toward training objectives and to continually adjust the training load to meet the athlete's changing physiological status. During the precompetitive and competitive phases, specific competitions are used as testing days. These competitions can reveal the athlete's progress toward specific objectives of the annual training plan.

Three or four medical evaluations during the annual training plan should be sufficient. The first should occur prior to the preparatory phase so that the athlete's health status is known before she begins a new training plan. Unhealthy individuals will require a different training plan structure that could include a prolonged regeneration and rest phase or a period of rehabilitation. Other medical control dates should be placed before and after the competitive phase. A long competitive phase may require at least one extra medical control date to effectively monitor the athlete's health status. Medical information collected during the last control can influence the length and type of transition phase used for each athlete. Medical controls should be conducted by a physician with a background in sport who understands the demands of training and the physiological responses to training.

The next section of the chart indicates locations of preparation during the annual plan. The coach can use different colors or, as in figure 6.23, draw an arrow to point out the training time at the club, in camps, or in semicamps. The chart should indicate periods of rest, including the transition phase. Sundays are not necessarily shown on the chart if they are the only days off. Two or three holidays or rest days (e.g., a religious holiday or the day after an important competition) are indicated by a narrow bar in the appropriate box.

Once most of the athlete's activities have been recorded on the chart, the percentage of each training factor per macrocycle can be calculated and placed on the chart. Once the percentages are established, the training component and peaking curves can be added to the chart. To distinguish quickly between each training factor, the coach may use different colors or symbols. The emphasis placed on each training factor depends on the specifics of the sport, the strengths and weaknesses of the athletes, and the phase of training. For example, during the first macrocycle of the annual plan the major emphasis usually is general physical preparation regardless of the sport. If the first macrocycle targets general physical preparation, then the second macrocycle will focus on specific physical preparation that is directly related to the demands of the sport. The factor that is focused on is the major emphasis, but other factors such as tactical or technical training are not excluded; rather these factors are trained but with a lower emphasis. This basic approach can be used with individual or team sports and allows for phase potentiation throughout the training plan.

Another important factor in deciding what weight to place on each training factor is performance level. The limiting factor of improvement for prospective athletes is generally considered to be technical proficiency. However, recent evidence suggests that muscular strength may be the most important factor because it is strongly related to technical abilities (79). Once basic technique is established, physical preparation, particularly specific physical preparation including the continued development of muscular strength, appears to be the limiting factor associated with performance improvements.

Athletes usually begin a new annual training program with workload percentages between 30% and 50% of maximal work capacity, depending on their performance levels. Using workload percentages lower than 30% during the initial stages of the annual plan commonly results in low levels of improvement across the year. However, in a year following the Olympic Games, participating athletes may allow themselves a longer rest period, so the volume of training for the new plan will be lower, possibly around 20% and 30% of maximal. An annual training program preceding the Olympics should begin with a volume of training of around 40%. The curve that represents the volume of training is progressively elevated through the preparatory phase, reaching its summit at the end of the general preparation phase and the beginning of the specific physical preparation phase. Conversely, during the competitive phase, the curve that represents the amount of endurance volume decreases progressively to below the curve that depicts intensity. This curve trails the training volume curve through the preparatory phase and then surpasses it by the middle of the competitive phase. Both curves undulate more during the macrocycles with many competitions. The intensity is generally higher during the early part of a microcycle that precedes a competition and decreases as the competition approaches to allow the athlete to rest and regenerate before the competition. When volume of training is high, intensity of training is generally lower. If both volume and intensity are high, the potential for overtraining increases markedly (16).

During the early part of the macrocycle before the main competition, volume increases, reflecting an emphasis on high-quality work. Toward the end of this macrocycle the volume decreases, usually in the last two microcycles prior to the next macrocycle. Training intensity is at first slightly lower than training volume but then elevates progressively as the competition approaches. During unloading, however, both curves may drop slightly depending on the type of taper being used. Traditionally, intensity is not elevated much for endurance sports, allowing both volume and intensity to be stressed equally. However, contemporary literature suggests that increasing intensity of endurance training with high-intensity interval training may allow for volume to be reduced while maintaining performance capacity (40). Sports characterized by dynamic activities that express high power outputs will require that intensity be elevated to levels higher than the training volume curve. As for the short subphase of competitions, volume is down and intensity is up, signifying that most competitions are intense.

The peaking curve, or preparatory curve as it is sometimes called, is a direct result of the interplay between volume and intensity that will affect the athlete's level of fitness or fatigue. The peaking curve generally trails both volume and intensity curves through the preparatory phase in response to the fatigue that is developed in this phase. The peaking curve then elevates during the precompetition and competitive subphases in response to the reduction of fatigue that occurs as volume is decreased. The peaking curve (preparatory curve) represents the athlete's potential for high-level performance as well as his level of fatigue.

In the sample chart for an annual plan (figure 6.23), the magnitude and not the percentage of each curve signifies the emphasis placed on volume and intensity. Expressing these curves in percentages rather than in relation to each other is more complicated; therefore, only experienced coaches training elite athletes should use that method of expression. Similarly, the stress curve is not included in the chart, because its shape is affected by (and therefore resembles) the intensity curve; competition dates also affect the stress curve.

Figure 6.24 presents a hypothetical monocycle for a volleyball team. In this example a main goal is to qualify for and win the finals of the provincial or state championship or the university conference championship in the United States. In the example, the team must qualify for the national championship tournament and place in the top three teams (third being the most realistic objective). Before the league games there are three exhibition games, which are a means of testing the team's abilities.

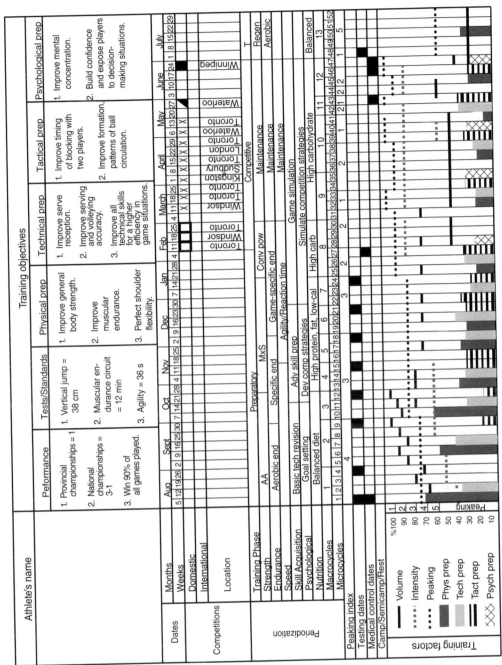

Figure 6.24 Monocycle annual training plan for a hypothetical volleyball team.
Prep = preparation, T = transition, AA = anatomical adaptation, MxS = maximal strength, Conv pow = conversion power, Regen = regenerate, end = endurance, tech = technical, Adv skill prep = advanced skill preparation, Dev comp strat = develop competitive strategies, cal = calories, carb = carbohydrates.

In the example presented in figure 6.24, the periodization section is expanded compared with figure 6.23. Included in this section are elements of periodization for strength, endurance, speed, and nutrition. The periodization section can be manipulated to include elements that meet the specific demands of the individual athlete or requirements of the sport.

The ratios between the training factors are different in figures 6.24 and 6.23 as a result of the specific requirements of a team sport. In this example, technical and tactical preparation has a higher emphasis. In the first macrocycle, physical preparation is the dominant factor, as it should be with most sports, especially when there is a long preparatory phase, because the athlete must first develop a physical foundation. Without solid physical development the athlete may not be able to perform the technical maneuvers required by the sport. For example, without significant muscular strength in the lower body, the athlete may not be able to generate enough force to jump high enough to spike the ball or block incoming balls.

The volume and intensity curves are presented as horizontal lines to represent a step-loading pattern and illustrate their percentages, compared with figure 6.23 where curves are used to show the need to stress the intensity component at a much earlier stage of preparation. In figure 6.24 the volume of training is elevated in the first four macrocycles, with the intensity curve elevating during the fifth macrocycle. This reflects the development of maximal strength and the emphasis on game-specific endurance, agility, and reaction time. Throughout the competitive phase, intensity remains high, reflecting training activities at this time and the stress of competitions.

Peaking Index

A new parameter is introduced in figure 6.24, the peaking or preparedness index (58, 79, 92). This index represents the athlete's level of preparedness to compete and reflects the athlete's physiological, technical, tactical, and psychological status (table 6.4). To modulate the athlete's level of preparedness, the training factors must be manipulated to dissipate fatigue, thus elevating the athlete's preparedness to perform. In this process competitions must be prioritized; it would be impossible to peak for every competition because fitness would begin to decline attributable to spending too much time at low volumes or intensities of training. Thus varying levels of emphasis should be placed on specific competitions. Except for high-priority competitions, it is not essential for the athlete (especially elite athletes and teams) to peak for every competition. In sports in which the competitive phase is long and there are many competitions, it is not feasible to achieve a true peak for each competition. The athlete should achieve his highest level of preparedness (peak) for the main competition at the end of the competitive phase. Therefore, it may be warranted to approach many of the competitions in the competitive phase of the annual training plan without peaking, thus effectively training through the competition and using minimal unloading strategies prior to these competitions. If peaking strategies that include unloading for every competition in the competitive phase (let's say 12 games over 6 months in American university football or 60 games over 10 months in premier league soccer) were used, significantly lower training volumes and intensities would occur in the competitive phase, which would reduce physiological function, muscular strength, physical preparation, and preparedness to perform across the season. However, this does not mean the athlete will not focus on each game. Rather the athlete and coach must determine the optimal approach to take or the degree of unloading to use prior to the competition.

Coaches should use the greatest amount of unloading when target-

Table 6.4 Description of the Peaking Index

Peaking index	Level of preparedness (%)
1	100
2	90
3	70-80
4	60
5	≤50

The peaking index will be modulated by alterations in training load (volume and intensity) and will reflect the athlete's level of fatigue, which directly affects preparedness. High levels of fatigue will decrease preparedness, whereas low levels of fatigue will increase preparedness. However, if fitness declines too much in response to prolonged periods of low volume and intensities of training, preparedness will decline.

ing the most important competitions or the three strongest opponents in the competitive schedule in team sports. In figure 6.24, this is indicated by the peaking index of 1 and represents a situation where the athlete's level of preparedness must be at its highest. To achieve this level of preparedness, the athlete would have to use specific peaking strategies (see chapter 7). Peaking index 2 represents a level of preparedness that is approximately 90% of that experienced in level 1. This index would be used when playing the top two thirds of the league, excluding the top three to five teams. To achieve this level of preparedness, the athlete would use less reduction in training volume and intensity compared with level 1. When playing against nothreatening teams in a league game or during precompetitive games, athletes would use a peaking index of 3 (70-80% of maximal preparedness). The training plan should emphasize technical and tactical objectives rather than winning during precompetitive games. It may be necessary to achieve this level of preparedness in the special preparation subphase of a bi-cycle or tri-cycle plan. Peaking index 4, indicated as 60% of maximal preparedness, represents a level of preparedness typically seen in the preparatory phase, when the athlete is undertaking high training loads and is not prepared to compete. A peaking index of 5, which represents 50% or less of maximal preparedness, is typically seen during the transition phase, where the training workload is at the lowest level during the annual plan, as are levels of fitness and fatigue.

The peaking index line in figure 6.24 represents the appropriate index for each macrocycle. At the bottom of this chart is a row for the peaking index, which serves as a guide by which the index curve is drawn. Although the lines drawn in this example are straight lines that express the index and magnitude for each macrocycle, the peaking index will actually fluctuate or undulate dramatically in parallel to the fatigue or stress levels generated by training.

Chart of a Bi-Cycle Annual Training Plan

An annual training plan for a hypothetical team that emphasizes tactical and technical preparations is presented in figure 6.25. This annual plan has a bi-cycle structure that contains two main competitions, the first competition being on February 25 and the more important competition being on August 26. The first preparatory phase is longer and the volume of training is much greater compared with the second preparatory phase. Less emphasis is placed on training intensity in the first preparatory phase, thus allowing the athlete to build a solid endurance and strength base. Because the February 25 competition is not as important as the August 26 event, the competition phase is shorter during the first cycle. Its duration and number of competitions suggest that the major emphasis during the first half of the training year is not placed on outstanding performances. Rather, the emphasis during this cycle is on improving the athlete's level of physical preparation in conjunction with increasing both technical and tactical capacity.

During the second cycle, training volume is dominant for six microcycles and slightly less important for the remaining 19 microcycles attributable to a longer competitive phase, throughout which the intensity of training is the major emphasis. Volume and intensity of training will vary in response to the training demands of each microcycle, with short unloading periods occurring before each important competition. The competitions in the first competitive cycle are organized in a cyclic manner, whereas those in the second competitive phase are structured using a grouping method. The approach used in the second cycle allows for training to be easily divided into training and competitions. After the first competitions (June 3, 10, and 17), the training microcycles that precede the two competitions in July can

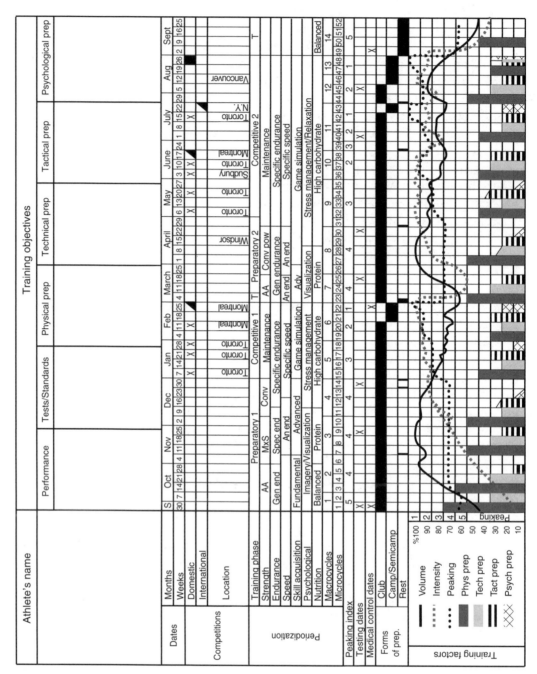

Figure 6.25 Bi-cycle annual training plan for a hypothetical team.
Prep = preparation, S = September, T = transition, AA = anatomical adaptation, MxS = maximal strength, Conv = conversion, Conv pow = conversion power, Gen end = general endurance, An end = anaerobic endurance, Adv = advanced.

be structured based on an evaluation of the athlete's performance, technique, and tactical proficiency during the initial competitions. A similar strategy can be used during the later stages of the second competitive phase.

Figure 6.25 shows a line on the periodization chart that specifies the 52 microcycles contained in the annual training plan. This parameter is significant, especially during the analysis of the previous year's training program. This analysis can provide information about the number of microcycles needed to achieve optimal performance. This analysis indicates that the current annual plan can accommodate the appropriate number of microcycles to achieve the highest possible level of performance.

Chart of a Tri-Cycle Annual Training Plan

Figure 6.26 is an example of an annual training plan with a tri-cycle structure in which three major competitions are targeted. This type of structure can be used for sports such as boxing, swimming, weightlifting, or wrestling, where competitions are spread evenly throughout the training year. Figure 6.26 is a generic example that does not reference a specific sport.

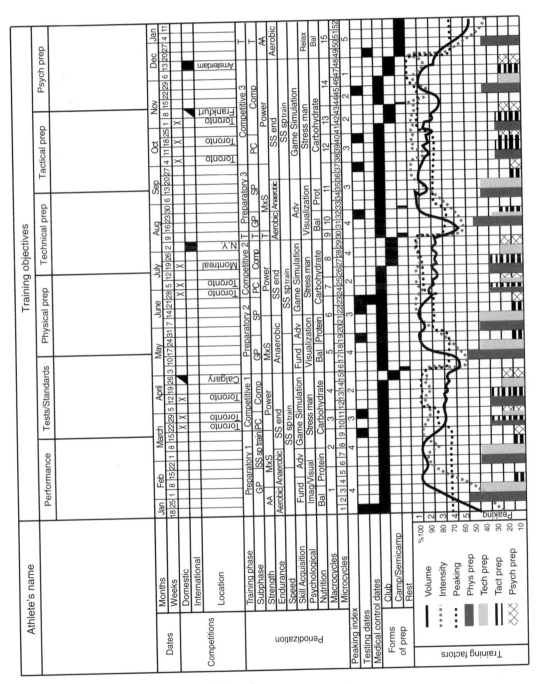

Figure 6.26 Tri-cycle annual training plan.

Prep = preparations, Comp = competitive, T = transition, GP = general preparatory phase, SS sp train = sport specific speed training, PC = precompetition phase, SP = specific preparatory phase, AA = anatomical adaptation, MxS = maximal strength, SS end = sport specific endurance, Fund = fundamental, Adv = advanced, Imag/visual = imagery and visualization, Stress man = stress management, Relax = relaxation, Bal = balanced.

In figure 6.26, no training objectives have been set and it is assumed that all training factors play an almost equal role in determining performance capacity. The first main competition (April 26) is a qualifying meet for the Pan American Games (August 2) and the World Championships (December 13). In this example, the athlete is projected to easily qualify (90% probability) for the first major competition, and therefore a peaking index of 2 is used. For the next two competitions, a peaking index of 1 is required to optimize performance at both international competitions.

The annual plan is appropriately organized for each competition and contains the classic training phases and subphases. However, a transition phase is not included after the qualifying meet (April 26) because a peaking index of 2 is used, thus indicating that the athlete was not taken to a peak. Instead of having a transition phase, the athlete undertakes 2 days of active rest before initiating a new preparatory phase for the August 2 international competition. A short transition phase, or full microcycle, is used following this competition after which the athlete begins a new preparatory and competitive phase. During the lead-up to the World Championships on December 13, the athlete participates in an invitation international meet (Frankfurt, November 8) to gain additional experience in European and international competition.

The first preparatory phase is slightly longer than the other two preparatory phases and places a greater emphasis on training volume to establish a solid foundation of general physical preparation. Although the general preparation phases of the other two cycles are shorter, they also provide enough training volume to continue to develop the training base. Collectively all three general preparatory phases develop the physiological characteristics necessary from which to elevate training intensity during the three competitive phases. The ratios of training factors across the different phases and subphases of the annual training plan indicate that physical preparation dominates each preparatory phase. In the macrocycles contained in the competitive phase, the ratio between the training factors is more balanced between the four training factors (physical, tactical, technical, and psychological).

Another example of an annual training plan with a tri-cycle format is presented in figure 6.27. As with the previous example, the planning chart depicts the periodization modeling of the dominant abilities as well as the psychological training factors across all phases of the training year. This example includes the volume of specific endurance work in meters per week. The curve of these activities evolves according to the training phases and follows the tenets of periodization. Because the volume of specific endurance per week is expressed in precise amounts, a critical element of objectivity is added to the planning of the training load.

Figure 6.28 on page 172 demonstrates an annual planning chart for swimming in which training volume and intensity are objectively defined. This example uses a bi-cycle structure and expresses the volume of training in kilometers per week and the intensity, in this case speed, as a percentage of maximum. This type of volume and intensity quantification works well for sports in which training load can be objectively measured. Examples of such sports include running, cycling, skiing, canoeing, rowing, and weightlifting. The concept may be modified for sports like gymnastics in which the training load can be specified by the number of half or full routines performed each week.

Chart of an Annual Training Plan for Artistic Sports

For sports that require perfect artistry, coordination, or very specific skills, the annual plan chart will be modified slightly. These types of plans can be structured as a monocycle, bi-cycle, or tri-cycle plan depending on the number and distribution of

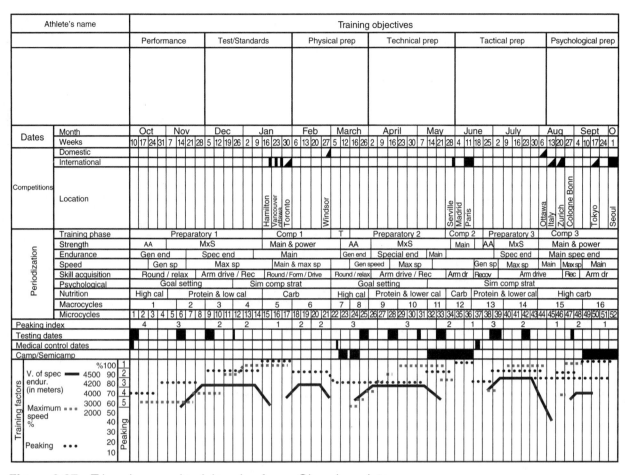

Figure 6.27 Tri-cycle annual training plan for an Olympic sprinter.

Prep = preparations, O = October, Comp = Competitive, T = Transition, AA = anatomical adaptation, MxS = maximal strength, Main & power = maintenance and power, Main = maintenance, Gen end = general endurance, Spec end = special endurance, Main spec end = maintenance of special endurance, Gen sp = general speed, Max sp = maximum speed, Main & max sp = maintenance and maximization of speed, Rec = recovery, Relax = relaxation, Sim comp strat = simulate competitive strategies, Cal = calories, Carb = carbohydrates.

competitions. Figure 6.29 on page 173 illustrates an annual training plan chart that contains a bi-cycle structure and is designed for gymnastics; however, this format could easily be applied to other sports such as figure skating, diving, or synchronized swimming. The first unique aspect of this chart is that the amount of time the gymnast will spend learning, repeating, and perfecting half and full routines is presented in the middle portion of the chart.

In this example there are two major competitions: the Olympic Games (July 20) and the World Cup (October 24-26). Before both contests, athletes participate in a competition to select the team or individual gymnasts. As a part of the normal training progression, the gymnasts participate in several exhibitions contests during the precompetitive subphase, one of which may be an international contest (May 25). After the completion of the Olympic Games, gymnasts have a short transition phase that contains 3 or 4 days of rest followed by light work.

The chart is based on hypothetical data; therefore, the phases when the athletes must learn technical elements, exercises, and routines are also supposition. Obviously, athletes acquire new elements and routines a year before a meet such as the Olympic Games or World Cup. When athletes begin perfecting an element, they retain only the

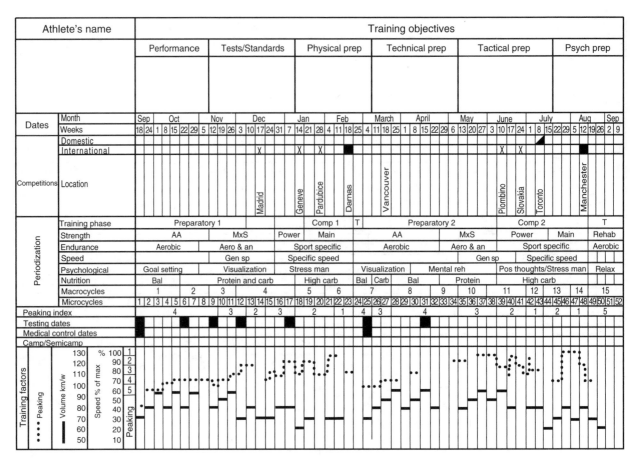

Figure 6.28   Bi-cycle annual training plan for a 100 m swimmer.

Prep = preparations, Comp = competitive, T = transition, AA = anatomical adaptation, MxS = maximal strength, Main = maintenance, Rehab = rehabilitation, Aero & an = aerobic and anaerobic endurance, Gen sp = general speed, Stress man = stress management, Ment reh = mental rehearsal, Pos thoughts/Stress man = positive thoughts and stress management, Relax = relaxation, Bal = balanced, Carb = carbohydrates.

elements that will be a part of the final routine. It is highly unlikely that new technical elements will be learned at this point because there is insufficient time to ensure that the skill is perfected by the time of competition. The elements that the athlete will learn and potentially include in the competitive routine should be established at least 1 year prior to the major contest. Only under special circumstances should a new skill be introduced in close proximity to a major competition. Such an instance might occur when a new element is invented or discovered that does not pose a learning problem or unduly stress the athlete.

The ratio between training factors is unique for gymnastics and other artistic sports because tactical training plays a minor role and is rarely noted on the annual training plan chart. In the first macrocycle, physical training should be the dominant training factor; the development of biomotor abilities such as specific strength is essential. The development of strength is essential for the gymnast because deficiencies here may impede the athlete's ability to develop or master specific technical skills (11). Beginning with the second macrocycle, technical training becomes the major emphasis along with continued development of physical preparation. This method is valid for all cycles of the training plan except the tenth, which marks the beginning of the second part of the annual training plan. The transition phase should be considered a maintenance phase for physical preparation in this example.

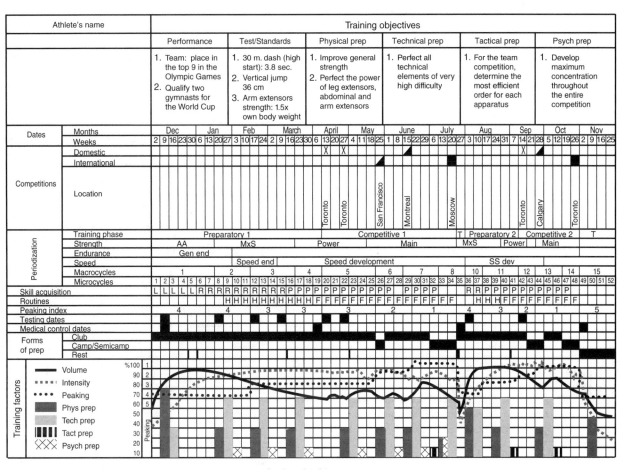

Figure 6.29 Tri-cycle annual training plan for a gymnast.

Prep = preparations, T = transition, AA = anatomical adaptation, MxS = maximal strength, Main = maintenance, Gen end = general endurance, Speed end = speed endurance, SS dev = specific speed development, L = learning, R = repetition for skill automatization, P = perfection, H = half routines or lines, F = full routines.

Individual Annual Training Plan

Most of the annual training plans that have been presented thus far can be used for either individual athletes or teams. These charts represent basic training structures that can serve as rough guidelines for preparing a year of training. However, although these plans offer specific training information, they do not present the individualized work necessary for each athlete. Therefore, the development of an individualized annual training plan as outlined in figure 6.30 (on page 174) might be warranted. This plan allows the coach to monitor the athlete's training plan in precise terms, because the plan incorporates all the means of training the individual athlete would use in training and more specifically the number of repetitions or mileage for a year of training.

The coach must know the competition schedule in order to create the training plan. Once the competition schedule is established, the periodization plan can be developed and the objectives for each macrocycle can be expressed according to the training phase for each training factor. In figure 6.30, a hypothetical individual training plan for a high jumper, anatomical adaptation, maximum strength, and power are developed during the first subphase of training (general preparation). As the program advances or approaches the competitive phase, the emphasis on other factors such as technique will increase. As the athlete moves into the transition phase

Figure 6.30 Individual training plan for a high jumper.

Prep = preparation, Comp = competitive, T = transition, GP = general preparatory phase, SP = specific preparatory phase, PC = precompetition phase, AA = anatomical adaptation, MxS power = maximal strength power, MxS tech = maximal strength technique, MxS PT = maximal strength power technique, Tech PT = technique power technique, MxS TP = maximal strength technique power, Tech P = technique power, GPP = general physical preparation, M = moderate, H = high, L = low.

of the annual training plan, general physical preparation becomes the dominant training objective.

Training intensity is specified in the annual plan because it will govern the amount and quality of work for each macrocycle. Intensity can be stated simply on a scale from low to high, as presented in figure 6.30, or more precisely using the scale presented in table 4.1 (1 = very low, 2 = low, 3 = medium, 4 = heavy, 5 = maximum, and 6 = supermaximal).

In figure 6.30, the most significant difference between the individual annual training plan and the other example plans presented in this chapter is the inclusion of a section that outlines the means of training. This section lists the dominant technical skills, drills, and exercises that are used to develop specific biomotor abilities. The repetitions, distance or time, volume load (kg), or kilogram force meters (kgm) that the athlete achieves during the whole training year are presented adjacent to each means of training. These figures are then divided per macrocycle, depending on the objectives and importance of each factor in the succeeding macrocycles. Some exercises are part of the entire year of training (e.g., ankle flexion), and others (exercises with medicine balls) are specific for the preparatory and precompetitive phases only.

In figure 6.30, all weight-training exercises are expressed in kilogram force meters, whereas other exercises specific to the development of power (plyometrics, explosive weight training) are expressed as the number of repetitions. For example, weight training that targets the generation of power is calculated as follows: 3,800 repetitions per year $\times$ 1 m, or distance traveled by the barbell $\times$ 70 kg, or the average load = 266,000 kgm. The bottom of the chart lists tests and corresponding standards with the progression to achieve those standards.

The individual annual training plan can be used for both individual and team sports. This type of plan appears to be best suited for individual sports, especially those with objective means of measurement. However, this plan can easily be adapted to the needs of team sports. For example, the number of repetitions of a specific skill set or series of tactical maneuvers can be planned. It is easy to include physical preparation, tests, and standards in the annual training plan of team sports athletes.

CRITERIA FOR COMPILING AN ANNUAL PLAN

Compiling an annual training plan is an essential part of the training process because this plan provides the guidelines by which training is directed. The ideal time to establish the annual training plan is at the end of the transition phase before the initiation of the next training year. After the athlete completes the main competition of the year, her improvement and physiological and psychological responses to the training plan can be analyzed and evaluated. Her rate of improvement or progress, competition performance, and tests also can be analyzed at this time. The information garnered from this analysis will influence the objectives established for the next training year as well as the structure of the training plan. The coach will use these observations coupled with the upcoming competitive schedule to establish the next year's training plan.

Each year's competitive schedule, including national and international events, is set by the national or international federation. Each regional organization bases its competition calendar on this schedule. These dates must be available by the transition phase of the previous year's annual training plan; otherwise, the next year's annual training plan cannot be established. Once the annual training plan is established, individual or small-group training plans can be developed. The annual training plan established by the coach should be clear and concise and must present the appropriate technical information.

The quality of an annual plan directly reflects the coach's methodological knowledge, her experience, and the latest innovations in training theory. The coach must stay abreast of these factors by reading scientific literature, attending conferences, networking with other coaches, and closely observing the training process of their athletes. The coach will modify and

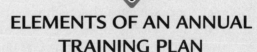

ELEMENTS OF AN ANNUAL TRAINING PLAN

1. Introduction

2. Retrospective analysis

3. Performance prediction

4. Objectives

5. Competition calendar

6. Tests and standards

7. Periodization model (including the chart of the annual plan and macrocycles)

8. Preparation model

9. Athlete or team organization and administration model (including budget and equipment needs)

adapt the annual training plan in parallel with her increased knowledge and experience. The more organized the coach, the easier this process will be.

In some instances the coach may be asked by the national sports association or funding organization to present a model of the next annual training plan. Such a model should be well organized and well thought out and must account for the main parameters of training. The following sections outline a model of an annual plan that contains all of the needed elements. An outline of the components contained in the presentation of a training program can be found on page 175.

Introduction

In the introduction, the first thing that should be presented is a needs analysis (13, 14) in which the scientific and methodological aspects of the sport are presented in the context of the training needs. For example, a soccer coach should discuss the magnitude of the physiological, technical, and tactical skills needed for success in the sport (27). This discussion may include information about the duration of the game (90 min) and the distance covered (~8-12 km) during a game (26). Further information about the contributions of strength and strength derivatives including acceleration, jumps, and sprints can be presented. For example, on average a soccer player will sprint for 2 to 4 s every 90 s, corresponding to 1% to 11% of the overall match distance (26). Elite players perform about 50 turns while maintaining balance and control of the ball (26). Thus, it can be demonstrated that soccer is a series of repetitive sprints that rely on energy supply from the phosphagen (ATP-PC) and glycolytic energy systems, which are interspersed with lower-intensity aerobic activities (26). The relationships among muscular strength, speed, power, and agility can be outlined as well (26, 28, 90). Finally, the coach should outline the duration of the annual training plan (e.g., September 15, 2009 to August 16, 2010) and present personal or team information (e.g., sport, gender, age, height, weight, body composition).

Retrospective Analysis

To properly elaborate the performance predictions and objectives for the upcoming year, the coach must thoroughly analyze performance and behavior in the past year. Performance achievements refer to competitive performance as well as performance on tests and standards. This information can be presented in a tabular form (table 6.5).

After analyzing the past year's competitive performances, objectives, and tests or standards, the coach can determine the athlete's state of preparation by analyzing each training factor. For physical preparation, the coach would analyze whether the

Table 6.5 Hypothetical Analysis of Test Results for a Female Javelin Thrower

	Performance	Planned	Achieved
Objectives	1. Distance thrown	51.50 m	52.57 m
	2. 30 m dash	4.80 s	4.7 s
	3. Standing long jump	2.40 m	2.36 m
	4. Chin-ups	8	7
	5. Baseball throw	60.00 m	61.36 m

Note: The factors presented are only examples; other factors such as markers of muscular strength (e.g., power clean, back squat, snatch), changes in body composition, or body mass would be presented.

indices of general, specific, and biomotor ability development corresponded with the specific needs of the sport and whether they adequately supported the technical, tactical, and psychological preparation. The coach can collect such information from competitions and test results, linking any improvement or decline in technical or tactical performance with the athlete's rate of progress or regress as reflected in test scores. Often, improvement will prevail during the preparation phase but regression occurs during the competitive phase as a result of inconsistent and inadequate physical preparation. Thus, the coach would continue specific physical preparation throughout the competitive phase and test the athlete's progress consistently in each macrocycle to collect objective data regarding the dynamics of physical preparation.

When examining technical preparation, the coach should evaluate the technical proficiency of the athlete and to what extent technical training and capacity affected the athlete's competitive performance. The coach should assess the effectiveness of past technical elements to determine whether to use them in the future. The time dedicated to improving technical elements directly reflects the athlete's level of technical proficiency and the fineness of the skill acquisition. Because muscular strength affects technical proficiency (11, 79), the coach should determine whether the athlete has sufficient strength to undertake the technical elements required by the sport.

An analysis of tactical preparation should reveal whether tactical maneuvers used were properly chosen, were suited to the characteristics of the team, and led to the solution of game problems. As a conclusion of the retrospective analysis, the coach should indicate which, if any, of the past year's strategic tools should be eliminated, maintained as part of the team's strategies, or perfected so that the team's efficiency will improve in the next training year.

The coach also has to investigate the athlete's psychological preparation and behavior and how these factors affected the final performance. In assessing the athlete's behavior, the coach would consider what happened during training and at all other times, because often the things that occur outside of training significantly affect training and competitive performance.

Finally, the coach needs to collaborate with training specialists (e.g., strength and conditioning coaches, exercise physiologists, sport scientists, nutritionists, physiotherapists) to determine how the strategies used in the previous year affected the athlete's performance capacity. The conclusions of the retrospective analysis are then used to predict future progress and performance and to establish specific training and competitive objectives for the new annual training plan.

Performance Prediction

One of the coach's important duties is determining the skills and abilities that need to be developed and the performances that need to be achieved between the date of planning and the main contests. Performance prediction is a reference from which the objectives and standards for the annual training plan are generated. Achieving these objectives and standards increases the athlete's likelihood of attaining the highest possible competitive performance. For instance, a gymnastics coach scores routines and technical elements to see whether they are difficult enough to warrant a 15.01 average score (total points of 120.1 in the all around), which is needed for a gymnast to place in the top six at the women's national championships. Following such an analysis, the coach decides what technical elements need to be incorporated from the following year's routines and the skills that may need to be added to achieve the predicted score during the next training year. This prediction must consider the gymnast's ability and skill level in order to be realistic.

Performance prediction for team sports is more difficult than for individual sports because there are many more factors that can affect performance. Among the few aspects that the coach can predict are the technical elements, tactical maneuvers, and level of ability that the players must acquire to improve performance during the next year's annual training plan.

For sports in which performance is objectively and precisely measured (e.g., track and field, weightlifting, track cycling), performance prediction is easier. With these sports the coach examines the best results achieved in the previous training year and uses the athlete's rate of improvement to predict the level that the athlete can attain in the next training year. For example, the performances of men rowing in a major regatta can be predicted with this process (table 6.6). Using these predictions and considering the athlete's abilities and potential for improvement, the coach can set the standards for his or her crews and the placing expectations for a specific regatta (table 6.7). Using performance prediction, the coach sets realistic objectives for each training factor and prepares the chart of the annual training plan.

Objectives

In both the annual training plan and the planning projection, the objectives must be presented in a methodological sequence with precise and concise language. The objectives are established based on past performances, test standards achieved, the

Table 6.6 Performance Prediction for the Places of Male Rowers in the Olympic Games (Events Listed in Speed Order)

Event	PERFORMANCE (MIN) AND PLACE			
	I	II-III	IV-VI	VI-IX
Eight	5:38	5:41	5:45	5:50
Quad	5:51	4:55	5:59	6:04
Coxless four	6:05	6:09	6:13	6:17
Coxed four	6:13	6:17	6:21	6:26
Double skull	6:23	6:27	6:31	6:36
Coxless pair	6:43	6:46	6:50	6:55
Single skull	7:03	7:07	7:11	7:16
Coxed pair	7:08	7:12	7:16	7:21

Table 6.7 Minimum Performance Prediction and Placing Expectation in a Major Regatta

Event	Performance (min)	Predicted place
Eight	5:45	VI-VIII
Quad	5:58	VI-VIII
Coxless four	6:12	III-V
Coxed four	6:20	VII-IX
Double skull	6:30	III-V
Coxless pair	6:50	V-VI
Single skull	7:10	VII-IX
Coxed pair	7:15	VI-IX

rate of improvement for both skills and performance, and the dates of the main competitions. In setting objectives, the coach must consider the dominant training factor and the factors that are poorly developed and thus limit the athlete's competitive and training potential. Then the coach determines the order of training priorities according to the limiting factors (e.g., physical, technical, or psychological preparation).

The methodological sequence and presentation of each training factor are as follows:

1. Performance objective
2. Physical preparation (e.g., strength, speed, endurance, flexibility, or coordination)
3. Technical preparation (offensive and defensive skills)
4. Tactical preparation (offensive and defensive individual and team tactics)
5. Psychological preparation
6. Theoretical preparation

This does not mean that the coach should stress each factor in this sequence. Rather he should give priority to those factors in which the athlete is proportionately underdeveloped and those that are primary to all athletes participating in the sport.

While setting objectives, the coach should consider and state the probability (percentage chance) of achieving them, especially the performance objective. Although this process relies on objective facts, it may be warranted to consider subjective assessments, such as the athlete's reserve, improvement potential, and psychological traits. Objectives for a hypothetical volleyball player are presented in table 6.8.

Table 6.8   Objectives for a Volleyball Player

PERFORMANCE FACTORS		
Item	**Objective**	**Probability of achievement (%)**
Performance	• Take first place in the junior national championships	80
	• Place in the top six in the senior national championships	50-60

TRAINING FACTORS		
Item	**Factor**	**Objective**
Physical preparation	Strength	Improve leg strength to improve jumping ability.
	Speed	Improve speed to facilitate quicker footwork for blocking and defense.
	Endurance	Improve muscular endurance required in long games and tournaments.
	Flexibility	Improve both shoulder and ankle flexibility.
Technical preparation	Serving	Improve serving consistency.
	Spiking	Improve spiking accuracy.
	Blocking	Improve blocking ability.
Tactical preparation	Offense	Improve spiking in a 6-0 system.
	Defense	Improve timing and quickness of blocking.
Psychological preparation		Develop the ability play calmly and with confidence following a mistake.
Theoretical preparation		Know all penalties that the referee may call.

Competition Calendar

Establishing the competition calendar is an important aspect of the annual training plan. The competitive schedule is established by the coach in accordance with the events scheduled by the national, conference, or international governing body. In this process competitions are selected that best suit the athlete's needs, level of development, performance capacity, skills, and psychological traits. Although athletes should contribute to the planning process, especially elite athletes, the coach has the decisive role in establishing the competitive schedule.

The major championship or main competitive objective of the training year is the central factor used to establish the periodized training plan and the competitive calendar. Other official and unofficial competitions should be of secondary importance. However, these competitions serve an important role in allowing the coach to assess the athlete's development and preparation level for the main competitions targeted by the annual plan. These competitions are spread over the competitive phase and are most prominent during the precompetitive subphase. Competitions should not be scheduled early in the preparatory phase because the focus during this phase is on physical preparation and skill development rather than performance. Ideally, major competitions and secondary competitions are alternated in the plan. Although team sports have many league or official games, competitions are sometimes scarce in individual sports. To maintain the unity of the annual training plan throughout the competitive phase, the coach should consider organizing preparatory competitions that can be integrated into the training plan.

When arranging the competitions in the annual plan the coach must consider the principle of progressive increase in training load, in which preparatory competitions of secondary importance must lead into major competitions that are more challenging. Although this method is ideal, it is not always possible especially in team sports in which sport governing bodies set the competition calendar. The number of competitions in the competition calendar can have a profound effect on the ability of the athlete to achieve the performance objectives. A heavy, demanding competition schedule, as often occurs in team sports, may result in a premature elevation in preparedness that in turn leads to a less than optimal performance at the end of the competitive phase when the major contest is planned. Conversely, participating in too few competitions can decrease preparedness and prevent the athlete from achieving the planned performance objective. Therefore, planning can become a delicate balancing act between too many and too few competitions in the calendar. Two important criteria can be used to establish the optimal number of competitions: the nature of the sport and the athlete's performance level or developmental status. For sports in which the effort is intense and for athletes with low performance capabilities, 15 to 25 competitions per year may suffice. With elite athletes, especially those involved in team sports (e.g., premier league soccer) more contests (>30) may be planned.

Once the competition schedule is established it should not be changed, because the entire annual training plan is based on this schedule. Coaches who work with high school or university athletes should not plan any competitions, especially important ones, during examination periods. Similarly, athletes should not participant in any official or demanding competitions during the last macrocycle before the main contest. During this last cycle, the coach and athlete should focus on training and make relatively few changes based on results of the previous secondary competition. Each contest, whether primary or secondary, will tax the athlete physically and mentally. Recovery and regeneration must be built into the training plan, especially after secondary contests that lead into the main competitions targeted by the annual training plan.

Tests and Standards

The evaluation of specific tests and standards related to a sport is a crucial part of developing a periodized training plan (79). These evaluations need to be organized, systematic, and consistently performed across the annual training plan to garner detailed information about the athlete's progress. Monitoring training by using tests and standards provides the coach an objective means with which to quantify the athlete's evolution, potential for stagnation, or risk of performance deterioration. By monitoring training, the coach can evaluate the dose–response relationship and thus optimize the training load to help the athlete achieve optimal performance at the appropriate time (79).

An athlete monitoring program can include specific physical tests that are periodically performed by the athlete to evaluate markers of the athlete's progress (see bottom of this page). More specific testing can be used to identify the athlete's strengths and weakness. Test results are then evaluated in relation to established performance standards. To ensure the effectiveness of a testing battery, the tests used must be valid (measure what they are supposed to measure), reliable (repeatable), and related to factors that affect the actual competitive performance. To truly understand the athlete's status, the coach must select diverse tests that evaluate more than just competitive performance results (66). For example, swimming performance is affected by basic speed, stroke mechanics, and start and turning ability. In addition, physiological factors such as anaerobic power and capacity, muscle power and flexibility, and basic and specific endurance affect swimming performance (66). Actual swim performance should also be evaluated, but time should not be the only focus. The coach should examine technical proficiency in conjunction with a competitive performance to gain insight into the athlete's progress (66). Therefore, to monitor a swimmer's preparation, the coach should periodically use tests that address these factors. A large amount of research has been conducted that correlates specific tests

MAIN OBJECTIVES OF THE TESTS CONTAINED IN AN ATHLETE MONITORING PROGRAM

- To monitor the athlete's rate of improvement in specific biomotor abilities or skills
- To determine skill status and ability level, which can then be used to guide training
- To determine the athlete's training content
- To determine the athlete's strengths, weaknesses, and limitations
- To test improvement in tactical skills or maneuvers
- To evaluate body mechanics and movement skill
- To determine appropriate standards in all training factors
- To evaluate and develop psychological attributes or traits
- To evaluate the athlete's potential for overtraining
- To monitor the dose–response relationship in the training plan

with performance in specific sporting activities, and this research can be used to establish performance-based testing procedures.

The testing battery should be based on metabolic specificity (bioenergetics), sport specificity (biomechanical or movement pattern), and the athlete's training status (25). Athletes should be familiarized with the testing procedures but should not directly train to master the test because this distorts the evaluative ability of the test. Obviously, the test may contain an activity that is germane to the training process and is frequently encountered during the training plan. For example, a common exercise used to train lower-body strength is the back squat, and this same exercise is often used to evaluate lower-body strength. So in this instance an athlete would train the back squat to develop leg strength and use a 1RM test with the back squat to evaluate maximal strength.

The testing battery should be concise (4-8 performance tests) and the tests should be highly related to the sport in question (20, 28, 33, 75-77). For example, Stone and colleagues (75) reported that maximal strength as assessed by the snatch and isometric midthigh pull is strongly related to both shot put- and weight bag–throwing ability in university throwers. Therefore, it makes sense to evaluate maximal strength throughout the annual training plan of university throwers. Haff and colleagues (21) used a biweekly testing battery that included assessments of body mass, body fat, lean body mass, hormonal responses to training, and force–time curve characteristics (peak force, rate of force development with isometric and dynamic movements) in elite women weightlifters. The testing battery was simple to perform, and changes in the force–time curve characteristics were related to the training plan. Interestingly, the maximization of peak force and peak rate of force development were shown to be related to weightlifting performance (20). Thus, this simple battery of tests was able to differentiate the level of preparedness of these athletes.

The tests used across the annual training plan and the dates of testing should be decided when the coach constructs the annual training plan. The first tests should occur during the first microcycle of the preparatory phase. By conducting the test at this time, the coach can determine the athlete's level of preparation and make any modifications to the annual training plan. Each macrocycle targets specific objectives, and testing can be conducted to determine whether these objectives are accomplished. Therefore, some form of testing should be conducted during 1 or 2 days at the end of each preparatory phase and precompetitive subphase macrocycle. This is done to evaluate the athlete's preparatory status during these phases. If the test results reveal consistent improvement, the original training structure should be maintained. Conversely, if the results indicate stagnation or decrease in the specific test measures, then the coach may need to modify the next training cycle. The coach must be careful when evaluating testing data, because the phase of training may cause expected decreases in specific performance characteristics. For example, during the general preparation phase where training volume, work load, and fatigue are the highest, one might suspect declines in markers of maximal power-generating capacity (71, 79). On the other hand, during the competitive phase one would expect elevations in power-generating capacity. During the competitive phase of the annual training plan, testing sessions should be planned only if the time between two competitions is 4 to 5 weeks. During this phase the competitions themselves provide ideal opportunities to evaluate the athlete's training status. Regardless of which phase of the annual training plan the testing sessions occur in, the coach must keep detailed records about the athlete's test results. The more organized the data, the easier it is to perform a longitudinal analysis of the athlete's rate of improvement and adaptation to the training plan.

In the written plan, the coach should indicate the test for each training factor using different colors or symbols. The coach should establish standards for each test, especially for physical and technical factors, while compiling the annual plan. Standards from the previous training year can serve as reference points for achieving each standard. This progression should reflect the athlete's rate of improvement and level of adaptation to the program. For novice athletes who are just beginning a structured training program, the results of the first testing session can be used as the reference point for further planning.

The coach must be careful when establishing standards because they provide incentives for preparation and progress. Standards must present a challenge but also must be realistic enough that the athlete can achieve them. For athletes who are aiming for high levels of performance, the standards must resemble those of other top athletes. There are two types of standards: Evolutionary standards are slightly superior to the athlete's potential and stimulate increases in performance, and maintenance standards that aim to preserve an optimal level of preparation. The time frame of training that progresses the athlete toward these standards should include a maximum of two macrocycles between each testing period. If the athlete has not achieved the standard within two macrocycles, the coach must determine why. For simplicity, the results of the tests and standards can be presented in a tabular format (table 6.9).

Periodization Model

The periodization of the annual plan provides the model to follow in training. The competition schedule can be used as a foundation from which the most suitable annual plan is constructed (mono-, bi-, or tri-cycle structure). After selecting the annual plan structure, the coach determines the duration of each phase and subphase of training. After sequencing each training phase, the coach designs the individual macrocycles contained in the annual plan. Within the macrocycles, the number, date, location, objectives, and methods to meet the stated objectives must be integrated

Table 6.9 Tests and Standard for a Preparatory Phase of Training in University Throwers

Tests	Measures		August 23	September 20	October 18
Biometrics	Body mass	(kg)	101.0	101.5	103.0
	Lean body mass	(kg)	78.3	78.8	80.2
	Body composition	(%)	21.9	21.5	21.5
Isometric midthigh pull	Peak force	(N)	2,881	2,894	3,002
	Peak rate of force development	(N/s)	15,047	18,873	18,000
Resistance training	Snatch		61.8	65.5	67.7
Throwing	Shot put	(m)	11.99	12.25	12.63
	Weight bag throw	(m)	11.55	12.43	12.97

Adapted from Stone et al. 2003 (75).

into the plan. The final step in creating the periodization model is the most difficult task in the planning process. In this step the coach inserts all athlete (team) activities into the chart of the annual training plan.

Preparation Model

The preparation model is a synopsis of the entire annual training plan. It delineates the main qualities and quantitative parameters used in training and the percentage increment per parameter between the current and previous annual plans. The coach must link the preparation model with the whole structure of the annual plan and its objectives. An experienced coach might predict the duration and number of workouts required to develop the necessary skills and abilities to accomplish the objectives. A preparation model can be structured as shown in table 6.10.

The model presented in table 6.10 assumes that to reach a higher performance level, the athlete must increase his aerobic and muscular endurance. This is accomplished by elevating training volume, prolonging the preparatory phase, and increasing the number of training lessons to correspond with an increase in the total number of hours spent training. Also, modifying the ratio between different methods and types of training will enhance muscular endurance and aerobic endurance.

Table 6.10 Preparatory Model for a 400 m Swimmer

Training factor	Symbol/ units	Volume (%)	Change over previous year (%)
Type of annual training plan	Monocycle		
Periodization			
Duration of annual plan (days)	322	100	>8
Preparatory phase (days)	182	56.5	<5
Competitive phase (days)	119	37	<3
Transition phase (days)	21	6.5	
Macrocycles (n)	9		
Microcycles (n)	46		
At the club	41		
At national camp	3		
Abroad	2		
Competitions (n)	7		
International	2		
National	4		
Regional	1		
Training lessons (n)	554		>6
Hours of training	1,122		<8.4
Tests (n)	16		
Medical controls (n)	3		
Specific training (days)	266	82.6	>3
Swimming (km)	2,436		>6
Nonspecific training (days)	14		>2
Running (km)	640	4.4	>2
Resistance training (kgm)	460,000		>14
Games (hr)	28		>1
Rest (days)	42	13	<8

To improve both aerobic and muscular endurance through resistance training and special water exercises, the training content can be altered with the guidelines presented in table 6.11. The breakdown per training phase may occur as in table 6.12. In addition to including these sections of an annual plan, the coach should consider the team or club's organizational and administration structure, including the budget and equipment needs.

Table 6.11   Model of Training Content for the Annual Plan and Alterations of Each Element Compared With the Previous Year

Content	Content of annual plan (%)	Change from previous year (%)
Anaerobic endurance and speed	2	<6
Muscular endurance	16	>2
Racing tempo endurance	32	No change
Aerobic endurance over medium distance	24	>2
Aerobic endurance over long distance	20	>2

Table 6.12   Alterations of Training Content and Its Percentage per Training Phase Between the Previous and Current Annual Plan

Content	Preparatory phase (%)	Change (%)	Competitive phase (%)	Change (%)
Anaerobic endurance and speed	5	<4	8	<2
Muscular endurance	10	>2	16	>3
Racing tempo endurance	20	<2	36	<2
Aerobic endurance over medium distance	30	>3	20	>2
Aerobic endurance over long distance	35	>5	20	>4

SUMMARY OF MAJOR CONCEPTS

The annual training plan and the microcyles contained in the plan are the cornerstones of a well-structured training program. Irrespective of the coach's knowledge of sport science, if his planning and organizational skills are poor his training effectiveness will be low. The fundamental concept for good annual planning is periodization, especially structuring the phases of biomotor abilities. The periodization of strength, speed, and endurance represents the manipulation of different training phases with specific goals, organized in a specific sequence, with the ultimate scope of creating sport-specific adaptation. When adaptation is complete, the athlete is physiologically equipped to perform at high levels.

A good understanding of periodization will help the coach produce better annual training plans, using the chart to schedule training activities. The competition schedule should guide the structure of the training phases. The periodization of nutrition and psychological training should be integrated into the annual training plan as well. The coach can use the blank charts supplied in the appendix to exercise and improve her skills in annual planning. The coach can also create her own charts to meet the needs of her athletes.

CHAPTER 7

PEAKING FOR COMPETITION

Athletes, coaches, and sport scientists work continually to facilitate the development of physiological adaptations that underlie optimal performance. Athletes undergo rigorous training plans that require them to train at high loads interspersed with unloading phases to optimize performance at major competitions. Peaking an athlete's performance usually is accomplished by reducing the training load for a predetermined time prior to major competitions. This period of reduced training is termed a *taper*. To optimize performance at the appropriate time, coaches and athletes must understand how to integrate tapers and competitions into the annual training plan.

PEAKING

The ultimate goal of an athlete's training plan is to optimize performance in specific competitions throughout the training year. This goal is accomplished through careful sequencing of the annual training plan. The foundation for peaking an athlete's performance is established during the preparatory and competition phases of training, when the athlete builds her physical, tactical, and technical training base (64, 65). During the later portions of the competition phase of training, the process of peaking an athlete for specific competition is initiated (figure 7.1). Peaking, or tapering as it is sometimes called (64, 65), is a complex process that can be affected by many factors including the training **volume**, frequency, and **intensity** (19). If implemented correctly, tapering or peaking occurs in response to the physiological and psychological adaptations induced by the training plan (19, 41). The **taper** is one of the most critical phases of an athlete's preparation for competition (19). Tapers are widely used by athletes from various sports to gain a performance edge over their competitors (10, 21, 24, 26, 34, 35, 38, 50, 63).

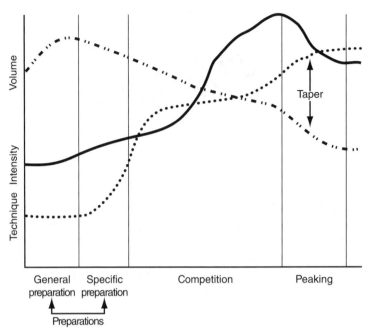

Figure 7.1 Generalized periodization model for strength and power training with a taper.

Adapted, by permission, from S.S. Plisk and M.H. Stone, 2003, "Periodization strategies," *Strength and Conditioning* 25:19-37.

DEFINING A TAPER

Many definitions have been used to describe how an athlete's training plan is modified in the final days before a competition (4, 39, 41, 44, 59, 62). When attempting to peak an athlete for competition, the coach reduces the workload prior to the competition (41). The reduction in workload that is used during this time is considered a taper (4, 41, 61). Traditionally, a *taper* is simply defined as a reduction in training workload prior to a competition (58). More recently, Mujika and Padilla (40) defined a taper as "a progressive non-linear reduction of the training load during a variable period of time, in an attempt to reduce the physiological and psychological stress of daily training and optimize sports performance" (p. 80). This definition expands on the traditional definition by including some implications for the design of the taper (41).

Primary Aim of a Taper

The goal of a taper is to optimize the athlete's performance at a specific time (4, 19, 41, 59). This is usually accomplished by systematically reducing the training load to reduce the cumulative fatigue, both physiological and psychological, that is generated in response to training while maintaining sport-specific fitness (41). The taper allows the athlete to recover from training, thus elevating performance (41, 61). This contention is supported in the scientific literature showing that accumulated fatigue is reduced during a taper period while fitness slightly increases (35), improving performance. As fatigue is dissipated in response to the taper the athlete may realize significant positive psychological alterations, such as a reduction in perception of effort, improved mood, a reduction in sense of fatigue, and an increased sense of vigor (20, 41, 56). These findings indicate that at the initiation of a taper, the physiological adaptations to the training program have already occurred (41) and are probably masked by accumulated fatigue (60), whereas the psychological adaptations will occur in response to the taper. Thus, the taper is a mechanism for decreasing both physiological and psychological fatigue, allowing for performance gains.

Premise of Tapering

The relationship between fitness and fatigue (figure 5.1 on p. 98) is a central concept underlying the appropriate implementation of a taper (5, 60). An athlete's preparedness is variable because it is directly affected by changes in the levels of fitness and fatigue generated in response to training (6, 64, 65). Preparedness is optimized by using training plans that maximize the fitness response while minimizing the development of fatigue (54). When training workload is high, preparedness is low as a result of a high level of accumulated fatigue.

The premise behind a taper is to dissipate accumulated fatigue while retaining fitness. Because the level of acquired fitness is relatively stable over several minutes, hours, and days, it is considered to be a slow-changing component of athletic preparedness. Conversely, fatigue is considered to be a fast-changing component because it is highly variable and is affected by physiological and psychological stressors (64, 65). Thus, when the training load is decreased during a taper the accumulated fatigue is dissipated somewhat rapidly, whereas the acquired fitness is maintained for a given duration depending on the type of taper used (4, 5).

Although the premise behind a taper is somewhat simple, the implementation of a taper is complex. If the duration of the taper is too long the fitness gains stimulated by the training program can dissipate, resulting in a state of detraining (40) and reducing preparedness (figures 7.2 and 7.3). One can consider the reduction in training load to be a compromise between the extent of the training reduction and the duration of this reduction (61), which combine to determine preparedness. If,

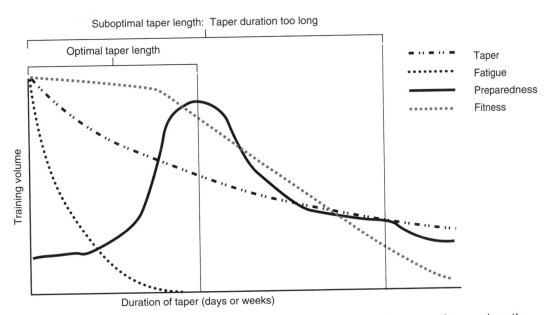

Figure 7.2 Relationships among fatigue, fitness, preparedness, and taper length. During the taper fatigue decreases rapidly, while fitness is maintained for a little longer depending on the composition of the taper. However, if the taper extends for too long, fitness will dissipate until detraining occurs.

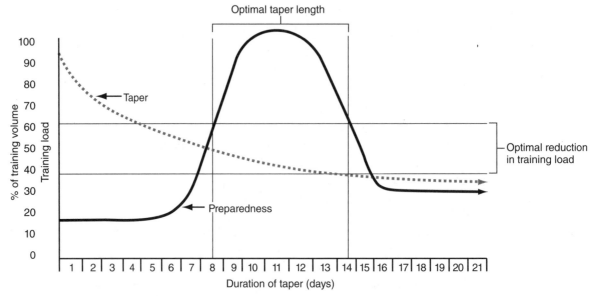

Figure 7.3 Relationship between preparedness and a taper.
Adapted from Bosquet, Leger, and Legros 2002 (4).

for example, the training load prior to the taper is very high, a greater reduction and duration of a taper will be necessary to maximize the decrease in fatigue required to elevate preparedness (30, 61). Thus, the taper is more than simply reducing the training load; it involves integrating many factors to elevate the athlete's preparedness and optimize performance.

Factors Affecting a Taper

There are many strategies for including a taper in an annual training plan (4). The key component of each of these strategies is to alter the training plan to reduce training load. Training load can be reduced during a taper by reducing training volume, intensity, or frequency (4, 41). The effectiveness of these reductions in training load will depend on the duration of the taper (59) and its relationship to the training load that preceded the taper (61). If the taper lasts too long, both fatigue and fitness will dissipate, which would lead to detraining (40) and decrease the athlete's preparedness. In this situation, performance would not increase and the taper would be deemed ineffective. Therefore, the coach must understand the interactions among training intensity, volume of training, training frequency, and the duration of the taper.

Training Intensity

The scientific literature indicates that when reducing volume and frequency during a taper it might be warranted to maintain or slightly elevate the training intensity (4, 24, 30, 34, 41, 50, 59). It appears that the training intensity during the taper is closely related to the ability to maintain training-induced performance adaptations during periods of reduced training load (17, 58). It has also been suggested that the training intensity is a key factor in maintaining training-induced physiological adaptations during the taper (4, 44). When examining endurance training studies, researchers have noted that lower training intensities ($\leq 70\%$ $\dot{V}O_2$max) during the taper period tend to result in a decrease or maintenance of endurance performance (25, 33). Conversely, when higher intensities ($\geq 90\%$ $\dot{V}O_2$max) are included in the taper, performance tends

RECOMMENDED TAPERING STRATEGIES

- Use taper strategies to dissipate fatigue, maintain fitness, elevate preparedness, and improve performance.

- Create individualized taper strategies that last between 1 and 4 weeks, with 8 to 14 days being optimal in most instances.

- Maintain moderate to high training intensities during the taper to avoid detraining.

- Decrease training volume by 41% to 60% of pretaper volumes. If extensive training precedes the taper, it may be warranted to decrease training volume by 60% to 90% of pretaper volumes.

- Maintain training frequency at 80% or more of pretaper frequencies.

- Use progressive, nonlinear taper models.

- Expect performance gains of approximately 3% in response to the taper.

Adapted from Mujika and Padilla 2003 (41), Mujika 1998 (34), and Bosquet et al. 2002 (4).

to increase (58). Similarly, when examining strength and power training, investigators have determined that maintaining intensity during the taper, while decreasing training volume, enhances strength but not power performance (11, 27). Thus, it seems warranted to maintain the training intensity during the taper period and adjust the workload by manipulating training volume or frequency or the duration of the taper (41, 59). See the top of this page for recommended tapering strategies.

Training Volume

Reducing training volume during a taper to reduce the training load is the method that is probably the most discussed in the scientific literature (4, 19, 34, 41, 59, 61). The volume of training can be decreased during a taper by reducing the duration of each training session, reducing training frequency, or both (4, 41). Decreasing the duration of each training session is preferable to reducing the training frequency, because the former appears to exert a greater effect on the effectiveness of a taper (4).

When attempting to create a taper by reducing training volume, the coach should consider that the training load (i.e., training volume and intensity) encountered prior to the taper will affect how much the training volume should be decreased and how long the taper should last (61). Because of this relationship, there are different recommendations for how much training volume must be decreased during the taper period to maximize performance outcomes (4, 41). Tapers that range between a 50% and 90% reduction in training volume have been reported in the scientific literature on swimming (28, 36, 37, 42, 62), running (22, 23, 25, 33, 38, 39, 58), cycling (32, 47, 48, 57), triathlon (2, 49, 63), and strength training (11, 27). In well-trained endurance athletes (e.g., cycling and running), a standardized 50% to 70% reduction in training volume has been reported to maintain or increase training-induced adaptations (22, 23, 25, 32, 33, 57). Progressive tapers that result in a 75% reduction in training volume appear to optimize taper-induced outcomes compared with a 50% reduction in training volume (38). It appears that low-volume tapers result in better physiological and performance outcomes compared with moderate-volume tapers (58).

The scientific literature indicates that a 41% to 60% reduction in training volume during the taper results in optimal performance improvements (4). However, the percentage reduction in training volume is related to the pretaper training load and the duration of the taper. If the training load prior to the taper is heavy, then a greater reduction in training volume, on the magnitude of 60% to 90% of pretaper loads, may

AP Photo/Rick Stevens

Tapering training can help an athlete peak for a key competition.

be warranted to dissipate fatigue (41, 61) (see the recommendations on p. 191). If training volume is substantially reduced, a shorter duration of taper may be warranted to offset the loss of training-induced adaptations that would result in a decrease in fitness and preparedness (30).

Training Frequency

Reducing training frequency is another popular method for reducing the training load during a taper (14, 18, 41, 59). Several studies report that reductions on the magnitude of 50% of pretaper training frequencies can increase performance (18, 28). Decreases in training frequency for 2 to 4 weeks have been shown to result in maintenance of training-induced physiological and performance outcomes in athletic groups (22, 23, 25, 32, 33, 41, 44, 50, 57). This literature indicates that modulating training frequencies might be a successful method for altering training volume.

However, performance seems to be only increased with tapers that use a high frequency of training, when compared to a moderate frequency of training in highly trained endurance runners (39). A recent meta-analysis indicated that a decrease in the frequency of training during a taper does not appear to improve performance (4). Although physiological adaptations can be maintained with 30% to 50% of pretaper training frequencies in moderately trained individuals, it has been suggested that highly trained athletes may need a greater frequency of training during the taper period to maintain technical proficiency (41). These findings indicate that training frequency should be maintained at 80% or more of pretaper training values to optimize performance outcomes and maintain technical proficiency (4, 41) (see the recommendations on p. 191).

Duration of Taper

The duration of a taper is probably one of the most difficult things to determine (41), because many factors affect the taper. For example, the pretaper training load can significantly affect the length of the taper necessary to dissipate training-induced fatigue and elevate preparedness (61). The amount of volume reduction or the pattern of reduction during the taper affects the duration needed to elevate preparedness while maintaining fitness. If a larger reduction in training volume is used, then a shorter duration of taper would be warranted (30, 61). Physiological, psychological, and performance improvements have been reported in the scientific literature for 1- to 4-week tapers (4). Several authors suggest that 8 to 14 days are necessary to dissipate fatigue and avoid the negative effects of detraining that might occur with a longer taper (4, 30). However, it appears that the duration of a taper is highly individualized

(4, 41) as a result of differences in physiological and psychological adaptations to reductions in training load (4, 35, 43). Therefore, it is recommended that the taper duration be individualized for each athlete (41) (see the recommendations on p. 191).

Types of Tapers

Various taper formats have been proposed in the literature (4, 41). Tapers can be broadly defined as either **progressive** or **nonprogressive**. A progressive taper is marked by a systematic and progressive reduction in training load, whereas a nonprogressive taper uses standardized reductions in training load (41). Different loading characteristics can exist within each category of taper.

In a progressive taper, the training load is reduced in either a linear or an exponential fashion. Progressive tapers can be classified into three types: a linear taper, a slow exponential taper, and a fast exponential taper (figure 7.4) (41). The linear taper normally contains higher training loads than those seen in either a slow or fast exponential taper. A slow exponential taper tends to have a slower reduction in training load and higher training loads than those seen in a fast exponential taper (41). Fast exponential tapers appear to result in greater performance gains than linear or slow exponential tapers (2, 41, 63). For example, a comparison between fast and slow exponential tapers revealed that the fast exponential taper resulted in a 3.9% to 4.1% greater increase in markers of performance (41).

The nonprogressive taper, also called a step taper (2, 34, 41, 63), is accomplished with standardized reductions in training. This taper is often marked by sudden decreases in training load (61), which can increase the potential for a loss of fitness during the taper (2). **Step tapers** have been shown by many studies to improve both physiological and performance adaptations to training (13, 17, 22, 23, 25, 32, 41, 51). However, the literature indicates that step tapers are less effective than either slow or fast progressive tapers (2, 4, 63). For example, Mujika and Padilla (41) reported that step tapers result in a 1.2% to 1.5% increase in markers of performance, whereas

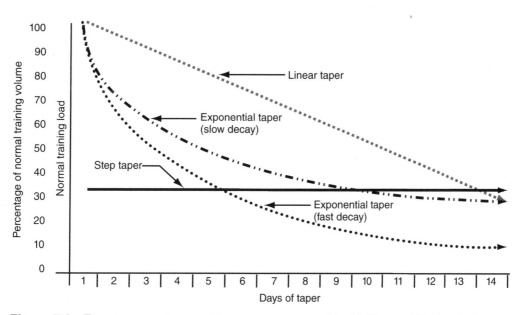

Figure 7.4   Four common types of tapers as proposed by Mujika and Padilla (41).
Adapted from Mujika and Padilla 2003 (41).

exponential tapers result in a 4.0% to 5.0% increase in performance. Authors usually recommend that an exponential taper be used when attempting to peak an athlete's performance for a competition (4, 41, 61).

The selection of the type of progressive taper used will depend on many factors including the training load prior to the taper (61) and the duration of the taper (19). However, it appears that the fast exponential tapers should be selected in most instances (41) (see the recommendations on p. 191).

Expected Performance Improvements

The primary goal of any taper is to elevate performance at the appropriate time (4, 34, 41). Small improvements in performance may result in distinct differences in placing at the Olympics. For example, Mujika and colleagues (43) reported that the difference between the gold medal and fourth place in swimming at the 2000 Sydney Olympics was only 1.62% and the difference between third and eighth place was only 2.02%. At the 2004 Athens Olympics the difference between first and third place in weightlifting was 1.96% (women = 2.21%; men = 1.73%). These data show that very small elevations in performance can have a great impact on performance outcomes and may differentiate between winning and losing.

When examining the scientific literature it has been reported that a properly implemented taper can result in significant improvements in performance (0.5-11.0%) and muscular strength and power (8-25%) in runners, triathletes, cyclists and swimmers (16, 24, 32, 38, 41, 48, 53, 58, 63). When looking specifically at competition measures it appears that a 0.5% to 6.0% (~3.0%) increase in performance can be expected in response to a preevent taper (41). Mujika and colleagues (43) reported that during a 3-week taper prior to the 2004 Sydney Olympics, swimming performance was elevated by 2.2%. Interestingly, the magnitude of this taper-induced increase in swimming performance was similar to the differences between first and fourth place (1.62%) and third and eighth place (2.02%) (4, 43).

Regarding muscular strength, it appears that a taper can result in a 2% to 8% increase in performance. Izquierdo and colleagues (27) reported that a taper protocol results in a 2.0% increase in back squat and bench press performance. A larger increase in strength performance in response to a taper protocol was reported by Coutts and colleagues (7), who found that 3RM back squat strength increased by 7.2% and 3RM bench press increased by 5.2%. Gibala and colleagues (11) reported a 3% to 8% increase in maximal isometric and dynamic force-generating capacity.

A properly implemented taper can result in significant increases in performance. The magnitude of the performance gains will be related to many factors, especially the type of taper selected (41). The appropriate taper may result in an elevation of performance (~3.0%) that differentiates between first and third place at the Olympic Games, because the magnitude of taper-induced gains in performance is similar to that of the difference between first and third place in many sports.

COMPETITION PHASE OF THE ANNUAL PLAN

The competition phase of the annual training plan is a complex period because it depends on the number of competitions that the athlete is undertaking (52), the primary goal of the training plan, and the preparedness of the athlete. This phase of training is designed to elevate the athlete's level of physiological, technical, and tactical preparedness, which should result in a peaking of performance. This process is facilitated by using the tapering methods mentioned previously at specific time points to elevate the athlete's performance at the appropriate time (major competitions such as regional, state, conference, national, and world championships or, most important, the Olympic Games). Although the competition period usually contains many competitions, a true peak of performance can only be maintained for about 2 to 3 weeks (60), suggesting that the competition phase must be planned carefully to optimize the athlete's performance.

Classifications of Competitions

Competitions can be classified into two broad categories: (1) major or official competitions and (2) preparatory or exhibition competitions.

Major competitions are the athlete's most important competitions (e.g., national championships, world championships, Olympic Games). These contests require the athlete to be at peak performance and often provide the guidelines for organizing the athlete's annual training plan, especially for individual sports. Preparations for a major competition usually include a taper to dissipate accumulated fatigue and enhance the athlete's preparedness.

© Human Kinetics

Minor competitions and exhibition events at the beginning of the competition calendar are good ways to gauge how a training plan is working. Coaches can use these events to analyze what parts of the training plan may need to be altered to prepare the athlete for major competitions and events.

Preparatory or exhibition competitions are used to test the athlete and attain feedback regarding specific aspects of training. These competitions are integral to the preparation of the athlete and are an important part of the training plan. Often athletes will train through these types of competitions without using any specific tapering strategies. Many coaches use these competitions to test some aspect of the athlete's development. For example, at a local competition a weightlifter may compete at very near maximal capacity in the snatch to test a technical change he has made in training. If this is his goal for this competition, he may use only moderate training loads for the clean and jerk and then undertake a training session after the contest. Victory is not always the focus of these types of competitions; rather they are undertaken as very high-intensity training sessions. However, victory in these competitions may yield valuable information about the athlete's level of preparedness that may warrant alterations to the training plan.

Planning for Competition

The most important step in developing the annual training plan is to establish the competitive schedule for the athlete or team and to determine which competitions require peak form. The competition schedule is established by the sport's governing body and culminates with the national or world championships. When determining the competitive schedule, the coach needs to select specific competitions that can be considered preparatory or exhibition contests and are scheduled to target specific training objectives. These contests are used as hard training days that target specific skill sets, so they can serve as important tools for preparing the athlete for major competitions. Because these contests are used as training days, specific tapering strategies usually are not used.

Many coaches make two very large mistakes when planning the competitive schedule for their athletes. The first mistake is to have the athlete participate in every available competition; this interrupts the athlete's training and her ability to develop the physiological, technical, and tactical skills required for major competitions. The second major mistake is attempting to peak the athlete for every competition. If the athlete attempts to peak too frequently, she likely will need a large number of restoration-based training sessions and will not undergo enough actual training to enhance physiological, tactical, or technical characteristics. It is recommended that the athlete attempt to peak by using specific tapering strategies for only a very few competitions (two or three) and that the remainder of the competitive schedule consist of specific training days or competitions of secondary emphasis (figure 7.5). Both of these common coaching errors can be avoided if the coach plans an appropriate competitive phase of training.

There are several ways to plan the competitive phase of training (52). If the athlete is preparing for one specific competition, the coach should use a *simple competition training period,* whereas if two or more competitions are being prepared for a *complex*

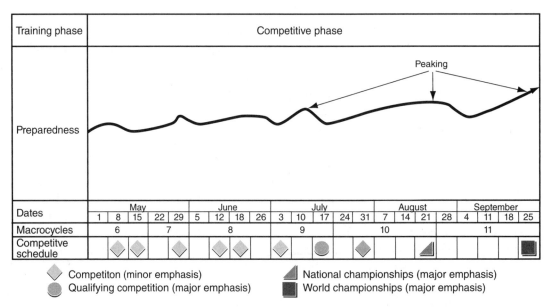

Figure 7.5 Competitive calendar showing emphasis on preparedness and peaking.

competition training period is used (52). The number of macrocycles in the competitive period is dictated by the complexity of the competition phase of training (simple vs. complex) and the athlete's needs (52).

Two methods for planning the competitive phase of the annual training plan are traditionally used: the grouping and the cyclic approach. The grouping approach is a method of planning 2 or 3 weeks in a row, during which the athlete takes part in tournaments or competitions or participates in several events or races per weekend. As illustrated in figure 7.6, this approach is usually followed by several microcycles (3 or 4 weeks) that are dedicated to training and allow the athlete to prepare for another 2 or 3 weeks of grouped competitions.

In the example illustrated in figure 7.6, the athlete or team participates in a group of competitions spread over a 2-week period during the early part of the competitive schedule. During these 2 weeks, races or games may be held during each weekend. The first microcycle following these competitions is of low intensity, with the first 2 or 3 days of the cycle targeting a low training load designed to stimulate regeneration. After the first 2 or 3 days of the cycle are completed the training load is increased, typically resulting in one peak at the end of the microcycle. The next two and a half microcycles are dedicated to hard training followed by a short 2- or 3-day unloading period that leads into the next 3 weeks of competitions. The next major competition occurs on August 21 and is designated as the qualifying competition for the championships that are held on September 25. Because the August 21 contest is a major competition that serves as a qualifier for the championships, an 8- to 14-day exponential taper is used to elevate performance. After the athlete completes the qualifying competition, she enters a regeneration microcycle that includes 2 to 2.5 weeks of hard training before undertaking another taper. If the schedule is structured correctly, performance will be optimized at the championships.

The grouping method usually is best suited for individual sports where only a few major competitions are undertaken throughout the annual training plan. With team sports, the grouping method may only be useful when teams approach national championships, international competitions, or official international tournaments. Coaches of most team sports use a cyclic approach to planning the competitive schedule.

In the cyclic approach, competitions are spaced at regular, repeating intervals (figure 7.7). In figure 7.7, the vast majority of the competitions occur each weekend during macrocycles 8 and 9. This pattern of competition is often seen in American football, where competitions usually occur each weekend throughout the fall. The last

Training phase	Competitive phase																				
Dates	May				June				July					August				September			
	1	8	15	22	29	5	12	19	26	3	10	17	24	31	7	14	21	28	4	11	18	25
Macrocycles	6			7			8			9					10				11			
Competitve schedule			◇	◇				◇	◇	◇							◢					◼

◇ Competiton (minor emphasis)

◢ Qualifying competition (major emphasis)

◼ Championships (major emphasis)

Figure 7.6 Competitive schedule based on the grouping approach.

two macrocycles (10 and 11) contain the two major competitions of this competition phase. In American university football, the competition in macrocycle 10 would be the conference championships, whereas the contest in macrocycle 11 would be a bowl game. Because each microcycle throughout macrocycle 8 and 9 ends with a game, a one-peak microcycle structure may be warranted. This peak or increased training load would occur on Tuesday or Wednesday. One or two days before each game, an unloading period would be used to dissipate fatigue and prepare the athlete for competition. Coaches who work with individual sports should consider using the cyclic approach in the lead-up to the major competitions (figure 7.8). In this approach the coach may take the athlete to several competitions that occur every 2 weeks to gain information about the athlete in competitive situations. This will allow the coach to modify the training plan based on the feedback garnered from the periodic competitions.

In the cyclic approach, the first half of the week after a competition would contain a lower training load to enhance recovery, whereas the second half of the week would contain higher training loads (figure 7.9). The microcycle preceding the next competition would be structured so that the higher training loads are encountered earlier in the week (i.e., Tuesday or Wednesday) and unloading would occur in the second half of the week to facilitate recovery for the weekend competition. However, this is only an example of how a microcycle could be formatted; many different formats are available based on the type of taper and the competitive season. Although these two major approaches are usually used to design the competitive phase of training, it is likely that the cyclic and grouped approaches can be combined when planning for competitions.

Training phase	Competitive phase																							
Dates	August					September				October					November				December			
	1	8	15	22	29	5	12	19	26	3	10	17	24	31	7	14	21	28	4	11	18	25
Macrocycles	7					8				9					10				11			
Competitve schedule		◇		◇		◇	◇	◇	◇	◇	◇	◇	◇	◇	◇			◢			◼	

◇ Competiton (minor emphasis)

◢ Qualifying competition (major emphasis)

◼ Championships (major emphasis)

Figure 7.7 Competition schedule for a team sport based on a cyclic approach.

Training phase	Competitive phase																							
Dates	November					December				January					February				March			
	1	8	15	22	29	5	12	19	26	3	10	17	24	31	7	14	21	28	4	11	18	25
Macrocycles																						
Competitve schedule	◇			◇		◇		◇		◇		◇					◢				◼	

◇ Competiton (minor emphasis)

◢ Qualifying competition (major emphasis)

◼ Championships (major emphasis)

Figure 7.8 Cyclic approach for a cross-country skier.

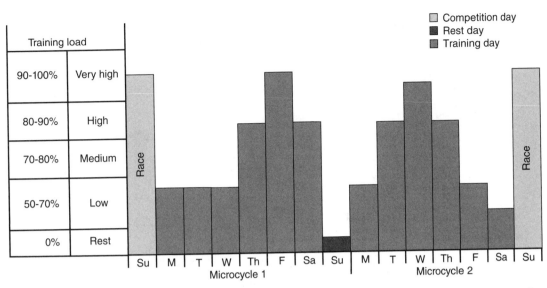

Figure 7.9 Microcycle structure for training between competitions during the cyclic approach.

Competition Frequency

Determining the frequency of competitions is a complex undertaking. Factors such as the athlete's characteristics, training age, and sport contribute to the frequency and number of competitions undertaken each year. The coach also must consider the length of the competition phase, given that a longer phase would allow a greater number of competitions.

A primary determinant of the number of competitions undertaken by athletes is their age and training experience (9). The less experienced the child or youth athlete, the less frequently she should compete (9). If the athlete's training is centered on multilateral development, the young athlete will increase the number of competitive starts progressively as her skills develop and her training plan increases the emphasis on specialization (45, 55). Kauhanen (29) suggested that as the young athlete becomes more trained, the number of major competitions should increase each year (table 7.1). During these years, secondary or minor competitions are still undertaken to help develop the athlete's skills in competition. With young athletes the primary emphasis is the development of the skills that will be used in competition as they become more trained.

A second factor determining the frequency of competitions is the characteristics of the sport. In team sports, the length of the season can have a great impact on the number of competitions held. For example, a top team in the FA Premier League may compete in roughly 60 competitions over approximately 270 days, which roughly equates to competing every 3 1/2 to 4 1/2 days (8). Individual sports athletes usually have greater flexibility in the selection of competitions because these athletes will probably compete less frequently than athletes in team sports. For example, an elite weightlifter may only compete in three or four major competitions per training year (1, 12). Dick (8) suggested that the build-up and principle competition period in track and field should consist of about 7 to 10 competitions. Any additional competitions would be used for lower-level training (8). Table 7.2 offers some very rough guidelines concerning the number of competitions for novice and advanced athletes. Regardless

Table 7.1 Frequency of Competitions in the Annual Training Plan of Junior Weightlifters

Training year	1	2	3	4	5
Age (years)	14-15	15-16	16-17	17-18	18-19
Total number of competitions	6-8	8-12	9-12	9-12	9-12
Major competitions	0	0-2	1-2	2-3	2-3
Secondary competitions	6-8	8-10	8-10	7-9	7-9

Adapted from H. Kauhanen 1998 (29).

Table 7.2 Suggested Number of Competitions Per Year in Athletics (Track and Field)

Event	NOVICE ATHLETES		ELITE ATHLETES	
	Winter	Summer	Winter	Summer
Sprinters, hurdlers, jumpers, and throwers				
Specialized event	3-4	12-16	3-5	16-20
Other events and sports	2-3	4-6	1-3	3-5
Middle distance				
800-1,500 m	—	4-8	2-3	10-16
Short distances	2-3	8-10	2-4	8-10
Distance running and walking				
Marathon	—	1	—	2-3
50K walk		6-8	—	8-10
Combined events				
Decathlon	—	1-2	—	2-3
Heptathlon	—	1-2	—	2-4
Individual events	2-4	10-12	3 -5	12-16

of the athlete or sport, the coach must consider the relationships among recovery, training, and peaking.

When constructing the training plan for the competitive phase, the coach must consider the sequence and frequency of competitions and how they relate to the time allowed for recovery after competition (46). The more frequently the athlete competes, the less time he will have to train for the next competition (8, 15). Therefore, overly frequent competitions can impede the athlete's development, because each competition undertaken can result in fatigue, which must be dealt with by reducing training loads.

The coach should plan for two to four major competitions during the competitive phase of the training year. These competitions will most likely include qualifying meets for the year's main competition. The training plan should also include secondary competitions that are used as hard training sessions and to test the athlete's ability. The coach and athlete should think of the competitive schedule as a build-up to the major competition (table 7.3). However, the schedule must allow time between the preparatory (exhibition) competitions and the major competitions. The precompetition training period can be sequenced in several ways (31) (figure 7.10). The optimal sequencing of training in this phase will depend on the time interval between each competition.

Table 7.3 Objectives for the Competitive Subphase

Competitive Subphase	Objectives	Means of implementation
Precompetition	1. Improve performance 2. Gain experience 3. Determine strengths and weaknesses 4. Test technique and tactics	1. Enter competitions of progressive difficulty 2. Increase density of competitions 3. Decrease training volume slightly
Specialized preparation for league competitions	1. Correct deficiencies revealed during precompetition subphase 2. Alter techniques and methods to improve competitive abilities	1. Include extensive training 2. Increase training volume 3. Participate in some competitions without altering training
League or official competitions	1. Elevate preparedness 2. Prepare for qualifying competitions	1. Reduce training volume and increase training intensity according to demands of the sport 2. Participate in competitions of increasing demands
Special preparation	1. Maximize preparedness 2. Compete at highest level in major competition	1. Use specialized preparation methods such as a taper to prepare for major competition

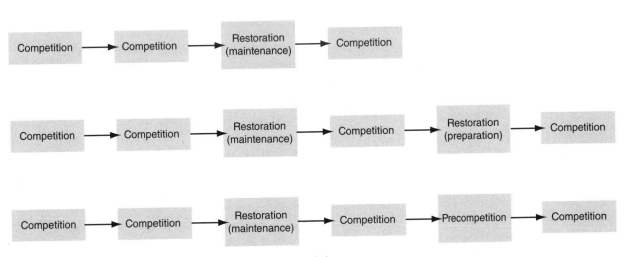

Figure 7.10 Three sequences of precompetition training.

Data from G.I. Kukushkin 1983 (31).

Regarding the time interval between competitions, Bompa (3) and Harre (15) recommended the following:

- Undertake competitions only when the athlete is capable of achieving set objectives for each training factor: physical, technical, tactical, and psychological.
- Carefully select and schedule competitions so that they progressively increase in difficulty.
- Select challenging competitions, because unchallenging competitions do not motivate the athlete.
- Challenge the athlete by placing her against opponents with superior capabilities.

- Avoid entering too many competitions. Participating in too many competitions, especially those that require substantial travel, will result in an improperly dosed competitive and training schedule, which will reduce physical and psychological potential.

- Sequence the competitive schedule in a progressive fashion, allowing for preparedness to be maximized at the main competition of the season. This will allow the athlete every possibility to perform at her highest level at this contest.

- Allocate adequate time between competitions to allow the athlete time to train and correct any technical flaws noted in secondary or exhibition competitions.

- Instruct the athlete to perform at her highest level only in the main competitions of the training year. Think of the other competitions as sequential progressive steps that bring the athlete's physiological capacity, technical skill, tactical ability, and psychological state, and thus performance, to the very highest level.

SUMMARY OF MAJOR CONCEPTS

The appropriate use of tapering strategies is essential for the athlete to achieve peak preparedness and performance. The athlete cannot achieve a true peak for every competition he enters. Therefore, the coach must carefully craft the competitive schedule to include two to four major competitions. All other competitions should be considered preparatory competitions in which the athlete uses the competitive environment as a training tool. If, however, a team sport athlete participates in competitions that occur in a cyclic pattern, the coach should consider training strategies that allow the athlete to recover, train, and dissipate fatigue before each contest. As with individual sports, the culmination of the competitive team sports calendar should be a major contest, such as conference or national championship, at which the athlete reaches a physiological and performance peak.

The goal of a tapering strategy is to reduce training-induced fatigue and elevate preparedness. When appropriately applied, the taper can improve performance approximately 3%, which can make a large difference in the competitive outcome. To implement the taper, the coach should decrease the training load in an exponential fashion and decrease training volume as well, by about 41% to 60% in most instances. If, however, the pretaper training load is very high, a greater reduction in training volume (60-90%) may be warranted. When training volume is reduced, training frequency should be maintained at 80% or more of the pretaper values. The taper should last approximately 8 to 14 days. If the pretaper training load is excessive, a longer taper may be warranted; however, another strategy is to use a fast exponential taper that involves larger decreases in volume. During the taper period the training intensity should be maintained or slightly increased to allow the athlete to maintain the physiological adaptations achieved during the pretaper training.

CHAPTER 8

TRAINING CYCLES

Training cycles can be structured into long-term plans such as the **quadrennial** (4-year) plan and the individual annual plan (1 year). Based on the methodological plans of the Germans preparing for the 1936 Olympics, the annual plan can be further subdivided into grosse (**macrocycle**) and kleine (**microcycle**) plans. Macrocycles can be structured in 2- to 7-week increments, whereas microcycles generally consist of 1 week or 3 to 7 days of training. Although some authors suggest that eight or nine microcycle variants exist, it is probably better to use five basic variants: developmental, shock, regeneration, competition, and tapering. Although the five basic microcycle types are used most of the time, it is likely that some coaches use variations of these broad categories.

MICROCYCLE

The term **microcycle** is rooted in the Greek word *micros,* which means "small," and the Latin word *cyclus,* which refers to a regular sequence of events. In training methodology, a microcycle is a weekly or 3 to 7- day training program within an annual program. The microcycle is the most important functional planning tool in the training process (16, 19, 20). The structure and content of the microcycle determine the quality of the training process. The microcycle is structured according to the objectives, volume, intensity, and methods that are the focus of the training phase. The physiological and psychological demands placed on the athlete cannot be steady; they must change according to the athlete's working capacity, the athlete's need for recovery, and the competition plan. The microcycle must be flexible enough that individual training sessions can be modified to address certain circumstances (20). When the microcycle is modified, subsequent training lessons must be modified to maintain the focus of the microcycle and ensure that the training objectives are achieved (22).

Constructing Microcycles

The microcycle has a strong historical precedence and can be found in the works of Philostratus, an ancient Greek scholar. Philostratus proposed a short-term plan that he called the *tetra system,* which was a 4-day training cycle that proceeded in the following order.

Day 1: Undertake a short and energetic program.

Day 2: Exercise intensely.

Day 3: Relax to revive the activity.

Day 4: Perform moderate exercise.

The tetra system structure was to be repeated continually. Such ancient training practices are the foundation of the microcycle structure.

The main criteria determining the microcycle structure are the training goal, training factors, and desired improvements in athletic performance. The appropriate microcycle structure will dictate the rate of improvement in the various training factors. The sequencing of the microcycle is of particular importance, because the fatigue generated in one session can significantly affect subsequent training sessions. For example, if a session that focuses on endurance development or contains a very intense stimulus precedes a technical training session, the fatigue generated by the first session will significantly impair the development of technique in the next session. Thus, the sequencing of the training stimuli throughout the microcycle must account for accumulated fatigue in order to maximize the development of specific performance or biomotor factors. The microcycle should be structured using the same concepts suggested for the training session plan:

© Human Kinetics

When structuring microcycles, the coach should include opportunities for the athlete to improve technical knowledge and develop speed, strength, and endurance.

- Technical or tactical training
- Development of speed, agility, or power
- Development of strength
- Development of specific endurance

Constructing a Microcycle

Repetition of a training stimulus is essential for the athlete to improve a technical element or develop a biomotor ability. *Repetitia mater studiorum ets* is a Roman phrase meaning "repetition is the mother of study." To maximize gains, exercises that target specific biomotor abilities must be undertaken with varying frequencies during the microcycle. Depending on the athlete's ability, targeted training sessions with similar objectives and content may need to be repeated two or three times during a microcycle to maximize the training effect. Of particular importance is the training stimulus used, because the amount of fatigue generated will affect the recovery required before that stimulus can be used again. For example, in strength training a 20RM load requires significantly more recovery than either a 5RM or a 10RM load (1). Thus a longer recovery period may be warranted before performing this type of strength training.

When the athlete and coach are targeting specific endurance with submaximal intensities, three training sessions per week will suffice. However, for specific endurance of maximum intensity during the competitive phase, the athlete should engage in endurance training twice a week and dedicate the remaining days to lower-intensity training. The athlete should use one or two training sessions per week to maintain **strength**, **flexibility**, and speed. It appears that 2 or 3 days a week are optimal for plyometric, **speed**, and **agility** training.

Various training loads should be alternated throughout the microcycle. The athlete should use maximal loads no more than twice a week, interspersed with low-intensity training days and active rest days. It is particularly important to schedule active rest and relaxation the day after a competition. Active rest or low-intensity exercise should be interspersed throughout the microcycle, especially after sessions that have high to maximal demand.

When planning the microcycles, the coach can repeat the basic structure across several microcycles, especially during the preparatory phase. Throughout a macrocycle, microcycles of similar nature (i.e., content and methods) can be repeated two or three times, which can result in qualitative improvements based on the athlete's adaptation. The types of microcycle fluctuations will vary depending on the athlete's level of development.

Structural Considerations

The long-term or annual training plan dictates the structure of the macrocycle and microcycle plans. The individual microcycle plans should be developed to meet the objectives of each phase of the annual and macrocycle training plans. One school of thought is to develop only two microcycles into the future, allowing the coach to modify the training structure in response to the athlete's improvement. A second school of thought is to construct and use macrocycle plans. The second approach must allow for flexibility in the training plan. In this approach the macrocycle is considered a guideline, and the plan can be altered to address the athlete's improvement rate or dynamics. Regardless of which school of thought is used, the microcycle should be constructed in accordance with the training objectives and the phase of training. When structuring the microcycles of the training plan, the coach should consider many factors:

- The objective of the microcycle and the dominant training factors.
- The training demand (e.g., number of sessions, number of hours, volume, intensity, and complexity) targeted during the microcycle.
- The intensity of the microcycle and the intensity fluctuations that are contained in the microcycle.
- The methods that will be used to induce the training stimulus in each training session.
- The days on which training and competition will occur (if applicable).
- The need to alter intensity each day. One possibility is to start the microcycle with a low- or medium-intensity training session and progress with increasing intensity.
- The timing of competitions in the context of the microcycle. When the microcycle leads into a competition, the highest intensity or peak training session should occur 3 to 5 days prior to the event.

The coach must determine whether the athlete should perform one or more sessions per day. If the athlete's development and work, school, or personal schedule allow for multiple training sessions, the coach should plan the timing of such sessions.

It is helpful to begin each microcycle with a meeting in which the coach and athlete discuss the objectives for each training factor contained in the microcycle and how those objectives will be achieved. The coach and athlete should discuss the volume and intensity of training, the number of training session contained in each training day, and where the most difficult training sessions will fall. The coach may want to target performance standards for the microcycle. Additional personalized information can be given to athletes at this time. Finally, if the microcycle is leading into a competition, the coach should give the athlete details about the upcoming contest and motivate the athlete to attain each competition goal.

If there is no competition at the end of microcycle, a short meeting should be held after the last training session of the microcycle to analyze whether the athlete achieved the microcycle training objectives and goals. The coach should use this meeting to critique the athlete's performance during training, making sure to highlight the positive aspects while targeting others for improvement. The coach can strengthen the evaluation of the microcycle by collecting input from the athlete. The coach should then take all information obtained from the meetings and training outcomes to formulate strategies for future microcycles with similar objectives and goals. The meeting following a microcycle is a tool with which coaches and athletes can coordinate their focus on performance outcomes.

Classifying Microcycles

Several different microcycle structures are presented in this chapter, but specific training circumstances result in an infinite number of structural variations. The dynamics of the microcycle is dictated by many factors including the phase of training, the developmental status of the athlete, and the training factor emphasis (e.g., technical, tactical, or physical preparation). One of the most important factors dictating the microcycle structure is the athlete's level of development and training capacity. For example, a highly trained athlete may be able to tolerate a greater density of training sessions performed at higher intensities than a novice or less-developed athlete. Athletes on the same team may have different work capacities and training needs, so individualization of microcycle structure may be warranted.

To create an individualized training stimulus, the coach must eliminate standardization and rigidity when structuring the microcycle. The microcycle should be flexible in the context of the training plan as well, which will allow the coach to change training factors as the athlete progresses through the training plan. This flexibility allows the coach to use information gathered from training, assessments, or competition to modify the training plan to help the athlete meet performance and training objectives.

One method for classifying microcycles centers on the number of training sessions per week. As stated previously, the number of training sessions that the athlete can tolerate without overtraining occurring is dictated by the athlete's level of development and physical preparation. Additionally, the microcycle structure will change depending on the available time for training and whether the athlete is participating in a training camp or undergoing regular training sessions.

There are a variety of microcycle structures: 3 days per week (figure 8.1), 4 days per week (figure 8.2), and 5 days per week (figure 8.3) are common structures. Advanced athletes who have a high work tolerance and can meet the time requirements can undergo eight training sessions per week (figures 8.4 and 8.5). Microcycles with

Session time	DAY						
	Monday	Tuesday	Wednesday	Thursday	Friday	Saturday	Sunday
a.m.							
p.m.	Training		Training		Training		

Figure 8.1   Microcycle with three training sessions per week.

Session time	DAY						
	Monday	Tuesday	Wednesday	Thursday	Friday	Saturday	Sunday
a.m.							
p.m.	Training	Training		Training		Training	

Figure 8.2   Microcycle with four training sessions per week. A variant is to have the fourth training session on Friday.

Session time	DAY						
	Monday	Tuesday	Wednesday	Thursday	Friday	Saturday	Sunday
a.m.							
p.m.	Training	Training		Training	Training	Training	

Figure 8.3   Microcycle with five sessions per week.

Session time	DAY						
	Monday	Tuesday	Wednesday	Thursday	Friday	Saturday	Sunday
a.m.	Training	Training		Training		Training	
p.m.	Training	Training		Training		Training	

Figure 8.4   Microcycle with eight sessions per week.

additional training session may be used during holidays or during training camps, when more time is available for training, or with more advanced athletes.

There are many ways to increase the number of training sessions. The athlete can use a 3+1 microcycle, training on three successive half days, followed by a half day of rest, for a total of 9 training sessions during the microcycle (figure 8.6). This model can be modified for an athlete whose training tolerance or potential is higher and can tolerate more intensive microcycles. A 5+1 microcycle (five sessions plus 1/2 day of rest) (figure 8.7) and a 5+1+1 microcycle (five sessions plus 1/2 day rest, followed by 1/2 day of work) are intensive microcycles (figure 8.8). The structure of these more intensive microcycles depends on the amount of time that is available and the type of training stimulus used during each session.

The microcycle structure can be further expanded by integrating multiple training sessions throughout the day that target different training factors. For example, a three-component microcycle may be constructed where a sprint–agility or a plyometric session is conducted in the morning and the main training session, which targets tactical or technical development followed by strength training, may be performed in the late afternoon or early evening (figure 8.9).

An additional aspect of the microcycle structure relates to the variations in training intensity and demand. The training dynamics should not be uniform across the microcycle. They should vary depending on the characteristics of the training, the type of microcycle used, the environmental conditions (e.g., climate, weather),

Session time	DAY						
	Monday	Tuesday	Wednesday	Thursday	Friday	Saturday	Sunday
a.m.						Training	Training
p.m.	Training	Training	Training	Training	Training	Training	

Figure 8.5 Alternative microcycle with eight sessions per week.

Session time	DAY						
	Monday	Tuesday	Wednesday	Thursday	Friday	Saturday	Sunday
a.m.	Training	Training	Training	Training	Training	Training	
p.m.	Training		Training		Training		

Figure 8.6 Microcycle with a 3+1 structure.

Session time	DAY						
	Monday	Tuesday	Wednesday	Thursday	Friday	Saturday	Sunday
a.m.	Training	Training	Training	Training	Training	Training	
p.m.	Training	Training		Training	Training		

Figure 8.7 Microcycle with a 5+1 structure.

Session time	DAY						
	Monday	Tuesday	Wednesday	Thursday	Friday	Saturday	Sunday
a.m.	Training	Training	Training	Training	Training	Training	Training
p.m.	Training	Training		Training	Training		

Figure 8.8 Microcycle with a 5+1+1 structure.

and the phase of the annual training plan. The intensity of training can alternate between the seven intensity zones, ranging from very high (90-100% of maximum) to a recovery session where no training is undertaken (table 8.1). These alterations are dictated by the objectives of the microcycle. For example, the objectives of an intensive microcycle may require one (figure 8.10), two (figures 8.11-8.15), or occasionally

Session time	DAY						
	Monday	Tuesday	Wednesday	Thursday	Friday	Saturday	Sunday
7:00 a.m.	Plyometric training	Sprint and agility training	Plyometric training	Sprint and agility training	Plyometric training	Sprint and agility training	
3:00 p.m.	Main training	Main training	Main training	Main training	Main training		
5:00 p.m.	Strength training		Strength training		Strength training		

Figure 8.9 Microcycle with the integration of multiple training factors.

Table 8.1   Intensity Zones and Training Demand

Intensity zone	Training demand	Percentage of maximum performance	Intensity
5	Very high	90-100	Maximum
4	High	80-90	Heavy
3	Medium	70-80	Medium
2	Low	50-70	Low
1	Very low	<50	Very low
Recovery	Recovery	No training	Recovery

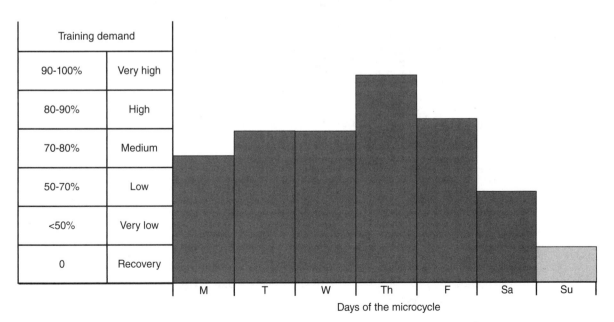

Figure 8.10 Microcycle with one peak.

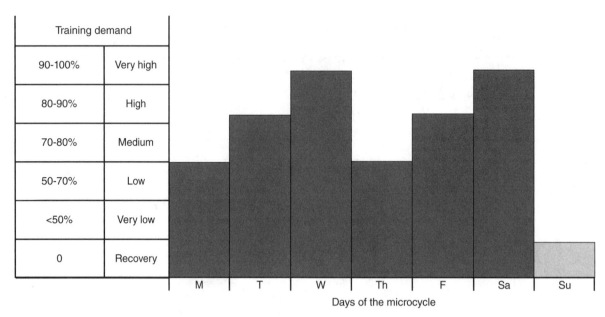

Figure 8.11 Two-peak microcycle.

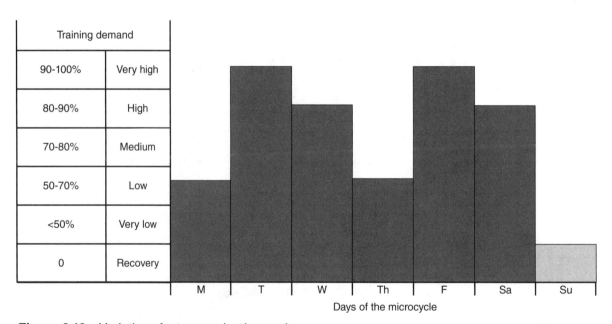

Figure 8.12 Variation of a two-peak microcycle.

three (figure 8.16) high-demand to very high-demand training days depending on the objective of the microcycle.

When planning the modulations of intensity or training demand within the microcycle, the coach should consider the principles of load progression. The microcycle usually should contain only one peak, which occurs somewhere during the middle 3 days of the week. In some instances a microcycle can contain two peaks that are followed by 1 or 2 days of regeneration sessions. An exception to this rule may occur when model training is being used; in this case, two peaks can occur on adjacent days to simulate a competitive situation.

The microcycle structure can be modified if the athlete is training at high altitude or has traveled a long distance and crossed several time zones (5-8 hr time difference).

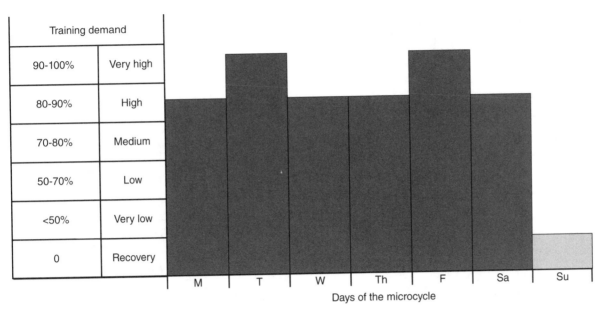

Figure 8.13 Two-peak microcycle with high demand.

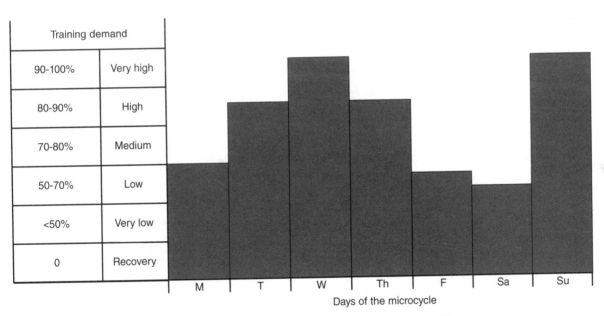

Figure 8.14 Two-peak microcycle in which the second peak is a competition.

In these situations it may be warranted to add an adaptation microcycle that does not contain a peak. The microcycle structure also should be altered when the athlete is training in a hot and humid climate. In this situation it is recommended that the peak occur at the beginning of the week when the athlete has more vigor.

The sample microcycles in figures 8.10 through 8.16 represent **total training demand** rather than the separate variables of volume and intensities. The use of total training demand allows for the microcycle structure to be used in a variety of sporting activities, because sports vary in their area of emphasis, with some being dominated by speed-power, maximal strength, or endurance. Additionally, team sports contain a complex interaction of many factors that can best represented by total training demand.

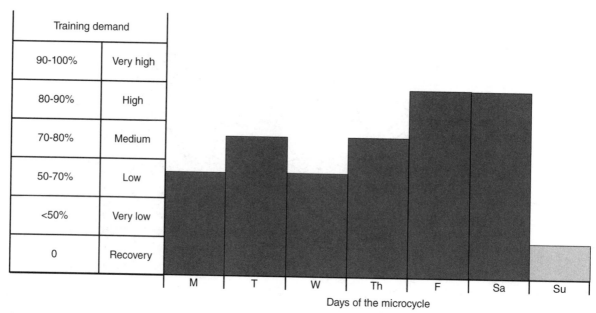

Figure 8.15   Microcycle model for two adjacent peaks.

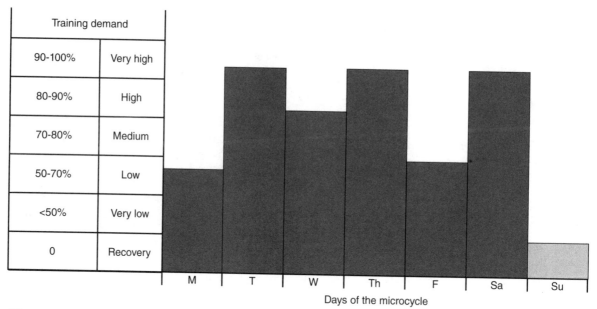

Figure 8.16   Three-peak microcycle with alternating training demands.

A microcycle can be structured many ways; some authors speculate that there are at least 22 possible microcycle structures. This number of microcycle variants may complicate the training and planning process, so it may be better for the coach to use the most common microcycle structures and adapt them to individual training needs.

The microcycle should be functional and, therefore, as simple as possible. The plan should specify the date, objectives, and content for each training session. The content should be succinct and easy to understand and should emphasize major items to target in the training session. Figure 8.17 shows a microcycle plan from the competition phase.

Sport/Event: Javelin	Microcyle # 29						
Date : 20.07-27-09	Objectives: 1. Perform 67:00 m 2. Perfect the rhythm of the last three strides under higher velocity conditions 3. Develop the ability to concentrate for the morning competition 4. Maintain leg and arm power						
Time	Mon.	Tues.	Wed.	Thurs.	Fri.	Sat.	Sun.
a.m. 10:00-11:00	• 15 min warm-up • Sprints: $\dfrac{20, 30, 40\ m}{\frac{2}{4}, \frac{3}{4}}$ 6	Competition warm-up: 6 throws		Same as Tuesday	Competition warm-up	Competition 10:45	
	• Warm-up: 20 min • Sprints: $\dfrac{30\ m}{\frac{4}{4}}$ 3 • Technique: • Last 3 strides • 30 throws with baseball • 15 medicine ball throws • 2 × 30 m bounds	• Warm-up: Competition • Throws: • 6 throws 4/4 • 15 throws, 3/4 with short approach • Warm-up: 7 min specific warm-up • Weight training: 30 min • Flexibility: 5 min	Basketball game: 2 × 15 min	Same as Monday	• Warm-up: Competition • Throws: 15 medium approach • Walk & throw: 15 min at different sports in the grass • Relaxation: Special exercises	Basketball game: 2 × 15 min	

Figure 8.17 Competition phase microcycle plan.

Classification of Microcycles Based on Training Objectives and Phase of Training

The structure of the microcycle depends on the training objectives and thus the training phase. From this point of view there are four general microcycle classifications: developmental, shock, recovery–regeneration, and peaking and unloading.

Developmental Microcycles

Developmental microcycles are specific to the preparatory phase of training. The objective is to increase the level of adaptation, improve skills, and develop biomotor abilities. Such cycles could have two or three peaks of medium and high demand. The microcycle can use a step loading or flat loading method, depending on the athlete's classification. Figure 8.18 illustrates a microcycle for the early part of the preparatory phase, presenting training sessions for early adaptation and development.

Shock Microcycle

A shock microcycle contains a sudden increase of training demands beyond those previously experienced. These microcycles may also be considered as planned over-reaching (20) or concentrated loading (20-22). A shock microcycle can be characterized by two to four peaks in training demand that most likely occur in the middle and second part of the preparatory phase. A shock microcycle is designed to apply a saturated stimulus that will elevate the athlete's preparedness in subsequent training blocks (16). This type of load will result in a significant level of physiological disturbance, which will facilitate further increases in preparedness and performance (5, 6, 15). However, the greater the training load programmed in a shock microcycle, the longer the delay before performance increases after the athlete returns to normal training loads (16, 19).

An example of a shock microcycle is presented in figure 8.19. In this example a three-peak microcycle has been constructed in which very high training demands are encountered. To facilitate recovery, two recovery days are planned (Thursday and

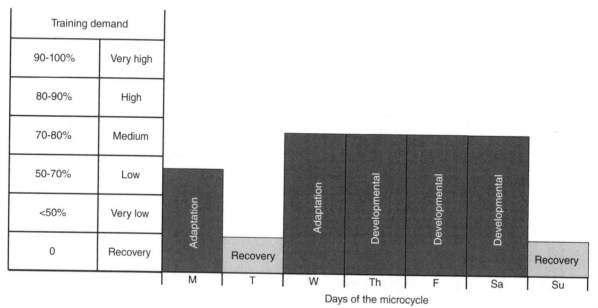

Figure 8.18 Developmental microcycle. The scope or focus of this microcycle is adaptation.

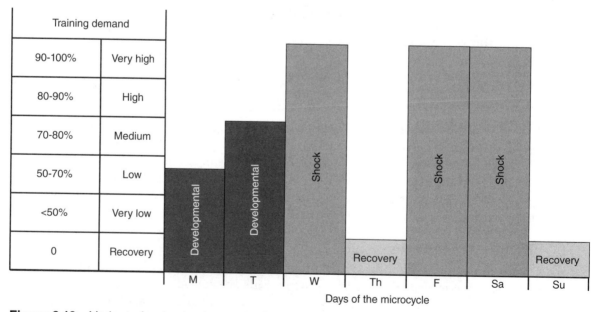

Figure 8.19 Variant of a shock microcycle. A variant of the shock microcycle presented may contain a light recovery training session on Thursday.

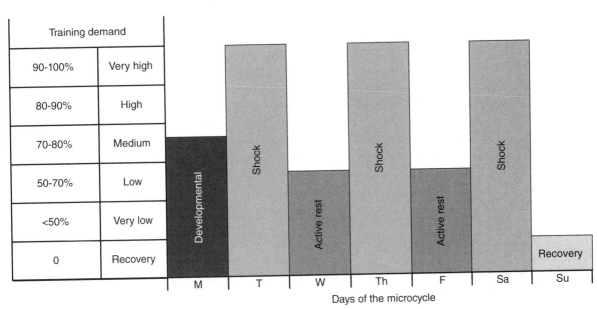

Figure 8.20 Variant of a shock microcycle interspersing high-intensity peaks with lower-intensity active rest.

Sunday). An alternative to this format is to intersperse the high-intensity peaks with lower-intensity active rest or regeneration workouts (figure 8.20). When using these types of cycles, the athlete must allow enough time for preparedness and performance to supercompensate. Therefore, these types of microcycles should not be used immediately before a competition or 2 to 3 weeks after a shock, regeneration, or unloading microcycle, when training intensity should be markedly lower.

Recovery–Regeneration Microcycle

The goal of a regeneration microcycle is to dissipate fatigue and elevate the athlete's level of preparedness, which ultimately will improve performance. This microcycle is marked by a significantly lower training demand, which can be created by decreasing training intensity, volume, or some combination of both. Another approach to using this type of microcycle is to include activities that train similar physiological characteristics as the targeted sport but are different than the typical training activities. The regeneration microcycle elevates performance and decreases the potential for overtraining.

Peaking and Unloading Microcycles

To dissipate fatigue and elevate performance, unloading or peaking microcycles need to be included in the annual training plan. (See chapter 7 for more information on peaking.) This type of microcycle is created by manipulating training demand (volume and intensity) to dissipate fatigue and elevate performance at the appropriate time. The reduction of training demand will result in physiological responses that allow supercompensation to occur.

Microcycle Dynamics During the Competitive Phase

The sequencing of individual microcycles depends on the competitive schedule. Timing of competitions also affects the placement of regeneration and unloading days within the microcycle. The format used when planning a competitive microcycle will be affected by the requirements of the sport. In team sports there may be several competitions in 1 week, whereas in individual sports (figure 8.21) competitions may occur over several consecutive weeks. With one competition per week, 1 or 2 days of rest and recovery should be included each week. The bulk of training will be conducted during the middle of the microcycle. In this example, a medium to high training demand is used. After the bulk of training is completed, unloading should then be planned for the 2 days prior to the next competition.

This basic competitive microcycle can be modified when the opponent is weaker or the competition is of little importance. Such a competition will not present a high physiological challenge, and the subsequent competition-induced fatigue will be markedly less than usual. It may be warranted in these situations to replace the recovery day that is planned for Monday in this example with an additional technical or tactical training session. Additionally, it is likely that only one unloading day would be needed before a minor competition. This schedule results in a net gain of 4 training days, with at least one of those days being of a high demand.

When teams have multiple competitions or games in one microcycle (see figure 8.22), Monday is as a short regeneration session that contains a very low to low training demand. The second session of the microcycle (Tuesday) is a tactical day that is used to elevate performance during the Wednesday competition. On Thursday a regeneration day is planned, and Friday is the only high-demand training session of the microcycle. To elevate performance for the Sunday game, an unloading day is planned for Saturday.

If the competitive schedule is organized over 2 days of a weekend (e.g., team sports tournament or several races in track and swimming) the microcycle can be organized as depicted in figure 8.23. Two unloading training sessions are used on the 2 days (Thursday and Friday) prior to the weekend competition so that fatigue is dissipated and supercompensation of preparedness occurs at the competition. The highest training demand occurs at the beginning of the microcycle (Tuesday), thus progressively decreasing the training demand across the microcycle.

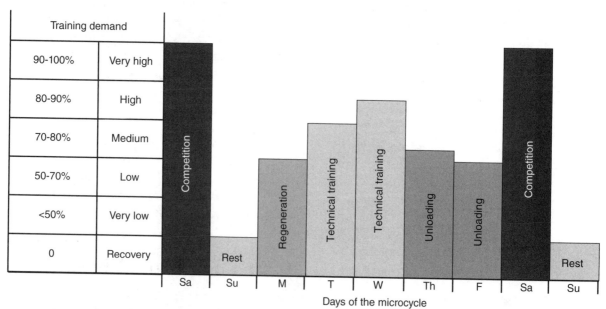

Figure 8.21 Microcycle with weekly competitions.

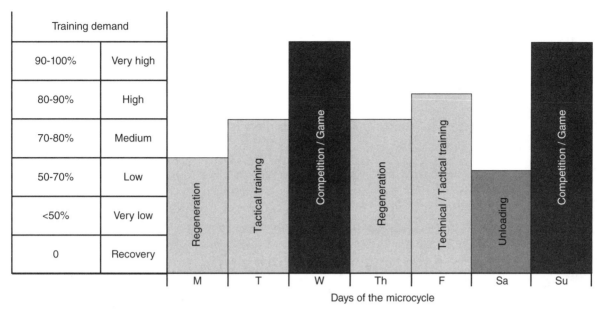

Figure 8.22 Competitive microcycle for a team sport with two games in 1 week.

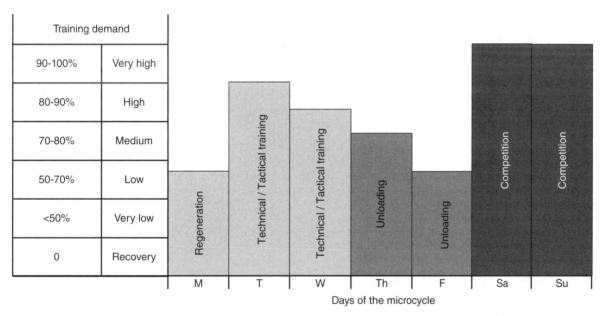

Figure 8.23 Competitive microcycle for a team sport with two games in one weekend.

If the microcycle contains a multiple-day tournament, the coach should plan regeneration activities that may include active recovery (see chapter 5 for information on rest and recovery). Active recovery performed at very low intensities can facilitate lactate removal (10, 13, 17), dampen central nervous system activity (18), and reduce muscle soreness (18). Active recovery should include very low intensities of exercise that do not significantly affect muscle glycogen stores. Tournament play can significantly affect glycogen (9), so glycogen stores must be replenished before the next competitive match. The best method for accomplishing this is to follow a postexercise supplementation regime and ensure adequate dietary intake of carbohydrate between matches (4, 8). A microcycle for a week-long tournament is presented in figure 8.24. Note that the morning after every game includes a very low-intensity

Time	DAYS OF THE MICROCYCLE						
	Mon.	Tues.	Weds.	Thurs.	Fri.	Sat.	Sun.
a.m.	Game	Regeneration	Game	Regeneration	Game	Regeneration	Game
p.m.		Tactical training		Tactical training		Tactical training	

Figure 8.24 Microcycle for a week-long team sport tournament.

regeneration session that is designed to speed recovery. Additionally, a low-intensity tactical training session is planned for the late afternoon on the day prior to each game. A microcycle formatted in this fashion will provide the athlete with the best potential to recover and maximize performance.

Model of a Microcycle for Competition

The vast majority of the microcycles in the annual training plan target the development of skills and abilities required by the sport. However, during the competitive phase, the focus of the training plan shifts to maximizing performance capacity during competition. This is accomplished by modifying the microcycle structure in accordance with the demands of the sport and the athlete's physiological and psychological needs. One strategy is to develop the microcycle based on a model of the competition. This model can be used repeatedly prior to main competition. The model should contain training sessions of various intensities and should alternate between active rest and recovery. The daily cycle should be identical to the day of the competition.

Many sports (e.g., track and field, swimming, tennis, some team sports, martial arts) have qualifying rounds followed by finals in the same day (e.g., Friday 10:00 a.m. and 6:00 p.m.). Models designed to address this competitive schedule would place the main training day on Friday, which would contain two training sessions that would occur at the same times as the targeted competition.

Other sports (e.g., some team sports, boxing, tennis, and wrestling) may contain 3 or 4 days of consecutive competitions. This type of competitive format can also be modeled by modifying the microcycle structure to correspond to the demands of the competition. This model should be repeated several times prior to the contest. However, the model should only be used every 2 or 3 weeks, with developmental microcycles placed between each microcycle containing this competitive model.

Some tournaments such as the Olympic Games, World Championships, or international competitions are organized over 4 to 9 days. It is not feasible to model this competitive format because such a model will create a large amount of physiological stress and significantly affect the time that can be dedicated to training. To prepare for larger tournaments, the athlete should participate in smaller tournaments that last 2 or 3 days and contain four or five competitive efforts. To prepare for these tournaments, the athlete should follow developmental microcycles and daily training structures that contain characteristics of the targeted tournament. It may also be warranted to familiarize the athlete with the competitive schedule by using the competitive model, altering between competition and recovery typically seen in a tournament. It may be recommended that training days that fall on the same day of a tournament involve higher demands, whereas the day after this session should be of lower intensity or contain a recovery session.

The athlete should alternate between simulated competitive days and rest and recovery days to maximize her ability to adapt to the competition schedule. Many athletes do not favor free days between competitions because performance during the second day of competition is sometimes not as good as expected. The decrease in performance seems to be based on postcompetition psychological reactions (such as overconfidence, conceit) rather than an accumulation of fatigue. To facilitate the athlete's ability to tolerate the rest days between competitions, the coach can include competition-based microcycles in all macrocycles contained in the competitive phase of the annual training plan. If the competitive phase is short, the coach can introduce the competitive model during the last part of the preparatory phase.

Although the competitive model can be used to prepare for a major competition, the athlete likely will participate in several additional competitions. Such competitions may occur on a different day of the microcycle than the major competition. The microcycle model usually should not be modified in these situations, especially if the athlete is likely to qualify for the major competition.

The main goal of the microcycles preceding the major competition is to allow the athlete to completely recover from the physiological and psychological stress of training so that peak performance occurs (for more information on peaking, see chapter 7). The athlete can peak by reducing the training load by approximately 40% to 60% across the microcycle (2) before the major competition. Another strategy is to manipulate the training load across two microcycles. In this situation peaking can be accomplished in 8 to 14 days with gradual reductions in training load. Several examples of peaking strategies are presented in chapter 7.

Recovery and Regeneration Microcycles

Elevations in preparedness and performance occur when fatigue is dissipated (19, 20, 24). One might argue that fatigue management is central to the actual training process (20). If fatigue is managed appropriately, a supercompensation effect will occur, elevating preparedness and performance.

Recovery and regeneration can be integrated into a microcycle in several fashions. For example, including rest days, variations in training intensity, and alternative methods of training can facilitate recovery between or within training sessions (20). A regeneration microcycle should be incorporated at the end of a macrocycle. Figure 8.25 presents a classic 4:1 (loading and unloading) step paradigm in which week 4 is an unloading or regeneration microcycle. These microcycles can be structured the same as a training microcycle, but the intensity, density, or frequency of training can be reduced.

Another restoration microcycle structure contains actual training sessions that are designed to stimulate recovery. These sessions can contain a slightly longer warm-up and a relatively short training session consisting of either light work applicable to the sport or complementary activities followed by a series of activities designed to facilitate recovery (see chapter 5 for more details). Table 8.2 gives an example regeneration session and several different regeneration techniques.

Regeneration microcycles are integral parts of the annual plan and are particularly important during the competition phase. During the competition phase of training for many sports, 2 or 3 microcycles can be included that contain a series of competitions. The use of many competitions will increase the amount of fatigue experienced by the athlete. To enable the athlete to tolerate this high amount of physiological and psychological stress, regeneration and recovery microcycle structures should be used.

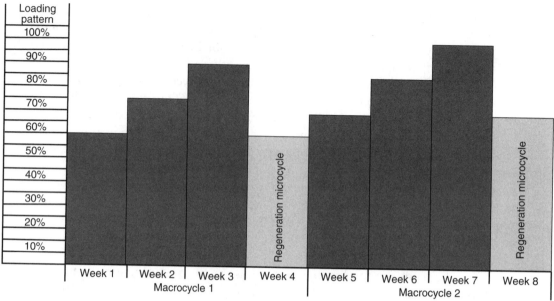

Figure 8.25 Placement of a recovery and regeneration microcycle.

Table 8.2 Regeneration Session

	Description	Duration (min)
Warm-up	General warm-up	10
	Specific warm-up	20
Training session	Low-intensity work from either the sport being trained for or a complementary activity	30
Cool-down	Static stretching	10
Regeneration	Warm water immersion • 37-39 °C for the whole body • 37-40 °C for the legs • 37-45 °C for the arms or hands	10-20
Alternative regeneration techniques	Total body massage	10-20
	Sauna • 60-140 °C; 5-15% humidity	30
	Contrast therapy • Thermotherapy: 37-44 °C • Cryotherapy: 7-20 °C	20 4 1
	Cold water immersion • 12-18 °C	20

An example of a regeneration microcycle is presented in figure 8.26. This microcycle is designed to remove physiological and psychological fatigue, aid in the replenishment of energy substrates, and supercompensate the athlete at the end of the cycle.

Quantifying Training

The coach and athlete should use objective methods to plan training intensities or loads. Too often training programs are based on subjective indicators. In the best-

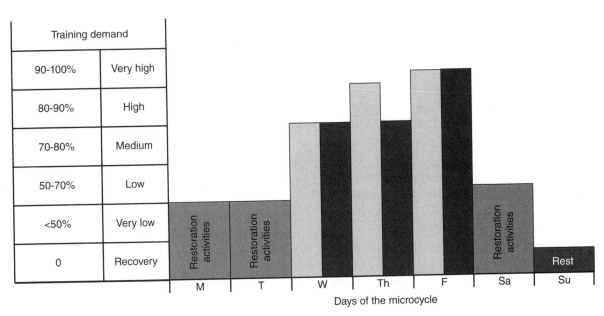

Figure 8.26   Regeneration microcycle.

case scenario the plan alternates heavy training days with easy days throughout the year. In the worst-case scenario, the plan uses a "no pain, no gain" philosophy and the loading or intensity of training is constantly very high, which ultimately leads to overtraining and high levels of fatigue.

Although few coaches quantify the loading parameters contained in their training programs, quantifying training is one of the most important parts of developing a training plan. In individual sports, such as track and field, swimming, and rowing, volume is often quantified using mileage (kilometers or miles per microcycle, macrocycle, or year of training). In the throwing events, volume may be quantified as the number of throws completed in the individual cycles. Intensity may be quantified as distance jumped or thrown, the percentage of maximum speed, or maximal power output or heart rate. In strength training, the volume of training is quantified as the **volume load** or tonnage lifted, whereas intensity is determined by the athlete's maximal strength or **1RM** (see chapter 10 for more information). **Training intensity** and **volume** are rarely quantified in team sports, which makes it difficult for coaches to monitor the athletes' training.

The quantification of training is often a difficult undertaking, which is easier to accomplish when the training program is designed for an athlete with whom the coach is very familiar. The coach should know the athlete's training background, abilities to tolerate physiological and psychological stress, strengths and weakness, and training environment. Because these characteristics are different for each athlete, training programs should not be shared by athletes. Understanding the athlete's needs and abilities is an essential component of designing a training plan. The intensity of training should be planned using established equations, and the volume of training should be quantified.

In all programs, the training intensity throughout the microcycle must be varied to enhance the athlete's physiological adaptation to the training load and stimulate regeneration after a training session. To quantify the training intensity, the coach may identify three to five training intensities based on the physiological demands of the sport. Each intensity must correlate with the activity's rhythm or tempo, the training type and method, and the athlete's heart rate response (plus or minus a few beats per minute). The intensity zones should be determined according to the bioenergetic characteristics of the sport or the percentage contribution of the various energy systems. After gathering this information, the coach can plan the percentage of each intensity level contained in the microcycle (table 8.3). The highest percentage of the training load should target the development of the dominant ability and the bioenergetic characteristics of the sport.

Tables 8.3 and 8.4 show this concept applied in a microcycle for rowing. In table 8.3, intensities 3 and 4 comprise 70% of the total training load for the competitive phase of the annual training plan. The same two intensities dominate the example in table 8.4, which shows the link between the theoretical concept and its application in the training of rowers.

If an objective means of quantifying training does not exist, the coach can subjectively divide skills and training into more difficult (pace of game, race, or match) and less difficult stratifications. The pace of the game, race, or match should be simulated with intensity number 2; this intensity should be used for at least 50% of the training time per week.

Table 8.3 Example of Intensity Zones for Rowing

	INTENSITY ZONES				
	1	**2**	**3**	**4**	**5**
Characteristics	Speed endurance	Power endurance	Specific racing endurance	Aerobic endurance of medium distance	Aerobic endurance of long distance
Rhythm of activity	Maximum	Very high, greater than the racing rate and rhythm	Rapid, the optimal rhythm and ratios	Moderate, lower than the racing rhythm	Low
Stroke rate	>40	37-40	32-36	24-32	<24
Type of training	Starts and sprints up to 15 s; rest 1.5 min	Repetitions of 250-1,000 m; rest 3-10 min	Races and controlled racing. Interval training of 3-4 min; rest 4-5 min	Long repetitions; variable rate and power. Long-distance rowing with sprints of 30-60 s	Long-distance (steady-state) technique
Heart rate (beats/min)	>180	170-180	150-170	120-150	<120
Bioenergetics (%)					
Anaerobic	80	65	25	1%	5
Aerobic	20	35	75	85	95
Total training volume (%)	10		70		20

Table 8.4   Example of Using Numeric-Based Intensity Zones to Construct a Microcycle for Rowing

Time		Mon.	Tues.	Wed.	Thurs.	Fri.	Sat.	Sun.
9:30-11:30 a.m.	Intensity	4	3	5	4	3	4	
	Distribution (km)	24	20	24	24	20	24	
	Training	Long repetitions: 8 × 2 km	Interval training: 10 × 3 min, work/rest ratio 1:1	Aerobic endurance, long distance	Variable rate, variable power	Interval training: 6 × 3 min, work/rest ratio 1:1.5	Aerobic endurance: 3 × 1 min	
16:00-18:00	Intensity	2	4		1	4	2	
	Distribution (km)	20	24		20	24	20	
	Training	Model training: 1 × 250 m, 2 × 500 m, 2 × 1,000 m, 2 × 500 m, 2 × 250 m	Variable rate, variable power		Sprints: 500 total strokes, rest 1.5 min	Long reps: 3 × 6 km, rest 5 min	Model training: 1 × 250 m, 6 × 1,000 m, 2 × 500 m, 2 × 250 m	
	Weight training	Maximum strength	Muscular endurance		Maximum strength	Muscular endurance		

A better quantification system contains five intensities, in which 5 is a low intensity to use for compensation between other intensities or to facilitate supercompensation. An example of a five-category stratification follows:

1. Maximum intensity
2. Higher than the pace of the game, race, or match
3. Pace of the game, race, or match
4. Lower than the pace of the game, race, or match
5. Compensation

In either case, the intensity higher than the pace of the game, race, or match is dominated by anaerobic energy supply, whereas aerobic energy supply dominates intensities that are below game, race, or match pace.

Whether using objective or subjective methods to quantify training, the coach should follow the correct sequence when planning the microcycle. The first step is to plan the intensity zones for each day of the week and indicate this on the training plan (table 8.4). Intensity zones should be chosen for each day of the week to provide variations in intensities, type of work, or energy system targeted. After this step of the planning process is completed, the training plan should be developed (step 2). For the best results, the coach should include several variables of work for each intensity, irrespective of whether this refers to technical, tactical, or physical training. Each plan should include one to three intensity symbols, which means it is possible to train at least two types of work that tax the same energy system. This suggestion is mostly valid for sports of high technical and tactical complexity. An example for a team sport illustrates this sequence. Table 8.5 is an example of a method for quantifying training; whereas table 8.6 is an example of how to plan intensity zones.

Table 8.5 Quantification of Training for Team Sports

	INTENSITY ZONES				
	1	**2**	**3**	**4**	**5**
Characteristics of training	T: complex; TA: lactic acid tolerance training	T/TA: suicide drills	TA: $\dot{V}O_2$max	T/TA: phosphagen	T: skills: accuracy in shooting, serving, passing
Duration	30-60 s	20-30 s	3-5 min	5-15 s	10 min (several bouts)
Rest interval (min)	3-5	3	2-3	1-2	1
Heart rate (beats/ min)	>180	>180	>170	>170	120-150
Bioenergetics (%)					
Anaerobic	80	90	40	90	10
Aerobic	20	10	60	10	90
Total training volume (5)	40		20	20	20

Note: T = technical; TA = tactical. During the rest interval, athletes can practice technical skills of low intensity (e.g., shooting the basketball).

Table 8.6 Example of Alternating Intensities During a Microcycle for a Team Sport

DAY						
Mon.	**Tues.**	**Wed.**	**Thurs.**	**Fri.**	**Sat.**	**Sun.**
3	2	4	3	4	5	
1	5	5	5	1		
5			2	5		

Note: Several intensities are planned for a given day.

Alternating Intensity and Energy System Focus During a Microcycle

Alternating training intensities during a microcycle is one of the most effective methods to prevent exhaustion, staleness, and **overtraining**. The higher the **intensity** or **power** output of the activity, the greater the reliance on anaerobic energy supply (phosphagen, **fast glycolytic**, and **slow glycolytic**). Thus, a plan that modulates the intensity of training will target a specific energy system, thus facilitating recovery and regeneration or stimulating adaptation. The structure of this variation will be dictated by the phase of training (preparatory vs. competitive) and the need to supercompensate a specific energy system prior to competition. This is best accomplished through creating microcycle variations based on the interaction of science and training methodology. A plan that is appropriately varied will greatly increase the athlete's probability of reaching peak performance at the appropriate time.

For most sports, the energy demand of the activity preferentially targets at least two energy systems (12, 20). Although the primary energy system targeted can be isolated, all of the energy systems are active at the same time and the intensity of the activity (i.e., power output) will dictate which energy systems are preferentially targeted (3). Therefore, a high intensity will increase the influence of the phosphagen and fast glycolytic systems, whereas a lower intensity will increase the emphasis on the slow glycolytic and oxidative systems (20). If the competition depletes the athlete's energy reserves, training intensity during the postcompetitive training days should be reduced. Reducing the intensity of training will dissipate cumulative **fatigue**, thus creating a microcycle that induces recovery and regeneration and thus prepares the athlete for subsequent training.

Although it is important to alternate work and regeneration, it is not always necessary for the athlete to be completely recovered for the next bout of training. For example, during the preparatory phase of training, when the major focus is to develop a strong physiological foundation, the athlete will not fully recover and performance will not supercompensate. When the training demand is lowered in later unloading microcycles, the athlete's level of preparedness will be elevated and performance will increase. Therefore, during the preparatory phase of training, the plan can include developmental and shock microcycles without allowing the athlete enough time to remove all of the accumulated fatigue. This process will challenge the athlete's physiological systems and result in greater performance improvements after future unloading microcycles. As a competition approaches, the fatigue generated in the preparatory phase can be reduced by alternating training intensities, thus stimulating physiological adaptations, removing fatigue, and allowing physical parameters to supercompensate.

Alternating the focus on intensity and energy systems can be very difficult with complex sports (such as team sports) in which multiple energy systems play a large role in performance and the technical and tactical skills are very intricate. Such activities can require the athlete to maximize strength, speed, and high-intensity endurance to be successful. Thus, planning involves a conundrum in which many tasks must be trained to meet the demands of the sport without inducing overtraining. The best approach is to vary intensities of training, thus changing the bioenergetic targets of training, to develop multiple facets of the athlete's physiology. A two-step process can be used to vary training intensities in an attempt to target specific energy systems.

The first step is to classify all the skills and types of training according to the energy systems that are taxed. Table 8.7 gives an example of how one might classify skills. Although table 8.7 can be used as a guideline for classifying skills, it may be warranted to systematically classify the skills and biomotor abilities that are germane to the sport. One method for planning the daily training session is to target a specific energy system with all skills and physical training activities. Conversely, the daily session can target one training option and leave the balance of the other activities for other days.

The second step is to plan a microcycle that alternates the training options from table 8.7 to target specific energy systems. The alterations in training loads coupled with appropriate nutrition will allow the athlete to restore energy sources, facilitating physiological adaptations that will eventually increase performance.

In terms of microcycles that alternate energy systems, these types of training cycles are not planned throughout the annual plan. During some phases of training fatigue must be dissipated to stimulate supercompensation, whereas in other phases high levels of fatigue are generated to challenge the athlete's physiology to adapt. Even though the training options are alternated in these microcycles, it is likely that the training demand will create a large amount of fatigue, which will decreases preparedness and ultimately suppress the supercompensation effect.

Several examples of how to manipulate the training demand are presented in this chapter (see the figures in the following sections). Alternating the training demand will challenge the athlete on some training days, which will produce a high level of fatigue, whereas on other days fatigue will be removed in response to a less-challenging training bout. Each sample microcycle contains a diagram of the dynamics of fatigue or supercompensation in response to various training sessions.

Team sports are very complex, and a single training session for these sports will stress multiple energy systems as well as the neuromuscular system (technique, maximum speed, strength and power). Figure 8.27 gives an example of how the microcycle can be varied. Monday's session taxes the neuromuscular, phosphagen, and glycolytic

Table 8.7 Classification of Skills and Physical Training for Alternating Energy Systems

ENERGY SYSTEM					
Phosphagen		**Glycolytic**		**Oxidative**	
Technical skills	1-10 s	Technical skills	10-60 s	Technical skills	Long duration
Tactical skills	5-10 s	Tactical skills	10-60 s	Tactical skills	Medium to long duration
Maximum speed		Speed training	10-60 s	Aerobic endurance	
Power training	Short duration	Power endurance		Muscle endurance	Medium to long duration
Maximum strength	1-2 sets with long rest intervals	Muscle endurance			

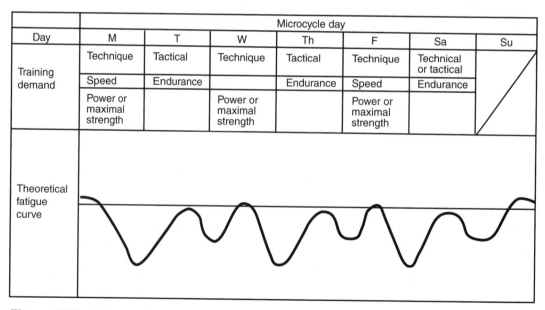

	Microcycle day						
Day	M	T	W	Th	F	Sa	Su
Training demand	Technique	Tactical	Technique	Tactical	Technique	Technical or tactical	
	Speed	Endurance		Endurance	Speed	Endurance	
	Power or maximal strength		Power or maximal strength		Power or maximal strength		
Theoretical fatigue curve							

Figure 8.27 Microcycle to be used at the end of the preparatory phase of training for a team sport.

energy systems. Activities involving speed, power, and maximum strength training performed for short durations rely on ATP-PCr as fuel. However, a large volume of these activities can cause significant glycolytic stress and can deplete glycogen stores. Depending on the volume and intensity of training, the rate of recovery from Monday's workout should be relatively quick, allowing the athlete to perform Tuesday's training session without much fatigue.

In a traditional plan in which the athlete experiences high levels of physiological stress almost every day, the demanding session occurring on Monday in figure 8.27 could nearly deplete the glycogen stores and produce a high level of accumulated fatigue. Alternating training intensities may help the athlete better manage this fatigue. For example, in figure 8.27 Monday is a training day with a high amount of physiological stress, whereas Tuesday's training session contains tactical and endurance training performed at a much lower intensity. The remainder of the microcycle alternates training stressors that modulate fatigue (or preparedness).

Another example of how one might alternate training stressors during a microcycle is presented in figure 8.28. This figure presents a hypothetical model for a sport in which speed and power are dominant. Speed and power training occurs on the same day as power endurance training, which is marked by repeating power exercises 10 to 25 times per set. Two high-intensity training days in which the phosphagen and glycolytic systems are taxed precede a training day that focuses on tempo training and the development of endurance.

Figure 8.29 is a microcycle for a sport that is dominated by aerobic endurance capacity and thus relies predominantly on **oxidative metabolism**. The training options in this plan tax the same energy system in the same day. The plan simultaneously includes types of strength training specific to endurance sports that tax the energy system on the particular day. Consequently, muscular endurance or high-volume (many repetitions) strength training is performed after the endurance training bout. Higher-intensity activities (maximal strength or power endurance training) occur on days that specifically tax the phosphagen and glycolytic systems. This type of targeted training is sometimes termed ergogenesis or ergogenic training.

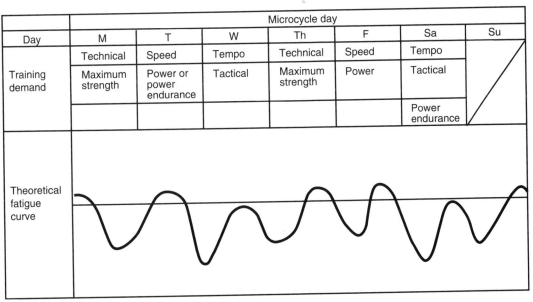

	Microcycle day						
Day	M	T	W	Th	F	Sa	Su
Training demand	Technical	Speed	Tempo	Technical	Speed	Tempo	
	Maximum strength	Power or power endurance	Tactical	Maximum strength	Power	Tactical	
						Power endurance	
Theoretical fatigue curve							

Figure 8.28 Alternating training stress for a sport that requires speed and power.

Figure 8.30 shows a microcycle structure for an endurance sport in which competition lasts between 4 and 6 min. In this example, high-intensity endurance that stresses both the phosphagen and glycolytic systems is important for a successful performance. Days that target the development of high-intensity endurance (i.e., produce significant glycolytic stress) are followed by low-intensity aerobic work that is used as a compensation activity. The goal is to develop the ability to produce high levels of lactic acid formation and then buffer this lactic acid and remove it quickly, inducing a faster recovery rate. In this example, days that follow high-intensity inter-

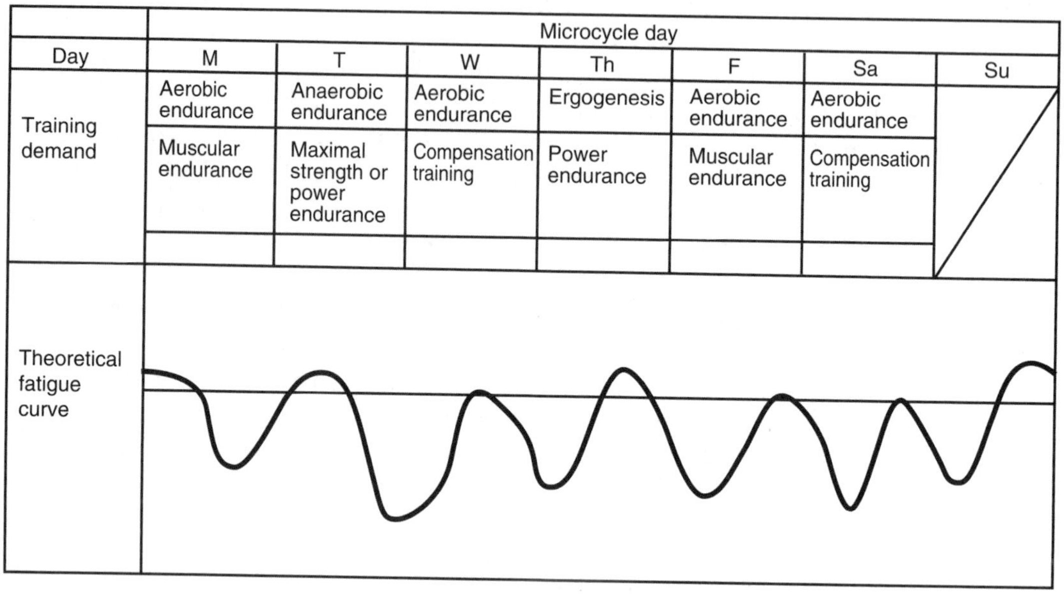

Figure 8.29 Alternating training stress for a sport that requires endurance.

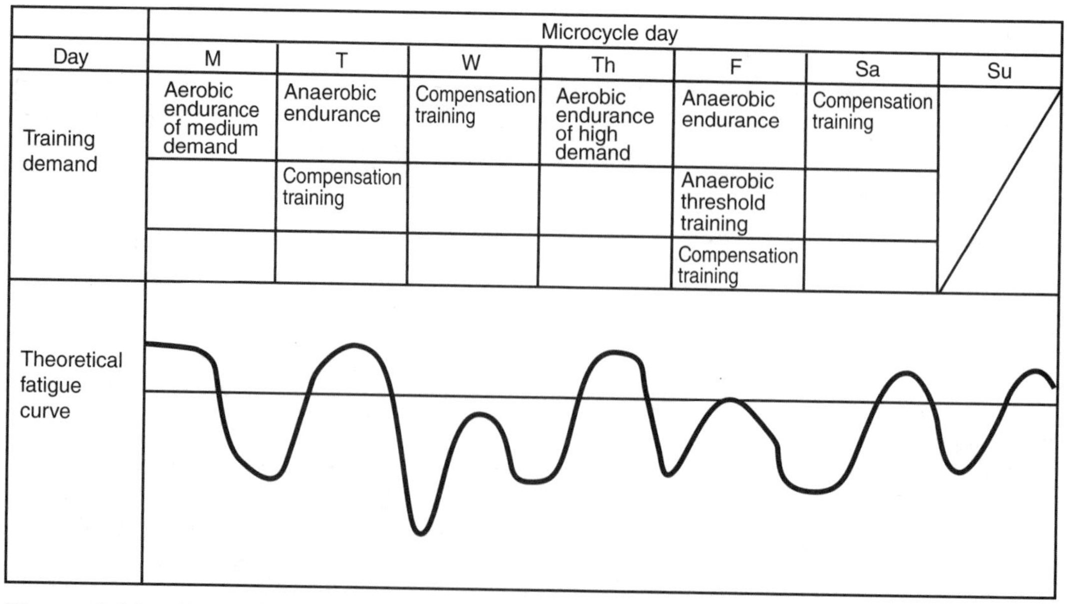

Figure 8.30 Alternating training stress for a sport that requires endurance for 4 to 6 min.

val training are always followed by compensation training days designed to enhance recovery.

MACROCYCLE

The term *macro* is derived from the Greek word *makros,* meaning "large." A training **macrocycle** is a phase that lasts 2 to 7 weeks. A macrocycle contains two to seven microcycles. The microcycle is used to plan for the immediate future, whereas the macrocycle projects the structure of a training program several weeks in advance. Therefore, one could think of the macrocycle as the general structure of training and the microcycle as the exact method used to accomplish the targeted goals.

Duration of a Macrocycle

Although the macrocycle plans used to prepare athletes for various sporting activities may have some similarities, it is likely that each sport will have requirements that must be addressed. These requirements will in most instances dictate the macrocycle structure. The loading paradigm and the duration of the macrocycles may be different depending on the sport and the phase of training. Therefore, the macrocycle must be carefully crafted to meet the individual athlete's training objectives. Table 8.8 presents a macrocycle structure for the strength training plan of an American university women's soccer team.

When establishing the length of the macrocycle, the coach must consider the phase of training. During the preparatory phase, the macrocycle is generally longer (4-7 weeks) than those in the competition phase to address the objectives of this portion of the annual training plan. In this context the macrocycle should be long enough

Table 8.8 Macrocycle Structures for the Strength Training of an American University Women's Soccer Team

Month	May	June	July	August		September	October	November
Phase	PREPARATORY			PRECOMPETITIVE		COMPETITIVE		
Focus	Strength endurance	Strength	Power	Technique	Maintenance	Reconditioning	Maintenance	Peaking
Number of microcycles	4	4	5	2	3	2	4	3
Emphasis on training objectives								
Muscular endurance	High	Moderate	Low	–	Low	High	Low	–
Strength	Moderate	High	Moderate	Low	Low	Moderate	Low	Low
Power	Low	Moderate	High	Moderate	Low	Low	Moderate	Low
Speed	–	Low	Moderate	High	Moderate	Moderate	Moderate	Moderate

to develop biomotor abilities, technical skills, or tactical elements. Therefore, one method for determining a macrocycle's length is the time necessary to perfect an ability or its components.

The macrocycle structure is also influenced by the competitive schedule. During the competitive phase of training in individual sports, macrocycles are structured in shorter blocks in accordance with the competitive schedule and contain two to four 1-week microcycles. Competitions should fall at the end of the macrocycle because this will give the coach information about the athlete's level of development and progress toward training objectives. If the competition phase contains several competitions during the month (possibly as many as eight), as typically seen in team sports, the coach must decide which competitions are the most important. In this type of macrocycle structure, less emphasis is placed on the minor competitions because they are simply used for training and to provide feedback on the athlete's preparation for the major contest. Therefore, the length of the macrocycle should allow for the last microcycle to lead into the major competition.

Another way to classify the macrocycle is based on the objective of training (24, 25). Zatsiorsky (24) suggested that there are three basic classifications for the macrocycle (i.e., mesocycles), called *accumulation, transmutation,* and *realization* macrocycles. The goal of the accumulation macrocycle is to elevate the athlete's potential by increasing her state of conditioning and improving her level of technical proficiency. In the transmutation macrocycle, the conditioning and technical base established in the accumulation phase is used to work on the athlete's preparedness for competitions. After the athlete's preparedness is elevated, the realization macrocycle is used to improve the athlete's competitive performance.

Structural Consideration for a Macrocycle

The development of the macrocycle structure is based on the objectives, the phase of training, and the competition schedule. Therefore, the macrocycles of the annual training plan should vary according to the training objectives for each phase of the plan (i.e., preparatory, competitive, and transition phases).

Macrocycles for the Preparatory Phase

The main objective of the preparatory phase is to induce physiological, psychological, and technical adaptations that will serve as the foundation for competitive performances. A disturbing trend in some sports is the use of year-round competitive schedules. This schedule will limit the athlete's performance capacity because too little time is dedicated to the preparatory phase of training. In an appropriately constructed annual training plan, the preparatory phase is a crucial part of the plan and is the foundation for competitive success.

Developmental and shock microcycles are well suited for the preparatory phase of training. The training demand of developmental macrocycles usually follows the step-loading method. Figure 8.31 depicts two step-loading examples, the 4:1 and the 3:1 loading patterns. In the 4:1 loading pattern, the training load is increased across four microcycles and unloading or regeneration is planned for the last microcycle. This loading pattern works well during the early part of the preparatory phase when the athlete is attempting to develop a physiological base, correct technical habits, and learn new technical or tactical skills. A 3:1 loading pattern is also well suited for the preparatory phase and is probably the most common loading plan. This loading pattern fits well with the body's natural biocycles (11, 16, 23, 24). The 3:1 loading pattern contains three microcycles with increasing workloads followed by a regeneration or unloading microcycle. If the level of fatigue is very high after the third microcycle, the load used in the fourth microcycle can be decreased even further or a second regeneration microcycle can be used to create a 3:2 loading pattern.

Shock macrocycles can be used in the preparatory phase to induce significant improvements in performance once fatigue is dissipated. Figure 8.32 shows two

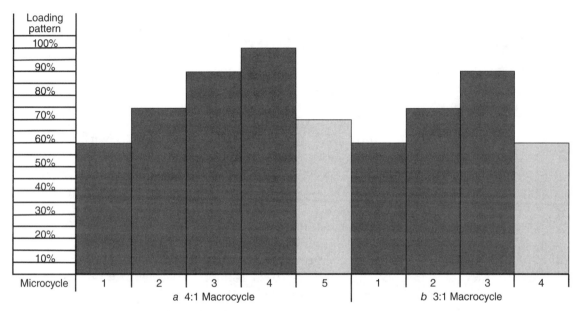

Figure 8.31   Two examples of developmental macrocycles: *(a)* 4:1 model and *(b)* 3:1 model.

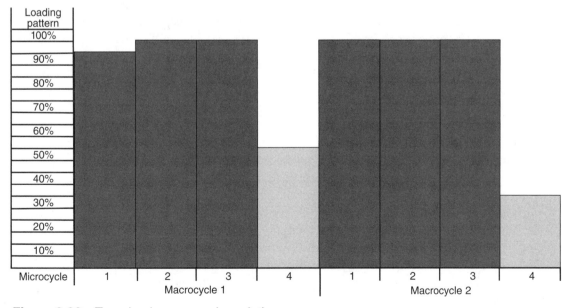

Figure 8.32   Two shock macrocycle variations.

examples of shock macrocycles in which high-demand microcycles are repeated three times. Performance improvements in this type of macrocycle are delayed: The higher the training stress during these macrocycles, the longer the time before the athlete shows improvement in performance or a supercompensation affect (7, 16, 20). For example, Halson and colleagues (7) reported that after 2 weeks of very high loading demands, 2 weeks of unloading are needed to return performance capacity to preloading levels. It is likely that additional unloading or regeneration weeks are needed for performance to supercompensate. Therefore, it may be appropriate to plan a regeneration or transition macrocycle after shock macrocycles to facilitate the supercompensation of performance. These types of macrocycles will help dissipate fatigue to promote adaptive responses to the shock macrocycle.

Macrocycles for the Competitive Phase

The dynamics of the competitive macrocycles are dictated by the competition calendar. Because of this relationship, there are numerous sport-specific macrocycle structures.

A steady loading pattern should be used throughout the competitive season with team sports in which there are one or two competitions per week. Within this structure, microcycles will vary in intensity and volume, especially microcycles that contain competitions. In these microcycles, the contests will be interspersed with regeneration days and training days that fluctuate between various levels of demand (low to high). To address the unique loading demands of team sports, coaches should consider using various microcycle loading patterns.

With individual sports the macrocycle loading pattern can be 4:1, 3:1, 2:1, 1:1, 2:2, or any other combination. One consideration regarding the structure of the macrocycle is the number of peaks contained in the cycle. For example, if two peaks or important competitions occur within the macrocycle, it may be warranted to plan for them to occur at the beginning and end of the macrocycle (figure 8.33). In the macrocycle presented in figure 8.33, the qualification competition occurs on July 9 and the main competition on August 14. No other competitions are planned in the microcycles between these two important dates. The results of the qualification contest are used as markers of progress toward the major contest and serve as guidelines for modifying before the major contest. If additional contests are planned between these two contests, this approach is impossible because the focus will be on performing well instead of training. Additionally, if the number of contests is increased during this macrocycle the athlete would experience a significant increase in fatigue, which might impede performance in the major contests at the end of the cycle.

In figure 8.33 there are two competitions, which are separated by several microcycles. The first microcycle after the qualifying competition is a regeneration microcycle designed to dissipate fatigue and allow the athlete to recover from the stress of the first competition. The next three microcycles are used to fine-tune technical skills, tactical strategies, and physical capacity. These microcycles are designed to build the athlete's confidence in his abilities and develop the motivational levels necessary to produce a maximal performance at the major event on August 14. The 8 to 14 days prior to the August 14 competition are used for peaking (see figure 7.3 on p. 190). During this time the training load is decreased to elevate preparedness as a result of decreased fatigue. If the peaking phase is structured correctly, performance will be significantly elevated.

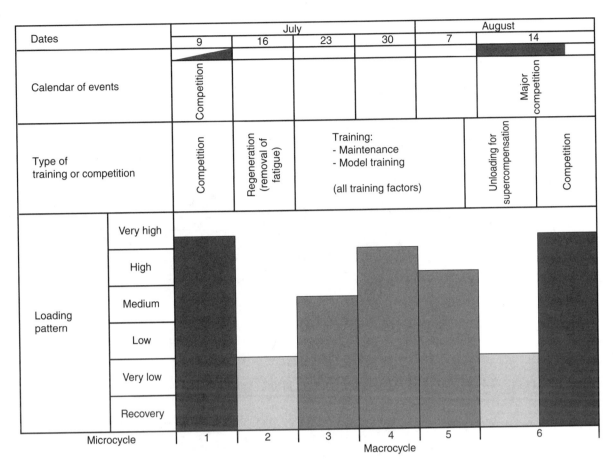

Figure 8.33   Macrocycle structure for two important competitions.

Macrocycles for Unloading and Tapering for Competitions

The goal of unloading and tapering macrocycles is to remove fatigue to stimulate a supercompensation of performance. Optimal taper or unloading durations appear to be between 8 and 14 days and require a decrease in training load of about 40% to 60% (see chapter 7) (2). Four strategies for decreasing the load are available: linear, slow decay, fast decay, or step taper (14). The type and duration of taper are largely determined by the training load encountered in the weeks before the taper period. For example, if the training load is high, the taper or unloading period may require a longer duration and a greater reduction in training load. The basic tapering strategies appear to be effective in many sports including weightlifting, track and field, and swimming. Additional information on tapering strategies can be found in chapter 7.

Macrocycles for the Transition Phase

The transition phase is an important part of the annual training plan. A basic macrocycle structure for a transition phase is presented in figure 8.34. More details about the structure of the transition phase are provided in chapter 6.

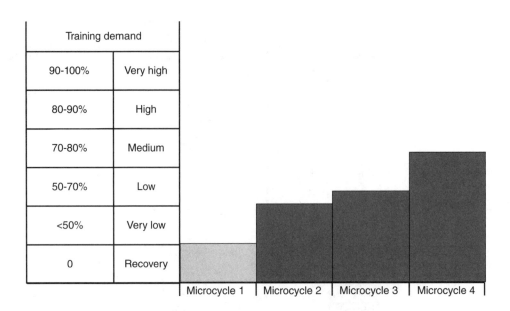

Training demand	
90-100%	Very high
80-90%	High
70-80%	Medium
50-70%	Low
<50%	Very low
0	Recovery

Microcycle 1 | Microcycle 2 | Microcycle 3 | Microcycle 4

Figure 8.34 Loading pattern for a transition macrocycle.

SUMMARY OF MAJOR CONCEPTS

The microcycle is the most important and functional part of the annual training plan. However, the macrocycle is only useful for dividing the annual training plan into smaller segments. Ultimately, the macrocycle directs the focus of the microcycle to fulfill the goals of the annual training plan.

A microcycle must provide variation in the training load (volume and intensity) to facilitate recovery. The technique used to create this variation in training load is based on the scientific principles related to the ability of the body to recover from training stress. The application of these microcycle models is based on many physiological factors that relate to the body's ability to tolerate, recover from, and adapt to training stress. If the training loads are varied appropriately, the athlete will be able to recover from and tolerate the training demand, which ultimately improves performance.

It is important to vary the loading patterns between the microcycles. This allows the training load to be varied across the macrocycle so the athlete can deal with accumulated fatigue and avoid overtraining. The coach must appropriately sequence developmental, shock, and regeneration microcycles. The shock microcycle should not be overused, because it creates large amounts of physiological and psychological stress coupled with high levels of fatigue. Overuse of the shock microcycle may increase the athlete's risk for overtraining.

The microcycle and macrocycle are structured to direct training so that the athlete will achieve a physiological and psychological peak at the appropriate time. The training plan should be based on the concepts of bioenergetic specificity of training, muscle physiology, hormonal physiology, and the body's response to training stress. To better guide the training program, the coach should consider quantifying the training stress with the numerical intensity and volume system outlined in this chapter.

CHAPTER

9

WORKOUT PLANNING

Workout planning has existed since the ancient Olympic Games. Evidence for this can be found in several manuals on planning and training written by Flavius Philostratus (AD 170-245) for Greek athletes. Although most of his work has been destroyed, his surviving manuals, the *Handbook for the Athletic Coach* and *Gymnasticus*, teach the reader how to train for competition and the importance of recovery. He suggests that the coach "should be a psychiatrist with considerable knowledge in anatomy and heritage." Even in ancient times, science was the foundation for the development of the training plan.

The earliest evidence of an organized training session plan is mentioned in *The Aeneid*, the great work of the Roman poet Virgil (Publius Virgilius Maro, 70-19 BC). In this poem, Virgil refers to the trip of Aeneas, a Trojan, who after the destruction of Troy, about 1000 BC, decided to migrate to Italy. During the trip Aeneas and his crew had to stop in several Mediterranean islands where they were challenged by the locals to rowing races. Virgil described how Aeneas organized a training session in which the rowers did some exercises, which might be considered a warm-up, and then proceeded to row for a while. After they had completed the rowing portion of their training session, they lifted stones to improve their strength, and then they concluded the training session with a bath and massage.

What is interesting about this passage is that the organization of the training session that Virgil describes is very similar to the composition of a modern training session. Even more interesting is that the Aeneas integrated strength training into the training session, which in modern times is still a topic of debate. It is clear that training is an evolutionary process that spans back to ancient times and is in continual flux. This evolution continues as a result of the tireless work of sport scientists who develop the scientific foundations of training and the training theorists and coaches who use this knowledge to continually improve the training process.

IMPORTANCE OF PLANNING

Planning is probably the most important tool a coach has. By using a methodical and scientifically based procedure, the coach can structure a training process that will allow the athlete to optimize performance at the appropriate times. The coach's ability to effectively guide the training process is dictated by her knowledge about the physiological responses of the body to training stimuli and her planning and organizational skills.

The organization and planning of training should be considered an art that is based on science (12, 69, 72). The implementation of a well-organized and scientifically based training plan eliminates random and aimless training practices, which are sometimes still practiced by ill-informed coaches. A well-devised training plan removes poor training concepts or philosophies such as "intensity all the way" and "no pain, no gain" and replaces them with practices that are logically devised, meticulously planned, and based on science. The goal of the training plan is to stimulate specific physiological responses according to a planned design so that certain performance outcomes are stimulated at the appropriate time (72). Nothing that occurs during training should happen by accident; responses should occur as a result of the design of the training plan. The old adage that "if you fail to plan, you plan to fail" is true of the training process.

Training consists of introducing a training stimulus, which causes a specific physiological response, and inducing recovery, which allows the athlete to adapt to the training stimulus (56, 72, 78, 79). One might also consider the training process as a fatigue management system in which intense periods of training are interspersed with periods of easier training or rest that are designed to allow the athlete to recover and adapt. The coach must consider how much fatigue a certain training intervention may stimulate, how the athlete will respond to that fatigue, and how that training stimulus relates to the training plan. The coach must try to predict the athlete's physiological and psychological responses to the training stimuli and the fatigue induced by that stimulus. Central to this prediction is an understanding of the physiological

A coach must have a thorough knowledge of training theory and athlete development to successfully help an athlete reach her potential.

responses to training and how different actions can modulate recovery and stimulate adaptation (see chapter 5). This line of reasoning suggests that it may be best to consider the planning of training as a process in which the training stimulus is systematically and logically manipulated to optimize the physiological adaptations to training. This process should be undertaken in accordance with the demands of the sport being trained for with the express goal of maximizing performance outcomes.

The effectiveness of the training plan is largely dictated by the coach's expertise and experience. The coach must understand many factors related to training theory and the development of athletes. A coach should understand the physiological responses of the body to training and exercise, the recovery process and techniques necessary to induce restoration, nutrition and its importance in training, motor learning and its application to skill development, and the psychological aspects of motivation. The greater the coach's knowledge base, the better prepared he will be to manage the training plan.

Because training is planned in accordance with the athlete's potential and rate of development, the training plan reflects the coach's knowledge base (52). To optimize an athlete's training plan, the coach must examine the athlete's test results, competitive results, progress in all training factors, and competition schedule. The training plan must evolve in accordance with the athlete's rate of progress and the coach's continually expanding knowledge.

PLANNING REQUIREMENTS

To create an effective training plan, the coach must establish a long-term path of development that optimizes the athlete's potential. To help the athlete achieve long-term training goals, the coach must monitor the athlete during training, at competitions, and periodically with specialized tests that can be interpreted and used to adjust the training stimuli.

Develop a Long-Term Plan

It can take 8 to 12 years of dedicated training to maximize an athlete's competitive performance (figure 9.1) (62). A long-term training plan is an essential component of the training process because it guides the athlete's development. A major goal of long-term planning is to facilitate the progressive and continual development of the athlete's skills and performance (52, 56). To accomplish this goal the coach must consider the athlete's rate of improvement and the athlete's potential to achieve performance and training goals. The long-term training plan is at best a prognostication (52), and the ultimate success of the plan depends on the coach's ability to forecast future developments and implement appropriate training objectives at the correct times.

Central to the athlete's success is the ability of the coach to design and implement annual training plans that fit into the context of the long-term training structure. The training plan must provide for continuity between the **microcycles** and **macrocycles** of the **annual** and long-term portions of the training plan. The plan also has to be flexible enough to account for factors like illness, professional business, weather, social issues, and changes to the sport (52). To ensure that the athlete is responding to the training plan and progressing appropriately, the coach must monitor training and performance outcomes throughout the training year, and the plan must include a comprehensive testing program. This type of training approach is appropriate for

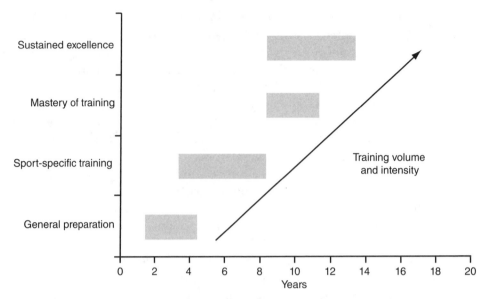

Figure 9.1 Paradigm of the long-term development of athletes.

Adapted, by permission, from A.S. Medvedev, 1986, *Sistema mnogoletnyei trenirovki V tyazheloi atletikye* (Fizkultura I Sport, Publishers), p. 222.

all levels of athletes because it can be tailored to individual athletes and can increase their ability to attain a high level of performance.

Integrate Periodic Testing and Monitoring Programs

An often overlooked but highly important part of the long-term plan is a comprehensive monitoring program in which periodic testing is conducted to track the athlete's development. The inclusion of a monitoring program eliminates the random approach to training that is sometimes present in modern athlete development. An inclusive monitoring program allows the coach to examine the effects of the training program and quantify factors that the scientific literature has shown to be related to performance.

The testing program should be completely integrated into the training plan and contain tests that target the athlete's development (55, 72) and focus on the athlete's objectives (i.e., performance outcomes). For example, a plan designed to monitor a weightlifter should include markers of maximal strength, given that strength is a major factor in weightlifting performance (70). The inclusion of tests that evaluate the isometric rate of force development and peak power output generated during a countermovement and static vertical jumps may be warranted, because recent research suggests that performance in these tests is significantly correlated with weightlifting performance (15, 29). The testing battery for any sport should include tests that reveal the athlete's progress toward his performance goals.

Monitoring should occur continuously and at periodic intervals throughout the training year (72). For example, testing should be conducted at the beginning of each new training phase, whereas daily monitoring of certain factors (e.g., resting heart rate, mood status, sleep patterns) can yield information about the athlete's tolerance for the training stimulus. An often-overlooked tool that can shed substantial light on the athlete's progress is the training log. The training log is a very simple tool to track daily responses to training stimuli; it yields a large amount of information that can give the coach great insight into the athlete's response to the training plan (72). The analysis of daily **training logs** coupled with data collected from specialized tests and performance results will allow the coach to help the athlete maximize her performance gains.

Establish and Emphasize the Main Training Factor

When establishing the training plan, the coach must carefully examine the results of the monitoring program to determine the athlete's weaknesses. Performance results and test data will reveal which training factors have not improved or have deteriorated as a result of the training plan. Training factors that fall behind the athlete's mean development rate are the weakest links in training and must be addressed via a redistribution of training efforts. The coach and athlete must determine the underlying reason for a lack of development. For example, in gymnastics, technical improvement depends on strength development. Thus, if a gymnast is not strong enough to perform a technical skill, the coach should increase training activities designed to improve muscular strength. Once the athlete's areas of weakness are determined, the training program should be designed to target training factors that address the athlete's weaknesses. This change in program focus must be implemented in conjunction with adjustments in volume and intensity of training dictated by the training plan.

TYPES OF TRAINING PLANS

The coach's ability to organize and use appropriate planning tools will dictate the success of the training plan. Many training tools are available, including the individual training session, microcycle, macrocycle, annual training plan, and long-term training plan. *Long-term plans* (8-16 years) are essential for the development of young athletes.

The terms used to describe the planning of training are not consistent throughout the world (22, 38, 43-45, 52, 55, 56, 63, 65, 66, 72, 73). For example, Russian scientists (43-45) and many other authors (22, 68, 72) refer to the annual plan as the **macrocycle** and training phases that range from 4 to 8 weeks as **mesocycles** (22, 38, 78). The current text uses the term **annual training plan** to describe a yearly training program, based upon Philostratus' work on yearly planning.

Annual plans are used as guides or training projections for the year to come and are constructed in the context of the long-term training goals and plans established by the coach. The annual plan is often broken into smaller phases, described by Russian scientists as mesocycles (22, 43-45) or in this text as macrocycles. The macrocycle structure is based on the annual plan and is designed in concert with the development of the **microcycle,** which is the most important functional tool for planning. The microcycle is a short training cycle that can range from 3 to 7 days depending on the phase of training (38, 78, 79).

The establishment of an annual training plan is the second step in the planning process. To effectively establish the annual training plan, the coach must first set long-term training goals and establish a general plan to accomplish those goals. As part of long-term planning, performance and *training objectives* are established for each year of the plan. Once this is established, the individual annual training plans can be created. At this point the annual training plan can be partitioned into macrocycles and microcycles (see chapter 6 for more information). The microcycle structure is the most important part of the plan (see chapter 8 to learn more) and is generally broken into individual training sessions, which are the shortest-term segments of training.

TRAINING SESSION

During an individual training session or lesson, the coach shares knowledge with the athlete, who then attempts to develop one or more training factors. The training session can be classified in several different fashions depending on the tasks and structure of the session.

Training Sessions Classified by Task

The training session can be classified based on the tasks within the session. There are four basic classifications of training sessions: learning, repetition, skill perfection, and assessment.

Learning Session

The athlete's main task in a learning session is to acquire new skills or tactical maneuvers. The coach uses a basic structure to organize this type of session. For example, the coach begins the session by explaining the objectives of the session and then directing the athlete through a warm-up session. After the warm-up, the athlete focuses on acquiring a specific skill set. After completing the main portion of the session, the athlete cools down and the coach gives the athlete pertinent information about her progress toward developing the skill.

Repetition Session

A repetition session is very similar to a learning session in that a specific skill set or tactical maneuver is practiced. The major difference is that during the repetition session, the athlete continues to learn the skill and attempts to improve the skill set.

Skill Perfection Session

The skill perfection session is an extension of the repetition session in that the athlete attempts to improve the overall skill set. The major difference is that at this point the skill has been learned and the athlete now attempts to perfect the skill to maximize performance.

Assessment Sessions

Assessment sessions should be conducted periodically. These sessions can include tests that evaluate the athlete's physiological responses to training and performance, or the sessions can include exhibition or practice competitions to gauge the athlete's preparedness. The results of these sessions can be used to fine-tune an athlete's training or as a tool for selecting athletes for competitions.

Training Sessions Classified by Structure

The coach may organize training sessions in several forms to accommodate individual and groups of athletes.

- **Group Sessions.** The group session is organized for several athletes although not necessarily an entire team. For example, the coach may work with the offensive linemen from an American-style football team or a group of athletes who compete in an individual sport. Although group sessions are not optimal for the individualization of training, they can be an effective tool for developing team spirit, especially before an important competition, and psychological qualities.

• **Individual Sessions.** Individual sessions allow the coach to focus attention on one athlete to address physical or psychological problems. This session provides the coach the opportunity to precisely evaluate the individual athlete and adjust her skill development. These sessions are most appropriate during the preparatory phase of the annual plan. Other types of sessions may be more appropriate during the competitive phase.

• **Mixed Sessions.** A mixed session is a combination of group and individual sessions. In this type of session the whole team may warm up together and then divide into individualized training sessions. After completing the individualized portion of the training session, the athletes come back together to either practice as a team or cool down together. During the cool-down, the coach discusses pertinent issues to reinforce certain aspects of the training session.

• **Free Sessions.** Free sessions minimize a coach's control over the athlete's training and can promote trust and confidence between the athlete and coach.

Sporting News/ZUMA Press/Icon SMI

Incorporating different types of training sessions in a training plan can foster team unity as well as individual growth.

This type of session develops the athlete's conscientious participation in training, stimulates his independence, and may increase his level of maturity. Free sessions can help the athlete develop problem-solving skills that can translate to the competitive arena, where the coach may not always be available. Although this type of session can greatly benefit the athlete, it should be used exclusively with advanced and elite athletes because less developed athletes may not possess the physical and psychological skills to handle such a session.

Sessions generally last approximately 2 hr, although they can last as long as 5 hr depending on the sport and the phase of the annual training plan. Training sessions for team sports are usually consistent in duration, whereas training sessions for individual sports tend to vary in duration. Training sessions fall into three categories of duration: (a) short sessions, which last between 30 and 90 min; (b) medium sessions, which last 2 to 3 hr; and (c) long sessions, which last longer than 3 hr. The duration of the training session depends on the tasks that are required during the session, the activities being performed, and the athlete's physical preparation. A sprinter may perform a training session that lasts only 1 to 1.5 hr during the competitive phase, whereas a marathon runner may undertake a 2 to 2.5 hr session. Training can also be broken into smaller subunits throughout the training day (1-4, 33). When a training session is broken into smaller subunits, the total time spent training may be slightly longer, about 2 to 2.5 hr. Integral to the length of the training session are the number of repetitions being performed and the rest intervals between repetitions and sets.

Structure of Training Sessions

A training session consists of several parts that are sequenced in a way that allows the coach and athlete to follow the principle of a progressive increase and decrease in work across the training session. The training session consists of three or four main structural components. A three-part training session contains a warm-up (preparation), the workout, and a cool-down (conclusion); a four-part training session consists of an introduction, a warm-up, the workout, and a cool-down period.

The selection of which structure to use in a training session depends on the training task and content, the phase of training, and the athlete's training level. The four-part structure is used during the preparatory phase of training for most athletes, especially beginners or novice athletes. Advanced athletes generally use the three-part model, especially during the competitive period of the annual training plan, because these athletes require less explanation and motivation and prefer to dedicate more time to the main body of the training session. The only substantial difference between the two structures is the inclusion of a directed introduction in the four-part model.

Introduction

The introduction of a training session is initiated by gathering the athletes into a group to facilitate communication. Several managerial tasks can be undertaken during this time, such as taking attendance (especially in team sports), relaying any information that is pertinent to the athletes' training or competitive schedules, and explaining the objectives of the training session. When discussing training objectives, the coach should explain the methods that will be used to accomplish these objectives. At this time the coach must attempt to increase the athletes' motivation and focus on the day's training tasks. After the general objectives are explained, the group should be broken into smaller subgroups according to individual or position-based goals.

The length of the introduction depends on the extent of the explanation and the level of the athlete. Beginner and novice athletes will require a 5 to 10 min introduction, but as the athletes become more developed the length of the introduction can be reduced.

The coach must always be prepared and organized when explaining the training objectives; some coaches find it useful to use audiovisual aids or handouts explaining parts of the session. Handouts may cover specific goals or objectives that need to be highlighted in the session and may be considered an expansion of the overall training plan. Athletes should receive the training plan well in advance of the training session so they can familiarize themselves with and prepare for the session. If this is done, the coach will only need to emphasize the important parts of the training session. The training plan should also be posted so that athletes can easily refer to it during the training session. Allowing the athletes to become familiar with the organization of the training session gives them a sense of shared responsibility and increases the likelihood that they will give a focused effort during training. It is also likely that this process will allow the athletes to develop dependability and willpower.

Warm-Up

It is widely accepted by athletes and coaches that a warm-up is essential for optimal performance during either training or competition (8). The contemporary scientific literature supports this contention and suggests that the composition of the warm-up can affect the degree of performance improvement (8, 9, 40, 60, 75-77). It is well documented that an appropriate warm-up will improve muscle function and prepare the athlete for the demands of exercise or competition (75).

Types of Warm-Up Warm-ups can be broadly classified as either passive or active (8, 75). A passive warm-up uses external means (e.g., saunas, hot showers, hot baths, heating pads, or diathermy) to elevate the muscle and core temperature without depleting energy substrates (8). An active warm-up involves using some form of physical activity to elevate muscle and core temperature (75). The active warm-up can be further divided into either general or specific types (65). General warm-up procedures include activities such as jogging, calisthenics, or cycling (8), whereas specific warm-ups use activities specific to the sport (8, 75). For most athletes it is impractical to use passive warm-up procedures; therefore, athletes who are preparing for training or competition typically use active warm-ups.

Structure of a Warm-Up The composition of a warm-up depends on factors such as the activity being prepared for, the athlete's physical capacity, the environmental conditions, and the restrictions of the sporting activity (9). During the general warm-up, the athlete should participate in activities that will elevate muscle and core temperature, such as light jogging, calisthenics, or cycling (75). For most athletes the general warm-up should be performed at low intensity (40-60% $\dot{V}O_2$max) and for 5 to 10 min (9). A low intensity is recommended because this level of activity will increase temperature while limiting the reduction in phosphate degradation (9). Additionally, temperature begins to elevate within 3 to 5 min of the initiation of the warm-up and plateaus at about 10 to 20 min (61). The coach may need to tailor the warm-up to the individual athlete, because poorly conditioned athletes can achieve the same degree of temperature elevation with less warm-up time. Conversely, highly trained athletes may need to increase the duration and intensity of the warm-up to achieve the appropriate elevation of temperature (75). A good guide to determine whether the athlete is adequately warmed up is the presence of perspiration (9, 75).

After completing the general warm-up, the athlete should shift to a specific warm-up. A specific warm-up is designed to prepare the athlete for a certain activity. The warm-up features progressively increasing intensities and may involve postactivation potentiation activities in some instances. For example, the inclusion of short, intense sprint activities has been shown to improve running (28) and kayak performance (10), provided sufficient recovery time is available between the cessation of the warm-up and the competition or training bout. It appears that at least 5 min of recovery is necessary when transitioning from the warm-up to training or competitions (9).

The specific warm-up is important when preparing for competition, because it includes specific skill sets. For example, a gymnast may include certain technical elements in the warm-up in order to prepare physically and mentally for the competition. It has been recommended that an athlete spend 10 to 15 min undergoing specific activities during the warm-up period (35). However, as the complexity of the sport increases, the athlete may need to spend more time on the specific warm-up. An example of a warm-up that contains all of these elements is presented in Table 9.1.

The total warm-up should take between 20 and 45 min and include a general warm-up designed to increase body temperature and a specific warm-up designed to prepare the athlete for his chosen sporting activity. The duration of the warm-up can be increased or decreased depending on the needs of the particular athlete. An athlete who participates in long-duration activities such as endurance running may

Table 9.1 Warm-Up Protocol for a Thrower

Type of warm-up	Activities contained in warm-up	Duration (min)
General	Walking ⇒ lunging ⇒ jogging ⇒ skipping ⇒ shuffling ⇒ carioca ⇒ backward running	10
Specific	Dynamic stretches	5-10
	Throwing drills, low-intensity practice drills	5-10
	Intermittent high-intensity activities (e.g., sprints or vertical jumps)	5-10
Transition to competition or training	Passive recovery	5
Total warm-up time		30-45

require up to 45 min to effectively warm up. Conversely, an athlete who is in poor shape will probably have to decrease the duration of the warm-up. An interesting application of the warm-up is to use longer warm-ups as conditioning tools during the preparatory phase of training.

Physiological Effects A wide variety of physiological factors are altered by an active warm-up (see below) (8, 75). The primary improvement associated with a warm-up is the elevation of muscle and core temperature (8, 9, 75). These elevations in temperature likely increase nerve conduction rate and speed metabolic reactions, which can increase the speed and force of muscle contractions (8, 9, 75). Additionally, as temperature elevates the amount of oxygen that is delivered to the muscle increases (6) as a result of increased vasodilation and blood flow (75). The release of oxygen from both **hemoglobin** and **myoglobin** increases as well, thus increasing oxygen delivery to the working muscle (7, 8).

Although most of the effects of a warm-up are related to increases in temperature, other factors have been suggested to be major contributors to performance improvement. Of particular interest is a postactivation potentiating effect created by the warm-up protocol (47, 71, 76). Postactivation potentiation has been defined as an increased contractile ability of a muscle after a contraction (47). Potentiation effects are most likely related to phosphorylation of myosin regulatory chains (26, 27, 34) or an elevation of calcium (Ca^{2+}) in the cytosol (5). The effects of postactivation potentiation appear to be most prevalent in strength and power performance (47, 57, 71, 76), and some investigators have found that these effects are limited to highly trained athletes (17).

POSSIBLE EFFECTS OF AN ACTIVE WARM-UP

- Increased resistance of muscle and joints
- Increased release of oxygen from hemoglobin and myoglobin
- Increased rate of metabolic reactions
- Increased nerve conduction rate
- Increased thermoregulatory strain
- Increased vasodilation and blood flow to the muscle
- Decreased internal viscosity
- Increased speed and force of muscle contractions
- Increased baseline oxygen consumption
- Increased preparedness for competition or training

Adapted from Bishop 2003 (9) and Woods, Bishop, and Jones 2007 (75).

Psychological Effects Another warm-up-induced response involves the athlete's psychological state (8). Investigators reported a lack of performance improvements when athletes were hypnotized to forget they had gone through a warm-up (42). Other investigators have shown that athletes who used mental imagery as a warm-up tool demonstrated enhanced physiological performance characteristics (41). It appears that the warm-up prepares the athlete not only physiologically but also psychologically.

Injury   It has been well documented that an appropriate warm-up will reduce rates of injury (75). It is likely that the increased temperature that occurs during a warm-up reduces the potential for injury. Support for this contention can be seen in animal studies demonstrating that a 1 °C increase in temperature reduces the occurrence of skeletal muscle injury.

Stretching   Contemporary scientific literature has demonstrated that only dynamic stretching should be performed during the warm-up period and that static stretching should always be avoided (64, 74). Performance decrements associated with static stretching are most noted in strength and power sports, but static stretching decreases performance in all activities (64). The warm-up should include dynamic stretching activities that involve sport-specific movements, whereas static stretching and attempts to increase flexibility should be reserved for the cool-down.

Main Body of the Session

Specific training objectives are addressed in the main body of the training session. This is when the athlete learns new skills and tactical maneuvers, develops specific biomotor abilities, and enhances psychological qualities.

The content of this part of the training session depends on many factors including the athlete's training status, gender, and age; the sporting activity; and the phase of training. The main body of the training session may stress technique while simultaneously focusing on biomotor abilities and psychological traits. For less advanced athletes, the following succession is a general recommendation:

1. Learn and perfect a technical or tactical element.
2. Develop speed and agility.
3. Develop strength.
4. Develop endurance.

The athlete should be well rested when learning new skills, and technical and tactical elements should be addressed early in the main body of the training session. This is particularly important because fatigue will impede the athlete's ability to master motor skills (53). When the athlete is attempting to sequence learning or perfect technical and tactical elements, she should consolidate elements or skills acquired in previous lessons. She should work on perfecting the most important technical elements or skills and then conclude by applying those skills in simulated competitions.

If perfecting a technique requires heavy, fatiguing work, the athlete should perform these activities later in the main body of the training session. It is advisable to precede these activities with speed exercises. This approach may be appropriate for weightlifters or track-and-field athletes.

Activities that are designed to improve speed and agility are usually of a high intensity and are undertaken for relatively short durations. These types of exercise are extremely taxing, and the athlete should perform them when well rested. These activities usually precede both strength and endurance training. However, the focus of the training session will change the relative order of activities. For example, if speed development is the primary focus of the session, then speed-based exercises should immediately follow the warm-up. If coordination or agility is the major focus, it should be addressed early in the training session because fatigue can significantly affect motor skills (53).

Strength-developing exercises usually are placed after technique development and speed exercises. Although this is appropriate for most athletes, it may not be advisable in some cases. For example, several studies suggest that preceding sprint activities with a heavy-load strength exercise (70-90% of 1RM) results in a postactivation potentiation response that manifests itself as an increase in running velocity (47, 76). This technique appears to be very effective at increasing sprint performance if the volume and intensity of the strength activity are not excessive. This method of sequencing strength training only appears to be effective with highly trained athletes (17).

Exercises for developing general or specific endurance should be placed in the last portion of the main body of the training session. These activities generate large amounts of fatigue, which will impede the athlete's ability to acquire or perfect movement or tactical skills, develop speed and agility, and maximize strength development. This sequencing should not be confused with the strategy of practicing certain drills under fatigue to prepare the athlete for a specific game scenario.

If learning is the dominant objective for beginning athletes, the training sequence should be technique, speed, strength, and endurance. However, a single training session should rarely include all four of these elements. This same general sequence for training can be used with elite athletes; however, advanced athletes may benefit from altering the order of training depending on the objectives of the individual training session and the objectives of the microcycle.

The structure of the main body of training will be dictated by the objectives established for the individual training session. Each training session should focus on only two or three objectives, because it is very difficult to effectively target more than three training objectives. Trying to target too many objectives will likely impair the athlete's rate of improvement and may result in the occurrence of overtraining. The individual training session objectives should be linked to the microcycle and macrocycle objectives, the athlete's performance level, and the athlete's potential. Although it may be advisable to plan objectives derived from different training factors (e.g., technical, tactical, physical, or psychological), these factors should be chosen based on the needs of the sport and the abilities of the athlete.

The coach can plan 15 to 20 min of supplementary physical development, or what is sometimes referred to as a conditioning program, to take place after the athlete has achieved the objectives of a given training session. This addition should be considered for less demanding training sessions that do not challenge the athlete. This supplementary development should be specific to the dominant **biomotor abilities** of the sport and should address factors that are limiting the athlete's rate of improvement.

Cool-Down

After the conclusion of the main portion of the training session, the athlete should undergo a cool-down period. The cool-down begins the recovery process and facilitates the body's return to homeostasis. As noted in chapter 5, the postexercise recovery period is a time when the body must remove waste products, replenish energy stores, and initiate tissue repair (37, 65). The body usually does not return to a resting state immediately after a training bout or competition. Depending on the intensity and volume of the session, recovery can require up to 38 hr (39, 48). To initiate and speed

Include a cool-down in your training plans. The cool-down period is an important part of a training workout.

the posttraining or competition recovery, the athlete needs to undergo a structured cool-down session that is designed to stimulate recovery. This portion of the training session is often overlooked, but when implemented correctly it is a very valuable tool for maximizing the recovery from and adaptation to a session.

The cool-down should last around 20 to 40 min and consist of two major parts. The first part entails active recovery exercise and lasts around 10 to 20 min (see chapter 5 for more detail). This active recovery exercise should be of a low intensity (<50% of the athlete's maximal heart rate). Although limited data are available in the scientific literature, it appears that active recovery is much more effective in inducing postexercise recovery than is passive recovery (11, 50, 51). The activities included in the active recovery will depend on the athlete's sport. A cyclist may use a 20 min continuous bout of very low-intensity cycling as the active exercise portion of the cool-down, whereas a soccer player might use very light jogging. A shot putter may use an interval series that contains low-intensity and short-duration jogging after a training session. Regardless of the sport, this portion of the cool-down should be of low intensity and should not overly tax the athlete.

The second part of the cool-down should contain 10 to 20 min of stretching. Although static stretching is not recommended during the warm-up, the cool-down is an excellent time for this activity (35). There are several reasons to include stretching in the postexercise period. First, stretching during the cool-down period can significantly improve flexibility without compromising performance. It appears that the stretching portion of a cool-down can improve range of motion (flexibility) as a result of increased muscle temperature (35). Second, the inclusion of a postexercise stretching protocol has been demonstrated to reduce the onset of muscle soreness that can be stimulated by a training session (16). Third, it has been reported that the combination of active recovery followed by a period of stretching significantly increases the rate of recovery from training and competitive stress (58).

While the athletes are stretching during the cool-down, the coach can ask them whether they achieved the training session's objectives and how they feel about the session; the coach also can use this time to further the athletes' understanding of training.

Duration of Each Part of the Lesson

The length of a training session depends on many factors, but sessions usually last about 2 hr (120 min) (table 9.2). The duration of each component of the session will depend on the athlete's age, gender, stage of development, and athletic experience; the type of session; the characteristics of the sport; and the phase of training in which the session occurs. For example, a novice athlete may not have the fitness to tolerate a 2 hr training session, and so the session will be modified to accommodate the athlete's training status. The coach can use either the three- or four-component structure discussed previously to modulate the time commitment to each element of the training session. Examples of the three- and four-component models are provided in table 9.2.

Fatigue and Methodological Guidelines for Lessons

From a holistic perspective fatigue is a multifactorial response to some sort of exercise, training, or competitive stress (36). Conceptually fatigue is defined as an acute impairment in exercise performance, which ultimately can impair the ability to produce maximal force or control motor function (36, 67). Fatigue can occur in response to an exercise bout or competition when one or more of the following situations arise: a reduction in energy substrate availability, an accumulation of metabolic by-products, neuromuscular transmission failure, impairments in Ca^{2+} handling by the sarcoplasmic reticulum, central disruption, and a response to conscious perception (24, 54, 67). Although there are numerous potential causes of **fatigue**, the two broad categories of peripheral and central fatigue are often discussed (19).

Table 9.2 Durations (Given in Minutes) for Each Part of a 2 Hr Training Session

Training session parts	Four-part training session	Three-part training session
Introduction	5	
Preparation	30	30
Main body	65	70
Conclusion	20	20
Total time	120	120

Peripheral fatigue has received the most attention in the scientific literature and generally is related to factors in the muscles themselves (18, 19, 24). These factors can include impairments in neuromuscular transmission, impulse propagation, sarcoplasmic reticulum failure, substrate depletion, and various other metabolic factors that can disrupt energy production and muscular contraction (19). Research exploring peripheral fatigue has centered on the availability of fuel substrates during a bout of exercise or competition (18). When exercise bouts are intense (31, 59) or undertaken for long durations (18), the availability of fuel substrates such as carbohydrates can become compromised. This can substantially reduce the athlete's ability to maintain high levels of performance (32).

The second type of fatigue that is discussed in the literature, central fatigue, is related to the brain (19). Central fatigue is often associated with a failure of the central nervous system to recruit skeletal muscle (54). It appears that fatigue-induced alterations in neurotransmitters such as dopamine, serotonin, and possibly acetylcholine have the potential to alter the ability of neural impulses to reach the muscle (20, 21, 54). For example, it has been suggested that exercise-induced increases in serotonin (5-HT) can lead to central fatigue and possibly mental fatigue, which could impair performance (19). Along these lines, it appears that the conscious perception of body functions such as breathing, increased cardiac output (pounding of the heart), body temperature, and sweating can affect fatigue (67). These cognitive sensations also are believed to affect motivation, which appears to be linked to previous exposure to similar situations (67).

It is clear that both central and peripheral fatigue can accumulate in response to a training or competitive bout. Gandelsman and Smirnov (25) suggested that there are two major phases of fatigue: latent and evident. In the early portions of a competition or training bout, physiological changes occur in order to meet the demands of the exercise bout. During this phase, latent fatigue can result in response to the increased neuromuscular activity and metabolic stress stimulated by the bout of exercise. If the exercise bout is prolonged at the same intensity, fatigue will accumulate, resulting in the occurrence of evident fatigue. Consequently, the athlete's ability to maintain maximal work capacity will progressively decrease.

Many strategies can be used to deal with fatigue, ranging from modifying the structure of the training session (30) to including dietary supplements to offset reductions in energy substrates (32). For example, increasing the length of the rest interval can decrease the occurrence of latent fatigue, which may facilitate the development of specific biomotor abilities such as power (30). Under some circumstances, training under conditions of latent fatigue can help prepare the athlete for the end of competitions, when fatigue is high. Such training also may enable the athlete to develop the psychological tools to deal with training-induced accumulation latent fatigue, which may improve her performance in the later stages of a competition (67). Strategies to deal with evident fatigue can include a structured cool-down period, as outlined previously in this chapter. Additionally, recovery techniques such as massage and contrast baths may alleviate this form of fatigue as well (see chapter 5).

The coach must consider fatigue when structuring a training session. For example, if the training session's major objective is to develop technical or tactical skills, technique can be addressed early in the session, when the athlete is least fatigued. In this type of session it may be warranted to include longer rest intervals during a session to alleviate latent fatigue.

The intensity of the training session will affect the amount of fatigue that is developed, and the session should be structured to address this. A session that contains high-intensity activities should have only a few objectives and be of short duration. Conversely, a session containing lower-intensity bouts of exercise could have multiple training objectives and last longer. For example, the session may focus on perfecting a technical element, incorporating those elements into the team's tactical scheme, and doing tactical drills with a high endurance component. Even with this format, athletes can experience latent fatigue as a result of the metabolic disturbances stimulated by the volume of work.

The athlete's ability to dissipate fatigue and recover from a training session or microcycle of intense training depends on many factors. The athlete's physical preparedness and training age may dictate his ability to tolerate training. For example, an athlete who lacks the appropriate physical development will experience greater levels of fatigue, which may result in an inability to tolerate training stress. Therefore, the coach must modify the training lesson to accommodate this athlete's deficiencies. This process may require more variations in the training plan with greater fluctuations in training intensity and volume in an attempt to dissipate fatigue and stimulate restoration. In the end, the recovery rate is proportional to the degree of physiological disturbance stimulated by the training session. The greater the training intensity and volume, the greater the accumulated fatigue and the more time needed before preparedness is elevated.

Supplementary Training Sessions

Most athletes want to maximize the time that they spend training while minimizing the occurrence of overtraining. One way to maximize training time and increase training volume is to use supplementary training sessions, which can consist of individual training sessions or special group sessions, such as training camps. These training sessions can be performed during the early morning, before school or work. Sometimes they are performed before breakfast, but it is probably advisable that the athlete consume a small amount of food before training, especially when the session lasts longer than 30 min (14). The time spent in these sessions depends on the athlete's schedule. Even though each session may be short in duration (30-60 min), over the course of the training year these small increases in training volume can result in a substantial increase in yearly training volume. For example, an athlete who trains an extra 30 to 60 min each day will accumulate 150 to 300 additional training hours per year, which could significantly improve her potential.

Although these sessions are considered supplemental, they must fit into the structure of the training plan designed by the coach. The coach will prescribe the content and dosage of these sessions in accordance with the athlete's objectives, weaknesses, and phase of training. These 20 to 40 min sessions can be structured to improve the athlete's general endurance, general or specific flexibility, and even general or specific strength. One use for supplemental training sessions might be to improve an area of weakness to enhance certain abilities. For example, an athlete who lacks flexibility can undertake a supplemental training session that directly targets flexibility. Any resulting improvement in flexibility could transfer to improve a technical aspect that the athlete is attempting to perfect.

A supplemental training session lends itself best to a three-part struc-

Table 9.3 Three-Part Supplemental Training Session

Training session part	Duration (min)
Warm-up	5-10
Main body	20-40
Cool-down	5-10
Total session time	30-60

ture (table 9.3). Because these training sessions may be undertaken independently of the coach, an introduction phase is not included. Therefore, these sessions contain the major components of a three-part training session: warm-up, main body, and cool-down. The goal and format of each session are no different than those of a regular training session. The main body of these sessions should have no more than two objectives; one objective is optimal.

Sample Training Plan

The training plan is a tool with which the coach can structure and guide the training session. The written version of the training plan should contain all pertinent information and be easy to follow. It is advisable to give the athlete a copy of the training plan well in advance of the training session. This allows the athlete to prepare for the training session mentally and physically. The coach should briefly introduce the plan during the introduction portion of the session and, if space is available, post the day's training plan so that the athletes can refer to it during the session.

There are many formats by which the training plan can be presented, but it should contain some basic elements. One of the most important items to include on a training plan for an individual session is the objective of that session. The session's objective guides the training session, allowing the athlete to understand what happens during the training session. The plan should include the date and location of the training session as well as the equipment needed. The training plan should specify the exercise, drills, and activities that the athlete must complete during each portion of the session. The plan should provide a detailed explanation of the dosage (repetitions, sets, duration) and intensity (percentage maximum strength, heart rate range, time, power) of the training session. Another item to include, especially when working with team sports, is a section detailing the most difficult drills an athlete can perform during the lesson. Finally, the training plan should note items that the athlete needs to focus on while performing the drills and exercises. These notes can be very specific to the individual athlete or address global needs of a group of athletes. A sample training session plan is presented in figure 9.2.

The length of a session plan will depend on the sport and the coach's experience. Inexperienced coaches need to be as specific as possible and include as much information as possible in the training plan. This provides them a blueprint to work from during the training session and decreases the chance they will forget an important aspect of the training session. More experienced coaches may be able to get away with a more generalized training plan, but it may still be warranted to present a detailed plan to the athletes so they can prepare mentally and physically for the training session.

DAILY CYCLE OF TRAINING

An important aspect of implementing a training plan is to organize the athlete's daily schedule to make optimum use of her time. It is important to strike a balance between training, personal free time, work schedules, and relaxation. This is best accomplished by organizing the training day into time allotments. The best organizational strategy appears to be multiple training lessons that occur on the same training day (33). Research by Häkkinen and Kallinen (33) suggests that splitting the day's training volume into two shorter sessions results in a greater improvement in performance compared with performing one long training session. This finding supports the practical observations of European coaches who have noted that long training sessions decrease the quality of training as a result of stimulating large

Training Lesson Plan 148

Date: June 14

Place: York Stadium

Equipment: Starting blocks

Barbells

Coach: _____

Objectives: Perfect start

Specific endurance

Power training

Part	Exercises	Dosage	Formations	Notes
Introduction	1. Describe the lesson's objectives.	3 min		
	2. Stress what the athletes should focus on during training.			John: Pay attention to arm work.
Warm-up	1. Warm-up duration	20 min		Rita: Put on two warm-up suits.
	2. Jogging	1,200 m		
	3. Calisthenics	8×		
	Arm rotations	8×		
	Upper-body rotations	12×		
	4. Hip flexibility	8-10×		Stress hip flexibility.
	5. Ankle flexibility	8-10×		
	6. Bounding exercises	4 × 20 m		Stress weak leg.
	7. Wind sprints	4 × 40-60 m		
Main body	1. Starts	12 × 30 m Rest 1 -2 min		Stress arm work.
	2. Specific endurance	8 × 120 m 3/4 (14 s)		Maintain a constant velocity throughout all repetitions.
	3. Power training	$\dfrac{60\ kg}{8\text{–}10\ reps}$ 4 sets		Between exercises, relax arms and legs.
Cool down	1. Jogging	800 m		Stay light and relaxed.
	2. Stretching	10-15 min		Focus on hip flexors.
	3. Massage	5-10 min		Work with partner.
Session notes	Remember that 8× = 8 times; 8-10× = 8-10 times			

Figure 9.2 Training session plan for a sprinter.

amounts of fatigue. This increase in fatigue appears to decrease the athlete's ability to develop biomotor abilities and perfect technical and tactical skills. Therefore, when possible the daily training volume should be broken into smaller subunits to maximally develop the athlete's capabilities.

The actual structure of the training day depends on many factors, including the time available for training, the developmental status of the athlete, and the avail-

STRUCTURE FOR MULTIPLE TRAINING SESSIONS PER DAY TRAINING

Two Training Sessions Per Day

Time	Activity
5:30-6:00 a.m.	Wake up, eat snack, prepare for training
6:00-7:30 a.m.	**First training session**
7:30-8:00 a.m.	Eat breakfast
8:00-8:30 a.m.	Prepare for work
8:30-9:00 a.m.	Travel to work
9:00-10:30 a.m.	Work
10:30-10:45 a.m.	Eat snack
10:45 a.m. to 12:30 p.m.	Work
12:30-1:00 p.m.	Eat lunch
1:00-5:00 p.m.	Work
5:00-5:30 p.m.	Travel to training
5:30-6:00 p.m.	Eat pretraining snack and prepare for training
6:00-7:30 p.m.	**Second training session**
7:30-8:00 p.m.	Travel home
8:00-8:30 p.m.	Eat dinner
8:30-10:00 p.m.	Have free time
10:00 p.m. to 5:30 a.m.	Sleep

Three Training Sessions Per Day

Time	Activity
6:30 a.m.	Wake up
7:00-8:00 a.m.	**First training session**
8:30-9:00 a.m.	Eat breakfast
9:00-10:00 a.m.	Rest
10:00 a.m. to 12:00 noon	**Second training session**
12:00-1:00 p.m.	Rest and recovery session
1:00-2:00 p.m.	Eat lunch
2:00-4:00 p.m.	Rest
4:00-6:00 p.m.	**Third training session**
6:00-7:00 p.m.	Rest and recovery session
7:00-7:30 p.m.	Eat dinner
7:30-10:00 p.m.	Have free time
10:00 p.m. to 6:30 a.m.	Sleep

Four Training Sessions Per Day

Time	Activity
6:30 a.m.	Wake up
7:00-8:00 a.m.	**First training session**
8:30-9:00 a.m.	Eat breakfast
9:00-10:00 a.m.	Rest
10:00 a.m. to 12:00 noon	**Second training session**
12:00-1:00 p.m.	Rest and recovery session
1:00-2:00 p.m.	Eat lunch
2:00-4:00 p.m.	Rest
4:00-5:30 p.m.	**Third training session**
5:30-6:30 p.m.	Rest and recovery session
6:30-7:30 p.m.	**Fourth training session**
7:30-8:00 p.m.	Recovery techniques
8:00-8:30 p.m.	Eat dinner
8:30-10:00 p.m.	Have free time
10:00 p.m. to 6:30 a.m.	Sleep

ability of training facilities. If the athlete is attending a training camp, the density of training sessions may be substantially greater. It appears that the training day can be broken into two training sessions, one in the morning and one in the evening. An example of how training might be structured for an athlete who is working full time and also training two times per day is shown above. When athletes attend training camps they will most likely undergo a greater density of training, such as three to four sessions per day or more, as shown above.

MODELING THE TRAINING SESSION PLAN

A training model is a simulation of a competition, the goal of which is to increase certain training adaptations and translate those adaptations to competitive performance. The modeling process can be thought of a method for creating a training session that mimics the physiological, technical, tactical, and psychological elements encountered during a competition. Any training session can be designed to coincide with the objectives of a given phase of training while modeling competitive performance (13).

The coach must avoid the temptation to structure the training session the same way all of the time. Variation of the training stimulus is very important in inducing physiological and performance gains (72). The model approach is one method for inserting a new or novel training stimulus into the training plan. This method can be used to increase the athlete's motivation, induce a new physiological challenge, and present the athlete with novel tasks that prepare her for competition. There are many ways to use the model approach, and coaches should modify the following examples to best suit their training objectives.

Model Training Session for Skill Acquisition

A model can be developed to enhance skill acquisition and refinement. New skills are best learned when fatigue is minimized. Additionally, cumulative fatigue makes it more difficult to retain skills that have already been acquired. Thus drills that are used to teach and develop skills should take place immediately after the warm-up. Table 9.4 presents an example of this type of model. This model can be used to develop speed, agility, and power.

Model Training for Skill Refinement Under Conditions of Fatigue

This type of model may be used to mimic the conditions that are encountered at the end of a game, match, or race, where the athlete may be required to perform certain skills under fatigue. Although mastery of skills is best addressed when the athlete is fresh, athletes must practice skills under the influence of fatigue. The objective in using this type of model is to create a situation of fatigue similar to that seen in the later part of a competition. To accomplish this objective, the coach should create technical and tactical drills that stress the glycolytic and oxidative energy systems in

Table 9.4 Model Training Session for Skill Acquisition

Training component	Time (min)	Goals
Warm-up	10-20	Get the athlete ready to train.
Tactical and technical drills	45-60	Improve and refine a specific skill set.
Physical training	30-45	Develop a specific biomotor ability in accordance with the daily plan.
Cool-down	10-20	Initiate the recovery.

Note: This basic model structure can be modified for agility, speed, and power training.

a way similar to that seen in competition (see chapter 1). This situation challenges the athlete's ability to cope with and overcome fatigue, both physically and psychologically (i.e., via determination, motivation, and willpower). An example of how this model may be incorporated into a training session is presented in table 9.5.

This model can also be adapted to challenge the abilities of the athlete to perform fast, agile, and powerful athletic movements under the condition of fatigue. This type of model may also be useful when preparing martial artists, racket sport players, athletes in contact sports, or any athlete to perform technical and tactical skills effectively during the last part of a sporting contest. The goal of this model is to improve performance at the end of the game, match, or competition when fatigue is at its highest. This model exposes the athlete to these conditions, allowing the athlete to physiologically and psychologically adapt to this scenario.

Model Training for Controlling Precontest Arousal

To achieve maximum effectiveness during an afternoon or evening competition, the athlete must be in a state of arousal and psychological alertness. A short morning (e.g., 10:00 a.m.) session may facilitate optimal arousal for the afternoon contest, reduce anxiety, and help the athlete overcome feelings of excitability, nervousness, and restlessness. This type of session should be used to promote calmness and controlled confidence. The session should be relatively short and contain a brief series of short, explosive movements (table 9.6). These short and non-fatigue-inducing actions

Table 9.5 Model Training Session for Skill Refinement Under the Condition of Fatigue

Training component	Time (min)	Goals
Warm-up	10-20	Get the athlete ready to train.
Fatigue-inducing tactical and technical drills	45-60	Stress the athlete's glycolytic and oxidative system. Induce a situation of fatigue under which the athlete must perform specific skills.
Technical and tactical drills	20-30	Improve the accuracy of passing and shooting. Develop precision and accuracy of shooting. Work on quickness and power under conditions of fatigue.
Cool-down	10-20	Initiate the recovery.

Note: This model can be adapted to challenge the athlete's ability to perform fast, agile and precise movements under the condition of fatigue.

Table 9.6 Model Training Session for Controlling Precontest Arousal

Training component	Time (min)	Goals
Warm-up	10-20	Short and light warm-up to get the athlete ready
Technical, tactical, or speed drills	10-15	Short technical, tactical, or speed drill separated by long rest intervals designed to prepare athlete for an afternoon competition
Cool-down	10-20	Initiate the recovery

can improve later performance by increasing the contractility of the major skeletal muscles used in the sporting movements (23). These activities must be of short duration and must not induce fatigue, because fatigue will decrease performance capacity. An additional strategy is to use long rest intervals between each activity bout to ensure recovery (46).

SUMMARY OF MAJOR CONCEPTS

This chapter emphasizes the benefits of organization and planning. Training effectiveness depends on the coach's and athlete's ability to organize and plan training from a single workout to a long-term plan. A workout plan is not difficult to construct, and it is a powerful tool that can maximize performance outcomes. The objectives and goals of the individual training sessions must be clearly outlined for the athlete. The athlete must receive feedback about his progress toward attaining these objectives.

The workout plan includes several key components. The warm-up is an often overlooked but essential component. This important segment prepares the athlete for the training session and should never be compromised or removed from the training plan. The warm-up should contain general dynamic activities and progress to dynamic muscle actions that are specific to the sporting activity. The athlete should avoid static stretching during this portion of the training session because the scientific literature suggests that static stretching at this time can impair performance.

The cool-down is another often-overlooked component that can influence the effectiveness of the training session. This portion of the session allows the body to return to homeostasis and initiate recovery. This is the ideal time to include static stretching and improve flexibility. If implemented correctly, the cool-down can be a very effective part of the training session.

Training Methods

A vast array of training methods can be employed in the development of a training plan. Probably the most important training method for almost all sports centers on the development of strength and power, which is discussed in Chapter 10. In many sports, the development of sport-specific endurance characteristics is essential for competitive success. Chapter 11 explores the various types of endurance that are required in sport and presents methods for the development of sport-specific endurance characteristics. Finally, Chapter 12 presents information about speed and agility training, paying specific attention to the sequencing of training and to maximizing these important sports performance characteristics.

CHAPTER 10

STRENGTH AND POWER DEVELOPMENT

Muscular strength and power-generating capacity are critical factors in determining success in a wide variety of sports. Muscular strength and power are generally acknowledged as being important in all team sports and sports that are dominated by speed. Contemporary scientific data reveal that muscular strength and power are important for sports with a large endurance component, such as long-distance running or cross-country skiing. Given the importance of muscular strength and power in so many sports, the coach and athlete must understand how the development of strength and power can affect performance. The coach and athlete need to understand the principles associated with resistance training to effectively use resistance training to enhance performance.

BIOMOTOR ABILITIES

Athletic performance is dominated by combinations of strength, speed, and endurance, which are **biomotor abilities**. Most sport activities can be classified as having a predominant biomotor ability. Figure 10.1 illustrates a theoretical paradigm where strength or force, speed, or endurance is the dominant biomotor ability (24, 51). For example, the dominant biomotor ability necessary for success in long-distance running is generally considered to be endurance (24). Every sporting activity has a dominant biomotor ability (figure 10.2). However, contemporary research suggests that sporting activities can be affected by several of the biomotor abilities (141, 144). This can be clearly seen by the fact that muscular **strength** appears to influence both running speed (18, 26, 37) and endurance (110). For example, leg strength and **power** appear to be significantly related to sprint **speed**, with the strongest and most powerful athletes being able to run the fastest (18, 26, 37). Support for the influence of strength on endurance can be seen in the literature demonstrating that adding resistance training to the training regimes of long-distance runners (110, 144), Nordic skiers (94, 94, 143, 145), or cyclists (20) results in significantly greater improvements in performance compared with focusing only on endurance training. Recent evidence suggests that stronger, more powerful athletes perform better on performance tests designed to evaluate agility (147). Based on this data, a hypothetical model can be constructed in which strength is connected with many of the factors that have been shown in the literature to effect performance in a variety of sporting activities (figure 10.3). Because strength affects the other biomotor abilities and almost all facets of athletic performance, strength should be considered as the crucial biomotor ability (24). Therefore, to maximize athletic performance strength should always be trained in concert with the other biomotor abilities.

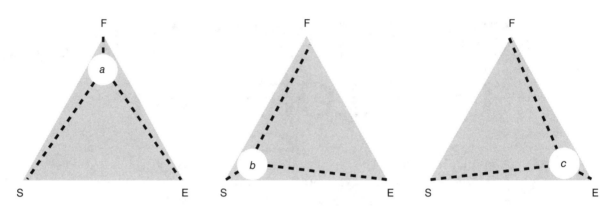

Figure 10.1   Relationship between the main biomotor abilities, in which *(a)* strength, *(b)* speed, and *(c)* endurance dominate (51). F = strength or force; S = speed; E = endurance.
From Florescu, Dumitrescu, and Predescu 1969 (51).

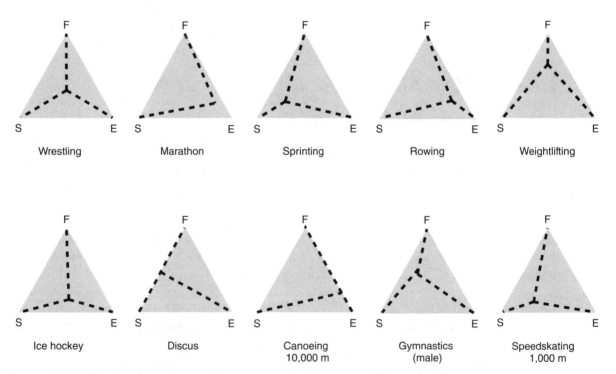

Figure 10.2   The dominant composition among the biomotor abilities of various sports.

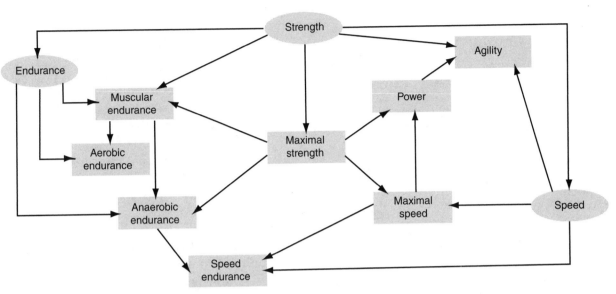

Figure 10.3 Interaction of biomotor abilities and various aspects of sport performance.

STRENGTH

Strength can be defined as the maximal force or **torque** (rotational force) a muscle or muscle group can generate (116, 117). Strength is better defined as the ability of the neuromuscular system to produce force against an external resistance (187). Contemporary literature suggests that high levels of muscular strength are significantly related to sport performance. For example, muscular strength has been related to sprint performance (18, 26, 37), American football performance (19, 57), soccer performance (34, 65, 93, 174), volleyball performance (48, 134), ice hockey performance (95), rugby league performance (60), and aerobic exercise performance (20, 94, 110, 144). These data seem to support the contention that muscular strength is a major contributor to most sporting activities. Therefore, the appropriate application of resistance training can alter the neuromuscular system in a way that improves the athlete's capacity to produce force and improves sports performance (73, 182, 183).

Force, Velocity, Rate of Force Development, and Power

When looking at sporting activities, one could argue that the ability to generate force against an external resistance is very important (129). Newton's second law of motion supports the importance of force-generating capacity (i.e., strength) (see the equations on p. 262), in that this law reveals that the product of mass and acceleration is equal to force (equation 1). If one rearranges this equation, it is easy to see that to increase the **acceleration** of an object one must apply a greater force. Because increases in acceleration result in increases in **velocity**, it is also easy to conclude that a high force-generating capacity or strength level is needed to achieve high velocities of movements (187). Support for this contention can be seen in the literature that demonstrates significant relationships between speed and muscular strength (18, 26, 37).

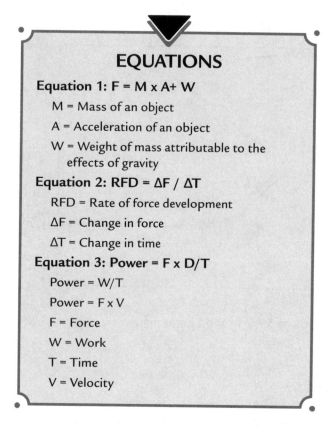

EQUATIONS

Equation 1: F = M x A+ W

M = Mass of an object

A = Acceleration of an object

W = Weight of mass attributable to the effects of gravity

Equation 2: RFD = ΔF / ΔT

RFD = Rate of force development

ΔF = Change in force

ΔT = Change in time

Equation 3: Power = F x D/T

Power = W/T

Power = F x V

F = Force

W = Work

T = Time

V = Velocity

Further examination of the interaction between force and velocity suggests that an inverse relationship exists, where as external resistance increases the movement velocity subsequently decreases (figure 10.4) (114, 212). The application of a periodized resistance training regime has the potential to alter the **force–velocity curve** (44, 107, 113, 114, 130, 138). The literature suggests that heavy resistance training induces adaptations that are different than those seen with explosive resistance training (79, 78, 114, 206). For example, the implementation of a resistance training program that focuses on the use of heavy loading has a greater potential to alter the high-force portion of the force–velocity curve (figure 10.5), whereas the implementation of explosive resistance training exercises will alter the high-velocity portion of the curve (figure 10.6) (114).

The effect of explosive resistance training on the high-velocity portion of the force–velocity curve is supported by evidence suggesting that explosive resistance training has the potential to alter an athlete's explosive muscle strength or **rate of force development** (RFD) (2, 70, 79, 80, 97). The RFD indicates how fast force is developed and is calculated by dividing the change in force by the change in time (198) (see equation 2 above). It appears that the ability to generate a high RFD is very important for sporting activities that involve explosive movements (e.g., sprinting, jumping, throwing) and require force to be generated during a limited time frame (~50-250 ms). This time is generally substantially less than the time to reach maximal

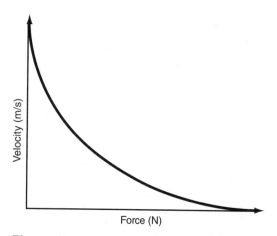

Figure 10.4 Force–velocity relationship.

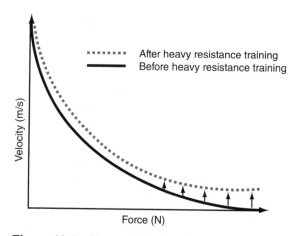

Figure 10.5 Theoretical alterations to the force-velocity curve by heavy resistance training.

force (>250 ms) (13, 71, 163). However, maximal strength and the RFD are interrelated (13, 136) and are both associated with sporting performance, as both variables appear to relate to the ability to cause acceleration, which affects movement velocity (187).

It appears that both force and velocity are important in human movement, because the product of these two variables is **power** (114, 187) (see equation 3 on p. 262). Maximal force-generating capacity appears to be a major effector of power-generating capacity (162, 163). Schmidtbleicher (162, 163) suggested that as the load being overcome decreases, the effect that **maximal strength** has on power generation also decreases. He suggested that as this occurs, the RFD

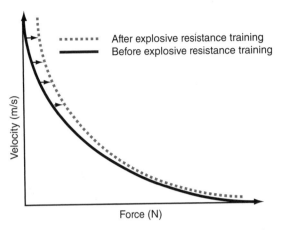

Figure 10.6 Theoretical alterations to the force–velocity curve by explosive resistance training.

becomes more important (162, 163, 187). Although Schmidtbleicher's theory is plausible, our understanding of the interrelationship between power, strength, and the RFD is incomplete (187).

It has been speculated that power-generating capacity or the rate of performing work is the single most important characteristic in sport (73, 114, 129, 162, 187). In fact, the power-generating capacity of various athletes appears to differentiate between levels of sporting performance (19, 57). Two types of power output are relevant in sporting performance: maximal power output and average power output. Maximal power output is most related to single-effort maximal performances such as jumping, sprinting, weightlifting, changing direction, and striking (16, 17, 73, 114, 129, 187, 193). Conversely, average power output is related to the performance of repetitive tasks such as endurance running (140), cycling (190), and Nordic skiing (143).

Factors Affecting Strength

Strength can be defined as the ability of the neuromuscular system to produce force against an external resistance (187). The maximal strength that an athlete can exhibit depends on seven key concepts: (a) the number of **motor units** involved (recruitment), (b) the motor unit firing rate (rate coding), (c) the amount of motor unit **synchronization**, (d) the use of the stretch shortening cycle, (e) the degree of neuromuscular inhibition, (f) the muscle fiber type, and (g) the degree of muscle **hypertrophy** (180, 187).

Motor Unit Recruitment

Motor unit recruitment relates to the number of motor units called into play (40, 88). When more motor units are activated, the amount of force generated by the muscle then increases (73). Recruitment usually occurs in an orderly pattern from smaller to larger motor units (88). Henneman and colleagues (88) in their seminal work established what is known as the Henneman **size principle,** which suggests that the size of the motor unit dictates its activation. This work established that larger motor units have a higher activation threshold and are activated after smaller motor units. It is also widely accepted that larger motor units are activated in response to higher external loads (49, 73). However, the motor unit recruitment pattern is affected not only by the force exerted (73) but also by the contraction speed (73), type of muscle contraction (45), and the metabolic state of the muscle (106, 137).

Motor Unit Rate Coding

Rate coding deals with the motor unit firing frequency (40). One unique aspect of rate coding is that the force generated by a muscle increases without recruiting additional motor units (73). Van Cutsem and colleagues (197) suggested that rate coding plays a significant role in determining the speed of voluntary contractions. Support for this contention can be seen in several investigations showing that higher motor unit firing rates are associated with higher rates of force development (2, 52, 197, 199). It appears that explosive high–power output exercises (e.g., weightlifting exercises, plyometrics, jump squats) have the potential to alter the rate coding of motor units because these exercises tend to increase the motor unit firing rate (40, 73).

Motor Unit Synchronization

Motor units fire in response to low-intensity muscle actions with brief dynamic twitches that result in an **asynchronous** motor unit firing patterns (187). Asynchronous motor unit firing occurs as a result of one motor unit deactivating while another activates. Conversely, motor unit **synchronization** occurs as a result of the simultaneous activation of numerous motor units (61, 119) and historically has been suggested to result in an increased force output (135). Recent research suggests that motor unit synchronization may not directly enhance maximal force output or maximal strength (164, 208). The relationship between motor unit synchronization and force production capacity is partially supported by literature demonstrating a higher incidence of motor unit synchronization in strength-trained athletes (166). However, it appears that motor unit synchronization may exert a stronger influence on the rate of force development (164). Support for this contention can be seen in recent research suggesting that motor unit synchronization plays a role in force development during rapid muscle contractions (164). Motor unit synchronization may exert its greatest influence on performance of activities that require the coactivation of multiple muscles at the same time (164).

Stretch Shortening Cycle

A **stretch shortening cycle (SSC)** is defined as a combination of eccentric and concentric muscle actions (117, 118). A stretch shortening cycle could be considered a plyometric muscle action (187) because an eccentric muscle action (lengthening of the muscle) occurs prior to the concentric muscle action (shortening of the muscle) (118). The most well-known effect of the stretch shortening cycle is an enhancement in performance (concentric muscle action) during the final phase of the cycle (38, 117, 118). The performance enhancement resulting from a stretch shortening cycle most likely occurs because of storage of elastic energy during the eccentric phase (30, 118), activation of the stretch reflex (119), and optimization of muscle activation (3, 23). Several investigations have suggested that strength training improves maximal strength as a result of an improved ability to activate stretch shortening cycles (3, 38).

Neuromuscular Inhibition

Neural inhibition can occur as a result of neural feedback from various muscle and joint receptors that can reduce force production (61, 187). For example, it appears that the **Golgi tendon organ**, which operates as a protective mechanism, prevents the generation of harmful muscular forces during maximal or near-maximal efforts (61). If neural activation patterns of these protective mechanisms are altered, disinhibition may occur and force-generating capacity may increase (111). Support for this argument can be seen in the work of Aagaard and colleagues (3), where 14 weeks of heavy resistance training significantly reduced neuromuscular inhibitory responses. The resultant decrease in inhibition may partially explain some of the increases in force-generating capacity seen as a result of training (3).

Strength is affected by many factors including fiber type and the degree of muscle hypertrophy.

AP Photo/Andres Leighton

Muscle Fiber Type

Cross-sectional studies suggest that strength and power athletes have high percentages of Type II (fast twitch) muscle fibers (53-60%) (58, 59, 81, 84, 153, 191). This is important because the muscle fiber type characteristics of an athlete play a significant role in the athlete's ability to exhibit maximal muscular strength and power-generating capacity (58, 59, 153, 154, 192). For example, Fry and colleagues (58) reported that the Type II fiber concentration of weightlifters is significantly correlated to the maximal weight lifted in the snatch (r = .94) and the clean and jerk (r = .78). The fiber type distribution of an athlete also appears to be significantly related to the athlete's vertical jump ability (r = .79). Conversely, athletes who participate in endurance sports generally have higher percentages of Type I (slow twitch) muscle fibers (21, 192), which have been shown to correspond to higher maximal oxygen consumption rates (21) and lower maximal force-generating capacities. Thus, the athlete who possesses higher concentrations of Type II muscle fibers appears to have an advantage in sporting activities that require high levels of strength and power. Conversely, having a higher percentage of Type I muscle fibers is advantageous to endurance exercise performance.

Muscle Hypertrophy

An increase in muscle cross-sectional area is thought to contribute to the increases in muscle **hypertrophy** seen in response to resistance training (1, 52). Increases in cross-sectional area of a muscle increases the amount of contractile units and thus increases force-generating potential (10, 52, 203). Type II muscle fibers exhibit a greater plasticity, which is demonstrated by the faster rate of hypertrophy seen in response to training and the faster rate of atrophy seen with detraining by these types of fibers (52, 82).

Physiological Adaptations to Strength Training

The physiological adaptations to a strength-training regime can be categorized as being either neurological or morphological (52). Neurological adaptations include factors such as changes in motor unit recruitment patterns (73), motor unit synchronization (112, 135, 165-167), motor unit firing rate (40), and reflex activation (52). Morphological changes relate to changes in whole muscle size (36), muscle hypertrophy (36, 142), muscle fiber type transitions (205), and alterations to muscle architecture (168). The degree to which these two broad categories contribute to adaptations can be influenced by many factors such as training status (161), type of exercises used in the training regime (31, 142), genetic makeup (25, 35, 103, 146, 194), age (104), and gender (104).

It has been suggested that the development of strength in the early phase of training is most affected by neurological factors, whereas in the longer term training adaptations are limited by the morphological factors (161, 201). The time when neurological factor adaptation predominates is between 6 and 20 weeks from the initiation of a resistance training regime depending on the type of exercise and the structure of the resistance training regime (31, 161, 201). This time frame can be altered depending on the complexity of the exercises used in the resistance training regime (31). Chilibeck and colleagues (31) suggested that complex exercises that involve more than one joint (e.g., squat, clean, snatch) may require more time for neural adaptations to be manifested, thus requiring a longer time frame before hypertrophy predominates. Those investigators noted that the neurological adaptations in the upper arm occurred very rapidly, because hypertrophy was noted after 10 weeks of performing the biceps curl. Conversely, significant hypertrophy was not noted in the legs until after 20 weeks of leg press training. These data indicate that the exercises used in the resistance training regime may mitigate the degree to which neurological or hypertrophic factors predominate.

Neurological Adaptations

With the initiation of a resistance training regimen, the primary adaptations that affect performance relate to motor learning and coordination (158). These adaptations appear to be very specific to the movement pattern and the sequence of muscle contraction (52), which suggests that the expression of strength requires a degree of skill.

Resistance training has the potential to alter the motor unit recruitment patterns (73, 197), motor unit rate coding (2, 40, 73), and degree of motor unit synchronization (166). The type of training undertaken in a resistance training regime plays a role in determining neurological adaptations. For example, explosive resistance training with high loads or heavy resistance training has been shown to lower the motor unit recruitment thresholds (73, 197) and increase the occurrence of motor unit rate coding (2, 40, 197). A heavy resistance training regime has the potential to increase motor unit synchronization (164) and reduce neural inhibition (3). These neurological adaptations appear to alter force-generating capacity and the rate of force generation, which both can affect sports performance.

Morphological Adaptations

The occurrence of muscle hypertrophy in response to a resistance training regime results in changes to the muscle architecture (168). These architectural alterations can increase contractile material, which in turn can increase force production capacity

(52). The most significant morphological change noted in most resistance training studies is an increase in muscle hypertrophy (3, 52, 75, 83, 89, 168, 178). Most short-term strength training studies demonstrate significant hypertrophy of Type II muscle fibers (1, 41, 98, 195, 203, 205), whereas long-term studies demonstrate hypertrophy of both Type II and Type I fibers (82, 125). Muscle hypertrophy is marked by significant increases in the cross-sectional area of the skeletal muscle fibers, which can result in an increase in contractile material (52) and an increase in the angle of pennation of the muscle (1). These two morphological adaptations significantly enhance muscular strength adaptations in response to a resistance training regime (1, 52).

A further consideration when looking at the morphological adaptations of the muscle is the training intervention (55). It appears that explosive strength training has the potential to significantly increase Type II fiber size, significantly altering the ratio of Type II to Type I muscle fiber cross-sectional area, which favors maximal strength and power-generating capacity (55, 74, 187). Support for this contention is presented by Fry (55), who demonstrated that the ratio of Type II to Type I content is greater in weightlifters than in powerlifters and bodybuilders. These data suggest that the type of resistance training used has the potential to dictate the types of morphological changes expressed by the skeletal muscle.

Another potential positive morphological adaptation to a resistance training program is an alteration in the muscle fiber type (52, 205). The most consistent fiber type adaptation seen in response to a resistance training regime is a reduction in Type IIx fiber distribution with a concomitant increase in Type IIa distribution (29, 83, 178, 205). The results of these studies may be predicated by the analytical techniques used. Newer analytical techniques suggest that muscles exhibit an even greater plasticity and thus may express greater alterations in response to training or detraining (62, 126, 196, 205).

Contemporary research has examined **myosin heavy chain** (MHC) content when identifying muscle composition (52, 55, 126, 205). Myosin heavy chain composition is closely associated with the classic fiber typing methods (55). However, current literature reveals that in addition to the major categories of myosin heavy chain (Type I, Type IIa, and Type IIx), there exists a pool of hybrid fibers (Type I/IIa, Type I/IIa/IIx, and Type IIa/IIx). This pool of hybrids can be altered by resistance training (205), endurance training (196), and bed rest (62). As this pool is modified, the percentage of Type IIx, IIa, or I fibers can be altered, which partially explains the fiber type compositions of different classifications of strength athletes (table 10.1).

Table 10.1   Fiber Type Distributions of Various Strength-Trained Athletes

Population	FIBER TYPE DISTRIBUTION (%)			
	I	**IIa**	**IIx**	**Hybrids**
Recreationally active young people (39, 172, 203)	41	33	6	20
Resistance-trained men (9, 172, 203, 205)	34	58	<1	8
Resistance-trained women (205)	35	53	<1	12
Bodybuilders (39)	27	47	9	17
Weightlifters (58)	35	64	1	NA

Note: All percentages based on myosin heavy chain data. NA = not available.

Type of Strength

Various types of strength can be targeted within a resistance training regime. Understanding the relationship between strength and the performance characteristics of the sport will allow the coach to construct training programs that transfer strength development into performance gains. Some types of strength to consider are as follows:

• *General Strength:* **General strength** refers to the strength of the whole muscular system. This strength is the foundation for the strength program and must be developed for ultimate performance to be achieved. Coaches can focus on general strength during the preparatory phase of training or during the first few years of training in novice athletes. If general strength is not adequately developed, the athlete's progress may be impeded.

• *Specific Strength:* **Specific strength** relates to the motor patterns of muscle groups that are essential to a sporting activity. Athletes usually work on specific strength at the end of the preparation phase.

• *Speed Strength:* **Speed strength** is the ability to develop force rapidly and at high velocities. Speed strength is important in most sports, especially team sports. This type of strength is best developed during the specific preparation phase and within the competition phase of training.

• *Maximum Strength:* **Maximum strength** refers to the highest force the neuromuscular system can generate during a maximum voluntary contraction. Maximal strength is demonstrated by the highest load that an athlete can lift one time. Maximal strength has been related to factors such as muscular endurance, weightlifting performance, and speed.

• *Muscular Endurance:* **Muscular endurance** is the ability of the neuromuscular system to produce force in a repetitive fashion over extended periods of time. The total number of repetitions that can be lifted with a specific load is a marker of muscular endurance.

• *Absolute Strength:* **Absolute strength** refers to the amount of force that can be generated regardless of body weight. In some sports (shot put, American football, or the super-heavy weight class in weightlifting and wrestling), the athlete must achieve a very high level of muscular strength. An athlete's absolute maximal strength capacity can be measured with one repetition maximum testing (1RM).

METHODS OF SCALING MAXIMAL STRENGTH

Ratio = AS/BW

Ratio = AS/LBM

Allometric scaling = load $\times$ $(BW^{0.67})^{-1}$

Height scaling = load $\times$ $(HT^{2.16})^{-1}$

Sinclair formula (men) = $10^{\wedge}0.845716976 \times (Log10(BW/168.091)^2)$

Sinclair formula (women) = $10^{\wedge}1.316081431 \times (Log10(BW/107.844)^2)$

Scaled value = load $\times$ Sinclair coefficient

AS = absolute strength; BW = body weight; LBM = lean body mass; HT = height.

Knowledge of the athlete's maximal capacity is necessary to calculate the training loads needed within a periodized training system.

• *Relative Strength:* **Relative strength** is the ratio between an athlete's maximal strength and his body weight or lean body mass. The ratio for evaluating relative strength is calculated by the athlete's absolute strength divided by his body weight (185). However, several researchers have suggested that simply dividing the absolute strength by body weight results in a misrepresentation of relative muscular strength because the relationship between strength and body mass is not linear (14, 139, 185). The ratio method usually results in a bias toward small individuals (14, 213). To avoid this bias several methods (53, 175, 185) have been suggested as alternatives for determining relative strength (see methods of scaling on p. 268). Comparisons of muscular strength show that allometric scaling techniques or the Sinclair formula (175) provide a better representation of an athlete's relative strength.

METHODS OF STRENGTH TRAINING

Strength training or resistance training entails using resistive loads to develop muscular strength and power. Depending on the goals of a strength training regime, various methods of applying resistance can be used (see Methods of Resistance Application on

METHODS OF RESISTANCE APPLICATION

• *Body Weight.* Body weight resistance can be used to increase strength because of the actions of gravity on the body. Body weight exercises include a vast variety of exercises, all of which use the body as a resistive load. Some examples are push-ups, pull-ups, chin-ups, dips, and stair climbing.

• *Elastic Bands.* When stretched, elastic bands create resistive forces. A potential problem with this resistive device is that the forces exerted on the body become greater as the band is stretched further (85). With activities such as jumping, these devices apply less force at the initiation of the jump and greater force after the athlete has left the ground, which does not model the loading patterns typically found in sport. Conversely, using a weighted vest or jumping with free weights applies the force consistently throughout the movement, which better translates to sports performance and is a more effective training practice (85).

• *Weighted Objects.* Weighted objects can include medicine balls, kettle balls, and bags of sand. Resistive force is created as a result of the interaction between gravity and the object's weight.

• *Weight Stack Machines.* With weight stack machines, resistance is provided by the action of gravity on the resistance. The direction of the force is controlled by the use of pulleys, cables, cams, and gears. It has been suggested that such machines do not match human strength curve patterns (85).

• *Fluid Resistance Machines.* Fluid resistance machines create resistive forces by moving the body or apparatus through a fluid, moving fluid past an object, moving fluid around an object, or moving fluid through an orifice (85). The fluid used in these devices can be either a liquid or a gas. One problem with fluid-based resistive devices is that they do not provide for eccentric muscle actions, which may limit the device's effectiveness (85). Power development is limited with these devices because of their limited ability to generate maximal velocities (85).

• *Free Weights.* Free weights, such as dumbbells and barbells, are considered the gold standard of resistance training. Free weights most closely match the human strength curve (85, 180) and use gravity to apply the resistive forces.

• *Isometric.* Isometric methods apply resistive forces in which the contractile forces equal the resistive forces. An example of an isometric muscle action is pushing with maximal forces against an immovable object.

p. 269). The preferred method of strength training combines the use of free weights with other methods of developing strength and power such as plyometrics, medicine ball work, and agility training. Using multijoint, large muscle mass exercises (e.g., cleans, snatches, pulls, squats, etc.) provides greater transfer to the athlete's sporting events compared with single-joint, small muscle mass exercises.

When designing a resistance training regime, the coach should consider the concept of progressive overload. In progressive overload, the loading paradigm is altered as the muscle adapts to the training stimulus (50). Progressive overload can be accomplished through the manipulation of many of the training variables, such as changing the resistance used, altering the number of repetitions or sets in the training program, varying the frequency of training, altering the rest interval between sets or repetitions, and changing the exercises in the training regime (12).

MANIPULATION OF TRAINING VARIABLES

An effective strength training regime systematically manipulates many training factors in a periodized fashion. Coaches can optimize the training plan by methodically managing the volume and the intensity of training. Early in the training plan, during the preparatory phase, volume will be higher, intensity will be lower, and sport-specific training will be minimized. As the athlete moves closer to the competitive season, there is a general downward shift in training volume, an increase in training intensity, and an increase in sport-specific training. Although the manipulation of volume and intensity of training is extremely important, it is also important to manipulate other variables associated with the training plan, such as the frequency of training, the order of exercises, the interset rest intervals, and the exercises selected.

Volume

Volume of training can be quantified as the amount of work performed and can incorporate total training hours, number of kilograms lifted, **metric ton** or **short tons** lifted per training session, phase of training or per year, and the number of **sets** and **repetitions** completed (24). In the literature, volume is traditionally represented as a metric ton (11, 46, 133) or **volume load** (180, 187), and several authors suggest that the metric ton (volume load) gives the best representation of the training volume (180, 187). A metric ton is equivalent to 1,000 kg, whereas a short ton is equal to 1,102.3 kg. The volume of a training session is calculated by multiplying the weight lifted by number of sets and the number of repetitions, which yields a volume load value (table 10.2).

Table 10.2 Example of Volume Calculation

Exercise	Sets	×	Repetitions	Load (kg)	Volume load (kg)	Metric ton	Short ton
Power clean	3	×	5	125	1,875	1.875	1.701
Clean pull (floor)	3	×	5	160	2,400	2.400	2.177
Clean pull (knee)	3	×	5	170	2,550	2.550	2.313
Clean grip Romanian deadlift	3	×	5	140	2,100	2.100	1.905
				Total	8,925	8.925	8.504

To calculate the number of metric tons divide the volume load by 1,000. To calculate the number of short tons, divide the volume load by 1,102.3.

Investigators have used different methods for calculating the volume load: Some authors calculate only attempts greater than 80% of 1RM (11, 150) whereas others calculate all of the repetitions performed in training (180). The total workload in an annual training plan can approach 3,726 metric tons for elite weightlifters (11), with 2,789 metric tons in the preparatory phase and 937 metric tons in the competition phase. The number of metric tons encountered in a training session depends on the sport being trained for, the developmental status of the athlete, and the phase of training. As the athlete becomes more developed, he can tolerate higher training session or microcycle volume loads. It is not uncommon for weightlifters to train with 10 to 60 metric tons in a microcycle (11, 46). The microcycle volume can vary drastically depending on the sport and the phase of training (table 10.3).

Table 10.3   Suggested Volume in Metric Tons of Strength Training Per Year

Sport or event	VOLUME PER MICROCYCLE			VOLUME PER YEAR	
	Preparatory	Competitive	Transition	Minimum	Maximum
Baseball and cricket	20-30	8-10	2-4	900	1,450
Basketball	12-24	4-6	2	450	850
Boxing and martial arts	8-14	3	1	380	500
Cycling	16-22	8-10	2-4	600	950
Downhill skiing	18-36	6-10	2-4	700	1,250
Figure skating	8-12	2-4	2	350	550
Football	30-40	10-12	6	900	1,400
Golf	4-6	2	1	250	300
Gymnastics	10-16	4	4	380	600
High jump	16-28	8-10	2-4	620	1,000
Ice hockey	15-25	6-8	2-4	600	950
Javelin	12-24	4	2	450	800
Jumps	20-30	8-10	2	800	1,200
Kayaking and canoeing	20-40	10-12	4	900	1,200
Lacrosse	14-22	4-8	2-4	500	900
Rowing	30-40	10-12	4	900	1,200
Rugby	10-20	4-6	4	320	600
Shot put	24-40	8-12	4-6	900	1,450
Speedskating	14-26	4-6	2-4	500	930
Sprinting	10-18	4	2	400	600
Squash	8-12	4	4	350	550
Swimming	20	8-10	2-4	700	1,200
Tennis	8-12	2-4	2	350	550
Triathlon	16-20	8-10	2-4	600	1,000
Volleyball	12-20	4	2	450	600
Wrestling	20-30	10	4	800	1,200

Adapted, by permission, from T.O. Bompa and M.C. Carrera, 2005, *Periodization training for sports: Science-based strength and conditioning plans for 20 sports,* 2nd ed. (Champaign, IL: Human Kinetics), 258.

Training Intensity

The **training intensity** or load relates to the amount of weight or resistance being used. The intensity of a training session can be calculated by dividing the volume load by the total number of repetitions completed (173).

The load used in resistance training is best expressed as a percentage of 1RM (115). Some strength and conditioning professionals suggest using repetitions to failure with repetition maximum zones (e.g., 1-3RM, 8-12RM, or 13-15RM) as a method for determining training intensity (29, 50). However, using training to failure in the development of maximal strength has been consistently questioned and is not the optimal method for loading during strength training (105, 148, 179). This contention is supported by research by Izquierdo and colleagues (105) suggesting that training to failure brings about fewer improvements in muscular strength compared with not training to failure. Additional support for this argument was offered by Peterson and colleagues (148), who clearly showed in their meta-analysis that training to failure does not maximize strength gains. Thus, it appears that loading is best determined as a percentage of 1RM.

Table 10.4 Intensity Zones for Strength Training

Intensity zone	Loading	Intensity (% of 1RM)	Muscle action
1	Supermaximal	>100	Eccentric overload Isometric
2	Maximum	90-100	Concentric
3	Heavy	80-90	Concentric
4	Medium	70-80	Concentric
5	Low	50-70	Concentric
6	Very low	30-50	Concentric

Adapted, by permission, from T.O. Bompa and M.C. Carrera, 2005, *Periodization training for sports: Science-based strength and conditioning plans for 20 sports*, 2nd ed. (Champaign, IL: Human Kinetics), 258.

By examining different percentages of 1RM, we can create a loading paradigm (table 10.4). In this paradigm, loading intensity zones (figure 10.7) can be quantified in relationship to their emphasis on muscular endurance, power generation, and maximal strength. Maximal strength is most likely emphasized with loads 80% of 1RM or greater (55), whereas muscular endurance is emphasized with loads between 20% and 80% of 1RM. Muscular power appears to be maximized somewhere between 30% and 80% of 1RM depending on the exercise (114).

Intensities between 100% and 125% of 1RM are classified as *supermaximal* loads; athletes can use these loads when attempting to establish new 1RM values or when using eccentric overload or forced repetition techniques (43). Although eccentric overload or forced repetition training appears to have a place in strength training, it may not result in significant increases in muscular strength compared with regular training (43). Supermaximal loads should be attempted only by highly strength trained athletes and should be used infrequently. Aján and Baroga (11) suggested that only 5% of the total yearly training volume be performed at intensities 100% of 1RM or greater.

Training loads that range from 90% to 100% of 1RM are classified as *maximum* loads. *Heavy* loads are intensities between 80% and 90% of 1RM. Loads of 50% to 80% of 1RM can be classified as *medium* intensities, whereas loads less than 50% are classified as *low* intensity. The vast majority of the loading should come from medium intensities (50-80% of 1RM). Support for this can be seen in the training loads undertaken by weightlifters, where the following intensity breakdown can be seen: low = 8%, medium =59%, heavy = 26% and maximum = 7% (211). The load encountered in training will vary depending on the training phase and the loading paradigm used.

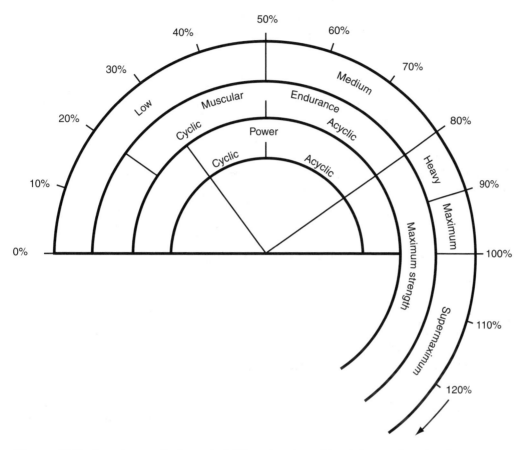

Figure 10.7 Load magnitude and abilities developed by using various loads.

Repetitions

The number of repetitions that can be performed is usually a function of the load used (table 10.5). The higher the load, the lower the number of repetitions that can be performed (90, 91, 171). However, it is difficult to make definitive connections between a percentage of 1RM and the number of repetitions that can be performed because it appears that training status, muscle mass engaged, gender, and type of exercise can change the number of repetitions that can be performed at a given load. For example, Shimano and colleagues (171) reported that at 60% of the 1RM, untrained individuals can perform 35.9 ± 13.4 repetitions in the back squat, 21.6 ± 4.2

Table 10.5 Load to Repetition Relationship

Percentage of 1RM	Number of repetitions
100	1
95	2-3
90	4
85	6
80	8-10
75	10-12
70	15
65	20-25
60	25
50	40-50
40	80-100
30	100-150

Adapted, by permission, from T.O. Bompa and M.C. Carrera, 2005, *Periodization training for sports: Science-based strength and conditioning plans for 20 sports,* 2nd ed. (Champaign, IL: Human Kinetics), 258.

repetitions in the bench press, and 17.2 ± 3.7 repetitions in the arm curl. Conversely, trained individuals were reported to have performed 29.9 ± 7.4 repetitions in the back squat, 21.7 ± 3.8 repetitions in the bench press, and 19.0 ± 2.9 repetitions in the arm curl at training loads that corresponded to 60% of 1RM. Hoeger and colleagues (91) reported that exercise type, training status, and gender resulted in differences in the number of repetitions that could be performed at various percentages of 1RM. For example, at an intensity of 40% of 1RM, untrained men performed 80.1 ± 47.9 repetitions on the leg press and 34.9 ± 8.8 repetitions on the machine bench press. When the same protocol was repeated with untrained women, 83.6 ± 38.6 repetitions were performed on the leg press; no repetitions were performed on the machine bench press because the load could not be set on the machine. The coach needs to consider the athlete's training status and gender, the muscle mass involved, and the mode of resistance training when determining how many repetitions can be performed at various percentages of 1RM.

The repetition scheme used results in specific physiological adaptations (29). As illustrated in figure 10.8, low-repetition schemes (1-6 repetitions) are better for the development of maximal muscular strength. Higher numbers of repetitions (>10 repetitions) appear to be more suited for stimulating muscular endurance (20, 29). High-intensity endurance (short duration) appears to be enhanced with repetition schemes of 10 to 15 (29, 50), whereas low-intensity endurance (long duration) is improved with more than 20 repetitions (29). Power-based adaptations are best realized with low-repetition schemes (1-3 repetitions) depending on the phase of training. The repetition scheme should be selected based on the goal of the phase of training and the loading scheme being used. In a periodized training plan, the repetition scheme is manipulated to facilitate specific adaptations.

Sets

Traditionally a set consists of a series of repetitions performed continuously followed by a rest interval (72). Contemporary literature clearly demonstrates that single-set training programs dramatically restrict the development of strength and that multiple-set protocols result in significantly greater adaptations in both athletes and nonathletes (148, 156). Peterson and colleagues (148) reported dose–response data suggesting that single-set protocols offer minimal stimulus for strength gains and that between four and eight sets are needed to optimize training-induced strength gains. Rhea and colleagues (156) also reported that a minimum of three sets are needed to maximize strength gains in both trained and untrained individuals. The literature

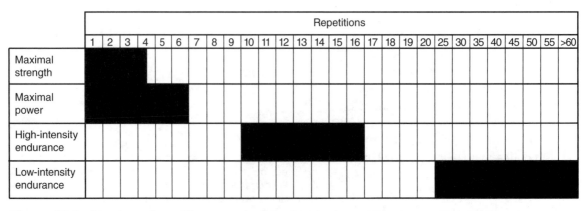

Figure 10.8 Number of repetitions required for developing various types of strength.

indicates that untrained individuals receive the most benefit from three or four sets, whereas trained individuals will gain the most adaptations from four to eight sets (148, 156). Therefore, when constructing a training program coaches must consider the training status of the individual, because highly trained athletes are able to tolerate and may benefit from higher numbers of sets. The more sets an athlete can tolerate, the greater the stimulus for adaptation and the greater the strength gains.

The traditional format of a set may be modified to change the training stimulus (72, 123, 124). Several researchers have suggested that the format of a traditional set can be modified by incorporating a short interrepetition rest interval to create what is termed a cluster set (72, 123, 124). During traditional set configurations, with each repetition there is a decrease in repetition velocity, power, and quality. The addition of a 10 to 30 s interrepetition rest interval can allow for partial recovery between each repetition (160), thus allowing for higher repetition quality (72). The interrepetition rest interval can be manipulated to target physiological responses. For example, if the athlete is focusing on power-generating capacity, she can use a 30 s interrepetition rest interval. Conversely, if high-intensity endurance is the target of training, the athlete may use a 10 s interrepetition rest interval.

Cluster sets can be structured in several different fashions depending on the goal of training (table 10.6). Additional variation in the cluster set can be accomplished by changing the loading paradigm (72). Three distinct repetition schemes can be constructed: a straight cluster set that uses the same intensity across all repetitions, an ascending cluster where the intensity of each repetition is increased, and an undulating cluster where loading is implemented in a pyramidal fashion (table 10.7). Contemporary literature suggests that the most effective use of the cluster set is with ballistic or explosive exercise (124) and that traditional sets may be better for the development of muscular hypertrophy or maximal muscular strength (157).

Table 10.6   Cluster Set Configurations Using Various Configurations for the Clean Pull

	Sets × repetitions	Interrepetition rest interval (s)	Repetition load (kg)									
Cluster	3 × 10/1	30	110	110	110	110	110	110	110	110	110	110
Cluster	3 × 10/2	30	110	110	110	110	110					
Cluster	3 × 10/5	30	110	110								

Note: 3 × 10/1 = three sets of 10 repetitions performed with 30 s rest between each repetition of the set; 3 × 10/2 = three sets of 10 repetitions with 30 s rest after every two repetitions; 3 × 10/5 = three sets of 10 repetitions with 30 s rest after 5 repetitions. Loads are based on of a 1RM clean of 150 kg.

Table 10.7   Intensity Variations for Cluster Set Configurations Using the Clean Pulls

	Sets × repetitions	Interrepetition rest interval (s)	Repetition load (kg)				
Cluster	3 × 5/1	30	120	120	120	120	120
Undulating cluster	3 × 5/1	30	120	130	140	130	120
Ascending cluster	3 × 5/1	30	120	130	140	150	160

Note: 3 × 5/1 = three sets of 5 repetitions performed with 30 s between each repetition of the set. Loads are based on of a 1RM clean of 150 kg.

Regardless of how the set is configured, the phase of training will dictate the makeup of the training set. For example, during the preparation phase of training when greater numbers of repetitions and exercises are performed, fewer sets may be performed. As the competitive phase approaches, the number of exercises will decrease whereas the number of sets usually increases. During the competitive phase everything will decrease, including the number of repetitions and number of sets, so that the athlete is recovered and can focus on technical and tactical training.

Interset Rest Intervals

The rest interval between sets is a function of the load being used, the goal of the training plan, the type of strength being developed, and the degree of explosiveness of the training exercise (24). The rest interval must be long enough to allow for the restoration of adenosine triphosphate (ATP) and phosphocreatine (PCr), the clearance of fatigue-inducing substrates, and the restoration of force production capacity (204).

The time selected for the interset rest interval may play a distinct role in the replenishment of substrates used during the set. After 30 s of rest, 70% of ATP has been restored, although complete ATP resynthesis does not occur until 3 to 5 min (99). Two minutes of rest is needed to restore approximately 84% of PCr, whereas 4 min of rest is need to restore approximately 89% of the PCr stores, and 8 min of rest is needed for complete restoration of PCr (87, 99, 100). Thus, during high-volume training, rest intervals of less than 1 min may not be long enough to allow for restoration of substrates and may result in inadequate recovery (204). Force- and power-generating capacity has been shown to be almost completely restored with 2 to 5 min of recovery between sets (8, 22, 160, 188). Conversely, when less than 1 min of recovery is allowed between sets, force- and power-generating capacity can be decreased by 12% to 44% (8, 149, 188). These data indicate that short recovery periods (<1 min) should be avoided in favor of longer recovery periods (2-5 min) when the athlete is attempting to maximize force- and power-generating capacity.

Clearly, short rest intervals do not allow for enough recovery to sustain training intensities across several sets and are not advantageous when the athlete is attempting to maximize muscular strength and power development (204). However, when the resistance training program is designed to emphasize muscular endurance, short rest intervals may be advantageous. It is plausible that when short rest intervals are coupled with high volumes of training, physiological adaptations occur that can facilitate endurance performance. These adaptations may include increases in capillary density, mitochondrial density, and buffer capacity (204). Very little research has been completed that examines the effects of different resistance training regimes on muscular endurance, but contemporary literature suggests that shorter rest intervals may be advantageous when targeting muscular endurance.

Short rest interval programs have also been suggested to result in significant hormonal responses that provide a greater stimulus for hypertrophy (67, 131, 204). In particular, it appears that when short rest intervals are included in a resistance training program that uses higher repetitions (~10 repetitions) with moderate loads, greater levels of growth hormone are released (67, 121, 131). However, high levels of growth hormone also have been reported in response to weightlifting, which uses longer rest intervals (2-5min) and multijoint exercises (e.g., snatch, clean, pulls) with moderate to very high intensities, for relatively low numbers of repetitions (120). Short rest intervals do not allow for complete recovery, and they decrease the total work load that the athlete can accomplish. Frobrose and colleagues (54) suggested the work accomplished (i.e., tonnage or volume load) is the primary stimulus for muscular hypertrophy. Thus, depending on the athlete's ability to recover, various rest interval lengths may be used when targeting muscular hypertrophy.

Order of Exercises

The order of exercises in a strength training program can significantly influence the effectiveness of the training session (12, 15, 169, 177). Large-mass, multijoint exercises should be placed early in the training session (12, 169, 177) because these exercises are fundamental to strength development and need to be trained when the athlete has a minimal amount of fatigue (177, 180). Vorobeyev (200) suggested that speed strength exercises (e.g., **power snatches**, **power cleans**), which are often large-mass, multijoint exercises, be performed first because they may exert a positive effect on subsequent exercise performance. After completing the large-mass, multijoint exercises, the athlete can then progress to smaller mass, single-joint exercises (12). Alternatively, it has been suggested that the athlete alternate between upper-body and lower-body exercises to facilitate recovery (202). This method of training may be useful with circuit-based training programs, but it has been shown to be inappropriate for training programs that emphasize strength and power development (181).

Another method of sequencing exercise that is popular in **bodybuilding** involves fatiguing the muscle group by using a large-mass, single-joint exercise prior to performing a related large-mass, multijoint exercise, creating what is termed a *pre-exhaustion complex* (15, 189). Current research suggests that the use of a pre-exhaustion exercise reduces strength gains and decreases muscle activation (15). This phenomenon most likely occurs as a result of fatigue negatively affecting the multijoint exercises that follow the single-joint pre-exhaustion exercise. Therefore, athletes who are trying to maximize maximal strength and power development should not use a pre-exhaustion complex.

When an athlete is attempting to maximize strength and power development, it may be advantageous to perform either an explosive exercise (130, 200) or a heavy-load, multijoint, large-mass exercise (130) before performing an explosive exercise such as a jump or a sprint. This can be termed a *postactivation potentiation complex*. Postactivation complexes have been shown to significantly increase the rate of force development (RFD), jumping height (210), sprinting performance (130), and sprint cycle performance (176). However, if the initial exercise creates large amounts of fatigue, performance most likely will be impaired during the second exercise of the series (32). The postactivation complex appears to be effective only when used with highly trained individuals (33). There are numerous examples of postactivation complexes in the scientific literature, but some examples that may have significant performance effects can be seen in table 10.8. Potentiation complexes need to have a heavy-load activity (≥90% 1RM) such as a back squat for minimal repetitions (one to three repetitions) performed 4 to 5 min prior to an explosive activity, such as jumping or sprinting.

Training Frequency

Training frequency is usually measured as the number of times per week a certain muscle group is trained or how often the athlete trains the whole body (12, 50, 180). The greater the training frequency, the greater the strength gains (64, 68, 102, 132,

Table 10.8 Postactivation Complexes

Study	Postactivation potentiation complex			Results
Chiu et al. (33)	Back squats 5 × 1 90% 1RM	18.5 min rest	Jump squats	Power output ⇑ with jumps at 30% 1RM
McBride et al. (128)	Back squat 1 × 3 90% 1RM	4 min rest	40 m sprint	0.87% ⇓ in sprint time
Smith et al. (176)	Back squats 10 × 1 90% 1RM	5 min rest	10 s sprint cycle test	4.8% ⇑ in average power output
Yetter and Moir (211)	Back squat 3 x 70% 1RM	4 min rest	40 m sprint	2.3% ⇓ in sprint time
Young et al. (210)	Backs squat 1 × 5RM	4 min rest	Loaded countermovement jump	2.8% ⇑ in jump height

Note: ⇓ = decrease; ⇑ = increase.

152). For novice and intermediate weight trainers who are training the whole body during each training session, training 2 or 3 days per week appears to be optimal, whereas intermediate weight trainers who base their training sessions on muscle groups should train 3 or 4 days per week with each muscle group being trained 1 or 2 days per week (12). As the athlete becomes more developed, the frequency of training may need to be increased.

Support for higher frequencies of training with advanced athletes can be found in the scientific literature. For example, university-level American football players who participated in four or five training sessions per week experienced significantly greater gains in muscular strength than those who participated in fewer training sessions (96). It appears that higher frequencies of training are necessary to maximize maximal muscular strength adaptations (12). This contention is supported by the fact that elite weightlifters have been reported to train with as many as 21 sessions per week (63, 211). This high frequency of training is often accomplished by breaking the training volume into short sessions that occur multiple times per day (4-7, 42, 63, 109). For example, the Greek (42) and former Soviet (63) weightlifting systems use two sessions in one training day, whereas the Bulgarian system of weightlifting uses as many as six 45 min sessions throughout the training day (4-7, 63). Aján and Baroga (11) suggested that multiple training sessions may be needed per day to maximize performance in competitive weightlifters. It is thought that breaking the training volume into short sessions, followed by periods of recovery in which dietary nutrients and supplements are supplied, will increase training quality. This concept is supported by the work of Häkkinen and Kallinen (76), who demonstrated that increasing the frequency of training to two sessions per day, even when the volume was maintained, resulted in significantly greater increases in muscle hypertrophy and neuromuscular adaptations compared with one training session per day.

The optimal frequency of training is determined by many factors. Training status, the type of strength needed, the phase of the periodized training plan, and the athlete's goal influence the frequency of strength training. For example, most athletes undertake strength training to improve their performance in other activities. Therefore, these athletes may perform three or four strength training sessions per week in conjunction with their other training activities. However, if the athlete's goal is to maximize strength and power-generating capabilities, more frequent training may be warranted. The phase of training must be considered when selecting a training frequency. For example, during the preparation phase, the frequency of training might be substantially higher than in the later portion of the competition phase. The number of training sessions often is reduced to taper training and dissipate fatigue.

Loading Patterns

The loading pattern used in the training regime is particularly important because it will stimulate physiological adaptations. The most effective loading pattern to stimulate maximal strength gains is the *flat pyramid* (24). In the flat pyramid, the athlete begins with several warm-up sets and works toward a prescribed load at which all of the training sets are performed, followed by a down set (table 10.9). The flat portion of the pyramid generally uses an intensity between 80% and 100% of maximum when the athlete is specifically targeting maximum strength (12, 66, 77). The down set may result in a postactivation potentiation effect that increases power output and movement velocity (186). It appears that performance is maximized when the majority of training is undertaken with intensities of about 70% to 85% of 1RM (66, 211). This is seen in the data presented by Zatsiorsky (211), who reported that 35% of the training volume of Soviet weightlifters was between 70% and 80% of 1RM, 26% of the training volume was between 80% and 90% of 1RM, and only 7% of the training volume was between 90% and 100% of 1RM throughout the training year. Conversely, Häkkinen and colleagues (77) reported that when training volume is increased in the 80% to 90% and 90% to 100% of 1RM, maximal strength increases significantly. When too much of the training volume is in the 90% to 100% range, performance may not be optimized and overtraining may occur (56).

A second loading pattern is the *pyramid* loading pattern (24, 173) or an *ascending pyramid* loading scheme. In this loading scheme, with each set the percentage of 1RM increases until a maximal attempt is made and with each set the number of repetitions decreases (table 10.10). The load range of the ascending pyramid has been suggested to range from 10% to 15% (24). Load ranges greater than 15% are not recommended because the cumulative fatigue that accumulates may impair strength development (24).

A modification of the ascending pyramid loading pattern is what some have termed the *double pyramid* (24, 69) or simply a *pyramid* (211, 212). In this loading pattern, the resistance is increased up to a maximal attempt and then the load is progressively decreased (211, 212). In conjunction with this loading pattern, two volume patterns

Table 10.9   Loading Pattern for a Flat Pyramid Using the Back Squat

	WARM-UP					TARGET SETS			DOWN SETS
Load (kg)	67.5	112.5	135	157.5	180	190	190	190	180.5
Repetitions	5	5	5	5	5	5	5	5	5
Percentage of 1RM	30	50	60	70	80	84	84	84	80

Note: Loading based on a maximum back squat of 225 kg

Adapted from Stone et al. 2006 (184).

Table 10.10 Loading Pattern for an Ascending Pyramid Using the Back Squat

	WARM-UP					PYRAMID			
Load (kg)	67.5	112.5	135	157.5	180	191	202.5	214	225
Repetitions	6	6	6	6	6	6	4	2	1
Percentage of 1RM	30	50	60	70	80	85	90	95	100

Note: Loading based upon a maximum back squat of 225 kg.

Adapted from Stone et al. 2006 (184).

Table 10.11 Loading Pattern for a Double Pyramid Using the Back Squat

	DOUBLE PYRAMID VERSION 1							
Load (kg)	180	191	202.5	214	214	202.5	191	180
Repetitions	4	3	2	1	1	2	3	4
Percentage of 1RM	80	85	90	95	95	90	85	80
	DOUBLE PYRAMID VERSION 2							
Load (kg)	180	191	202.5	214	214	202.5	191	180
Repetitions	1	1	1	1	1	1	1	1
Percentage of 1RM	80	85	90	95	95	90	85	80

Note: Loading based on a maximum back squat of 225 kg. An appropriate warm-up is required to prepare the athlete for the training bout.

Adapted from Stone et al. 2006 (184).

have been suggested (table 10.11). In one volume pattern, the number of repetitions decreases as the intensity increases and increases as the intensity is lowered on the descending sets (24, 69). Another volume pattern leaves the volume constant, typically at one repetition, and then uses an ascending intensity pattern followed by a descending pattern (211, 212). Proponents of these loading patterns suggest that there is a potentiation effect on the descending intensity portion of the pyramid. However, it is likely that the amount of fatigue established in this type of loading paradigm will result in a lack of potentiation (32). Zatsiorsky (211) and Zatsiorsky and Kraemer (212) suggested that this type of loading paradigm is not popular and has been abandoned by most Olympic-caliber athletes.

Another modification to the pyramid loading pattern is the *skewed pyramid*. This modification is considered to be an improvement on the double pyramid loading model (24). In this loading structure, the intensity is increased for a series of sets and on the last set a down set is performed (table 10.12). Decreasing the intensity of the last set should induce a postactivation potentiation effect (186). This concept is supported by work by Stone and colleagues (186), which demonstrates that greater barbell velocities are achieved during the down set. These data suggest that the skewed pyramid may be useful when attempting to create potentiation complexes.

Yet another loading pattern is the *wave-loading* model (189), which is sometimes referred to as segment work (108). In this model the training load increases in an undulating or wave-like fashion (table 10.13). The wave-loading method may be useful

Table 10.12 Loading Pattern for a Skewed Pyramid Using the Midthigh Clean Pull

	SKEWED PYRAMID				
Load (kg)	60	140	180	220	140
Repetitions	2	2	2	2	2
Percentage of 1RM	30	65	85	105	65

Note: Loading based on a maximum clean of 212 kg. An appropriate warm-up is required to prepare the athlete for the training bout.

Adapted from Stone et al. 2008 (186).

Table 10.13 Wave-Loading and Double Stimulation Models Using the Snatch

	WARM-UP			WAVE SEGMENT				
Load (kg)	84	98	105	112	119	105	112	119
Repetitions[a]	5	3	2	3	2	3	3	2
Percentage of 1RMa	60	70	75	80	85	75	80	85

	WARM-UP			DOUBLE STIMULATION SEGMENT				
Load (kg)	135	157.5	180	202.5	180	202.5	180	202.5
Repetitions[b]	5	5	5	1	5	1	5	1
Percentage of 1RMb	60	70	80	90	80	90	80	90

[a]Data calculated for a 1RM snatch of 140 kg.

[b]Data calculated for a 1RM squat of 225 kg.

Adapted from Jones 1992 (108).

because it allows for a potentiating effect, because a light load is undertaken after a heavy load; however, the occurrence of a postactivation potentiation effect with this model has yet to be investigated in the scientific literature. The wave-loading model appears to work best with weightlifting exercises (e.g., snatches, power snatches, cleans, power cleans). A variant of the wave-loading model is the *double stimulation* model (108). In this model the athlete alternates a set of high repetitions with a single repetition that is performed at 10% to 15% greater intensity. The double stimulation model appears to work best with strength exercises (e.g., back squat, pulls) but has yet to be explored in the scientific literature.

IMPLEMENTATION OF A STRENGTH TRAINING REGIMEN

Continual monitoring of the training process is an often overlooked but essential part of implementing a periodized strength training plan (187). Monitoring the athlete's progress allows the coach to determine whether the goals of the training plan are being achieved. The following steps will allow the coach to conceptualize, design, and implement a periodized strength training regimen.

1. ***Determine the Training Goal:*** The most important step in establishing a periodized strength training regimen is to determine the goal of the training program. In this step, the coach and athlete determine the points during the competitive season at which the athlete needs to give her best performance.

2. ***Determine the Phases of Training:*** Like any other periodized training plan, a strength training program has preparatory, competitive, and transition phases of training. Each phase is essential to maximize training outcomes. This concept can be considered phase potentiation (86, 151), which suggests that activities of the general preparatory phase facilitate the athlete's development in the specific preparatory phase (86) and the competition phase. Thus, the coach must structure the phases of training so the athlete develops the appropriate biomotor abilities.

3. ***Determine the Athlete's Needs:*** The coach needs to perform a *needs analysis* in which she determines the types of strength needed by the sport, the types of movement patterns, prime movers associated with the sport, bioenergetic demands of the sport, and any deficit or area of concern (50). The coach must understand the physiological demands of the sporting activity to establish a reference point from which to design the strength training plan.

© Human Kinetics

To develop a successful strength training plan, a coach must understand what kind of strength the athlete needs for his sport.

4. ***Consider the Characteristics of All Components of the Training Plan:*** A resistance training plan must not be implemented randomly. For the resistance training plan to be effective, all training factors must be integrated (187). Therefore, in team sports, for example, the coach must consider the strength training regimen, the conditioning program, the agility component, and the tactical training activities as an overall unit of training. If these factors are not considered as a whole, the potential for overtraining is substantially increased and the optimization of performance is left up to chance.

5. ***Select the Exercises to Be Used in the Training Plan:*** The training exercises selected must be related to the requirements of the sport. When examining a sport during the needs analysis, the coach can determine the muscles that act as prime movers and match exercises to these activities. For example, watching a 100 m sprinter shows that lower-body strength is essential for optimal performance outcomes. Thus, the coach may select exercises such as back squats and power cleans in an attempt to target the prime movers of this activity. Support for this idea can be seen in several studies suggesting that maximal strength capacity in the back squat and power clean is significantly related to running performance (18, 26, 37).

An additional consideration when selecting exercises is the phase of training. Certain exercises are best used at specific times during the periodized plan (86, 151, 187). For example, early in the general preparation phase of training it may be warranted to use fewer technical lifts because fatigue may impair technical performance, which can increase the injury risk and decrease performance gains. As the athlete moves toward the specific preparation and competitive phase of training, more technical lifts can be used because the reduction in training volume will reduce accumulative fatigue. Another way to look at this is that exercises that target conditioning are central to the goals of the general preparation phase, whereas exercises that target strength and power development are appropriate during the specific preparation and competition phases.

6. ***Test Performance:*** After selecting the exercises that are needed to develop the performance attributes needed by the athlete, the coach must test the athlete's maximal strength. Knowledge of the athlete's 1RM capabilities in at least the primary or dominant exercises will allow the coach to establish the training loads. The 1RM will continually change as the athlete adapts to the physiological stressors of the training regime. Therefore, the athlete must be tested periodically to individualize the loading parameters.

Many coaches wrongly believe that performing a 1RM test is dangerous and will increase the athlete's risk of injury (28, 122, 127, 155). In fact, 1RM testing is very safe for most populations (159, 170) and is considered the gold standard in the assessment of muscular strength (101). Some authors suggest that testing strength with multiple repetition tests is a better way to establish the training intensity (27, 28, 47, 127), but it has been consistently shown that many of the prediction equations misrepresent the 1RM (127). This is a major problem because using an estimate of 1RM capabilities that is too high may increase injury risk during training or induce high-intensity overtraining from consistently training at high intensities (56). Conversely, training with an intensity that is underpredicted will result in inadequate strength development because the athlete will train using suboptimal loads.

7. ***Develop the Resistance Training Program:*** After establishing the athlete's physical performance capabilities, the coach can establish the number of exercises, sets, repetitions, and loading (percentage of 1RM) that will be used during the microcycles and macrocycle. Throughout the training plan the coach probably will need to alter volume, intensity, and the exercises selected to allow for continued physiological adaptations that will lead to increases in muscular strength. As muscular strength increases across the macrocycle, the coach will need to periodically retest the 1RM to optimize the training load. It is essential for the coach to test the 1RM before each new macrocycle.

8. ***Record the Training Plan:*** The coach must record the exercises, number of sets, number of repetitions, and training load (table 10.14). The load, number of repetitions, and sets usually are noted as follows:

% of 1RM / number of repetitions

Noting the load as a percentage of 1RM is useful when working with many athletes, because this allows the coach to calculate the load for every athlete. By using a percentage notation, the coach can individualize the program for each athlete and athletes will use their own 1RM to establish their training loads.

Table 10.14 Sample Chart of a Strength Training Program

Exercise number	Exercise	Loading	Rest interval
1	Clean	$\frac{80}{4}$	3
2	Back squat	$\frac{80}{2}$ $\frac{85}{3}$	3
3	Push press	$\frac{75}{2}$	3

Notes: loading = $\frac{\text{\% 1-RM}}{\text{repetitions}}$

9. *Create a Training Log:* One of the most important steps is to record what was done in the training sessions. If the coach and athlete keep detailed records, they will be able to evaluate the athlete's progress and chart her performance. Things to record in the training log include the exercise, the number of repetitions completed, the number of sets performed, the load lifted in kilograms, and the duration of the training session (figure 10.9). This record will allow the coach to calculate the volume load, metric tons, and training intensity (volume load divided by total repetitions performed). By using a spreadsheet software program such as Excel, the coach can easily calculate the volume load, metric tons, and training intensity and create figures depicting the volume and intensity of training. If the training log is accurate and inclusive, it provides an excellent tool for monitoring training (187).

SUMMARY OF MAJOR CONCEPTS

Strength is one of the most important biomotor abilities for most sports. Strength is the foundation for both generating maximal power and maintaining repetitive muscular contractions, in other words, muscular endurance. A periodized strength training regime can be an excellent tool for maximizing performance outcomes. The physiological adaptations to the neuromuscular system that resistance training can bring about are very specific to the training program that the athlete uses. Athletic performance can be maximized only if the training regime provides appropriate variation. Many methods for inducing training variation are available, and many of them can result in very specific physiological adaptations. Finally, to truly maximize the effectiveness of a strength training regime, it must be integrated into the comprehensive periodized training plan developed for the athlete. Simply adding strength training to an athlete's training plan without considering the other training activities will not maximize performance outcomes.

Name: ______________________ Time in: ____________

Day: ______________________ Time out: ____________

Date: ______________________

Exercise		Set 1	Set 2	Set 3	Set 4	Set 5	Set 6	Set 7	Set 8	Set 9	Set 10	Volume load	Training intensity
Back squat	Weight	60	80	110	130	130	130					6,400	106.67
	Repetitions	10	10	10	10	10	10						
1/3 front squat	Weight	160	160	160								4,800	160.00
	Repetitions	10	10	10									
Military press	Weight	60	60	60								1,800	60.00
	Repetitions	10	10	1									
Incline bench press	Weight	70	70	70								2,100	70.00
	Repetitions	10	10	10									
	Weight Repetitions Weight												
	Repetitions Weight												
	Repetitions Weight												
Notes:								Total volume load				15,100	
								Metric tons				15.1	
										Training intensity			99.167

Figure 10.9 Training log for a single training session.

CHAPTER 11

ENDURANCE TRAINING

Endurance can be classified several ways. For example, aerobic endurance, sometimes called low-intensity exercise endurance, allows a person to perform activities continually for a long duration, whereas anaerobic endurance, or high-intensity exercise endurance, provides the ability to repetitively perform bouts of high-intensity exercise. Although most sports rely on some form of endurance, the type of endurance developed (high or low intensity) can significantly affect performance outcomes. Therefore, the coach and athlete must consider the type of endurance that the athlete needs for the sport and how the appropriate endurance will be targeted within the training plan. The coach and athlete must also consider the athlete's physiological responses to the methods for developing endurance. Once the type of endurance and the physiological responses are understood, the coach can develop a training plan to enhance sport-specific endurance.

CLASSIFICATION OF ENDURANCE

The concept of endurance differs distinctly between various sporting activities and thus can be defined in several different ways. For example, the type of endurance that an elite marathon runner needs provides the ability to continuously perform at a specific power output or velocity for a long duration of time. Conversely, an elite ice hockey player needs to repetitively perform periods of high-velocity movements for 30 to 80 s interspersed with periods of recovery lasting between 4 and 5 min (106). Although some form of endurance affects both athletes' performance, the development of endurance in these athletes will be distinctly different. If the wrong type of endurance training is implemented, the athlete might develop endurance characteristics that do not meet the needs of the sport, and thus performance capacity can be reduced (45, 147). To understand the correct application of endurance training, the coach and athlete must differentiate between the two major types of endurance reported in the contemporary literature: **low-intensity exercise endurance (LIEE)** and **high-intensity exercise endurance (HIEE)** (147).

Low-Intensity Exercise Endurance

Activities that are predominated by aerobic energy supply tend to exhibit lower peak powers and thus can be classified as being of lower intensities (29, 148). These activities require the athlete to perform continually, at a low intensity, for a substantial duration

(148). Thus, this type of endurance is often termed LIEE (148) or aerobic endurance. Many activities rely predominantly on oxidative or aerobic metabolism (see chapter 1 and table 1.2 on p. 28) and require the athlete to develop a high level of LIEE. For such activities, developing LIEE can greatly improve the athlete's performance.

Conversely, the development of LIEE in sports that rely on anaerobic energy supply (e.g., weightlifting, sprinting, American football, ice hockey, volleyball) can result in several maladaptations that reduce the athlete's performance capacity (45). When LIEE is used to improve endurance in athletes who participate in sports that rely predominantly on anaerobic energy supply, marked decreases in power-generating capacity are noted and performance usually is impaired (42, 45, 63, 83). One reason that has been proposed to explain this impaired anaerobic performance is that the development of LIEE can reduce the athlete's ability to produce force in the high-velocity, low-frequency region of the force–velocity curve (12). Changes to this region of the force–velocity curve can interfere with the athlete's ability to develop explosive strength, which is required by many anaerobic activities (45). In particular, the ability to achieve high rates of force development and to generate high levels of peak force can be impaired by the implementation of an LIEE regime (figure 11.1). There also appears to be a fiber type shift resulting in a decrease in the number of Type II muscle fibers and an increase in Type I fibers when LIEE is the focus of the endurance development program (154). LIEE training can also impede muscular growth (108), which will impair an athlete's ability to generate high rates of force development (81), maximize peak force-generating capacity (81), and optimize peak power generation (45). The contemporary literature indicates that LIEE training should not be used for athletes in sports that predominantly rely on anaerobic energy supply, require high levels of force production, require high rates of force development, call for fast velocities of movement, or require high levels of power output. LIEE training should be restricted to long-duration activities that rely on aerobic energy supply, whereas other methods for developing endurance should be used by athletes in other types of sports.

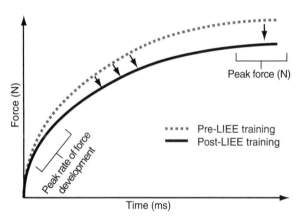

Figure 11.1 Force–time curve alterations to the development of low-intensity exercise endurance .
Adapted from Häkkinen and Myllyla 1990 (61) and Häkkinen et al. 1989 (60).

High-Intensity Exercise Endurance

Sports that rely on anaerobic metabolism (see chapter 1 and table 1.2 on p. 28) usually require high power outputs or the repetitive performance of high-velocity movements. Because anaerobic activities require higher power outputs than those seen in aerobic activities, anaerobic activities can be classified as being of high intensity (29, 148). Therefore, the ability to sustain and repeat high-intensity exercise bouts is considered to be HIEE (147). The development of HIEE does not impair strength and power-generating capacity, as typically occurs when LIEE is developed. One explanation why HIEE does not reduce maximal strength and power development is that

HIEE training tends to increase Type II muscle fiber content (38). Because Type II fiber content is related to the maximal rate of force development (81, 85), maximal force generation capacity (81), and the ability to generate peak power outputs (149), it is easy to conclude that HIEE may be more beneficial for sports that rely on these performance factors, especially if high-velocity or high-power movements are performed repetitively. Several authors report that the use of high-intensity intervals can significantly increase markers of both anaerobic and aerobic exercise endurance (95, 126, 152). Therefore, it is recommended that an HIEE or interval training approach be used to develop endurance for sports that require the repetitive performance of high-intensity exercise (e.g., American football, soccer, basketball, ice hockey)(147).

HIEE training should not be limited to the development of anaerobic endurance, because this type of training also has the potential to improve LIEE (87). The development of HIEE with the use of high-intensity interval training appears to have a profound effect on aerobic activities that typically rely on LIEE. For example, it has been shown that 3K (+3%) (142) and 10K (4) running performance can be significantly improved with high-intensity interval training. As well, 40 km cycle time-trial performance has been increased significantly (+2.1-4.5%) with high-intensity interval training (144, 145, 158). Several authors have suggested that increasing the quantity of traditional LIEE training with elite athletes may not result in the necessary physiological adaptations needed to improve performance (31, 64). Laursen and Jenkins (87) suggested that high-intensity interval training or HIEE training may be warranted for athletes who have established an LIEE training base. Therefore, it may be beneficial to consider using HIEE training methods for athletes who participate in aerobic sports that require repetitive performance over a long duration of time.

FACTORS AFFECTING AEROBIC ENDURANCE PERFORMANCE

Several aspects of aerobic endurance are central in determining the athlete's endurance capacity (35, 75). These factors include the athlete's aerobic power, lactate threshold, economy of movement, and muscle fiber type (figure 11.2). Each factor can be improved significantly with appropriate training methods (75, 87). To develop appropriate aerobic endurance training programs, the coach and athlete must understand the physiological responses associated with endurance performance.

Aerobic Power

Maximal **aerobic power** has long been considered to be a major factor in determining success in endurance sports (33, 131). However, aerobic power is not the only determinant of sport performance (92). Aerobic power is measured as the highest rate at which oxygen can be taken up and used by the body during maximal exercise (56) and can also be defined as maximal oxygen uptake ($\dot{V}O_2$max) (9, 35). $\dot{V}O_2$max values between 70 and 85 ml·kg^{-1}·min^{-1} have been reported for elite endurance athletes (34, 76) with women exhibiting an approximately 10% lower $\dot{V}O_2$max than their male counterparts as a result of lower **hemoglobin** concentrations and higher body fat percentages. Regardless of gender, the ability to achieve a high $\dot{V}O_2$max appears to be affected by the functioning of the pulmonary system, the maximum cardiac output, the oxygen-carrying capacity, and factors associated with the skeletal muscle system (figure 11.3) (9).

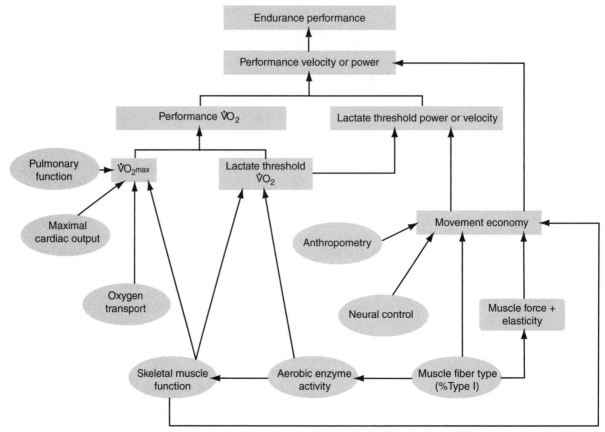

Figure 11.2 Model of the relationships between physiological factors and endurance performance.
Adapted from Bassett and Howley 2000 (9), Coyle 1995 (35), Paavolainen et al. 1999 (110), and Joyner and Coyle 2008 (76).

Pulmonary System

The **pulmonary system** appears to limit $\dot{V}O_2$max in very specific circumstances (9, 120). For example, oxygen (O_2) desaturation can occur in elite athletes who are performing maximal work (39), because a high exercise **cardiac output** (Q = **stroke volume** × heart rate) decreases the red blood cell (RBC) transit time through the pulmonary capillary (9, 39). The decreased transit time for the RBC decreases the time available to saturate the blood with O_2, potentially limiting performance. Support for the contention that the pulmonary system can limit $\dot{V}O_2$max can be seen in studies that have explored the effects of hyperoxia (120). If supplemental O_2 is supplied, there is an increased O_2 "driving force," which elevates $\dot{V}O_2$max as a result of increased oxygen saturation (109, 120).

Similar performance impairments can be seen when exercise is performed at moderately high altitudes (3,000-5,000 m) (9, 49). This altitude-induced reduction in performance can be experienced in response to short-term (1-3 days) altitude exposure, which can stimulate a reduction in O_2 saturation (23). A similar reduction in performance and oxygen desaturation response can be seen in individuals who have asthma (9). Like athletes, people with asthma who use supplemental O_2 experience an increased driving force for O_2 diffusion (9). These data suggest that pulmonary gas exchange can significantly limit an athlete's ability to express a high $\dot{V}O_2$max (9).

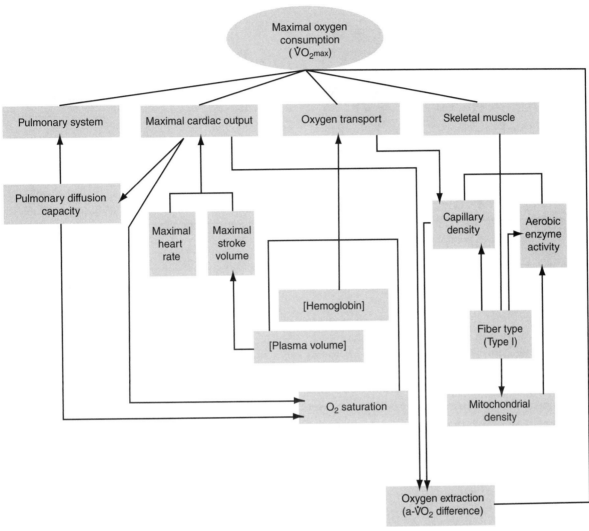

Figure 11.3 Factors affecting maximal aerobic power or maximal oxygen consumption.
(a-$\dot{V}O_2$ difference) = arterial–mixed venous oxygen difference.
Adapted from Bassett and Howley 2000 (9), Coyle 1995 (35), and Joyner and Coyle 2008 (76).

Cardiac Output

Maximal aerobic power is strongly related to maximal cardiac output (Qmax) (75). This relationship can be seen when comparing the typical Qmax and $\dot{V}O_2$max of athletes with those values in untrained individuals (figure 11.4) (164). The Qmax is a function of both the maximal heart rate and the volume of blood (stroke volume) pumped by the heart (92, 164). Lower-level athletes and untrained individuals exhibit a linear increase in both stroke volume and exercise heart rate until approximately 40% of $\dot{V}O_2$max (119, 160, 164), after which stroke volume plateaus or slightly increases, and increases in heart rate determine increases in cardiac output (164). It is believed that the plateau in cardiac output is a direct function of a decreased left ventricular diastolic filling time, which can be seen with increasing exercise intensity (128). Conversely, elite endurance athletes exhibit increases in both heart rate and cardiac output in response to increasing exercise intensity (59, 164). The reason for this discrepancy in stroke volume response between elite endurance athletes and trained or

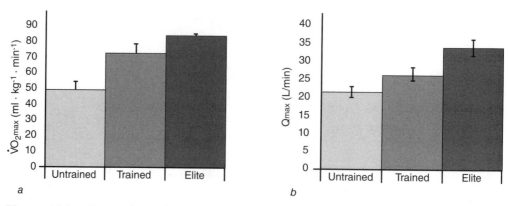

Figure 11.4 Comparison of (a) maximal oxygen consumption and (b) maximal cardiac output between untrained, trained, and elite male distance runners.
Parts a-b adapted from Zhou et al. 2001 (164).

untrained individuals has yet to be determined, but it is generally accepted that elite athletes exhibit higher Qmax values (9).

Because elite athletes exhibit a higher Qmax, it might be speculated that the difference between elite athletes, trained athletes, and untrained individuals rests in either the ability to achieve maximal heart rates or the ability to increase stroke volume (9, 92). Maximum heart rate is slightly lower in elite athletes compared with nonathletes (92, 164); therefore, it is likely that the main factor differentiating the Qmax between athletes and nonathletes is the training-induced alterations in stroke volume (92). The increase in **stroke volume** seen in athletes is likely related to an increase in end-diastolic volume that occurs as a result of improved cardiac chamber compliance or an increase in the distensibility of the pericardium (92). These data indicate that the Qmax partially explains the differences in $\dot{V}O_2$max between athletes and nonathletes.

Oxygen Transport

Another factor that can explain individual differences in $\dot{V}O_2$max is the capacity of the cardiorespiratory system to *transport oxygen* (9). Alterations to the **hemoglobin (Hb)** concentration can have a profound effect on O_2 transport to the working muscle (15). For example, if athletes use blood transfusions to artificially increase their Hb concentrations, a concomitant increase in $\dot{V}O_2$max and Qmax is seen (44). These relationships among Hb concentration, $\dot{V}O_2$max, and Qmax partially explain why blood doping is effective (15). Although doping appears to exert a profound effect on the body's ability to transport oxygen (15), it also appears that aerobic endurance training can alter this ability (134).

Endurance training appears to reduce Hb concentration, hematocrit (Hct), and red blood cell (RBC) count as a result of plasma volume expansion, which can begin to occur after several days of prolonged training (135). Although there is a general decrease in Hct and Hb concentration in response to endurance training, there is an absolute increase in the Hb mass (133). The plasma volume increase noted with endurance training decreases blood viscosity, which increases $\dot{V}O_2$max as a result of an increase in cardiac output that improves oxygen delivery to the working muscles (134).

Skeletal Muscle

The skeletal muscle can play a very important role in determining an athlete's $\dot{V}O_2$max (9). The $\dot{V}O_2$max appears to be related to the rate at which O_2 can be delivered to the mitochondria (100). Several factors associated with skeletal muscles can affect their ability to use O_2, including the skeletal muscle fiber type (Type I vs. Type II), mitochondrial density, and capillary density.

Muscle Fiber Type   Muscle fiber type appears to be significantly related to the $\dot{V}O_2$max of elite athletes (98). Athletes who express higher $\dot{V}O_2$max values also appear to have higher Type I fiber content. This phenomenon may be related to the different capillary densities, mitochondrial content, and aerobic enzyme capacities seen between Type I and Type II fibers. Type I fibers, which have a higher oxidative capacity, have a greater capillary to fiber ratio as a result of being surrounded by more capillaries compared with Type II fibers (165). Type I fibers also display a greater mitochondrial density (127) and a greater reliance on aerobic enzyme activity (51, 70, 156). Finally, there appears to be a general shift from Type II to Type I fiber content, an increase in mitochondrial content, and an increased reliance on aerobic metabolism in response to endurance training (127, 154). These endurance training–induced adaptations appear to be related to the athlete's training age; athletes who have trained longer experience greater increases in capillary density and Type I fiber content and a greater reliance on aerobic enzyme activity (127).

Mitochondrial Density   The **mitochondria** are the sites within the muscle where O_2 is consumed during oxidative metabolism (9). An increase in mitochondrial content of the skeletal muscle may contribute to an increased $\dot{V}O_2$max as a result of a greater extraction of O_2 from the blood (69). Exercise appears to be a powerful stimulator for mitochondrial biogenesis (69, 161), and exercise-induced increases in mitochondrial density may partially explain the improvements in $\dot{V}O_2$max seen with endurance training (69). Theoretically, if the mitochondrial density is increased, a proportional increase in O_2 extraction from the blood should occur (9). However, this does not appear to be the case, because only modest increases in $\dot{V}O_2$max occur in response to training (20-40%) even though there are marked increases in mitochondrial enzymes (69). It is likely that training induces increases in mitochondrial enzymes, which improves endurance performance (9). These enzymatic adaptations may improve endurance performance via decreased lactate production during exercise and an increase in fat oxidation, which results in a sparing of muscle glycogen and blood glucose (69). Although mitochondrial enzyme adaptations to training result in increases in endurance $\dot{V}O_2$max during whole-body exercise, it appears that performance is most affected by oxygen delivery, not mitochondrial density (9).

Capillary Density   Investigators have reported that a greater capillary density or number corresponds to a higher $\dot{V}O_2$max (9, 26, 35, 132). It has been speculated that $\dot{V}O_2$max depends on capillary density, or the number of capillaries per unit of cross-sectional area of muscle (100). An increase in capillary density allows for a maintenance or elongation of the RBC's transient time through the capillary bed (130), which would increase O_2 extraction at the tissue, called the **arteriovenous oxygen difference**, or $(a-\bar{v})O_2$ difference, even when blood flow is elevated (9). Investigators also have reported that athletes who possess higher capillary densities are able to exercise for longer durations as a result of being able to tolerate anaerobic metabolism and lactate formation better than athletes with lower capillary densities (76). This suggests that capillary density plays an important role in the delivery of O_2 to working tissue and the removal of waste products created by the muscle.

Capillary density is increased in response to endurance training (36, 71, 130, 136, 151). This increase in capillary density appears to be tightly linked to the training age of the athlete, where a greater training age relates to greater increases in capillary density (127).

Lactate Threshold

It is well accepted that $\dot{V}O_2$max plays a role in endurance performance capabilities. However, with elite athletes there is a narrow range between the $\dot{V}O_2$max of individual athletes (18, 27), thus suggesting that the $\dot{V}O_2$max does not differentiate between the performances of these athletes (14, 18). If, for example, two elite athletes with different $\dot{V}O_2$max values are competing, the athlete who possess the lower $\dot{V}O_2$max may be able to compensate for this by working at a higher percentage of her maximal capacity (figure 11.5) (18, 33, 140). The percentage of $\dot{V}O_2$max at which an athlete can work may be a more accurate predictor of performance. This percentage is called the *per-*

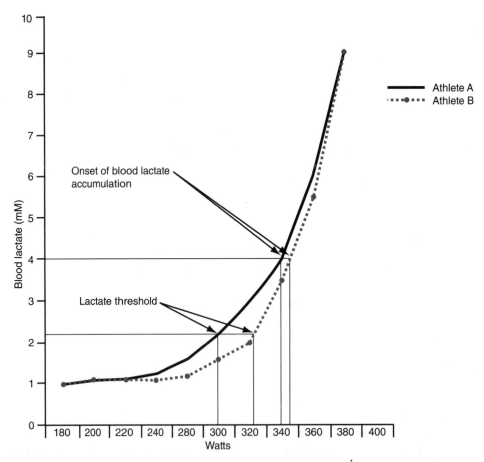

Figure 11.5 Comparison of two athletes with the same $\dot{V}O_2$max with different lactate threshold and onset of blood lactate accumulation (OBLA) values.

Note: Athlete A can produce 300 W at his lactate threshold, whereas athlete B can produce 320 W. Thus, athlete B can work at a 6.7% higher work load. Power at lactate threshold has been strongly correlated to endurance performance capacity (75).

formance oxygen uptake, and it is limited by a combination of the individual's **lactate threshold** and $\dot{V}O_2$max (14, 35).

The performance oxygen uptake can also be considered as the highest amount of work at which an equilibrium between lactate formation and buffering exists. This equilibrium has also been termed the ***maximal lactate steady state*** (150). The point at which this equilibrium becomes out of balance and lactate accumulation begins to outweigh buffering capabilities is the ***anaerobic threshold*** (150). The anaerobic threshold represents an intensity of exercise at which the body cannot meet its energy demand through aerobic mechanisms, and anaerobic energy supply begins to increase to maintain the intensity of exercise. In this scenario, the increase in lactate production occurs as a result of an increased rate of formation of pyruvate from the glycolytic system, which cannot be incorporated into oxidative metabolism, being rapidly converted into lactic acid and then lactate (150).

A graded exercise test in which intensity is periodically increased coupled with blood sampling can be used to create a **lactate** accumulation curve (figure 11.6). The lactate accumulation curve shows that breakpoints in the formation of lactate occur as the intensity of exercise increases (148). The intensity of exercise at which a substantial increase in lactate accumulation begins to occur has been termed the *lactate threshold* (14, 148, 150). The lactate threshold is defined as a 1 mM increase in blood lactate accumulation above resting levels in response to a graded exercise test

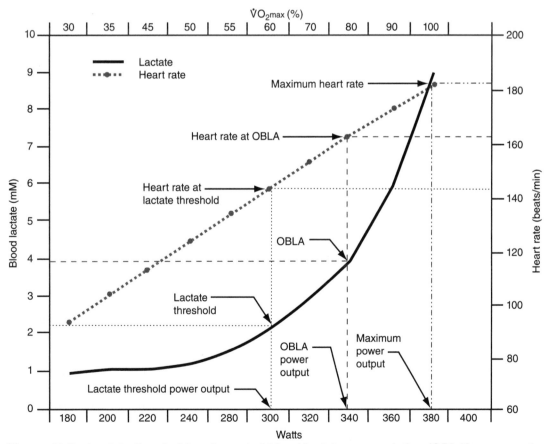

Figure 11.6 Lactate threshold and onset of blood lactate accumulation (OBLA) response to a graded cycle ergometer test.

(35, 162). In untrained subjects the lactate threshold occurs at approximately 50% to 60% of $\dot{V}O_2max$ (25, 76, 148), whereas in trained subjects the lactate threshold can occur between 75% and 90% of $\dot{V}O_2max$ (76). The power output or velocity of movement that can be maintained at the lactate threshold is a strong predictor of endurance performance (43, 75). Dumke and colleagues (43) reported that the heart rate at lactate threshold is similar to the heart rate during a 60 min cycle time trial performed by trained cyclists. Strong evidence exists suggesting that the speed or power output at the lactate threshold explains the vast majority of performance variance seen in distance racing (9, 47, 48). It appears that coaches who work with endurance athletes should quantify the lactate threshold and the heart rate and power or velocity values associated with it.

A second breakpoint on the lactate accumulation curve is called the **onset of blood lactate accumulation (OBLA),** which occurs at a fixed lactate value of 4 mM (138) (figure 11.6). OBLA is much higher than the lactate threshold and corresponds to an intensity of exercise that is much higher than that seen at the lactate threshold. As with the lactate threshold, OBLA has been suggested to be a strong indicator of endurance performance capabilities (14, 43, 79). Dumke and colleagues (43) reported that the heart rate at OBLA is similar to the heart rate during a 30 min time trial.

Both the lactate threshold and OBLA are sensitive to training (40, 75). Endurance training has been shown to shift the lactate threshold to the right, which suggests that a greater intensity of exercise (power or speed) can be performed without the accumulation of lactate (75). It appears that continuous training at or slightly above the lactate threshold is important to improve endurance performance as a result of shifting OBLA and the lactate threshold (24, 65, 78, 139, 157). Anecdotal evidence suggests that a well-balanced endurance training plan requires periodic training at the lactate threshold via the use of "threshold" or "tempo" training to optimize performance (75).

The lactate threshold and OBLA can also be shifted in response to high-intensity interval training performed at intensities that are substantially higher than the lactate threshold power, velocity, or heart rate (40, 65). High-intensity interval training can require multiple high-intensity efforts (>80% of peak aerobic power) of various durations (30 s to 8 min) interspersed with lower-intensity recovery (60 s to 4.5 min) (87). The use of resistance training in the preparation of endurance athletes also has been shown to improve the lactate threshold (77).

The lactate threshold is a primary determinant of endurance performance, and understanding what heart rate, power, or velocity corresponds to the lactate threshold can be very useful in designing endurance training programs.

Economy of Movement

Exercise economy is a key factor dictating endurance exercise performance. Exercise or movement economy has been defined as the oxygen uptake required to perform exercise at a given intensity (75) or the ratio of mechanical work done to energy expended (9). The economy of movement and its effect on the energy cost of an exercise bout may partially explain some of the differences in performance noted between athletes who possess similar $\dot{V}O_2max$ values (10). Close examination of athletes with similar $\dot{V}O_2max$ values suggests that there is a large interindividual variability in the oxygen cost of submaximal exercise (75).

This large interindividual difference is clearly seen when examining the variations among oxygen costs when individuals run at a given submaximal speed (9, 19, 107).

These individual differences appear to be affected by training status, because running economy is significantly related to training status (75, 97, 103, 107). Trained individuals express a greater exercise economy compared with their untrained counterparts (107). In fact, the number of training years appears to be significantly correlated ($p < .05$, $r = .62$) with running economy (97). It is speculated that over time, running economy improves as a result of long-term skeletal muscle adaptations, such as the transition of Type II fibers to Type I (117, 154), and metabolic changes that reduce the energy cost for developing a particular repetitive level of force (103). Long-term training has also been suggested to affect running economy as a result of changes to anthropometric, biomechanical, and technical factors (5).

Training stimulus appears to play a significant role in the development of exercise economy (9, 75, 103). The highest movement economies appear to occur at the speeds or power outputs at which the athlete usually trains (75). It has been suggested that these changes to running economy are related to the athlete's volume of training (75). This is clearly seen by the fact that more experienced athletes or athletes who have accumulated more training miles express higher levels of exercise economy (74, 75).

High-intensity interval training has been suggested to significantly improve running economy and $\dot{V}O_2$max, which are usually associated with improvements in endurance performance (87). Performing interval running with intensities that range between 93% and 106% of $\dot{V}O_2$max has been shown to improve running economy (103). Support for this contention can be found in the work of Franch and colleagues (53);

© Human Kinetics

High-intensity interval training can improve running economy, increase $\dot{V}O_2$max, raise the lactate threshold, and improve soccer playing ability.

in that study, 6 weeks of long intervals, which consisted of four to six sets of 4 min intervals (4.6 m/s) separated by 2 min rest, resulted in a 6.0% increase in $\dot{V}O_2max$ and a 3% increase in running economy. In a study of soccer players, 8 weeks of aerobic interval training that consisted of four sets of 4 min sprint intervals (90-95% of maximum heart rate) separated by 3 min of light jogging performed two times per week resulted in a 6.7% increase in running economy, a 10.7% increase in $\dot{V}O_2max$, a 15.9% increase in the lactate threshold, a 24% increase in involvements with the ball during a game, and a 3.5% increase in the ability to perform at a higher average heart rate during a soccer match (62). Although this preliminary data suggest that high-intensity intervals can improve running economy, more research is needed to clarify the types of interval training that are most effective. It does appear that high-intensity interval training should be incorporated into the training plans of both team sport athletes and more traditional endurance athletes.

Another method for improving running economy in distance runners is the addition of strength or plyometric training (73, 110, 155). These improvements in running economy may occur as a result of an increased mechanical efficiency caused by improved motor unit recruitment patterns, increased muscular strength, enhanced rates of force development, and increases in tendon stiffness (73, 110, 155). Although strength training appears to offer a great benefit for the endurance athlete, many athletes worry about gaining weight because of training (103). This, however, should not be of major concern because the contemporary literature on cell signaling suggests that endurance training blunts the signaling pathways that would need to be activated to induce significant gains in muscle mass (108). This can be clearly seen in the literature exploring the effects of strength training on endurance performance, where athletes typically see less than 1.0% increase in body mass as a result of an increase in lean body mass (68, 110). Therefore, it may be warranted for endurance athletes to include strength and plyometric training to optimize exercise economy and ultimately endurance performance.

FACTORS AFFECTING ANAEROBIC ENDURANCE PERFORMANCE

Several factors affect the athlete's ability to repetitively perform high-intensity, anaerobic bouts of exercise (3, 50, 84). These factors include the ability to preferentially activate the anaerobic energy systems, the ability to buffer lactic acid, the functioning of the cardiovascular system, and the ability to maintain neuromuscular characteristics related to performance.

Bioenergetics

HIEE depends on the ability to repetitively perform high–power output activities that preferentially activate the anaerobic energy systems (113). When the athlete incorporates HIEE training into his training plan, he will experience physiological adaptations that increase the concentration or activity of key enzymes of the phosphagen and glycolytic energy systems (3, 50).

Increases in muscular stores of ATP, phosphocreatine (PCr), and muscle **glycogen** have been reported to occur in response to sprint or interval training (3, 50, 84). These alterations in enzymatic properties appear to allow for a more rapid supply of energy during high-intensity bouts of exercise, thus allowing the athlete to maintain a higher level of performance.

Lactatic Acid–Buffering Capacity

One of the most important factors affecting an athlete's ability to develop HIEE is the ability to buffer lactic acid to lactate. The ability to buffer lactic acid or H^+ ions has been suggested to be related to sprint performance ability (93, 159). It is well documented that increases in H^+ ion concentration result in an inhibitory effect on **phosphofructokinase (PFK)** (143). If these H^+ ions are not buffered, the concomitant reduction in PFK activity will reduce the ATP yield from glycolysis, thus reducing the power output that can be maintained during the activity (87).

HIEE training methods such as sprint or interval training have been demonstrated to increase the athlete's buffering capacities (101, 159). These increases in buffering capacity enable the body to maintain energetic flux at a rapid rate and thus maintain high-power performance typically seen in sports that rely on HIEE. Therefore, if the bioenergetic profile of the sporting activity indicates a need for HIEE, the training program must include interventions that increase the athlete's ability to buffer lactic acid while maintaining the rate of energetic flux.

LIEE or aerobic training does not allow for the maximal development of the lactic acid–buffering capacity (113). To increase this buffering capacity, the training plan must stimulate the accumulation of H^+ ions, which only occurs if the fast glycolytic systems are repetitively stimulated. Because LIEE primarily activates the aerobic energy supply systems, especially when undertaken at intensities under the lactate threshold, this training method holds little merit for the athlete who requires HIEE. In fact, it is likely that incorporating LIEE training methods in the training plans of anaerobic athletes will decrease HIEE (125).

Cardiovascular System

Oxidative metabolism and the cardiovascular system play an integral role in recovery from high-intensity interval training, such as resistance or sprint interval training (148). However, athletes who participate in sports that rely on HIEE should not undergo LIEE training, because this training impairs anaerobic performance capacity (45).

Recent evidence clearly demonstrates that high-intensity interval training can increase $\dot{V}O_2max$, stroke volume, and the ability to use oxidative metabolism during recovery from interval training (87, 113). These adaptations appear to play an integral role in the athlete's ability to recover from repetitive bouts of high-intensity exercise. Interestingly, the use of high-intensity interval training does not impair anaerobic energetic supply during exercise or alter the neuromuscular activation patterns typically seen in response to LIEE. Therefore, high-intensity interval training, when implemented correctly, will allow for the cardiovascular system adaptations needed for the development of HIEE. Accordingly, athletes who require HIEE in their sports should not use LIEE training methods because high-intensity interval training will supply the necessary adaptive stimulus need to optimize performance.

Neuromuscular System

High-intensity interval training does not interfere with the development of high force or power outputs necessary for performance in sports that rely on HIEE. Conversely, LIEE training decreases the athlete's ability to produce force at the high-velocity, low-frequency region of the force–velocity curve (13, 45). The force–time curve can be shifted in response to LIEE training (figure 11.1). The impact of HIEE and LIEE training can be clearly seen in the differences in the force–time curve and electromyographic activation patterns seen in endurance, strength, and power athletes (61).

The **rate of force development (RFD)** appears to be affected by the type of training used. For example, LIEE methods will substantially decrease the RFD and the ability to generate peak forces (61). The ability to express high RFD appears to depend on the energy system activated, the muscle fiber type, and the neuromuscular recruitment pattern (45, 61).

The ability to rapidly release energy from ATP depends on the activity of adenosine triphosphatase (ATPase), which is related to the **myosin heavy chain (MHC)** isoforms (fiber type) (163). Muscle fibers that contain MHC Type X and IIa are considerably faster than those containing MHC Type I (55). Endurance athletes usually contain a higher MHC Type I concentration than sprint or strength athletes (163). LIEE training appears to increase MHC Type I isoforms (154), which could decrease the rate of ATPase activity. This shift would impair the athlete's ability to produce the high-force and high-velocity movements that are necessary to maintain HIEE capabilities. Conversely, the use of interval training methods will increase MHC Type IIa isoforms, which allows the athlete to maintain force- and power-generating capacities (45). The ability to generate force rapidly is an important component of HIEE. Thus, sprints and interval training are the preferred methods of developing endurance for athletes who participate in strength- and power-based sports.

METHODS FOR DEVELOPING ENDURANCE

Athletes can develop endurance by using a variety of methods that produce very specific physiological and performance responses. When developing a training plan, the coach must determine the type of endurance that the plan will target, because methods of developing endurance are vastly different in their implementation and physiological outcomes. For example, traditional methods to develop LIEE call for continuous training performed at a variety of intensities ranging from 60% to 100% of maximal heart rate (141). The use of high-intensity intervals has been reported to improve LIEE (20, 21, 57, 58, 86-91), thus increasing the training options available to the coach and athlete. Conversely, LIEE training methods appear to decrease HIEE capacity, which would ultimately impede the performance of athletes who must perform repetitive high-intensity or high-power movements during competition. The coach and athlete must be aware of the different methods used to develop both LIEE and HIEE and which kind of endurance is needed for various sports.

Low-Intensity or Aerobic Exercise

Several methods are available to develop endurance, and the choice usually depends on the time of year and the athlete's training goals (table 11.1). The development of LIEE is a function of stimulating physiological adaptations that improve performance. Traditionally, aerobic endurance is developed via the use of recovery exercise and long slow distance training. However, other methods such as pace or tempo, interval, and resistance training appear can be used to develop LIEE.

Active Rest

Active rest or recovery exercise is often used to stimulate recovery from high-intensity training or competition. This type of activity requires a low exercise heart rate (<65%

Table 11.1   Methods Used to Develop Low-intensity Exercise Endurance

Training method	Recommended frequency (times per week)*	Duration of training portion	Intensity Heart rate (% max)	$\dot{V}O_2$ max (% max)
Active rest	1 or 2	30-60 min	<60%	<55%
Long slow distance (LSD)	1 or 2	≥30 min (race distance or longer)	60-70%	55-65%
Continuous pace or tempo training	1 or 2	20-30 min	At lactate threshold heart rate and $\dot{V}O_2$	
Interval training				
Aerobic intervals	1 or 2	30-40 min total time (depending on structure)	80-85% or maximum	100% Pmax
Anaerobic intervals	1 or 2	<2 min work bouts (work rest interval 1:1-1:5)	Maximum	Supermaximal
Fartlek	1	>30 min	Varies	Varies

*Other training days contain other training methods or rest and recovery. Pmax= peak power at $\dot{V}O_2$max.

of maximum) and lasts around 30 to 60 min (1, 141). One example of a recovery exercise bout is running in water, which would couple active recovery with water immersion (122, 123). This technique can be used several times per week depending on the structure of the microcycle.

Long Slow Distance (LSD)

Long slow distance (LSD) training can be considered "conversation" exercise, where the athlete is able to carry on a conversation without undue respiratory stress (118). LSD training involves relatively high training mileages or distances that are performed for a long duration (30-120 min or greater depending on the sport) at moderate to low intensities (66-80% maximum heart rate; 55-75% $\dot{V}O_2$max) (103, 118, 129). LSD training has been suggested to improve cardiovascular function, thermoregulatory abilities, mitochondrial energy production, and oxidative capacity of the skeletal muscle (30, 32, 41, 52, 69, 80, 118). These physiological adaptations to LSD training have been consistently demonstrated in untrained individuals (87); however, these physiological changes do not appear to occur as readily in highly trained endurance athletes (31, 64, 87). It is likely that advanced endurance athletes will need higher intensities of training, which may be accomplished via the use of interval training methods (87).

The intensity of exercise during LSD training is markedly lower than that experienced during competition (118). Thus suggesting that higher-intensity training methods, such as interval and Fartlek training, must be included in the training plan to optimize performance. This is not to say that LSD training should be excluded from the training plan of endurance athletes; this type of training appears to be very important in developing aerobic endurance (46). For example, Esteve-Lanao (46) suggested that LSD training should make up a large portion of the training volume, provided that high-intensity training is sufficient.

During the preparatory phase of an endurance training program, the main objective is to establish a physiological base (54, 141). The development of this physiological base is accomplished via the use of long slow distance and aerobic interval training (steady pace or tempo training) interspersed with active rest, passive rest, and resistance training. A microcycle with an emphasis on establishing a base is presented in table 11.2.

Interval Training

Interval training involves the repeated performance of short to long bouts of exercise usually performed at or above the lactate threshold, or at the maximal lactate steady state, interspersed with periods of low-intensity exercise or complete rest (16). Although interval training was first made popular in the 1950s (124) and is definitely not a new concept (16), contemporary sport science literature (20, 21, 86, 87, 91) has stimulated an increased interest in the concept. This literature has revealed many physiological reasons why interval training should be an integral part of the annual training plan for athletes ranging from novice to elite (87).

Interval training can be subdivided into two broad categories: aerobic and anaerobic intervals (16, 17).

Aerobic Intervals

Aerobic interval training preferentially stresses the aerobic energy system (16) and involves intensities that are at or slightly above the lactate threshold or those seen during competition (118). Aerobic interval training has also been termed *threshold training* or *pace or tempo training* (118). Pace or tempo training can be performed continuously or intermittently. For example, in a continuous pace or tempo training session, the athlete would maintain a steady pace at or slightly above the lactate threshold for the duration of the exercise bout. Conversely, pace or tempo intervals contain periods of steady-state exercise similar to that seen in the continuous model, but in this model the bouts are shorter and interspersed with brief periods of recovery (118). Examples of aerobic interval workouts are presented in tables 11.3 and 11.4.

When the coach is designing an aerobic interval workout, it is recommended that a graded exercise test be performed to establish the athlete's maximal heart rate, maximal power output or velocity, and lactate threshold. Integral to this process is determining the time at which peak power or maximal velocity can be maintained, which has been termed the **Tmax** (87, 91). Once the Tmax and the maximal power output or velocity are established, then the interval durations and intensities can be determined. It has been recommended that the duration of each interval correspond to 60% of Tmax and be performed at peak power or velocity (91). The rest interval will then be set as the time to reach 65% of the athlete's maximal heart rate.

Aerobic intervals can also be set by prescribing a heart rate range or power range that is performed for a predetermined duration (145). The rest interval can be preset to specifically target the development of the aerobic system. For example, an athlete may perform eight sets of aerobic intervals that last 5 min and are separated by 1 min of low-intensity active recovery. The intensity for this type of interval would

Table 11.2   General Preparation Microcycle Emphasizing Long Slow Distance

Day	Monday	Tuesday	Wednesday	Thursday	Friday	Saturday	Sunday
Workout	Rest day						
Endurance training		LSD	Recovery	Aerobic intervals	Recovery	LSD	Fartlek
Resistance training			Resistance training		Resistance training		
Total duration (min)		120	60	80	60	150	60-120
Interval duration (min)		120	60	15	60	150	—
Recovery (min)		0	0	5	0	0	—
Work/rest ratio		1:0	1:0	3:1	1:0	1:0	—
Intensity (beats/min)		131-139	<131	140-146	<131	131-139	—

Note: The microcycle example is based on a weekly training volume of 10 hr, where the athlete's heart rate at the lactate threshold is 153 beats/min. LSD = long slow distance.

Based on Friel 2006 (54) and Potteiger 2000 (118).

Table 11.3   Two Aerobic Interval Workouts

	AEROBIC INTERVAL FORMAT	
	Interval series 1	Interval series 2
Warm-up	10-15 min	10-15 min
Number of work intervals	8	8
Intensity	80% peak power* 80-85% maximum heart rate	100% peak power (413 W)
Duration	5 min	60% Tmax (~4 min)
Rest interval	1 min	Time to achieve 65% max heart rate (~2-4 min)
Work/rest interval	5:1	1:0.5-1:1
Cool-down	10-15 min	10-15 min
Total workout time	67-77 min	66-90 min
Frequency (times per week)	1 or 2	1 or 2

Note: Tmax = time to exhaustion at maximal velocity or power output.

*Peak power at $\dot{V}O_2$max.

Adapted from Stepto et al. 2001 (145) and Laursen et al. 2005 (89).

be between 80% and 85% of maximal heart rate or some percentage of the lactate threshold heart rate.

Regardless of the method used, aerobic intervals can stimulate significant performance gains and concomitant physiological adaptations when performed two times a week for up to 4 weeks (87, 91, 145). Because of the large amount of physiological and psychological stress that can be generated by aerobic interval training, the coach should integrate recovery methods and lower-intensity training into the microcycle to avoid overtraining the athlete. A sample microcycle is presented in table 11.5.

Table 11.4 Pace or Tempo Workouts

	Continuous pace or tempo training	Intermittent pace or tempo training
Warm-up (min)	15-20	15-20
Work bouts		
Number	1	2
Duration (min)	30	10
Intensity (beats/min)	153-156	153-156
Recovery bouts		
Number	0	2
Duration (min)	0	10
Intensity (beats/min)	<131	<131

Note: Based on a lactate threshold heart rate of 153 beats/min.

Adapted from Potteiger 2000 (118) and USA Cycling 2002 (1).

Table 11.5 Microcycle With Aerobic Intervals or Pace or Tempo Training

Day	Monday	Tuesday	Wednesday	Thursday	Friday	Saturday	Sunday
Workout	Rest day						
Endurance training		LSD	Pace tempo ride	Recovery	Fartlek	Aerobic intervals	LSD
Resistance training							
Total duration (min)		120	80	60	60-120	65	150
Interval duration (min)		120	15	60	—	5	150
Recovery (min)		0	5	0	—	1	0
Work/rest ratio		1:0	3:1	1:0	—	5:1	1:0
Intensity (beats/min)		131-139	140-146	<131	—	80-85% HRmax	131-139 beats/min

Notes: This microcycle is based on a weekly training volume of 9-10 r, where the athlete's heart rate at the lactate threshold is 153 beats/min. LSD = long slow distance; HRmax = heart rate maximum.

Adapted from Friel 2006 (54) and Potteiger 2000 (118).

Anaerobic Intervals

Anaerobic interval training for the endurance athlete has recently received a large amount of attention in the scientific literature (86-91). In this type of interval training, the work duration is very short (<2 min) and the intensity is supramaximal (all-out or above the power output achieved during the assessment of $\dot{V}O_2max$) (87). Anaerobic interval training bouts that use 4 to 10 sets of 15 to 30 s of all-out work interspersed with 45 s to 12 min of recovery have been shown to significantly increase $\dot{V}O_2max$, anaerobic endurance, and stimulate many physiological adaptations that improve performance in as little as 2 weeks (87). These types of training sessions are usually very intense and require the use of recovery methods and appropriate program variations to avoid overtraining. It is likely that this type of training can be very effective when performed one or two times per week and integrated into the training plan. A microcycle that incorporates anaerobic intervals is presented in table 11.6.

Repetition

Another interval training method has been termed the *repetition method*. The distances used with this method can be either longer or shorter than the distance seen in competition. Longer-duration intervals will shift the emphasis toward the development of the aerobic energy systems, similar to aerobic interval training. Conversely, intervals of shorter duration will increase the stress on the anaerobic energy systems, similar to anaerobic interval training. Short bouts of very high intensity will require longer rest intervals (118). The repetition method allows the athlete to improve running speed, running economy, and HIEE.

Fartlek

Fartlek is the Swedish word for "speed play" and is a classic method for developing endurance (98). This method of training is a rather unscientific combination of interval and continuous training. For example, a runner may intersperse period of fast running with slow running (98, 118, 141). This type of training can be undertaken on flat ground or up and down hills (141). Fartlek does not call for specific workloads or heart rates. Instead, this type of training relies on the subjective sense of how the bout feels (98). Fartlek training may be most useful during the general conditioning or preparatory phase of the annual training plan because it challenges

Table 11.6 Microcycle for a 10K Runner With Anaerobic Interval Training

Day	Monday	Tuesday	Wednesday	Thursday	Friday	Saturday	Sunday
Workout	Rest day						
Endurance training		Interval	Recovery	LSD	Interval	LSD	Fartlek
Resistance training							
Total duration		30-40 min*	60 min	120 min	30-40 min*	45 min	45-60 min
Interval duration		30 s	60 min	120 min	30 s	45 min	—
Recovery		60 s	0	0	60 s	0	—
Number of intervals		6			6		
Work/rest ratio		1:2	1:0	1:0	1:2	1:0	—
Intensity		Maximal	<131 beats/min	131-139 beats/min	Maximal	131-139 beats/min	—

Note: This microcycle is based on a weekly training volume of 5-6 hr, where the athlete's heart rate at the lactate threshold is 153 beats/min. LSD = long slow distance; HRmax = heart rate maximum.

*Includes 15 min of warm-up and cool-down.

Adapted from Friel 2006 (54) and Potteiger 2000 (118).

the physiological systems of the body while eliminating the boredom and monotony associated with daily training (98, 118).

Resistance Training

Resistance training can enhance the development of endurance. Traditionally, resistance training has not been considered to be a very important part of the development of LIEE (77). However, recent research evidence suggests that resistance training has the potential to improve cycling (11, 96), running (73, 110, 153), and Nordic skiing (68, 111) performance. Resistance training has been suggested to affect $\dot{V}O_2max$, the lactate threshold, economy of movement, and neuromuscular characteristics of endurance athletes depending on their levels of training (77). For example, untrained individuals can experience improvements in LIEE as a result of improvements in $\dot{V}O_2max$, lactate threshold, and movement economy (77). In highly trained endurance athletes, improvements in LIEE performance are most likely related to changes in the lactate threshold (96), improvements in movement economy (110), and alterations to neuromuscular function (104, 153) (figure 11.7). It appears that incorporating resistance training into the annual training plan for the endurance athlete holds some merit.

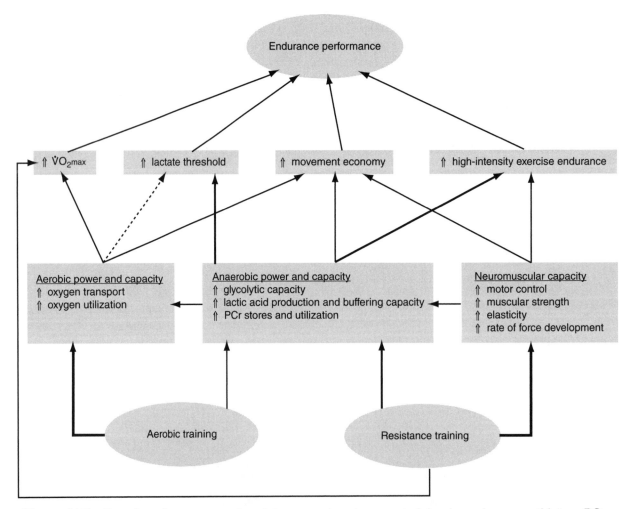

Figure 11.7 Paradigm for concurrent resistance and endurance training in endurance athletes. PCr = phosphocreatine.

Adapted from Paavolainen et al. 1999 (110) and Stone et al. 2006 (147).

Incorporating resistance training into the annual training plan of an endurance athlete appears to produce favorable performance responses (77, 147, 153). However, care must be taken when introducing resistance training in an attempt to improve LIEE performance. When resistance training is simply added to the preexisting endurance training plan, performance usually is not improved (72). It is likely that adding the resistance training load to the overall training load results in excessive training stress, elevating fatigue and decreasing preparedness. Support for this contention can be seen in the work of Jackson and colleagues (72), who reported that the addition of resistance training to a cycling program resulted in a higher sense of fatigue, which corresponded to a lack of performance gains. Investigators who report enhancement of LIEE performance with concurrent resistance and endurance training typically reduce some of the endurance training volume to accommodate the resistance training load (11, 104, 110). It is likely that a 19% to 37% reduction in endurance training load is warranted when adding resistance training to the overall training plan to stimulate performance gains (11, 104, 110).

METHODS FOR DEVELOPING HIGH-INTENSITY EXERCISE ENDURANCE

The use of LIEE techniques will decrease performance capacity for athletes who participate in sports that require the ability to repetitively produce high power outputs (28, 45). Power-based sports fall into two classifications: (a) sports such as American football and baseball, which require brief intermittent tasks that involve very large power outputs and derive most of their energy from phosphate energy system, and (b) sports such as soccer and basketball, which require repetitive high-intensity activities and derive energy predominantly from phosphate and glycolytic energy systems (45). In both types of sports, oxidative metabolism is important during recovery because the replenishment of phosphocreatine and removal of lactate is an oxidative process (22, 45). This reliance on oxidative metabolism during recovery is the foundation for the classic argument that LIEE techniques are needed by athletes who participate in anaerobic-based sports (28, 45). Although LIEE training enhances several physiological factors that may improve the rate of recovery between bouts of exercise, the corresponding decreases in anaerobic abilities and corresponding performance capacities appear to outweigh the benefits of this training intervention (45). Anaerobic athletes should avoid LIEE training and use other strategies that enhance performance and recovery (113, 115). However, the development of HIEE can actually improve LIEE performance, and thus the methods used by anaerobic athletes may benefit the aerobic endurance athlete (87, 147).

One strategy for developing endurance that has recently been recommended is the use of high-intensity interval training, because this allows for improvements in anaerobic capacity, anaerobic power, and also aerobic capacity (87, 113). Interval training is usually conducted by using sets of repetitions of sprints interspersed with recovery intervals. The duration of these recovery intervals varies depending on the bioenergetic system being targeted (28) (table 11.7). For example, an interval training program with a work-to-rest ratio of 1:1 would target the oxidative system (50), whereas a work-to-rest ratio of 1:20 would target the phosphagen system (28, 148). The use of an interval training program will be dictated by several factors including the bioenergetic demands of the sport, the performance model established for the sport, and the phase of the annual training plan. These factors can be addressed via the

Table 11.7 Bioenergetic Characteristics of Interval Training

Interval ratio (work to rest)	TYPICAL INTERVAL FORMAT		SAMPLE INTERVAL FORMAT		Primary energy system used	Maximum power (%)
	Work (s)	Rest (s)	Work (s)	Rest (s)		
1:12-1:20	5-10	60-200	5	60	ATP-PC	90-100
1:3-1:5	15-30	45-150	30	75	Fast glycolysis	75-90
1:3-1:4	60-180	180-720	60	180	Fast glycolysis, slow glycolysis, and oxidative*	30-75
1:1-1:3	>180	>180	180	180	Oxidative metabolism	20-35

*The primary energy system used will vary depending on the length of the interval and the duration of recovery.

Adapted from Conley 2000 (28) and Stone, Stone, and Sands 2007 (148).

manipulation of work-to-rest intervals, interval intensities, interval duration or distance, interval exercise volume, interval training duration, interval training frequency, interval training progression, in-season maintenance, and resistance training.

Work-to-Rest Intervals

The work-to-rest interval may be dictated by the demands of the sport (113, 115). It has been reported that the average work-to-rest interval in American football is around 1:6, which is depicted as a work/rest (seconds/seconds) interval of 4.3:27.9 for rushing plays and 5.8:36.8 for passing plays (115). One study reported that there were 12 to 13 plays per game (3.1-3.3 per quarter) with an average play length of 2 to 12 s (113). The vast majority of the plays lasted between 3 and 6 s (113) for an average play length of around 4 s (112). This information led Plisk and Gambetta (115) to suggest that a series of 10 to 16 sprints performed with a 3 to 5 s work interval and a 20 to 45 s recovery (1:6 work-to-rest interval) was an ideal interval training program for this population.

Soccer provides another example of matching the work-to-rest interval in training. The literature suggests that a work-to-rest ratio of 1:6 is similar to that seen in competition (7, 8) and demonstrates similar speed decrements as seen in a soccer match (94). Soccer demonstrates work-to-rest ratios of approximately 1:7 to 8 with 3 to 4 s of work interspersed with lower-intensity exercise (94). Little and Williams (94) suggested that 40 sets of 15 m sprints performed at a 1:6 work-to-rest ratio simulated the physiological stress seen in soccer match play. The work-to-rest interval should be prescribed based on the individual demands of the sport and in the context of the phase of the training plan.

Once the coach has determined the work-to-rest interval required by a sport, she can choose from several ways to implement an interval session into the training plan. The first method is to use predetermined performance times to calculate the appropriate rest interval duration (50, 113). Another method for determining the rest interval is to use the time to a specific heart rate, such as 110 to 120 beats/min (116). The rest intervals should be individualized as much as possible to give each athlete the appropriate recovery duration and allow for the training stimulus needed to target the bioenergetic factors specified by the training plan.

A classic mistake that many coaches make is to train all their athletes in one large group and base the recovery duration on the fastest athlete. If this practice is undertaken, the slower athletes will most likely be forced to work at a lower work/rest ratio than the fastest athlete, which would result in a harder training session and shift the bioenergetic focus of the training session for these athletes (table 11.8). This practice can increase the chance of overtraining and impedes an athlete's development. It may be warranted to group the athletes by sprinting ability and then create rest interval durations that are individualized for each group. This practice will ensure that each athlete is using the appropriate work-to-rest ratio and receiving the planned physiological stimulus.

Table 11.8 Comparison of Two Athletes' Interval Training Plans

Variable	Athlete A	Athlete B
Intended work-to-rest ratio	1:4	1:4
Maximal 40 m time (s)	5.2	6.0
Recovery duration (s)	20.8	20.8
Actual work-to-rest ratio	1:4	1:3

These athletes are performing five sets of 40 m sprints, and the time for recovery is based on the faster athlete. Athlete B is experiencing a harder training session because she has a shorter recovery period.

Interval Intensities

The prescription of interval training intensities can significantly affect the performance outcomes stimulated by the training plan. Using heart rate as an indicator of performance intensity during an anaerobic interval training program is not recommended because heart rate is poorly related to intensity in this scenario (113). It is better to set training time goals based on the individual athlete's maximal capacity, which would then allow the coach to manipulate training intensity and determine the rest interval (50, 113). For example, when attempting to develop a fitness base the athlete may perform a high volume of sprints at 60% to 80% of maximal capacity. Conversely, when shifting to more specific work in the later stages of the preparatory phase of training, the athlete could increase the intensity of interval training to 80% to 90% of maximal or competitive needs (116).

Establishing target times for a specific distance is an excellent tool for individualizing the intensity of the training bout. However, the athlete should be tested periodically so the coach can adjust the intensity of training. When using this method to determine interval intensities, the coach should group athletes of similar capacities (e.g., sprint times) because this will help the coach determine the appropriate work-to-rest intervals and maximize each athlete's physiological and performance gains.

Interval Duration or Distance

The quality of HIEE training is more important than the quantity (113). The duration and distance of the work portion of the interval training plan will depend on the tactical model established for the individual sport (114). For example, Plisk (114) reported that three sets of six or seven repeated 40 yd sprints with a work-to-rest ratio of 1:6 would meet the metabolic demands of American football. It appears that this intensity targets the phosphagen and glycolytic energy supply mechanisms better than does the duration (148), so extending the duration or distance beyond that required by the sport would be impractical and would likely induce maladaptive responses (113). Therefore, the distance or duration of the interval should be matched to the competitive model established for the sporting activity.

Interval Exercise Volume

The interval training volume will be dictated by the phase of the annual training plan, the targeted physiological adaptations, and the sport. The volume of interval training will be higher during the early preparatory phase and decrease during the competitive phase of the annual training plan. The scientific literature provides limited information about the optimal volume of interval training needed to induce physiological and performance adaptations.

Investigators have explored interval training volume schemes that require between 2 and 24 repetitions (87, 94) and as high as 40 repetitions (94). Some empirical evidence has suggested that sprinters need between 10 and 20 repetitions per workout, whereas middle-distance runners may need between 1.5 and 2.0 repetitions when performing fast intervals and 2 to 3 repetitions when performing slow interval workouts (113). Not enough scientific evidence is available regarding the effects of different interval training volumes on performance to make volume-based recommendations. Therefore, decisions about how to manipulate the training volume should be based on the athlete's needs and training-induced stress.

Interval Training Duration

Anaerobic interval training has been shown to stimulate significant physiological adaptations in 2 to 15 weeks in previously untrained individuals depending on the frequency, duration, and intensity of the interval program used (87). Elite cyclists have demonstrated significant physiological adaptations and performance gains in as little as 2 weeks of using a high-intensity interval training plan (86, 87, 144). Although the literature has shown significant performance enhancement in both cyclists and runners as a result of as little as 2 weeks of high-intensity interval training, further research is needed to establish guidelines for the duration of training needed to optimize performance.

Interval Training Frequency

The scientific literature on high-intensity interval training has explored a variety of training frequencies ranging from 2 to 7 days per week (87). However, little research exists that defines the optimal frequency of interval training and how it relates to the individual portions of a periodized annual plan. Empirical evidence suggests that it may be practical to limit HIEE training to 2 or 3 days per week (113). This general recommendation is warranted because HIEE training must be considered in conjunction with the other training modalities (e.g., strength, plyometric, agility, tactical, and technical training) that are included in the annual training plan. If integrated appropriately, HIEE can be addressed with skill, technique, or agility drills that can also stimulate improvements in endurance (113). The coach should modulate the training stimulus to allow for appropriate restoration while continuing to stimulate physiological and performance-based adaptations across the annual training plan.

Interval Training Progression

Creating an HIEE training plan involves integrating several training factors (e.g., tactical, technical, strength, power, endurance) into the periodized program. The coach can establish the basic progression of training after determining the work-to-rest interval and endurance demands of the sport (114). The intensities and volumes used in the interval training plan depend on the phase of the annual training plan and the method being used to develop HIEE. When the athlete is attempting to develop a fitness base during the early portion of the preparatory phase of training, the interval intensities should be lower and contain more extensive methods (table 11.9) (113). As the athlete progresses toward the season, she can use higher intensities and lower volumes of training (table 11.9) (113, 114). In the later stages of the preparatory phase and the early part of the competition phase of the annual training plan, the athlete will begin to incorporate elements from the competitive trial method of developing HIEE, which has also been termed *special endurance* (114, 116) (table 11.10). As the competitive phase of the season progresses, the athlete uses specific strategies, including various interval training and competitive trial methods, to maintain HIEE capacity across the season.

Table 11.9   Interval Characteristics for the Development of Speed Endurance

Interval method	Variable	CHARACTERISTIC	
		Novice athlete	Advanced athlete
Extensive	Relative intensity	60-80% of competitive speed	60-80% of competitive speed
	Intensity classification	Low to medium	Low to medium
	Duration or distance	17-100 s or 100-400 m	14-180 s or 100-1,000 m
	Volume	5-12 repetitions	8-40 repetitions
	Target recovery heart rate	110-120 beats/min	125-130 beats/min
	Recovery duration	60-120 s	45-90 s
Intensive	Relative intensity	80-90% of competitive speed	80-90% of competitive speed
	Intensity classification	High	High
	Duration or distance	14-95 s or 100-400 m	13-180 s or 100-1,000 m
	Volume	4-8 repetitions	4-12 repetitions
	Target recovery heart rate	110-120 beats/min	125-130 beats/min
	Recovery duration	120-240 s	90-180 s

Adapted from Plisk and Stone 2003 (116).

Table 11.10   Competitive Trial Methods of Developing High-Intensity Exercise Endurance

Method	Intensity	Duration or distance	Example for a 200 m sprinter
Supramaximal training	> Competition	< Competition	100 m sprint intervals
Maximal training	≤ Competition	= Competition	200 m sprint intervals
Submaximal training	< Competition	> Competition	400 m sprint intervals

Adapted from Plisk and Stone 2003 (116) and Plisk 2008 (114).

In-Season Maintenance

Over the course of the competitive season, the athlete can fall into a state of deconditioning if special attention is not paid to integrating conditioning activities into her competitive training schedule (84, 105, 113, 137). Support for this contention can be found in the scientific literature, which suggests that when the volume of anaerobic interval training (e.g., sprint and agility training) is significantly reduced or when this training is eliminated altogether during the competitive season, there is a concomitant reduction in markers of fitness and muscle mass (105). The magnitude of these decreases is likely to be different when comparing starters and nonstarters (84). Thus specific HIEE conditioning strategies must be implemented in the in-season training plan.

When examining in-season responses, the coach must first consider what happened in the 6 to 8 weeks before the initiation of the season. If acute overtraining is induced during this time, a general catabolic state will predominate during the season and performance capacity will decline (84). Even if the preseason training plan is implemented appropriately, performance can decline during the season if the HIEE is not appropriately incorporated into the in-season training plan (105). The best approach is to include a combination of sport-specific practices, strength training, and HIEE-based conditioning (137).

It is likely that HIEE can be trained in conjunction with sport-specific skills to maximize training time. In soccer, for example, soccer-specific drills can be used as a conditioning tool (121). Rampinini and colleagues (121) reported that using a

© Human Kinetics

In-season training is an important part of any training plan. Do not let deconditioning occur during the competitive season.

three-sided training game on a large pitch can increase the exercise intensity to a level similar to that seen in actual game play. Using this type of strategy will allow the athlete to develop specific endurance that is closely related to the demands of a soccer game. The training stimulus can be modified by manipulating the field dimensions, number of players, and skills used during a small-sided soccer game in an attempt to target conditioning goals while still practicing sport-specific skills in an environment that models game play (121).

Although skill-based conditioning drills are important, it is equally important to include strength training (105) in conjunction with HIEE and sprint agility training to avoid the typical losses in performance capacity seen across a season (137). Different training factors (e.g., HIEE, drills, and strength training) should be integrated to avoid overtraining, because overtraining would only compound the typical degradation in performance seen across the season. The coach must allow for recovery (see chapter 5 for techniques that can aid in recovery and regeneration) between training sessions and competitive events (113). The coach must perform a balancing act by providing an adequate training stimulus to maintain fitness and performance while avoiding overtraining.

Resistance Training

Investigators have repeatedly shown that resistance training improves HIEE (66, 67, 99, 125, 147). Improvements in HIEE performance are likely related to increases in muscular strength (2), morphological adaptations (113), or metabolic adaptations that increase buffering capacity (102, 125).

HIEE performance is improved when the training plan includes resistance training with 12 or more repetitions per set (125). This improvement in performance is most noted as the intensity of exercise is increased (66). Higher repetitions per set (more than eight repetitions) performed for multiple sets appear to improve HIEE more than do lower-repetition protocols or single-set protocols (51, 99, 146). HIEE performance seems to be improved to a greater extent with high volumes (volume loads) of resistance training.

Several authors have suggested that short rest intervals between sets of resistance training can increase HIEE capacity (51, 146). This theory was recently supported by Hill-Haas and colleagues (67), who demonstrated that a resistance training program that included short rest intervals (20 s) resulted in significantly greater HIEE performance gains (+12.5%) compared with a resistance training program that used longer rest intervals (80 s). It is likely that the program that included short rest intervals increased the lactate-buffering capacity in response to resistance training as a result of repeated exposure to high lactate levels that allowed for a greater HIEE performance. Conversely, Robinson and colleagues (125) reported that short rest intervals (30 s) did not result in greater improvements in HIEE performance compared with longer rest intervals (180 s). Their findings suggested that simply increasing the volume of resistance training was more effective at improving HIEE without comprising other training-induced adaptations.

Both studies found muted strength gains in response to short rest intervals (67, 125). Because sprinting speed is highly correlated with muscular strength (6, 37), the validity of decreasing the rest interval between sets may be questionable because increasing volume and intensity of training appears to improve HIEE (99, 125). Therefore, the coach and athlete should be cautious when manipulating rest interval lengths because drastic decreases in interset rest intervals appear to impair the development of strength.

SUMMARY OF MAJOR CONCEPTS

All sports require some level of endurance, and the coach must determine the type of endurance needed to optimize performance in a given sport. Endurance is classified as low-intensity exercise endurance (LIEE) and high-intensity exercise endurance (HIEE). LIEE is typically needed in aerobic sports that require work to be continually performed for a long duration. Conversely, HIEE requires the repetitive performance of high-intensity activities interspersed with periods of recovery. Sports that rely on HIEE also appear to rely on the ability to express high power outputs or generate high levels of force. Interestingly, HIEE training methods appear to improve LIEE performance, but LIEE training methods can reduce HIEE performance. Therefore, the coach and athlete must understand the methods of training that optimize HIEE and LIEE capacity.

CHAPTER 12

SPEED AND AGILITY TRAINING

Speed, agility, and speed endurance are crucial abilities that can affect performance in a variety of sports. These abilities are related and depend in large part on the athlete's muscular strength. Integrating speed, agility, and speed endurance training into the annual training plan and manipulating specific training variables can optimize performance capacity. Therefore, understanding the factors that affect speed, agility, and speed endurance enables coaches to develop sport-specific training plans that maximize performance.

SPEED TRAINING

Speed is the ability to cover a distance quickly. The ability to move quickly in a straight line is an integral component of successful performance in a wide variety of sports (69, 81, 121, 120). Straight-line sprinting can be broken down into three phases: acceleration, attainment of maximal speed, and maintenance of maximal speed (27, 81).

Acceleration is the ability to increase movement **velocity** in a minimum amount of time (69). Acceleration determines sprint performance abilities over short distances (e.g., 5 m and 10 m) and is usually measured as a velocity (e.g., m/s) or as a unit of time (e.g., seconds or minutes) (83). The ability to accelerate differentiates between athletes for a variety of sports (2, 27, 81). For example, during a 100 m race, untrained sprinters achieve maximal speed within 10 to 36 m (27), whereas highly trained sprinters do not attain maximal speed until around 80 m (2). It is likely that maximal strength levels for the knee extensors partially explains the acceleratory abilities of various athletes, because strength is strongly related to sprinting ability (6, 10, 18, 78, 79, 119). Support for this contention can be garnered from the literature, which reports that faster sprinters are significantly stronger and are able to accelerate at faster rates than their slower counterparts (6, 24, 74).

In many sports, such as soccer, the ability to accelerate underlies successful game play (69, 83). During soccer game play, the average distance sprinted is around 17 m and ranges between 1.5 and 105 m (9). Often these sprints are initiated while the athlete is moving at slower speeds (119) or when the athlete is making a breakaway

AP Photo/Matt Dunham

Speed training isn't just for track athletes. It should be incorporated into training plans for athletes in all sports.

or initiating a tackle (83, 95). Therefore, the ability to accelerate rapidly in the first few steps is essential to effective game play (83). These data reveal that a sprint training program that targets the acceleration phase should develop specific strength characteristics and mechanical skills (119).

After completing the acceleration phase of a sprint, the athlete achieves maximal running velocity. Athletes may have great acceleratory capacity but lack the ability to achieve and maintain high velocities in this phase of a sprint (119), which suggests that acceleration and the maximal speed of running are very specific sprinting qualities (26). Differences in the kinematics of the acceleratory and maximal velocity portions of a sprint support this observation and suggest that running mechanics (83, 119) and specific strength qualities (74) play a role in developing maximal running speed.

The final phase of a straight-line sprint requires the athlete to maintain maximal speed (27, 81). Although the athlete is moving at maximal speed, the development of **fatigue** begins to affect the athlete's ability to maintain force output, effective running mechanics, and thus speed (91). The fatigue generated during a bout of maximal sprinting appears related to the body's ability to buffer the lactic acid that is formed in response to the rapid glycolytic rate (97). As **lactic acid** increases there is an accumulation of hydrogen ions (H^+), which can reduce the athlete's capacity to exert force (106) and lead to a breakdown in running mechanics and mechanical efficiency. Short- and long-interval-based sprinting programs appear effective in improving muscle buffering capacity and reducing fatigue (25, 62, 97).

Speed is the expression of a set of skills and abilities that allow for high movement velocities (91). Although it is often suggested that skills and abilities are unrelated, they are highly related and thus can be developed with specific training practices (91, 97, 98). The application of appropriate sprint training methods in conjunction with a periodized training plan can improve sprint performance (e.g., acceleration, achievement of maximal velocities, and maintenance of high velocities) and thus improve competitive performance (81, 97).

Factors Affecting the Expression of Speed

To develop speed, the coach and athlete must understand the factors that affect one's ability to generate high movement speeds. Sprinting ability is affected by several physiological and performance factors, as described in the following paragraphs.

Energy Systems

Sprinting involves a rapid release of energy that allows for a high rate of cross-bridge cycling within the muscle and a rapid and repetitive production of muscular force. The body meets the energy demands of muscle under sprinting conditions by (a) altering the enzymatic activity of specific energy-producing pathways, (b) increasing the amount of energy stored within the muscle, and (c) increasing the muscles' ability to overcome the accumulation of fatigue-inducing metabolites (97).

Enzymatic Activity   All three of the body's energy systems (e.g., phosphagen, glycolytic, and oxidative) contribute to energy supply (72). However, the **phosphagen** and **glycolytic** systems predominate during most sprinting activities (22). The degree of contribution of the **oxidative energy system** depends on the duration, length, and number of sprints performed as well as the rest interval between efforts (97). For example, if the sprinting activity is long ($\geq$30 s in duration) and repeated several times with short rest intervals between bouts, the contribution of the oxidative energy system will progressively increase (72). Therefore the enzymatic adaptations will be very specific to the sprinting tasks performed in training (97).

The phosphagen system's (ATP-PC) response to sprinting activities shows that muscular stores of adenosine triphosphate (ATP) and phosphocreatine (PCr) can be significantly reduced in response to bouts of sprint training (47). The rate of PCr breakdown is significantly higher in the fastest sprinters (47), which may occur as a result of an increased rate of **creatine phosphokinase (CPK)** activity in response to sprint training (83, 87, 109). To meet the increased demand for ATP during sprint training, an increased **myokinase (MK)** enzyme activity is stimulated, which may increase the rate of ATP resynthesis (25, 97). This increase in MK activity has been reported to occur in response to training with both short- and long-duration sprints (25, 87).

Several key enzymes associated with the glycolytic system also are affected by various forms of sprint training (97). For example, glycogen **phosphorylase (PHOS),** the enzyme responsible for stimulating muscle glycogen breakdown, is increased in response to both short (<10 s) and long (>10 s) bouts of sprinting (25, 55, 71, 87, 97). **Phosophofructokinase (PFK)** activity (the enzyme that regulates the rate of the glycolytic system) appears to increase in response to short-duration, long-duration, or combination sprinting activities (19, 51, 71, 87, 96, 97). Changes in PFK activity may be of particular importance because the rate of PFK activity has been related to performance in high-intensity exercise such as sprinting (108). Finally, lactate dehydrogenase (LDH) activity has been shown to increase in response to both short- and long-duration sprinting (19, 51, 71, 84, 94, 97).

The contribution of the oxidative system to an acute 10 s bout of sprinting is considered to be minimal (~13%) (13). However, during multiple sprints of a longer duration ($\geq$30 s) there is a significant decrease in the glycolytic energetic supply and a concomitant decrease in maximal power output and speed (12), which may occur in response to elevated H^+ concentrations slowing the glycolytic rate and allowing for a decreased production of **lactate**. To meet the energy demands of the exercising muscle, the contribution of oxidative metabolism increases (8, 12, 104). However, the contribution of oxidative metabolism to the energy supply is affected largely by the duration of the sprint (8, 104) and the rest interval between bouts (7). For example, longer sprints performed multiple times with short rest intervals will increase the contribution of the oxidative systems to energy supply. With this increased energy supply from oxidative metabolism, it is not surprising that there are increases in succinate dehydrogenase and citrate synthase activity (key enzymes of the oxidative system) in response to sprinting (19, 51, 71).

Short and long sprint interval training bouts can significantly increase the athlete's aerobic power ($\dot{V}O_2$max) (62, 104). Thus high-intensity interval training is an important tool for the development of sport-specific fitness for sports dominated by both anaerobic (e.g., soccer, American football, basketball) and aerobic (e.g., long-distance running, cycling, skiing) energy supplies. Although repetitive sprint bouts, similar to those seen in competition, may have a large aerobic contribution, this does not mean that long-distance aerobic training is the best way to develop fitness (46, 48). For example, Helgerud and colleagues (46) reported that high-intensity interval training resulted in significantly greater increases in $\dot{V}O_2$max than traditional aerobic training. This interval-based training increase in $\dot{V}O_2$max was related to significant increases in running economy, distances covered, number of involvements with the ball, and average work intensity during a soccer match (45).

The enzymatic alterations stimulated by sprint training may play an integral role in facilitating rapid muscular contractions by allowing for a faster rate of ATP supply from the glycolytic systems. Adaptation to multiple bouts of high-intensity sprint intervals seems to produce a superior training stimulus, which appears to translate to team sports play better than does traditional endurance training.

Energy Substrate Storage   An increased availability of metabolic substrates (e.g., PCr, ATP, and glycogen) prior to the initiation of an exercise bout may enhance the athlete's ability to perform or maintain high-intensity exercise (97, 113). Parra and colleagues (87) reported that a short sprint protocol elevated resting PCr and glycogen levels, whereas a long protocol elevated only resting glycogen levels. This suggests that the sprint training program may alter the energy substrates stored in the muscle. These changes to energy substrate storage may have contributed to the increases in sprint performance noted in the investigation (87).

Accumulation of Fatigue Inducing Metabolites   Lactic acid accumulation as a result of multiple sprint bouts appears to contribute to impaired sprinting performance (68, 114). With an increase in lactic acid accumulation, there is an increase in H^+ ion concentration (which can inhibit PFK activity) (43), a decrease in the Ca^+ transport rate (65), and a decrease in the rate of cross bridge cycling within the skeletal muscle (107). If the H^+ ions are not buffered, the ability to sprint, and more importantly to repetitively sprint, will be impaired (62).

The use of high-intensity interval training has been demonstrated to result in an increased buffering capacity (75, 114). With this increased buffering capacity, there is an increased ability to maintain energetic flux and thus to maintain high power output performance, such as sprinting. Thererfore, when developing a physiological base for sprint and agility performance, it is important to include high-intensity interval training in the overall training plan as it has the ability to increase buffering capacity, which allows the body to deal with the accumulation of metabolic fatigue inducing factors such as lactic acid or H^+. For more information on the increasing endurance and buffering capacity, refer to chapter 11 of this text.

Neuromuscular Systems

The morphological characteristics of the muscle as well as adaptations to neural activation patterns can play a significant role in the expression of high-velocity movements. Traditional literature has suggested that performance in sprinting activities depends largely on genetic factors, but recent literature suggests that muscle fiber characteristics as well as neural activation patterns can be altered in response to various training stimuli (98, 110-112, 116, 117).

Muscle Composition   The muscle fiber type or composition appears to play a role in determining sprint performance abilities. A higher percentage of Type IIb or IIx **myosin heavy chain (MHC)** isoforms (fast twitch) is advantageous for activities that require the expression of high power outputs or forces (17, 88), such as those seen in sprinting. A continuum of muscle fiber MHC isoforms ranging from Type I (slow twitch) to Type IIa, IIb, or IIx can be delineated, along with specific hybrids that exist as transitional states (e.g., I/IIa, I/IIa/IIx, IIa/IIx) between the major subtypes (5, 89, 116). Within this continuum of individual MHC isoforms, a spectrum of force- and power-generating capacity can be created (figure 12.1) in which Type I fibers exhibit the lowest force- and power-generating capacity, whereas Type IIb or IIx MHC isoforms are associated with the highest power- and force-generating capacity (16, 17).

Because of the relationships among power, force, and fiber type, it appears that sprinting performance capacity may be partially explained by the athlete's fiber type. Support for this contention can be seen in the scientific literature, which suggests that sprint performance is significantly correlated with the athlete's percentage of Type II fibers (25, 32, 78). Sprint-trained athletes appear to exhibit greater rates of force development and force output than either untrained or endurance trained individuals (41, 73), which may be related to a higher percentage of Type II fibers. In fact, sprinters have been shown to have a high percentage of Type II fibers (23). Thus, a potential explanation for improved sprinting performance may center on specific training-induced adaptations to the muscle fiber composition.

The ability of sprint training to alter the muscle fiber depends partially on individual differences and genetic predisposition to different types of training (31, 65, 67, 97). Prolonged endurance training usually induces a shift from Type II to a Type I fiber composition (e.g., IIx or IIb $\Rightarrow$ IIa $\Rightarrow$ I), which is disadvantageous for sprinting performance (111). Conversely, sprint training can increase Type II fiber content (25, 31, 51, 52). Some types of sprint training induce a bidirectional shift toward

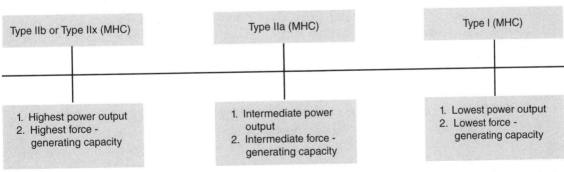

Figure 12.1   Power output and force-generating capacity by muscle fiber myosin heavy chain (MHC) subtype.

Type IIa fibers (I $\Rightarrow$ IIa $\Leftarrow$ IIb or IIx) (3, 4, 97). However, it appears that this favorable adaptation to the muscle fiber composition can be muted if endurance training is included in the training plan (97). Providing insufficient rest between repetitions or sets of sprinting efforts (44, 66, 97) and including only long-duration sprints (19, 64, 97, 103) result in a fiber type transition similar to that seen with endurance training. Given this information, coaches must carefully consider the content of the periodized training program. The first program concern is that traditional endurance training, such as long slow distance work, should be avoided by athletes who must express high levels of sprinting speed. Second, depending on the needs of the athlete and the sport being trained for, the use of short rest intervals and longer sprinting bouts should be reserved for the general preparatory phase of the annual training plan. As the athlete progresses through the specific preparatory phase and into the competitive phase, the use of shorter sprints with longer rest intervals will help the athlete produce higher speeds of movement.

Neural Factors   High-velocity movement, such as that used during maximal intensity sprint performance, requires a high level of neural activation (29, 56, 86, 98). Several neural factors influence sprinting ability, include the sequencing of muscle activation, the stretch reflex, and the development of neural fatigue (98).

Muscle Activation   When performing a sprinting motion a multitude of different muscles are activated at specific times and intensities to optimize movement speed (98). It appears that training results in a refinement of neural innervations' patterns and a more developed and efficient motor program (76, 98). It appears that the ratio of contribution of co-agonist muscles is altered with changes in muscle contraction speed (20, 98). Alterations to the **stretch shortening cycle (SSC)** have also been reported (98) and appear to contribute to propulsive forces during running (29). Finally, the ability to fully or selectively recruit Type II muscle fibers may be important when optimizing sprint performance capacity (98). Engaging in training practices that use ballistic or explosive activities such as sprinting, weightlifting, and plyometrics may alter the **motor unit** recruitment pattern so that Type II fibers are recruited sooner (40).

Stretch Reflex   Short latency stretch reflexes appear to influence sprint running performance (98). In particular, the **stretch reflex** appears to enhance force production when the athlete is sprinting. During the nonsupport phase of sprinting (discussed further in the section titled Technical Systems), the numerous muscles involved in the development of force are activated (36) and there is an increase in muscle spindle sensitivity (37, 42, 98). Training-induced adaptations to muscle spindle sensitivity may occur in response to sprint training (58, 59) and can improve muscle stiffness upon ground contact (98). Increases in the tendomuscular system stiffness appear to be related to both maximal running velocity and speed maintenance (21, 70). Increases in tendomuscular system stiffness appear to decrease contact time during the support phase of sprinting by increasing the rate of force development and the peak forces generated during this time (98).

Neural Fatigue   Neural fatigue can affect sprint performance by reducing voluntary force-generating capacity (94). As fatigue manifests itself during a maximal 100 m sprint there is a slight decline in speed, especially in the later stages of the race, which corresponds to a decrease in stride rate (2, 98). Ross and colleagues (98) suggested that this reduction in stride rate is the result of neural fatigue, whereby motor unit recruitment patterns are altered and change the motor unit firing rate (98).

During sprinting, such as a 100 m dash, there is a preferential recruitment of Type II (fast twitch) fibers, which are particularly susceptible to acute neural fatigue as a result of their short contraction times and high axial conduction velocities (80). As the 100 m dash progresses, there is a progressive reduction in recruitment that probably occurs as a result of a less than optimal output from the motor cortex (98). A 4.9% to 8.7% reduction in muscle activation has been noted once maximal velocity has been achieved during a 100 m dash. This reduction in recruitment may have occurred as a result of fatigue of the neuromuscular junction, a decreased firing rate, or a reduction in the recruitment of higher threshold motor units (Type IIb or IIx) (98).

Ross and colleagues (98) postulated that acute neural fatigue may decrease reflex sensitivity. Even though it has yet to be demonstrated in response to sprint exercise, it is possible that large volumes of traumatic stretch shortening can reduce reflex sensitivity, which could reduce force output during running (98). This reduction in force output could impair sprint performance.

Technical Systems

Sprinting is a ballistic activity in which a series of running strides launch the body forward with maximal acceleration or velocity over some distance (91). Sprinting contains two major phases: a nonsupport or flight phase and a support phase (1). The nonsupport phase contains recovery and ground preparations, whereas the support phase includes both eccentric breaking and concentric propulsion subphases (1, 91). As an athlete sprints, she alternates between the nonsupport and support phases. As the athlete enters the support phase, an eccentric breaking action precedes an

The combination of a large stride length and a high stride rate can impact sprinting performance.

explosive concentric contraction. With increasing running speeds, the time spent in the nonsupport phase generally increases and the time spent in the support phase decreases (1). As the time spent in the support phase decreases, it becomes particularly important that the athlete demonstrate high rates of force development very quickly to maintain or continue to elevate running speed.

The speed at which an athlete runs or sprints depends largely on an interaction between stride rate and stride length (61, 91, 119). As the athlete accelerates and approaches maximal velocity, stride rate increases to a greater extent than stride length (91). Stride rate appears to be more trainable than stride length (91), because stride length is related to body height and length and appears to be very individualized (77). However, elite sprinters tend to achieve a greater stride rate and stride length in a shorter amount of time (91), suggesting that both stride rate and length can be optimized with appropriate training interventions.

The phases of a sprint are the start, the acceleration, and the maximal velocity phase.

Start Plisk (91) suggested that the optimal starting position is a medium heel-to-toe stance, regardless of whether the athlete is in a two-point (standing) or three- or four-point (crouching) stance. Initiating a sprint from the starting stance is then accomplished by overcoming inertia through the explosive application of force with the legs. The front leg extends while the rear leg is swung forward to the front of the body to ready the body for a ground strike. At the same time the arm opposite the leg that is swinging forward moves frontward and up with the elbow flexed at approximately 90° and the hand moves toward the forehead (91). As the front leg moves through the support phase and extends, the opposite arm should initially swing backward prior to swinging forward (91). When the start is performed correctly, the body moves forward and is at an angle of 45° or less from horizontal (91). Figure 12.2 shows the sprinting technique for the starting position.

Acceleration During the initial acceleration period from a static start, both stride rate and length will increase during the first 15 to 20 m or 8 to 10 strides (91, 119). However, it appears that stride frequency is of primary importance during this phase (83). During the preliminary portion of the acceleration period, the body will have a forward lean (≤45°), which will progressively move to a more upright position as the athlete approaches maximal velocity (119). Plisk (91) suggested that the forward lean during the acceleration period allows the leg to be in what is termed a *power line* position at the end of the drive phase. While in the power line position, the leg is fully extended and is in line with the body's longitudinal axis. Recovery from this position

Figure 12.2 Technique for the starting and acceleration subphases of sprinting.
Reprinted, by permission, from G. Schmolinsky, ed., 1993, *Track and field: The East German textbook of athletics* (Toronto: Sport Books).

is initiated by punching the knee in front of the hip to achieve a position in which the thigh is perpendicular to the trunk while the lower leg is parallel to the trunk. As the leg enters the support phase, it extends downward and back (91). During the support phase the athlete will transition between an eccentric and concentric subphase with the use of a stretch shortening cycle action (91). As the athlete accelerates, greater vertical ground reaction forces must be developed to continue to accelerate (57). These data seem to suggest that strength training, especially activities that improve the rate of force development, is an essential component of a training program designed to enhance sprinting performance.

The arm action during acceleration occurs with the arm flexed at approximately 90° and requires that the arm opposite the leg entering the support phase move close to the body as the hand swings up and forward from the hip to shoulder height (53, 63, 91). The arm motion should always originate from the shoulder and move forward and back (63). These arm motions offset the axial momentum generated by the contralateral leg and hip (91). The positions used in the acceleration phase are shown in figure 12.2.

Maximal Velocity   When maximal velocity is achieved (~15-20 m or 8-10 strides), the trunk position will be more upright (figure 12.3) (91, 119) and the stride rate and length will both contribute to the velocity of movement (81). During this phase, the time spent in the nonsupport phase will be maximized by the application of vertical ground reaction forces during the initial support phase to allow sufficient time for the swinging leg to be repositioned in preparation for the transition into the next support phase (115). Athletes who are able to apply higher vertical ground reaction forces during the support phase of the maximal velocity portion of a sprint are able to reach and maintain higher velocities of movement (81, 115). This further strengthens the contention that muscular strength and strength training are essential components of a periodized training plan that emphasizes speed development.

As the athlete enters the support phase, she will contact the ground directly beneath or slightly in front of her center of gravity (91). While moving into the support phase, the athlete will transition from an eccentric braking action into a concentric action with the use of a stretch shortening cycle action (1, 91). During the concentric phase, the athlete will perform a "triple extension" of the hip, knee, and ankle to properly apply forces to the ground. After the triple extension is performed, the athlete will then initiate a triple flexion of the ankle, knee, and hip, which will place the heel

Figure 12.3   Technique for sprinting at maximal velocity.

Notes: I = early nonsupport, ii = mid nonsupport, iii = late nonsupport, iv = early support and v = late support.
Reprinted, by permission, from G. Schmolinsky, ed., 1993, *Track and field: The East German textbook of athletics* (Toronto: Sport Books).

close to the buttocks. This triple flexion motion allows the athlete to rapidly move the knee to a position in front of the hip, effectively positioning the leg on the front side of the body. This movement prepares the foot for a rapid descent and allows of the athlete to maximize ground reaction forces as the foot moves down and back during ground strike (91).

Fatigue

During sprint training, the athlete should be conscious of fatigue because the development of fatigue can reduce sprint performance capacity. As fatigue is manifested, stride rate can be decreased while stride length increases and the duration of the ground support phase can increase. These events effectively decrease the effectiveness of the stretch shortening cycle that is applied between the eccentric and concentric subphases of the support phase (91). High levels of fatigue may also reduce ranges of leg extension (91). These breakdowns in running mechanics may be partially explained by the occurrence of metabolic fatigue (97).

Fatigue can reduce sprinting capacity, especially when a series of maximal sprints are performed (98). This type of fatigue may occur as a result of supraspinal failure, segmental afferent inhibition, depression of motor neuron excitability, loss of excitation branch points, and a decreased ability of the neuromuscular junction to fully activate the muscle (98). Neuromuscular fatigue can play a large role in reducing sprinting speed.

Methods for Developing Speed and Speed Endurance

Speed and speed endurance can be developed by manipulating a multitude of training factors. For example, the acceleration phase can be developed by targeting the ATP-PC system and performing short sprints (20-80 m) at 90% to 95% of maximum with longer recovery periods between repetitions and sets (33). Conversely, tempo work in which longer distances (>200 m) are covered and lower intensities (<70% of maximum) are interspersed with short rest intervals (<45 s) will develop the athlete's aerobic capacity (33). Table 12.1 gives examples of manipulations for the development of several different aspects of speed and speed endurance.

AGILITY TRAINING

It is commonly accepted that the development of straight-line sprinting ability is important for track-and-field athletes and athletes who participate in other field- or court-based sports (e.g., soccer, American football, baseball) (101). As mentioned previously, this type of speed is developed by drills and activities that target acceleration, maximal speed, and speed endurance (61, 91, 101). Although the ability to rapidly accelerate is an important skill, the athlete must also be able to rapidly change direction in response to the sporting environment (11, 69).

The abilities to stop, rapidly change direction, and accelerate in response to an external cue are required by many sports (11, 34, 69). These abilities can be considered as an expression of agility (35, 69). Some literature uses the term *quickness* synonymously with *agility* or *change-of-direction speed* (82, 101). However, Sheppard and Young (101) suggested that the definition of *quickness* does not consider deceleration or a change of direction and that quickness in and of itself contributes to agility. The term *cutting* has been used to describe change-of-direction capabilities (101) and is sometimes

Table 12.1 Methods for Developing Speed and Speed Endurance

Type of training		TARGET ENERGY SYSTEM		Objectives	Distance (m)	% of Best	RECOVERY TIME	
		Global	Specific				Repetitions	Sets
Speed		Anaerobic	ATP-PC	Speed	20-80	90-95	3-5 min	6-8 min
			Glycolytic	Anaerobic power	20-80	95-100	3-5 min	6-8 min
Speed endurance		Anaerobic	ATP-PC	Short speed endurance	50-80	90-95	1-2 min	5-7 min
				Power	50-80	95-100	2-3 min	7-10 min
			Glycolytic	Short speed endurance	< 80	90-95	1 min	3-4 min
				Power	< 80	95-100	1 min	4 min
			ATP-PC and glycolytic	Speed endurance	80-150	90-95	5-6 min	
Tempo	**Extensive**	Aerobic	Oxidative metabolism	Aerobic capacity	> 200	< 70	<45 s	<2 min
				Aerobic power	> 100	70-79	30-90 s	2-3 m
	Intensive	Mix	Glycolytic Oxidative	Anaerobic capacity	> 80	80-90	30 s to 5 min	2-3 min
Special endurance		Anaerobic	ATP-PC and glycolytic	Long speed endurance	150-300	90-95	10-12 min	
			Glycolytic	Anaerobic power	150-300	95-100	12-15 min	Full
			Glycolytic	Lactate tolerance	300-600	95-100	Full	Full

Adapted, by permission, from W.H. Freeman, 2001, *Peak when it counts: Periodization for American track & field,* 4th ed. (Mountain View, CA: Tafnews Press), 147.

falsely used to describe **agility**. This term only considers the change of direction, but the change of direction is initiated by the foot's ground contact (101). The literature indicates that agility must consider not only speed but also the ability to decelerate, change direction, and reaccelerate in response to stimuli.

Agility is a complex set of interdependent skills that converge for the athlete to respond to an external stimulus with a rapid deceleration, change of direction, and reacceleration (101, 120). Young and colleagues (120) and Sheppard and Young (101) suggested that agility is affected by the athlete's perceptual and decision-making ability and her ability to quickly change direction (figure 12.4).

Perceptual and Decision-Making Factors

During competition, the athlete must be able to perceive a situation, make a decision, and then change his direction of movement and speed in response to some external stimulus. The ability to engage this process involves a complex interaction of visual interpretation, anticipation, recognition of patterns, and knowledge of tactical situations (101, 120).

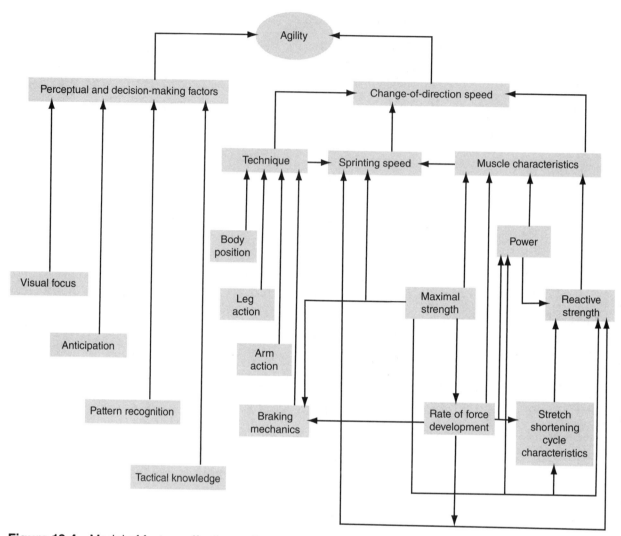

Figure 12.4 Model of factors affecting agility.

Adapted from Young, James, and Montgomery 2002 (120), Sheppard and Young 2006 (101), and Plisk 2008 (91).

The ability to visually scan or focus while performing multidirectional tasks appears to affect performance (90, 91). The ability to visually recognize a specific action, process the ramifications of that action, and respond with the appropriate change-of-direction or movement pattern differentiates between athletes (101). Knowledge of the tactical situation and the ability to anticipate the potential movements of the opponent also affect athlete's ability to appropriately change direction (101). Although it appears that perceptual decision-making factors can affect competition agility, there is a paucity of scientific data on this relationship.

Because there appears to be a relationship between visual interpretation and changes in direction, it may be warranted to include activities or drills that require the athlete to perform a specific movement in response to a visual or auditory stimulus (64). These activities can be integrated into both speed and agility training and may translate into competitive play. However, research exploring the efficacy of such training practices is limited.

Change-of-Direction Speed

Three key factors affect the athlete's ability to perform change-of-direction tasks: technique, sprinting speed, and muscle characteristics (101, 120).

Technique

Leg action, arm action, and braking mechanics can all affect an athlete's ability to express agility in movements (91). When the athlete is accelerating or decelerating, the body lean must increase to allow the base of support to move away from the athlete's center of gravity (91) while the center of gravity is lowered (101). These actions allow the athlete to maintain dynamic stability (91) and change direction rapidly (101). When initiating the deceleration action prior to the change of direction, the athlete will decrease his stride length (99). Upon reacceleration, the athlete will progressively increase both stride length and rate while the body position becomes more vertical (91). It may be warranted for the athlete to run with a lower center of gravity and a more pronounced forward lean when participating in sports that require frequent changes in direction (99, 101).

Powerful arm actions are a fundamental component of multidirectional movements (90, 91). As stated previously, the actions of the arm affect the athlete's leg drive when accelerating. When the athlete initiates a change in direction, the powerful actions of the arms contribute to the leg drive (90, 91). If the arm drive is not properly performed or is mistimed, speed may be reduced as a result of an inefficient movement pattern (90, 91).

A key component in the ability to change direction is the ability to tolerate the high eccentric forces that are generated when the athlete attempts to decelerate (91). Several techniques can be used to develop the athlete's ability to tolerate these eccentric breaking loads. For example, the ability to tolerate eccentric forces is related to muscular strength (49) and the technique used to initiate the change of direction (90). It is recommended that the athlete contact the ground with the full foot to maximize the surface area that is contacting the ground and reducing the eccentric load by engaging the entire lower extremity (90).

Sprinting Speed

Some coaches believe that straight-line sprinting ability directly affects the athlete's ability to change direction (101). This is why many coaches use a lot of straight-line sprinting to prepare their athletes. However, this practice may not be the best when working with athletes in sports that require multidirectional tasks (121), such as soccer or rugby. Straight-line sprinting ability explains only a small amount of the variance seen with change-of-direction activities (101, 121, 120). It has been shown that to maximize improvements in change-of-direction ability, the athlete must incorporate these types of activities into his training (118, 121). When only straight-line sprinting is used, there is virtually no improvement in performance of multidirectional change-of-direction tasks (101, 121). The addition of the ball (e.g., soccer or basketball) can significantly alter the athlete's ability to perform multidirectional tasks such as change-of-direction movements (101). Therefore, both straight-line sprinting and change-of-direction tasks with and without implements (e.g., balls, gloves) must be incorporated at various stages of the athlete's development and preparation for competition.

Muscle Characteristics

It is commonly accepted that muscular strength and power characteristics are related to the ability to sprint (6, 24, 49, 100, 101). There appears to be a relationship between muscular strength and power and change-of-direction performance (34, 49, 84). For example, Hori and colleagues (49) reported significant relationships between change-of-direction performance and the hang power clean and maximal front squat. The literature indicates that this relationship may be stronger with distinct change-of-direction movements than with directional changes performed at speed over longer durations (e.g., soccer forward) (101). The athlete should always strive to become stronger and more powerful because this will translate into change-of-direction ability. Although it appears that the athlete's muscular strength and power-generating capacity plays a major role in change-of-direction performance, more research is needed to elucidate this relationship.

Reactive strength or the ability to engage the stretch shortening cycle also appears to contribute to the athlete's ability to change direction (34, 120). The ability to engage the stretch shortening cycle in response to eccentric loading allows for greater forces to be generated during the concentric phase of a change-of-direction task (59). The ability to engage this mechanism may allow for a more rapid acceleration when changing direction. Therefore, it may be warranted to use plyometric activities, given their strong relationship to change-of-direction performance (120), in the development of athletes.

PROGRAM DESIGN

Developing a training plan involves planning at several distinct levels. These include the **microcycle** (short term), the **macrocycle** (intermediate term), and the **annual training plan** (long term). At each level of planning the coach must consider the principles of developing speed and agility and understand the physiological and performance responses to specific training variables.

Principles of Speed and Agility Development

When considering the development of speed, several principles must be considered (28).

Quality Over Quantity

Speed training places a large physiological stress on the athlete (28). To maximize training effects, speed training needs to be meticulously dosed and incorporate low training volumes interspersed with long periods of restoration. Excessive use of sprint activities will eventually result in overtraining. It is not wise to perform sprint and agility training under conditions of excessive fatigue or with excessively short rest intervals (91).

Proper Technique at All Times

To develop the appropriate movement patterns, the coach must emphasize proper technique in all training activities. If the athlete performs drills with inadequate technique, he will stabilize inappropriate movement patterns that will hinder the development of speed and the expression of agility. Focus on proper technique should begin during the warm-up and continue into the main body of the training session.

If excessive fatigue causes technical breakdowns, it may be warranted to reduce the training volume of that session.

Specificity of Speed and Agility Development

When developing speed and agility, the athlete should develop skills in relationship to the demands of her sport. For example, it may be warranted for soccer players to perform speed and agility activities with a ball because this will be a major component of competitive performance. Coaches also should consider the bioenergetics, the work-to-rest ratio, and the dynamics of the targeted sport when designing specific sprint and agility sessions. The coach should develop specific sprint and agility activities based on the needs of the sport. For example, the coach can use short side games or the "dribble track" (see figure 6.18 on p. 144) in soccer because these activities will more closely model what occurs in competition (47).

Develop the Supporting Characteristics

Many factors can contribute to the athlete's ability to exhibit speed and effectively perform change-of-direction movements (28, 49, 101, 120). Coaches must understand the bioenergetic demands of different sprint and agility training activities and how they relate to the athlete's targeted sport. Additional things to consider are the role of strength training in the expression of speed and the development of change-of-direction abilities.

© Human Kinetics

Cater agility training to your sport. That way, you'll develop sport-specific skills at the same time you develop speed and agility.

Feedback

It is important that the athlete is given objective and subjective feedback throughout the training process. Objective feedback can include recorded times and video analysis of performance, whereas subjective feedback may include the concept of perceived maximum speed (28). With novice athletes or when the skill set is complex, the coach should provide constant feedback and reinforcement. This feedback appears to be essential during the early stages of skills development, but as the athlete develops less feedback is necessary. Consider providing information on proper performance and methods for correcting errors. As the skill develops, feedback should be less frequent and progress from qualitative to quantitative (91).

Motivation

To develop speed or agility, the athlete must be highly motivated (28). Sprint and agility training produces a large amount of fatigue, especially when targeting **speed endurance** (90, 91), and a motivated athlete is more likely to tolerate this type of training. Motivation can be cultivated by providing feedback, especially feedback that emphasizes the positive aspects of the athlete's training, and by including the athlete in the planning process. If the plan is implemented correctly, the athlete will be more likely to push herself to higher levels.

Variables Associated With Training for Speed or Agility

When integrating speed or agility training into the annual periodized training plan, the coach should consider manipulating several training variables (91):

Density

The **density of training** is the amount of training that occurs within a given time period (107). When considering a sprint, sprint endurance, or agility session, the density is a ratio of the interval of exercise and relief within a set or series of sprints (91).

Duration and Distance

A run can be calculated in either seconds or minutes to determine the duration of exercise. The distance traveled can also be quantified in meters or yards. For example, if an athlete sprints 100 m (distance) in 22 s (duration), both distance and duration have been determined and can be used to calculate an intensity factor.

The duration or distance of an activity determines the bioenergetic pathway targeted as well as the specific quality targeted. Short-duration or short-distance activities tend to target the phosphagen system and the development of acceleration or speed. For example, acceleration is emphasized when the athlete runs short sprints (10-20 m) whereas maximum speed is targeted with longer sprints (>20 m). Elite sprinters appear to reach maximal velocities after 5 to 6 s in about 45 to 55 m, whereas novice sprinters attain top speeds by 20 to 30 m (91). If the sprint is extended, reliance on the oxidative energy system will increase. Therefore, the distance and duration of the sprint are important considerations when one is targeting acceleration, maximal speed, or endurance characteristics.

Exercise Order

The exercise order is the sequence in which specific training tasks are performed (91). When prescribing the order of exercises in a speed, speed endurance, or agility session, the coach must consider both the management of fatigue and the development of fitness. Because sprint and agility training activities impose large metabolic, neuromuscular, and coordinative demands, they should be conducted when the athlete has a minimal level of fatigue. The activities are best undertaken after a dynamic warm-up that primes that athlete for the training bout and before more fatiguing bouts of training are undertaken (60, 91). It is recommended that speed and agility training be conducted after a recovery day or after a light technical workout to maximize the training benefits while the athlete is under a minimal amount of fatigue (60).

Plisk (91) suggested that speed and agility training sessions are best structured with brief work periods separated by frequent rest intervals that last between 2 and 3 min or contain a work-to-rest ratio between 1:12 and 1:20. An effective method for performing this type of activity is the *repetition method,* which contains very short, high-intensity work bouts performed for low volumes and long rest intervals that maximize recovery and the development of speed and technical proficiency (91). (See chapter 11 for more information on different interval methods.) It is possible to create sessions that target speed and speed endurance, but the coach must take care in ordering the exercises in these sessions.

Intensity

When an athlete is training for speed, speed endurance, or agility, the intensity is often quantified in relation to maximal velocity or speed of movement.

$$\text{Intensity } (m \cdot s^{-1}) = \frac{\text{Distance (m)}}{\text{Time (s)}}$$

According to this equation, if an athlete runs 100 m in 22 s she would have an intensity of 4.5 m/s. Additional examples of the calculation of intensity for individual sprints are presented in tables 12.2 and 12.3. The coach must consider that short sprints performed at high velocities provide a higher-intensity bout of exercise.

Table 12.2   Determination of Volume Load and Average Intensity for a Sprint Training Session

WORKOUT 1				WORKOUT 2			
Distance (m)	Time (s)	Intensity (m/s)	Volume load	Distance (m)	Time (s)	Intensity (m/s)	Volume load
200	48	4.17	833.33	400	79	5.06	2,025.32
200	35	5.71	1,142.86	400	89	4.49	1,797.75
200	36	5.56	1,111.11	200	42	4.76	952.38
200	39	5.13	1,025.64	200	40	5.00	1,000.00
Training intensity =		5.14		Training intensity =		4.83	
Training session volume load =			4,112.94	**Training session volume load =**			5,775.45

Note: Volume load is in arbitrary units. Training intensity is the average velocity of the workout. Concept based on methods presented by Plisk (91).

Table 12.3 Training Zone Intensities for Sprint Training

Zone	Percentage maximal	Velocity (m/s)	Times (s)	Intensity
6	>100	>4.5	>22.0	Supermaximal
5	90-100	4.1-4.5	24.4-22.0	Maximum
4	80-90	3.6-4.1	27.5-24.5	Heavy
3	70-80	3.2-3.6	31.4-27.5	Medium
2	50-70	2.3-3.3	44.0-31.4	Low
1	<50	<2.3	<44.0	Very low

Note: Times are based on a best 100 m time of 22 s.

When designing the training plan, the coach can establish intensity zones based on the athlete's best times in a prescribed distance (table 12.3). To create the intensity zones, the coach would use the following formula to determine the percentage maximum intensity (velocity):

$$\text{Percent maximum velocity (m/s)} = \text{max intensity} \times \text{percent}$$

If the athlete had a maximum 100 m time of 22 s, her 90% max intensity would be

$$90\% \text{ maximum velocity (m/s)} = 4.5 \text{ (m/s)} \times (0.90) = 4.1 \text{ (m/s)}$$

If the training zone was set at 90% to 100% of maximum, the limits for time would be calculated with the following equation:

$$\text{Training time (s)} = \text{distance (m)}/\text{percentage maximum velocity (m/s)}$$

$$90\% \text{ training time (s)} = 100 \text{ (m)}/4.1 \text{ (m/s)} = 24.4 \text{ (s)}$$

Therefore, the training zone for a maximum day (90-100%) for this athlete would require her to run 100 m in a time between 24.4 and 22.0 s. Further examples of the training zones can be found in table 12.3.

Rest Intervals

Manipulation of the interrepetition and interset rest interval can significantly affect the physiological stress and performance outcomes of a speed, speed endurance, or agility training session. Long rest intervals (work/rest = 1:12-1:20) should be used when targeting the development of absolute speed because they allow for a greater replenishment of stored phosphagens and allow for the expression of maximal power outputs. When targeting high-intensity interval endurance, the coach should use shorter rest intervals (work/rest = 1:3-1:5). Finally, short rest intervals (work/rest = 1:1-1:3) are used when targeting the oxidative system (aerobic) (22, 92, 107). A summary of the effect of manipulating rest intervals can be found in chapter 11 and in tables 11.7 to 11.9 (pp. 308-311).

When establishing the work-to-rest ratio, the coach can examine the work-to-rest ratios that occur in the sporting event. For example, the work-to-rest ratio in rugby games is between 1:1-1.9 and 1-1.9:1 (30), whereas American football generally has a work-to-rest ratio of 1:6 (92) and soccer exhibits a 1:7 to 1:8 work-to-rest ratio (69). By determining these ratios, the coach can design the training program to target the metabolic demands of the sport while also developing the appropriate speed characteristics required for successful performance.

Sequenced Training Strategies

A multitude of factors that can contribute to the generation of fatigue should be considered when sequencing a training session, microcycle, or **block** of training. It may be advisable to separate the training session into specific segments within the daily training plan (60, 91). For example, the morning session (7:00 a.m.) after a recovery day may focus on speed training and the afternoon session (4:00 p.m.) may target speed endurance or strength training. Kurz (60) suggested allowing a minimum of 4 hr between sessions when structuring training in this fashion.

Plisk (91) suggested that speed and agility training has the potential to create a large amount of neuromuscular and metabolic fatigue. Fatigue can hinder the development of either speed or agility, so it is recommended that speed and agility training be performed early in the training session and after a day of rest or a light technical training day (60). Manipulating the daily training structure will allow the athlete to better manage the fatigue developed in response to training. One strategy that can elevate fitness and preparedness while minimizing fatigue is termed *block training* (50) or *sequenced training* (91).

Sequenced training (or block training) is based on the idea that the delayed training effects of activities can modify the responses of other training activities (50, 91, 102). The idea that different abilities (aerobic endurance, maximal strength, anaerobic endurance, strength endurance, and maximal speed) exhibit different rates of decay (**involution**) is central to the sequencing of training (50). The length of time dedicated to the preparation period will influence the rate of decay of training factors. The longer the training program, or the preparation subphase of the annual training plan, the more stable the physiological and performance adaptations and residuals (91). This allows the athlete to maintain adaptations created in one training subphase with a minimal emphasis or small volume load of training in the next training subphase. This enables the athlete to place the major emphasis during the next subphase on another training focus (14, 15, 50, 91, 102).

Sequenced training involves alternating the use of accumulation, transmutation, and realization blocks or subphases of training to emphasize one major training factor while minimizing the focus on other factors (table 12.4) (50). For example,

Table 12.4   Example Sequenced Training for Speed Development

Factor	TRAINING BLOCKS AND SEQUENCE		
	Accumulation	**Transmutation**	**Restitution**
Primary focus	Maximal strength	Muscular power	Speed and agility
Secondary focus	Muscular power	Speed and agility	Muscular power
Tertiary focus	Speed and agility	Maximal strength	Maximal strength
Duration (weeks)	2-4	2-4	1-2

Adapted from Issurin 2008 (50) and Plisk 2008 (91).

during the accumulation period training may focus on the development of maximal strength, whereas maintenance loads are used to develop muscular power and speed and agility loads (50, 91). As the athlete moves to the next block (transmutation), the emphasis shifts to developing muscular power while using maintenance loads for both maximal strength and speed agility. Speed agility is emphasized during the realization block, whereas maintenance loads are used for maximal strength- and power-generating capacity. The sequenced training model is intended to alleviate the cumulative fatigue problems that are typically seen when parallel training models are used (91). The sequenced training model adapts well to sports that require a large number of competitions or a long competitive phase (50).

Sequenced training is a major departure from traditional concurrent training strategies (50, 91). It is essential that the blocks of training be sequenced appropriately to allow each block to potentiate the next block (phase potentiation) because inappropriate sequencing will result in maladaptive responses that reduce the athlete's preparedness (91). Although this strategy of training is highly effective, it is best suited for experienced athletes and should be avoided with novice or beginners (93, 91, 107). With novice and beginners, traditional concurrent training strategies are recommended.

Training Intensity

The training intensity is associated with the rate of performing work or the rate at which energy is expended (107). The higher the training intensity, the higher the rate of performing work, which corresponds to higher energy expenditures. The training intensity during sprint and agility training can be calculated as follows:

$$\text{Training intensity (m} \cdot \text{s}^{-1}) = \frac{\text{Training session volume load}}{\text{Total distance covered in training}}$$

In table 12.2, an example training series is presented in which an athlete's volume load is 4,112.94 and the total distance covered during the training session is 800 m.

$$\text{Training intensity (m} \cdot \text{s}^{-1}) = \frac{41192.94}{800} = 5.14 \text{m} \cdot \text{s}^{-1}$$

Therefore, the training intensity of this session is 5.14 m/s. Note that as the volume load increases, there is a general trend for the intensity or velocity of movement to decrease.

Volume

The volume of training represents the amount of work performed in a training bout and is often expressed as the total repetitions of a prescribed workload or task assignment. The most accurate method for determining the volume of workload completed in a training session is the **volume load**, which is a product of the intensity and distance completed per repetition (91).

Volume Load

When looking at the interactive effects of intensity and volume, coaches and athletes must have a quantifiable method for estimating training stress (91). Volume load is an excellent indicator of training stress and is generally calculated as a product of work volume and intensity (91, 107). In the context of sprint or agility training, the volume load of training can be determined using running speeds (intensity) and distances covered (91), and in the following formula:

$$\text{Sprint or agility training volume load} = \text{velocity (m/s)} \times \text{distance (m)}$$

As with resistance training (see chapter 10), when the intensity (speed) of the session decreases the volume load will increase. An example calculation of volume load can be found in table 12.2.

When the coach is designing the training plan, it may be warranted to predict the volume load fluctuations for sprint training and integrate those volume loads with those established for resistance training activities. If done appropriately, the integration of the training loads will allow for a superior management of fatigue while maximizing fitness and preparedness for competition.

Periodization for Speed and Agility Training

A key aspect of implementing a speed and agility training plan is ensuring that the training factors are integrated to allow the athlete to attain the training goals. The annual training plan must be established and then broken into macrocycle and microcycle structures. Developing a sprint program for a track athlete is somewhat easier than developing a plan for a team sport athlete that must include agility, technical skills, and tactics.

Annual Training Plan

Developing a plan for speed and agility training begins with the development of the annual training plan. As noted in chapter 6, key information is needed when developing the annual plan includes dates of important competitions and the individual preparation, competition, and transition phases. The annual training plan will be structured based on the sport's characteristics. For example, a sprinter will typically use a bi-cycle annual training plan, whereas a team sport athlete may not, depending on league requirements.

The annual training plan for an elite sprinter uses a bi-cycle model in which two major peaks are planned, whereas a mono-cycle structure may be warranted for less developed sprinters (33). In the bi-cycle model presented in figure 12.5 the first peak, for the indoor season, occurs on March 10, whereas the second peak, for the outdoor season, is planned for September 1. This structure divides the training plan into two distinct parts, or cycles, separated by a 3-week transition phase.

The dynamics of the annual plan structure for team sports can be vastly different compared with an individual sports athlete, such as a sprinter. The competitive phase is generally dictated by the league or conference in which the athlete's team competes. One of the rationales for using sequenced training models is to allow the athlete to tolerate a longer competitive season (50). This is accomplished by rotating through various blocks of training that are divided into various primary, secondary, and tertiary emphases (table 12.5) (50, 91).

Figure 12.6 is an example of a sequenced annual training plan for a collegiate soccer program. The annual training plan presented in figure 12.6 has a bi-cycle structure in which major competitive emphasis occurs in competition phase 1. Note that as with traditional annual training plans, the year is broken into preparation, competition, and transition phases.

Figure 12.5 Periodization model for a sprinter.

First half (October–March)

Dates	October	November	December	January	February	March
Weekends	7 14 21 28	4 11 18 25	2 9 16 23 30	6 13 20 27	3 10 17 24	3 10 17 24 31

Calendar of competitions (Location): Oregon (Jan), NY (Feb 3), LA (Feb 17), Worlds (Mar 10)

Periodization:
- Phase: Preparation phase 1 | Competition phase 1
- Subphase: General preparation | Specific preparation | Precompetition. | Main competition
- Strength: Anatomical adaptation | Maximal strength | Power | Maintenance
- Endurance: Tempo | Speed endurance development | Maintenance of speed endurance
- Speed: Technique work | Foundation speed development | Maximum speed development
- Transition 1

Second half (April–September)

Dates	April	May	June	July	August	September
Weekends	7 14 21 28	6 12 19 26	2 9 16 23	30 7 14 21	29 4 11 18 24	1 9 17 24

Calendar of competitions (Location): Seville (June 9), Moscow (June 23), Berlin (July 7), Oslo (July 21), Zurich (Aug 4), Tokyo (Sept 1)

Periodization:
- Training phase: Preparation phase 2 | Competition phase 2
- Subphase: General preparation | Specific preparation | Precompetition | Main competition
- Strength: Anatomical adaptation | Maximal strength | Power | Maintenance
- Endurance: Tempo | Speed endurance development | Maintenance of speed endurance
- Speed: Technique work | Foundation speed development | Maximum speed development
- Transition 2 | Other activities

Adapted from W.H. Freeman 2001 (33).

336

Table 12.5 Annual Training Plan Phase Emphases for a Sprinter

| Emphasis | PHASE OF THE ANNUAL TRAINING PLAN | | |
	General preparation	Specific preparation	Competition
Primary emphasis	General endurance Strength endurance	Anaerobic endurance Short speed endurance General strength	Speed Speed endurance Long speed endurance
Secondary emphasis	Aerobic capacity Aerobic power Flexibility	Specific strength Speed Running technique	Special endurance Tactics Running technique
Tertiary emphasis	Speed Anaerobic capacity	General endurance Aerobic power Aerobic capacity Flexibility	General strength Specific strength Aerobic power Flexibility

Adapted, by permission, from W.H. Freeman, 2001, *Peak when it counts: Periodization for American track & field* (Mountain View, CA: Tafnews Press), 147.

Macrocycle

In the annual training plan presented for a sprinter in figure 12.5, preparation phase 1 is substantially longer than preparation phase 2, as discussed in chapter 6. Preparation phase 1 contains two subphases, which are classified as general and specific preparation. The general preparation phase targets conditioning with an emphasis on anatomical adaptation or what is also referred to as strength endurance. A secondary emphasis is placed on tempo work, which targets both anaerobic and aerobic development. In the early part of the general preparation work, long tempo work or aerobic intervals are completed, whereas in the later stages of the phase short-duration tempo work (anaerobic intervals) is used. As the athlete transitions into the specific preparation subphase, a greater emphasis is placed on the development of maximal strength and the use of anaerobic interval work. Anaerobic interval work is then used to develop repetitive speed endurance. As the athlete transitions into the competitive phase, the focus shifts to developing maximal speed while increasing power-generating capacity and maintaining speed endurance.

The annual training plan can be structured to target aspects of the athlete's development depending on the phase of training. For example, during the general preparation phase the primary emphasis is developing strength and general endurance, whereas in the specific preparation phase anaerobic endurance as well as short speed endurance is emphasized. When structuring the phases of the annual training plan, the coach must consider the goals of each phase because this will dictate which factors associated with sprinting are targeted. Table 12.5 gives an example of the factors targeted in each phase of the annual training plan for a sprinter. Using this table as a guide, one can then select different training activities from table 12.1 when establishing a training plan. For example, in the general preparation phase, aerobic capacity and power development is a secondary development emphasis. Selecting extensive tempo work early in the phase would accomplish this goal. As the athlete progresses through the phase, the distance covered can be shortened and intensive tempo work can be used to tap both aerobic and anaerobic energy supply. Once the

Figure 12.6 — Annual training plan for an American university soccer team.

Category	May			June					July				August				September					October			
Week starting	12	19	24	2	9	16	23	30	7	14	21	28	4	11	18	25	1	8	15	22	29	6	13	20	27
Competitions																									
Training phase	Preparation phase 1															Competition phase 1									
Subphase	General preparation			Specific preparation									Precompetition			Competitive									
Macrocycles	1				2								3			4			5		6			7	
Microcycles	1	2	3	4	5	6	7	8	9	10	11	12	13	14	15	16	17	18	19	20	21	22	23	24	25
Primary focus (strength)	Strength endurance				Maximal strength				Power				Technique			Maintenance						Peaking			
Sessions	3	3	3	3	3	3	3	3	3	3	3	3	3	2	2	2	2	2	3	3	2	2	2	2	2
Strength endurance	M	H	M	M	M	M	L	-	H	L	L	L	-	-	-	L	L	L	H	H	L	L	L	-	L
Strength	M	M	M	M	H	H	H	M	M	M	M	M	M	L	M	M	M	L	L	L	M	M	M	M	L
Power	L	L	L	L	L	M	M	L	-	H	H	H	H	M	M	M	M	H	M	M	M	M	M	M	M
Speed	-	-	L	L	L	L	L	M	-	L	M	M	H	H	H	M	M	H	M	M	M	M	M	H	H
Primary focus (endurance)	SA and SA endurance				SA endurance				Endurance				Tactics			Tactics, maintenance, and recovery									
Endurance	L	L	L	L	M	M	M	M	H	H	H	H	M	M	M	L	L	L	M	M	L	L	L	L	L
Speed and agility Endurance	M	M	M	M	H	H	H	M	M	M	M	M	M	L	L	M	M	M	M	M	M	L	L	L	L
Speed and agility	M	M	M	M	L	L	L	M	L	L	M	L	L	M	M	L	L	L	L	L	L	L	L	L	L
Technical	M	M	M	M	M	M	M	M	L	M	M	L	M	L	L	L	L	L	L	L	L	L	L	L	L
Tactical	L	L	L	M	L	L	L	L	L	M	M	M	H	H	H	H	H	H	H	H	H	H	H	H	M
Recovery	L	L	L	L	L	L	L	M	L	L	M	M	M	L	M	M	M	M	L	M	M	H	M	H	M

Figure 12.6 Annual training plan for an American university soccer team.

Figure 12.6 Annual training plan for an American university soccer team. (rotated table)

Dates		November				December					January				February				March					April			
	Months	November				December					January				February				March					April			
	Week starting	3	10	17	24	1	8	15	22	29	5	12	19	26	2	9	16	23	2	9	16	23	30	6	13	20	27
	Competitions		■																■								■
Periodization	Training phase	Competition phase 1		Transition phase 1		Preparation phase 2													Competition phase 2								
	Subphase	Comp.		Transition		General preparation						Specific preparation							Precompetitive	Competitive							
	Macrocycles	7		8		9					10				11				12		13				14		
	Microcycles	26	27	28	29	30	31	32	33	34	35	36	37	38	39	40	41	42	43	44	45	46	47	48	49	50	51
Strength training	Primary focus	Peaking		Recovery		Technique			Strength endurance			Maximal strength							Recovery	Power				Speed			
	Sessions	2	1	0	0	2	2	3	3	3	3	4	4	4	4	4	4	4	3	3	3	3	3	3	3	3	3
	Strength endurance	-	-	-	-	M	M	H	H	H	M	M	M	M	L	L	L	M	H	-	M	L	L	-	-	-	-
	Strength	L	-	L	-	L	M	M	M	M	L	H	M	H	M	H	H	H	M	M	M	M	L	L	L	L	L
	Power	L	L	-	-	-	-	-	-	L	L	-	L	L	M	M	M	M	L	H	H	H	H	M	M	M	M
	Speed	H	M	-	-	L	M	M	M	L	H	-	L	L	L	L	M	M	M	M	H	M	M	H	M	M	H
Endurance, speed and agility, technical, and tactical training	Primary focus	Maintenance		Recovery		Endurance development						Speed and agility			Speed and agility endurance				Recovery and tactical	Speed and agility							
	Endurance	M	L	-	-	H	H	M	M	M	M	M	M	M	L	H	H	H	L	-	L	M	L	L	L	L	-
	Speed and agility endurance	-	-	-	-	L	L	L	-	L	L	L	-	L	H	M	H	L	-	-	M	-	-	-	L	-	-
	Speed/agility	L	L	-	-	L	M	M	M	L	H	H	M	H	M	M	L	L	L	H	H	M	H	L	M	H	L
	Technical	L	L	-	-	M	M	L	M	M	H	H	M	L	L	M	L	L	L	L	L	M	M	M	H	L	L
	Tactical	H	M	-	-	L	L	L	L	L	L	L	L	M	H	H	H	H	H	H	H	H	M	H	H	H	L
	Recovery	H	H	H	H	L	M	M	M	H	H	M	M	M	H	M	L	H	H	M	M	M	M	M	H	M	H

Figure 12.6 *(continued)* Annual training plan for an American university soccer team.

Note: H = high emphasis; m = moderate emphasis; L = low emphasis; - = not trained; SA = speed and agility
Adapted from Gray and Stone 2008 (38).

athlete shifts into the specific preparation phase, speed endurance activities such as short speed activities can be selected.

One important factor to consider is that the use of long slow distance to develop aerobic capacity is detrimental to the development of speed (92). It is best to develop aerobic capacity and power or speed endurance by using extensive and intensive tempo methods, which may also be termed *aerobic* and *anaerobic intervals* (92, 91). Recent research suggests that these methods results in physiological adaptations that improve speed endurance performance (62).

The dynamics of working with team sports creates additional issues at the macrocycle level because the training plan must include both technical and tactical activities in conjunction with activities that are designed to develop endurance, strength, and sprint and agility capabilities. In the team sport example presented in figure 12.6, preparation phase 1 and competition phase 1 are significantly longer than preparation phase 2 or competition phase 2. Preparation phase 1 contains a shorter general preparation subphase with a greater emphasis placed on specific preparation. Conversely, preparation phase 2 contains a significantly longer general preparation phase. Each subphase is broken into macrocycles that contain blocks of training that have specific primary emphases (focus in figure 12.6). For example, in macrocycle 1 the primary emphasis is placed on strength endurance, speed and agility, and speed and agility endurance. Macrocycle 2 is broken into two blocks, with the first block focusing primarily on maximal strength and speed and agility endurance and the second block focusing primarily on power and endurance. Remember that although each block has a primary focus, a major tenet of the sequenced or block system is to use maintenance loads for other factors, as can be seen in figure 12.6.

An additional example of a sequenced training plan has been presented by Plisk (91). Figure 12.7 shows a preparatory phase of training for a university or professional American football team based on Plisk's work. Each block (macrocycle) is distinguished by different frequencies and densities of training in regard to training content (strength training, speed and agility, and speed endurance). In macrocycle 1 there is a large emphasis on strength training with 12 sessions (4 per microcycle), whereas a secondary emphasis is placed on speed and agility and speed endurance (2 per microcycle). The speed and agility and speed endurance work are done in the same session, with emphasis being varied between sessions or in separate sessions

Dates	Months	May			June				July					August	
	Week starting	11	18	26	2	9	16	23	30	7	14	21	28	4	11
Periodization	Macrocycles	1			2				3			4			
	Microcycles	1	2	3	4	5	6	7	8	9	10	11	12	13	14
Strength training	Sessions	4	4	4	3	3	3	3	4	4	4	3	3	3	3
Speed and agility	Sessions	2	2	2	3	3	3	3	2	2	2	3	3	3	3
Speed endurance	Sessions	2	2	2	3	3	3	3	2	2	2	-	-	-	-
Special endurance	Session	-	-	-	-	-	-	-	-	-	-	3	3	3	3

Figure 12.7 14-week sequenced preparation phase of training plan for university or professional American football.

Adapted from Plisk 2008 (91) and Haff et al. 2004 (39).

depending on time restraints. Speed endurance is developed in accordance with the strategies of tactical metabolic training (92) where three or four repetitive bouts of exercise that last no longer than 10 min are used to develop oxidative capacity and the ability to buffer lactate (91). The durations used for speed endurance are similar to the intensive tempo runs presented in table 12.1.

During macrocycle 2 the emphasis shifts, with a decreasing density and frequency of strength training (12 sessions: 3 per microcycle) and an increase in the density and frequency of both speed and agility training and speed endurance training. In this macrocycle major emphasis is the development of speed endurance via the use of 2 or 3 min interval bouts that are separated by 8 to 10 min of recovery (91). These types of intervals are similar to the special endurance training practices presented in table 12.1.

Once macrocycle 3 is initiated, the density and frequency of training increase for strength training, whereas the density of both speed and agility training and special endurance training decreases (activities that model the specifics of American football). Activities such as intensive tempo training are used in this macrocycle to maintain the oxidative and glycolytic adaptations established in previous macrocycles. This is accomplished by using simulated quarters in which the exercise work-to-rest patterns closely match what is seen in a game of American football (39, 91, 92). In the last macrocycle the density and frequency of strength training are reduced, whereas the density and frequency of speed and agility training and special endurance training (e.g., activities used in macrocycle 3) are maintained.

Microcycle

Once the characteristics of the macrocycle are established, the individual microcycles can be constructed. One of the main factors dictating the construction of the microcycles contained in a speed, agility, or speed endurance portion of an annual training plan is the management of fatigue (91). The management of fatigue is important because high levels of fatigue can affect the athlete's ability to effectively perform speed- and agility-based drills with appropriate technique. It is advisable that the athlete perform speed- and agility-based activities under a minimal amount of fatigue to maximize technical proficiency and allow for the mastery of skills. This requires that the athlete perform these activities after completing an appropriate warm-up that emphasizes a combination of general and specific warm-up activities (54); as well, the coach must incorporate adequate rest between repetitions or sets. It may be warranted to organize the different training components into multiple sessions within the training day (figure 12.8).

Unlike speed and agility training, speed endurance training is designed to increase the athlete's ability to resist and tolerate fatigue. This is accomplished by specifically taxing the metabolic systems (92, 91) by manipulating training variables such as the work-to-rest interval, duration, and intensity of the sprint bout. Increasing the volume of multiple bouts of sprinting can result in very specific metabolic adaptations that can aid in the development of speed endurance.

When expanding the macrocycle structure for the American football example presented in figure 12.7, the coach can construct a microcycle model (figure 12.8). In this model sequenced training blocks are used with alterations in the density and frequency of training for each training factor. Because multiple factors are trained on the same day, fatigue management is important, so splitting the factors into distinct training sessions within the day is warranted.

Month	Macrocycle	Weeks	Emphasis	Monday	Tuesday	Wednesday	Thursday	Friday	Saturday	Sunday
May	1	1-3	Strength training	ST	ST		ST	ST		
			Speed and agility		SA			SA		
			Speed endurance	SE			SE			
			Special endurance							
June	2	4-7	Strength training	ST		ST		ST		
			Speed and agility		SA		SA		SA	
			Speed endurance	SE		SE		SE		
			Special endurance							
July	3	8-10	Strength training	ST	ST		ST	ST		
			Speed and agility		SA			SA		
			Speed endurance							
			Special endurance	SPE		SPE		SPE		
August	4	11-14	Strength training	ST		ST		ST		
			Speed and agility		SA		SA		SA	
			Speed endurance							
			Special endurance	SPE		SPE		SPE		

Figure 12.8 Microcycle structure for a 14-week sequenced preparation phase of training plan for university or professional American football.

ST = strength training; SA= speed agility, SE= speed endurance, and SPE= special endurance. On days when multiple activities are scheduled, the activities must be separated so that one factor is addressed in a morning session and the other at least 4 hr later. If time constraints dictate that both factors must be trained in the same session, the priority item should be addressed first. On days when SA and ST occur, the ST generally for this session focuses on upper-body activities.
Adapted from Plisk 2008 (91) and Haff et al. 2004 (39).

SUMMARY OF MAJOR CONCEPTS

The development of speed, agility, and speed endurance is important for the majority of sports, so these important sport performance characteristics must be integrated into the periodized training plan. Long-distance training methods will impede the development of both speed and agility and should be avoided when attempting to maximize these performance abilities. Both maximal strength and power are important characteristics, which emphasizes the need for an integrated strength training program for athletes who are attempting to maximize speed performance.

Some very specific movement mechanics are essential to maximizing an athlete's speed of movement (see Plisk 91) and facilitate change-of-direction activities. Although speed plays a role in change-of-direction performance, change-of-direction or agility activities must be included in the periodized training plan. Simply practicing straight-line running will not significantly improve agility. Many athletes spend large amounts of time performing straight-line training tasks, but it may be warranted to use more change-of-direction tasks that emphasize acceleration, deceleration, changes in direction, and reacceleration activities. It also may be warranted to include the implements used in competition (e.g., soccer ball, basketball).

Appendix

▼

BLANK CHARTS FOR ANNUAL AND FOUR-YEAR PLANS

These blank charts can be photocopied and reused as you create annual and four-year plans.

Chart of the Annual Plan

Type: ___ Year: ___ Coach: ___

Athlete's name

Training objectives

Performance	Tests/Standards	Physical prep	Technical prep	Tactical prep	Psychological prep

Dates: Months, Weeks

Competitions: Domestic, International, Location

Periodization: Training phase, Strength, Endurance, Speed, Psychological, Nutrition, Macrocycles, Microcycles

Microcycles: 1 2 3 4 5 6 7 8 9 10 11 12 13 14 15 16 17 18 19 20 21 22 23 24 25 26 27 28 29 30 31 32 33 34 35 36 37 38 39 40 41 42 43 44 45 46 47 48 49 50 51 52

Peaking index

Testing dates

Medical control dates

Camp/Semicamp

Peaking index scale: %100 1, 90 2, 80 3, 70 4, 60 5, 50, 40, 30, 20, 10, Peaking

Training factors
- Volume
- Intensity
- Peaking
- Phys prep
- Tech prep
- Tact prep
- Psych prep

From T.O. Bompa and G.G. Haff, 2009, *Periodization: Theory and methodology of training* 5th ed. (Champaign, IL: Human Kinetics).

344

Chart of the Annual Plan

Type:

Year:

Coach:

		1	2	3	4	5	6	7	8	9	10	11	12	13	14	15	16	17	18	19	20	21	22	23	24	25	26	27	28	29	30	31	32	33	34	35	36	37	38	39	40	41	42	43	44	45	46	47	48	49	50	51	52
Dates	Months																																																						
	Weeks																																																						
Competitions	Domestic		
	International		
	Location		
Periodization	Training phase		
	Strength		
	Endurance		
	Speed		
	Psychological		
	Nutrition		
	Macrocycles		
	Microcycles		
Peaking index			
Testing dates			
Medical control dates			
Camp/Semicamp			

%100	1
90	2
80	3
70	4
60	5
50	
40	
30	Peaking
20	
10	

Training factors

| Volume |
| Intensity |
| Peaking |
| Phys prep |
| Tech prep |
| Tact prep |
| Psych prep |

From T.O. Bompa and G.G. Haff, 2009, *Periodization: Theory and methodology of training* 5th ed. (Champaign, IL: Human Kinetics).

Chart of the Annual Plan

Type: _____ Year: _____ Coach: _____

Athlete's name		Training objectives					
		Performance	Tests/Standards	Physical prep	Technical prep	Tactical prep	Psychological prep

Dates	Months		
	Weeks		
Competitions	Domestic		
	International		
	Location		
Periodization	Training phase		
	Strength		
	Endurance		
	Speed		
	Psychological		
	Nutrition		
	Macrocycles		
	Microcycles	1 2 3 4 5 6 7 8 9 10 11 12 13 14 15 16 17 18 19 20 21 22 23 24 25 26 27 28 29 30 31 32 33 34 35 36 37 38 39 40 41 42 43 44 45 46 47 48 49 50 51 52	
Training factors	Optional exercises		
	Skill acquisition		
	Routines		
	Peaking index		
	Testing dates		
	Medical control dates		
	Camp/Semicamp		

Legend:

%100	1
90	2
80	3
70	4
60	5
50	
40	
30	Peaking
20	
10	

— Volume
----- Intensity
..... Peaking
▮ Phys prep
▮ Tech prep
‖ Tact prep
XXX Psych prep

From T.O. Bompa and G.G. Haff, 2009, *Periodization: Theory and methodology of training* 5th ed. (Champaign, IL: Human Kinetics).

346

Chart of the Annual Plan

Year: Coach:

Dates	Months	
	Weeks	
Competitions	Domestic	
	International	
	Location	
Periodization	Training phase	
	Strength	
	Endurance	
	Speed	
	Psychological	
	Nutrition	
	Macrocycles	
	Microcycles	1 2 3 4 5 6 7 8 9 10 11 12 13 14 15 16 17 18 19 20 21 22 23 24 25 26 27 28 29 30 31 32 33 34 35 36 37 38 39 40 41 42 43 44 45 46 47 48 49 50 51 52
Peaking index		
Testing dates		
Medical control dates		
Camp/Semicamp		

Training factors

| | 1 | 2 | 3 | 4 | 5 |

Peaking

Speed (% of mx.) - - - -

Volume (km/wk) ——

Peaking - - - -

From T.O. Bompa and G.G. Haff, 2009, *Periodization: Theory and methodology of training* 5th ed. (Champaign, IL: Human Kinetics).

347

Chart of the Annual Plan

Year: _____   Coach: _____

		1	2	3	4	5	6	7	8	9	10	11	12	13	14	15	16	17	18	19	20	21	22	23	24	25	26	27	28	29	30	31	32	33	34	35	36	37	38	39	40	41	42	43	44	45	46	47	48	49	50	51	52
Dates	Months																																																					
	Weeks																																																					
Competitions	Domestic																																																					
	International																																																					
	Location																																																					
Periodization	Training phase																																																					
	Strength																																																					
	Endurance																																																					
	Speed																																																					
	Psychological																																																					
	Nutrition																																																					
	Macrocycles																																																					
	Microcycles																																																					
Peaking index																																																						
Testing dates																																																						
Medical control dates																																																						
Camp/Semicamp																																																						

Training factors

Peaking | 1 2 3 4 5

······ Peaking
—— Volume
------ Intensity

Training factors

Peaking | 1 2 3 4 5

······ Peaking
—— Volume
------ Intensity

Training factors

Peaking | 1 2 3 4 5

······ Peaking
—— Volume
------ Intensity

From T.O. Bompa and G.G. Haff, 2009, *Periodization: Theory and methodology of training* 5th ed. (Champaign, IL: Human Kinetics).

Objectives					
Year	20	20	20	20	20
Performance					
Physical preparation					
Technical preparation					
Tactical preparation					
Psychological preparation					
Tests and standards					

Training factors

Volume	%100
Intensity	90
Peaking	80
Phys prep	70
Tech prep	60
Tact prep	50
Psych prep	40
	30
	20
	10

From T.O. Bompa and G.G. Haff, 2009, *Periodization: Theory and methodology of training* 5th ed. (Champaign, IL: Human Kinetics).

Glossary

▼

absolute strength—The amount of force that can be generated regardless of body size.

acceleration—The ability to increase movement velocity in a minimum amount of time.

acidosis—Condition in which an accumulation of H^+ increases muscles acidity.

acyclic combined skills—Cyclic skills followed by an acyclic skill.

acyclic skills—Integral functions performed in one action.

acute fatigue—Short-term fatigue that results from training stress.

adenosine diphosphate (ADP)—A high-energy phosphate compound that can be used to form ATP.

adenosine triphosphate (ATP)—A high-energy phosphate compound that allows for the release of energy when its phosphate bounds are broken.

aerobic intervals—Intervals that are designed to stress the aerobic system and are also referred to as pace-tempo training. Aerobic intervals can be performed in a continuous or intermittent fashion.

aerobic power—See *maximal aerobic capacity.*

agility—Ability to rapidly change direction and accelerate in response to an external cue.

anabolic—An environment in which building of tissue can occur.

anabolism—The building of body tissue or the constructive phase of metabolism.

anaerobic intervals—Form of interval training where very high-intensity bouts are retentively performed for short periods of time with periods of rest interspersed between efforts.

anaerobic threshold—The intensity of exercise at which the body cannot meet its energy demand with aerobic means; the point at which lactate production outweighs buffering capacities.

annual training plan—A long-term training plan that typically lasts for 1 year.

arteriovenous oxygen difference (a-VO₂ difference)—The oxygen difference between the arterial and mixed venous blood. Reflects the amount of oxygen used by the tissue.

asynchronous—Asynchronous motor unit firing occurs as a result of one motor unit deactivating while another activates.

bi-cycle plan—An annual training plan with two major peaks.

bioenergetics—Process by which the body converts foods such as carbohydrates, proteins, and fats into a biologically useable form of energy.

bioenergetic specificity—Training the specific bioenergetic characteristics of a specified sport or activity.

biological age—An indication of age based upon sexual maturation.

biomotor abilities—Abilities whereby the body can perform a range of activities, such as strength, speed, and endurance. They are influenced by training and may be genetically determined.

block—A period of training usually last 4 weeks in duration, sometimes referred to as a mesocycle.

block training—A sequential approach to structuring training in which individual blocks of training which contain a distinct focus are linked together.

bodybuilding—Sport in which muscle size, definition, and symmetry determine the winner.

capillarization—An increase in the capillary networks that bring oxygen and nutrients to the tissues of the body.

carbohydrate—A compound composed of carbon, hydrogen, and oxygen.

cardiac output (Q)—The volume of blood pumped by the heart per minute. Calculated as stroke volume multiplied by heart rate.

chronic fatigue—A long-term manifestation of fatigue from which the athlete cannot easily recovery.

chronological age—The age of the individual.

cluster set—A series of repetitions interspersed with a short rest interval.

complexity—Degree of sophistication and biomechanical difficulty of a skill.

concentrated loading—A short-term period where training loads are increased dramatically.

conjugated sequence—A method of sequencing training to take advantage of training residuals developed with periods of concentrated loading; also called the coupled successive system.

cortisol—A corticosteroid hormone released from the adrenal cortex that stimulates the catabolism of proteins, the sparing of glucose utilization, an increase in gluconeogenesis, and an increase in free fatty acid mobilization.

creatine phosphokinase (CPK)—An enzyme contained in the phosphagen system that adds a phosphate to taken from phosphocreatine to and adenosine diphospate to create ATP.

cross-bridges—Projections around the myosin filament that latch onto the binding site on actin.

cyclic skills—Sporting activities that contain repetitive movements of the same motor skill.

delayed-onset muscle soreness (DOMS)—Muscle soreness or pain that occurs 24 to 48 hr after a heavy bout of exercise.

density of training—The frequency of training within a given time frame.

detraining—Reversal of the adaptations stimulated by training. The effects of detraining can occur very rapidly when work loads are significantly reduced.

detraining syndrome—Syndrome that occurs when training is intentionally or unintentionally stopped and results in several maladaptations including insomnia, anxiety, depression, and alterations to the cardiovascular system. Also known as relaxation syndrome, exercise abstinence, or exercise dependency syndrome.

differentiation—Process of dissecting skill into subunits and determining where errors are.

enzyme—A protein compound that speeds a chemical reaction.

excess postexercise oxygen consumption (EPOC)—The oxygen debt; an oxygen consumption that is elevated above resting after exercise.

fartlek—The Swedish word for "speed play"; a classic method for developing endurance.

fast glycolysis—One of the two ways in which glycolysis proceeds. Fast glycolysis results in the formation of lactic acid from the breakdown of glucose and has a faster rate of energy supply when compared to slow glycolysis.

fatigue—A general sense of tiredness that is often accompanied by a decrease in muscular performance.

fitness-fatigue relationship—The relationship between fitness and fatigue and how they modulate athlete preparedness. This concept is a major factor associated with periodization.

force-velocity curve—A graphic representation of the relationship between force and velocity.

general adaptive syndrome (GAS)—A syndrome conceptualized by Hans Selye that explains the body's response to stressors, including physiological and psychological stress. The GAS is often cited as being a foundational component of periodization theory.

general strength—The strength of the whole muscular system.

glucose—The most common mechanism for transporting carbohydrates in the body; primarily broken down by the glycolytic energy system.

glucose transporter-4 (GLUT4)—Contraction-sensitive glucose transport protein that aids in the uptake of glucose by working skeletal muscle.

glycogen—A storage form of carbohydrate that is found in the skeletal muscle and liver.

glycogenolytic—The breakdown of glycogen.

glycolytic system—The energy system that provides energy via the breakdown of glucose. Generally supplies energy for higher-intensity activities lasting 20 s to 2 min. Also known as glycolysis.

Golgi tendon organ—A sensory receptor that monitors tension and is located in the muscle tendon.

growth hormone—Also known as somatotropin; an anabolic hormone that can enhance cellular amino acid uptake and stimulate protein synthesis.

hemoglobin (Hb)—The iron-containing compound in blood that binds oxygen.

high-intensity exercise endurance (HIEE)—A type of endurance that requires the athlete to sustain or repeat high-intensity or high-power movements with exercise durations lasting 2 min or less.

hypertrophy—An increase in size. For example, muscle can undergo hypertrophy and increase in size.

inflammation—A local cellular response that is marked by leukocytic infiltration, pain, swelling, and often loss of function.

insulin—An anabolic hormone that facilitates the uptake of glucose and can stimulate protein synthesis.

integration—A process of constructing whole skills.

intensity—The qualitative element of training such as speed, maximum strength, and power. In strength training, intensity is often expressed in load related to the 1RM.

interexercise recovery—The form of recovery that occurs during the exercise bout and relates to the bioenergetics of the activity being performed.

interval training—The repeated performance of short to long bouts of exercise usually performed at or above the lactate threshold interspersed with periods of rest or low-intensity exercise.

involution—Also known as a decay or detraining.

lactate—A salt formed from lactic acid. Lactate is not believed to be associated with fatigue but can be used to create energy.

lactate dehydrogenase—An enzyme contained in the glycolytic energy system that converts pyruvate to lactate.

lactate threshold (LT)—The point at which lactate formation begins to abruptly increase above baseline.

lactic acid—The end product of the fast glycolytic system that is often associated with fatigue because it can inhibit calcium binding to troponin or interfere with cross-bridge formation.

long slow distance (LSD)—Endurance training that can be classified as conversational exercise, where the athlete can carry on a conversation without respiratory stress.

long-term recovery—A form of recovery that occurs in response to the training plan.

low-intensity exercise endurance (LIEE)—A form of endurance that relates to the ability to continually perform work for a long duration of time.

macrocycle—A medium-term training cycle that lasts between 2 and 8 weeks.

maximal aerobic capacity—The maximal capacity for oxygen consumption. Also known as the $\dot{V}O_2max$, maximal oxygen uptake, or maximal aerobic power.

maximum lactate steady state—A balance between lactate production and lactate buffering.

maximum strength—The highest force that the neuromuscular system can generate during a maximal voluntary contraction.

mesocycle—In the Russian literature, a medium-term training cycle that lasts between 2 and 8 weeks.

metabolism—The sum of the anabolic and catabolic reactions occurring in the body.

Metric ton—A *tonne*, which is equivalent to 1,000 kg.

microcycle—A short training cycle that lasts 3 to 7 days.

mitochondria—Specialized cell organelles in which oxidative production of ATP occurs.

monocycle—An annual training plan with one major peak.

monotonous program overtraining—A form of overtraining that occurs in response to a lack of training variation and results in a reduction or stagnation of performance gains.

motor unit—The motor nerve and all of the muscle fibers it innervates.

muscular endurance—The ability of the neuromuscular system to produce force in a repetitive manner.

myoglobin—A compound found in muscle that carries oxygen from the cell membrane to the mitochondria.

myokinase (MK)—An enzyme of the phosphagen system that takes a phosphate from and adenosine diphosphate and adds the phosphate and adenosine diphosphate to make adenosine triphosphate.

myosin heavy chain (MHC)—Consists primarily of the head of the cross-bridge and typically associated with the fiber type of the muscle.

nonprogressive taper—A taper that is marked by standardized reductions in training load. Also known as a step taper.

nonsteroidal anti-inflammatory drugs (NSAIDs)—A class of drugs that are often prescribed to reduce inflammatory responses.

onset of blood lactate (OBLA)—Point at which the blood lactate concentration reaches 4 mmol/L.

overreaching—A short-term period during which the athlete intentionally overtrains.

overtraining—A long-term decrement in performance that occurs in response to accumulation of training and non-training stressors.

oxidative system—The primary source of ATP at rest and during low-intensity exercise. Occurs in the mitochondria and requires oxygen to make energy. Also known as the aerobic system.

oxygen deficit—The anaerobic contribution to the total energy cost of an exercise.

periodization—The logical and systematic sequencing of training factors in an integrative fashion in order to optimize specific training outcomes at pre-determined time points.

phosphagen system (ATP-PC)—An anaerobic energy system that primarily provides energy for short-term, high-intensity activities and contains three major enzymatic reactions including the ATPase, creatine kinase, and myokinase reactions.

phosphocreatine (PCr)—A component of the ATP-PC system that provides energy for muscle actions by maintaining ATP stores.

phosphofructokinase (PFK)—The rate-limiting enzyme of the glycolytic system.

phosphorylase (PHOS)—The enzyme responsible for stimulating muscle glycogen breakdown.

postexercise recovery—A form of recovery that occurs after the cessation of exercise.

power—A unit of work expressed per unit of time (i.e., power = work/time), often considered a factor of intensity. May also be calculated by multiplying force × displacement.

power clean—A weightlifting movement in which the barbell is lifted from the ground to the shoulders in one movement.

power snatch—A weightlifting movement in which the barbell is lifted from the ground to a position arms length over head in one movement.

preparedness—A state that if elevated will lead to performance increases; if suppressed, preparedness will correspond to decreases in performance.

progressive overload—A progressive increase in the training load (i.e., intensity, volume) above a normal magnitude.

progressive taper—A systematic reduction in training load.

proteins—Combinations of linked amino acids all of which contain nitrogen.

pulmonary system—A series of structures that work together to ventilate the body.

quadrennial plan—A 4 year training plan, typically used with high school, collegiate and Olympic athletes.

rate coding—The firing rate of a motor unit.

rate of force development (RFD)—The rate at which force is developed; calculated by dividing the change in force by the change in time.

recovery—Process of returning to preexercise state.

relative strength—The ratio between the athlete's maximal strength and his body weight or lean body mass.

repetitions—The number of work intervals within a set.

repetition maximum (RM)—The heaviest weight that can be lifted for a predetermined number of repetitions. A 1RM is the heaviest weight that can be lifted 1 time, whereas a 10RM is the heaviest weight that can be lifted 10 times.

sarcoplasmic reticulum—An extensive complex of latticelike longitudinal network of tubules and structures that store Ca^{2+}.

sequenced training—See block training.

set—The total number of repetitions an athlete performs before taking a rest.

short ton—Unit that equals 1,102.3 kg.

size principle—Principle suggesting that the size of the motor unit dictates its activation.

slow glycolysis—One of the two ways in which glycolysis proceeds. Slow glycolysis results in the formation of pyruvate from the breakdown of glucose and proceeds with a rate slower than fast glycolysis.

specific strength—Strength that is related to the movement patterns of a specific sport.

speed—The ability to cover a distance in the fastest time possible.

speed endurance—The ability to maintain speed or repetitively express high speeds of movements.

speed strength—The ability to develop force rapidly and at high velocities

step taper—See *nonprogressive taper.*

strength—The maximal force or torque a muscle or muscle group can generate.

stretch reflex—The contraction of a muscle in response to a stretch; also known as the myototic reflex.

stretch shortening cycle (SSC)—A combination of eccentric and concentric muscle actions.

stroke volume (SV)—The amount of blood ejected from the left ventricle during contraction.

sympathetic nervous system—The part of the automatic nervous system that effects, among other things, the cardiovascular system. Releases norepinephrine from its post ganglionic nerve endings.

synchronization—The simultaneous activation of numerous motor units.

taper—An unloading phase of training prior to a major competition that generally lasts between 8 and 14 days.

testosterone—The predominant male sex hormone, which is produced in the testes in men and the adrenal cortex and ovaries in women. Testosterone is often used as an index of anabolism or the anabolic status of the body.

testosterone/cortisol ratio (T:C ratio)—An indicator of the anabolic to catabolic balance.

Tmax—The duration at which maximal velocity or power can be maintained during an endurance bout.

training age—The number of years and individual has been training.

training effect—A physiological, performance, or psychological response to a training program.

tri-cycle plan—An annual training plan that contains three major peaks.

tonne—A metric ton, which is equivalent to 1,000 kg.

torque—The rotational force a muscle or muscle group can generate.

total training demand—A summation of all the training factors contained in the plan.

training—A structured exercise program that is designed to develop specific performance characteristics related to sports performance.

training frequency—The number of times per week training workouts occur.

training intensity—Intensity determined by dividing the total volume load by the total number of repetitions.

training log—A document used to record training information.

Type I muscle fiber—Fibers that have a low force-generating capacity; also known as slow-twitch fibers. These fibers tend to be smaller, have higher concentrations of oxidative enzymes, and are more fatigue resistant than Type II fibers.

Type II muscle fiber—Fibers that have a high force-generating capacity; also known as fast-twitch fibers. These fibers tend to be larger, have higher concentrations of anaerobic enzymes, and are more fatigue sensitive than Type I fibers.

velocity—The speed of movement of the body or an object.

volume—A quantitative element of training that can be measured as time or duration of training, the distance covered, the volume load of resistance training, or the number of repetitions performed.

volume load—A method for quantifying volume in resistance training; calculated by multiplying the number of repetitions performed by the number of sets and the resistance in kilograms used.

work—Calculated by multiplying force by displacement.

References

Chapter 1

1. ABERNETHY, P.J., J. JURIMAE, P.A. LOGAN, A.W. TAYLOR, and R.E. THAYER. Acute and chronic response of skeletal muscle to resistance exercise. *Sports Med* 17:22-38, 1994.

2. ABERNETHY, P.J., R. THAYER, and A.W. TAYLOR. Acute and chronic responses of skeletal muscle to endurance and sprint exercise: a review. *Sports Med* 10:365-389, 1990.

3. AHTIAINEN, J.P., A. PAKARINEN, W.J. KRAEMER, and K. HÄKKINEN. Acute hormonal and neuromuscular responses and recovery to forced vs maximum repetitions multiple resistance exercises. *Int J Sports Med* 24:410-418, 2003.

4. Alpine Canada Alpin. *Physiological Profile of Skiing Events.* Alpine Canada News Letter 32, Calgary, Alberta, Canada, 1990.

5. BAAR, K. Training for endurance and strength: lessons from cell signaling. *Med Sci Sports Exerc* 38:1939-1944, 2006.

6. BALOG, E.M., B.R. FRUEN, P.K. KANE, and C.F. LOUIS. Mechanisms of P(i) regulation of the skeletal muscle SR Ca(2+) release channel. *Am J Physiol Cell Physiol* 278:C601-611, 2000.

7. BANGSBO, J. The physiology of soccer—with special reference to intense intermittent exercise. *Acta Physiol Scand Suppl* 619:1-155, 1994.

8. BISHOP, D., and M. SPENCER. Determinants of repeated-sprint ability in well-trained team-sport athletes and endurance-trained athletes. *J Sports Med Phys Fitness* 44:1-7, 2004.

9. BONDARCHUK, A.P. Constructing a Training System. *Track Tech.* 102:254-269, 1988.

10. BROOKS, G.A., T.D. FAHEY, T.P. WHITE, and K.M. BALDWIN. *Exercise Physiology: Human Bioenergetics and Its Application.* 3rd ed. Mountain View, CA: Mayfield, 2000.

11. BURGOMASTER, K.A., G.J. HEIGENHAUSER, and M.J. GIBALA. Effect of short-term sprint interval training on human skeletal muscle carbohydrate metabolism during exercise and time-trial performance. *J Appl Physiol* 100:2041-2047, 2006.

12. BURKE, L.M. Nutrition for post-exercise recovery. *Aus J Sci Med Sport* 29:3-10, 1996.

13. BURKE, L., and V. DEAKIN. *Clincial Sports Nutrition.* Roseville, Australia: McGraw-Hill Australia, 2000.

14. BURLESON, M.A., Jr., H.S. O'BRYANT, M.H. STONE, M.A. COLLINS, and T. TRIPLETT-MCBRIDE. Effect of weight training exercise and treadmill exercise on post-exercise oxygen consumption. *Med Sci Sports Exerc* 30:518-522, 1998.

15. CAREY, D.G., M.M. DRAKE, G.J. PLIEGO, and R.L. RAYMOND. Do hockey players need aerobic fitness? Relation between VO2max and fatigue during high-intensity intermittent ice skating. *J Strength Cond Res* 21:963-966, 2007.

16. CERRETELLI, P., G. AMBROSOLI, and M. FUMAGALLI. Anaerobic recovery in man. *Eur J Appl Physiol Occup Physiol* 34:141-148, 1975.

17. CHESLEY, A., J.D. MACDOUGALL, M.A. TARNOPOLSKY, S.A. ATKINSON, and K. SMITH. Changes in human muscle protein synthesis after resistance exercise. *J Appl Physiol* 73:1383-1388, 1992.

18. CLOSE, G.L., T. ASHTON, A. MCARDLE, and D.P. MACLAREN. The emerging role of free radicals in delayed onset muscle soreness and contraction-induced muscle injury. *Comp Biochem Physiol* 142:257-266, 2005.

19. COFFEY, V.G., and J.A. HAWLEY. The molecular bases of training adaptation. *Sports Med* 37:737-763, 2007.

20. CONLEY, M. Bioenergetics of exercise training. In: *Essentials of Strength Training and Conditioning.* T.R. Baechle and R.W. Earle, eds. Champaign, IL: Human Kinetics, 2000, pp. 73-90.

21. COOKE, S.R., S.R. PETERSEN, and H.A. QUINNEY. The influence of maximal aerobic power on recovery of skeletal muscle following anaerobic exercise. *Eur J Appl Physiol Occup Physiol* 75:512-519, 1997.

22. COOPER, H.K. *The New Aerobics.* New York, NY: M. Evans and Company, 1970.

23. COSTILL, D.L., P.D. GOLLNICK, E.D. JANSSON, B. SALTIN, and E.M. STEIN. Glycogen depletion pattern in human muscle fibres during distance running. *Acta Physiol Scand* 89:374-383, 1973.

24. COSTILL, D.L., and J.M. MILLER. Nutrition for endurance sport: carbohydrate and fluid balance. *Int J Sports Med* 1:2-14, 1980.

25. COSTILL, D.L., D.D. PASCOE, W.J. FINK, R.A. ROBERGS, S.I. BARR, and D. PEARSON. Impaired muscle glycogen resynthesis after eccentric exercise. *J Appl Physiol* 69:46-50, 1990.

26. COSTILL, D.L., W.M. SHERMAN, W.J. FINK, C. MARESH, M. WITTEN, and J.M. MILLER. The role of dietary carbohydrates in muscle glycogen resynthesis after strenuous running. *Am J Clin Nutr* 34:1831-1836, 1981.

27. COYLE, E.F. Physical activity as a metabolic stressor. *Am J Clin Nutr* 72:512S-520S, 2000.

28. COYLE, E.F. Substrate utilization during exercise in active people. *Am J Clin Nutr* 61:968S-979S, 1995.

29. COYLE, E.F. Timing and method of increased carbohydrate intake to cope with heavy training, competition and recovery. *J Sports Sci* 9(Spec No):29-51, discussion 51-22, 1991.

30. DAHLSTEDT, A.J., A. KATZ, B. WIERINGA, and H. WESTERBLAD. Is creatine kinase responsible for fatigue? Studies of isolated skeletal muscle deficient in creatine kinase. *FASEB J* 14:982-990, 2000.

31. DAL MONTE, A. *The functional values of sport*. Firente: Sansoni, 1983.

32. DAVIS, J.M. Central and peripheral factors in fatigue. *J Sports Sci* 13(Spec No):S49-S53, 1995.

33. DAVIS, J.M., Z. ZHAO, H.S. STOCK, K.A. MEHL, J. BUGGY, and G.A. HAND. Central nervous system effects of caffeine and adenosine on fatigue. *Am J Physiol Regul Integr Comp Physiol* 284:R399-R404, 2003.

34. DI PRAMPERO, P.E., L. PEETERS, and R. MARGARIA. Alactic O 2 debt and lactic acid production after exhausting exercise in man. *J Appl Physiol* 34:628-632, 1973.

35. DUMKE, C.L., D.W. BROCK, B.H. HELMS, and G.G. HAFF. Heart rate at lactate threshold and cycling time trials. *J Strength Cond Res* 20:601-607, 2006.

36. DUNLAVY, J.K., W.A. SANDS, J.R. MCNEAL, M.H. STONE, S.A. SMITH, M. JEMNI, and G.G. HAFF. Strength performance assessment in a simulated men's gymnastics still rings cross. *J. Sports. Sci. Medicine* 6:93-97, 2007.

37. EDGE, J., D. BISHOP, C. GOODMAN, and B. DAWSON. Effects of high- and moderate-intensity training on metabolism and repeated sprints. *Med Sci Sports Exerc* 37:1975-1982, 2005.

38. ENDEMANN, F. Teaching Throwing Events. In: *The Throws: Contemporary Theory, Technique, and Training*. J. Jarver, ed. Mountain View, CA: Tafnews Press, 2000. pp. 11-14.

39. ESFARJANI, F., and P.B. LAURSEN. Manipulating high-intensity interval training: effects on VO_{2max}, the lactate threshold and 3000 m running performance in moderately trained males. *J Sci Med Sport* 10:27-35, 2007.

40. FEBBRAIO, M.A., and J. DANCEY. Skeletal muscle energy metabolism during prolonged, fatiguing exercise. *J Appl Physiol* 87:2341-2347, 1999.

41. FRY, A.C. The role of training intensity in resistance exercise overtraining and overreaching. In: *Overtraining in Sport*. R.B. Kreider, A.C. Fry, and M.L. O'Toole, eds. Champaign, IL: Human Kinetics, 1998, pp. 107-127.

42. FRY, A.C., and W.J. KRAEMER. Resistance exercise overtraining and overreaching: neuroendocrine responses. *Sports Med* 23:106-129, 1997.

43. FRY, A.C., W.J. KRAEMER, M.H. STONE, B.J. WARREN, S.J. FLECK, J.T. KEARNEY, and S.E. GORDON. Endocrine responses to overreaching before and after 1 year of weightlifting. *Can J Appl Physiol* 19:400-410, 1994.

44. FRY, A.C., W.J. KRAEMER, F. VAN BORSELEN, J.M. LYNCH, J.L. MARSIT, E.P. ROY, N.T. TRIPLETT, and H.G. KNUTTGEN. Performance decrements with high-intensity resistance exercise overtraining. *Med Sci Sports Exerc* 26:1165-1173, 1994.

45. FRY, A.C., B.K. SCHILLING, L.W. WEISS, and L.Z. CHIU. Beta2-Adrenergic receptor downregulation and performance decrements during high-intensity resistance exercise overtraining. *J Appl Physiol* 101:1664-1672, 2006.

46. GALLIVEN, E.A., A. SINGH, D. MICHELSON, S. BINA, P.W. GOLD, and P.A. DEUSTER. Hormonal and metabolic responses to exercise across time of day and menstrual cycle phase. *J Appl Physiol* 83:1822-1831, 1997.

47. GARCIA-LOPEZ, D., J.A. DE PAZ, R. JIMENEZ-JIMENEZ, G. BRESCIANI, F. DE SOUZA-TEIXEIRA, J.A. HERRERO, I. ALVEAR-ORDENES, and J. GONZALEZ-GALLEGO. Early explosive force reduction associated with exercise-induced muscle damage. *J Physiol Biochem* 62:163-169, 2006.

48. GARRANDES, F., S.S. COLSON, M. PENSINI, and P. LEGROS. Time course of mechanical and neuromuscular characteristics of cyclists and triathletes during a fatiguing exercise. *Int J Sports Med* 28:148-156, 2007.

49. GARRANDES, F., S.S. COLSON, M. PENSINI, O. SEYNNES, and P. LEGROS. Neuromuscular fatigue profile in endurance-trained and power-trained athletes. *Med Sci Sports Exerc* 39:149-158, 2007.

50. GILLAM, G.M. Effects of frequency of weight training on muscle strength enhancement. *J Sports Med* 21:432-436, 1981.

51. GOLLNICK, P.D., R.B. ARMSTRONG, B. SALTIN, C.W.T. SAUBERT, W.L. SEMBROWICH, and R.E. SHEPHERD. Effect of training on enzyme activity and fiber composition of human skeletal muscle. *J Appl Physiol* 34:107-111, 1973.

52. GOTO, K., M. HIGASHIYAMA, N. ISHII, and K. TAKAMATSU. Prior endurance exercise attenuates growth hormone response to subsequent resistance exercise. *Eur J Appl Physiol* 94:333-338, 2005.

53. GRANTIN, K. Contributions regarding the systematization of physical exercises. *Theory and Practice of Physical Culture* 9:27-37, 1940.

54. GUEZENNEC, Y., L. LEGER, F. LHOSTE, M. AYMONOD, and P.C. PESQUIES. Hormone and metabolite response to weight-lifting training sessions. *Int J Sports Med* 7:100-105, 1986.

55. HAFF, G.G., A.J. KOCH, J.A. POTTEIGER, K.E. KUPHAL, L.M. MAGEE, S.B. GREEN, and J.J. JAKICIC. Carbohydrate supplementation attenuates muscle glycogen loss during acute bouts of resistance exercise. *Int J Sport Nutr Exerc Metab* 10:326-339, 2000.

56. HAFF, G.G., M.J. LEHMKUHL, L.B. MCCOY, and M.H. STONE. Carbohydrate supplementation and resistance training. *J Strength Cond Res* 17:187-196, 2003.

57. HAFF, G.G., and A. WHITLEY. Low-carbohydrate diets and high-intensity anaerobic exercise. *Strength Cond* 24:42-53, 2002.

58. HALSON, S.L., M.W. BRIDGE, R. MEEUSEN, B. BUSSCHAERT, M. GLEESON, D.A. JONES, and A.E. JEUKENDRUP. Time course of performance changes and fatigue markers during intensified training in trained cyclists. *J Appl Physiol* 93:947-956, 2002.

59. HARE, D. *Principles of sports training*. Berlin, Germany: Democratic Republic: Sportverlag, 1982.

60. HARRIS, R.C., R.H. EDWARDS, E. HULTMAN, L.O. NORDESJO, B. NYLIND, and K. SAHLIN. The time course of phosphorylcreatine resynthesis during recovery of the quadriceps muscle in man. *Pflugers Arch* 367:137-142, 1976.

61. HEIDT, R.S., JR., L.M. SWEETERMAN, R.L. CARLONAS, J.A. TRAUB, and F.X. TEKULVE. Avoidance of soccer injuries with preseason conditioning. *Am J Sports Med* 28:659-662, 2000.

62. HEPBURN, D., and R.J. MAUGHAN. Glycogen availability as a limiting factor in performance of isometric exercise. *J Physiol* 342:52P-53P, 1982.

63. HERMANSEN, L., and I. STENSVOLD. Production and removal of lactate during exercise in man. *Acta Physiol Scand* 86:191-201, 1972.

64. HIRVONEN, J., S. REHUNEN, H. RUSKO, and M. HARKONEN. Breakdown of high-energy phosphate compounds and lactate accumulation during short supramaximal exercise. *Eur J Appl Physiol* 56:253-259, 1987.

65. HULTMAN, E., J. BERGSTROM, and N.M. ANDERSON. Breakdown and resynthesis of phosphorylcreatine and adenosine triphosphate in connection with muscular work in man. *Scand J Clin Lab Invest* 19:56-66, 1967.

66. HULTMAN, E., and H. SJØHOLM. Biochemical causes of fatigue. In: *Human Muscle Power*. N.L. Jones, ed. Champaign, IL: Human Kinetics, 1986, pp. 343-363.

67. IMPELLIZZERI, F., A. SASSI, M. RODRIGUEZ-ALONSO, P. MOGNONI, and S. MARCORA. Exercise intensity during off-road cycling competitions. *Med Sci Sports Exerc* 34:1808-1813, 2002.

68. IVY, J.L., A.L. KATZ, C.L. CUTLER, W.M. SHERMAN, and E.F. COYLE. Muscle glycogen synthesis after exercise: effect of time of carbohydrate ingestion. *J Appl Physiol* 64:1480-1485, 1988.

69. IZQUIERDO, M., J. IBANEZ, J.J. GONZALEZ-BADILLO, K. HÄKKINEN, N.A. RATAMESS, W.J. KRAEMER, D.N. FRENCH, J. ESLAVA, A. ALTADILL, X. ASIAIN, and E.M. GOROSTIAGA. Differential effects of strength training leading to failure versus not to failure on hormonal responses, strength, and muscle power gains. *J Appl Physiol* 100:1647-1656, 2006.

70. JACOBS, I. Lactate, muscle glycogen and exercise performance in man. *Acta Physiol Scand Suppl* 495:1-35, 1981.

71. JAMURTAS, A.Z., Y. KOUTEDAKIS, V. PASCHALIS, T. TOFAS, C. YFANTI, A. TSIOKANOS, G. KOUKOULIS, D. KOURETAS, and D. LOUPOS. The effects of a single bout of exercise on resting energy expenditure and respiratory exchange ratio. *Eur J Appl Physiol* 92:393-398, 2004.

72. KARLSSON, J. Lactate in working muscles after prolonged exercise. *Acta Physiol Scand* 82:123-130, 1971.

73. KARLSSON, J., L.O. NORDESJÖ, L. JORFELDT, and B. SALTIN. Muscle lactate, ATP, and CP levels during exercise after physical training in man. *J Appl Physiol* 33:199-203, 1972.

74. KARLSSON, J., and B. OLLANDER. Muscle metabolites with exhaustive static exercise of different duration. *Acta Physiol Scand* 86:309-314, 1972.

75. KJAER, M., B. KIENS, M. HARGREAVES, and E.A. RICHTER. Influence of active muscle mass on glucose homeostasis during exercise in humans. *J Appl Physiol* 71:552-557, 1991.

76. KRAEMER, W.J., B.J. NOBLE, M.J. CLARK, and B.W. CULVER. Physiologic responses to heavy-resistance exercise with very short rest periods. *Int J Sports Med* 8:247-252, 1987.

77. LAFORGIA, J., R.T. WITHERS, and C.J. GORE. Effects of exercise intensity and duration on the excess post-exercise oxygen consumption. *J Sports Sci* 24:1247-1264, 2006.

78. LAURSEN, P.B., and D.G. JENKINS. The scientific basis for high-intensity interval training: optimising training programmes and maximising performance in highly trained endurance athletes. *Sports Med* 32:53-73, 2002.

79. LAURSEN, P.B., C.M. SHING, J.M. PEAKE, J.S. COOMBES, and D.G. JENKINS. Interval training program optimization in highly trained endurance cyclists. *Med Sci Sports Exerc* 34:1801-1807, 2002.

80. LEBON, V., S. DUFOUR, K.F. PETERSEN, J. REN, B.M. JUCKER, L.A. SLEZAK, G.W. CLINE, D.L. ROTHMAN, and G.I. SHULMAN. Effect of triiodothyronine on mitochondrial energy coupling in human skeletal muscle. *J Clin Invest* 108:733-737, 2001.

81. MACDOUGALL, J.D., M.J. GIBALA, M.A. TARNOPOLSKY, J.R. MACDONALD, S.A. INTERISANO, and K.E. YARASHESKI. The time course for elevated muscle protein synthesis following heavy resistance exercise. *Can J Appl Physiol* 20:480-486, 1995.

82. MACDOUGALL, J.D., A.L. HICKS, J.R. MACDONALD, R.S. MCKELVIE, H.J. GREEN, and K.M. SMITH. Muscle performance and enzymatic adaptations to sprint interval training. *J Appl Physiol* 84:2138-2142, 1998.

83. MACDOUGALL, J.D., S. RAY, D.G. SALE, N. MCCARTNEY, P. LEE, and S. GARNER. Muscle substrate utilization and lactate production during weightlifting. *Can J Appl Physiol* 24:209-215, 1999.

84. MACINTOSH, B.R., and D.E. RASSIER. What is fatigue? *Can J Appl Physiol* 27:42-55, 2002.

85. MACINTYRE, D.L., S. SORICHTER, J. MAIR, A. BERG, and D.C. MCKENZIE. Markers of inflammation and myofibrillar proteins following eccentric exercise in humans. *Eur J Appl Physiol* 84:180-186, 2001.

86. MATHEWS, D., and E. FOX. *The Physiological Basis of Physical Education and Athletics.* Philadelphia: Saunders, 1976.

87. MAUGHAN, R., and M. GLEESON. *The Biochemical Basis of Sports Performance.* New York: Oxford University Press, 2004.

88. MCARDLE, W.D., F.I. KATCH, and V.L. KATCH. *Exercise Physiology: Energy, Nutrition, and Human Performance.* 6th ed. Baltimore: Lippincott, Williams & Wilkins, 2007.

89. MCCANN, D.J., P.A. MOLE, and J.R. CATON. Phosphocreatine kinetics in humans during exercise and recovery. *Med Sci Sports Exerc* 27:378-389, 1995.

90. MCMILLAN, J.L., M.H. STONE, J. SARTIN, R. KEITH, D. MARPLE, C. BROWN, and R.D. LEWIS. 20-hour physiological responses to a single weight-training session. *J Strength Cond Res* 7:9-21, 1993.

91. MELBY, C., C. SCHOLL, G. EDWARDS, and R. BULLOUGH. Effect of acute resistance exercise on postexercise energy expenditure and resting metabolic rate. *J Appl Physiol* 75:1847-1853, 1993.

92. MICHAUT, A., M. POUSSON, G. MILLET, J. BELLEVILLE, and J. VAN HOECKE. Maximal voluntary eccentric, isometric and concentric torque recovery following a concentric isokinetic exercise. *Int J Sports Med* 24:51-56, 2003.

93. NICOL, C., J. AVELA, and P.V. KOMI. The stretch-shortening cycle: a model to study naturally occurring neuromuscular fatigue. *Sports Med* 36:977-999, 2006.

94. NIEMAN, D.C., and B.K. PEDERSEN. Exercise and immune function: recent developments. *Sports Med* 27:73-80, 1999.

95. PADILLA, S., I. MUJIKA, F. ANGULO, and J.J. GOIRIENA. Scientific approach to the 1-h cycling world record: a case study. *J Appl Physiol* 89:1522-1527, 2000.

96. PAROLIN, M.L., A. CHESLEY, M.P. MATSOS, L.L. SPRIET, N.L. JONES, and G.J. HEIGENHAUSER. Regulation of skeletal muscle glycogen phosphorylase and PDH during maximal intermittent exercise. *Am J Physiol* 277:E890-E900, 1999.

97. PETERSON, M.D., M.R. RHEA, and B.A. ALVAR. Applications of the dose-response for muscular strength development: a review of meta-analytic efficacy and reliability for designing training prescription. *J Strength Cond Res* 19:950-958, 2005.

98. PINCIVERO, D.M., and T.O. BOMPA. A physiological review of American football. *Sports Med* 23:247-260, 1997.

99. PLISK, S.S. Anaerobic metabolic conditioning: a brief review of theory, strategy and practical application. *J Appl Sport Sci Res* 5:22-34, 1991.

100. PLISK, S.S., and V. GAMBETTA. Tactical metabolic training: part 1. *Strength Cond* 19:44-53, 1997.

101. POWERS, S.K., and E.T. HOWLEY. *Exercise Physiology: Theory and Application to Fitness and Performance.* 5th ed. New York: McGraw-Hill, 2004.

102. PRATLEY, R., B. NICKLAS, M. RUBIN, J. MILLER, A. SMITH, M. SMITH, B. HURLEY, and A. GOLDBERG. Strength training increases resting metabolic rate and norepinephrine levels in healthy 50- to 65-yr-old men. *J Appl Physiol* 76:133-137, 1994.

103. RAHNAMA, N., T. REILLY, and A. LEES. Injury risk associated with playing actions during competitive soccer. *Br J Sports Med* 36:354-359, 2002.

104. SELYE, H. *The Stress of Life.* New York: McGraw-Hill, 1956.

105. SHERMAN, W.M. Carbohydrates, muscle glycogen, and muscle glycogen supercompensation. In: *Ergogenic Aids in Sport.* M.H. Williams, ed. Champaign IL: Human Kinetics, 1983, pp. 3-26.

106. SHERMAN, W.M., and G.S. WIMER. Insufficient dietary carbohydrate during training: does it impair athletic performance? *Int J Sport Nutr* 1:28-44, 1991.

107. SIFF, M.C., and Y.U. VERKHOSHANSKY. *Supertraining.* Denver, CO: Supertraining International, 1999.

108. STEPTO, N.K., D.T. MARTIN, K.E. FALLON, and J.A. HAWLEY. Metabolic demands of intense aerobic interval training in competitive cyclists. *Med Sci Sports Exerc* 33:303-310, 2001.

109. STONE, M.H., M.E. STONE, and W.A. SANDS. *Principles and Practice of Resistance Training.* Champaign, IL: Human Kinetics, 2007.

110. STONE, M.H., W.A. SANDS, and M.E. STONE. The downfall of sports science in the United States. *Strength and Cond J* 26:72-75, 2004.

111. SUH, S.H., I.Y. PAIK, and K. JACOBS. Regulation of blood glucose homeostasis during prolonged exercise. *Mol Cells* 23:272-279, 2007.

112. TESCH, P. Muscle fatigue in man: with special reference to lactate accumulation during short term intense exercise. *Acta Physiol Scand Suppl* 480:1-40, 1980.

113. TESCH, P.A., L.L. PLOUTZ-SNYDER, L. YSTRÖM, M. CASTRO, and G. DUDLEY. Skeletal muscle glycogen loss evoked by resistance exercise. *J Strength Cond Res* 12:67-73, 1998.

114. TOMLIN, D.L., and H.A. WENGER. The relationship between aerobic fitness and recovery from high intensity intermittent exercise. *Sports Med* 31:1-11, 2001.

115. WADLEY, G., and P. LE ROSSIGNOL. The relationship between repeated sprint ability and the aerobic and

anaerobic energy systems. *J Sci Med Sport* 1:100-110, 1998.

116. WESTERBLAD, H., D.G. ALLEN, and J. LANNERGREN. Muscle fatigue: lactic acid or inorganic phosphate the major cause? *News Physiol Sci* 17:17-21, 2002.

117. YASPELKIS, B.B.D., J.G. PATTERSON, P.A. ANDERLA, Z. DING, and J.L. IVY. Carbohydrate supplementation spares muscle glycogen during variable-intensity exercise. *J Appl Physiol* 75:1477-1485, 1993.

118. ZAINUDDIN, Z., P. SACCO, M. NEWTON, and K. NOSAKA. Light concentric exercise has a temporarily analgesic effect on delayed-onset muscle soreness, but no effect on recovery from eccentric exercise. *Appl Physiol Nutr Metab* 31:126-134, 2006.

119. ZATSIORSKY, V.M., and W.J. KRAEMER. *Science and Practice of Strength Training.* 2nd ed. Champaign, IL: Human Kinetics, 2006.

Chapter 2

1. ABERNETHY, P.J., J. JURIMAE, P.A. LOGAN, A.W. TAYLOR, and R.E. THAYER. Acute and chronic response of skeletal muscle to resistance exercise. *Sports Med* 17:22-38, 1994.

2. ABERNETHY, P.J., R. THAYER, and A.W. TAYLOR. Acute and chronic responses of skeletal muscle to endurance and sprint exercise: a review. *Sports Med* 10:365-389, 1990.

3. ARMSTRONG, N., B.J. KIRBY, A.M. MCMANUS, and J.R. WELSMAN. Aerobic fitness of prepubescent children. *Ann Hum Biol* 22:427-441, 1995.

4. ATHERTON, P.J., J. BABRAJ, K. SMITH, J. SINGH, M.J. RENNIE, and H. WACKERHAGE. Selective activation of AMPK-PGC-1alpha or PKB-TSC2-mTOR signaling can explain specific adaptive responses to endurance or resistance training-like electrical muscle stimulation. *FASEB J* 19:786-788, 2005.

5. AVALOS, M., P. HELLARD, and J.C. CHATARD. Modeling the training-performance relationship using a mixed model in elite swimmers. *Med Sci Sports Exerc* 35:838-846, 2003.

6. BAAR, K. Training for endurance and strength: lessons from cell signaling. *Med Sci Sports Exerc* 38:1939-1944, 2006.

7. BAAR, K., G. NADER, and S. BODINE. Resistance exercise, muscle loading/unloading and the control of muscle mass. *Essays Biochem* 42:61-74, 2006.

8. BAKER, D. Cycle-length variants in periodized strength/power training. *Strength Cond* 29:10-17, 2007.

9. BALYI, I., and A. HAMILTON. Long-term athlete development: trainability in childhood and adolescence. *Olympic Coach* 16:4-9, 1993.

10. BANISTER, E.W., T.W. CALVERT, M.V. SAVAGE, and A. BACK. A system model of training for athletic performance. *Aus J Sports Med* 7:170-176, 1975.

11. BILLAT, L.V., J.P. KORALSZTEIN, and R.H. MORTON. Time in human endurance models: from empirical models to physiological models. *Sports Med* 27:359-379, 1999.

12. BREWER, C. Athlete development: principles into practice. In: *SPEC: Coaches and Sports Sciences Symposium.* Johnson City, TN: East Tennessee State University, 2007, pp. 1-44.

13. BRUIN, G., H. KUIPERS, H.A. KEIZER, and G.J. VANDER VUSSE. Adaptation and overtraining in horses subjected to increasing training loads. *J Appl Physiol* 76:1908-1913, 1994.

14. BUSHMAN, B., G. MASTERSON, and J. NELSEN. Anaerobic power performance and the menstrual cycle: eumenorrheic and oral contraceptive users. *J Sports Med Phys Fitness* 46:132-137, 2006.

15. CAINE, D.J., and J. BROEKHOFF. Maturity assessment: available preventive measure against physical and psychological insult to the young athlete? *Phys Sportsmed.* 15:70, 1987.

16. CALVERT, T.W., E.W. BANISTER, and M.V. SAVAGE. A systems model of the effects of training on physical performance. *SMS Systems, Man, and Cybernetics* 2:94-102, 1976.

17. CAO, W. Training differences between males and females. In: *Proceedings of the Weightlifting Symposium: Ancient Olympia, Greece,* A. Lukácsfalvi and F. Takács, eds. International Weightlifting Federation: Budapest, Hungary. 1993, pp. 97-101.

18. CARLSON, R. The socialization of elite tennis players in Sweden: an analysis of the players' background and development. *Sociol Sport J* 5:241-256, 1988.

19. CHEUVRONT, S.N., R. CARTER, K.C. DERUISSEAU, and R.J. MOFFATT. Running performance differences between men and women: an update. *Sports Med* 35:1017-1024, 2005.

20. COAST, J.R., J.S. BLEVINS, and B.A. WILSON. Do gender differences in running performance disappear with distance? *Can J Appl Physiol* 29:139-145, 2004.

21. COFFEY, V.G., and J.A. HAWLEY. The molecular bases of training adaptation. *Sports Med* 37:737-763, 2007.

22. COLIBABA, E.D., and I. BOTA. *Jocurile Sportive: Teoria si Medodica.* Bucuresti: Editura Aldin, 1998.

23. COUTTS, A.J., L.K. WALLACE, and K.M. SLATTERY. Monitoring changes in performance, physiology, biochemistry, and psychology during overreaching and recovery in triathletes. *Int J Sports Med* 28:125-134, 2007.

24. DENCKER, M., O. THORSSON, M.K. KARLSSON, C. LINDEN, S. EIBERG, P. WOLLMER, and L.B. ANDERSEN. Gender differences and determinants of aerobic fitness in children aged 8-11 years. *Eur J Appl Physiol* 99:19-26, 2007.

25. DRABIK, J. *Children and Sports Training.* Island Pond, VT: Stadion, 1995.

26. FAIGENBAUM, A.D. Strength training for children and adolescents. *Clin Sports Med* 19:593-619, 2000.

27. FAIGENBAUM, A.D., and W.L. WESTCOTT. *Strength and Power for Young Athletes*. Champaign, IL: Human Kinetics, 2000.

28. FLECK, S., and W.J. KRAEMER. *Designing Resistance Training Programs*. 3rd ed. Champaign, IL: Human Kinetics, 2004.

29. FORD, L.E., A.J. DETTERLINE, K.K. HO, and W. CAO. Gender- and height-related limits of muscle strength in world weightlifting champions. *J Appl Physiol* 89:1061-1064, 2000.

30. FOSTER, C. Monitoring training in athletes with reference to overtraining syndrome. *Med Sci Sports Exerc* 30:1164-1168, 1998.

31. FRY, A.C. The role of training intensity in resistance exercise overtraining and overreaching. In: *Overtraining in Sport*. R.B. Kreider, A.C. Fry, and M.L. O'Toole, eds. Champaign, IL: Human Kinetics, 1998, pp. 107-127.

32. FRY, A.C., and W.J. KRAEMER. Resistance exercise overtraining and overreaching: neuroendocrine responses. *Sports Med* 23:106-129, 1997.

33. FRY, A.C., W.J. KRAEMER, M.H. STONE, L.P. KOZIRIS, J.T. THRUSH, and S.J. FLECK. Relationships between serum testosterone, cortisol, and weightlifting performance. *J Strength Cond Res.* 14:338-343, 2000.

34. FRY, A.C., W.J. KRAEMER, M.H. STONE, B.J. WARREN, S.J. FLECK, J.T. KEARNEY, and S.E. GORDON. Endocrine responses to overreaching before and after 1 year of weightlifting. *Can J Appl Physiol* 19:400-410, 1994.

35. FUSTER, V., A. JEREZ, and A. ORTEGA. Anthropometry and strength relationship: male-female differences. *Anthropol Anz* 56:49-56, 1998.

36. GARHAMMER, J. A comparison of maximal power outputs between elite male and female weightlifters in competition. *Int J Sport Biomech* 7:3-11, 1991.

37. GRGANTOV, Z., D. NEDOVIC, and R. KATIC. Integration of technical and situation efficacy into the morphological system in young female volleyball players. *Coll Antropol* 31:267-273, 2007.

38. GURD, B., and P. KLENTROU. Physical and pubertal development in young male gymnasts. *J Appl Physiol* 95:1011-1015, 2003.

39. HAFF, G.G., M. BURGENER, A.D. FAIGENBAUM, J.L. KILGORE, M.E. LAVALLE, M. NITKA, M. RIPPETOE, and C. PROULX. Roundtable discussion: youth resistance training. *Strength Cond J* 25:49-64, 2003.

40. HÄKKINEN, K. Neuromuscular and hormonal adaptations during strength and power training: a review. *J Sports Med Phys Fitness* 29:9-26, 1989.

41. HÄKKINEN, K., and M. KALLINEN. Distribution of strength training volume into one or two daily sessions and neuromuscular adaptations in female athletes. *Electromyogr Clin Neurophysiol* 34:117-124, 1994.

42. HÄKKINEN, K., K.L. KESKINEN, M. ALEN, P.V. KOMI, and H. KAUHANEN. Serum hormone concentrations during prolonged training in elite endurance-trained and strength-trained athletes. *Eur J Appl Physiol* 59:233-238, 1989.

43. HÄKKINEN, K., A. PAKARINEN, M. ALEN, H. KAUHANEN, and P.V. KOMI. Daily hormonal and neuromuscular responses to intensive strength training in 1 week. *Int J Sports Med* 9:422-428, 1988.

44. HÄKKINEN, K., A. PAKARINEN, M. ALEN, H. KAUHANEN, and P.V. KOMI. Neuromuscular and hormonal adaptations in athletes to strength training in two years. *J Appl Physiol* 65:2406-2412, 1988.

45. HALSON, S.L., M.W. BRIDGE, R. MEEUSEN, B. BUSSCHAERT, M. GLEESON, D.A. JONES, and A.E. JEUKENDRUP. Time course of performance changes and fatigue markers during intensified training in trained cyclists. *J Appl Physiol* 93:947-956, 2002.

46. HARRE, D. *Trainingslehre*. Berlin, Germany: Sportverlag, 1982.

47. HARRIS, G.R., M.H. STONE, H.S. O'BRYANT, C.M. PROULX, and R.L. JOHNSON. Short-term performance effects of high power, high force, or combined weight-training methods. *J Strength Cond Res* 14:14-20, 2000.

48. HAWLEY, J.A. Adaptations of skeletal muscle to prolonged, intense endurance training. *Clin Exp Pharmacol Physiol* 29:218-222, 2002.

49. HELLARD, P., M. AVALOS, L. LACOSTE, F. BARALE, J.C. CHATARD, and G.P. MILLET. Assessing the limitations of the Banister model in monitoring training. *J Sports Sci* 24:509-520, 2006.

50. HELLEBRANDT, F., and S. HOUTZ. Mechanisms of muscle training in man: experimental demonstration of the overload principle. *Phys Ther Rev* 36:371-383, 1956.

51. HODGES, N.J., S. HAYES, R.R. HORN, and A.M. WILLIAMS. Changes in coordination, control and outcome as a result of extended practice on a novel motor skill. *Ergonomics* 48:1672-1685, 2005.

52. HOFFMAN, J.R., M. WENDELL, J. COOPER, and J. KANG. Comparison between linear and nonlinear in-season training programs in freshman football players. *J Strength Cond Res* 17:561-565, 2003.

53. JANSE DE JONGE, X.A. Effects of the menstrual cycle on exercise performance. *Sports Med* 33:833-851, 2003.

54. JANSSEN, I., S.B. HEYMSFIELD, Z.M. WANG, and R. ROSS. Skeletal muscle mass and distribution in 468 men and women aged 18-88 yr. *J Appl Physiol* 89:81-88, 2000.

55. KALLINEN, M., and A. MARKKU. Aging, physical activity and sports injuries: an overview of common sports injuries in the elderly. *Sports Med* 20:41-52, 1995.

56. KATIC, R., M. CAVALA, and V. SRHOJ. Biomotor structures in elite female handball players. *Coll Antropol* 31:795-801, 2007.

57. KRAEMER, W.J., S.A. MAZZETTI, B.C. NINDL, L.A. GOTSHALK, J.S. VOLEK, J.A. BUSH, J.O. MARX, K.

DOHI, A.L. GOMEZ, M. MILES, S.J. FLECK, R.U. NEWTON, and K. HÄKKINEN. Effect of resistance training on women's strength/power and occupational performances. *Med Sci Sports Exerc* 33:1011-1025, 2001.

58. KURZ, T. *Science of Sports Training*. 2nd ed. Island Pond, VT: Stadion, 2001.

59. LANGE, L. *Uber Funktionelle Anpassung*. Berlin, Germany: Springer Verlag, 1919.

60. LAUGHLIN, N.T., and P.L. BUSK. Relationships between selected muscle endurance tasks and gender. *J Strength Cond Res* 21:400-404, 2007.

61. MACKINNON, L.T., and S.L. HOOPER. Overtraining and overreaching: causes effects and prevention. In: *Exercise and Sport Science*. W.E. Garrett and D.T. Kirkendall, eds. Philadelphia: Lippincott Williams & Wilkins, 2000, pp. 487-498.

62. MATVEYEV, L.P. *Fundamentals of Sports Training*. Moscow: Fizkultua i Sport, 1977.

63. MATVEYEV, L.P. *Periodisterung Des Sportlichen Trainings*. Moscow: Fizkultura i Sport, 1972.

64. MAUD, P.J., and B.B. SHULTZ. Gender comparisons in anaerobic power and anaerobic capacity tests. *Br J Sports Med* 20:51-54, 1986.

65. MERO, A., H. KAUHANEN, E. PELTOLA, T. VUORIMAA, and P.V. KOMI. Physiological performance capacity in different prepubescent athletic groups. *J Sports Med Phys Fitness* 30:57-66, 1990.

66. MILLER, A.E., J.D. MACDOUGALL, M.A. TARNOPOLSKY, and D.G. SALE. Gender differences in strength and muscle fiber characteristics. *Eur J Appl Physiol Occup Physiol* 66:254-262, 1993.

67. NADER, G.A. Concurrent strength and endurance training: from molecules to man. *Med Sci Sports Exerc* 38:1965-1970, 2006.

68. NADER, G.A., T.J. MCLOUGHLIN, and K.A. ESSER. mTOR function in skeletal muscle hypertrophy: increased ribosomal RNA via cell cycle regulators. *Am J Physiol Cell Physiol* 289:C1457-C1465, 2005.

69. NÁDORI, L., and I. GRANEK. *Theoretical and Methodological Basis of Training Planning With Special Considerations Within a Microcycle*. Lincoln, NE: NSCA, 1989.

70. O'TOOLE, M.L. Overreaching and overtraining in endurance athletes. In: *Overtraining in Sport*. R.B. Kreider, A.C. Fry, and M.L. O'Toole, eds. Champaign, IL: Human Kinetics, 1998, pp. 3-18.

71. PLISK, S.S., and V. GAMBETTA. Tactical metabolic training: part 1. *Strength Cond* 19:44-53, 1997.

72. PLISK, S.S., and M.H. STONE. Periodization strategies. *Strength Cond* 25:19-37, 2003.

73. POLIQUIN, C. Five steps to increasing the effectiveness of your strength training program. *NSCA J*. 10:34-39, 1988.

74. RATEL, S., N. LAZAAR, C.A. WILLIAMS, M. BEDU, and P. DUCHE. Age differences in human skeletal muscle fatigue during high-intensity intermittent exercise. *Acta Paediatr* 92:1248-1254, 2003.

75. RHEA, M.R., R.L. HUNTER, and T.J. HUNTER. Competition modeling of American football: observational data and implications for high school, collegiate, and professional player conditioning. *J Strength Cond Res* 20:58-61, 2006.

76. RILLING, J.K., C.M. WORTHMAN, B.C. CAMPBELL, J.F. STALLINGS, and M. MBIZVA. Ratios of plasma and salivary testosterone throughout puberty: production versus bioavailability. *Steroids* 61:374-378, 1996.

77. ROBAZZA, C., L. BORTOLI, and Y. HANIN. Perceived effects of emotion intensity on athletic performance: a contingency-based individualized approach. *Res Q Exerc Sport* 77:372-385, 2006.

78. SATORI, J., and P. TSCHIENE. The further development of training theory: new elements and tendencies. *Sci Period Res Technol Sport* 8:Physical Training 8(4):W-1. 1988.

79. SCHMOLINSKY, G. *Track and Field: The East German Textbook of Athletics*. Toronto, ON, Canada: Sports Book Publisher, 2004.

80. SEILER, K.S., and G.O. KJERLAND. Quantifying training intensity distribution in elite endurance athletes: is there evidence for an "optimal" distribution? *Scand J Med Sci Sports* 16:49-56, 2006.

81. SEILER, S., J.J. DE KONING, and C. FOSTER. The fall and rise of the gender difference in elite anaerobic performance 1952-2006. *Med Sci Sports Exerc* 39:534-540, 2007.

82. SHARP, M.A., J.F. PATTON, J.J. KNAPIK, K. HAURET, R.P. MELLO, M. ITO, and P.N. FRYKMAN. Comparison of the physical fitness of men and women entering the U.S. Army: 1978-1998. *Med Sci Sports Exerc* 34:356-363, 2002.

83. SIFF, M.C., and Y.U. VERKHOSHANSKY. *Supertraining*. Denver, CO: Supertraining International, 1999.

84. SMITH, D.J. A framework for understanding the training process leading to elite performance. *Sports Med* 33:1103-1126, 2003.

85. STEYERS, J. *Liukin good at 18*. www.nbcolympics.com/gymnastics/news/newsid=100218.html.

86. STONE, M.H., and A.C. FRY. Increased training volume in strength/power athletes. In: *Overtraining in Sport*. R.B. Kreider, A.C. Fry, and M.L. O'Toole, eds. Champaign, IL: Human Kinetics, 1998, pp. 87-106.

87. STONE, M.H., R. KEITH, J.T. KEARNEY, G.D. WILSON, and S. FLECK, J. Overtraining: a review of the signs and symptoms of overtraining. *J Appl Sport Sci Res* 5:35-50, 1991.

88. STONE, M.H., and H.O. O'BRYANT. *Weight Training: A Scientific Approach*. Edina, MN: Burgess, 1987.

89. STONE, M.H., H. O'BRYANT, and J. GARHAMMER. A hypothetical model for strength training. *J. Sports Med* 21:342-351, 1981.

90. STONE, M.H., K. SANBORN, H.S. O'BRYANT, M. HARTMAN, M.E. STONE, C. PROULX, B. WARD, and J. HRUBY. Maximum strength-power-performance relationships in collegiate throwers. *J Strength Cond Res* 17:739-745, 2003.

91. STONE, M.H., M.E. STONE, and W.A. SANDS. *Principles and Practice of Resistance Training.* Champaign, IL: Human Kinetics, 2007.

92. SUZUKI, S., T. SATO, A. MAEDA, and Y. TAKAHASHI. Program design based on a mathematical model using rating of perceived exertion for an elite Japanese sprinter: a case study. *J Strength Cond Res* 20:36-42, 2006.

93. TANAKA, H., and D.R. SEALS. Endurance exercise performance in masters athletes: age-associated changes and underlying physiological mechanisms. *J Physiol* 586:55-63, 2008.

94. TSCHIENE, P. A necessary direction in training: the integration of biological adaptation in the training program. *Coach Sport Sci J* 1:2-14, 1995.

95. VANDERBURGH, P.M., M. KUSANO, M. SHARP, and B. NINDL. Gender differences in muscular strength: an allometric model approach. *Biomed Sci Instrum* 33:100-105, 1997.

96. VERKHOSHANSKY, Y.U. *Fundamentals of Special Strength Training in Sport.* Livonia, MI: Sportivy Press, 1986.

97. VERKHOSHANSKY, Y.U. *Programming and Organization of Training.* Moscow: Fizkultura i Sport, 1985.

98. VIRU, A. *Adaptations in Sports Training.* Boca Raton, FL: CRC Press, 1995.

99. VIRU, A., and M. VIRU. *Biochemical Monitoring of Sport Training.* Champaign, IL: Human Kinetics, 2001.

100. WERCHOSHANSKI, J. Specific training principles for power. *Mod Athlete Coach* 17:11-13, 1979.

101. WILMORE, J.H., D.L. COSTILL, and W.L. KENNEY. *Physiology of Sport and Exercise.* 4th ed. Champaign, IL: Human Kinetics, 2008.

102. ZANCHI, N.E., and A.H. LANCHA, JR. Mechanical stimuli of skeletal muscle: implications on mTOR/p70s6k and protein synthesis. *Eur J Appl Physiol* 102:253-263, 2008.

103. ZATSIORSKY, V.M. *Science and Practice of Strength Training.* Champaign, IL: Human Kinetics, 1995.

104. ZATSIORSKY, V.M., and W.J. KRAEMER. *Science and Practice of Strength Training.* 2nd ed. Champaign, IL: Human Kinetics, 2006.

Chapter 3

1. BAKER, D., and S. NANCE. The relation between running speed and measures of strength and power in professional rugby league players. *J Strength Cond Res* 13:230-235, 1999.

2. BOMPA, T.O. *Periodization: Theory and Methodology of Training.* 4th ed. Champaign, IL: Human Kinetics, 1999.

3. Bompa, T.O. *Total training for coaching team sports.* Toronto: Sport Books Publisher, 2006, page 22.

4. BRAVO, D.F., F.M. IMPELLIZZERI, E. RAMPININI, C. CASTAGNA, D. BISHOP, and U. WISLOFF. Sprint vs. interval training in football. *Int J Sports Med* 29:668-674, 2008.

5. BRET, C., A. RAHMANI, A.B. DUFOUR, L. MESSONNIER, and J.R. LACOUR. Leg strength and stiffness as ability factors in 100 m sprint running. *J Sports Med Phys Fitness* 42:274-281, 2002.

6. BURGOMASTER, K.A., G.J. HEIGENHAUSER, and M.J. GIBALA. Effect of short-term sprint interval training on human skeletal muscle carbohydrate metabolism during exercise and time-trial performance. *J Appl Physiol* 100:2041-2047, 2006.

7. BURGOMASTER, K.A., S.C. HUGHES, G.J. HEIGENHAUSER, S.N. BRADWELL, and M.J. GIBALA. Six sessions of sprint interval training increases muscle oxidative potential and cycle endurance capacity in humans. *J Appl Physiol* 98:1985-1990, 2005.

8. CAVANAGH, P.R., and K.R. WILLIAMS. The effect of stride length variation on oxygen uptake during distance running. *Med Sci Sports Exerc* 14:30-35, 1982.

9. CHIU, L.Z., A.C. FRY, B.K. SCHILLING, E.J. JOHNSON, and L.W. WEISS. Neuromuscular fatigue and potentiation following two successive high intensity resistance exercise sessions. *Eur J Appl Physiol* 92:385-392, 2004.

10. CONLEY, D.L., and G. KRAHENBUHL. Running economy and distance running performance of highly trained athletes. *Med Sci Sports Exerc* 14:357-360, 1980.

11. CRONIN, J.B., and K.T. HANSEN. Strength and power predictors of sports speed. *J Strength Cond Res* 19:349-357, 2005.

12. CURY, F., S. BIDDLE, P. SARRAZIN, and J.P. FAMOSE. Achievement goals and perceived ability predict investment in learning a sport task. *Br J Educ Psychol* 67:293-309, 1997.

13. DALLEAU, G., A. BELLI, M. BOURDIN, and J.R. LACOUR. The spring-mass model and the energy cost of treadmill running. *Eur J Appl Physiol Occup Physiol* 77:257-263, 1998.

14. DANIELS, J.T. A physiologist's view of running economy. *Med Sci Sports Exerc* 17:332-338, 1985.

15. DICK, F.W. *Sports Training Principles.* 4th ed. London: A & C Black, 2002.

16. DUNLAVY, J.K., W.A. SANDS, J.R. MCNEAL, M.H. STONE, S.A. SMITH, M. JEMNI, and G.G. HAFF. Strength performance assessment in a simulated men's gymnastics still rings cross. *J Sports Sci Med* 6:93-97, 2007.

17. ENDEMANN, F. Teaching throwing events. In: *The Throws: Contemporary Theory, Technique, and Training.* J. Jarver, ed. Mountain View, CA: Tafnews Press, 2000, pp. 11-14.

18. FLORESCU, C., V. DUMITRESCU, and A. PREDESCU. *Metodologia Desvoltari Calitatilor Fizice* [The Methodology of Developing Physical Qualities]. Bucharest: National Sports Council, 1969.

19. GIBALA, M.J., J.P. LITTLE, M. VAN ESSEN, G.P. WILKIN, K.A. BURGOMASTER, A. SAFDAR, S. RAHA, and M.A. TARNOPOLSKY. Short-term sprint interval versus traditional endurance training: similar

initial adaptations in human skeletal muscle and exercise performance. *J Physiol* 575:901-911, 2006.

20. GODFREY, R.J. Cross-training. *Sports Exercise & Injury* 4:50-56, 1998.

21. HEISE, G.D., and P.E. MARTIN. Are variations in running economy in humans associated with ground reaction force characteristics? *Eur J Appl Physiol* 84:438-442, 2001.

22. HODGES, N.J., S. HAYES, R.R. HORN, and A.M. WILLIAMS. Changes in coordination, control and outcome as a result of extended practice on a novel motor skill. *Ergonomics* 48:1672-1685, 2005.

23. HUGHES, M.D., and R.M. BARTLETT. The use of performance indicators in performance analysis. *J Sports Sci* 20:739-754, 2002.

24. KANEKO, M., A. ITO, T. FUCHIMOTO, Y. SHISHI-KURA, and J. TOYOOKA. Influence of running speed on the mechanical efficiency of sprinters and distance runners. In: *Biomechanics IX-B*. D.A. Winter et al., eds. Champaign, IL: Human Kinetics, 1985, pp. 307-312.

25. LAURSEN, P.B., C.M. SHING, J.M. PEAKE, J.S. COOMBES, and D.G. JENKINS. Interval training program optimization in highly trained endurance cyclists. *Med Sci Sports Exerc* 34:1801-1807, 2002.

26. MALTSEVA, N. Instructing young throwers. In: *The Throws: Contemporary Theory, Technique, and Training*. J. Jarver, ed. Mountain View, CA: Tafnews Press, 2000, pp. 15-17.

27. MATVEYEV, L.P. *Periodisterung Des Sportlichen Trainings*. Moscow: Fizkultura i Sport, 1972.

28. MEDVEDEV, A.S. *Sistema Mnogoletnyei Trenirovki V Tyazheloi Atletikye*. Moscow: Fizkultura i Sport, 1986.

29. MORGAN, D.W., and M. CRAIB. Physiological aspects of running economy. *Med Sci Sports Exerc* 24:456-461, 1992.

30. NÁDORI, L. *Training and Competition*. Budapest: Sport, 1962.

31. NÁDORI, L., and I. GRANEK. *Theoretical and Methodological Basis of Training Planning With Special Considerations Within a Microcycle*. Lincoln, NE: NSCA, 1989.

32. NUMMELA, A., T. KERANEN, and L.O. MIKKELS-SON. Factors related to top running speed and economy. *Int J Sports Med* 28:655-661, 2007.

33. PLISK, S.S., and V. GAMBETTA. Tactical metabolic training: part 1. *Strength Cond* 19:44-53, 1997.

34. PLISK, S.S., and M.H. STONE. Periodization strategies. *Strength Cond* 25:19-37, 2003.

35. RAGLIN, J.S. The psychology of the marathoner: of one mind and many. *Sports Med* 37:404-407, 2007.

36. ROBINSON, J.M., M.H. STONE, R.L. JOHNSON, C.M. PENLAND, B.J. WARREN, and R.D. LEWIS. Effects of different weight training exercise/rest intervals on strength, power, and high intensity exercise endurance. *J. Strength Cond Res* 9:216-221, 1995.

37. SCHMIDT, R.A., and C.A. WRISBERG. *Motor Learning and Performance*. 3rd ed. Champaign, IL: Human Kinetics, 2004.

38. SCHMOLINSKY, G. *Track and Field: The East German Textbook of Athletics*. Toronto, ON, Canada: Sports Book Publisher, 2004.

39. SIFF, M.C., and Y.U. VERKHOSHANSKY. *Supertraining*. Denver, CO: Supertraining International, 1999.

40. SINITSIN, A. A few hints for novice discus throwers. In: *The Throws: Contemporary Theory, Technique, and Training*. J. Jarver, ed. Mountain View, CA: Tafnews, 2000, pp. 95-97.

41. SMITH, D.J. A framework for understanding the training process leading to elite performance. *Sports Med* 33:1103-1126, 2003.

42. STONE, M.H., and H.O. O'BRYANT. *Weight Training: A Scientific Approach*. Edina, MN: Burgess, 1987.

43. STONE, M.H., R. KEITH, J.T. KEARNEY, G.D. WILSON, and S. FLECK, J. Overtraining: a review of the signs and symptoms of overtraining. *J Appl Sport Sci Res* 5:35-50, 1991.

44. STONE, M.H., W.A. SANDS, K.C. PIERCE, R.U. NEWTON, G.G. HAFF, and J. CARLOCK. Maximum strength and strength training: a relationship to endurance? *Strength Cond J* 28:44-53, 2006.

45. STONE, M.H., M.E. STONE, and W.A. SANDS. *Principles and Practice of Resistance Training*. Champaign, IL: Human Kinetics, 2007.

46. SUINN, R.M. Mental practice in sport psychology: where have we been, where do we go? *Clin Psychol Sci Pract* 4:189-207, 1997.

47. TAN, J.C., and M.R. YEADON. Why do high jumpers use a curved approach? *J Sport Sci* 23:775-780, 2005.

48. TEODORESCU, L., and C. FLORESCU. Some directions regarding the perfection and mastery of technique and strategy. In: *The Content and Methodology of Training*. E. Ghibu, ed. Bucharest, Hungary: Stadion, 1971, pp. 66-81.

49. VAN-YPEREN, N.W., and J.L. DUDA. Goal orientations, beliefs about success, and performance improvement among young elite Dutch soccer players. *Scand J Med Sci Sports* 9:358-364, 1999.

50. WILLIAMS, S.J., and L.R. KENDALL. A profile of sports science research (1983-2003). *J Sci Med Sport* 10:193-200, 2007.

51. ZATSIORSKY, V.M. *Science and Practice of Strength Training*. Champaign, IL: Human Kinetics, 1995.

Chapter 4

1. *2002 USA Cycling Club Coach Manual*. Colorado Springs, CO: USA Cycling, 2002.

2. ABADEJEV, I. Basic training principles for Bulgarian elite. *Int Olympic Lifter* 3:12-13, 1976.

3. ABADEJEV, I. Basic training principles for Bulgarian elite. *Canadian Weightlifting Federation Official Newsletter* 5:13-18, 1976.

4. ABADEJEV, I. Basic training principles for Bulgarian elite. *New Brunswick Weightlifting Association Newsletter* 4:19-24, 1977.

5. ABADEJEV, I. Preparation of the Bulgarian weightlifters for the Olympic Games 1984. *Australian Weightlifter* October:25-29, 1981.

6. ABADJIEV, I., and B. FARADJIEV. *Training of Weight Lifters*. Sofia, Bulgaria: Medicina i Fizkultura, 1986.

7. ABERNETHY, P.J., J. JURIMAE, P.A. LOGAN, A.W. TAYLOR, and R.E. THAYER. Acute and chronic response of skeletal muscle to resistance exercise. *Sports Med* 17:22-38, 1994.

8. ABERNETHY, P.J., R. THAYER, and A.W. TAYLOR. Acute and chronic responses of skeletal muscle to endurance and sprint exercise: a review. *Sports Med* 10:365-389, 1990.

9. ACEVEDO, E.O., and A.H. GOLDFARB. Increased training intensity effects on plasma lactate, ventilatory threshold, and endurance. *Med Sci Sports Exerc* 21:563-568, 1989.

10. AJÁN, T., and L. BAROGA. *Weightlifting: Fitness for All Sports*. Budapest: International Weightlifting Federation, 1988.

11. ALLEN, H., and A.R. COGGAN. *Training and Racing with a Power Meter*. Boulder, CO: Velo Press, 2006.

12. BARNETT, A. Using recovery modalities between training sessions in elite athletes: does it help? *Sports Med* 36:781-796, 2006.

13. BEN ABDELKRIM, N., S. EL FAZAA, and J. EL ATI. Time-motion analysis and physiological data of elite under-19-year-old basketball players during competition. *Br J Sports Med* 41:69-75; discussion 75, 2007.

14. BILLAT, V.L., B. FLECHET, B. PETIT, G. MURIAUX, and J.P. KORALSZTEIN. Interval training at VO2max: effects on aerobic performance and overtraining markers. *Med Sci Sports Exerc* 31:156-163, 1999.

15. BOMPA, T.O. *Periodization: Theory and Methodology of Training*. 4th ed. Champaign, IL: Human Kinetics, 1999.

16. BOMPA, T.O., and M.C. CARRERA. *Periodization Training for Sports: Science-Based Strength and Conditioning Plans for 20 Sports*. 2nd ed. Champaign, IL: Human Kinetics, 2005.

17. BROOKS, G.A., T.D. FAHEY, T.P. WHITE, and K.M. BALDWIN. *Exercise Physiology: Human Bioenergetics and Its Application*. 3rd ed. Mountain View, CA: Mayfield, 2000.

18. BURKE, L., and V. DEAKIN. *Clincial Sports Nutrition*. Roseville, Australia: McGraw-Hill Australia, 2000.

19. COFFEY, V.G., and J.A. HAWLEY. The molecular bases of training adaptation. *Sports Med* 37:737-763, 2007.

20. CONLEY, M. Bioenergetics of exercise training. In: *Essentials of Strength Training and Conditioning*. T.R. Baechle and R.W. Earle, eds. Champaign, IL: Human Kinetics, 2000, pp. 73-90.

21. CONLEY, M.S., M.H. STONE, H.S. O'BRYANT, R.L. JOHNSON, D.R. HONEYCUTT, and T.P. HOKE. Peak power versus power at maximal oxygen uptake. In: *Proceedings of the National Strength and Conditioning Association Annual Convention*, Las Vegas, NV, 1993.

22. CRAIG, N., C. WALSH, D.T. MARTIN, S. WOOLFORD, P. BOURDON, T. STANEF, P. BARNES, and B. SAVAGE. Protocols for the physiological assessment of high-performance track, road, and mountain cyclists. In: *Physiological Tests for Elite Athletes*. C.J. Gore, ed. Champaign, IL: Human Kinetics, 2000, pp. 258-277.

23. DEDRICK, M.E., and P.M. CLARKSON. The effects of eccentric exercise on motor performance in young and older women. *Eur J Appl Physiol Occup Physiol* 60:183-186, 1990.

24. DRESCHLER, A. *The Weightlifting Encyclopedia: A Guide to World Class Performance*. Flushing, NY: A IS A Communications, 1998.

25. ENISELER, N. Heart rate and blood lactate concentrations as predictors of physiological load on elite soccer players during various soccer training activities. *J Strength Cond Res* 19:799-804, 2005.

26. FARIA, E.W., D.L. PARKER, and I.E. FARIA. The science of cycling: physiology and training—part 1. *Sports Med* 35:285-312, 2005.

27. FARIA, E.W., D.L. PARKER, and I.E. FARIA. The science of cycling: factors affecting performance—part 2. *Sports Med* 35:313-337, 2005.

28. FISKERSTRAND, Å., and K.S. SEILER. Training and performance characteristics among Norwegian international rowers 1970-2001. *Scand J Med Sci Sports* 14:303-310, 2004.

29. FLECK, S., and W.J. KRAEMER. *Designing Resistance Training Programs*. 3rd ed. Champaign, IL: Human Kinetics, 2004.

30. FROBÖSE, I., A. VERDONCK, F. DUESBERG, and C. MUCHA. Effects of various load intensities in the framework of postoperative stationary endurance training on performance deficit of the quadriceps muscle of the thigh. *Z Orthop Ihre Grenzgeb* 131:164-167, 1993.

31. FRY, A.C., and W.J. KRAEMER. Resistance exercise overtraining and overreaching: neuroendocrine responses. *Sports Med* 23:106-129, 1997.

32. FRY, R.W., A.R. MORTON, and D. KEAST. Overtraining in athletes: an update. *Sports Med* 12:32-65, 1991.

33. GABBETT, T.J. Science of rugby league football: a review. *J Sports Sci* 23:961-976, 2005.

34. GARHAMMER, J., and B. TAKANO. Training for weightlifting. In: *Strength and Power in Sport*. P.V. Komi, ed. Oxford, UK: Blackwell Scientific, 2003, pp. 502-515.

35. GILLAM, G.M. Effects of frequency of weight training on muscle strength enhancement. *J Sports Med* 21:432-436, 1981.

36. HAFF, G.G., A. WHITLEY, and J.A. POTTEIGER. A brief review: explosive exercises and sports performance. *Natl Strength Cond Assoc* 23:13-20, 2001.

37. HÄKKINEN, K., and M. KALLINEN. Distribution of strength training volume into one or two daily sessions and neuromuscular adaptations in female athletes. *Electromyogr Clin Neurophysiol* 34:117-124, 1994.

38. HARRE, D. *Trainingslehre*. Berlin, Germany: Sportverlag, 1982.

39. HAUSSWIRTH, C., D. LEHENAFF, P. DREANO, and K. SAVONEN. Effects of cycling alone or in a sheltered position on subsequent running performance during a triathlon. *Med Sci Sports Exerc* 31:599-604, 1999.

40. HOWE, C., and A.R. COGGAN, *The Road Cyclist's Guide to Training by Power*. 2003, Training Smart Online. http://www.trainingsmartonline.com/images/Free_Triathlon_Articles/Power_Cycling_Training.pdf

41. ILIUTA, G., and C. DUMITRESCU. Medical and physiological criteria for the assessing and directing of athletes' training. *Sportul de Performanta Bucareti* 53:49-64, 1998.

42. JONES, L. Training programs: do Bulgarian methods lead the way for the USA? *Weightlifting USA* 9:10-11, 1991.

43. KOMI, P.V. *Strength and Power in Sport*. Oxford, UK: Blackwell Scientific, 1991.

44. KOMI, P.V. *Strength and Power in Sport*. 2nd ed. Malden, MA: Blackwell Scientific, 2003.

45. LANIER, A.B. Use of nonsteroidal anti-inflammatory drugs following exercise-induced muscle injury. *Sports Med* 33:177-186, 2003.

46. LAURSEN, P.B., and D.G. JENKINS. The scientific basis for high-intensity interval training: optimising training programmes and maximising performance in highly trained endurance athletes. *Sports Med* 32:53-73, 2002.

47. LAURSEN, P.B., C.M. SHING, J.M. PEAKE, J.S. COOMBES, and D.G. JENKINS. Interval training program optimization in highly trained endurance cyclists. *Med Sci Sports Exerc* 34:1801-1807, 2002.

48. LAURSEN, P.B., C.M. SHING, J.M. PEAKE, J.S. COOMBES, and D.G. JENKINS. Influence of high-intensity interval training on adaptations in well-trained cyclists. *J Strength Cond Res* 19:527-533, 2005.

49. LEUTSHENKO, A.V., and A.L. BERESTOVSKAYA. The main elements in the planning of training for elite discus throwers. In: *The Throws: Contemporary Theory, Technique, and Training*. J. Jarver, ed. Mountain View, CA: Tafnews Press, 2000, pp. 106-108.

50. LUEBBERS, P.E., J.A. POTTEIGER, M.W. HULVER, J.P. THYFAULT, M.J. CARPER, and R.H. LOCKWOOD. Effects of plyometric training and recovery on vertical jump performance and anaerobic power. *J Strength Cond Res* 17:704-709, 2003.

51. LYMAN, S., G.S. FLEISIG, J.W. WATERBOR, E.M. FUNKHOUSER, L. PULLEY, J.R. ANDREWS, E.D. OSINSKI, and J.M. ROSEMAN. Longitudinal study of elbow and shoulder pain in youth baseball pitchers. *Med Sci Sports Exerc* 33:1803-1810, 2001.

52. MATVEYEV, L.P. *Fundamentals of Sports Training*. Moscow: Fizkultua i Sport, 1977.

53. MAUGHAN, R., and M. GLEESON. *The Biochemical Basis of Sports Performance*. New York: Oxford University Press, 2004.

54. MCARDLE, W.D., F.I. KATCH, and V.L. KATCH. *Exercise Physiology: Energy, Nutrition, and Human Performance*. 6th ed. Baltimore: Lippincott, Williams & Wilkins, 2007.

55. MONEDERO, J., and B. DONNE. Effect of recovery interventions on lactate removal and subsequent performance. *Int J Sports Med* 21:593-597, 2000.

56. MORTON, R.H., J.R. FITZ-CLARKE, and E.W. BANISTER. Modeling human performance in running. *J Appl Physiol* 69:1171-1177, 1990.

57. MUJIKA, I., and S. PADILLA. Detraining: loss of training-induced physiological and performance adaptations: part I: short term insufficient training stimulus. *Sports Med* 30:79-87, 2000.

58. MUJIKA, I., and S. PADILLA. Detraining: loss of training-induced physiological and performance adaptations: part II: long term insufficient training stimulus. *Sports Med* 30:145-154, 2000.

59. NADER, G.A. Concurrent strength and endurance training: from molecules to man. *Med Sci Sports Exerc* 38:1965-1970, 2006.

60. NÁDORI, L., and I. GRANEK. *Theoretical and Methodological Basis of Training Planning With Special Considerations Within a Microcycle*. Lincoln, NE: NSCA, 1989.

61. NOAKES, T.D. *Lore of Running*. 4th ed. Champaign, IL: Human Kinetics, 2001.

62. OLBRECT, J. *The Science of Winning: Planning, Periodizing, and Optimizing Swim Training*. Luton, UK: Swimshop, 2000.

63. PETERSON, M.D., M.R. RHEA, and B.A. ALVAR. Applications of the dose-response for muscular strength development: a review of meta-analytic efficacy and reliability for designing training prescription. *J Strength Cond Res* 19:950-958, 2005.

64. PLATONOV, V.N. *Teoria General del Entrenamiento Deportivo Olimpico*. Badalona, Spain: Paidotribo Editorial, 2002.

65. PLISK, S.S., and M.H. STONE. Periodization strategies. *Strength Cond* 25:19-37, 2003.

66. POTTEIGER, J.A. Aerobic endurance exercise training. In: *Essentials of Strength Training and Conditioning*. T.R. Baechle and R.W. Earle, eds. Champaign, IL: Human Kinetics, 2000, pp. 495-509.

67. RHEA, M.R., B.A. ALVAR, L.N. BURKETT, and S.D. BALL. A meta-analysis to determine the dose response for strength development. *Med Sci Sports Exerc* 35:456-464, 2003.

68. SCHMOLINSKY, G. *Track and Field: The East German Textbook of Athletics*. Toronto, ON, Canada: Sports Book Publisher, 2004.

69. SIFF, M.C., and Y.U. VERKHOSHANSKY. *Supertraining*. Denver, CO: Supertraining International, 1999.

70. SIMONEAU, J.A., G. LORTIE, M.R. BOULAY, M. MARCOTTE, M.C. THIBAULT, and C. BOUCHARD. Effects of two high-intensity intermittent training programs interspaced by detraining on human skeletal muscle and performance. *Eur J Appl Physiol Occup Physiol* 56:516-521, 1987.

71. SKURVYDAS, A., V. DUDONIENE, A. KALVENAS, and A. ZUOZA. Skeletal muscle fatigue in long-distance runners, sprinters and untrained men after repeated drop jumps performed at maximal intensity. *Scand J Med Sci Sports* 12:34-39, 2002.

72. SMITH, D.J. A framework for understanding the training process leading to elite performance. *Sports Med* 33:1103-1126, 2003.

73. SMITH, T.P., L.R. MCNAUGHTON, and K.J. MARSHALL. Effects of 4-wk training using Vmax/Tmax on VO$_2$max and performance in athletes. *Med Sci Sports Exerc* 31:892-896, 1999.

74. SPENCER, M., D. BISHOP, B. DAWSON, and C. GOODMAN. Physiological and metabolic responses of repeated-sprint activities: specific to field-based team sports. *Sports Med* 35:1025-1044, 2005.

75. STEPTO, N.K., D.T. MARTIN, K.E. FALLON, and J.A. HAWLEY. Metabolic demands of intense aerobic interval training in competitive cyclists. *Med Sci Sports Exerc* 33:303-310, 2001.

76. STOLEN, T., K. CHAMARI, C. CASTAGNA, and U. WISLOFF. Physiology of soccer: an update. *Sports Med* 35:501-536, 2005.

77. STONE, M.H., R. KEITH, J.T. KEARNEY, G.D. WILSON, and S. FLECK, J. Overtraining: a review of the signs and symptoms of overtraining. *J Appl Sport Sci Res* 5:35-50, 1991.

78. STONE, M.H., and H.O. O'BRYANT. *Weight Training: A Scientific Approach*. Edina, MN: Burgess, 1987.

79. STONE, M.H., M.E. STONE, and W.A. SANDS. *Principles and Practice of Resistance Training*. Champaign, IL: Human Kinetics, 2007.

80. WERNBOM, M., J. AUGUSTSSON, and R. THOMEE. The influence of frequency, intensity, volume and mode of strength training on whole muscle cross-sectional area in humans. *Sports Med* 37:225-264, 2007.

81. ZATSIORSKY, V.M. Intensity of strength training fact and theory: Russian and Eastern European approach. *NSCA J* 14:46-57, 1992.

82. ZATSIORSKY, V.M. *Science and Practice of Strength Training*. Champaign, IL: Human Kinetics, 1995.

83. ZATSIORSKY, V.M. and W.J. KRAEMER. *Science and Practice of Strength Training*. 2nd ed. Champaign, IL: Human Kinetics, 2006.

Chapter 5

1. ABERNETHY, P.J., R. THAYER, and A.W. TAYLOR. Acute and chronic responses of skeletal muscle to endurance and sprint exercise: a review. *Sports Med* 10:365-389, 1990.

2. ALLEN, D.G., A.A. KABBARA, and H. WESTERBLAD. Muscle fatigue: the role of intracellular calcium stores. *Can J Appl Physiol* 27:83-96, 2002.

3. ANGUS, S. Massage therapy for sprinters and runners. *Clin Podiatr Med Surg* 18:329-336, 2001.

4. BALE, P., and H. JAMES. Massage, warmdown and rest as recuperative measures after short term performance. *Physiother Sport* 13:4-7, 1991.

5. BARNES, M., L.M. GIBSON, and D.G. STEPHENSON. Increased muscle glycogen content is associated with increased capacity to respond to T-system depolarisation in mechanically skinned skeletal muscle fibres from the rat. *Pflugers Arch* 442:101-106, 2001.

6. BARNETT, A. Using recovery modalities between training sessions in elite athletes: does it help? *Sports Med* 36:781-796, 2006.

7. BATY, J.J., H. HWANG, Z. DING, J.R. BERNARD, B. WANG, B. KWON, and J.L. IVY. The effect of a carbohydrate and protein supplement on resistance exercise performance, hormonal response, and muscle damage. *J Strength Cond Res* 21:321-329, 2007.

8. BERGLUND, B., and H. SAFSTROM. Psychological monitoring and modulation of training load of world-class canoeists. *Med Sci Sports Exerc* 26:1036-1040, 1994.

9. BIOLO, G., R.Y. DECLAN FLEMING, and R.R. WOLFE. Physiologic hyperinsulinemia stimulates protein synthesis and enhances transport of selected amino acids in human skeletal muscle. *J Clin Invest* 95:811-819, 1995.

10. BIOLO, G., B.D. WILLIAMS, R.Y. FLEMING, and R.R. WOLFE. Insulin action on muscle protein kinetics and amino acid transport during recovery after resistance exercise. *Diabetes* 48:949-957, 1999.

11. BIRK, T.J., A. MCGRADY, R.D. MACARTHUR, and S. KHUDER. The effects of massage therapy alone and in combination with other complementary therapies on immune system measures and quality of life in human immunodeficiency virus. *J Altern Complement Med* 6:405-414, 2000.

12. BLEAKLEY, C., S. MCDONOUGH, and D. MACAULEY. The use of ice in the treatment of acute soft-tissue injury: a systematic review of randomized controlled trials. *Am J Sports Med* 32:251-261, 2004.

13. BLOM, P.C., A.T. HOSTMARK, O. VAAGE, K.R. KARDEL, and S. MAEHLUM. Effect of different post-exercise sugar diets on the rate of muscle glycogen synthesis. *Med Sci Sports Exerc* 19:491-496, 1987.

14. BOGDANIS, G.C., M.E. NEVILL, H.K. LAKOMY, C.M. GRAHAM, and G. LOUIS. Effects of active recovery on power output during repeated maximal sprint cycling. *Eur J Appl Physiol Occup Physiol* 74:461-469, 1996.

15. BOND, V., B. BALKISSOON, B.D. FRANKS, R. BROWNLOW, M. CAPRAROLA, D. BARTLEY, and M. BANKS. Effects of sleep deprivation on performance during submaximal and maximal exercise. *J Sports Med Phys Fitness* 26:169-174, 1986.

16. BONDE-PETERSEN, F., L. SCHULTZ-PEDERSEN, and N. DRAGSTED. Peripheral and central blood flow in man during cold, thermoneutral, and hot water immersion. *Aviat Space Environ Med* 63:346-350, 1992.

17. BONEN, A., G.W. NESS, A.N. BELCASTRO, and R.L. KIRBY. Mild exercise impedes glycogen repletion in muscle. *J Appl Physiol* 58:1622-1629, 1985.

18. BRUKNER, P., and K. KHAN. *Clinical Sports Medicine*. 2nd ed. Sydney: McGraw-Hill, 2001.

19. BULBULIAN, R., J.H. HEANEY, C.N. LEAKE, A.A. SUCEC, and N.T. SJOHOLM. The effect of sleep deprivation and exercise load on isokinetic leg strength and endurance. *Eur J Appl Physiol Occup Physiol* 73:273-277, 1996.

20. BURKE, L. Nutrition for recovery after competition and training. In: *Clinical Sports Nutrition*. L. Burke and V. Deakin, eds. Roseville, Australia: McGraw-Hill Australia, 2000, p. 759.

21. BURKE, L.M. Nutrition strategies for the marathon: fuel for training and racing. *Sports Med* 37:344-347, 2007.

22. BURKE, L., and V. DEAKIN. *Clinical Sports Nutrition*. Roseville, Australia: McGraw-Hill Australia, 2000.

23. BUSSO, T., K. HÄKKINEN, A. PAKARINEN, H. KAUHANEN, P.V. KOMI, and J.R. LACOUR. Hormonal adaptations and modeled responses in elite weightlifters during 6 weeks of training. *Eur J Appl Physiol* 64:381-386, 1992.

24. CALDER, A. Recovery training. In: *Training for Speed and Endurance*. P. Reaburn and D. Jenkins, eds. Sydney: Allen and Unwin, 1996.

25. CHANDLER, R.M., H.K. BYRNE, J.G. PATTERSON, and J.L. IVY. Dietary supplements affect the anabolic hormones after weight-training exercise. *J Appl Physiol* 76:839-845, 1994.

26. CHEUNG, K., P. HUME, and L. MAXWELL. Delayed onset muscle soreness: treatment strategies and performance factors. *Sports Med* 33:145-164, 2003.

27. CHIN, E.R., and D.G. ALLEN. Effects of reduced muscle glycogen concentration on force, Ca2+ release and contractile protein function in intact mouse skeletal muscle. *J Physiol* 498(pt 1):17-29, 1997.

28. CHOI, D., K.J. COLE, B.H. GOODPASTER, W.J. FINK, and D.L. COSTILL. Effect of passive and active recovery on the resynthesis of muscle glycogen. *Med Sci Sports Exerc* 26:992-996, 1994.

29. COCHRANE, D.J. Alternating hot and cold water immersion for athlete recovery: a review. *Phys Ther Sport* 5:26-32, 2004.

30. COFFEY, V., M. LEVERITT, and N. GILL. Effect of recovery modality on 4-hour repeated treadmill running performance and changes in physiological variables. *J Sci Med Sport* 7:1-10, 2004.

31. COGGAN, A.R., and E.F. COYLE. Carbohydrate ingestion during prolonged exercise: effects on metabolism and performance. *Exerc Sport Sci Rev* 19:1-40, 1991.

32. CONLEY, M. Bioenergetics of exercise training. In: *Essentials of Strength Training and Conditioning*. T.R. Baechle and R.W. Earle, eds. Champaign, IL: Human Kinetics, 2000, pp. 73-90.

33. COSTILL, D.L., and J.M. MILLER. Nutrition for endurance sport: carbohydrate and fluid balance. *Int J Sports Med* 1:2-14, 1980.

34. COSTILL, D.L., D.D. PASCOE, W.J. FINK, R.A. ROBERGS, S.I. BARR, and D. PEARSON. Impaired muscle glycogen resynthesis after eccentric exercise. *J Appl Physiol* 69:46-50, 1990.

35. COSTILL, D.L., W.M. SHERMAN, W.J. FINK, C. MARESH, M. WITTEN, and J.M. MILLER. The role of dietary carbohydrates in muscle glycogen resynthesis after strenuous running. *Am J Clin Nutr* 34:1831-1836, 1981.

36. COTE, D.J., W.E. PRENTICE, JR., D.N. HOOKER, and E.W. SHIELDS. Comparison of three treatment procedures for minimizing ankle sprain swelling. *Phys Ther* 68:1072-1076, 1988.

37. COYLE, E.F. Physical activity as a metabolic stressor. *Am J Clin Nutr* 72:512S-520S, 2000.

38. COYLE, E.F. Timing and method of increased carbohydrate intake to cope with heavy training, competition and recovery. *J Sports Sci* 9(spec no):29-51; discussion 51-52, 1991.

39. CREER, A., P. GALLAGHER, D. SLIVKA, B. JEMIOLO, W. FINK, and S. TRAPPE. Influence of muscle glycogen availability on ERK1/2 and Akt signaling after resistance exercise in human skeletal muscle. *J Appl Physiol* 99:950-956, 2005.

40. CROWE, M.J., D. O'CONNOR, and D. RUDD. Cold water recovery reduces anaerobic performance. *Int J Sports Med* 28:994-998, 2007.

41. DEDRICK, M.E., and P.M. CLARKSON. The effects of eccentric exercise on motor performance in young and older women. *Eur J Appl Physiol Occup Physiol* 60:183-186, 1990.

42. DI PRAMPERO, P.E., L. PEETERS, and R. MARGARIA. Alactic O 2 debt and lactic acid production after exhausting exercise in man. *J Appl Physiol* 34:628-632, 1973.

43. ESTON, R., and D. PETERS. Effects of cold water immersion on the symptoms of exercise-induced muscle damage. *J Sports Sci* 17:231-238, 1999.

44. FISCUS, K.A., T.W. KAMINSKI, and M.E. POWERS. Changes in lower-leg blood flow during warm-, cold-, and contrast-water therapy. *Arch Phys Med Rehabil* 86:1404-1410, 2005.

45. FLANNAGAN, T.E., C. PRUSCINO, J. PIHAN, R. MARSHALL, A. HEALY, M. BAUM, and M. MERRICK. Brisbane Tour 1998: achieving recovery during major tournaments. In: *Success in Sport and Life*. Melbourne: Victorian Institute of Sport, 1998.

46. FRIDEN, J., and R.L. LIEBER. Eccentric exercise-induced injuries to contractile and cytoskeletal muscle fibre components. *Acta Physiol Scand* 171:321-326, 2001.

47. FRY, A.C. The role of training intensity in resistance exercise overtraining and overreaching. In: *Overtraining in Sport*. R.B. Kreider, A.C. Fry, and M.L. O'Toole, eds. Champaign, IL: Human Kinetics, 1998, pp. 107-127.

48. FRY, A.C., W.J. KRAEMER, M.H. STONE, L.P. KOZIRIS, J.T. THRUSH, and S.J. FLECK. Relationships between serum testosterone, cortisol, and weightlifting performance. *J Strength Cond Res* 14:338-343, 2000.

49. FRY, A.C., W.J. KRAEMER, F. VAN BORSELEN, J.M. LYNCH, J.L. MARSIT, E.P. ROY, N.T. TRIPLETT, and

H.G. KNUTTGEN. Performance decrements with high-intensity resistance exercise overtraining. *Med Sci Sports Exerc* 26:1165-1173, 1994.

50. FRY, R.W., A.R. MORTON, and D. KEAST. Overtraining in athletes: an update. *Sports Med* 12:32-65, 1991.

51. GABRIELSEN, A., R. VIDEBAEK, L.B. JOHANSEN, J. WARBERG, N.J. CHRISTENSEN, B. PUMP, and P. NORSK. Forearm vascular and neuroendocrine responses to graded water immersion in humans. *Acta Physiol Scand* 169:87-94, 2000.

52. GILL, N.D., C.M. BEAVEN, and C. COOK. Effectiveness of post-match recovery strategies in rugby players. *Br J Sports Med* 40:260-263, 2006.

53. GULICK, D.T., I.F. KIMURA, M. SITLER, A. PAOLONE, and J.D. KELLY. Various treatment techniques on signs and symptoms of delayed onset muscle soreness. *J Athl Train* 31:145-152, 1996.

54. HAFF, G.G., M.J. LEHMKUHL, L.B. MCCOY, and M.H. STONE. Carbohydrate supplementation and resistance training. *J Strength Cond Res* 17:187-196, 2003.

55. HAHN, A.G. Training, recovery and overtraining—the role of the autonomic nervous system. *Sports Coach*:29-30, 1994.

56. HALSON, S.L., M.W. BRIDGE, R. MEEUSEN, B. BUSSCHAERT, M. GLEESON, D.A. JONES, and A.E. JEUKENDRUP. Time course of performance changes and fatigue markers during intensified training in trained cyclists. *J Appl Physiol* 93:947-956, 2002.

57. HALSON, S.L., and A.E. JEUKENDRUP. Does overtraining exist? An analysis of overreaching and overtraining research. *Sports Med* 34:967-981, 2004.

58. HARRIS, R.C., R.H. EDWARDS, E. HULTMAN, L.O. NORDESJO, B. NYLIND, and K. SAHLIN. The time course of phosphorylcreatine resynthesis during recovery of the quadriceps muscle in man. *Pflugers Arch* 367:137-142, 1976.

59. HAWLEY, J.A. Interaction of exercise and diet to maximise training adaptation. *Asia Pac J Clin Nutr* 14:S35, 2005.

60. HAWLEY, J.A., K.D. TIPTON, and M.L. MILLARD-STAFFORD. Promoting training adaptations through nutritional interventions. *J Sports Sci* 24:709-721, 2006.

61. HEMMINGS, B. Psychological and immunological effects of massage after sport. *Br J Ther Rehabil* 7:516-519, 2000.

62. HEMMINGS, B., M. SMITH, J. GRAYDON, and R. DYSON. Effects of massage on physiological restoration, perceived recovery, and repeated sports performance. *Br J Sports Med* 34:109-114; discussion 115, 2000.

63. HIGGINS, D., and T.W. KAMINSKI. Contrast therapy does not cause fluctuations in human gastrocnemius intramuscular temperature. *J Athl Train* 33:336-340, 1998.

64. HINGHOFER-SZALKAY, H., M.H. HARRISON, and J.E. GREENLEAF. Early fluid and protein shifts in men during water immersion. *Eur J Appl Physiol Occup Physiol* 56:673-678, 1987.

65. HIRVONEN, J., S. REHUNEN, H. RUSKO, and M. HARKONEN. Breakdown of high-energy phosphate compounds and lactate accumulation during short supramaximal exercise. *Eur J Appl Physiol* 56:253-259, 1987.

66. HOOPER, S.L., and L.T. MACKINNON. Monitoring overtraining in athletes: recommendations. *Sports Med* 20:321-327, 1995.

67. HOOPER, S.L., L.T. MACKINNON, and S. HANRAHAN. Mood states as an indication of staleness and recovery. *Int J Sport Psychol* 20:1-12, 1997.

68. HOOPER, S.L., L.T. MACKINNON, A. HOWARD, R.D. GORDON, and A.W. BACHMANN. Markers for monitoring overtraining and recovery. *Med Sci Sports Exerc* 27:106-112, 1995.

69. HOWATSON, G., and K.A. VAN SOMEREN. Ice massage: effects on exercise-induced muscle damage. *J Sports Med Phys Fitness* 43:500-505, 2003.

70. HULTMAN, E., J. BERGSTROM, and N.M. ANDERSON. Breakdown and resynthesis of phosphorylcreatine and adenosine triphosphate in connection with muscular work in man. *Scand J Clin Lab Invest* 19:56-66, 1967.

71. HULTMAN, E., and K. SAHLIN. Acid-base balance during exercise. *Exerc Sport Sci Rev* 8:41-128, 1980.

72. HULTMAN, E., and H. SJOHOLM. Biochemical causes of fatigue. In: *Human Muscle Power*. N.L. Jones, ed. Champaign, IL: Human Kinetics, 1986, pp. 343-363.

73. HUNTER, S.K., J. DUCHATEAU, and R.M. ENOKA. Muscle fatigue and the mechanisms of task failure. *Exerc Sport Sci Rev* 32:44-49, 2004.

74. IVY, J.L., A.L. KATZ, C.L. CUTLER, W.M. SHERMAN, and E.F. COYLE. Muscle glycogen synthesis after exercise: effect of time of carbohydrate ingestion. *J Appl Physiol* 64:1480-1485, 1988.

75. IVY, J.L., M.C. LEE, J.T. BROZINICK, JR., and M.J. REED. Muscle glycogen storage after different amounts of carbohydrate ingestion. *J Appl Physiol* 65:2018-2023, 1988.

76. IVY, J., and R. PORTMAN. *The Future of Sports Nutrition: Nutrient Timing*. North Bergan, NJ: Basic Health, 2004.

77. IVY, J.L., P.T. RES, R.C. SPRAGUE, and M.O. WIDZER. Effect of a carbohydrate-protein supplement on endurance performance during exercise of varying intensity. *Int J Sport Nutr Exerc Metab* 13:382-395, 2003.

78. JENTJENS, R., and A. JEUKENDRUP. Determinants of post-exercise glycogen synthesis during short-term recovery. *Sports Med* 33:117-144, 2003.

79. JOHANSEN, L.B., T.U. JENSEN, B. PUMP, and P. NORSK. Contribution of abdomen and legs to central blood volume expansion in humans during immersion. *J Appl Physiol* 83:695-699, 1997.

80. JONES, N.A., and T. FIELD. Massage and music therapies attenuate frontal EEG asymmetry in depressed adolescents. *Adolescence* 34:529-534, 1999.

81. KARLSSON, J. Lactate in working muscles after prolonged exercise. *Acta Physiol Scand* 82:123-130, 1971.

82. KENTTA, G., and P. HASSMEN. Overtraining and recovery: a conceptual model. *Sports Med* 26:1-16, 1998.

83. KHOSLA, S.S., and A.B. DUBOIS. Fluid shifts during initial phase of immersion diuresis in man. *J Appl Physiol* 46:703-708, 1979.

84. KREIDER, R.B., A.C. FRY, and M.L. O'TOOLE. *Overtraining in Sport*. Champaign, IL: Human Kinetics, 1998.

85. KUIPERS, H., and H.A. KEIZER. Overtraining in elite athletes: review and directions for the future. *Sports Med* 6:79-92, 1988.

86. KULIGOWSKI, L.A., S.M. LEPHART, F.P. GIANNAN-TONIO, and R.O. BLANC. Effect of whirlpool therapy on the signs and symptoms of delayed-onset muscle soreness. *J Athl Train* 33:222-228, 1998.

87. KURZ, T. *Science of Sports Training*. 2nd ed. Island Pond, VT: Stadion, 2001.

88. LAFORGIA, J., R.T. WITHERS, and C.J. GORE. Effects of exercise intensity and duration on the excess post-exercise oxygen consumption. *J Sports Sci* 24:1247-1264, 2006.

89. LANE, K.N., and H.A. WENGER. Effect of selected recovery conditions on performance of repeated bouts of intermittent cycling separated by 24 hours. *J Strength Cond Res* 18:855-860, 2004.

90. LANIER, A.B. Use of nonsteroidal anti-inflammatory drugs following exercise-induced muscle injury. *Sports Med* 33:177-186, 2003.

91. LAPOINTE, B.M., P. FREMONT, and C.H. COTE. Adaptation to lengthening contractions is independent of voluntary muscle recruitment but relies on inflammation. *Am J Physiol Regul Integr Comp Physiol* 282:R323-R329, 2002.

92. LEES, S.J., and J.H. WILLIAMS. Skeletal muscle sarcoplasmic reticulum glycogen status influences Ca2+ uptake supported by endogenously synthesized ATP. *Am J Physiol Cell Physiol* 286:C97-C104, 2004.

93. LEGG, S.J., and J.F. PATTON. Effects of sustained manual work and partial sleep deprivation on muscular strength and endurance. *Eur J Appl Physiol Occup Physiol* 56:64-68, 1987.

94. LEHMANN, M., C. FOSTER, and J. KEUL. Overtraining in endurance athletes: a brief review. *Med Sci Sports Exerc* 25:854-862, 1993.

95. LEHMANN, M., E. JAKOB, U. GASTMANN, J.M. STEINACKER, and J. KEUL. Unaccustomed high mileage compared to intensity training-related neuromuscular excitability in distance runners. *Eur J Appl Physiol Occup Physiol* 70:457-461, 1995.

96. LEIVADI, S., M. HERNANDEZ-REIF, T. FIELD, and E. AL. Massage therapy and relaxation effects on university dance students. *J Dance Med Sci* 3:108-112, 1999.

97. LI, J.L., X.N. WANG, S.F. FRASER, M.F. CAREY, T.V. WRIGLEY, and M.J. MCKENNA. Effects of fatigue and training on sarcoplasmic reticulum Ca(2+) regulation in human skeletal muscle. *J Appl Physiol* 92:912-922, 2002.

98. LI, T.L., and M. GLEESON. The effects of carbohydrate supplementation during the second of two prolonged cycling bouts on immunoendocrine responses. *Eur J Appl Physiol* 95:391-399, 2005.

99. LINNAMO, V., R.U. NEWTON, K. HAKKINEN, P.V. KOMI, A. DAVIE, M. MCGUIGAN, and T. TRIPLETT-MCBRIDE. Neuromuscular responses to explosive and heavy resistance loading. *J Electromyogr Kinesiol* 10:417-424, 2000.

100. LLOYD, E.L. ABC of sports medicine: temperature and performance. I: cold. *BMJ* 309:531-534, 1994.

101. LOAT, C.E., and E.C. RHODES. Jet-lag and human performance. *Sports Med* 8:226-238, 1989.

102. MACKINNON, L.T., and S.L. HOOPER. Overtraining and overreaching: causes effects and prevention. In: *Exercise and Sport Science*. W.E. Garrett and D.T. Kirkendall, eds. Philadelphia: Lippincott Williams & Wilkins, 2000, pp. 487-498.

103. MANCINELLI, C.A., D.S. DAVIS, L. ABOULHOSN, M. BRADY, J. EISENHOFER, and S. FOUTTY. The effects of massage on delayed onset muscle soreness and physical performance in female college athletes. *Phys Ther Sport* 7:5-13, 2006.

104. MARTIN, N.A., R.F. ZOELLER, R.J. ROBERTSON, and S.M. LEPHART. The comparative effects of sports massage, active recovery, and rest in promoting blood lactate clearance after supramaximal leg exercise. *J Athl Train* 33:30-35, 1998.

105. MCARDLE, W.D., F.I. KATCH, and V.L. KATCH. *Exercise Physiology: Energy, Nutrition, and Human Performance*. 6th ed. Baltimore: Lippincott Williams & Wilkins, 2007, p 1067.

106. MCMILLAN, J.L., M.H. STONE, J. SARTIN, R. KEITH, D. MARPLE, C. BROWN, and R.D. LEWIS. 20-hour physiological responses to a single weight-training session. *J Strength Cond Res* 7:9-21, 1993.

107. MEEUSEN, R., M. DUCLOS, M. GLEESON, G. RIETJENS, J.M. STEINACKER, and A. URHAUSEN. Prevention, diagnosis and treatment of overtraining syndrome. *Eur J Sport Sci* 6:1-14, 2006.

108. MIKA, A., P. MIKA, B. FERNHALL, and V.B. UNNI-THAN. Comparison of recovery strategies on muscle performance after fatiguing exercise. *Am J Phys Med Rehabil* 86:474-481, 2007.

109. MILLER, S.L., K.D. TIPTON, D.L. CHINKES, S.E. WOLF, and R.R. WOLFE. Independent and combined effects of amino acids and glucose after resistance exercise. *Med Sci Sports Exerc* 35:449-455, 2003.

110. MONEDERO, J., and B. DONNE. Effect of recovery interventions on lactate removal and subsequent performance. *Int J Sports Med* 21:593-597, 2000.

111. MOUGIN, F., D. DAVENNE, M.L. SIMON-RIGAUD, A. RENAUD, A. GARNIER, and P. MAGNIN. Disturbance of sports performance after partial sleep deprivation. *CR Seances Soc Biol Fil* 183:461-466, 1989.

112. MYRER, J.W., D.O. DRAPER, and E. DURRANT. Contrast therapy and intramuscular temperature in the human leg. *J Athl Train* 29:318-322, 1994.

113. NAKAMURA, K., H. TAKAHASHI, S. SHIMAI, and M. TANAKA. Effects of immersion in tepid bath water on recovery from fatigue after submaximal exercise in man. *Ergonomics* 39:257-266, 1996.

114. NIEMAN, D.C. *Exercise Testing and Prescription: A Health Related Approach.* 4th ed. Mountain View, CA: Mayfield, 1999, p. 708.

115. PADDON-JONES, D.J., and B.M. QUIGLEY. Effect of cryotherapy on muscle soreness and strength following eccentric exercise. *Int J Sports Med* 18:588-593, 1997.

116. PARKIN, J.A., M.F. CAREY, I.K. MARTIN, L. STOJANOVSKA, and M.A. FEBBRAIO. Muscle glycogen storage following prolonged exercise: effect of timing of ingestion of high glycemic index food. *Med Sci Sports Exerc* 29:220-224, 1997.

117. PICHOT, V., F. ROCHE, J.M. GASPOZ, F. ENJOLRAS, A. ANTONIADIS, P. MININI, F. COSTES, T. BUSSO, J.R. LACOUR, and J.C. BARTHELEMY. Relation between heart rate variability and training load in middle-distance runners. *Med Sci Sports Exerc* 32:1729-1736, 2000.

118. PLYLEY, M.J., R.J. SHEPHARD, G.M. DAVIS, and R.C. GOODE. Sleep deprivation and cardiorespiratory function: influence of intermittent submaximal exercise. *Eur J Appl Physiol Occup Physiol* 56:338-344, 1987.

119. PRENTICE, W.E. *Therapeutic Modalities for Physical Therapists.* 2nd ed. New York: McGraw-Hill, 2002.

120. PRENTICE, W.E. *Therapeutic Modalities in Sports Medicine.* 4th ed. Boston: WCB/McGraw-Hill, 1999.

121. RAGLIN, J.S., and W.P. MORGAN. Development of a scale for use in monitoring training-induced distress in athletes. *Int J Sports Med* 15:84-88, 1994.

122. RASMUSSEN, B.B., K.D. TIPTON, S.L. MILLER, S.E. WOLF, and R.R. WOLFE. An oral essential amino acid-carbohydrate supplement enhances muscle protein anabolism after resistance exercise. *J Appl Physiol* 88:386-392, 2000.

123. REILLY, T., and G.A. BROOKS. Exercise and the circadian variation in body temperature measures. *Int J Sports Med* 7:358-362, 1986.

124. REILLY, T., N.T. CABLE, and C.N. DOWZER. The efficacy of deep-water running. In: *Contemporary Ergonomics.* P.T. McCabe, ed. London: Taylor & Francis, 2002, pp. 162-166.

125. REILLY, T., and B. EDWARDS. Altered sleep-wake cycles and physical performance in athletes. *Physiol Behav* 90:274-284, 2007.

126. REILLY, T., and B. EKBLOM. The use of recovery methods post-exercise. *J Sports Sci* 23:619-627, 2005.

127. REILLY, T., and M. PIERCY. The effect of partial sleep deprivation on weight-lifting performance. *Ergonomics* 37:107-115, 1994.

128. REILLY, T., and M. RIGBY. Effect of an active warm-down following competitive soccer. In: *Science and Football IV.* W. Spinks, T. Reilly, and A. Murphy, eds. London: Routledge, 2002, pp. 226-229.

129. REILLY, T., J. WATERHOUSE, and B. EDWARDS. Jet lag and air travel: implications for performance. *Clin Sports Med* 24:367-380, xii, 2005.

130. REXILIUS, S.J., C. MUNDT, M. ERICKSON MEGEL, and S. AGRAWAL. Therapeutic effects of massage therapy and handling touch on caregivers of patients undergoing autologous hematopoietic stem cell transplant. *Oncol Nurs Forum* 29:E35-E44, 2002.

131. ROTH, S.M., G.F. MARTEL, F.M. IVEY, J.T. LEMMER, E.J. METTER, B.F. HURLEY, and M.A. ROGERS. High-volume, heavy-resistance strength training and muscle damage in young and older women. *J Appl Physiol* 88:1112-1118, 2000.

132. ROWBOTTOM, D.G. Periodization of training. In: *Exercise and Sport Science.* W.E. Garrett and D.T. Kirkendall, eds. Philadelphia: Lippincott Williams & Wilkins, 2000, pp. 499-512.

133. ROWLAND, T.W. Developmental aspects of physiological function relating to aerobic exercise in children. *Sports Med* 10:255-266, 1990.

134. ROY, B.D., M.A. TARNOPOLSKY, J.D. MACDOUGALL, J. FOWLES, and K.E. YARASHESKI. Effect of glucose supplement timing on protein metabolism after resistance training. *J Appl Physiol* 82:1882-1888, 1997.

135. RUTKOVE, S.B. Effects of temperature on neuromuscular electrophysiology. *Muscle Nerve* 24:867-882, 2001.

136. SANDS, W.A. Monitoring elite female gymnasts. *Natl Strength Cond Assoc* 13:66-71, 1991.

137. SCHNIEPP, J., T.S. CAMPBELL, K.L. POWELL, and D.M. PINCIVERO. The effects of cold-water immersion on power output and heart rate in elite cyclists. *J Strength Cond Res* 16:561-566, 2002.

138. SCOON, G.S., W.G. HOPKINS, S. MAYHEW, and J.D. COTTER. Effect of post-exercise sauna bathing on the endurance performance of competitive male runners. *J Sci Med Sport* 10:259-262, 2007.

139. SHIRAISHI, M., M. SCHOU, M. GYBEL, N.J. CHRISTENSEN, and P. NORSK. Comparison of acute cardiovascular responses to water immersion and head-down tilt in humans. *J Appl Physiol* 92:264-268, 2002.

140. SIFF, M.C., and Y.U. VERKHOSHANSKY. *Supertraining.* Denver, CO: Supertraining International, 1999.

141. SKURVYDAS, A., V. DUDONIENE, A. KALVENAS, and A. ZUOZA. Skeletal muscle fatigue in long-distance runners, sprinters and untrained men after repeated drop jumps performed at maximal intensity. *Scand J Med Sci Sports* 12:34-39, 2002.

142. SNYDER, A.C. Overtraining and glycogen depletion hypothesis. *Med Sci Sports Exerc* 30:1146-1150, 1998.

143. SNYDER, A.C., H. KUIPERS, B. CHENG, R. SERVAIS, and E. FRANSEN. Overtraining following intensified training with normal muscle glycogen. *Med Sci Sports Exerc* 27:1063-1070, 1995.

144. SOLTOW, Q.A., J.L. BETTERS, J.E. SELLMAN, V.A. LIRA, J.H. LONG, and D.S. CRISWELL. Ibuprofen inhibits skeletal muscle hypertrophy in rats. *Med Sci Sports Exerc* 38:840-846, 2006.

145. SOUISSI, N., B. SESBOUE, A. GAUTHIER, J. LARUE, and D. DAVENNE. Effects of one night's sleep deprivation on anaerobic performance the following day. *Eur J Appl Physiol* 89:359-366, 2003.

146. SPENCER, M., D. BISHOP, B. DAWSON, C. GOODMAN, and R. DUFFIELD. Metabolism and performance in repeated cycle sprints: active versus passive recovery. *Med Sci Sports Exerc* 38:1492-1499, 2006.

147. STACKHOUSE, S.K., D.S. REISMAN, and S.A. BINDER-MACLEOD. Challenging the role of pH in skeletal muscle fatigue. *Phys Ther* 81:1897-1903, 2001.

148. STONE, M.H., and A.C. FRY. Increased training volume in strength/power athletes. In: *Overtraining in Sport.* R.B. Kreider, A.C. Fry, and M.L. O'Toole, eds. Champaign, IL: Human Kinetics, 1998, pp. 87-106.

149. STONE, M.H., R. KEITH, J.T. KEARNEY, G.D. WILSON, and S. FLECK, J. Overtraining: a review of the signs and symptoms of overtraining. *J Appl Sport Sci Res* 5:35-50, 1991.

150. STONE, M.H., H.S. O'BRYANT, L. MCCOY, R. COGLIANESE, M. LEHMKUHL, and B. SCHILLING. Power and maximum strength relationships during performance of dynamic and static weighted jumps. *J Strength Cond Res* 17:140-147, 2003.

151. STONE, M.H., M.E. STONE, and W.A. SANDS. *Principles and Practice of Resistance Training.* Champaign, IL: Human Kinetics, 2007.

152. TAOUTAOU, Z., P. GRANIER, B. MERCIER, J. MERCIER, S. AHMAIDI, and C. PREFAUT. Lactate kinetics during passive and partially active recovery in endurance and sprint athletes. *Eur J Appl Physiol Occup Physiol* 73:465-470, 1996.

153. THYFAULT, J.P., M.J. CARPER, S.R. RICHMOND, M.W. HULVER, and J.A. POTTEIGER. Effects of liquid carbohydrate ingestion on markers of anabolism following high-intensity resistance exercise. *J Strength Cond Res* 18:174-179, 2004.

154. TIETZEL, A.J., and L.C. LACK. The recuperative value of brief and ultra-brief naps on alertness and cognitive performance. *J Sleep Res* 11:213-218, 2002.

155. TIKUISIS, P., I. JACOBS, D. MOROZ, A.L. VALLERAND, and L. MARTINEAU. Comparison of thermoregulatory responses between men and women immersed in cold water. *J Appl Physiol* 89:1403-1411, 2000.

156. TOMASIK, M. Effect of hydromassage on changes in blood electrolyte and lactic acid levels and haematocrit value after maximal effort. *Acta Physiol Pol* 34:257-261, 1983.

157. TONER, M.M., M.N. SAWKA, M.E. FOLEY, and K.B. PANDOLF. Effects of body mass and morphology on thermal responses in water. *J Appl Physiol* 60:521-525, 1986.

158. TRAPPE, T.A., F. WHITE, C.P. LAMBERT, D. CESAR, M. HELLERSTEIN, and W.J. EVANS. Effect of ibuprofen and acetaminophen on postexercise muscle protein synthesis. *Am J Physiol Endocrinol Metab* 282:E551-E556, 2002.

159. VAILE, J.M., N.D. GILL, and A.J. BLAZEVICH. The effect of contrast water therapy on symptoms of delayed onset muscle soreness. *J Strength Cond Res* 21:697-702, 2007.

160. VAN LOON, L.J., M. KRUIJSHOOP, H. VERHAGEN, W.H. SARIS, and A.J. WAGENMAKERS. Ingestion of protein hydrolysate and amino acid-carbohydrate mixtures increases postexercise plasma insulin responses in men. *J Nutr* 130:2508-2513, 2000.

161. VAN LOON, L.J., W.H. SARIS, M. KRUIJSHOOP, and A.J. WAGENMAKERS. Maximizing postexercise muscle glycogen synthesis: carbohydrate supplementation and the application of amino acid or protein hydrolysate mixtures. *Am J Clin Nutr* 72:106-111, 2000.

162. VERKHOSHANSKY, Y.U. *Programming and Organization of Training.* Moscow: Fizkultura i Sport, 1985.

163. VIITASALO, J.T., K. NIEMELA, R. KAAPPOLA, T. KORJUS, M. LEVOLA, H.V. MONONEN, H.K. RUSKO, and T.E. TAKALA. Warm underwater water-jet massage improves recovery from intense physical exercise. *Eur J Appl Physiol Occup Physiol* 71:431-438, 1995.

164. VOLLESTAD, N.K., I. TABATA, and J.I. MEDBO. Glycogen breakdown in different human muscle fibre types during exhaustive exercise of short duration. *Acta Physiol Scand* 144:135-141, 1992.

165. WARDEN, S.J. Cyclo-oxygenase-2 inhibitors: beneficial or detrimental for athletes with acute musculoskeletal injuries? *Sports Med* 35:271-283, 2005.

166. WATERHOUSE, J., T. REILLY, G. ATKINSON, and B. EDWARDS. Jet lag: trends and coping strategies. *Lancet* 369:1117-1129, 2007.

167. WATERHOUSE, J., T. REILLY, and B. EDWARDS. The stress of travel. *J Sports Sci* 22:946-965; discussion 965-946, 2004.

168. WATTS, P.B., M. DAGGETT, P. GALLAGHER, and B. WILKINS. Metabolic response during sport rock climbing and the effects of active versus passive recovery. *Int J Sports Med* 21:185-190, 2000.

169. WEERAPONG, P., P.A. HUME, and G.S. KOLT. The mechanisms of massage and effects on performance, muscle recovery and injury prevention. *Sports Med* 35:235-256, 2005.

170. WEINBER, R., A. JACKSON, and K. KOLODNY. The relationship of massage and exercise to mood enhancement. *Sport Psychol* 2:202-211, 1988.

171. WESTERBLAD, H., D.G. ALLEN, and J. LANNERGREN. Muscle fatigue: lactic acid or inorganic

phosphate the major cause? *News Physiol Sci* 17:17-21, 2002.

172. WESTON, C.F., J.P. O'HARE, J.M. EVANS, and R.J. CORRALL. Haemodynamic changes in man during immersion in water at different temperatures. *Clin Sci (Lond)* 73:613-616, 1987.

173. WHITNEY, J.D., and M.M. WICKLINE. Treating chronic and acute wounds with warming: Review of the science and practice implications. *J Wound Ostomy Continence Nurs* 30:199-209, 2003.

174. WILCOCK, I.M., J.B. CRONIN, and W.A. HING. Physiological response to water immersion: a method for sport recovery? *Sports Med* 36:747-765, 2006.

175. WILCOCK, I.M., J.B. CRONIN, and W.A. HING. Water immersion: does it enhance recovery from exercise? *Int J Sports Physiol Perf* 1:195-206, 2006.

176. YAMANE, M., H. TERUYA, M. NAKANO, R. OGAI, N. OHNISHI, and M. KOSAKA. Post-exercise leg and forearm flexor muscle cooling in humans attenuates endurance and resistance training effects on muscle performance and on circulatory adaptation. *Eur J Appl Physiol* 96:572-580, 2006.

177. YANAGISAWA, O., Y. MIYANAGA, H. SHIRAKI, H. SHIMOJO, N. MUKAI, M. NIITSU, and Y. ITAI. The effects of various therapeutic measures on shoulder strength and muscle soreness after baseball pitching. *J Sports Med Phys Fitness* 43:189-201, 2003.

178. YONA, M. Effects of cold stimulation of human skin on motor unit activity. *Jpn J Physiol* 47:341-348, 1997.

179. ZAINUDDIN, Z., M. NEWTON, P. SACCO, and K. NOSAKA. Effects of massage on delayed-onset muscle soreness, swelling, and recovery of muscle function. *J Athl Train* 40:174-180, 2005.

180. ZALESSKY, M. Pedagogical, physiological, and psychological means of restoration. *Legkaya Atletika* 7:20-22, 1979.

181. ZATSIORSKY, V.M., and W.J. KRAEMER. *Science and Practice of Strength Training*. 2nd ed. Champaign, IL: Human Kinetics, 2006.

182. ZEITLIN, D., S.E. KELLER, S.C. SHIFLETT, S.J. SCHLEIFER, and J.A. BARTLETT. Immunological effects of massage therapy during academic stress. *Psychosom Med* 62:83-84, 2000.

183. ZEMKE, J.E., J.C. ANDERSEN, W.K. GUION, J. MCMILLAN, and A.B. JOYNER. Intramuscular temperature responses in the human leg to two forms of cryotherapy: ice massage and ice bag. *J Orthop Sports Phys Ther* 27:301-307, 1998.

Chapter 6

1. ANDERSEN, L.L., J.L. ANDERSEN, S.P. MAGNUSSON, C. SUETTA, J.L. MADSEN, L.R. CHRISTENSEN, and P. AAGAARD. Changes in the human muscle force-velocity relationship in response to resistance training and subsequent detraining. *J Appl Physiol* 99:87-94, 2005.

2. BOMPA, T.O. *Periodization: Theory and Methodology of Training*. 4th ed. Champaign, IL: Human Kinetics, 1999.

3. BOMPA, T.O. *Theory and Methodology of Training: The Key to Athletic Performance*. Dubuque, IA: Kendall/Hunt, 1994.

4. BOMPA, T.O. *Total Trainng for Coaching Team Sports: A Self Help Guide*. Toronto, CA: Sports Books Publisher, 2006.

5. BOMPA, T.O., and M.C. CARRERA. *Periodization Training For Sports: Science-Based Strength and Conditioning Plans for 20 Sports*. 2nd ed. Champaign, IL: Human Kinetics, 2005.

5. BONDERCHUK, A. Periodization of sports training. *Legkaya Atletika* 12:8-9, 1986.

6. BONDARCHUK, A.P. *Track and Field Training*. Kiev: Zdotovye, 1986.

8. BOSQUET, L., L. LEGER, and P. LEGROS. Methods to determine aerobic endurance. *Sports Med* 32:675-700, 2002.

9. COYLE, E.F., W.H. MARTIN, III, D.R. SINACORE, M.J. JOYNER, J.M. HAGBERG, and J.O. HOLLOSZY. Time course of loss of adaptations after stopping prolonged intense endurance training. *J Appl Physiol* 57:1857-1864, 1984.

10. DICK, F.W. *Sports Training Principles*. 4th ed. London: A & C Black, 2002.

11. DUNLAVY, J.K., W.A. SANDS, J.R. MCNEAL, M.H. STONE, S.A. SMITH, M. JEMNI, and G.G. HAFF. Strength performance assessment in a simulated men's gymnastics still rings cross. *J Sports Sci Med* 6:93-97, 2007.

12. FARROW, D., W. YOUNG, and L. BRUCE. The development of a test of reactive agility for netball: a new methodology. *J Sci Med Sport* 8:52-60, 2005.

13. FLECK, S.J., and W.J. KRAEMER. *Designing Resistance Training Programs*. 2nd ed. Champaign, IL: Human Kinetics, 1997.

14. FLECK, S., and W.J. KRAEMER. *Designing Resistance Training Programs*. 3rd ed. Champaign, IL: Human Kinetics, 2004.

15. FREEMAN, W.H. *Peak When It Counts: Periodization for American Track & Field*. 4th ed. Mountain View, CA: Tafnews Press, 2001.

16. FRY, A.C. The role of training intensity in resistance exercise overtraining and overreaching. In: *Overtraining in Sport*. R.B. Kreider, A.C. Fry, and M.L. O'Toole, eds. Champaign, IL: Human Kinetics, 1998. pp. 107-127.

17. FRY, R.W., A.R. MORTON, and D. KEAST. Overtraining in athletes: an update. *Sports Med* 12:32-65, 1991.

18. GABBETT, T.J. Skill-based conditioning games as an alternative to traditional conditioning for rugby league players. *J Strength Cond Res* 20:309-315, 2006.

19. GABBETT, T.J., J.N. KELLY, and J.M. SHEPPARD. Speed, change of direction speed, and reactive agility of rugby league players. *J Strength Cond Res* 22:174-181, 2008.

20. HAFF, G.G., J.M. CARLOCK, M.J. HARTMAN, J.L. KILGORE, N. KAWAMORI, J.R. JACKSON, R.T. MORRIS, W.A. SANDS, and M.H. STONE. Force-time curve characteristics of dynamic and isometric

muscle actions of elite women Olympic weightlifters. *J Strength Cond Res* 19:741-748, 2005.

21. HAFF, G.G., J.R. JACKSON, N. KAWAMORI, J.M. CARLOCK, M.J. HARTMAN, J.L. KILGORE, R.T. MORRIS, M.W. RAMSEY, W.A. SANDS, and M.H. STONE. Force-time curve characteristics and hormonal alterations during an eleven-week training period in elite women weightlifters. *J Strength Cond Res* 22:433-446, 2008.

22. HÄKKINEN, K., M. ALEN, and P.V. KOMI. Changes in isometric force- and relaxation-time, electromyographic and muscle fibre characteristics of human skeletal muscle during strength training and detraining. *Acta Physiol Scand* 125:573-585, 1985.

23. HÄKKINEN, K., and P.V. KOMI. Electromyographic changes during strength training and detraining. *Med Sci Sports Exerc* 15:455-460, 1983.

24. HÄKKINEN, K., P.V. KOMI, and P.A. TESCH. Effect of combined concentric and eccentric strength training and detraining on force-time, muscle fiber and metabolic characteristics of leg extensor muscles. *Scand J Sports Sci* 3:50-58, 1981.

25. HARMAN, E., and C. PANDORF. Principles of test selection and administration. In: *Essentials of Strength Training and Conditioning*. T.R. Baechle and R.W. Earle, eds. Champaign, IL: Human Kinetics, 2000, pp. 275-286.

26. HOFF, J., and J. HELGERUD. Endurance and strength training for soccer players: physiological considerations. *Sports Med* 34:165-180, 2004.

27. HOFF, J., U. WISLØFF, L.C. ENGEN, O.J. KEMI, and J. HELGERUD. Soccer specific aerobic endurance training. *Br J Sports Med* 36:218-221, 2002.

28. HORI, N., R.U. NEWTON, W.A. ANDREWS, N. KAWAMORI, M.R. MCGUIGAN, and K. NOSAKA. Does performance of hang power clean differentiate performance of jumping, sprinting, and changing of direction? *J Strength Cond Res* 22:412-418, 2008.

29. HORTOBAGYI, T., J.A. HOUMARD, J.R. STEVENSON, D.D. FRASER, R.A. JOHNS, and R.G. ISRAEL. The effects of detraining on power athletes. *Med Sci Sports Exerc* 25:929-935, 1993.

30. HOUMARD, J.A., T. HORTOBAGYI, R.A. JOHNS, N.J. BRUNO, C.C. NUTE, M.H. SHINEBARGER, and J.W. WELBORN. Effect of short-term training cessation on performance measures in distance runners. *Int J Sports Med* 13:572-576, 1992.

31. HOUMARD, J.A., and R.A. JOHNS. Effects of taper on swim performance: practical implications. *Sports Med* 17:224-232, 1994.

32. IZQUIERDO, M., J. IBANEZ, J.J. GONZALEZ-BADILLO, N.A. RATAMESS, W.J. KRAEMER, K. HÄKKINEN, H. BONNABAU, C. GRANADOS, D.N. FRENCH, and E.M. GOROSTIAGA. Detraining and tapering effects on hormonal responses and strength performance. *J Strength Cond Res* 21:768-775, 2007.

33. KAWAMORI, N., S.J. ROSSI, B.D. JUSTICE, E.E. HAFF, E.E. PISTILLI, H.S. O'BRYANT, M.H. STONE, and G.G. HAFF. Peak force and rate of force development during isometric and dynamic mid-thigh clean pulls performed at various intensities. *J Strength Cond Res* 20:483-491, 2006.

34. KRAEMER, W.J., D.N. FRENCH, N.J. PAXTON, K. HÄKKINEN, J.S. VOLEK, W.J. SEBASTIANELLI, M. PUTUKIAN, R.U. NEWTON, M.R. RUBIN, A.L. GOMEZ, J.D. VESCOVI, N.A. RATAMESS, S.J. FLECK, J.M. LYNCH, and H.G. KNUTTGEN. Changes in exercise performance and hormonal concentrations over a big ten soccer season in starters and nonstarters. *J Strength Cond Res* 18:121-128, 2004.

35. KRAEMER, W.J., L.P. KOZIRIS, N.A. RATAMESS, K. HÄKKINEN, T.R.-M. NT, A.C. FRY, S.E. GORDON, J.S. VOLEK, D.N. FRENCH, M.R. RUBIN, A.L. GOMEZ, M.J. SHARMAN, J. MICHAEL LYNCH, M. IZQUIERDO, R.U. NEWTON, and S.J. FLECK. Detraining produces minimal changes in physical performance and hormonal variables in recreationally strength-trained men. *J Strength Cond Res* 16:373-382, 2002.

36. KRAEMER, W.J., J.S. VOLEK, J.A. BUSH, M. PUTUKIAN, and W.J. SEBASTIANELLI. Hormonal responses to consecutive days of heavy-resistance exercise with or without nutritional supplementation. *J Appl Physiol* 85:1544-1555, 1998.

37. KUBUKELI, Z.N., T.D. NOAKES, and S.C. DENNIS. Training techniques to improve endurance exercise performances. *Sports Med* 32:489-509, 2002.

38. KUIPERS, H., and H.A. KEIZER. Overtraining in elite athletes: review and directions for the future. *Sports Med* 6:79-92, 1988.

39. KURZ, T. *Science of Sports Training*. 2nd ed. Island Pond, VT: Stadion, 2001.

40. LAURSEN, P.B., and D.G. JENKINS. The scientific basis for high-intensity interval training: optimising training programmes and maximising performance in highly trained endurance athletes. *Sports Med* 32:53-73, 2002.

41. MALLO, J., and E. NAVARRO. Physical load imposed on soccer players during small-sided training games. *J Sports Med Phys Fitness* 48:166-171, 2008.

42. MATVEYEV, L.P. *Fundamentals of Sports Training*. Moscow: Fizkultua i Sport, 1977.

43. MATVEYEV, L.P. *Periodisterung Des Sportlichen Trainings*. Moscow: Fizkultura i Sport, 1972.

44. MATVEYEV, L. *Periodization of Sports Training*. Moscow: Fizkultura i Sport, 1965.

45. MAUGHAN, R. Physiology of sport. *Br J Hosp Med (Lond)* 68:376-379, 2007.

46. MAUGHAN, R., and M. GLEESON. *The Biochemical Basis of Sports Performance*. New York: Oxford University Press, 2004.

47. MIKKOLA, J., H. RUSKO, A. NUMMELA, T. POLLARI, and K. HÄKKINEN. Concurrent endurance and explosive type strength training improves neuromuscular and anaerobic characteristics in young distance runners. *Int J Sports Med* 28:602-611, 2007.

48. MUJIKA, I., A. GOYA, E. RUIZ, A. GRIJALBA, J. SANTISTEBAN, and S. PADILLA. Physiological and

performance responses to a 6-day taper in middle-distance runners: influence of training frequency. *Int J Sports Med* 23:367-373, 2002.

49. MUJIKA, I., and S. PADILLA. Detraining: loss of training-induced physiological and performance adaptations: part I: short term insufficient training stimulus. *Sports Med* 30:79-87, 2000.

50. MUJIKA, I., and S. PADILLA. Detraining: loss of training-induced physiological and performance adaptations: part II: Long term insufficient training stimulus. *Sports Med* 30:145-154, 2000.

51. MUJIKA, I., and S. PADILLA. Muscular characteristics of detraining in humans. *Med Sci Sports Exerc* 33:1297-1303, 2001.

52. NÁDORI, L. *Training and Competition.* Budapest: Sport, 1962.

53. NÁDORI, L., and I. GRANEK. *Theoretical and Methodological Basis of Training Planning With Special Considerations Within a Microcycle.* Lincoln, NE: NSCA, 1989.

54. NEUMAIR, A. The faculty of sports sciences: a multidisciplinary approach to sports. *Eur J Sport Sci* 3:1-3, 2003.

55. OZOLIN, N. *Sovremennaia Systema Sportivnoi Trenirovky* [Athlete's Training System for Competition]. Moscow: Fizkultura i Sport, 1971.

56. PAAVOLAINEN, L., K. HÄKKINEN, I. HAMALAINEN, A. NUMMELA, and H. RUSKO. Explosive-strength training improves 5-km running time by improving running economy and muscle power. *J Appl Physiol* 86:1527-1533, 1999.

57. PLISK, S.S., and V. GAMBETTA. Tactical metabolic training: part 1. *Strength Cond* 19:44-53, 1997.

58. PLISK, S.S., and M.H. STONE. Periodization strategies. *Strength Cond* 25:19-37, 2003.

59. REILLY, T., B. DRUST, and N. CLARKE. Muscle fatigue during football match-play. *Sports Med* 38:357-367, 2008.

60. SANNA, G., and K.M. O'CONNOR. Fatigue-related changes in stance leg mechanics during sidestep cutting maneuvers. *Clin Biomech (Bristol, Avon)* 23:946:954, 2008.

61. SHEPPARD, J.M., W.B. YOUNG, T.L. DOYLE, T.A. SHEPPARD, and R.U. NEWTON. An evaluation of a new test of reactive agility and its relationship to sprint speed and change of direction speed. *J Sci Med Sport* 9:342-349, 2006.

62. SIEGLER, J., S. GASKILL, and B. RUBY. Changes evaluated in soccer-specific power endurance either with or without a 10-week, in-season, intermittent, high-intensity training protocol. *J Strength Cond Res* 17:379-387, 2003.

63. SIFF, M.C. *Supertraining.* 6th ed. Denver, CO: Supertraining Institute, 2003.

64. SIFF, M.C., and Y.U. VERKHOSHANSKY. *Supertraining.* Denver, CO: Supertraining International, 1999.

65. SILVESTRE, R., W.J. KRAEMER, C. WEST, D.A. JUDELSON, B.A. SPIERING, J.L. VINGREN, D.L. HATFIELD, J.M. ANDERSON, and C.M. MARESH. Body composition and physical performance during a National Collegiate Athletic Association Division I men's soccer season. *J Strength Cond Res* 20:962-970, 2006.

66. SMITH, D.J., S.R. NORRIS, and J.M. HOGG. Performance evaluation of swimmers: scientific tools. *Sports Med* 32:539-554, 2002.

67. STARON, R.S., M.J. LEONARDI, D.L. KARAPONDO, E.S. MALICKY, J.E. FALKEL, F.C. HAGERMAN, and R.S. HIKIDA. Strength and skeletal muscle adaptations in heavy-resistance-trained women after detraining and retraining. *J Appl Physiol* 70:631-640, 1991.

68. STONE, M.H., and C. KARATZEFERI. Connective tissue and bone response to strength training. In: *Encyclopaedia of Sports Medicine: Strength and Power in Sports.* P.V. Komi, ed. Oxford, UK: Blackwell, 2003. pp. 343-360.

69. STONE, M.H., R. KEITH, J.T. KEARNEY, G.D. WILSON, and S. FLECK, J. Overtraining: a review of the signs and symptoms of overtraining. *J Appl Sport Sci Res* 5:35-50, 1991.

70. STONE, M.H., and H.S. O'BRYANT. Letter to the editor. *J Strength Cond Res* 9:125-127, 1995.

71. STONE, M.H., and H.O. O'BRYANT. *Weight Training: A Scientific Approach.* Edina, MN: Burgess, 1987.

72. STONE, M.H., H. O'BRYANT, and J. GARHAMMER. A hypothetical model for strength training. *J. Sports Med.* 21:342-351, 1981.

73. STONE, M.H., H.S. O'BRYANT, and J. GARHAMMER. A theoretical model of strength training. *NSCA J.* 3:36-39, 1982.

74. STONE, M.H., H.S. O'BRYANT, L. MCCOY, R. COGLIANESE, M. LEHMKUHL, and B. SCHILLING. Power and maximum strength relationships during performance of dynamic and static weighted jumps. *J Strength Cond Res* 17:140-147, 2003.

75. STONE, M.H., K. SANBORN, H.S. O'BRYANT, M. HARTMAN, M.E. STONE, C. PROULX, B. WARD, and J. HRUBY. Maximum strength-power-performance relationships in collegiate throwers. *J Strength Cond Res* 17:739-745, 2003.

76. STONE, M.H., W.A. SANDS, J. CARLOCK, S. CALLAN, D. DICKIE, K. DAIGLE, J. COTTON, S.L. SMITH, and M. HARTMAN. The importance of isometric maximum strength and peak rate-of-force development in sprint cycling. *J Strength Cond Res* 18:878-884, 2004.

77. STONE, M.H., W.A. SANDS, K.C. PIERCE, J. CARLOCK, M. CARDINALE, and R.U. NEWTON. Relationship of maximum strength to weightlifting performance. *Med Sci Sports Exerc* 37:1037-1043, 2005.

78. STONE, M.H., W.A. SANDS, K.C. PIERCE, R.U. NEWTON, G.G. HAFF, and J. CARLOCK. Maximum strength and strength training: a relationship to endurance? *Strength Cond J* 28:44-53, 2006.

79. STONE, M.H., M.E. STONE, and W.A. SANDS. *Principles and Practice of Resistance Training.* Champaign, IL: Human Kinetics, 2007.

80. TANAKA, H., and T. SWENSEN. Impact of resistance training on endurance performance: a new form of cross-training? *Sports Med* 25:191-200, 1998.

81. TSCHIENE, P. Finally a theory of training to overcome doping. In *Second IAAF World Symposium on Doping in Sport.* Monte Carlo, 1989.

82. VERKHOSHANSKY, Y.U. *Fundamentals of Special Strength Training in Sport.* Livonia, MI: Sportivy Press, 1986.

83. VERKHOSHANSKY, Y.U. Perspectives in the development of speed-strength preparation in the development of jumpers. *Track and Field* 9:11-12, 1966.

84. VERKHOSHANSKY, Y.U. *Programming and Organization of Training.* Moscow: Fizkultura i Sport, 1985.

85. VERKHOSHANSKY, Y.U. *Special Strength Training: A Practical Manual for Coaches.* Muskegon, MI: Ultimate Athlete Concepts, 2006.

86. VIRU, A. *Adaptations in Sports Training.* Boca Raton, FL: CRC Press, 1995.

87. VIVES, D., and J. ROBERTS. Quickness and reaction-time training. In: *Training for Speed, Agility, and Quickness.* L.E. Brown and V.A. Ferrigno, eds. Champaign, IL: Human Kinetics, 2005, pp. 137-222.

88. WESTGARTH-TAYLOR, C., J.A. HAWLEY, S. RICKARD, K.H. MYBURGH, T.D. NOAKES, and S.C. DENNIS. Metabolic and performance adaptations to interval training in endurance- trained cyclists. *Eur J Appl Physiol* 75:298-304, 1997.

89. WILLIAMS, S.J., and L.R. KENDALL. A profile of sports science research (1983-2003). *J Sci Med Sport* 10:193-200, 2007.

90. YOUNG, W.B., R. JAMES, and I. MONTGOMERY. Is muscle power related to running speed with changes of direction? *J Sports Med Phys Fitness* 42:282-288, 2002.

91. YOUNG, W.B., M.H. MCDOWELL, and B.J. SCARLETT. Specificity of sprint and agility training methods. *J Strength Cond Res* 15:315-319, 2001.

92. ZATSIORSKY, V.M., and W.J. KRAEMER. *Science and Practice of Strength Training.* 2nd ed. Champaign, IL: Human Kinetics, 2006.

Chapter 7

1. AJÁN, T., and L. BAROGA. *Weightlifting: Fitness for All Sports.* Budapest: International Weightlifting Federation, 1988.

2. BANISTER, E.W., J.B. CARTER, and P.C. ZARKADAS. Training theory and taper: validation in triathlon athletes. *Eur J Appl Physiol Occup Physiol* 79:182-191, 1999.

3. BOMPA, T.O. *Theory and Methodology of Training: The Key to Athletic Performance.* Dubuque, IA: Kendall/Hunt, 1994.

4. BOSQUET, L., L. LEGER, and P. LEGROS. Methods to determine aerobic endurance. *Sports Med* 32:675-700, 2002.

5. BUSSO, T. Variable dose-response relationship between exercise training and performance. *Med Sci Sports Exerc* 35:1188-1195, 2003.

6. BUSSO, T., K. HÄKKINEN, A. PAKARINEN, H. KAUHANEN, P.V. KOMI, and J.R. LACOUR. Hormonal adaptations and modeled responses in elite weightlifters during 6 weeks of training. *Eur J Appl Physiol* 64:381-386, 1992.

7. COUTTS, A., P. REABURN, T.J. PIVA, and A. MURPHY. Changes in selected biochemical, muscular strength, power, and endurance measures during deliberate overreaching and tapering in rugby league players. *Int J Sports Med* 28:116-124, 2007.

8. DICK, F.W. *Sports Training Principles.* 4th ed. London: A & C Black, 2002.

9. DRABIK, J. *Children and Sports Training.* Island Pond, VT: Stadion, 1995.

10. FLYNN, M.G., F.X. PIZZA, J.B. BOONE, JR., F.F. ANDRES, T.A. MICHAUD, and J.R. RODRIGUEZ-ZAYAS. Indices of training stress during competitive running and swimming seasons. *Int J Sports Med* 15:21-26, 1994.

11. GIBALA, M.J., J.D. MACDOUGALL, and D.G. SALE. The effects of tapering on strength performance in trained athletes. *Int J Sports Med* 15:492-497, 1994.

12. GJURKOW, D. Annual competition and training program for senior weightlifters. In: *Proceedings of the Weightlifting Symposium: Ancient Olympia/Greece 1993.* Á. Lukácsfalvi and F. Takács, eds. Budapest: International Weightlifting Federation, 1993, pp. 103-115.

13. GRAVES, J.E., M.L. POLLOCK, D. FOSTER, S.H. LEGGETT, D.M. CARPENTER, R. VUOSO, and A. JONES. Effect of training frequency and specificity on isometric lumbar extension strength. *Spine* 15:504-509, 1990.

14. GRAVES, J.E., M.L. POLLOCK, S.H. LEGGETT, R.W. BRAITH, D.M. CARPENTER, and L.E. BISHOP. Effect of reduced training frequency on muscular strength. *Int J Sports Med* 9:316-319, 1988.

15. HARRE, D. *Trainingslehre.* Berlin, Germany: Sportverlag, 1982.

16. HELLARD, P., M. AVALOS, G. MILLET, L. LACOSTE, F. BARALE, and J.C. CHATARD. Modeling the residual effects and threshold saturation of training: a case study of Olympic swimmers. *J Strength Cond Res* 19:67-75, 2005.

17. HICKSON, R.C., C. FOSTER, M.L. POLLOCK, T.M. GALASSI, and S. RICH. Reduced training intensities and loss of aerobic power, endurance, and cardiac growth. *J Appl Physiol* 58:492-499, 1985.

18. HICKSON, R.C., and M.A. ROSENKOETTER. Reduced training frequencies and maintenance of increased aerobic power. *Med Sci Sports Exerc* 13:13-16, 1981.

19. HOOPER, S.L., L.T. MACKINNON, and E.M. GINN. Effects of three tapering techniques on the performance, forces and psychometric measures of competitive swimmers. *Eur J Appl Physiol Occup Physiol* 78:258-263, 1998.

20. HOOPER, S.L., L.T. MACKINNON, and A. HOWARD. Physiological and psychometric variables for monitoring recovery during tapering for major competition. *Med Sci Sports Exerc* 31:1205-1210, 1999.

21. HOUMARD, J.A. Tapering for the competitive cyclist. *Performance Conditioning for Cyclists* 2:1-8, 1996.

22. HOUMARD, J.A., D.L. COSTILL, J.B. MITCHELL, S.H. PARK, W.J. FINK, and J.M. BURNS. Testosterone, cortisol, and creatine kinase levels in male distance runners during reduced training. *Int J Sports Med* 11:41-45, 1990.

23. HOUMARD, J.A., D.L. COSTILL, J.B. MITCHELL, S.H. PARK, R.C. HICKNER, and J.N. ROEMMICH. Reduced training maintains performance in distance runners. *Int J Sports Med* 11:46-52, 1990.

24. HOUMARD, J.A., and R.A. JOHNS. Effects of taper on swim performance: practical implications. *Sports Med* 17:224-232, 1994.

25. HOUMARD, J.A., J.P. KIRWAN, M.G. FLYNN, and J.B. MITCHELL. Effects of reduced training on submaximal and maximal running responses. *Int J Sports Med* 10:30-33, 1989.

26. HOUMARD, J.A., B.K. SCOTT, C.L. JUSTICE, and T.C. CHENIER. The effects of taper on performance in distance runners. *Med Sci Sports Exerc* 26:624-631, 1994.

27. IZQUIERDO, M., J. IBANEZ, J.J. GONZALEZ-BADILLO, N.A. RATAMESS, W.J. KRAEMER, K. HÄKKINEN, H. BONNABAU, C. GRANADOS, D.N. FRENCH, and E.M. GOROSTIAGA. Detraining and tapering effects on hormonal responses and strength performance. *J Strength Cond Res* 21:768-775, 2007.

28. JOHNS, R.A., J.A. HOUMARD, R.W. KOBE, T. HORTOBAGYI, N.J. BRUNO, J.M. WELLS, and M.H. SHINEBARGER. Effects of taper on swim power, stroke distance, and performance. *Med Sci Sports Exerc* 24:1141-1146, 1992.

29. KAUHANEN, H. Organization of the coaching system of young weightlifters in Finland. In: *Proceedings of International Conference on Weightlifting and Strength Training*. Lahti, Finland, 1998, p. 137-140.

30. KUBUKELI, Z.N., T.D. NOAKES, and S.C. DENNIS. Training techniques to improve endurance exercise performances. *Sports Med* 32:489-509, 2002.

31. KUKUSHKIN, G.I. *System of Physical Education in the USSR.* Moscow: Raduga, 1983.

32. MARTIN, D.T., J.C. SCIFRES, S.D. ZIMMERMAN, and J.G. WILKINSON. Effects of interval training and a taper on cycling performance and isokinetic leg strength. *Int J Sports Med* 15:485-491, 1994.

33. MCCONELL, G.K., D.L. COSTILL, J.J. WIDRICK, M.S. HICKEY, H. TANAKA, and P.B. GASTIN. Reduced training volume and intensity maintain aerobic capacity but not performance in distance runners. *Int J Sports Med* 14:33-37, 1993.

34. MUJIKA, I. The influence of training characteristics and tapering on the adaptation in highly trained individuals: a review. *Int J Sports Med* 19:439-446, 1998.

35. MUJIKA, I., T. BUSSO, L. LACOSTE, F. BARALE, A. GEYSSANT, and J.C. CHATARD. Modeled responses to training and taper in competitive swimmers. *Med Sci Sports Exerc* 28:251-258, 1996.

36. MUJIKA, I., J.C. CHATARD, and A. GEYSSANT. Effects of training and taper on blood leucocyte populations in competitive swimmers: relationships with cortisol and performance. *Int J Sports Med* 17:213-217, 1996.

37. MUJIKA, I., J.C. CHATARD, S. PADILLA, C.Y. GUEZENNEC, and A. GEYSSANT. Hormonal responses to training and its tapering off in competitive swimmers: relationships with performance. *Eur J Appl Physiol Occup Physiol* 74:361-366, 1996.

38. MUJIKA, I., A. GOYA, S. PADILLA, A. GRIJALBA, E. GOROSTIAGA, and J. IBANEZ. Physiological responses to a 6-d taper in middle-distance runners: influence of training intensity and volume. *Med Sci Sports Exerc* 32:511-517, 2000.

39. MUJIKA, I., A. GOYA, E. RUIZ, A. GRIJALBA, J. SANTISTEBAN, and S. PADILLA. Physiological and performance responses to a 6-day taper in middle-distance runners: influence of training frequency. *Int J Sports Med* 23:367-373, 2002.

40. MUJIKA, I., and S. PADILLA. Detraining: loss of training-induced physiological and performance adaptations: part I: short term insufficient training stimulus. *Sports Med* 30:79-87, 2000.

41. MUJIKA, I., and S. PADILLA. Scientific bases for precompetition tapering strategies. *Med Sci Sports Exerc* 35:1182-1187, 2003.

42. MUJIKA, I., S. PADILLA, A. GEYSSANT, and J.C. CHATARD. Hematological responses to training and taper in competitive swimmers: relationships with performance. *Arch Physiol Biochem* 105:379-385, 1998.

43. MUJIKA, I., S. PADILLA, and D. PYNE. Swimming performance changes during the final 3 weeks of training leading to the Sydney 2000 Olympic Games. *Int J Sports Med* 23:582-587, 2002.

44. MUJIKA, I., S. PADILLA, D. PYNE, and T. BUSSO. Physiological changes associated with the pre-event taper in athletes. *Sports Med* 34:891-927, 2004.

45. NABATNIKOWAS, M.Y. *Osnovy upravlienya podgotovki yunyky sportsmenov.* Moscow: Fizkultura i Sport, 1982.

46. NÁDORI, L., and I. GRANEK. *Theoretical and Methodological Basis of Training Planning With Special Considerations Within a Microcycle.* Lincoln, NE: NSCA, 1989.

47. NEARY, J.P., Y.N. BHAMBHANI, and D.C. MCKENZIE. Effects of different stepwise reduction taper protocols on cycling performance. *Can J Appl Physiol* 28:576-587, 2003.

48. NEARY, J.P., T.P. MARTIN, and H.A. QUINNEY. Effects of taper on endurance cycling capacity and single muscle fiber properties. *Med Sci Sports Exerc* 35:1875-1881, 2003.

49. NEARY, J.P., T.P. MARTIN, D.C. REID, R. BURNHAM, and H.A. QUINNEY. The effects of a reduced exercise duration taper programme on performance and muscle enzymes of endurance cyclists. *Eur J Appl Physiol Occup Physiol* 65:30-36, 1992.

50. NEUFER, P.D. The effect of detraining and reduced training on the physiological adaptations to aerobic exercise training. *Sports Med* 8:302-320, 1989.

51. NEUFER, P.D., D.L. COSTILL, R.A. FIELDING, M.G. FLYNN, and J.P. KIRWAN. Effect of reduced training on muscular strength and endurance in competitive swimmers. *Med Sci Sports Exerc* 19:486-490, 1987.

52. OLBRECT, J. *The Science of Winning: Planning, Periodizing, and Optimizing Swim Training.* Luton, UK: Swimshop, 2000.

53. PAPOTI, M., L.E. MARTINS, S.A. CUNHA, A.M. ZAGATTO, and C.A. GOBATTO. Effects of taper on swimming force and swimmer performance after an experimental ten-week training program. *J Strength Cond Res* 21:538-542, 2007.

54. PLISK, S.S., and M.H. STONE. Periodization strategies. *Strength Cond* 25:19-37, 2003.

55. RACKZEK, J. *Szkolenie mlodziezy w systemie sportu wyczynowego.* Katowice: AWF, 1989.

56. RAGLIN, J.S., D.M. KOCEJA, J.M. STAGER, and C.A. HARMS. Mood, neuromuscular function, and performance during training in female swimmers. *Med Sci Sports Exerc* 28:372-377, 1996.

57. RIETJENS, G.J., H.A. KEIZER, H. KUIPERS, and W.H. SARIS. A reduction in training volume and intensity for 21 days does not impair performance in cyclists. *Br J Sports Med* 35:431-434, 2001.

58. SHEPLEY, B., J.D. MACDOUGALL, N. CIPRIANO, J.R. SUTTON, M.A. TARNOPOLSKY, and G. COATES. Physiological effects of tapering in highly trained athletes. *J Appl Physiol* 72:706-711, 1992.

59. SMITH, D.J. A framework for understanding the training process leading to elite performance. *Sports Med* 33:1103-1126, 2003.

60. STONE, M.H., M.E. STONE, and W.A. SANDS. *Principles and Practice of Resistance Training.* Champaign, IL: Human Kinetics, 2007.

61. THOMAS, L., and T. BUSSO. A theoretical study of taper characteristics to optimize performance. *Med Sci Sports Exerc* 37:1615-1621, 2005.

62. TRAPPE, S., D. COSTILL, and R. THOMAS. Effect of swim taper on whole muscle and single muscle fiber contractile properties. *Med Sci Sports Exerc* 32:48-56, 2000.

63. ZARKADAS, P.C., J.B. CARTER, and E.W. BANISTER. Modelling the effect of taper on performance, maximal oxygen uptake, and the anaerobic threshold in endurance triathletes. *Adv Exp Med Biol* 393:179-186, 1995.

64. ZATSIORSKY, V.M. *Science and Practice of Strength Training.* Champaign, IL: Human Kinetics, 1995.

65. ZATSIORSKY, V.M., and W.J. KRAEMER. *Science and Practice of Strength Training.* 2nd ed. Champaign, IL: Human Kinetics, 2006.

Chapter 8

1. BEHM, D.G., G. REARDON, J. FITZGERALD, and E. DRINKWATER. The effect of 5, 10, and 20 repetition maximums on the recovery of voluntary and evoked contractile properties. *J Strength Cond Res* 16:209-218, 2002.

2. BOSQUET, L., J. MONTPETIT, D. ARVISAIS, and I. MUJIKA. Effects of tapering on performance: a meta-analysis. *Med Sci Sports Exerc* 39:1358-1365, 2007.

3. BROOKS, G.A., T.D. FAHEY, T.P. WHITE, and K.M. BALDWIN. *Exercise Physiology: Human Bioenergetics and Its Application.* 3rd ed. Mountain View, CA: Mayfield, 2000.

4. BURKE, L., and V. DEAKIN. *Clinical Sports Nutrition.* Roseville, Australia: McGraw-Hill Australia, 2000.

5. FRY, A.C. The role of training intensity in resistance exercise overtraining and overreaching. In: *Overtraining in Sport.* R.B. Kreider, A.C. Fry, and M.L. O'Toole, eds. Champaign, IL: Human Kinetics, 1998, pp. 107-127.

6. FRY, A.C., W.J. KRAEMER, M.H. STONE, B.J. WARREN, S.J. FLECK, J.T. KEARNEY, and S.E. GORDON. Endocrine responses to overreaching before and after 1 year of weightlifting. *Can J Appl Physiol* 19:400-410, 1994.

7. HALSON, S.L., M.W. BRIDGE, R. MEEUSEN, B. BUSSCHAERT, M. GLEESON, D.A. JONES, and A.E. JEUKENDRUP. Time course of performance changes and fatigue markers during intensified training in trained cyclists. *J Appl Physiol* 93:947-956, 2002.

8. IVY, J., and R. PORTMAN. *The Future of Sports Nutrition: Nutrient Timing.* North Bergan, NJ: Basic Health, 2004.

9. KRUSTRUP, P., M. MOHR, A. STEENSBERG, J. BENCKE, M. KJAER, and J. BANGSBO. Muscle and blood metabolites during a soccer game: implications for sprint performance. *Med Sci Sports Exerc* 38:1165-1174, 2006.

10. MARTIN, N.A., R.F. ZOELLER, R.J. ROBERTSON, and S.M. LEPHART. The comparative effects of sports massage, active recovery, and rest in promoting blood lactate clearance after supramaximal leg exercise. *J Athl Train* 33:30-35, 1998.

11. MATVEYEV, L.P. *Periodisterung Des Sportlichen Trainings.* Moscow: Fizkultura i Sport, 1972.

12. MCARDLE, W.D., F.I. KATCH, and V.L. KATCH. *Exercise Physiology: Energy, Nutrition, and Human Performance.* 6th ed. Baltimore: Lippincott Williams & Wilkins, 2007.

13. MONEDERO, J., and B. DONNE. Effect of recovery interventions on lactate removal and subsequent performance. *Int J Sports Med* 21:593-597, 2000.

14. MUJIKA, I., and S. PADILLA. Scientific bases for pre-competition tapering strategies. *Med Sci Sports Exerc* 35:1182-1187, 2003.

15. O'TOOLE, M.L. Overreaching and overtraining in endurance athletes. In: *Overtraining in Sport.* R.B. Kreider, A.C. Fry, and M.L. O'Toole, eds. Champaign, IL: Human Kinetics, 1998, pp. 3-18.

16. PLISK, S.S., and M.H. STONE. Periodization strategies. *Strength Cond* 25:19-37, 2003.

17. REILLY, T., and B. EKBLOM. The use of recovery methods post-exercise. *J Sport Sci* 23:619-627, 2005.

18. REILLY, T., and M. RIGBY. Effect of an active warm-down following competitive soccer. In: *Science and Football IV.* W. Spinks, T. Reilly, and A. Murphy, eds. London: Routledge, 2002, pp. 226-229.

19. SIFF, M.C., and Y.U. VERKHOSHANSKY. *Supertraining.* Denver, CO: Supertraining International, 1999.

20. STONE, M.H., M.E. STONE, and W.A. SANDS. *Principles and Practice of Resistance Training.* Champaign, IL: Human Kinetics, 2007.

21. VERKHOSHANSKY, Y.U. *Fundamentals of Special Strength Training in Sport.* Livonia, MI: Sportivy Press, 1986.

22. VERKHOSHANSKY, Y.U. *Programming and Organization of Training.* Moscow: Fizkultura i Sport, 1985.

23. VIRU, A. *Adaptations in Sports Training.* Boca Raton, FL: CRC Press, 1995.

24. ZATSIORSKY, V.M. *Science and Practice of Strength Training.* Champaign, IL: Human Kinetics, 1995.

25. ZATSIORSKY, V.M., and W.J. KRAEMER. *Science and Practice of Strength Training.* 2nd ed. Champaign, IL: Human Kinetics, 2006.

Chapter 9

1. ABADEJEV, I. Basic training principles for Bulgarian elite. *Can Weightlifting Fed Official Newsletter* 5:13-18, 1976.

2. ABADEJEV, I. Basic training principles for Bulgarian elite. *Int Olympic Lifter* 3:12-13, 1976.

3. ABADEJEV, I. Basic training principles for Bulgarian elite. *New Brunswick Weightlifting Association Newsletter* 4:19-24, 1977.

4. ABADEJEV, I. Preparation of the Bulgarian weightlifters for the Olympic Games 1984. *Australian Weightlifter* October:25-29, 1981.

5. ALLEN, D.G., J.A. LEE, and H. WESTERBLAD. Intracellular calcium and tension during fatigue in isolated single muscle fibres from Xenopus laevis. *J Physiol* 415:433-458, 1989.

6. BARCROFT, H., and O.G. EDHOLM. The effect of temperature on blood flow and deep temperature in the human forearm. *J Physiol* 102:5-20, 1943.

7. BARCROFT, J., and W.O. KING. The effect of temperature on the dissociation curve of blood. *J Physiol* 39:374-384, 1909.

8. BISHOP, D. Warm up I: potential mechanisms and the effects of passive warm up on exercise performance. *Sports Med* 33:439-454, 2003.

9. BISHOP, D. Warm up II: performance changes following active warm up and how to structure the warm up. *Sports Med* 33:483-498, 2003.

10. BISHOP, D., D. BONETTI, and M. SPENCER. The effect of an intermittent, high-intensity warm-up on supramaximal kayak ergometer performance. *J Sports Sci* 21:13-20, 2003.

11. BOGDANIS, G.C., M.E. NEVILL, H.K. LAKOMY, C.M. GRAHAM, and G. LOUIS. Effects of active recovery on power output during repeated maximal sprint cycling. *Eur J Appl Physiol Occup Physiol* 74:461-469, 1996.

12. BOMPA, T.O. *Periodization: Theory and Methodology of Training.* 4th ed. Champaign, IL: Human Kinetics, 1999.

13. BOMPA, T.O. *Total Training for Coaching Team Sports: A Self Help Guide.* Toronto, ON, Canada: Sports Books Publisher, 2006.

14. BURKE, L., and V. DEAKIN. *Clinical Sports Nutrition.* Roseville, Australia: McGraw-Hill Australia, 2000.

15. CARLOCK, J., A. SMITH, M. HARTMAN, R. MORRIS, D. CIROSLAN, K.C. PIERCE, R.U. NEWTON, and M.H. STONE. The relationship between vertical jump power estimates and weightlifting ability: a field test approach. *J Strength Cond Res* 18:534-539, 2004.

16. CHEUNG, K., P. HUME, and L. MAXWELL. Delayed onset muscle soreness: treatment strategies and performance factors. *Sports Med* 33:145-164, 2003.

17. CHIU, L.Z., A.C. FRY, L.W. WEISS, B.K. SCHILLING, L.E. BROWN, and S.L. SMITH. Postactivation potentiation response in athletic and recreationally trained individuals. *J Strength Cond Res* 17:671-677, 2003.

18. COGGAN, A.R., and E.F. COYLE. Carbohydrate ingestion during prolonged exercise: effects on metabolism and performance. *Exerc Sport Sci Rev* 19:1-40, 1991.

19. DAVIS, J.M. Central and peripheral factors in fatigue. *J Sports Sci* 13(spec no):S49-S53, 1995.

20. DAVIS, J.M., N.L. ALDERSON, and R.S. WELSH. Serotonin and central nervous system fatigue: nutritional considerations. *Am J Clin Nutr* 72:573S-578S, 2000.

21. DAVIS, J.M., and S.P. BAILEY. Possible mechanisms of central nervous system fatigue during exercise. *Med Sci Sports Exerc* 29:45-57, 1997.

22. DICK, F.W. *Sports Training Principles.* 4th ed. London: A & C Black, 2002.

23. ENOKA, R.M. Activation order of motor axons in electrically evoked contractions. *Muscle Nerve* 25:763-764, 2002.

24. ENOKA, R.M., and D.G. STUART. Neurobiology of muscle fatigue. *J Appl Physiol* 72:1631-1648, 1992.

25. GANDELSMAN, A., and K. SMIRNOV. *Physiologicheskie Osnovi Metodiki Sportivnoi Trenirovki* [The Physiological Foundations of Training]. Moscow: Fizkultura i Sport, 1970.

26. GRANGE, R.W., C.R. CORY, R. VANDENBOOM, and M.E. HOUSTON. Myosin phosphorylation augments force-displacement and force-velocity relationships of mouse fast muscle. *Am J Physiol* 269:C713-C724, 1995.

27. GRANGE, R.W., R. VANDENBOOM, J. XENI, and M.E. HOUSTON. Potentiation of in vitro concentric work in mouse fast muscle. *J Appl Physiol* 84:236-243, 1998.

28. GRODJINOVSKY, A., and J.R. MAGEL. Effect of warming up on running performance. *Res Q Exerc Sport* 41:116-119.

29. HAFF, G.G., J.M. CARLOCK, M.J. HARTMAN, J.L. KILGORE, N. KAWAMORI, J.R. JACKSON, R.T. MORRIS, W.A. SANDS, and M.H. STONE. Force-time curve characteristics of dynamic and isometric muscle actions of elite women Olympic weightlifters. *J Strength Cond Res* 19:741-748, 2005.

30. HAFF, G.G., R.T. HOBBS, E.E. HAFF, W.A. SANDS, K.C. PIERCE, and M.H. STONE. Cluster training: a novel method for introducing training program variation. *Strength Cond* 30:67-76, 2008.

31. HAFF, G.G., A.J. KOCH, J.A. POTTEIGER, K.E. KUPHAL, L.M. MAGEE, S.B. GREEN, and J.J. JAKICIC. Carbohydrate supplementation attenuates muscle glycogen loss during acute bouts of resistance exercise. *Int J Sport Nutr Exerc Metab* 10:326-339, 2000.

32. HAFF, G.G., M.J. LEHMKUHL, L.B. MCCOY, and M.H. STONE. Carbohydrate supplementation and resistance training. *J Strength Cond Res* 17:187-196, 2003.

33. HÄKKINEN, K., and M. KALLINEN. Distribution of strength training volume into one or two daily sessions and neuromuscular adaptations in female athletes. *Electromyogr Clin Neurophysiol* 34:117-124, 1994.

34. HODGSON, M., D. DOCHERTY, and D. ROBBINS. Post-activation potentiation: underlying physiology and implications for motor performance. *Sports Med* 35:585-595, 2005.

35. HOLCOMB, W.R. Stretching and warm-up. In: *Essentials of Strength and Conditioning*. T.R. Baechle and R.W. Earle, eds. Champaign, IL: Human Kinetics, 2000. pp. 321-342.

36. HORNERY, D.J., D. FARROW, I. MUJIKA, and W. YOUNG. Fatigue in tennis: mechanisms of fatigue and effect on performance. *Sports Med* 37:199-212, 2007.

37. IVY, J., and R. PORTMAN. *The Future of Sports Nutrition: Nutrient Timing*. North Bergan, NJ: Basic Health, 2004.

38. KURZ, T. *Science of Sports Training*. 2nd ed. Island Pond, VT: Stadion, 2001.

39. LAFORGIA, J., R.T. WITHERS, and C.J. GORE. Effects of exercise intensity and duration on the excess post-exercise oxygen consumption. *J Sports Sci* 24:1247-1264, 2006.

40. LITTLE, T., and A.G. WILLIAMS. Effects of differential stretching protocols during warm-ups on high-speed motor capacities in professional soccer players. *J Strength Cond Res* 20:203-207, 2006.

41. MALAREKI, I. Investigation of physiological justification of so-called "warming up." *Acta Physiol Pol* 5:543-546, 1954.

42. MASSEY, B.H., W.R. JOHNSON, and G.F. KRAMER. Effect of warm-up exercise upon muscular performance using hypnosis to control the psychological variable. *Re. Q Exerc Sport* 32:63-71, 1961.

43. MATVEYEV, L. About the construction of training. *Modern Athlete and Coach* 32:12-16, 1994.

44. MATVEYEV, L.P. *Fundamentals of Sports Training*. Moscow: Fizkultua i Sport, 1977.

45. MATVEYEV, L.P. *Periodisterung Des Sportlichen Trainings*. Moscow: Fizkultura i Sport, 1972.

46. MAUGHAN, R., and M. GLEESON. *The Biochemical Basis of Sports Performance*. New York: Oxford University Press, 2004.

47. MCBRIDE, J.M., S. NIMPHIUS, and T.M. ERICKSON. The acute effects of heavy-load squats and loaded countermovement jumps on sprint performance. *J Strength Cond Res* 19:893-897, 2005.

48. MCMILLAN, J.L., M.H. STONE, J. SARTIN, R. KEITH, D. MARPLE, C. BROWN, and R.D. LEWIS. 20-hour physiological responses to a single weight-training session. *J Strength Cond Res* 7:9-21, 1993.

49. MEDVEDEV, A.S. *Sistema Mnogoletnyei Trenirovki V Tyazheloi Atletikye*. Moscow: Fizkultura i Sport, 1986.

50. MIKA, A., P. MIKA, B. FERNHALL, and V.B. UNNITHAN. Comparison of recovery strategies on muscle performance after fatiguing exercise. *Am J Phys Med Rehabil* 86:474-481, 2007.

51. MONEDERO, J., and B. DONNE. Effect of recovery interventions on lactate removal and subsequent performance. *Int J Sports Med* 21:593-597, 2000.

52. NÁDORI, L., and I. GRANEK. *Theoretical and Methodological Basis of Training Planning With Special Considerations Within a Microcycle*. Lincoln, NE: NSCA, 1989.

53. NAGANE, M. Relationship of subjective chronic fatigue to academic performance. *Psychol Rep* 95:48-52, 2004.

54. NOAKES, T.D. Physiological models to understand exercise fatigue and the adaptations that predict or enhance athletic performance. *Scand J Med Sci Sports* 10:123-145, 2000.

55. OLBRECT, J. *The Science of Winning: Planning, Periodizing, and Optimizing Swim Training*. Luton, UK: Swimshop, 2000.

56. PLISK, S.S., and M.H. STONE. Periodization strategies. *Strength Cond* 25:19-37, 2003.

57. RADCLIFFE, J.C., and J.L. RADCLIFFE. Effects of different warm-up protocols on peak power output during a single response jump task [abstract]. *Med Sci Sports Exerc* 28:S189, 1996.

58. REILLY, T., and B. EKBLOM. The use of recovery methods post-exercise. *J Sport Sci* 23:619-627, 2005.

59. ROBERGS, R.A., D.R. PEARSON, D.L. COSTILL, W.J. FINK, D.D. PASCOE, M.A. BENEDICT, C.P. LAMBERT, and J.J. ZACHWEIJA. Muscle glycogenolysis during differing intensities of weight-resistance exercise. *J Appl Physiol* 70:1700-1706, 1991.

60. SAEZ SAEZ DE VILLARREAL, E., J.J. GONZALEZ-BADILLO, and M. IZQUIERDO. Optimal warm-up stimuli of muscle activation to enhance short and long-term acute jumping performance. *Eur J Appl Physiol* 100:393-401, 2007.

61. SALTIN, B., A.P. GAGGE, and J.A. STOLWIJK. Muscle temperature during submaximal exercise in man. *J Appl Physiol* 25:679-688, 1968.

62. SATORI, J., and P. TSCHIENE. The further development of training theory: new elements and tendencies. *Sci Period Res Technol Sport* 8:Physical Training W-1, 1988.

63. SCHMOLINSKY, G. *Track and Field: The East German Textbook of Athletics.* Toronto, ON, Canada: Sports Book Publisher, 2004.

64. SHRIER, I. Does stretching improve performance? A systematic and critical review of the literature. *Clin J Sports Med* 14:267-273, 2004.

65. SIFF, M.C., and Y.U. VERKHOSHANSKY. *Supertraining.* Denver, CO: Supertraining International, 1999.

66. SMITH, D.J. A framework for understanding the training process leading to elite performance. *Sports Med* 33:1103-1126, 2003.

67. ST CLAIR GIBSON, A., D.A. BADEN, M.I. LAMBERT, E.V. LAMBERT, Y.X. HARLEY, D. HAMPSON, V.A. RUSSELL, and T.D. NOAKES. The conscious perception of the sensation of fatigue. *Sports Med* 33:167-176, 2003.

68. STONE, M.H., and H.O. O'BRYANT. *Weight Training: A Scientific Approach.* Edina, MN: Burgess, 1987.

69. STONE, M.H., H.S. O'BRYANT, B.K. SCHILLING, R.L. JOHNSON, K.C. PIERCE, G.G. HAFF, A.J. KOCH, and M. STONE. Periodization: effects of manipulating volume and intensity: part 1. *Strength Cond* 21:56-62, 1999.

70. STONE, M.H., W.A. SANDS, K.C. PIERCE, J. CARLOCK, M. CARDINALE, and R.U. NEWTON. Relationship of maximum strength to weightlifting performance. *Med Sci Sports Exerc* 37:1037-1043, 2005.

71. STONE, M.H., W.A. SANDS, K.C. PIERCE, M.W. RAMSEY, and G.G. HAFF. Power and power potentiation among strength power athletes: preliminary study. *Int J Sports Physiol Perf* 3:55-67, 2008.

72. STONE, M.H., M.E. STONE, and W.A. SANDS. *Principles and Practice of Resistance Training.* Champaign, IL: Human Kinetics, 2007.

73. VERKHOSHANSKY, Y.U. *Special Strength Training: A Practical Manual for Coaches.* MI: Ultimate Athlete Concepts, 2006.

74. WINCHESTER, J.B., A.G. NELSON, D. LANDIN, M.A. YOUNG, and I.C. SCHEXNAYDER. Static stretching impairs sprint performance in collegiate track and field athletes. *J Strength Cond Res* 22:13-19, 2008.

75. WOODS, K., P. BISHOP, and E. JONES. Warm-up and stretching in the prevention of muscular injury. *Sports Med* 37:1089-1099, 2007.

76. YETTER, M., and G.L. MOIR. The acute effects of heavy back and front squats on speed during forty-meter sprint trials. *J Strength Cond Res* 22:159-165, 2008.

77. YOUNG, W.B., and D.G. BEHM. Effects of running, static stretching and practice jumps on explosive force production and jumping performance. *J Sports Med Phys Fitness* 43:21-27, 2003.

78. ZATSIORSKY, V.M. *Science and Practice of Strength Training.* Champaign, IL: Human Kinetics, 1995.

79. ZATSIORSKY, V.M., and W.J. KRAEMER. Science and Practice of Strength Training. 2nd ed. Champaign, IL: Human Kinetics, 2006.

Chapter 10

1. AAGAARD, P., J.L. ANDERSEN, P. DYHRE-POULSEN, A.M. LEFFERS, A. WAGNER, S.P. MAGNUSSON, J. HALKJAER-KRISTENSEN, and E.B. SIMONSEN. A mechanism for increased contractile strength of human pennate muscle in response to strength training: changes in muscle architecture. *J Physiol* 534:613-623, 2001.

2. AAGAARD, P., E.B. SIMONSEN, J.L. ANDERSEN, P. MAGNUSSON, and P. DYHRE-POULSEN. Increased rate of force development and neural drive of human skeletal muscle following resistance training. *J Appl Physiol* 93:1318-1326, 2002.

3. AAGAARD, P., E.B. SIMONSEN, J.L. ANDERSEN, S.P. MAGNUSSON, J. HALKJAER-KRISTENSEN, and P. DYHRE-POULSEN. Neural inhibition during maximal eccentric and concentric quadriceps contraction: effects of resistance training *J Appl Physiol* 89:2249-2257, 2000.

4. ABADEJEV, I. Basic training principles for Bulgarian elite. *Can Weightlifting Fed Official Newsletter* 5:13-18, 1976.

5. ABADEJEV, I. Basic training principles for Bulgarian elite. *Int Olympic Lifter* 3:12-13, 1976.

6. ABADEJEV, I. Basic training principles for Bulgarian elite. *New Brunswick Weightlifting Association Newsletter* 4:19-24, 1977.

7. ABADEJEV, I. Preparation of the Bulgarian weightlifters for the Olympic Games 1984. *Australian Weightlifter* October:25-29, 1981.

8. ABDESSEMED, D., P. DUCHE, C. HAUTIER, G. POUMARAT, and M. BEDU. Effect of recovery duration on muscular power and blood lactate during the bench press exercise. *Int J Sports Med* 20:368-373, 1999.

9. ADAMS, G.R., B.M. HATHER, K.M. BALDWIN, and G.A. DUDLEY. Skeletal muscle myosin heavy chain composition and resistance training. *J Appl Physiol* 74:911-915, 1993.

10. AHTIAINEN, J.P., A. PAKARINEN, M. ALEN, W.J. KRAEMER, and K. HÄKKINEN. Muscle hypertrophy, hormonal adaptations and strength development during strength training in strength-trained and untrained men. *Eur J Appl Physiol* 89:555-563, 2003.

11. AJÁN, T., and L. BAROGA. *Weightlifting: Fitness for All Sports.* Budapest: International Weightlifting Federation, 1988.

12. American College of Sports Medicine position stand: progressive models in resistance training for healthy adults. *Med Sci Sports Exerc* 34:364-380, 2002.

13. ANDERSEN, L.L., and P. AAGAARD. Influence of maximal muscle strength and intrinsic muscle contractile properties on contractile rate of force development. *Eur J Appl Physiol* 96:46-52, 2006.

14. ATKINS, S.J. Normalizing expressions of strength in elite rugby league players. *J Strength Cond Res* 18:53-58, 2004.

15. AUGUSTSSON, J., R. THOMEE, P. HORNSTEDT, J. LINDBLOM, J. KARLSSON, and G. GRIMBY. Effect of pre-exhaustion exercise on lower-extremity muscle activation during a leg press exercise. *J Strength Cond Res* 17:411-416, 2003.

16. BAKER, D. Comparison of upper-body strength and power between professional and college-aged rugby league players. *J Strength Cond Res* 15:30-35, 2001.

17. BAKER, D. A series of studies on the training of high-intensity muscle power in rugby league football players. *J Strength Cond Res* 15:198-209, 2001.

18. BAKER, D., and S. NANCE. The relation between running speed and measures of strength and power in professional rugby league players. *J Strength Cond Res* 13:230-235, 1999.

19. BARKER, M., T.J. WYATT, R.L. JOHNSON, M.H. STONE, H.S. O'BRYANT, C. POE, and M. KENT. Performance factors, physiological assessment, physical characteristic, and football playing ability. *J Strength Cond Res* 7:224-233, 1993.

20. BASTIAANS, J.J., A.B. VAN DIEMEN, T. VENEBERG, and A.E. JEUKENDRUP. The effects of replacing a portion of endurance training by explosive strength training on performance in trained cyclists. *Eur J Appl Physiol* 86:79-84, 2001.

21. BERGH, U., A. THORSTENSSON, B. SJODIN, B. HULTEN, K. PIEHL, and J. KARLSSON. Maximal oxygen uptake and muscle fiber types in trained and untrained humans. *Med Sci Sports* 10:151-154, 1978.

22. BILCHECK, H.M., W.J. KRAEMER, C.M. MARESH, and Z. M.A. The effect of isokinetic fatigue on recovery of maximal isokinetic concentric and eccentric strength in women. *J Strength Cond Res* 7:43-50, 1993.

23. BOBBERT, M.F., and A.J. VAN SOEST. Why do people jump the way they do? *Exerc Sport Sci Rev* 29:95-102, 2001.

24. BOMPA, T.O., and M.C. CARRERA. Periodization Training For Sports: Science-Based Strength and Conditioning Plans for 20 Sports. 2nd ed. Champaign, IL: Human Kinetics, 2005.

25. BOUCHARD, C., F.T. DIONNE, J.A. SIMONEAU, and M.R. BOULAY. Genetics of aerobic and anaerobic performances. *Exerc Sport Sci Rev* 20:27-58, 1992.

26. BRET, C., A. RAHMANI, A.B. DUFOUR, L. MESSONNIER, and J.R. LACOUR. Leg strength and stiffness as ability factors in 100 m sprint running. *J Sports Med Phys Fitness* 42:274-281, 2002.

27. BRYZYCHI, M. Assessing Strength. *Fitness Manage* June:34-37, 2000.

28. BRYZYCHI, M. Strength testing: predicting a one rep max from reps to fatigue. *JOPERD* 64:88-90, 1993.

29. CAMPOS, G.E., T.J. LUECKE, H.K. WENDELN, K. TOMA, F.C. HAGERMAN, T.F. MURRAY, K.E. RAGG, N.A. RATAMESS, W.J. KRAEMER, and R.S. STARON. Muscular adaptations in response to three different resistance-training regimens: specificity of repetition maximum training zones. *Eur J Appl Physiol* 88:50-60, 2002.

30. CAVAGNA, G.A., F.P. SAIBENE, and R. MARGARIA. Effect of negative work on the amount of positive work performed by an isolated muscle. *J Appl Physiol* 20:157-158, 1965.

31. CHILIBECK, P.D., A.W. CALDER, D.G. SALE, and C.E. WEBBER. A comparison of strength and muscle mass increases during resistance training in young women. *Eur J Appl Physiol* 77:170-175, 1998.

32. CHIU, L.Z., A.C. FRY, B.K. SCHILLING, E.J. JOHNSON, and L.W. WEISS. Neuromuscular fatigue and potentiation following two successive high intensity resistance exercise sessions. *Eur J Appl Physiol* 92:385-392, 2004.

33. CHIU, L.Z., A.C. FRY, L.W. WEISS, B.K. SCHILLING, L.E. BROWN, and S.L. SMITH. Postactivation potentiation response in athletic and recreationally trained individuals. *J Strength Cond Res* 17:671-677, 2003.

34. CHRISTOU, M., I. SMILIOS, K. SOTIROPOULOS, K. VOLAKLIS, T. PILIANIDIS, and S.P. TOKMAKIDIS. Effects of resistance training on the physical capacities of adolescent soccer players. *J Strength Cond Res* 20:783-791, 2006.

35. CLARKSON, P.M., J.M. DEVANEY, H. GORDISH-DRESSMAN, P.D. THOMPSON, M.J. HUBAL, M. URSO, T.B. PRICE, T.J. ANGELOPOULOS, P.M. GORDON, N.M. MOYNA, L.S. PESCATELLO, P.S. VISICH, R.F. ZOELLER, R.L. SEIP, and E.P. HOFFMAN. ACTN3 genotype is associated with increases in muscle strength in response to resistance training in women. *J Appl Physiol* 99:154-163, 2005.

36. COFFEY, V.G., and J.A. HAWLEY. The molecular bases of training adaptation. *Sports Med* 37:737-763, 2007.

37. CRONIN, J.B., and K.T. HANSEN. Strength and power predictors of sports speed. *J Strength Cond Res* 19:349-357, 2005.

38. CRONIN, J.B., P.J. MCNAIR, and R.N. MARSHALL. The role of maximal strength and load on initial power production. *Med Sci Sports Exerc* 32:1763-1769, 2000.

39. D'ANTONA, G., F. LANFRANCONI, M.A. PELLEGRINO, L. BROCCA, R. ADAMI, R. ROSSI, G. MORO, D. MIOTTI, M. CANEPARI, and R. BOTTINELLI. Skeletal muscle hypertrophy and structure and function of skeletal muscle fibres in male body builders. *J Physiol* 570:611-627, 2006.

40. DESCHENES, M. Short review: rate coding and motor unit recruitment patterns. *J Appl Sports Sci Res* 3:33-39, 1989.

41. DONS, B., K. BOLLERUP, F. BONDE-PETERSEN, and S. HANCKE. The effect of weight-lifting exercise related to muscle fiber composition and muscle cross-sectional area in humans. *Eur J Appl Physiol* 40:95-106, 1979.

42. DRESCHLER, A. The Weightlifting Encyclopedia: A Guide to World Class Performance. Flushing, NY: A IS A Communications, 1998.

43. DRINKWATER, E.J., T.W. LAWTON, M.J. MCKENNA, R.P. LINDSELL, P.H. HUNT, and D.B. PYNE. Increased number of forced repetitions does not enhance strength development with resistance training. *J Strength Cond Res* 21:841-847, 2007.

44. DUCHATEAU, J., and K. HAINAUT. Isometric or dynamic training: differential effects on mechanical properties of a human muscle. *J Appl Physiol* 56:296-301, 1984.

45. DUCHATEAU, J., J.G. SEMMLER, and R.M. ENOKA. Training adaptations in the behavior of human motor units. *J Appl Physiol* 101:1766-1775, 2006.

46. EL-HEWIE, M.F. Essentials of Weightlifting & Strength Training. Lodi, NJ: Shaymaa, 2003.

47. EPLEY, B. *The Path to Athletic Power*. Champaigne, IL: Human Kinetics, 307-312. 2004.

48. FERRIS, D.P., J.F. SIGNORILE, and J.F. CARUSO. The relationship between physical and physiological variables and volleyball spiking velocity. *J Strength Cond Res* 9:32-36, 1995.

49. FLECK, S.J., and W.J. KRAEMER. *Designing Resistance Training Programs*. 2 ed. Champaign, IL: Human Kinetics, 1997.

59. FLECK, S., and W.J. KRAEMER. *Designing Resistance Training Programs*. 3rd ed. Champaign, IL: Human Kinetics, 2004.

51. FLORESCU, C., V. DUMITRESCU, and A. PREDESCU. *Metodologia Desvoltari Calitatilor Fizice* [The Methodology of Developing Physical Qualities]. Bucharest: National Sports Council, 1969.

52. FOLLAND, J.P., and A.G. WILLIAMS. The adaptations to strength training: morphological and neurological contributions to increased strength. *Sports Med* 37:145-168, 2007.

53. FORD, L.E., A.J. DETTERLINE, K.K. HO, and W. CAO. Gender- and height-related limits of muscle strength in world weightlifting champions. *J Appl Physiol* 89:1061-1064, 2000.

54. FROBOSE, I., A. VERDONCK, F. DUESBERG, and C. MUCHA. Effects of various load intensities in the framework of postoperative stationary endurance training on performance deficit of the quadriceps muscle of the thigh. *Z Orthop Ihre Grenzgeb* 131:164-167, 1993.

55. FRY, A.C. The role of resistance exercise intensity on muscle fibre adaptations. *Sports Med* 34:663-679, 2004.

56. FRY, A.C. The role of training intensity in resistance exercise overtraining and overreaching. In: *Overtraining in Sport*. R.B. Kreider, A.C. Fry, and M.L. O'Toole, eds. Champaign, IL: Human Kinetics, 1998. pp. 107-127.

57. FRY, A.C., and W.J. KRAEMER. Physical performance characteristics of American collegiate football players. *J Appl Sport Sci Res* 5:126-138, 1991.

58. FRY, A.C., B.K. SCHILLING, R.S. STARON, F.C. HAGERMAN, R.S. HIKIDA, and J.T. THRUSH. Muscle fiber characteristics and performance correlates of male Olympic-style weightlifters. *J Strength Cond Res* 17:746-754, 2003.

59. FRY, A.C., J.M. WEBBER, L.W. WEISS, M.P. HARBER, M. VACZI, and N.A. PATTISON. Muscle fiber characteristics of competitive power lifters. *J Strength Cond Res* 17:402-410, 2003.

60. GABBETT, T.J. Science of rugby league football: a review. *J Sports Sci* 23:961-976, 2005.

61. GABRIEL, D.A., G. KAMEN, and G. FROST. Neural adaptations to resistive exercise: mechanisms and recommendations for training practices. *Sports Med* 36:133-149, 2006.

62. GALLAGHER, P., S. TRAPPE, M. HARBER, A. CREER, S. MAZZETTI, T. TRAPPE, B. ALKNER, and P. TESCH. Effects of 84-days of bedrest and resistance training on single muscle fibre myosin heavy chain distribution in human vastus lateralis and soleus muscles. *Acta Physiol Scand* 185:61-69, 2005.

63. GARHAMMER, J., and B. TAKANO. Training for weightlifting. In: *Strength and Power in Sport*. P.V. Komi, ed. Oxford, UK: Blackwell Scientific, 2003, pp. 502-515.

64. GILLAM, G.M. Effects of frequency of weight training on muscle strength enhancement. *J Sports Med* 21:432-436, 1981.

65. GISSIS, I., C. PAPADOPOULOS, V.I. KALAPOTHARAKOS, A. SOTIROPOULOS, G. KOMSIS, and E. MANOLOPOULOS. Strength and speed characteristics of elite, subelite, and recreational young soccer players. *Res Sports Med* 14:205-214, 2006.

66. GONZALEZ-BADILLO, J.J., M. IZQUIERDO, and E.M. GOROSTIAGA. Moderate volume of high relative training intensity produces greater strength gains compared with low and high volumes in competitive weightlifters. *J Strength Cond Res* 20:73-81, 2006.

67. GOTO, K., M. NAGASAWA, O. YANAGISAWA, T. KIZUKA, N. ISHII, and K. TAKAMATSU. Muscular adaptations to combinations of high- and low-intensity resistance exercises. *J Strength Cond Res* 18:730-737, 2004.

68. GRAVES, J.E., M.L. POLLOCK, S.H. LEGGETT, R.W. BRAITH, D.M. CARPENTER, and L.E. BISHOP. Effect of reduced training frequency on muscular strength. *Int J Sports Med* 9:316-319, 1988.

69. GROSSER, M., and A. NEUMEIER. *Tecnicas de Entrenamiento* [Training Techniques]. Barcelona, Spain: Martinez Roca, 1986.

70. HAFF, G.G., J.M. CARLOCK, M.J. HARTMAN, J.L. KILGORE, N. KAWAMORI, J.R. JACKSON, R.T. MORRIS, W.A. SANDS, and M.H. STONE. Force-time curve characteristics of dynamic and isometric muscle actions of elite women Olympic weightlifters. *J Strength Cond Res* 19:741-748, 2005.

71. HAFF, G.G., M.H. STONE, H.S. O'BRYANT, E. HARMAN, C.N. DINAN, R. JOHNSON, and K.H. HAN. Force-time dependent characteristics of dynamic and isometric muscle actions. *J Strength Cond Res* 11:269-272, 1997.

72. HAFF, G.G., A. WHITLEY, L.B. MCCOY, H.S. O'BRYANT, J.L. KILGORE, E.E. HAFF, K. PIERCE, and M.H. STONE. Effects of different set configurations on barbell velocity and displacement during a clean pull. *J Strength Cond Res* 17:95-103, 2003.

73. HAFF, G.G., A. WHITLEY, and J.A. POTTEIGER. A brief review: explosive exercises and sports performance. *Natl Strength Cond Assoc* 23:13-20, 2001.

74. HÄKKINEN, K. Neuromuscular adaptations during strength training, aging, detraining, and immobilization. *Crit Rev Phys Rehabil Med* 6:161-198, 1994.

75. HÄKKINEN, K., M. ALEN, M. KALLINEN, M. IZQUI-ERDO, K. JOKELAINEN, H. LASSILA, E. MALKIA, W.J. KRAEMER, and R.U. NEWTON. Muscle CSA, force production, and activation of leg extensors during isometric and dynamic muscle actions in middle-aged and elderly men and women. *J Aging Phys Act* 6:232-247, 1998.

76. HÄKKINEN, K., and M. KALLINEN. Distribution of strength training volume into one or two daily sessions and neuromuscular adaptations in female athletes. *Electromyogr Clin Neurophysiol* 34:117-124, 1994.

77. HÄKKINEN, K., H. KAUHANEN, and T. KUOPPA. Neural, muscular and hormonal adaptations, changes in muscle strength and weightlifting results with respect to variations in training during one year follow-up period in Finnish elite weightlifters. *World Weightlifting (IWF)* 87:2-10, 1987.

78. HÄKKINEN, K., and P.V. KOMI. Changes in electrical and mechanical behavior of leg extensor muscles during heavy resistance strength training. *Scand J Sports Sci* 7:55-64, 1985.

79. HÄKKINEN, K., and P.V. KOMI. Effect of explosive type strength training on electromyographic and force production characteristics of leg extensor muscles during concentric and various stretch-shortening cycle exercises. *Scand J Sports Sci* 7:65-76, 1985.

80. HÄKKINEN, K., and P.V. KOMI. Training-induced changes in neuromuscular performance under voluntary and reflex conditions. *Eur J Appl Physiol Occup Physiol* 55:147-155, 1986.

81. HÄKKINEN, K., P.V. KOMI, M. ALEN, and H. KAUHANEN. EMG, muscle fibre and force production characteristics during a 1 year training period in elite weight-lifters. *Eur J Appl Physiol* 56:419-427, 1987.

82. HÄKKINEN, K., P.V. KOMI, and P.A. TESCH. Effect of combined concentric and eccentric strength training and detraining on force-time, muscle fiber and metabolic characteristics of leg extensor muscles. *Scand J Sports Sci* 3:50-58, 1981.

83. HÄKKINEN, K., R.U. NEWTON, S.E. GORDON, M. MCCORMICK, J.S. VOLEK, B.C. NINDL, L.A. GOTSHALK, W.W. CAMPBELL, W.J. EVANS, A. HÄKKINEN, B.J. HUMPHRIES, and W.J. KRAEMER. Changes in muscle morphology, electromyographic activity, and force production characteristics during progressive strength training in young and older men. *J Gerontol A Biol Sci Med Sci* 53:B415-423, 1998.

84. HÄKKINEN, K., A. PAKARINEN, M. ALEN, H. KAUHANEN, and P.V. KOMI. Neuromuscular and hormonal adaptations in athletes to strength training in two years. *J Appl Physiol* 65:2406-2412, 1988.

85. HARMAN, E. Resistance training modes: a biomechanical perspective. *Strength Cond* 16:59-65, 1994.

86. HARRIS, G.R., M.H. STONE, H.S. O'BRYANT, C.M. PROULX, and R.L. JOHNSON. Short-term performance effects of high power, high force, or combined weight-training methods. *J Strength Cond Res* 14:14-20, 2000.

87. HARRIS, R.C., R.H. EDWARDS, E. HULTMAN, L.O. NORDESJO, B. NYLIND, and K. SAHLIN. The time course of phosphorylcreatine resynthesis during recovery of the quadriceps muscle in man. *Pflugers Arch* 367:137-142, 1976.

88. HENNEMAN, E., G. SOMJEN, and D.O. CARPENTER. Excitability and inhibitability of motoneurons of different sizes. *J Neurophysiol* 28:599-620, 1965.

89. HIGBIE, E.J., K.J. CURETON, G.L. WARREN, III, and B.M. PRIOR. Effects of concentric and eccentric training on muscle strength, cross-sectional area, and neural activation. *J Appl Physiol* 81:2173-2181, 1996.

90. HOEGER, W.W.K., S.L. BARETTE, D.F. HALE, and D.R. HOPKINS. Relationship between repetitions and selected percentages of one repetition maximum. *J Appl Sport Sci Res* 1:11-13, 1987.

91. HOEGER, W.W.K., D.R. HOPKINS, S.L. BARETTE, and D.F. HALE. Relationship between repetitions and selected percentages of one repetition maximum: a comparison between untrained and trained males and females. *J Appl Sport Sci Res* 4:47-54, 1990.

92. HOFF, J., A. GRAN, and J. HELGERUD. Maximal strength training improves aerobic endurance performance. *Scand J Med Sci Sports* 12:288-295, 2002.

93. HOFF, J., and J. HELGERUD. Endurance and strength training for soccer players: physiological considerations. *Sports Med* 34:165-180, 2004.

94. HOFF, J., J. HELGERUD, and U. WISLOFF. Maximal strength training improves work economy in trained female cross-country skiers. *Med Sci Sports Exerc* 31:870-877, 1999.

95. HOFF, J., O.J. KEMI, and J. HELGERUD. Strength and endurance differences between elite and junior elite ice hockey players: the importance of allometric scaling. *Int J Sports Med* 26:537-541, 2005.

96. HOFFMAN, J.R., W.J. KRAEMER, A.C. FRY, M. DESCHENES, and M. KEMP. The effects of self-selection for frequency of training in a winter conditioning program for football. *J Appl Sport Sci Res* 4:76-82, 1990.

97. HOLTERMANN, A., K. ROELEVELD, B. VEREIJKEN, and G. ETTEMA. The effect of rate of force development on maximal force production: acute and training-related aspects. *Eur J Appl Physiol* 99:605-613, 2007.

98. HOUSTON, M.E., E.A. FROESE, S.P. VALERIOTE, H.J. GREEN, and D.A. RANNEY. Muscle performance, morphology and metabolic capacity during strength training and detraining: a one leg model. *Eur J Appl Physiol* 51:25-35, 1983.

99. HULTMAN, E., J. BERGSTROM, and N.M. ANDERSON. Breakdown and resynthesis of phosphorylcreatine and adenosine triphosphate in connection with muscular work in man. *Scand J Clin Lab Invest* 19:56-66, 1967.

100. HULTMAN, E., and H. SJOHOLM. Biochemical causes of fatigue. In: *Human Muscle Power*. N.L. Jones, ed. Champaign, IL: Human Kinetics, 1986, pp. 343-363.

101. HUMPHRIES, B., E. DUGAN, and T.L. DOYLE. Muscular fitness. In: *ACSM's Resource Manual for Guidelines for Exercise Testing and Prescription*. L.A. Kaminsky, ed. Baltimore: Lippincott Williams & Wilkins, 2006, pp. 206-224.

102. HUNTER, G.R. Changes in body composition, body build and performance associated with different weight training frequencies in males and females. *NSCA J* 7:26-28, 1985.

103. HUYGENS, W., M.A. THOMIS, M.W. PEETERS, R.F. VLIETINCK, and G.P. BEUNEN. Determinants and upper-limit heritabilities of skeletal muscle mass and strength. *Can J Appl Physiol* 29:186-200, 2004.

104. IVEY, F.M., S.M. ROTH, R.E. FERRELL, B.L. TRACY, J.T. LEMMER, D.E. HURLBUT, G.F. MARTEL, E.L. SIEGEL, J.L. FOZARD, E. JEFFREY METTER, J.L. FLEG, and B.F. HURLEY. Effects of age, gender, and myostatin genotype on the hypertrophic response to heavy resistance strength training. *J Gerontol A Biol Sci Med Sci* 55:M641-M648, 2000.

105. IZQUIERDO, M., J. IBANEZ, J.J. GONZALEZ-BADILLO, K. HÄKKINEN, N.A. RATAMESS, W.J. KRAEMER, D.N. FRENCH, J. ESLAVA, A. ALTADILL, X. ASIAIN, and E.M. GOROSTIAGA. Differential effects of strength training leading to failure versus not to failure on hormonal responses, strength, and muscle power gains. *J Appl Physiol* 100:1647-1656, 2006.

106. JENSEN, B.R., M. PILEGAARD, and G. SJOGAARD. Motor unit recruitment and rate coding in response to fatiguing shoulder abductions and subsequent recovery. *Eur J Appl Physiol* 83:190-199, 2000.

107. JONES, K., P. BISHOP, G. HUNTER, and G. FLEISIG. The effects of varying resistance-training loads on intermediate- and high-velocity-specific adaptations. *J Strength Cond Res* 15:349-356, 2001.

108. JONES, L. Coaching platform: advanced training programs. *Weightlifting USA* volume x issue 4: 8-11, 1992.

109. JONES, L. Training programs: do Bulgarian methods lead the way for the USA? *Weightlifting USA* 9:10-11, 1991.

110. JUNG, A.P. The impact of resistance training on distance running performance. *Sports Med* 33:539-552, 2003.

111. KAMEN, G. The acquisition of maximal isometric plantar flexor strength: a force-time curve analysis. *J Motor Behav* 15:63-73, 1983.

112. KAMEN, G., and A. ROY. Motor unit synchronization in young and elderly adults. *Eur J Appl Physiol* 81:403-410, 2000.

113. KANEKO, M., T. FUCHIMOTO, H. TOJI, and K. SUEI. Training effect of different loads on the force–velocity relationship and mechanical power output in human muscle. *Scand J Sports Sci* 5:50-55, 1983.

114. KAWAMORI, N., and G.G. HAFF. The optimal training load for the development of muscular power. *J Strength Cond Res* 18:675-684, 2004.

115. KEMMLER, W.K., D. LAUBER, A. WASSERMANN, and J.L. MAYHEW. Predicting maximal strength in trained postmenopausal woman. *J Strength Cond Res* 20:838-842, 2006.

116. KOMI, P.V. *Strength and Power in Sport*. Oxford, UK: Blackwell Scientific, 1991.

117. KOMI, P.V. *Strength and Power in Sport*. 2nd ed. Malden, MA: Blackwell Scientific, 2003.

118. KOMI, P.V. Stretch-shortening cycle: a powerful model to study normal and fatigued muscle. *J Biomech* 33:1197-1206, 2000.

119. KOMI, P.V. Training of muscle strength and power: interaction of neuromotoric, hypertrophic, and mechanical factors. *Int J Sports Med* 7:10-15, 1986.

120. KRAEMER, W.J., A.C. FRY, B.J. WARREN, M.H. STONE, S.J. FLECK, J.T. KEARNEY, B.P. CONROY, C.M. MARESH, C.A. WESEMAN, N.T. TRIPLETT, and S.E. GORDON. Acute hormonal responses in elite junior weightlifters. *Int J Sports Med* 13:103-109, 1992.

121. KRAEMER, W.J., L. MARCHITELLI, S.E. GORDON, E. HARMAN, J.E. DZIADOS, R. MELLO, P. FRYKMAN, D. MCCURRY, and S.J. FLECK. Hormonal and growth factor responses to heavy resistance exercise protocols. *J Appl Physiol* 69:1442-1450, 1990.

122. KRAVITZ, L., C. AKALAN, K. NOWICKI, and S.J. KINZEY. Prediction of 1 repetition maximum in high-school power lifters. *J Strength Cond Res* 17:167-172, 2003.

123. LAWTON, T., J. CRONIN, E. DRINKWATER, R. LINDSELL, and D. PYNE. The effect of continuous repetition training and intra-set rest training on bench press strength and power. *J Sports Med Phys Fitness* 44:361-367, 2004.

124. LAWTON, T.W., J.B. CRONIN, and R.P. LINDSELL. Effect of interrepetition rest intervals on weight

training repetition power output. *J Strength Cond Res* 20:172-176, 2006.

125. MACDOUGALL, J.D., G.C. ELDER, D.G. SALE, J.R. MOROZ, and J.R. SUTTON. Effects of strength training and immobilization on human muscle fibres. *Eur J Appl Physiol* 43:25-34, 1980.

126. MALISOUX, L., M. FRANCAUX, and D. THEISEN. What do single-fiber studies tell us about exercise training? *Med Sci Sports Exerc* 39:1051-1060, 2007.

127. MAYHEW, J.L., J.L. PRINSTER, J.S. WARE, D.L. ZIMMER, J.R. ARABAS, and M.G. BEMBEN. Muscular endurance repetitions to predict bench press strength in men of different training levels. *J Sports Med Phys Fitness* 35:108-113, 1995.

128. MCBRIDE, J.M., S. NIMPHIUS, and T.M. ERICKSON. The acute effects of heavy-load squats and loaded countermovement jumps on sprint performance. *J Strength Cond Res* 19:893-897, 2005.

129. MCBRIDE, J.M., T. TRIPLETT-MCBRIDE, A. DAVIE, and R.U. NEWTON. A comparison of strength and power characteristics between power lifters, Olympic lifters, and sprinters. *J Strength Cond Res* 13:58-66, 1999.

130. MCBRIDE, J.M., T. TRIPLETT-MCBRIDE, A. DAVIE, and R.U. NEWTON. The effect of heavy- vs. light-load jump squats on the development of strength, power, and speed. *J Strength Cond Res* 16:75-82, 2002.

131. MCCALL, G.E., W.C. BYRNES, S.J. FLECK, A. DICKINSON, and W.J. KRAEMER. Acute and chronic hormonal responses to resistance training designed to promote muscle hypertrophy. *Can J Appl Physiol* 24:96-107, 1999.

132. MCLESTER, J.R., P. BISHOP, and M.E. GUILLIAMS. Comparison of 1 day and 3 day per week of equal volume resistance training in experienced subjects. *J Strength Cond Res* 14:273-281, 2000.

133. MEDVEDEV, A.S. *Sistema Mnogoletnyei Trenirovki V Tyazheloi Atletikye*. Moscow: Fizkultura i Sport, 1986.

134. MELROSE, D.R., F.J. SPANIOL, M.E. BOHLING, and R.A. BONNETTE. Physiological and performance characteristics of adolescent club volleyball players. *J Strength Cond Res* 21:481-486, 2007.

135. MILNER-BROWN, H.S., R.B. STEIN, and R.G. LEE. Synchronization of human motor units: possible roles of exercise and supraspinal reflexes. *Electroencephalogr Clin Neurophysiol* 38:245-254, 1975.

136. MIRKOV, D.M., A. NEDELJKOVIC, S. MILANOVIC, and S. JARIC. Muscle strength testing: evaluation of tests of explosive force production. *Eur J Appl Physiol* 91:147-154, 2004.

137. MORITANI, T., W.M. SHERMAN, M. SHIBATA, T. MATSUMOTO, and M. SHINOHARA. Oxygen availability and motor unit activity in humans. *Eur J Appl Physiol Occup Physiol* 64:552-556, 1992.

138. MOSS, B.M., P.E. REFSNES, A. ABILDGAARD, K. NICOLAYSEN, and J. JENSEN. Effects of maximal effort strength training with different loads on dynamic strength, cross-sectional area, load-power and load-velocity relationships. *Eur J Appl Physiol* 75:193-199, 1997.

139. NEVILL, A.M., and R.L. HOLDER. Scaling, normalizing, and per ratio standards: an allometric modeling approach. *J Appl Physiol* 79:1027-1031, 1995.

140. NOAKES, T.D. Implications of exercise testing for prediction of athletic performance: a contemporary perspective. *Med Sci Sports Exerc* 20:319-330, 1988.

141. NOAKES, T.D., K.H. MYBURGH, and R. SCHALL. Peak treadmill running velocity during the VO2 max test predicts running performance. *J Sports Sci* 8:35-45, 1990.

142. NORRBRAND, L., J.D. FLUCKEY, M. POZZO, and P.A. TESCH. Resistance training using eccentric overload induces early adaptations in skeletal muscle size. *Eur J Appl Physiol* 102:271-281, 2008.

143. ØSTERÅS, H., J. HELGERUD, and J. HOFF. Maximal strength-training effects on force–velocity and force–power relationships explain increases in aerobic performance in humans. *Eur J Appl Physiol* 88:255-263, 2002.

144. PAAVOLAINEN, L., K. HÄKKINEN, I. HAMALAINEN, A. NUMMELA, and H. RUSKO. Explosive-strength training improves 5-km running time by improving running economy and muscle power. *J Appl Physiol* 86:1527-1533, 1999.

145. PAAVOLAINEN, L., K. HÄKKINEN, and H. RUSKO. Effects of explosive type strength training on physical performance characteristics in cross-country skiers. *Eur J Appl Physiol Occup Physiol* 62:251-255, 1991.

146. PAPADIMITRIOU, I.D., C. PAPADOPOULOS, A. KOUVATSI, and C. TRIANTAPHYLLIDIS. The ACTN3 gene in elite Greek track and field athletes. *Int J Sports Med* 29:352-355, 2008.

147. PETERSON, M.D., B.A. ALVAR, and M.R. RHEA. The contribution of maximal force production to explosive movement among young collegiate athletes. *J Strength Cond Res* 20:867-873, 2006.

148. PETERSON, M.D., M.R. RHEA, and B.A. ALVAR. Applications of the dose-response for muscular strength development: a review of meta-analytic efficacy and reliability for designing training prescription. *J Strength Cond Res* 19:950-958, 2005.

149. PINCIVERO, D.M., W.S. GEAR, N.M. MOYNA, and R.J. ROBERTSON. The effects of rest interval on quadriceps torque and perceived exertion in healthy males. *J Sports Med Phys Fitness* 39:294-299, 1999.

150. PISTILLI, E.E., D.E. KAMINSKY, L. TOTTEN, and D. MILLER. An 8-week periodized mesocycle leading to a national level weightlifting competition. *Strength Cond J* 26:62-68, 2004.

151. PLISK, S.S., and M.H. STONE. Periodization strategies. *Strength Cond* 25:19-37, 2003.

152. POLLOCK, M.L., J.E. GRAVES, M.M. BAMMAN, S.H. LEGGETT, D.M. CARPENTER, C. CARR, J. CIRULLI, J. MATKOZICH, and M. FULTON. Frequency and volume of resistance training: effect on cervical extension strength. *Arch Phys Med Rehabil* 74:1080-1086, 1993.

153. PRINCE, F.P., R.S. HIKIDA, and F.C. HAGERMAN. Human muscle fiber types in power lifters, distance runners and untrained subjects. *Pflugers Arch* 363:19-26, 1976.

154. PRINCE, F.P., R.S. HIKIDA, F.C. HAGERMAN, R.S. STARON, and W.H. ALLEN. A morphometric analysis of human muscle fibers with relation to fiber types and adaptations to exercise. *J Neurol Sci* 49:165-179, 1981.

155. REYNOLDS, J.M., T.J. GORDON, and R.A. ROBERGS. Prediction of one repetition maximum strength from multiple repetition maximum testing and anthropometry. *J Strength Cond Res* 20:584-592, 2006.

156. RHEA, M.R., B.A. ALVAR, L.N. BURKETT, and S.D. BALL. A meta-analysis to determine the dose response for strength development. *Med Sci Sports Exerc* 35:456-464, 2003.

157. ROONEY, K.J., R.D. HERBERT, and R.J. BALNAVE. Fatigue contributes to the strength training stimulus. *Med Sci Sports Exerc* 26:1160-1164, 1994.

158. RUTHERFORD, O.M. and D.A. JONES. The role of learning and coordination in strength training. *Eur J Appl Physiol Occup Physiol* 55:100-105, 1986.

159. RYDWIK, E., C. KARLSSON, K. FRANDIN, and G. AKNER. Muscle strength testing with one repetition maximum in the arm/shoulder for people aged 75 +: test-retest reliability. *Clin Rehabil* 21:258-265, 2007.

160. SAHLIN, K., and J.M. REN. Relationship of contraction capacity to metabolic changes during recovery from a fatiguing contraction. *J Appl Physiol* 67:648-654, 1989.

161. SALE, D.G. Neural adaptation to resistance training. *Med Sci Sports Exerc* 20:S135-S145, 1988.

162. SCHMIDTBLEICHER, D. Strength training, part 2: structural analysis of motor strength qualities and its application to training. *Science Periodical on Research and Technology* 5:1-10, 1985.

163. SCHMIDTBLEICHER, D. Training for power events. In: *Strength and Power in Sport*. P.V. Komi, ed. Oxford, UK: Blackwell, 1992, pp. 381-385.

164. SEMMLER, J.G. Motor unit synchronization and neuromuscular performance. *Exerc Sport Sci Rev* 30:8-14, 2002.

165. SEMMLER, J.G., K.W. KORNATZ, D.V. DINENNO, S. ZHOU, and R.M. ENOKA. Motor unit synchronisation is enhanced during slow lengthening contractions of a hand muscle. *J Physiol* 545:681-695, 2002.

166. SEMMLER, J.G., and M.A. NORDSTROM. Motor unit discharge and force tremor in skill- and strength-trained individuals. *Exp Brain Res* 119:27-38, 1998.

167. SEMMLER, J.G., M.V. SALE, F.G. MEYER, and M.A. NORDSTROM. Motor-unit coherence and its relation with synchrony are influenced by training. *J Neurophysiol* 92:3320-3331, 2004.

168. SEYNNES, O.R., M. DE BOER, and M.V. NARICI. Early skeletal muscle hypertrophy and architectural changes in response to high-intensity resistance training. *J Appl Physiol* 102:368-373, 2007.

169. SFORZO, G.A., and P.R. TOUEY. Manipulating exercise order affects muscular performance during a resistance exercise training session. *J Strength Cond Res* 10:20-24, 1996.

170. SHAW, C.E., K.K. MCCULLY, and J.D. POSNER. Injuries during the one repetition maximum assessment in the elderly. *J Cardiopulm Rehabil* 15:283-287, 1995.

171. SHIMANO, T., W.J. KRAEMER, B.A. SPIERING, J.S. VOLEK, D.L. HATFIELD, R. SILVESTRE, J.L. VINGREN, M.S. FRAGALA, C.M. MARESH, S.J. FLECK, R.U. NEWTON, L.P. SPREUWENBERG, and K. HÄKKINEN. Relationship between the number of repetitions and selected percentages of one repetition maximum in free weight exercises in trained and untrained men. *J Strength Cond Res* 20:819-823, 2006.

172. SHOEPE, T.C., J.E. STELZER, D.P. GARNER, and J.J. WIDRICK. Functional adaptability of muscle fibers to long-term resistance exercise. *Med Sci Sports Exerc* 35:944-951, 2003.

173. SIFF, M.C., and Y.U. VERKHOSHANSKY. *Supertraining*. Denver, CO: Supertraining International, 1999.

174. SILVESTRE, R., W.J. KRAEMER, C. WEST, D.A. JUDELSON, B.A. SPIERING, J.L. VINGREN, D.L. HATFIELD, J.M. ANDERSON, and C.M. MARESH. Body composition and physical performance during a National Collegiate Athletic Association Division I men's soccer season. *J Strength Cond Res* 20:962-970, 2006.

175. SINCLAIR, R.G. Normalizing the performances of athletes in Olympic weightlifting. *Can J Appl Sport Sci* 10:94-98, 1985.

176. SMITH, J.C., A.C. FRY, L.W. WEISS, Y. LI, and S.J. KINZEY. The effects of high-intensity exercise on a 10-second sprint cycle test. *J Strength Cond Res* 15:344-348, 2001.

177. SPREUWENBERG, L.P., W.J. KRAEMER, B.A. SPIERING, J.S. VOLEK, D.L. HATFIELD, R. SILVESTRE, J.L. VINGREN, M.S. FRAGALA, K. HÄKKINEN, R.U. NEWTON, C.M. MARESH, and S.J. FLECK. Influence of exercise order in a resistance-training exercise session. *J Strength Cond Res* 20:141-144, 2006.

178. STARON, R.S., E.S. MALICKY, M.J. LEONARDI, J.E. FALKEL, F.C. HAGERMAN, and G.A. DUDLEY. Muscle hypertrophy and fast fiber type conversions in heavy resistance-trained women. *Eur J Appl Physiol* 60:71-79, 1990.

179. STONE, M.H., T.J. CHANDLER, M.S. CONLEY, J.B. KRAMER, and M.E. STONE. Training to muscular failure: is it necessary? *Strength Cond* 18:44-51, 1996.

180. STONE, M.H., and H.O. O'BRYANT. *Weight Training: A Scientific Approach*. Edina, MN: Burgess, 1987.

181. STONE, M.H., H.S. O'BRYANT, and J. GARHAMMER. A theoretical model of strength training. *NSCA J.* 3:36-39, 1982.

182. STONE, M.H., H.S. O'BRYANT, B.K. SCHILLING, R.L. JOHNSON, K.C. PIERCE, G.G. HAFF, A.J. KOCH, and M. STONE. Periodization: effects of manipulat-

ing volume and intensity, part 1. *Strength Cond* 21:56-62, 1999.

183. STONE, M.H., H.S. O'BRYANT, B.K. SCHILLING, R.L. JOHNSON, K.C. PIERCE, G.G. HAFF, A.J. KOCH, and M. STONE. Periodization: effects of manipulating volume and intensity, part 2. *Strength Cond J* 21:54-60, 1999.

184. STONE, M.H., K. PIERCE, W.A. SANDS, and M. STONE. Weightlifting: program design. *Strength Cond* 28:10-17, 2006.

185. STONE, M.H., W.A. SANDS, K.C. PIERCE, J. CARLOCK, M. CARDINALE, and R.U. NEWTON. Relationship of maximum strength to weightlifting performance. *Med Sci Sports Exerc* 37:1037-1043, 2005.

186. STONE, M.H., W.A. SANDS, K.C. PIERCE, M.W. RAMSEY, and G.G. HAFF. Power and power potentiation among strength power athletes: preliminary study. *Int J Sports Physiol Perf* in press.

187. STONE, M.H., M.E. STONE, and W.A. SANDS. *Principles and Practice of Resistance Training*. Champaign, IL: Human Kinetics, 2007.

188. STULL, G.A., and D.H. CLARKE. Patterns of recovery following isometric and isotonic strength decrement. *Med Sci Sports* 3:135-139, 1971.

189. TAN, B. Manipulating resistance training program variables to optimize maximum strength in men: a review. *J Strength Cond Res* 13:289-304, 1999.

190. TANAKA, H., and T. SWENSEN. Impact of resistance training on endurance performance: a new form of cross-training? *Sports Med* 25:191-200, 1998.

191. TERZIS, G., G. GEORGIADIS, E. VASSILIADOU, and P. MANTA. Relationship between shot put performance and triceps brachia fiber type composition and power production. *Eur J Appl Physiol* 90:10-15, 2003.

192. TESCH, P.A., and J. KARLSSON. Muscle fiber types and size in trained and untrained muscles of elite athletes. *J Appl Physiol* 59:1716-1720, 1985.

193. THOMAS, M., M.A. FIATARONE, and R.A. FIELDING. Leg power in young women: relationship to body composition, strength, and function. *Med Sci Sports Exerc* 28:1321-1326, 1996.

194. THOMPSON, P.D., N. MOYNA, R. SEIP, T. PRICE, P. CLARKSON, T. ANGELOPOULOS, P. GORDON, L. PESCATELLO, P. VISICH, R. ZOELLER, J.M. DEVANEY, H. GORDISH, S. BILBIE, and E.P. HOFFMAN. Functional polymorphisms associated with human muscle size and strength. *Med Sci Sports Exerc* 36:1132-1139, 2004.

195. THORSTENSSON, A., B. HULTEN, W. VON DOBELN, and J. KARLSSON. Effect of strength training on enzyme activities and fibre characteristics in human skeletal muscle. *Acta Physiol Scand* 96:392-398, 1976.

196. TRAPPE, S., M. HARBER, A. CREER, P. GALLAGHER, D. SLIVKA, K. MINCHEV, and D. WHITSETT. Single muscle fiber adaptations with marathon training. *J Appl Physiol* 101:721-727, 2006.

197. VAN CUTSEM, M., J. DUCHATEAU, and K. HAINAUT. Changes in single motor unit behaviour contribute to the increase in contraction speed after dynamic training in humans. *J Physiol* 513 (pt 1):295-305, 1998.

198. VIITASALO, J.T. Rate of force development, muscle structure and fatigue. In: *Biomechanics VII-A: Proceedings of the 7th International Congress of Biomechanics*. A. Morecki, et al. eds. Warsaw Poland, 1981, pp. 136-141.

199. VIITASALO, J.T., and P.V. KOMI. Interrelationships between electromyographic, mechanical, muscle structure and reflex time measurements in man. *Acta Physiol Scand* 111:97-103, 1981.

200. VOROBYEV, A.N. *A Textbook on Weightlifting*. Budapest: International Weightlifting Federation, 1978.

201. WERNBOM, M., J. AUGUSTSSON, and R. THOMEE. The influence of frequency, intensity, volume and mode of strength training on whole muscle cross-sectional area in humans. *Sports Med* 37:225-264, 2007.

202. WESTCOTT, W.L. *Strength Fitness*. Boston: Allyn & Bacon, 1982.

203. WIDRICK, J.J., J.E. STELZER, T.C. SHOEPE, and D.P. GARNER. Functional properties of human muscle fibers after short-term resistance exercise training. *Am J Physiol Regul Integr Comp Physiol* 283:R408-R416, 2002.

204. WILLARDSON, J.M. A brief review: factors affecting the length of the rest interval between resistance exercise sets. *J Strength Cond Res* 20:978-984, 2006.

205. WILLIAMSON, D.L., P.M. GALLAGHER, C.C. CARROLL, U. RAUE, and S.W. TRAPPE. Reduction in hybrid single muscle fiber proportions with resistance training in humans. *J Appl Physiol* 91:1955-1961, 2001.

206. WILSON, G.J., R.U. NEWTON, A.J. MURPHY, and B.J. HUMPHRIES. The optimal training load for the development of dynamic athletic performance. *Med Sci Sports Exerc* 25:1279-1286, 1993.

207. YAMAMOTO, L.M., R.M. LOPEZ, J.F. KLAU, D.J. CASA, W.J. KRAEMER, and C.M. MARESH. The effects of resistance training on endurance distance running performance among highly trained runners: a systematic review. *J Strength Cond Res* 22:2036-2044. 2008.

208. YAO, W., R.J. FUGLEVAND, and R.M. ENOKA. Motor-unit synchronization increases EMG amplitude and decreases force steadiness of simulated contractions. *J Neurophysiol* 83:441-452, 2000.

209. YETTER, M. and G.L. MOIR. The acute effects of heavy back and front squats on speed during forty-meter sprint trials. *J Strength Cond Res* 22:159-165. 2008.

210. YOUNG, W.B., A. JENNER, and K. GRIFFITHS. Acute enhancement of power performance from heavy load squats. *J. Strength Cond Res* 12:82-84, 1998.

211. ZATSIORSKY, V.M. *Science and Practice of Strength Training*. Champaign, IL: Human Kinetics, 1995.

212. ZATSIORSKY, V.M., and W.J. KRAEMER. *Science and Practice of Strength Training.* 2nd ed. Champaign, IL: Human Kinetics, 2006.

213. ZOELLER, R.F., E.D. RYAN, H. GORDISH-DRESSMAN, T.B. PRICE, R.L. SEIP, T.J. ANGELOPOULOS, N.M. MOYNA, P.M. GORDON, P.D. THOMPSON, and E.P. HOFFMAN. Allometric scaling of biceps strength before and after resistance training in men. *Med Sci Sports Exerc* 39:1013-1019, 2007.

Chapter 11

1. *2002 USA Cycling Club Coach Manual.* Colorado Springs, CO: USA Cycling, 2002.

2. AAGAARD, P., E.B. SIMONSEN, J.L. ANDERSEN, P. MAGNUSSON, and P. DYHRE-POULSEN. Increased rate of force development and neural drive of human skeletal muscle following resistance training. *J Appl Physiol* 93:1318-1326, 2002.

3. ABERNETHY, P.J., R. THAYER, and A.W. TAYLOR. Acute and chronic responses of skeletal muscle to endurance and sprint exercise. A review. *Sports Med* 10:365-389, 1990.

4. ACEVEDO, E.O., and A.H. GOLDFARB. Increased training intensity effects on plasma lactate, ventilatory threshold, and endurance. *Med Sci Sports Exerc* 21:563-568, 1989.

5. BAILEY, S.P., and R.R. PATE. Feasibility of improving running economy. *Sports Med* 12:228-236, 1991.

6. BAKER, D., and S. NANCE. The relation between running speed and measures of strength and power in professional rugby league players. *J Strength Cond Res* 13:230-235, 1999.

7. BALSOM, P.D., J.Y. SEGER, B. SJÖDIN, and B. EKBLOM. Maximal-intensity intermittent exercise: effect of recovery duration. *Int J Sports Med* 13:528-533, 1992.

8. BALSOM, P.D., J.Y. SEGER, B. SJÖDIN, and B. EKBLOM. Physiological responses to maximal intensity intermittent exercise. *Eur J Appl Physiol* 65:144-149, 1992.

9. BASSETT, D.R., Jr., and E.T. HOWLEY. Limiting factors for maximum oxygen uptake and determinants of endurance performance. *Med Sci Sports Exerc* 32:70-84, 2000.

10. BASSETT, D.R., Jr., and E.T. HOWLEY. Maximal oxygen uptake: "classical" versus "contemporary: viewpoints. *Med Sci Sports Exerc* 29:591-603, 1997.

11. BASTIAANS, J.J., A.B. VAN DIEMEN, T. VENEBERG, and A.E. JEUKENDRUP. The effects of replacing a portion of endurance training by explosive strength training on performance in trained cyclists. *Eur J Appl Physiol* 86:79-84, 2001.

12. BEHM, D.G., and D.G. SALE. Intended rather than actual movement velocity determines velocity-specific training response. *J Appl Physiol* 74:359-368, 1993.

13. BEHM, D.G., and D.G. SALE. Velocity specificity of resistance training. *Sports Med* 15:374-388, 1993.

14. BENTLEY, D.J., J. NEWELL, and D. BISHOP. Incremental exercise test design and analysis: implications for performance diagnostics in endurance athletes. *Sports Med* 37:575-586, 2007.

15. BERGLUND, B., B. EKBLOM, E. EKBLOM, L. BERGLUND, A. KALLNER, P. REINEBO, and S. LINDEBERG. The Swedish Blood Pass project. *Scand J Med Sci Sports* 17:292-297, 2007.

16. BILLAT, L.V. Interval training for performance: a scientific and empirical practice. Special recommendations for middle- and long-distance running. Part I: aerobic interval training. *Sports Med* 31:13-31, 2001.

17. BILLAT, L.V. Interval training for performance: a scientific and empirical practice. Special recommendations for middle- and long-distance running. Part II: anaerobic interval training. *Sports Med* 31:75-90, 2001.

18. BOSQUET, L., L. LEGER, and P. LEGROS. Methods to determine aerobic endurance. *Sports Med* 32:675-700, 2002.

19. BRANSFORD, D.R., and E.T. HOWLEY. Oxygen cost of running in trained and untrained men and women. *Med Sci Sports* 9:41-44, 1977.

20. BURGOMASTER, K.A., G.J. HEIGENHAUSER, and M.J. GIBALA. Effect of short-term sprint interval training on human skeletal muscle carbohydrate metabolism during exercise and time-trial performance. *J Appl Physiol* 100:2041-2047, 2006.

21. BURGOMASTER, K.A., S.C. HUGHES, G.J. HEIGENHAUSER, S.N. BRADWELL, and M.J. GIBALA. Six sessions of sprint interval training increases muscle oxidative potential and cycle endurance capacity in humans. *J Appl Physiol* 98:1985-1990, 2005.

22. BURLESON, M.A., JR., H.S. O'BRYANT, M.H. STONE, M.A. COLLINS, and T. TRIPLETT-MCBRIDE. Effect of weight training exercise and treadmill exercise on post-exercise oxygen consumption. *Med Sci Sports Exerc* 30:518-522, 1998.

23. BURTSCHER, M., M. FAULHABER, M. FLATZ, R. LIKAR, and W. NACHBAUER. Effects of short-term acclimatization to altitude (3200 m) on aerobic and anaerobic exercise performance. *Int J Sports Med* 27:629-635, 2006.

24. CARTER, H., A.M. JONES, and J.H. DOUST. Effect of 6 weeks of endurance training on the lactate minimum speed. *J Sports Sci* 17:957-967, 1999.

25. CERRETELLI, P., G. AMBROSOLI, and M. FUMAGALLI. Anaerobic recovery in man. *Eur J Appl Physiol Occup Physiol* 34:141-148, 1975.

26. COGGAN, A.R., R.J. SPINA, M.A. ROGERS, D.S. KING, M. BROWN, P.M. NEMETH, and J.O. HOLLOSZY. Histochemical and enzymatic characteristics of skeletal muscle in master athletes. *J Appl Physiol* 68:1896-1901, 1990.

27. CONLEY, D.L., and G.S. KRAHENBUHL. Running economy and distance running performance of highly trained athletes. *Med Sci Sports Exerc* 12:357-360, 1980.

28. CONLEY, M. Bioenergetics of Exercise Training. In: *Essentials of Strength Training and Conditioning.* T.R.

Baechle and R.W. Earle, eds. Champaign, IL: Human Kinetics, 2000, pp. 73-90.

29. CONLEY, M.S., M.H. STONE, H.S. O'BRYANT, R.L. JOHNSON, D.R. HONEYCUTT, and T.P. HOKE. Peak power versus power at maximal oxygen uptake. In: *Proceedings of National Strength and Conditioning Association Annual Convention*. Las Vegas, NV, 1993.

30. COSTILL, D.L., W.J. FINK, and M.L. POLLOCK. Muscle fiber composition and enzyme activities of elite distance runners. *Med Sci Sports* 8:96-100, 1976.

31. COSTILL, D.L., M.G. FLYNN, J.P. KIRWAN, J.A. HOUMARD, J.B. MITCHELL, R. THOMAS, and S.H. PARK. Effects of repeated days of intensified training on muscle glycogen and swimming performance. *Med Sci Sports Exerc* 20:249-254, 1988.

32. COSTILL, D.L., R. THOMAS, R.A. ROBERGS, D. PASCOE, C. LAMBERT, S. BARR, and W.J. FINK. Adaptations to swimming training: influence of training volume. *Med Sci Sports Exerc* 23:371-377, 1991.

33. COSTILL, D.L., H. THOMASON, and E. ROBERTS. Fractional utilization of the aerobic capacity during distance running. *Med Sci Sports* 5:248-252, 1973.

34. COYLE, E.F. Improved muscular efficiency displayed as Tour de France champion matures. *J Appl Physiol* 98:2191-2196, 2005.

35. COYLE, E.F. Integration of the physiological factors determining endurance performance ability. *Exerc Sport Sci Rev* 23:25-63, 1995.

36. COYLE, E.F., A.R. COGGAN, M.K. HOPPER, and T.J. WALTERS. Determinants of endurance in well-trained cyclists. *J Appl Physiol* 64:2622-2630, 1988.

37. CRONIN, J.B. and K.T. HANSEN. Strength and power predictors of sports speed. *J Strength Cond Res* 19:349-357, 2005.

38. DAWSON, B., M. FITZSIMONS, S. GREEN, C. GOODMAN, M. CAREY, and K. COLE. Changes in performance, muscle metabolites, enzymes and fibre types after short sprint training. *Eur J Appl Physiol* 78:163-169, 1998.

39. DEMPSEY, J.A., P.G. HANSON, and K.S. HENDERSON. Exercise-induced arterial hypoxaemia in healthy human subjects at sea level. *J Physiol* 355:161-175, 1984.

40. DENADAI, B.S., M.J. ORTIZ, C.C. GRECO, and M.T. DE MELLO. Interval training at 95% and 100% of the velocity at VO2 max: effects on aerobic physiological indexes and running performance. *Appl Physiol Nutr Metab* 31:737-743, 2006.

41. DUDLEY, G.A., W.M. ABRAHAM, and R.L. TERJUNG. Influence of exercise intensity and duration on biochemical adaptations in skeletal muscle. *J Appl Physiol* 53:844-850, 1982.

42. DUDLEY, G.A., and R. DJAMIL. Incompatibility of endurance- and strength-training modes of exercise. *J Appl Physiol* 59:1446-1451, 1985.

43. DUMKE, C.L., D.W. BROCK, B.H. HELMS, and G.G. HAFF. Heart rate at lactate threshold and cycling time trials. *J Strength Cond Res* 20:601-607, 2006.

44. EKBLOM, B., G. WILSON, and P.O. ASTRAND. Central circulation during exercise after venesection and reinfusion of red blood cells. *J Appl Physiol* 40:379-383, 1976.

45. ELLIOTT, M.C., P.P. WAGNER, and L. CHIU. Power athletes and distance training: physiological and biomechanical rationale for change. *Sports Med* 37:47-57, 2007.

46. ESTEVE-LANAO, J., C. FOSTER, S. SEILER, and A. LUCIA. Impact of training intensity distribution on performance in endurance athletes. *J Strength Cond Res* 21:943-949, 2007.

47. FARRELL, P.A., J.H. WILMORE, E.F. COYLE, J.E. BILLING, and D.L. COSTILL. Plasma lactate accumulation and distance running performance. *Med Sci Sports* 11:338-344, 1979.

48. FARRELL, P.A., J.H. WILMORE, E.F. COYLE, J.E. BILLING, and D.L. COSTILL. Plasma lactate accumulation and distance running performance. 1979. *Med Sci Sports Exerc* 25:1091-1097; discussion 1089-1090, 1993.

49. FAULKNER, J.A., J. KOLLIAS, C.B. FAVOUR, E.R. BUSKIRK, and B. BALKE. Maximum aerobic capacity and running performance at altitude. *J Appl Physiol* 24:685-691, 1968.

50. FLECK, S. Bridging the gap: interval training: physiological basis. *NSCA J* 5:40-63, 1983.

51. FLECK, S., and W.J. KRAEMER. *Designing Resistance Training Programs*. 3rd ed. Champaign, IL: Human Kinetics, 2004.

52. FOSTER, C., L.L. HECTOR, R. WELSH, M. SCHRAGER, M.A. GREEN, and A.C. SNYDER. Effects of specific versus cross-training on running performance. *Eur J Appl Physiol Occup Physiol* 70:367-372, 1995.

53. FRANCH, J., K. MADSEN, M.S. DJURHUUS, and P.K. PEDERSEN. Improved running economy following intensified training correlates with reduced ventilatory demands. *Med Sci Sports Exerc* 30:1250-1256, 1998.

54. FRIEL, J. *Total Heart Rate Training*. Berkley, CA: Ulysses Press, 2006.

55. FRY, A.C., C.A. ALLEMEIER, and R.S. STARON. Correlation between percentage fiber type area and myosin heavy chain content in human skeletal muscle. *Eur J Appl Physiol Occup Physiol* 68:246-251, 1994.

56. GABBETT, T., T. KING, and D. JENKINS. Applied physiology of rugby league. *Sports Med* 38:119-138, 2008.

57. GIBALA, M.J. High-intensity interval training: a time-efficient strategy for health promotion? *Curr Sports Med Rep* 6:211-213, 2007.

58. GIBALA, M.J., J.P. LITTLE, M. VAN ESSEN, G.P. WILKIN, K.A. BURGOMASTER, A. SAFDAR, S. RAHA, and M.A. TARNOPOLSKY. Short-term sprint interval versus traditional endurance training: similar initial adaptations in human skeletal muscle and exercise performance. *J Physiol* 575:901-911, 2006.

59. GLEDHILL, N., D. COX, and R. JAMNIK. Endurance athletes' stroke volume does not plateau: major advantage is diastolic function. *Med Sci Sports Exerc* 26:1116-1121, 1994.

60. HÄKKINEN, K., A. MERO, and H. KAUHANEN. Specificity of endurance, sprint and strength training on physical performance capacity in young athletes. *J Sports Med Phys Fitness* 29:27-35, 1989.

61. HÄKKINEN, K. and E. MYLLYLA. Acute effects of muscle fatigue and recovery on force production and relaxation in endurance, power and strength athletes. *J Sports Med Phys Fitness* 30:5-12, 1990.

62. HELGERUD, J., L.C. ENGEN, U. WISLOFF, and J. HOFF. Aerobic endurance training improves soccer performance. *Med Sci Sports Exerc* 33:1925-1931, 2001.

63. HENNESSY, L.C. and A.W.S. WATSON. The interference effects of training for strength and endurance simultaneously. *J Strength Cond Res* 8:12-19, 1994.

64. HENRIKSSON, J. Effects of physical training on the metabolism of skeletal muscle. *Diabetes Care* 15:1701-1711, 1992.

65. HENRITZE, J., A. WELTMAN, R.L. SCHURRER, and K. BARLOW. Effects of training at and above the lactate threshold on the lactate threshold and maximal oxygen uptake. *Eur J Appl Physiol Occup Physiol* 54:84-88, 1985.

66. HICKSON, R.C., B.A. DVORAK, E.M. GOROSTIAGA, T.T. KUROWSKI, and C. FOSTER. Potential for strength and endurance training to amplify endurance performance. *J Appl Physiol* 65:2285-2290, 1988.

67. HILL-HAAS, S., D. BISHOP, B. DAWSON, C. GOODMAN, and J. EDGE. Effects of rest interval during high-repetition resistance training on strength, aerobic fitness, and repeated-sprint ability. *J Sports Sci* 25:619-628, 2007.

68. HOFF, J., A. GRAN, and J. HELGERUD. Maximal strength training improves aerobic endurance performance. *Scand J Med Sci Sports* 12:288-295. 2002.

69. HOLLOSZY, J.O. and E.F. COYLE. Adaptations of skeletal muscle to endurance exercise and their metabolic consequences. *J Appl Physiol* 56:831-838, 1984.

70. HOWALD, H., H. HOPPELER, H. CLAASSEN, O. MATHIEU, and R. STRAUB. Influences of endurance training on the ultrastructural composition of the different muscle fiber types in humans. *Pflugers Arch* 403:369-376, 1985.

71. INGJER, F. Capillary supply and mitochondrial content of different skeletal muscle fiber types in untrained and endurance-trained men. A histochemical and ultrastructural study. *Eur J Appl Physiol Occup Physiol* 40:197-209, 1979.

72. JACKSON, N.P., M.S. HICKEY, and R.F. REISER, II. High resistance/low repetition vs. low resistance/high repetition training: effects on performance of trained cyclists. *J Strength Cond Res* 21:289-295, 2007.

73. JOHNSTON, R.E., T.J. QUINN, R. KERTZER, and N.B. VROMAN. Strength training in female distance runners: impact on running economy. *J Strength Cond Res* 11:224-229, 1997.

74. JONES, A.M. A five year physiological case study of an Olympic runner. *Br J Sports Med* 32:39-43, 1998.

75. JONES, A.M., and H. CARTER. The effect of endurance training on parameters of aerobic fitness. *Sports Med* 29:373-386, 2000.

76. JOYNER, M.J., and E.F. COYLE. Endurance exercise performance: the physiology of champions. *J Physiol* 586:35-44, 2008.

77. JUNG, A.P. The impact of resistance training on distance running performance. *Sports Med* 33:539-552, 2003.

78. KEITH, S.P., I. JACOBS, and T.M. MCLELLAN. Adaptations to training at the individual anaerobic threshold. *Eur J Appl Physiol Occup Physiol* 65:316-323, 1992.

79. KINDERMANN, W., G. SIMON, and J. KEUL. The significance of the aerobic-anaerobic transition for the determination of work load intensities during endurance training. *Eur J Appl Physiol Occup Physiol* 42:25-34, 1979.

80. KLAUSEN, K., L.B. ANDERSEN, and I. PELLE. Adaptive changes in work capacity, skeletal muscle capillarization and enzyme levels during training and detraining. *Acta Physiol Scand* 113:9-16, 1981.

81. KORHONEN, M.T., A. CRISTEA, M. ALEN, K. HAKKINEN, S. SIPILA, A. MERO, J.T. VIITASALO, L. LARSSON, and H. SUOMINEN. Aging, muscle fiber type, and contractile function in sprint-trained athletes. *J Appl Physiol* 101:906-917, 2006.

82. KRAEMER, W.J., D.N. FRENCH, N.J. PAXTON, K. HÄKKINEN, J.S. VOLEK, W.J. SEBASTIANELLI, M. PUTUKIAN, R.U. NEWTON, M.R. RUBIN, A.L. GOMEZ, J.D. VESCOVI, N.A. RATAMESS, S.J. FLECK, J.M. LYNCH, and H.G. KNUTTGEN. Changes in exercise performance and hormonal concentrations over a big ten soccer season in starters and nonstarters. *J Strength Cond Res* 18:121-128, 2004.

83. KRAEMER, W.J., J.F. PATTON, S.E. GORDON, E.A. HARMAN, M.R. DESCHENES, K. REYNOLDS, R.U. NEWTON, N.T. TRIPLETT, and J.E. DZIADOS. Compatibility of high-intensity strength and endurance training on hormonal and skeletal muscle adaptations. *J Appl Physiol* 78:976-989, 1995.

84. KUBUKELI, Z.N., T.D. NOAKES, and S.C. DENNIS. Training techniques to improve endurance exercise performances. *Sports Med* 32:489-509, 2002.

85. KYROLAINEN, H., J. AVELA, J.M. MCBRIDE, S. KOSKINEN, J.L. ANDERSEN, S. SIPILA, T.E. TAKALA, and P.V. KOMI. Effects of power training on muscle structure and neuromuscular performance. *Scand J Med Sci Sports* 15:58-64, 2005.

86. LAURSEN, P.B., M.A. BLANCHARD, and D.G. JENKINS. Acute high-intensity interval training improves Tvent and peak power output in highly trained males. *Can J Appl Physiol* 27:336-348, 2002.

87. LAURSEN, P.B., and D.G. JENKINS. The scientific basis for high-intensity interval training: optimising training programmes and maximising performance in highly trained endurance athletes. *Sports Med* 32:53-73, 2002.

88. LAURSEN, P.B., E.C. RHODES, R.H. LANGILL, D.C. MCKENZIE, and J.E. TAUNTON. Relationship of exercise test variables to cycling performance in an Ironman triathlon. *Eur J Appl Physiol* 87:433-440, 2002.

89. LAURSEN, P.B., E.C. RHODES, R.H. LANGILL, J.E. TAUNTON, and D.C. MCKENZIE. Exercise-induced arterial hypoxemia is not different during cycling and running in triathletes. *Scand J Med Sci Sports* 15:113-117, 2005.

90. LAURSEN, P.B., C.M. SHING, J.M. PEAKE, J.S. COOMBES, and D.G. JENKINS. Influence of high-intensity interval training on adaptations in well-trained cyclists. *J Strength Cond Res* 19:527-533, 2005.

91. LAURSEN, P.B., C.M. SHING, J.M. PEAKE, J.S. COOMBES, and D.G. JENKINS. Interval training program optimization in highly trained endurance cyclists. *Med Sci Sports Exerc* 34:1801-1807, 2002.

92. LEVINE, B.D. VO2max: what do we know, and what do we still need to know? *J Physiol* 586:25-34, 2008.

93. LINOSSIER, M.T., D. DORMOIS, C. PERIER, J. FREY, A. GEYSSANT, and C. DENIS. Enzyme adaptations of human skeletal muscle during bicycle short-sprint training and detraining. *Acta Physiol Scand* 161:439-445, 1997.

94. LITTLE, T., and A.G. WILLIAMS. Effects of sprint duration and exercise: rest ratio on repeated sprint performance and physiological responses in professional soccer players. *J Strength Cond Res* 21:646-648, 2007.

95. MACDOUGALL, J.D., A.L. HICKS, J.R. MACDONALD, R.S. MCKELVIE, H.J. GREEN, and K.M. SMITH. Muscle performance and enzymatic adaptations to sprint interval training. *J Appl Physiol* 84:2138-2142, 1998.

96. MARCINIK, E.J., J. POTTS, G. SCHLABACH, S. WILL, P. DAWSON, and B.F. HURLEY. Effects of strength training on lactate threshold and endurance performance. *Med Sci Sports Exerc* 23:739-743, 1991.

97. MAYHEW, J.L. Oxygen cost and energy expenditure of running in trained runners. *Br J Sports Med* 11:116-121, 1977.

98. MCARDLE, W.D., F.I. KATCH, and V.L. KATCH. *Exercise Physiology: Energy, Nutrition, and Human Performance*. 6th ed. Baltimore: Lippincott Williams & Wilkins, 2007.

99. MCGEE, D., T.C. JESSEE, M.H. STONE, and D. BLESSING. Leg and hip endurance adaptations to three weight-training programs. *J Appl Sport Sci Res* 6:92-85, 1992.

100. MCGUIRE, B.J., and T.W. SECOMB. Estimation of capillary density in human skeletal muscle based on maximal oxygen consumption rates. *Am J Physiol Heart Circ Physiol* 285:H2382-2391, 2003.

101. MCKENNA, M.J., A.R. HARMER, S.F. FRASER, and J.L. LI. Effects of training on potassium, calcium and hydrogen ion regulation in skeletal muscle and blood during exercise. *Acta Physiol Scand* 156:335-346, 1996.

102. MEDBO, J.I., and S. BURGERS. Effect of training on the anaerobic capacity. *Med Sci Sports Exerc* 22:501-507, 1990.

103. MIDGLEY, A.W., L.R. MCNAUGHTON, and A.M. JONES. Training to enhance the physiological determinants of long-distance running performance: can valid recommendations be given to runners and coaches based on current scientific knowledge? *Sports Med* 37:857-880, 2007.

104. MIKKOLA, J., H. RUSKO, A. NUMMELA, T. POLLARI, and K. HÄKKINEN. Concurrent endurance and explosive type strength training improves neuromuscular and anaerobic characteristics in young distance runners. *Int J Sports Med* 28:602-611, 2007.

105. MILLER, T.A., R. THIERRY-AGUILERA, J.J. CONGLETON, A.A. AMENDOLA, M.J. CLARK, S.F. CROUSE, S.M. MARTIN, and O.C. JENKINS. Seasonal changes in VO2max among Division 1A collegiate women soccer players. *J Strength Cond Res* 21:48-51, 2007.

106. MONTGOMERY, D.L. Physiology of ice hockey. *Sports Med* 5:99-126, 1988.

107. MORGAN, D.W., D.R. BRANSFORD, D.L. COSTILL, J.T. DANIELS, E.T. HOWLEY, and G.S. KRAHENBUHL. Variation in the aerobic demand of running among trained and untrained subjects. *Med Sci Sports Exerc* 27:404-409, 1995.

108. NADER, G.A. Concurrent strength and endurance training: from molecules to man. *Med Sci Sports Exerc* 38:1965-1970, 2006.

109. NIELSEN, H.B. Arterial desaturation during exercise in man: implication for O2 uptake and work capacity. *Scand J Med Sci Sports* 13:339-358, 2003.

110. PAAVOLAINEN, L., K. HÄKKINEN, I. HAMALAINEN, A. NUMMELA, and H. RUSKO. Explosive-strength training improves 5-km running time by improving running economy and muscle power. *J Appl Physiol* 86:1527-1533, 1999.

111. PAAVOLAINEN, L., K. HÄKKINEN, and H. RUSKO. Effects of explosive type strength training on physical performance characteristics in cross-country skiers. *Eur J Appl Physiol Occup Physiol* 62:251-255, 1991.

112. PINCIVERO, D.M., and T.O. BOMPA. A physiological review of American football. *Sports Med* 23:247-260, 1997.

113. PLISK, S.S. Anaerobic metabolic conditioning: a brief review of theory, strategy and practical application. *J Appl Sport Sci Res* 5:22-34, 1991.

114. PLISK, S.S. Speed, agility, and speed-endurance development. In: *Essentials of Strength Training and Conditioning*. T.R. Baechle and R.W. Earle, eds. Champaign, IL: Human Kinetics, 2008.

115. PLISK, S.S., and V. GAMBETTA. Tactical metabolic training: part 1. *Strength Cond* 19:44-53, 1997.

116. PLISK, S.S., and M.H. STONE. Periodization strategies. *Strength Cond* 25:19-37, 2003.

117. POLLOCK, M.L. The quantification of endurance training programs. *Exerc Sport Sci Rev* 1:155-188, 1973.

118. POTTEIGER, J.A. Aerobic endurance exercise training. In: *Essentials of Strength Training and Conditioning.* T.R. Baechle and R.W. Earle, eds. Champaign, IL: Human Kinetics, 2000, pp. 495-509.

119. POWERS, S.K., and E.T. HOWLEY. *Exercise Physiology: Theory and Application to Fitness and Performance.* 5th ed. New York: McGraw-Hill, 2004.

120. POWERS, S.K., J. LAWLER, J.A. DEMPSEY, S. DODD, and G. LANDRY. Effects of incomplete pulmonary gas exchange on VO2 max. *J Appl Physiol* 66:2491-2495, 1989.

121. RAMPININI, E., F.M. IMPELLIZZERI, C. CASTAGNA, G. ABT, K. CHAMARI, A. SASSI, and S.M. MARCORA. Factors influencing physiological responses to small-sided soccer games. *J Sports Sci* 25:659-666, 2007.

122. REILLY, T., C.N. DOWZER, and N.T. CABLE. The physiology of deep-water running. *J Sports Sci* 21:959-972, 2003.

123. REILLY, T., and B. EKBLOM. The use of recovery methods post-exercise. *J Sports Sci* 23:619-627, 2005.

124. REINDELL, H., and H. ROSKAMM. Ein Beitrag zu den physiologischen Grundlagen des Intervall training unter besonderer Berücksichtigug des Kreilaufes. *Schweiz Z Sportmed* 7:1-8, 1959.

125. ROBINSON, J.M., M.H. STONE, R.L. JOHNSON, C.M. PENLAND, B.J. WARREN, and R.D. LEWIS. Effects of different weight training exercise/rest intervals on strength, power, and high intensity exercise endurance. *J Strength Cond Res* 9:216-221, 1995.

126. RODAS, G., J.L. VENTURA, J.A. CADEFAU, R. CUSSO, and J. PARRA. A short training programme for the rapid improvement of both aerobic and anaerobic metabolism. *Eur J Appl Physiol* 82:480-486, 2000.

127. RODRIGUEZ, L.P., J. LOPEZ-REGO, J.A. CALBET, R. VALERO, E. VARELA, and J. PONCE. Effects of training status on fibers of the musculus vastus lateralis in professional road cyclists. *Am J Phys Med Rehabil* 81:651-660, 2002.

128. RUBAL, B.J., J.M. MOODY, S. DAMORE, S.R. BUNKER, and N.M. DIAZ. Left ventricular performance of the athletic heart during upright exercise: a heart rate-controlled study. *Med Sci Sports Exerc* 18:134-140, 1986.

129. RUBIO, J. Devising an efficient training plan. In: *Run Strong.* K. Beck, ed. Champaign, IL: Human Kinetics, 2005, pp. 41-58.

130. SALTIN, B. Hemodynamic adaptations to exercise. *Am J Cardiol* 55:42D-47D, 1985.

131. SALTIN, B., and P.O. ASTRAND. Maximal oxygen uptake in athletes. *J Appl Physiol* 23:353-358, 1967.

132. SALTIN, B., J. HENRIKSSON, E. NYGAARD, P. ANDERSEN, and E. JANSSON. Fiber types and metabolic potentials of skeletal muscles in sedentary man and endurance runners. *Ann N Y Acad Sci* 301:3-29, 1977.

133. SCHMIDT, W., N. MAASSEN, U. TEGTBUR, and K.M. BRAUMANN. Changes in plasma volume and red cell formation after a marathon competition. *Eur J Appl Physiol Occup Physiol* 58:453-458, 1989.

134. SCHUMACHER, Y.O., D. GRATHWOHL, J.M. BARTUREN, M. WOLLENWEBER, L. HEINRICH, A. SCHMID, G. HUBER, and J. KEUL. Haemoglobin, haematocrit and red blood cell indices in elite cyclists. Are the control values for blood testing valid? *Int J Sports Med* 21:380-385, 2000.

135. SCHUMACHER, Y.O., A. SCHMID, D. GRATHWOHL, D. BULTERMANN, and A. BERG. Hematological indices and iron status in athletes of various sports and performances. *Med Sci Sports Exerc* 34:869-875, 2002.

136. SHONO, N., H. URATA, B. SALTIN, M. MIZUNO, T. HARADA, M. SHINDO, and H. TANAKA. Effects of low intensity aerobic training on skeletal muscle capillary and blood lipoprotein profiles. *J Atheroscler Thromb* 9:78-85, 2002.

137. SILVESTRE, R., W.J. KRAEMER, C. WEST, D.A. JUDELSON, B.A. SPIERING, J.L. VINGREN, D.L. HATFIELD, J.M. ANDERSON, and C.M. MARESH. Body composition and physical performance during a National Collegiate Athletic Association Division I men's soccer season. *J Strength Cond Res* 20:962-970, 2006.

138. SJÖDIN, B., and I. JACOBS. Onset of blood lactate accumulation and marathon running performance. *Int J Sports Med* 2:23-26, 1981.

139. SJÖDIN, B., I. JACOBS, and J. SVEDENHAG. Changes in onset of blood lactate accumulation (OBLA) and muscle enzymes after training at OBLA. *Eur J Appl Physiol Occup Physiol* 49:45-57, 1982.

140. SJÖDIN, B, and J. SVEDENHAG. Applied physiology of marathon running. *Sports Med* 2:83-99, 1985.

141. SLEAMAKER, R., and R. BROWNING. *Serious Training for Endurance Athletes.* 2nd ed. Champaign, IL: Human Kinetics, 1996.

142. SMITH, T.P., L.R. MCNAUGHTON, and K.J. MARSHALL. Effects of 4-wk training using Vmax/Tmax on VO2max and performance in athletes. *Med Sci Sports Exerc* 31:892-896, 1999.

143. SPRIET, L.L., M.I. LINDINGER, R.S. MCKELVIE, G.J. HEIGENHAUSER, and N.L. JONES. Muscle glycogenolysis and H+ concentration during maximal intermittent cycling. *J Appl Physiol* 66:8-13, 1989.

144. STEPTO, N.K., J.A. HAWLEY, S.C. DENNIS, and W.G. HOPKINS. Effects of different interval-training programs on cycling time-trial performance. *Med Sci Sports Exerc* 31:736-741, 1999.

145. STEPTO, N.K., D.T. MARTIN, K.E. FALLON, and J.A. HAWLEY. Metabolic demands of intense aerobic

interval training in competitive cyclists. *Med Sci Sports Exerc* 33:303-310, 2001.

146. STONE, M.H., and H.O. O'BRYANT. *Weight Training: A Scientific Approach*. Edina, MN: Burgess, 1987.

147. STONE, M.H., W.A. SANDS, K.C. PIERCE, R.U. NEWTON, G.G. HAFF, and J. CARLOCK. Maximum strength and strength training: a relationship to endurance? *Strength Cond J* 28:44-53, 2006.

148. STONE, M.H., M.E. STONE, and W.A. SANDS. *Principles and Practice of Resistance Training*. Champaign, IL: Human Kinetics, 2007.

149. SUTER, E., W. HERZOG, J. SOKOLOSKY, J.P. WILEY, and B.R. MACINTOSH. Muscle fiber type distribution as estimated by Cybex testing and by muscle biopsy. *Med Sci Sports Exerc* 25:363-370, 1993.

150. SVEDAHL, K., and B.R. MACINTOSH. Anaerobic threshold: the concept and methods of measurement. *Can J Appl Physiol* 28:299-323, 2003.

151. SVEDENHAG, J., J. HENRIKSSON, and A. JUHLIN-DANNFELT. Beta-adrenergic blockade and training in human subjects: effects on muscle metabolic capacity. *Am J Physiol* 247:E305-311, 1984.

152. TABATA, I., K. IRISAWA, M. KOUZAKI, K. NISHIMURA, F. OGITA, and M. MIYACHI. Metabolic profile of high intensity intermittent exercises. *Med Sci Sports Exerc* 29:390-395, 1997.

153. TANAKA, H., and T. SWENSEN. Impact of resistance training on endurance performance. A new form of cross-training? *Sports Med* 25:191-200, 1998.

154. TRAPPE, S., M. HARBER, A. CREER, P. GALLAGHER, D. SLIVKA, K. MINCHEV, and D. WHITSETT. Single muscle fiber adaptations with marathon training. *J Appl Physiol* 101:721-727, 2006.

155. TURNER, A.M., M. OWINGS, and J.A. SCHWANE. Improvement in running economy after 6 weeks of plyometric training. *J Strength Cond Res* 17:60-67, 2003.

156. WANG, N., R.S. HIKIDA, R.S. STARON, and J.A. SIMONEAU. Muscle fiber types of women after resistance training–quantitative ultrastructure and enzyme activity. *Pflugers Arch* 424:494-502, 1993.

157. WELTMAN, A., R.L. SEIP, D. SNEAD, J.Y. WELTMAN, E.M. HASKVITZ, W.S. EVANS, J.D. VELDHUIS, and A.D. ROGOL. Exercise training at and above the lactate threshold in previously untrained women. *Int J Sports Med* 13:257-263, 1992.

158. WESTGARTH-TAYLOR, C., J.A. HAWLEY, S. RICKARD, K.H. MYBURGH, T.D. NOAKES, and S.C. DENNIS. Metabolic and performance adaptations to interval training in endurance- trained cyclists. *Eur J Appl Physiol* 75:298-304, 1997.

159. WESTON, A.R., K.H. MYBURGH, F.H. LINDSAY, S.C. DENNIS, T.D. NOAKES, and J.A. HAWLEY. Skeletal muscle buffering capacity and endurance performance after high-intensity interval training by well-trained cyclists. *Eur J Appl Physiol Occup Physiol* 75:7-13, 1997.

160. WILMORE, J.H., D.L. COSTILL, and W.L. KENNEY. *Physiology of Sport and Exercise*. 4th ed. Champaign, IL: Human Kinetics, 2008.

161. WRIGHT, D.C., D.H. HAN, P.M. GARCIA-ROVES, P.C. GEIGER, T.E. JONES, and J.O. HOLLOSZY. Exercise-induced mitochondrial biogenesis begins before the increase in muscle PGC-1 alpha expression. *J Biol Chem* 282:194-199, 2007.

162. YOSHIDA, T., M. CHIDA, M. ICHIOKA, and Y. SUDA. Blood lactate parameters related to aerobic capacity and endurance performance. *Eur J Appl Physiol Occup Physiol* 56:7-11, 1987.

163. ZAWADOWSKA, B., J. MAJERCZAK, D. SEMIK, J. KARASINSKI, L. KOLODZIEJSKI, W.M. KILARSKI, K. DUDA, and J.A. ZOLADZ. Characteristics of myosin profile in human vastus lateralis muscle in relation to training background. *Folia Histochem Cytobiol* 42:181-190, 2004.

164. ZHOU, B., R.K. CONLEE, R. JENSEN, G.W. FELLINGHAM, J.D. GEORGE, and A.G. FISHER. Stroke volume does not plateau during graded exercise in elite male distance runners. *Med Sci Sports Exerc* 33:1849-1854, 2001.

165. ZOLADZ, J.A., D. SEMIK, B. ZAWADOWSKA, J. MAJERCZAK, J. KARASINSKI, L. KOLODZIEJSKI, K. DUDA, and W.M. KILARSKI. Capillary density and capillary-to-fibre ratio in vastus lateralis muscle of untrained and trained men. *Folia Histochem Cytobiol* 43:11-17, 2005.

Chapter 12

1. ADRIAN, M.J., and J.M. COOPER. *Biomechanics of Human Movement*. 2nd ed. New York: WCB McGraw-Hill, 1995.

2. AE, M., A. ITO, and M. SUZUKI. The men's 100 metres. *New Studies in Athletics* 7:47-52, 1992.

3. ALLEMEIER, C.A., A.C. FRY, P. JOHNSON, R.S. HIKIDA, F.C. HAGERMAN, and R.S. STARON. Effects of sprint cycle training on human skeletal muscle. *J Appl Physiol* 77:2385-2390, 1994.

4. ANDERSEN, J.L., H. KLITGAARD, and B. SALTIN. Myosin heavy chain isoforms in single fibres from m. vastus lateralis of sprinters: influence of training. *Acta Physiol Scand* 151:135-142, 1994.

5. ANDERSEN, J.L., and S. SCHIAFFINO. Mismatch between myosin heavy chain mRNA and protein distribution in human skeletal muscle fibers. *Am J Physiol* 272:C1881-1889, 1997.

6. BAKER, D., and S. NANCE. The relation between running speed and measures of strength and power in professional rugby league players. *J. Strength Cond. Res* 13:230-235, 1999.

7. BALSOM, P.D., J.Y. SEGER, B. SJODIN, and B. EKBLOM. Maximal-intensity intermittent exercise: effect of recovery duration. *Int J Sports Med* 13:528-533, 1992.

8. BALSOM, P.D., J.Y. SEGER, B. SJODIN, and B. EKBLOM. Physiological responses to maximal

intensity intermittent exercise. *Eur J Appl Physiol* 65:144-149, 1992.

9. BANGSBO, J. The physiology of soccer–with special reference to intense intermittent exercise. *Acta Physiol Scand Suppl* 619:1-155, 1994.

10. BERTHOIN, S., G. DUPONT, P. MARY, and M. GERBEAUX. Predicting sprint kinematic parameters from anaerobic field tests in physical education students. *J Strength Cond Res* 15:75-80, 2001.

11. BLOOMFIELD, J., R. POLMAN, P. O'DONOGHUE, and L. MCNAUGHTON. Effective speed and agility conditioning methodology for random intermittent dynamic type sports. *J Strength Cond Res* 21:1093-1100, 2007.

12. BOGDANIS, G.C., M.E. NEVILL, L.H. BOOBIS, and H.K. LAKOMY. Contribution of phosphocreatine and aerobic metabolism to energy supply during repeated sprint exercise. *J Appl Physiol* 80:876-884, 1996.

13. BOGDANIS, G.C., M.E. NEVILL, H.K. LAKOMY, and L.H. BOOBIS. Power output and muscle metabolism during and following recovery from 10 and 20 s of maximal sprint exercise in humans. *Acta Physiol Scand* 163:261-272, 1998.

14. BONDARCHUK, A.P. The role and sequence of using different training-load intensities. *Fit Sports Rev Int* 29:202-204, 1994.

15. BONDARCHUK, A.P. *Track and Field Training.* Kiev: Zdotovye, 1986.

16. BOTTINELLI, R., M.A. PELLEGRINO, M. CANEPARI, R. ROSSI, and C. REGGIANI. Specific contributions of various muscle fibre types to human muscle performance: an in vitro study. *J Electromyogr Kinesiol* 9:87-95, 1999.

17. BOTTINELLI, R., S. SCHIAFFINO, and C. REGGIANI. Force-velocity relations and myosin heavy chain isoform compositions of skinned fibres from rat skeletal muscle. *J Physiol* 437:655-672, 1991.

18. BRET, C., A. RAHMANI, A.B. DUFOUR, L. MESSONNIER, and J.R. LACOUR. Leg strength and stiffness as ability factors in 100 m sprint running. *J Sports Med Phys Fitness* 42:274-281, 2002.

19. CADEFAU, J., J. CASADEMONT, J.M. GRAU, J. FERNANDEZ, A. BALAGUER, M. VERNET, R. CUSSO, and A. URBANO-MARQUEZ. Biochemical and histochemical adaptation to sprint training in young athletes. *Acta Physiol Scand* 140:341-351, 1990.

20. CARPENTIER, A., J. DUCHATEAU, and K. HAINAUT. Velocity dependent muscle strategy during plantarflexion in humans. *J Electromyogr Kinesiol* 6:225-233, 1996.

21. CHELLY, S.M., and C. DENIS. Leg power and hopping stiffness: relationship with sprint running performance. *Med Sci Sports Exerc* 33:326-333, 2001.

22. CONLEY, M. Bioenergetics of exercise training. In: *Essentials of Strength Training and Conditioning.* T.R. Baechle and R.W. Earle, eds. Champaign, IL: Human Kinetics, 2000, pp. 73-90.

23. COSTILL, D.L., J. DANIELS, W. EVANS, W. FINK, G. KRAHENBUHL, and B. SALTIN. Skeletal muscle enzymes and fiber composition in male and female track athletes. *J Appl Physiol* 40:149-154, 1976.

24. CRONIN, J.B., and K.T. HANSEN. Strength and power predictors of sports speed. *J Strength Cond Res* 19:349-357, 2005.

25. DAWSON, B., M. FITZSIMONS, S. GREEN, C. GOODMAN, M. CAREY, and K. COLE. Changes in performance, muscle metabolites, enzymes and fibre types after short sprint training. *Eur J Appl Physiol* 78:163-169, 1998.

26. DELECLUSE, C. Influence of strength training on sprint running performance. Current findings and implications for training. *Sports Med* 24:147-156, 1997.

27. DELECLUSE, C.H., H. VAN COPPENOLLE, E. WILLEMS, R. DIELS, M. GORIS, M. VAN LEEMPUTTE, and M. VUYLSTEKE. Analysis of 100 m sprint performance as a multi-dimensional skill. *Journal of Human Movement Studies* 28:87-101, 1995.

28. DICK, F.W. Planning the programme. In: *Sports Training Principles.* London: A&C Black, 1997, pp. 253-304.

29. DIETZ, V., D. SCHMIDTBLEICHER, and J. NOTH. Neuronal mechanisms of human locomotion. *J Neurophysiol* 42:1212-1222, 1979.

30. DUTHIE, G., D. PYNE, and S. HOOPER. Applied physiology and game analysis of rugby union. *Sports Med* 33:973-991, 2003.

31. ESBJORNSSON, M., Y. HELLSTEN-WESTING, P.D. BALSOM, B. SJODIN, and E. JANSSON. Muscle fibre type changes with sprint training: effect of training pattern. *Acta Physiol Scand* 149:245-246, 1993.

32. ESBJORNSSON, M., C. SYLVEN, I. HOLM, and E. JANSSON. Fast twitch fibres may predict anaerobic performance in both females and males. *Int J Sports Med* 14:257-263, 1993.

33. FREEMAN, W.H. *Peak When it Counts: Periodization for American Track & Field.* 4th ed. Mountain View, CA: Tafnews Press, 2001.

34. GABBETT, T.J., J.N. KELLY, and J.M. SHEPPARD. Speed, change of direction speed, and reactive agility of rugby league players. *J Strength Cond Res* 22:174-181, 2008.

35. GAMBETTA, V. How to develop sport-specific speed. *Sports Coach* 19:22-24, 1996.

36. GOLLHOFER, A., A. SCHOPP, W. RAPP, and V. STROINIK. Changes in reflex excitability following isometric contraction in humans. *Eur J Appl Physiol Occup Physiol* 77:89-97, 1998.

37. GOTTLIEB, G.L., G.C. AGARWAL, and R.J. JAEGER. Response to sudden torques about ankle in man. IV. A functional role of alpha-gamma linkage. *J Neurophysiol* 46:179-190, 1981.

38. GRAY, H., and M.H. STONE. *Players Guide to ETSU Men's Soccer: Athlete Development.* Johnson City, TN: East Tennessee State University, 2008, p. 40.

39. HAFF, G.G., W.J. KRAEMER, H.S. O'BRYANT, G. PENDLAY, S. PLISK, and M.H. STONE. Roundtable discussion: periodization of training–part 2. *NSCA J* 26:56-70, 2004.

40. HAFF, G.G., A. WHITLEY, and J.A. POTTEIGER. A brief review: explosive exercises and sports performance. *Natl Strength Cond Assoc* 23:13-20, 2001.

41. HÄKKINEN, K. and E. MYLLYLA. Acute effects of muscle fatigue and recovery on force production and relaxation in endurance, power and strength athletes. *J Sports Med Phys Fitness* 30:5-12, 1990.

42. HAMADA, T., D.G. SALE, and J.D. MACDOUGALL. Postactivation potentiation in endurance-trained male athletes. *Med Sci Sports Exerc* 32:403-411, 2000.

43. HARGREAVES, M., M.J. MCKENNA, D.G. JENKINS, S.A. WARMINGTON, J.L. LI, R.J. SNOW, and M.A. FEBBRAIO. Muscle metabolites and performance during high-intensity, intermittent exercise. *J Appl Physiol* 84:1687-1691, 1998.

44. HARRIDGE, S.D., R. BOTTINELLI, M. CANEPARI, M. PELLEGRINO, C. REGGIANI, M. ESBJORNSSON, P.D. BALSOM, and B. SALTIN. Sprint training, in vitro and in vivo muscle function, and myosin heavy chain expression. *J Appl Physiol* 84:442-449, 1998.

45. HELGERUD, J., L.C. ENGEN, U. WISLØFF, and J. HOFF. Aerobic endurance training improves soccer performance. *Med Sci Sports Exerc* 33:1925-1931, 2001.

46. HELGERUD, J., K. HOYDAL, E. WANG, T. KARLSEN, P. BERG, M. BJERKAAS, T. SIMONSEN, C. HELGESEN, N. HJORTH, R. BACH, and J. HOFF. Aerobic high-intensity intervals improve VO2max more than moderate training. *Med Sci Sports Exerc* 39:665-671, 2007.

47. HIRVONEN, J., S. REHUNEN, H. RUSKO, and M. HARKONEN. Breakdown of high-energy phosphate compounds and lactate accumulation during short supramaximal exercise. *Eur J Appl Physiol* 56:253-259, 1987.

48. HOFF, J., U. WISLØFF, L.C. ENGEN, O.J. KEMI, and J. HELGERUD. Soccer specific aerobic endurance training. *Br J Sports Med* 36:218-221, 2002.

49. HORI, N., R.U. NEWTON, W.A. ANDREWS, N. KAWAMORI, M.R. MCGUIGAN, and K. NOSAKA. Does performance of hang power clean differentiate performance of jumping, sprinting, and changing of direction? *J Strength Cond Res* 22:412-418, 2008.

50. ISSURIN, V. Block periodization versus traditional training theory: a review. *J Sports Med Phys Fitness* 48:65-75, 2008.

51. JACOBS, I., M. ESBJORNSSON, C. SYLVEN, I. HOLM, and E. JANSSON. Sprint training effects on muscle myoglobin, enzymes, fiber types, and blood lactate. *Med Sci Sports Exerc* 19:368-374, 1987.

52. JANSSON, E., M. ESBJORNSSON, I. HOLM, and I. JACOBS. Increase in the proportion of fast-twitch muscle fibres by sprint training in males. *Acta Physiol Scand* 140:359-363, 1990.

53. JEFFREYS, I. *Total Soccer Fitness*. Monterey, CA: Coaches Choice, 2007.

54. JEFFREYS, I. Warm-up and stretching. In: *Essentials of Strength Training and Conditioning*. T.R. Baechle and R.W. Earle, eds. Champaign, IL: Human Kinetics, 2008, pp. 296-276.

55. JENKINS, D.G., S. BROOKS, and C. WILLIAMS. Improvements in multiple sprint ability with three weeks of training. *NZ J Sports Med* 22:2-5, 1994.

56. JONHAGEN, S., M.O. ERICSON, G. NEMETH, and E. ERIKSSON. Amplitude and timing of electromyographic activity during sprinting. *Scand J Med Sci Sports* 6:15-21, 1996.

57. KELLER, T.S., A.M. WEISBERGER, J.L. RAY, S.S. HASAN, R.G. SHIAVI, and D.M. SPENGLER. Relationship between vertical ground reaction force and speed during walking, slow jogging, and running. *Clin Biomech (Bristol, Avon)* 11:253-259, 1996.

58. KOMI, P.V. Stretch-shortening cycle. In: *Strength and Power in Sport*. P.V. Komi, ed. Oxford, UK: Blackwell Science, 2003, pp. 184-202.

59. KOMI, P.V. Training of muscle strength and power: interaction of neuromotoric, hypertrophic, and mechanical factors. *Int J Sports Med* 7(suppl 1):10-15, 1986.

60. KURZ, T. *Science of Sports Training*. 2nd ed. Island Pond, VT: Stadion, 2001.

61. KYRÖLÄINEN, H., P.V. KOMI, and A. BELLI. Changes in muscle activity patterns and kinetics with increasing speed. *J Strength Cond Res* 13:400-406, 1999.

62. LAURSEN, P.B., and D.G. JENKINS. The scientific basis for high-intensity interval training: optimising training programmes and maximising performance in highly trained endurance athletes. *Sports Med* 32:53-73, 2002.

63. LENTZ, D. and A. HARDYK. Speed training. In: *Training for Speed, Agility, and Quickness*. L.E. Brown and V.A. Ferrigno, eds. Champaign, IL: Human Kinetics, 2005, pp. 17-70.

64. LILJEDAHL, M.E., I. HOLM, C. SYLVEN, and E. JANSSON. Different responses of skeletal muscle following sprint training in men and women. *Eur J Appl Physiol* 74:375-383, 1996.

65. LINNAMO, V., K. HAKKINEN, and P.V. KOMI. Neuromuscular fatigue and recovery in maximal compared to explosive strength loading. *Eur J Appl Physiol Occup Physiol* 77:176-181. 1998.

66. LINOSSIER, M.T., C. DENIS, D. DORMOIS, A. GEYSSANT, and J.R. LACOUR. Ergometric and metabolic adaptation to a 5-s sprint training programme. *Eur J Appl Physiol* 67:408-414, 1993.

67. LINOSSIER, M.T., D. DORMOIS, A. GEYSSANT, and C. DENIS. Performance and fibre characteristics of human skeletal muscle during short sprint training and detraining on a cycle ergometer. *Eur J Appl Physiol* 75:491-498, 1997.

68. LINOSSIER, M.T., D. DORMOIS, C. PERIER, J. FREY, A. GEYSSANT, and C. DENIS. Enzyme adaptations of human skeletal muscle during bicycle short-sprint training and detraining. *Acta Physiol Scand* 161:439-445, 1997.

69. LITTLE, T., and A.G. WILLIAMS. Specificity of acceleration, maximum speed, and agility in professional soccer players. *J Strength Cond Res* 19:76-78, 2005.

70. LOCATELLI, E. The importance of anaerobic glycolysis and stiffness in the sprints (60, 100, 200 metres) *N. Stud Athletics* 11:121-125, 1996.

71. MACDOUGALL, J.D., A.L. HICKS, J.R. MACDONALD, R.S. MCKELVIE, H.J. GREEN, and K.M. SMITH. Muscle performance and enzymatic adaptations to sprint interval training. *J Appl Physiol* 84:2138-2142, 1998.

72. MAUGHAN, R., and M. GLEESON. *The Biochemical Basis of Sports Performance.* New York: Oxford University Press, 2004.

73. MCBRIDE, J.M., T. TRIPLETT-MCBRIDE, A. DAVIE, and R.U. NEWTON. A comparison of strength and power characteristics between power lifters, Olympic lifters, and sprinters. *J Strength Cond Res* 13:58-66, 1999.

74. MCBRIDE, J.M., T. TRIPLETT-MCBRIDE, A. DAVIE, and R.U. NEWTON. The effect of heavy- vs. light-load jump squats on the development of strength, power, and speed. *J Strength Cond Res* 16:75-82, 2002.

75. MCKENNA, M.J., A.R. HARMER, S.F. FRASER, and J.L. LI. Effects of training on potassium, calcium and hydrogen ion regulation in skeletal muscle and blood during exercise. *Acta Physiol Scand* 156:335-346, 1996.

76. MERO, A., and P.V. KOMI. Effects of supramaximal velocity on biomechanical variables in sprinting. *Int J Sport Biomech* 1:240-252, 1985.

77. MERO, A., P.V. KOMI, and R.J. GREGOR. Biomechanics of sprint running. A review. *Sports Med* 13:376-392, 1992.

78. MERO, A., P. LUHTANEN, J.T. VIITASALO, and P.V. KOMI. Relationships between maximal running velocity, muscle fiber characteristics, force production and force relaxation of sprinters. *Scand J Sports Sci* 3:16-22, 1981.

79. MERO, A., and E. PELTOLA. Neural activation fatigued and non-fatigued conditions of short and long sprint running. *Biol Sport* 6:43-58, 1989.

80. MILLER, R.G., R.S. MOUSSAVI, A.T. GREEN, P.J. CARSON, and M.W. WEINER. The fatigue of rapid repetitive movements. *Neurology* 43:755-761, 1993.

81. MOIR, G., R. SANDERS, C. BUTTON, and M. GLAISTER. The effect of periodized resistance training on accelerative sprint performance. *Sports Biomech* 6:285-300, 2007.

82. MORENO, E. Developing quickness, part II. *Strength Cond J* 17:38-39, 1995.

83. MURPHY, A.J., R.G. LOCKIE, and A.J. COUTTS. Kinematic determinants of early acceleration in field sport athletes. *J Sports Sci Med* 2:144-150, 2003.

84. NEGRETE, R., and J. BROPHY. The relationship between isokinetic open and closed chain lower extremity strength and functional performance. *J Sport Rehabil* 9:46-61, 2000.

85. NEVILL, M.E., L.H. BOOBIS, S. BROOKS, and C. WILLIAMS. Effect of training on muscle metabolism during treadmill sprinting. *J Appl Physiol* 67:2376-2382, 1989.

86. NUMMELA, A., H. RUSKO, and A. MERO. EMG activities and ground reaction forces during fatigued and nonfatigued sprinting. *Med Sci Sports Exerc* 26:605-609, 1994.

87. PARRA, J., J.A. CADEFAU, G. RODAS, N. AMIGO, and R. CUSSO. The distribution of rest periods affects performance and adaptations of energy metabolism induced by high-intensity training in human muscle. *Acta Physiol Scand* 169:157-165, 2000.

88. PETTE, D. The adaptive potential of skeletal muscle fibers. *Can J Appl Physiol* 27:423-448, 2002.

89. PETTE, D., and R.S. STARON. Myosin isoforms, muscle fiber types, and transitions. *Microsc Res Tech* 50:500-509, 2000.

90. PLISK, S.S. The angle on agility. *Training and Conditioning* 10:37-43, 2000.

91. PLISK, S.S. Speed, agility, and speed-endurance development. In: *Essentials of Strength Training and Conditioning.* T.R. Baechle and R.W. Earle, eds. Champaign, IL: Human Kinetics, 2008.

92. PLISK, S.S., and V. GAMBETTA. Tactical metabolic training: part 1. *Strength Cond* 19:44-53, 1997.

93. PLISK, S.S., and M.H. STONE. Periodization strategies. *Strength Cond* 25:19-37, 2003.

94. RACINAIS, S., D. BISHOP, R. DENIS, G. LATTIER, A. MENDEZ-VILLANEUVA, and S. PERREY. Muscle deoxygenation and neural drive to the muscle during repeated sprint cycling. *Med Sci Sports Exerc* 39:268-274, 2007.

95. RIENZI, E., B. DRUST, T. REILLY, J.E. CARTER, and A. MARTIN. Investigation of anthropometric and work-rate profiles of elite South American international soccer players. *J Sports Med Phys Fitness* 40:162-169, 2000.

96. ROBERTS, A.D., R. BILLETER, and H. HOWALD. Anaerobic muscle enzyme changes after interval training. *Int J Sports Med* 3:18-21, 1982.

97. ROSS, A., and M. LEVERITT. Long-term metabolic and skeletal muscle adaptations to short-sprint training: implications for sprint training and tapering. *Sports Med* 31:1063-1082, 2001.

98. ROSS, A., M. LEVERITT, and S. RIEK. Neural influences on sprint running: training adaptations and acute responses. *Sports Med* 31:409-425, 2001.

99. SAYERS, M. Running technique for field sport players. *Sports Coach* Autumn:26-27, 2000.

100. SHEPPARD, J.M. Strength and conditioning exercise selection in speed development. *NSCA J* 25:26-30, 2003.

101. SHEPPARD, J.M., and W.B. YOUNG. Agility literature review: classifications, training and testing. *J Sports Sci* 24:919-932, 2006.

102. SIFF, M.C. *Supertraining.* 6th ed. Denver, CO: Supertraining Institute, 2003.

103. SIMONEAU, J.A., G. LORTIE, M.R. BOULAY, M. MARCOTTE, M.C. THIBAULT, and C. BOUCHARD. Human skeletal muscle fiber type alteration with high-intensity intermittent training. *Eur J Appl Physiol Occup Physiol* 54:250-253, 1985.

104. SPENCER, M., D. BISHOP, B. DAWSON, and C. GOODMAN. Physiological and metabolic responses of repeated-sprint activities : specific to field-based team sports. *Sports Med* 35:1025-1044, 2005.

105. SPRIET, L.L., M.I. LINDINGER, R.S. MCKELVIE, G.J. HEIGENHAUSER, and N.L. JONES. Muscle glycogenolysis and H+ concentration during maximal intermittent cycling. *J Appl Physiol* 66:8-13, 1989.

106. STACKHOUSE, S.K., D.S. REISMAN, and S.A. BINDER-MACLEOD. Challenging the role of pH in skeletal muscle fatigue. *Phys Ther* 81:1897-1903, 2001.

107. STONE, M.H., M.E. STONE, and W.A. SANDS. *Principles and Practice of Resistance Training.* Champaign, IL: Human Kinetics, 2007.

108. TESCH, P.A., J.E. WRIGHT, J.A. VOGEL, W.L. DANIELS, D.S. SHARP, and B. SJODIN. The influence of muscle metabolic characteristics on physical performance. *Eur J Appl Physiol Occup Physiol* 54:237-243, 1985.

109. THORSTENSSON, A., B. SJÖDIN, and J. KARLSSON. Enzyme activities and muscle strength after "sprint training" in man. *Acta Physiol Scand* 94:313-318, 1975.

110. TRAPPE, S., M. GODARD, P. GALLAGHER, C. CARROLL, G. ROWDEN, and D. PORTER. Resistance training improves single muscle fiber contractile function in older women. *Am J Physiol Cell Physiol* 281:C398-406, 2001.

111. TRAPPE, S., M. HARBER, A. CREER, P. GALLAGHER, D. SLIVKA, K. MINCHEV, and D. WHITSETT. Single muscle fiber adaptations with marathon training. *J Appl Physiol* 101:721-727, 2006.

112. TRAPPE, S., D. WILLIAMSON, M. GODARD, D. PORTER, G. ROWDEN, and D. COSTILL. Effect of resistance training on single muscle fiber contractile function in older men. *J Appl Physiol* 89:143-152, 2000.

113. VOLEK, J.S., and W.J. KRAEMER. Creatine supplementation: its effect on human muscular performance and body composition. *J Strength Cond Res* 10:200-210, 1996.

114. WESTON, A.R., K.H. MYBURGH, F.H. LINDSAY, S.C. DENNIS, T.D. NOAKES, and J.A. HAWLEY. Skeletal muscle buffering capacity and endurance performance after high-intensity interval training by well-trained cyclists. *Eur J Appl Physiol Occup Physiol* 75:7-13, 1997.

115. WEYAND, P.G., D.B. STERNLIGHT, M.J. BELLIZZI, and S. WRIGHT. Faster top running speeds are achieved with greater ground forces not more rapid leg movements. *J Appl Physiol* 89:1991-1999, 2000.

116. WILLIAMSON, D.L., P.M. GALLAGHER, C.C. CARROLL, U. RAUE, and S.W. TRAPPE. Reduction in hybrid single muscle fiber proportions with resistance training in humans. *J Appl Physiol* 91:1955-1961, 2001.

117. WILLIAMSON, D.L., M.P. GODARD, D.A. PORTER, D.L. COSTILL, and S.W. TRAPPE. Progressive resistance training reduces myosin heavy chain coexpression in single muscle fibers from older men. *J Appl Physiol* 88:627-633, 2000.

118. YOUNG, W.B. Transfer of strength and power training to sports performance. *Int J Sports Physiol Perf* 1:74-83, 2006.

119. YOUNG, W., D. BENTON, G. DUTHIE, and J. PRYOR. Resistance training for short sprints and maximum-speed sprints. *Strength Cond* 23:7-13, 2001.

120. YOUNG, W.B., R. JAMES, and I. MONTGOMERY. Is muscle power related to running speed with changes of direction? *J Sports Med Phys Fitness* 42:282-288, 2002.

121. YOUNG, W.B., M.H. MCDOWELL, and B.J. SCARLETT. Specificity of sprint and agility training methods. *J Strength Cond Res* 15:315-319, 2001.

Index

Note: The italicized *f* and *t* following page numbers refer to figures and tables, respectively.

A

Aagaard, P. 265
Abadjiev, I. 81
absolute intensity 86
absolute volume 80
acceleration 315
accumulation 230
active recovery 108-109
active rest 300-301
acute fatigue 99
adaptation 8-12
  recovery and 98*f*
  specificity 9-12, 10*f*, 11*f*
  standard load 9*f*
  threshold 11*f*
adenosine diphosphate (ADP) 21
adenosine triphosphate (ATP) 10, 21
aerobic endurance 142-143
  performance 289-298
  phase 144-145
aerobic exercise 300
aerobic intervals 302-304
  workouts 303*t*
aerobic power 289-294
age
  of high performance in sports 36*t*-37*t*
  recovery and 106
agility
  annual training plan 335-342
  development 328-330
  factors model 326*f*
  macrocycle 337-341
  microcycle 341-342
  training 324-328
Aján, T. 272, 278

alternating intensities microcycle team sport 224*t*
alternating maximal-and low-intensity stimuli 20*f*
alternating training stress
  endurance sports 228*f*
  speed and power sports 227*f*
anaerobic
  endurance performance 298-300
  endurance phase 144-145
  intervals 304-305
  interval training microcycle for runner 305*t*
anatomical adaptations 140
annual training plan 125
agility 335-342
  chart 160-175
  classification 129-135
  competition calendar 180-181
  competition phase 194-202
  criteria 175-185
  elements 175
  introduction 176
  objectives 178-179
  Olympic Games 161*f*
  performance prediction 177-178
  periodization model 183-184
  phases and characteristics 146-160
  with phases and cycles of training 127*f*
  phases for sprinter 337*t*
  physical training development 58*f*
  preparation model 184-185

preparatory phase 148-151
  retrospective analysis 176-177
  soccer 338*f*-339*f*
  standards 181-183
  tests 181-183
arteriovenous oxygen difference 293
artistic sports annual training plan chart 170-173
athletes
  comparison 294*f*
  performance level 91
  performing skill incorrectly 75-76
athletic training, history of 31
Australian Institute of Sport, heart rate training zones male cyclists 85*t*
auxiliary sciences 4*f*

B

Baroga, L. 272, 278
bi-cycle annual training plan 133, 168*f*
  chart 167-168
  swimming 172*f*
bi-cycle periodization swimming 139*f*
bi-cycle plan for track and field 132*f*
bioenergetics 24, 42, 298
  characteristics of interval training 308*t*
bioenergetic specificity, work-to-rest intervals and 94*t*
biological age 38
biomotor abilities 4, 259-261
  interaction 261*f*

About the Authors

Courtesy of Tudor Bompa.

Tudor O. Bompa, PhD, is recognized as the world's foremost expert on periodization training. He developed the concept of periodization of strength in Romania in 1963 as he helped the Eastern Bloc countries rise to dominance in the athletic world. Since then, Bompa has used his system in training 11 Olympic and world championship medalists and elite athletes.

Professor emeritus at York University in Toronto, Bompa has authored several books on physical conditioning, including the second edition of *Serious Strength Training, Periodization Training for Sports,* and *Total Training for Young Champions* as well as numerous articles on the subject. He has made presentations on periodization training in more than 30 countries. His publications, conferences, and ideas are highly regarded and sought out by many top professional athletes and training specialists. Bompa and his wife, Tamara, live in Sharon, Ontario.

Courtesy of Greg Haff.

G. Gregory Haff, PhD, is an assistant professor of exercise physiology in the School of Medicine at West Virginia University in Morgantown. Haff has published more than 50 articles, centering his research on performance effects in the areas of strength training, cycling, and nutritional supplementation.

A frequent presenter at national conferences on the topic of periodization, Haff was invited to present his research on the periodization of strength training in the United Kingdom in 2008. Haff also received a Distinguished Teaching Award from West Virginia University School of Medicine in 2008. In 2001, he was the recipient of the National Strength and Conditioning Association (NSCA) Young Investigator of the Year Award.

Haff applies his research as a regional weightlifting coach, level 3 cycling coach, and certified strength and conditioning specialist with distinction. He has also worked as a coach and consultant for national-level and international-level weightlifters and cyclists as well as numerous collegiate athletes.

A fellow of the NSCA, Haff has served on the association's board of directors since 2007. He is also a member of the European College of Sports Science. Haff served on the USA Weightlifting Sports Medicine Committee (1998-2004), USA Weightlifting Sport Science Committee (1997-2004), NSCA Research Committee (2000-2006), and United States Olympic Committee Performance Enhancement Team for Weightlifting (2003-2004).

A competitive weightlifter at the national level for 14 years, Haff continues to enjoy weightlifting in his free time as well as cycling and cooking. Haff resides in Morgantown, West Virginia, with his wife, Erin.

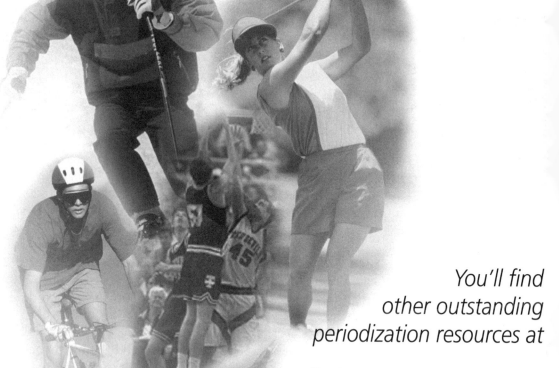

You'll find
other outstanding
periodization resources at

www.HumanKinetics.com

In the U.S. call

1-800-747-4457

Australia..08 8372 0999
Canada 1-800-465-7301
Europe...+44 (0) 113 255 5665
New Zealand.......................................0064 9 448 1207

 HUMAN KINETICS
The Information Leader in Physical Activity
P.O. Box 5076 • Champaign, IL 61825-5076 USA